Great News! These books are available online!
To get to these articles online, follow these easy steps:

1. Go to the TCC Library homepage at http:\\library.tccd.edu
2. Click the BOOKS tab
3. Type **Short Stories for Students [insert short story name]**
Example: Novels for Students Catch 22
4. Click on View Online
5. Click on Open Source In a New Window
6. Type the Novel Title in the
In the Publication box on the left side of the page

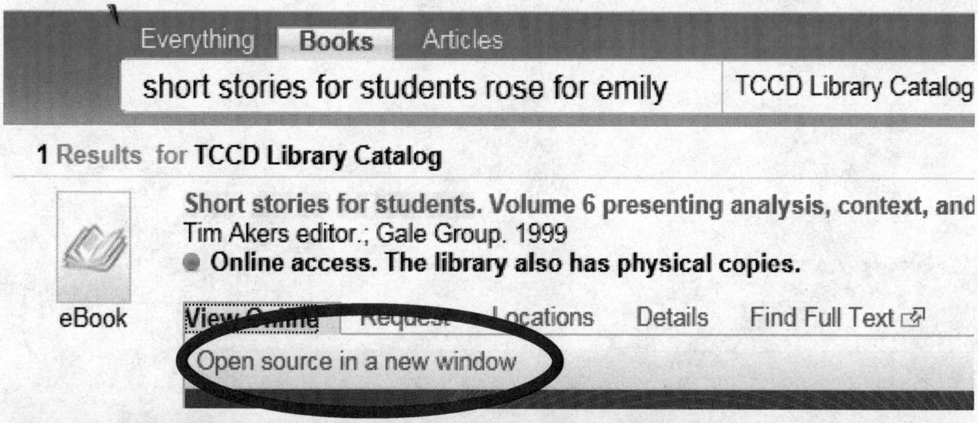

SHORT STORIES *for Students*

Advisors

Erik France: Adjunct Instructor of English, Macomb Community College, Warren, Michigan. B.A. and M.S.L.S. from University of North Carolina, Chapel Hill; Ph.D. from Temple University.

Kate Hamill: Grade 12 English Teacher, Catonsville High School, Catonsville, Maryland.

Joseph McGeary: English Teacher, Germantown Friends School, Philadelphia, Pennsylvania. Ph.D. in English from Duke University.

Timothy Showalter: English Department Chair, Franklin High School, Reisterstown, Maryland. Certified teacher by the Maryland State Department of Education. Member of the National Council of Teachers of English.

Amy Spade Silverman: English Department Chair, Kehillah Jewish High School, Palo Alto, California. Member of National Council of Teachers of English (NCTE), Teachers and Writers, and NCTE Opinion Panel. Exam Reader, Advanced Placement Literature and Composition. Poet, published in *North American Review, Nimrod,* and *Michigan Quarterly Review,* among other publications.

Jody Stefansson: Director of Boswell Library and Study Center and Upper School Learning Specialist, Polytechnic School, Pasadena, California. Board member, Children's Literature Council of Southern California. Member of American Library Association, Association of Independent School Librarians, and Association of Educational Therapists.

Laura Jean Waters: Certified School Library Media Specialist, Wilton High School, Wilton, Connecticut. B.A. from Fordham University; M.A. from Fairfield University.

SHORT STORIES *for Students*

Presenting Analysis, Context, and Criticism on Commonly Studied Short Stories

VOLUME 27

GALE
CENGAGE Learning™

Detroit • New York • San Francisco • New Haven, Conn • Waterville, Maine • London

GALE
CENGAGE Learning

Short Stories for Students, Volume 27

Project Editor: Sara Constantakis

Rights Acquisition and Management: Margaret Abendroth, Scott Bragg, Sara Teller, Robyn Young

Composition: Evi Abou-El-Seoud

Manufacturing: Drew Kalasky

Imaging: John Watkins

Product Design: Pamela A. E. Galbreath, Jennifer Wahi

Content Conversion: Civie Green, Katrina Coach

Product Manager: Meggin Condino

Gale
27500 Drake Rd.
Farmington Hills, MI, 48331-3535

ISBN-13: 978-1-4144-2185-8
ISBN-10: 1-4144-2185-0

ISSN 1092-7735

This title is also available as an e-book.
ISBN-13: 978-1-4144-4958-6
ISBN-10: 1-4144-4958-5
Contact your Gale, a part of Cengage Learning sales representative for ordering information.

Printed in the United States of America
1 2 3 4 5 6 7 13 12 11 10 09

Table of Contents

ADVISORS ii

WHY STUDY LITERATURE AT ALL? ix
(by Thomas E. Barden)

INTRODUCTION xi

LITERARY CHRONOLOGY xv

ACKNOWLEDGMENTS xvii

CONTRIBUTORS xix

AFTER TWENTY YEARS
(by O. Henry). 1
Author Biography 2
Plot Summary. 2
Characters 3
Themes 4
Style 6
Historical Context 7
Critical Overview. 8
Criticism. 9
Sources 23
Further Reading 23

AMERICAN HISTORY
(by Judith Ortiz Cofer) 24
Author Biography 24
Plot Summary. 25
Characters 27

Themes 28
Style 30
Historical Context 32
Critical Overview. 34
Criticism. 34
Sources 43
Further Reading 43

ANXIETY
(by Grace Paley). 45
Author Biography 46
Plot Summary. 47
Characters 48
Themes 50
Style 51
Historical Context 52
Critical Overview. 55
Criticism. 55
Sources 66
Further Reading 67

CHARLES
(by Shirley Jackson). 69
Author Biography 70
Plot Summary. 71
Characters 72
Themes 73
Style 75
Historical Context 76
Critical Overview. 78
Criticism. 79
Sources 84
Further Reading 85

ELEVEN
(by Sandra Cisneros). 86
Author Biography 87
Plot Summary. 88
Characters 89
Themes 90
Style 92
Historical Context 94
Critical Overview. 96
Criticism. 96
Sources 110
Further Reading 111

A HORSEMAN IN THE SKY
(by Ambrose Bierce). 112
Author Biography 113
Plot Summary. 113
Characters 115
Themes 117
Style 118
Historical Context 120
Critical Overview. 122
Criticism. 123
Sources 137
Further Reading 138

JIM BAKER'S BLUE JAY YARN
(by Mark Twain). 139
Author Biography 140
Plot Summary. 141
Characters 142
Themes 143
Style 145
Historical Context 146
Critical Overview. 147
Criticism. 148
Sources 157
Further Reading 157

LIBERTY
(by Julia Alvarez). 158
Author Biography 158
Plot Summary. 160
Characters 161
Themes 162
Style 164
Historical Context 165
Critical Overview. 166
Criticism. 167
Sources 175
Further Reading 175

RACE AT MORNING
(by William Faulkner) 176
Author Biography 176
Plot Summary. 178
Characters 181
Themes 184
Style 186
Historical Context 186
Critical Overview. 188
Criticism. 188
Sources 204
Further Reading 204

THIS BLESSED HOUSE
(by Jhumpa Lahiri) 206
Author Biography 207
Plot Summary. 207
Characters 209
Themes 210
Style 212
Historical Context 212
Critical Overview. 213

Criticism. 214
Sources 224
Further Reading 224

THE USE OF FORCE
(by William Carlos Williams) 225
Author Biography 226
Plot Summary 227
Characters 228
Themes 229
Style 231
Historical Context 232
Critical Overview. 234
Criticism. 235
Sources 240
Further Reading 240

A WAGNER MATINEE
(by Willa Cather). 241
Author Biography 242
Plot Summary 242
Characters 243
Themes 245
Style 247
Historical Context 248
Critical Overview. 250
Criticism. 250
Sources 262
Further Reading 262

THE WRITER IN THE FAMILY
(by E. L. Doctorow) 263
Author Biography 264
Plot Summary 264
Characters 267
Themes 268
Style 270
Historical Context 271
Critical Overview. 272
Criticism. 273
Sources 283
Further Reading 283

ZLATEH THE GOAT
(by Isaac Bashevis Singer) 284
Author Biography 284
Plot Summary 286
Characters 287
Themes 290
Style 292
Historical Context 292
Critical Overview. 294
Criticism. 294
Sources 307
Further Reading 308

GLOSSARY OF LITERARY TERMS. 309

CUMULATIVE AUTHOR/TITLE INDEX . . 321

CUMULATIVE NATIONALITY/ ETHNICITY INDEX 329

SUBJECT/THEME INDEX 337

Why Study Literature At All?

Short Stories for Students is designed to provide readers with information and discussion about a wide range of important contemporary and historical works of short fiction, and it does that job very well. However, I want to use this guest foreword to address a question that it does *not* take up. It is a fundamental question that is often ignored in high school and college English classes as well as research texts, and one that causes frustration among students at all levels, namely why study literature at all? Isn't it enough to read a story, enjoy it, and go about one's business? My answer (to be expected from a literary professional, I suppose) is no. It is not enough. It is a start; but it is not enough. Here's why.

First, literature is the only part of the educational curriculum that deals directly with the actual world of lived experience. The philosopher Edmund Husserl used the apt German term *die Lebenswelt*, "the living world," to denote this realm. All the other content areas of the modern American educational system avoid the subjective, present reality of everyday life. Science (both the natural and the social varieties) objectifies, the fine arts create and/or perform, history reconstructs. Only literary study persists in posing those questions we all asked before our schooling taught us to give up on them. Only literature gives credibility to personal perceptions, feelings, dreams, and the "stream of consciousness" that is our inner voice. Literature wonders about infinity, wonders why God permits evil, wonders what will happen to us after we die. Literature admits that we get our hearts broken, that people sometimes cheat and get away with it, that the world is a strange and probably incomprehensible place. Literature, in other words, takes on all the big and small issues of what it means to be human. So my first answer is that of the humanist we should read literature and study it and take it seriously because it enriches us as human beings. We develop our moral imagination, our capacity to sympathize with other people, and our ability to understand our existence through the experience of fiction.

My second answer is more practical. By studying literature we can learn how to explore and analyze texts. Fiction may be about *die Lebenswelt*, but it is a construct of words put together in a certain order by an artist using the medium of language. By examining and studying those constructions, we can learn about language as a medium. We can become more sophisticated about word associations and connotations, about the manipulation of symbols, and about style and atmosphere. We can grasp how ambiguous language is and how important context and texture is to meaning. In our first encounter with a work of literature, of course, we are not supposed to catch all of these things. We are spellbound, just as the writer wanted us to be. It is as serious students of the writer's art that we begin to see how the tricks are done.

Seeing the tricks, which is another way of saying "developing analytical and close reading skills," is important above and beyond its intrinsic literary educational value. These skills transfer to other fields and enhance critical thinking of any kind. Understanding how language is used to construct texts is powerful knowledge. It makes engineers better problem solvers, lawyers better advocates and courtroom practitioners, politicians better rhetoricians, marketing and advertising agents better sellers, and citizens more aware consumers as well as better participants in democracy. This last point is especially important, because rhetorical skill works both ways when we learn how language is manipulated in the making of texts the result is that we become less susceptible when language is used to manipulate us.

My third reason is related to the second. When we begin to see literature as created artifacts of language, we become more sensitive to good writing in general. We get a stronger sense of the importance of individual words, even the sounds of words and word combinations. We begin to understand Mark Twain's delicious proverb "The difference between the right word and the almost right word is the difference between lightning and a lightning bug." Getting beyond the "enjoyment only" stage of literature gets us closer to becoming makers of word art ourselves. I am not saying that studying fiction will turn every student into a Faulkner or a Shakespeare. But it will make us more adaptable and effective writers, even if our art form ends up being the office memo or the corporate annual report.

Studying short stories, then, can help students become better readers, better writers, and even better human beings. But I want to close with a warning. If your study and exploration of the craft, history, context, symbolism, or anything else about a story starts to rob it of the magic you felt when you first read it, it is time to stop. Take a break, study another subject, shoot some hoops, or go for a run. Love of reading is too important to be ruined by school. The early twentieth century writer Willa Cather, in her novel *My Antonia*, has her narrator Jack Burden tell a story that he and Antonia heard from two old Russian immigrants when they were teenagers. These immigrants, Pavel and Peter, told about an incident from their youth back in Russia that the narrator could recall in vivid detail thirty years later. It was a harrowing story of a wedding party starting home in sleds and being chased by starving wolves. Hundreds of wolves attacked the group's sleds one by one as they sped across the snow trying to reach their village. In a horrible revelation, the old Russians revealed that the groom eventually threw his own bride to the wolves to save himself. There was even a hint that one of the old immigrants might have been the groom mentioned in the story. Cather has her narrator conclude with his feelings about the story. "We did not tell Pavel's secret to anyone, but guarded it jealously as if the wolves of the Ukraine had gathered that night long ago, and the wedding party had been sacrificed, just to give us a painful and peculiar pleasure." That feeling, that painful and peculiar pleasure, is the most important thing about literature. Study and research should enhance that feeling and never be allowed to overwhelm it.

Thomas E. Barden
Professor of English and Director of Graduate English Studies, The University of Toledo

Introduction

Purpose of the Book

The purpose of *Short Stories for Students* (*SSfS*) is to provide readers with a guide to understanding, enjoying, and studying short stories by giving them easy access to information about the work. Part of Gale's "For Students" Literature line, *SSfS* is specifically designed to meet the curricular needs of high school and undergraduate college students and their teachers, as well as the interests of general readers and researchers considering specific short fiction. While each volume contains entries on "classic"stories frequently studied in classrooms, there are also entries containing hard-to-find information on contemporary stories, including works by multicultural, international, and women writers.

The information covered in each entry includes an introduction to the story and the story's author; a plot summary, to help readers unravel and understand the events in the work; descriptions of important characters, including explanation of a given character's role in the narrative as well as discussion about that character's relationship to other characters in the story; analysis of important themes in the story; and an explanation of important literary techniques and movements as they are demonstrated in the work.

In addition to this material, which helps the readers analyze the story itself, students are also provided with important information on the literary and historical background informing each work. This includes a historical context essay, a box comparing the time or place the story was written to modern Western culture, a critical overview essay, and excerpts from critical essays on the story or author. A unique feature of *SSfS* is a specially commissioned critical essay on each story, targeted toward the student reader.

To further aid the student in studying and enjoying each story, information on media adaptations is provided (if available), as well as reading suggestions for works of fiction and nonfiction on similar themes and topics. Classroom aids include ideas for research papers and lists of critical sources that provide additional material on the work.

Selection Criteria

The titles for each volume of *SSfS* were selected by surveying numerous sources on teaching literature and analyzing course curricula for various school districts. Some of the sources surveyed include: literature anthologies, *Reading Lists for College-Bound Students: The Books Most Recommended by America's Top Colleges*; *Teaching the Short Story: A Guide to Using Stories from around the World*, by the National Council of Teachers of English (NCTE); and "A Study of High School Literature Anthologies," conducted by Arthur Applebee at the Center for the Learning and Teaching of Literature and sponsored by the National Endowment for the

Arts and the Office of Educational Research and Improvement.

Input was also solicited from our advisory board, as well as educators from various areas. From these discussions, it was determined that each volume should have a mix of "classic" stories (those works commonly taught in literature classes) and contemporary stories for which information is often hard to find. Because of the interest in expanding the canon of literature, an emphasis was also placed on including works by international, multicultural, and women authors. Our advisory board members—educational professionals—helped pare down the list for each volume. Works not selected for the present volume were noted as possibilities for future volumes. As always, the editor welcomes suggestions for titles to be included in future volumes.

How Each Entry Is Organized

Each entry, or chapter, in *SSfS* focuses on one story. Each entry heading lists the title of the story, the author's name, and the date of the story's publication. The following elements are contained in each entry:

Introduction: a brief overview of the story which provides information about its first appearance, its literary standing, any controversies surrounding the work, and major conflicts or themes within the work.

Author Biography: this section includes basic facts about the author's life, and focuses on events and times in the author's life that may have inspired the story in question.

Plot Summary: a description of the events in the story. Lengthy summaries are broken down with subheads.

Characters: an alphabetical listing of the characters who appear in the story. Each character name is followed by a brief to an extensive description of the character's role in the story, as well as discussion of the character's actions, relationships, and possible motivation.

Characters are listed alphabetically by last name. If a character is unnamed—for instance, the narrator in "The Eatonville Anthology"—the character is listed as "The Narrator" and alphabetized as "Narrator." If a character's first name is the only one given, the name will appear alphabetically by that name.

Themes: a thorough overview of how the topics, themes, and issues are addressed within the story. Each theme discussed appears in a separate subhead, and is easily accessed through the boldface entries in the Subject/Theme Index.

Style: this section addresses important style elements of the story, such as setting, point of view, and narration; important literary devices used, such as imagery, foreshadowing, symbolism; and, if applicable, genres to which the work might have belonged, such as Gothicism or Romanticism. Literary terms are explained within the entry, but can also be found in the Glossary.

Historical Context: this section outlines the social, political, and cultural climate *in which the author lived and the work was created.* This section may include descriptions of related historical events, pertinent aspects of daily life in the culture, and the artistic and literary sensibilities of the time in which the work was written. If the story is historical in nature, information regarding the time in which the story is set is also included. Long sections are broken down with helpful subheads.

Critical Overview: this section provides background on the critical reputation of the author and the story, including bannings or any other public controversies surrounding the work. For older works, this section may include a history of how the story was first received and how perceptions of it may have changed over the years; for more recent works, direct quotes from early reviews may also be included.

Criticism: an essay commissioned by *SSfS* which specifically deals with the story and is written specifically for the student audience, as well as excerpts from previously published criticism on the work (if available).

Sources: an alphabetical list of critical material used in compiling the entry, with bibliographical information.

Further Reading: an alphabetical list of other critical sources which may prove useful for the student. Includes full bibliographical information and a brief annotation.

In addition, each entry contains the following highlighted sections, set apart from the main text as sidebars:

Media Adaptations: if availablee, a list of film and television adaptations of the story, including source information. The list also includes stage adaptations, audio recordings, musical adaptations, etc.

Topics for Further Study: a list of potential study questions or research topics dealing with the story. This section includes questions related to other disciplines the student may be studying, such as American history, world history, science, math, government, business, geography, economics, psychology, etc.

Compare and Contrast: an "at-a-glance" comparison of the cultural and historical differences between the author's time and culture and late twentieth century or early twenty-first century Western culture. This box includes pertinent parallels between the major scientific, political, and cultural movements of the time or place the story was written, the time or place the story was set (if a historical work), and modern Western culture. Works written after 1990 may not have this box.

What Do I Read Next?: a list of works that might complement the featured story or serve as a contrast to it. This includes works by the same author and others, works of fiction and nonfiction, and works from various genres, cultures, and eras.

Other Features

SSfS includes "Why Study Literature At All?," a foreword by Thomas E. Barden, Professor of English and Director of Graduate English Studies at the University of Toledo. This essay provides a number of very fundamental reasons for studying literature and, therefore, reasons why a book such as *SSfS*, designed to facilitate the study of literture, is useful.

A Cumulative Author/Title Index lists the authors and titles covered in each volume of the *SSfS* series.

A Cumulative Nationality/Ethnicity Index breaks down the authors and titles covered in each volume of the *SSfS* series by nationality and ethnicity.

A Subject/Theme Index, specific to each volume, provides easy reference for users who may be studying a particular subject or theme rather than a single work. Significant subjects from events to broad themes are included, and the entries pointing to the specific theme discussions in each entry are indicated in **boldface**.

Each entry may include illustrations, including photo of the author, stills from film adaptations (if available), maps, and/or photos of key historical events.

Citing Short Stories for Students

When writing papers, students who quote directly from any volume of *SSfS* may use the following general forms to document their source. These examples are based on MLA style; teachers may request that students adhere to a different style, thus, the following examples may be adapted as needed.

When citing text from *SSfS* that is not attributed to a particular author (for example, the Themes, Style, Historical Context sections, etc.), the following format may be used:

> "The Celebrated Jumping Frog of Calavaras County." *Short Stories for Students*. Ed. Kathleen Wilson. Vol. 1. Detroit: Gale, 1997. 19–20.

When quoting the specially commissioned essay from *SSfS* (usually the first essay under the Criticism subhead), the following format may be used:

> Korb, Rena. Critical Essay on "Children of the Sea." *Short Stories for Students*. Ed. Kathleen Wilson. Vol. 1. Detroit: Gale, 1997. 39–42.

When quoting a journal or newspaper essay that is reprinted in a volume of *Short Stories for Students*, the following form may be used:

> Schmidt, Paul. "The Deadpan on Simon Wheeler." *Southwest Review* 41.3 (Summer, 1956): 270–77. Excerpted and reprinted in *Short Stories for Students*. Vol. 1. Ed. Kathleen Wilson. Detroit: Gale, 1997. 29–31.

When quoting material from a book that is reprinted in a volume of *SSfS*, the following form may be used:

> Bell-Villada, Gene H. "The Master of Short Forms." *García Márquez: The Man and His Work*. University of North Carolina Press, 1990. 119–36. Excerpted and reprinted in *Short Stories for Students*. Vol. 1. Ed. Kathleen Wilson. Detroit: Gale, 1997. 89–90.

We Welcome Your Suggestions

The editorial staff of *Short Stories for Students* welcomes your comments and ideas. Readers who wish to suggest short stories to appear in future volumes, or who have other suggestions, are cordially invited to contact the editor. You may contact the editor via E-mail at: **ForStudentsEditors@cengage.com.** Or write to the editor at:

Editor, *Short Stories for Students*
Gale
27500 Drake Road
Farmington Hills, MI 48331-3535

Literary Chronology

1835: Mark Twain is born Samuel Langhorne Clemens on November 30, in Florida, Missouri.

1842: Ambrose Bierce is born Ambrose Gwinnett Bierce on June 24, in Megis County, Ohio.

1862: O. Henry is born William Sydney Porter on September 11, in Greensboro, North Carolina.

1873: Willa Cather is born on December 7, near Winchester, Virginia.

1880: Mark Twain's "Jim Baker's Blue Jay Yarn" is published.

1883: William Carlos Williams is born on September 17, in Rutherford, New Jersey.

1889: Ambrose Bierce's "A Horseman in the Sky" is published.

1897: William Faulkner is born William Cuthbert Falkner on September 25, in New Albany, Mississippi.

1904: Isaac Bashevis Singer is born Icek-Hersz Zynger on July 14, in Radzymin (some sources say Leoncin), Poland, near Warsaw. Some sources claim that Singer was born on November 21, 1902.

1904: Willa Cather's "A Wagner Matinee" is published.

1906: O. Henry's "After Twenty Years" is published.

1910: Mark Twain dies of failing health on April 21, in Redding, Connecticut.

1910: O. Henry dies of cirrhosis of the liver on June 5, in New York, New York.

1914: Ambrose Bierce is presumed to have died shortly after disappearing in Mexico.

1916: Shirley Jackson is born Shirley Hardie Jackson on December 14, in San Francisco, California.

1922: Grace Paley is born Grace Goodside on December 11, in New York, New York.

1931: E. L. Doctorow is born Edgar Lawrence Doctorow on January 6, in New York, New York.

1936: William Carlos Williams's "The Use of Force" is published.

1947: Willa Cather dies of a massive cerebral hemorrhage on April 24, in New York, New York.

1948: Shirley Jackson's "Charles" is published.

1949: William Faulkner is awarded the Nobel Prize in Literature.

1950: Julia Alvarez is born on March 27, in New York, New York.

1952: Judith Ortiz Cofer is born in Hormigueros, Puerto Rico.

1954: Sandra Cisneros is born on December 20, in Chicago, Illinois.

1955: William Faulkner is awarded the Pulitzer Prize for Fiction for *A Fable*.

1955: William Faulkner's "Race at Morning" is published.

1962: William Faulkner dies of a heart attack on July 6, in Byhalia, Mississippi.

1963: William Carlos Williams is awarded the Pulitzer Prize for Poetry for *Pictures from Brueghel and Other Poems*.

1963: William Carlos Williams dies of pulmonary illness on March 4, in Rutherford, New Jersey.

1963: William Faulkner is posthumously awarded the Pulitzer Prize for Fiction for *The Reivers*.

1965: Shirley Jackson dies of heart failure on August 8, in North Bennington, Vermont.

1966: Isaac Bashevis Singer's "Zlateh the Goat," is published.

1967: Jhumpa Lahiri is born in London, England.

1978: Isaac Bashevis Singer is awarded the Nobel Prize in Literature.

1984: E. L. Doctorow's "The Writer in the Family" is published.

1985: Grace Paley's "Anxiety" is published.

1991: Isaac Bashevis Singer dies following a series of strokes on July 24, in Surfside, Florida.

1991: Sandra Cisneros's "Eleven" is published.

1993: Judith Ortiz Cofer's "American History" is published.

1996: Julia Alvarez's "Liberty" is published.

1999: Jhumpa Lahiri's "This Blessed House" is published.

2000: Jhumpa Lahiri is awarded the Pulitzer Prize for Fiction for *Interpreter of Maladies*.

2007: Grace Paley dies of breast cancer on August 22, in Thetford Hills, Vermont.

Acknowledgments

The editors wish to thank the copyright holders of the excerpted criticism included in this volume and the permissions managers of many book and magazine publishing companies for assisting us in securing reproduction rights. We are also grateful to the staffs of the Detroit Public Library, the Library of Congress, the University of Detroit Mercy Library, Wayne State University Purdy/Kresge Library Complex, and the University of Michigan Libraries for making their resources available to us. Following is a list of the copyright holders who have granted us permission to reproduce material in this volume of *SSFS*. Every effort has been made to trace copyright, but if omissions have been made, please let us know.

COPYRIGHTED EXCERPTS IN *SSFS*, VOLUME 27, WERE REPRODUCED FROM THE FOLLOWING PERIODICALS:

American Literature, v. 26, January, 1955. Copyright © 1955 Duke University Press. Copyright © renewed 1983 by Duke University Press. All rights reserved. Used by permission of the publisher.—***Américas*** (English Edition), v. 59, March-April, 2007. Copyright © 2007 *Américas*. Reprinted by permission of *Américas*, a bimonthly magazine published by the General Secretariat of the Organization of American States in English and Spanish.—***CEA Critic***, v. 34, May, 1972 for "Further Freudian Implications in William Carlos Williams' 'The Use of Force,'" by Fergal Gallagher. Copyright © 1972 by the College English Association, Inc. Reproduced by permission of the publisher and the author.—***Critique***, v. 34, 1993. Copyright © 1993 by Helen Dwight Reid Educational Foundation. Reproduced with permission of the Helen Dwight Reid Educational Foundation, published by Heldref Publications, 1319 18th Street, NW, Washington, DC 20036-1802.—***European Journal of American Culture***, v. 21, 2002. Copyright © Intellect Ltd. 2002. Reproduced by permission.—***The Explicator***, v. 37, fall, 1978; v. 62, winter, 2004. Copyright © 1978, 2004 by Helen Dwight Reid Educational Foundation. Both reproduced with permission of the Helen Dwight Reid Educational Foundation, published by Heldref Publications, 1319 18th Street, NW, Washington, DC 20036-1802.—***Geographical Review***, v. 67, January, 1977. Copyright © 1977 by the American Geographical Society of New York. Reproduced by permission.—***The Lion and the Unicorn***, v. 27, September, 2003. Copyright © 2003 by The Johns Hopkins University Press. Reproduced by permission.—***Los Angeles Times Book Review***, April 28, 1991. Reproduced by permission.—***Mark Twain Journal***, v. 21, fall, 1983. Reproduced by permission.—***MELUS***, v. 19, spring, 1994; v. 22, fall, 1997; v. 29, fall-winter, 2004. Copyright © 1994, 1997, 2004 *MELUS: The Society for the Study of Multi-Ethnic Literature of the United States*. All reproduced by permission.—***Meridians: Feminism, Race, Transnationalism***, v. 3, spring, 2003. Reproduced by permission of Indiana University Press.—***Midamerica***, v. 14, 1987 for "Nebraska's Cultural Desert: Willa Cather's Early Short Stories," by Bruce P. Baker. Copyright © 1987 by the Society for the Study of Midwestern Literature. All rights reserved. Reproduced by permission of the publisher and the author.—***Midwest Modern Language Association***, v. 33, autumn-winter, 2001 for "Envisioning the Jewish Community in Children's Literature: Maurice Sendak and Isaac Singer," by Jill P. May. Copyright © 2001 by The Midwest Modern Language Association. Reproduced by permission of the publisher and the author.—***Midwest Quarterly***, v. IV, January, 1964. Copyright © 1964 by *The Midwest Quarterly*, Pittsburgh State University. Reproduced by permission.—***Mississippi Quarterly***, v. 36, summer, 1983; v. 49, summer, 1996. Copyright © 1983, 1996 Mississippi State University. Both reproduced by permission.—***The Nation***, v. 252, May 6, 1991. Copyright © 1991 by The Nation Magazine/The Nation Company, Inc. Reproduced by permission.—***Publishers Weekly***, April 5, 1985. Copyright © 1985 by Xerox Corporation./v. 238, March 29, 1991; v. 243, December 16, 1996. Copyright © 1991, 1996 by Reed Publishing USA. All reproduced from *Publishers Weekly*, published by the Bowker Magazine Group of Cahners Publishing Co., a division of Reed Publishing USA, by permission.—***Studies in American Fiction***, v. 19, autumn, 1991. Copyright © 1991 Northeastern University. Reproduced by permission.—***Studies in Short Fiction***, v. 31, 1994. Copyright © 1994 by *Studies in Short Fiction*. Reproduced by permission.—***The Women's Review of Books***, v. 11, July, 1994. Reproduced by permission.

COPYRIGHTED EXCERPTS IN *SSFS*, VOLUME 27, WERE REPRODUCED FROM THE FOLLOWING BOOKS:

Allison, Alida. From "Manuscript and Metaphor: Translating Isaac Bashevis Singer's Children's Stories," in ***Critical Essays on Isaac Bashevis Singer***. Edited by Grace Farrell. G. K. Hall & Co., 1996. Copyright © 1996 by G. K. Hall & Co. Reproduced by permission of Gale, a part of Cengage Learning.—Éjxenbaum, B. M. From ***O. Henry and the Theory of the Short Story***. Translated by I. R. Titunik. University of Michigan Press, 1968. Copyright © 1968 by the University of Michigan. All rights reserved. Reproduced by permission.—Kevane, Bridget. From "The Poetic Truth: An Interview with Judith Ortiz Cofer," in ***Latina Self-Portraits: Interviews with Contemporary Women Writers***. Edited by Bridget Kevane and Juanita Heredia. University of New Mexico Press, 2000. Copyright © 2000 by the University of New Mexico Press. All rights reserved. Reproduced by permission.—Langford, Gerald. From ***Alias O. Henry: A Biography of William Sydney Porter***. The Macmillan Company, 1957. Copyright © 1957 Gerald Langford. Copyright © renewed 1985 by Gerald Langford. Reproduced by permission of the author.—Madsen, Deborah L. From ***Understanding Contemporary Chicano Literature***. University of South Carolina Press, 2000. Copyright © 2000 University of South Carolina. Reproduced by permission.—Morris, Roy, Jr. From ***Ambrose Bierce: Alone in Bad Company***. Crown Publishers, Inc., 1995. Copyright © 1995 by Roy Morris, Jr. All rights reserved. Used by permission of the author.—Murphy, Bernice M. From "Introduction: 'Do You Know Who I Am?': Reconsidering Shirley Jackson," in ***Shirley Jackson: Essays on the Literary Legacy***. Edited by Bernice M. Murphy. McFarland and Company, Inc., 2005. Copyright © 2005 Bernice M. Murphy. All rights reserved. Reproduced by permission of McFarland & Company, Inc., P.O. Box 611, Jefferson NC 28640, *www.mcfarlandpub.com*.—Prewitt, Wiley C., Jr. From "Return of the Big Woods: Hunting and Habitat in Yoknapatawpha," in ***Faulkner and the Natural World: Faulkner and Yoknapatawpha, 1996***. Edited by Donald M. Kartiganer and Ann J. Abadie. University Press of Mississippi, 1999. Copyright © 1999 by University Press of Mississippi. All rights reserved. Reproduced by permission.—Stout, Janis P. From ***Willa Cather: The Writer and Her World***. University Press of Virginia, 2000. Copyright © 2000 by the University of Virginia Press. All rights reserved. Reproduced with permission of the University of Virginia Press.—Tokarczyk, Michelle M. From ***E.L. Doctorow's Skeptical Commitment***. Peter Lang, 2000. Copyright © 2000 Peter Lang Publishing, Inc., New York. All rights reserved. Reproduced by permission.—Wilson, James D. From ***A Reader's Guide to the Short Stories of Mark Twain***. G. K. Hall & Co., 1987. Copyright © 1987 by James D. Wilson. Reproduced by permission of Gale, a part of Cengage Learning.—Woodruff, Stuart C. From ***The Short Stories of Ambrose Bierce: A Study In Polarity***. University of Pittsburgh Press, 1964. Copyright © 1964 University of Pittsburgh Press. All rights reserved. Reproduced by permission.

Contributors

Bryan Aubrey: Aubrey holds a Ph.D. in English. Entries on "Liberty" and "This Blessed House." Original essays on "Liberty" and "This Blessed House."

Jennifer Bussey: Bussey is a freelance writer specializing in literature. Entry on "Jim Baker's Blue Jay Yarn." Original essay on "Jim Baker's Blue Jay Yarn."

Catherine Dominic: Dominic is a novelist and a freelance writer and editor. Entry on "A Wagner Matinee." Original essay on "A Wagner Matinee."

Joyce M. Hart: Hart is a freelance writer and the author of literary essays and several books. Entry on "American History." Original essay on "American History."

Neil Heims: Heims is the author of over two dozen books on literature and literary figures. Entry on "The Writer in the Family." Original essay on "The Writer in the Family."

Diane Andrews Henningfeld: Henningfeld is a professor of English who publishes widely on literary topics. Entry on "Eleven." Original essay on "Eleven."

Sheri Metzger Karmiol: Karmiol has a doctorate in English Renaissance literature. She teaches literature and drama at the University of New Mexico, where she is a lecturer in the University Honors Program. Karmiol is also a professional writer and the author of several reference texts on poetry and drama. Entry on "Anxiety." Original essay on "Anxiety."

David Kelly: Kelly is a writer and instructor of creative writing and literature at two colleges in Illinois. Entries on "After Twenty Years" and "The Use of Force." Original essays on "After Twenty Years" and "The Use of Force."

Claire Robinson: Robinson has an M.A. in English. She is an English literature and creative writing teacher and a freelance writer and editor. Entry on "Charles." Original essay on "Charles."

Bradley A. Skeen: Skeen is a classics professor. Entry on "A Horseman in the Sky." Original essay on "A Horseman in the Sky."

Leah Tieger: Tieger is a freelance writer and editor. Entries on "Race at Morning" and "Zlateh the Goat." Original essays on "Race at Morning" and "Zlateh the Goat."

After Twenty Years

O. HENRY

1906

O. Henry is one writer whose style is familiar to generations of readers the world over, and "After Twenty Years" presents a prime example of this style. A typical O. Henry story will involve two people with an emotional connection to each other that is put under stress by the circumstances they face. At the end of the story, a strange twist generally occurs. Sometimes it is a twist of fate, but sometimes the twist is a piece of information that was not previously available to the reader and that sheds a new light on all that has come before it. Though some readers feel that the twist shows an overly sentimental view of the human condition, many readers enjoy the way O. Henry's stories affirm the best things about the human condition.

The situation in "After Twenty Years" is simple and clearly defined: a man stands on a New York street, waiting for a friend that he agreed to meet twenty years earlier, and he explains his story to a passing policeman. It is a situation that can be understood by cultures all over the world, by one generation after the next.

The enduring popularity of O. Henry has given him a degree of public recognition that is unusual for a writer. The naming of the Oh Henry candy bar, first introduced in 1920, was almost certainly influenced by the public's familiarity with the writer's name. On a more serious note, one of the most prestigious literary prizes

O. Henry *(The Library of Congress)*

awarded each year is the O. Henry Award, given to writers who show excellence in the short story form.

"After Twenty Years" is frequently included in anthologies of short stories. It was originally published in O. Henry's 1906 collection *The Four Million*, which was reissued in 2003 by Wildside Press.

AUTHOR BIOGRAPHY

O. Henry was born William Sydney Porter in Greensboro, North Carolina, on September 11, 1862. His father was a physician. His mother died of tuberculosis when he was three, and responsibility for raising the child fell to his aunt and his grandmother. He was educated at his Aunt Lina's private school until he was fifteen, and in his teen years he worked at his uncle's pharmacy and became a licensed pharmacist.

When he was nineteen years old, health concerns forced Porter to move to Texas, where he lived on a sheep ranch belonging to Richard Hall, a family friend. He lived on the ranch for two years and then moved to Austin, where he spent several years working a variety of jobs, including real estate agent, draftsman, and teller at the First National Bank. Around that time he met Athol Estes, a seventeen-year-old woman from a wealthy family. Because of Porter's social position and the fact that Athol was ill with tuberculosis, her family opposed their romance. Porter eloped with her in 1887, and they went on to have three children, though one died soon after birth. Porter left First National Bank in the early 1890s to start a weekly humor magazine, the *Rolling Stone*. The magazine quickly failed, and in 1895, Porter and his young family moved to Houston where he began writing columns for the *Houston Daily Post*.

While he was working for the *Post*, he was charged with embezzlement after an investigation at the First National Bank. During his trial he left his wife and children behind and escaped to Honduras. Two years later, news reached him that Athol's tuberculosis had worsened significantly, so he returned to Austin. She died in 1898, and Porter's trial went on. He was found guilty of embezzling and on March 25, 1898, began a three-year sentence in an Ohio prison.

It was while he was in prison in Columbus, Ohio, that Porter began writing in earnest. He had stories published in *McClure's* and the *Outlook*, writing under the name O. Henry to hide his true identity. After his release from prison, he was living in poverty in Pittsburgh when the editors of *Ainslee's Magazine* offered him a guaranteed income if he would move to New York. He moved in 1902 and began publishing stories frequently in all of the top magazines. Within eight years he became one of the most widely read authors in America. During this period, "After Twenty Years" was first published as part of the collection *The Four Million*, in 1906.

His personal life was less successful, plagued by drinking and debts. In 1907 he married his childhood sweetheart, Sarah Lindsay Coleman of Weaverville, North Carolina, but they separated a year later. He died in New York City of cirrhosis of the liver on June 5, 1910.

PLOT SUMMARY

"After Twenty Years" takes place on a street in New York City around the turn of the twentieth century. Many of the businesses on the block are closed for the day. A policeman walks along the block, testing the doorknobs of businesses, making sure that they are locked and secure against

MEDIA ADAPTATIONS

- "After Twenty Years" is one of the short stories included in the audiotape collection *O. Henry Favorites*, released in 1987 by Listening Library of Old Greenwich, Connecticut. Readings in this collection are by Robert Donley and Jack Whitaker.
- This story is also one of five O. Henry stories included in the 2001 Naxos AudioBooks compact disc collection *Classic American Short Stories*, read by William Roberts.
- A short film titled *After Twenty Years* and starring Richard Keats and Glen Thompson was released on VHS videocassette by Coronet/MTI Film and Video in 1989.

burglars. In the doorway of a hardware store that is closed, he comes across a man who has an unlit cigar in his mouth. Before the officer can begin to question him, the man assures him that he is not a burglar, that he is merely waiting for a friend. He goes on to light his cigar and tell the officer why he and his friend are meeting at such a dark and desolate place.

Twenty years earlier, he explains, he and his friend had dinner at a restaurant called "Big Joe" Brady's, which used to be located where the hardware store stands. The officer confirms that this was the site of the restaurant up until five years earlier, when it was torn down. At the time of their last meal together, the man continues, he was eighteen years old and his friend Jimmy was twenty. The two had grown up together and were the closest of friends, but the man was leaving the next morning to go out to the West to find his fortune, and Jimmy was the type of person who would never leave New York. After eating their dinner that night, they agreed that no matter where they were or what they were doing, they would both do all they could to return to that same spot at that exact same time, ten o'clock, exactly twenty years later.

The officer expresses interest, asking why they had been in contact so seldom over the past twenty years. The man briefly explains that he has been busy in the West trying to make his fortune. He checks the time on his watch, which is adorned with diamonds, indicating that he has been successful in his business endeavors. The time is three minutes before ten o'clock, the precise moment that they are scheduled to meet. The officer stays a few minutes more, and it is after ten o'clock when he says goodbye and leaves.

The man waits twenty minutes more. Finally, another man approaches, bundled up against the light rain that has started to fall. The new man calls the man in the doorway Bob and answers to the name of Jimmy Wells. As they chat, Jimmy points out that he has not done as well financially as Bob: he has a position in a city department. He suggests that they go to a place that he knows of nearby, where they can get out of the rain and have a long talk about old times.

When they pass through the light emanating from the window of a drug store that is still open, Bob looks at the man he is with and exclaims with certainty that he is not Jimmy Wells. Though a man can change much in twenty years, he explains, the shape of his nose could never be so drastically altered. The other man says that he is in fact a plainclothes police officer, and that the man, whom he now refers to as "Silky" Bob, has been under arrest since they met ten minutes ago for warrants issued in Chicago.

He gives Bob a note and says that it is from "Patrolman Wells." In the note, the real Jimmy Wells explains that he was in fact the officer who was with Bob at the site of "Big Joe" Brady's restaurant at ten o'clock, but that when Bob struck a match to light his cigar, he recognized Bob's face as the one wanted in Chicago. Jimmy did not have the nerve to arrest his old friend, so he had left before he could be recognized and found a plainclothes officer to arrest him.

CHARACTERS

Bob

When he first appears in this story, Bob seems to have a sinister presence: he is standing in the shadows of a store that is closed, on a street that is deserted. He has a good explanation for why he is there, however, and he seems comfortable in the presence of the police officer who is on the lookout for suspicious activities. His story about going out to the West and successfully pursuing his fortune is supported by the diamonds on his watch and scarfpin, which show that he is a wealthy man and not a vagrant. His story is also supported by his knowledge of "Big Joe" Brady's restaurant, which had been torn down five years earlier.

Because he is in New York for a legitimate purpose, to see a friend from before his days as a criminal, Bob does not think about the fact that he is wanted by the police. He chats openly with the policeman, unaware that his picture has been forwarded from Chicago and that the policeman has seen it. While his innocence makes him miss some details, his criminal past also blinds him to the realities of the situation. He knows that he looks suspicious standing in a darkened doorway on a deserted street, and so he is not at all surprised that a policeman would approach him. Looking at the situation from a criminal point of view, he is conscious of looking like a law breaker, which makes Bob blind to the idea that the person who approaches him at ten o'clock on the appointed night at the appointed place might be the person whom he is scheduled to meet.

Throughout the story, Bob never explains what he has done out West to earn his fortune, only that life out there has given him everything he ever wanted. Readers never learn what crimes "Silky" Bob is wanted for in Chicago, only that he is established enough as a criminal to earn a criminal nickname.

The Plainclothes Officer

The plainclothes officer, not given a name in this story, is sent to trick the criminal known by the Chicago police as "Silky" Bob by pretending that he is Jimmy Wells. The real Jimmy has apparently briefed him on the situation: the officer mentions the restaurant that they were to meet at, the plan to have dinner there once again, and the fact that Bob has been living in the West. When asked about his own life, he truthfully states that he works for the city, avoiding mention of the police force. He leads Bob off to a place he knows of without indicating what that place might be.

He could have arrested Bob the minute that he approached him. The quiet, nonviolent way that he carefully leads him toward the police station is in keeping with Jimmy Wells's sorrow about having his friend arrested: the plainclothes officer allows Bob the dignity of walking along the street and believing himself to be a free man for just a few minutes longer.

The Policeman

See Jimmy Wells

Jimmy Wells

When he is first mentioned in the story, the man later identified as Jimmy is described as twirling his nightstick expertly, establishing that he has been a policeman for a considerable length of time. By referring to him only as "the policeman," O. Henry keeps Jimmy's identity a secret from the reader as well as from Bob.

Bob does not recognize his old friend on the darkened street because he is distracted by the uniform that Jimmy wears. Though he does not say so, the story implies that the Jimmy that Bob knew, twenty years earlier, was not the type one would expect to join the police force. Bob explains why he is there, and Jimmy, who needs no explanation, listens for a while. He does not reveal his true identity to his friend because the match that Bob ignites to light his cigar illuminates his face and shows him to be a wanted man. Jimmy is a conscientious officer in several ways. For one thing, he has paid close attention to the photos of wanted criminals that are sent to the New York police department from other parts of the country. More importantly, though, is the fact that Jimmy knows, as he listens to Bob reminisce about his old friend, that he will have to have Bob arrested.

Although he is more dedicated to the law than to his old friend, Jimmy still cannot forget his connection to Bob. The sentimental bond between them is so strong that Jimmy cannot arrest Bob himself, so he leaves and sends another officer to do it. He also takes the time to write a note to Bob, explaining himself, so that Bob will not think that Jimmy forgot about him after twenty years. His note is terse and offers no apology for having Bob arrested, but that is the best that Jimmy can do when he and a man who was once his best friend are on opposite sides of the law.

THEMES

Friendship

Friendship is at the heart of "After Twenty Years." The character who does the most talking, Bob, seems to be genuinely enthusiastic

TOPICS FOR FURTHER STUDY

- Study old newspapers, phone books, or other sources to find the name and location of a restaurant that was in business near you a hundred years ago. Prepare a multimedia presentation or collection of pictures to show how that location or nearby locations have changed over time.
- This story takes place in the first years of the twentieth century. Create a CD of songs that would have been popular then and might have been playing in the drug store where Bob and the plainclothes officer stop. Prepare a booklet that contains background information about the historical significance of the recordings you have chosen.
- Compile a collection of at least ten different shapes of noses, including the "Roman" and "pug" mentioned in the story. Have classmates work in groups to classify their own noses according to the forms you provide.
- In his note at the end of the story, Jimmy Wells explains that he went to find another policeman when he recognized Bob as a wanted criminal. Write a dialogue that they might have had if Jimmy had not recognized Bob as a criminal and if Bob had first realized that his old friend had grown up to be a policeman.

about seeing his old friend Jimmy. He speaks glowingly about what a great friend Jimmy was and relates that he has traveled across the country, over a thousand miles, to see him again. When he is questioned about whether Jimmy might forget about an appointment that was made so long ago, he says that Jimmy was the kind of friend who would remain true to the promise he once gave, despite whatever changes might have come to his life over the course of twenty years. Jimmy Wells also takes the bond of his old friendship with Bob seriously. He turns up at the appointed time to see his old friend, and, finding that his friend must be arrested, he leaves because he is emotionally incapable of performing the arrest himself.

Although this story does not discuss the nature of the friendship of these two men, it does present some implicit assumptions about friendship. First, it suggests that friendship can last for decades, even when the two friends have no contact with one another. Bob casually mentions that they have not even written letters to one another in a long time. Furthermore, the story suggests that friendship can be powerful enough to make a criminal like Bob sentimental for the days before his financial success, showing his faith in the Jimmy Wells that he remembers. Though his time in the West has obviously changed Bob in some ways, he is willing to forget his current status briefly in the memory of his old friendship.

Crime

O. Henry does not tell readers what crimes Bob is wanted for in this story, leaving them to piece together clues to determine what sort of man he might be. His criminal nickname, "Silky" Bob, indicates that he probably is not known for violent crimes, but for crimes that involve cunning and deception. The diamond-encrusted watch that he carries indicates that he finds it important to show off his wealth, which suggests that he may be a con artist, involved in crimes that require gaining the confidence of his victims by making them think he is rich.

One thing that is fairly clear is that Bob is a criminal of some significance. The police in Chicago have been unable to capture him, but they have watched him closely enough to make an educated guess about the fact that he is headed to New York. The telegraph that they sent with the description of "Silky" Bob was broadly distributed in the New York police department, given so much priority that a patrolman like Jimmy Wells would read it and memorize its details. When Bob talks about living out West, he first talks about making his fortune, but later he ominously suggests that the life that he has been leading has put a "razor-edge" on him, indicating that it has made him tough.

Duty and Responsibility

O. Henry puts the focus of "After Twenty Years" on the friendship between Bob and Jimmy, keeping readers interested in the fact that their relationship could survive even though they have not

New York City in the 1890s (© ClassicStock / Alamy)

been in contact for such a long time. While paying attention to their long separation and admiring the devotion that would drive Bob a thousand miles to visit a friend who might have forgotten about him, readers are distracted from other aspects that might interfere with the friendship between these two men. The fact that Jimmy turns out to be the patrolman that Bob told his story to is a surprise twist, but even more surprising is the fact that Jimmy could not reveal his identity because he felt obliged to have his friend arrested.

Jimmy's note, reproduced in the story's last paragraph, explains his moral situation: he still has a lingering emotional attachment to his old friend, but he also is responsible for upholding the law. His responsibility to the law takes precedence, and he arranges to have Bob arrested, though his emotional bond is still strong enough to prevent him from making the arrest himself. The note that he sends Bob might not help a criminal understand a police officer's sense of civic duty, but it does show Bob that turning him in is not an easy decision for Jimmy.

STYLE

Situational Irony

Situational irony is a plot device used in plays and in fiction in which the outcome is unexpected to the audience or reader. In "After Twenty Years," readers do not discover that Bob is a criminal until the last few lines of the story, when he is arrested. Rather, they are led to think of him as a loyal friend and successful businessman. Furthermore the story does not explain that the person referred to as "the policeman" is actually the same Jimmy Wells that Bob has been describing to the policeman until the arresting officer calls him "Officer Wells."

Although these final revelations change the story's meaning, astute readers have reasons to anticipate such a reversal of expectations. Readers who are familiar with O. Henry's fiction know that his stories commonly feature a surprise ending, and they read his stories trying to guess what it will be. In "After Twenty Years," readers can look back after reaching the last line and feel that the clues to the shift in situation are there all along: O. Henry has the policeman show up at the same time that Jimmy Wells was expected, and he has Bob mention the fact that he has scrabbled to make his fortune in the West. When it turns out that Bob is a criminal and that Jimmy is the officer he was talking to, many readers may be surprised and find it ironic that they could not see this logical outcome all along.

Third-Person, Limited Point of View

This story is told from a restricted third-person point of view. It does not offer readers insight into the thoughts of any of the characters but instead relates facts that anyone present could observe. The narration in this story is further limited to things that Bob can observe, such as the policeman who approaches twirling his club, and the stranger who approaches him later. The reader is not told that the person who Bob thinks is Jimmy is actually someone else until the moment that Bob says it out loud.

Because the point of view does not offer insight into Bob's mind, readers are kept from knowing that he is a wanted fugitive: they only know what he tells the police officer about himself. The limited point of view stays with him when the officer leaves, so readers do not know that the first officer has gone to phone a plainclothes officer. By carefully limiting the scope of the narrative, O. Henry is able to leave out information that would reveal the story's surprise ending without making reader aware that information has been left out.

HISTORICAL CONTEXT

In the first decade of the twentieth century, when this story was published, the social characteristics of the different geographic regions of the United States were much more distinct than they are in the twenty-first century. The Northeast, as the area originally settled by Europeans, continued to carry identifiable traces of European social structure. The South was an agricultural power that was still weakened after the Civil War thirty-five years earlier. The Midwest was built by immigrant labor during the Industrial Revolution of the late nineteenth century, and the Great Plains were known as a land of widely dispersed, lonely farms. At this time in the nation's history, the West was already shrouded in mythology as an open, untamed land where people with no social prospects could go, build fortunes, and create new personalities for themselves.

Since Europeans had moved from east to west across the continent, the area west of the settlement boundaries was considered the frontier. By the middle of the nineteenth century, the reach of the U.S. government had extended to the Pacific coast, with California becoming a state in 1850. California's early development is attributed to the discovery of gold ore there in 1848, along with its accessibility by ocean. The area between the Rocky Mountains and California developed more slowly over the second half of the century.

After the Civil War ended in 1865, the U.S. government took an active role in encouraging the development of the West. Settlers were able to claim hundreds of acres of land for free or for little money. U.S. Army troops were sent to protect the settlers by fighting wars against Native American tribes such as the Cheyenne, the Apache, the Kiowa, and the Comanche. Railroads were allotted massive land grants to unite the East and West Coasts.

The development of the West offered much to people who had little invested in the traditional social order, attracting a higher proportion of rough, antisocial lawbreakers than did the areas already settled. In addition, the quick development of such a wide-open area made law enforcement difficult to maintain. This led to an environment that encouraged lawlessness, earning the region the nickname "the Wild West." Common among men hired for their ability to do difficult work such as clearing timber, cultivating land, laying railroad track, fur trading, mining, and tending livestock were guns and alcohol, which often led to violence and criminal activity.

By the 1880s, the West's reputation for lawlessness had been absorbed into popular culture and was even glorified by it. William "Buffalo Bill" Cody, who made his reputation as a scout, put together a carnival-like traveling show that purported to bring the Wild West experience to cities. Outlaws like Jesse James and lawmen like Wyatt Earp became the heroes of legends, celebrated in the popular media of the day: popular songs and cheap, quickly published dime novels cranked out by anonymous writers. More serious writers, including William Sydney Porter (who would go on to write as O. Henry), Mark Twain, and William S. Hart brought interest in the lawless frontier into the literary salons of the East.

The census of 1890 made it clear that by that time the "wild" days were through, the West was

COMPARE & CONTRAST

- **1906:** O. Henry names the collection that this story comes from *The Four Million* in reference to the four million people crowding New York City.

  Today: New York's population tops eight million at the turn of the twenty-first century.

- **1906:** Criminals are identified by their appearance. Fingerprinting, which uses traits that are unique to the individual, is introduced to the United States in 1906.

  Today: Fingerprinting is still used to confirm a person's identity. DNA testing is also regularly used to link a person to a crime scene.

- **1906:** Rail travel is the fastest way to go across the country. A person traveling from the West to New York has to travel for several days.

  Today: A person can fly across the country, meet a friend, and be back home within a day.

- **1906:** Friends living far apart seldom send photographs. Photographic equipment is only owned by photographers, and pictures must be sent through the mail.

  Today: A picture taken on one end of the continent can show up on a friend's phone or computer on the other coast within seconds.

- **1906:** Many police officers in major cities patrol by foot, making them aware of suspicious loiterers.

  Today: Although police officers are trained to look for unusual characters, their vantage from patrol cars makes them focus on more obvious suspects.

- **1906:** Only a few businesses are open in New York City after ten o'clock at night.

  Today: New York, like any major city, has an abundance of stores and restaurants that are open throughout the night.

settled. Since then, though, that area of the country has continued to represent a time in America's history when laws were a matter of strength and conscience and individuals struggled with nature as much as they did with their fellow humans. Though the country has become more homogenized by mass communication and transportation, so that a mall in New Mexico is nearly identical to one in Maine or Florida or Michigan, many Americans still recognize the historical significance of the area referred to as "the West." As O. Henry does in "After Twenty Years," television shows and movies use the West of the 1880s to represent a time when a man with nothing could create his own fortune, often by breaking the law.

CRITICAL OVERVIEW

O. Henry was a very popular writer in the first decade of the twentieth century. From the publication of his first book, *Cabbages and Kings*, in 1904, to his death in 1910, he published hundreds of stories. In the decade after his death, his publisher put out five more collections of his works in an attempt to keep up with popular demand. His works have been translated into dozens of languages and published in millions of volumes. They were particularly familiar in the Soviet Union, where O. Henry achieved almost cultlike status.

In the United States, critical praise for O. Henry faded at about the same time that his general popularity began to wane. This shift in the interest of the literary community was foreseen by Hyder E. Rollins, who complimented the writer's use of slang in his dialog in a 1914 article in the *Sewanee Review*, stating that "in his unexcelled mastery of slang our author was quite effective." But, Rollins noted, "taste changes and, what is more pertinent, slang itself changes, so that his constant use of slang will some day count heavily against him." He summarized the fading of O. Henry's reputation this way: "That

O. Henry's piquant audacities of style are attractive is indisputable, but they are certain to lose their piquancy and to lower his rank in literature."

In 1924, fourteen years after O. Henry's death, N. Bryllion Fagin suggested in *Short Story Writing: An Art or a Trade?* that looking at O. Henry's stories when

> not blinded by hero-worship and popular esteem, discloses at best an occasional brave peep at life, hasty, superficial and dazzlingly flippant: an idea, raw, unassimilated, timidly works its way to the surface only to be promptly suppressed by a hand skilled in producing sensational effects. At its worst, his work is no more than a series of cheap jokes renovated and expanded. But over all there is the unmistakable charm of a master trickster, of a facile player with incidents and words.

Over a hundred years later, O. Henry is often forgotten by popular audiences, who by definition tend to turn their attention to contemporary works. He does, however, maintain a loyal base of support along with a small, focused group of fans. Literary critics tend to respect his storytelling skills more than they admire any particular stories.

CRITICISM

David Kelly

Kelly is a writer and instructor of creative writing and literature at two colleges in Illinois. In this essay, he uses "After Twenty Years" to explore the schism between readers who love O. Henry's works and those who find them lacking.

In the last decade of his life and in the years following his death in 1910, O. Henry, the pen name chosen by William Sydney Porter, was a household name throughout the United States. This was, of course, an easier feat for a writer to achieve back then, before the age of electronic communication, when newspapers were a primary source of popular entertainment. Many of O. Henry's stories appeared in newspapers before being anthologized in collections under his name. When motion pictures made storytelling a popular visual and aural enterprise, the general interest in printed stories dropped, and the subsequent ascension of radio, television, and the Internet drove the popular imagination further and further away from published fiction. In the modern atmosphere of media saturation, it is not at all certain that O. Henry would be the national success that he was during his lifetime.

> "O. HENRY WAS A TALENTED CRAFTSMAN WHO KNEW HOW TO ACHIEVE THE EFFECTS HE WANTED, BUT HE WAS ALSO A COMPROMISED ARTIST WHO USED HIS TALENTS TO ACHIEVE MUCH LESS THAN COULD HAVE BEEN GOTTEN WITH THEM."

Still, after a hundred years, he maintains a strong fan base. Collections of his books are still in print, and faithful readers have stood by him through many changes in understanding of what the short story is and can be. The fact that O. Henry's style of writing is continually gaining new readers can be viewed in two ways. Some people would maintain that he was a populist writer whose knowledge of how to use flat characters and manipulate sentimentality to reach the lowest common denominator would speak to audiences in any generation. Others see his longevity as a sign that Porter was such a keen observer of the human condition that time could only dim, but not erase, the impact of his talent.

Proponents of either argument would agree on one thing: that standards and expectations in the short story have changed. Most of O. Henry's stories are plot driven, relying on a surprise reversal of situation at the end that he used so regularly it earned its own name, the "O. Henry twist." The twist made his stories entertaining at a time when readers looked to stories to be entertained. However, as the main function of fiction shifted from entertainment to art in the late twentieth century, short stories came to be judged by the artistic elements they had to offer, such as character analysis or explorations on the nature of fiction itself. It would not be fair to judge O. Henry's writing by standards that he was not trying to meet, but then, there is the constant question of whether or not literary standards exist that should apply to all works of all times.

There are some very good reasons to admire O. Henry's writing. He had a masterful control of his stories and their intended effects. It takes

WHAT DO I READ NEXT?

- The author of "After Twenty Years" is the protagonist of Steven Saylor's novel *A Twist at the End: A Novel of O. Henry*, published in 2000. In this book, Saylor imagines a murder mystery involving William Sydney Porter in 1885 that later comes back to haunt Porter, now O. Henry, as he is living in New York in 2006.
- O. Henry's best-known and frequently reprinted short story is "The Gift of the Magi," about a poor young couple in New York and the sacrifices they undergo to buy Christmas presents for each other. This story, like "After Twenty Years," was originally published in *The Four Million* in 1906, and it is available in *41 Stories by O. Henry*, a Signet Classic book published in 2007.
- In his lifetime, O. Henry was often compared with the French writer Guy de Maupassant, whose stories, written in the late 1800s, also often included a surprise twist at the end. De Maupassant's famous and frequently anthologized story "The Necklace" is about a vain woman who borrows an expensive necklace and then loses it. First published in 1884, it is included in the Penguin Popular Classics collection of de Maupassant's *Selected Short Stories*, published in 1998.
- When O. Henry was alive, critics compared his works to those of Frank Norris, one of the writers often associated with American naturalism. Norris is remembered as a muckraking journalist who used his fiction to expose society's injustices, but he also wrote moving short stories about the human condition. Norris's autobiographical story "Dying Fires," written around the turn of the century and published in *The Third Circle* in 1909, is available in *The Best Short Stories of Frank Norris*, published in 1998 by Ironweed Press.
- Another writer with whom O. Henry is frequently compared is the British author Saki, which is the pen name used by Hector Hugh Munro. Writing around the same time as O. Henry, Saki also often ended his short stories with surprising plot twists, though his stories take place in upper-class England and his style is much more acerbic and macabre. One of Saki's best-known stories, "Tobermory," is about a cat who develops the power of speech and ends up telling all of the secrets of the residents of a manor house. Published in the collection *The Chronicles of Clovis* in 1912, it can be found in *The Complete Saki*, a Penguin Twentieth-Century Classics edition published in 1998.
- O. Henry's colorful life story has fascinated generations of his fans. The definitive biography of the author is Gerald Langford's 1957 book *Alias O. Henry: A Biography of William Sydney Porter*, first published by the Macmillan Company in 1957 and released in a revised edition in 1983.
- Angela M. Blake's book *How New York Became American, 1890–1924* examines how the city, considered by many to be dark and overrun with crime at the turn of the century, transformed its image with careful management of its urban identity to a tourist destination. Published by the Johns Hopkins University Press in 2006, this book offers an excellent academic examination of the city's status at the time when O. Henry wrote.

nothing short of mastery to pull off the surprise ending, not just once or twice, but time and time again, to lull readers into a sense of security and then trick them even when they think they are braced for the coming reversal. The twist relies on a careful balance of skillful language, particular characters, and a strong authorial discernment that controls which details are revealed and which are withheld. On the other hand, readers looking for art would question his decision to end the story with a twist at all, charging that it forces him to present highly sentimentalized, unrealistic characters in unlikely situations, offering readers little to learn about their lives. Looking at a typical O. Henry story like "After Twenty Years" shows just how correct both sides were. O. Henry was a talented craftsman who knew how to achieve the effects he wanted, but he was also a compromised artist who used his talents to achieve much less than could have been gotten with them.

"After Twenty Years" takes place in a simple setting—it stays within a unified time frame, over the course of half an hour or less, in one spot, a doorway, until the characters stroll a few doors up the block at the end. The characters have simple and easily identifiable motives: friendship, trust, and duty. The situation presented is not quite a situation that many people are likely to encounter in their lives, but that is no reason to criticize it. Fiction, as much as television and movies, often features characters in particular professions, such as law enforcement, legal practice, and medicine, because individuals in these fields deal with serious matters of life and death, guilt and innocence, or, as in this story, personal loyalties and social order. A little divergence from reality is sometimes necessary for an author to make a point.

Therefore, the problem is not that O. Henry uses an artificial situation to make a point but that he does not have any particular point to make. He uses the situation solely to surprise the reader with plot twists. Twists can be interesting, and the way that the story surprises readers can be looked at as an intellectual puzzle, but they do little to engage the reader on an emotional level.

There are three twists in "After Twenty Years," working with varying degrees of success. The first surprise for readers is that the person walking beside Bob at the end is not his old friend Jimmy. Astute readers might be able to anticipate this turn of events if they notice the evasive language that O. Henry uses: not only does he have the man who walks up fail to answer the direct question "Is that you, Jimmy Wells?" but the narrator also refers to him indirectly, as "the new arrival" and "the other," instead of simply calling him by name. This is the kind of reversal that readers will blame themselves for not expecting; therein lies the delight of a well-designed puzzle. Readers will say that they did not see it coming, but should have.

The second twist comes as a bigger surprise, and it is deftly played. It is the fact that Bob, who has been doing much of the talking throughout the story, is actually a wanted criminal. The reason it surprises readers is that Bob, for all his talking by the time this fact comes up, has said nothing that could let readers predict it. Bob does have a diamond-laden watch, but there are certainly enough legitimate businesses in the West of the 1880s, such as mining, cattle, or lumber, that could make a man rich. There would be no way for even a careful reader to predict that the fortune that Bob has made for himself was attained through crime. Although this plot twist seems to come from nowhere, however, it is the most satisfying because of the way that O. Henry springs it on his readers. Bob is under arrest before readers even know that he is a criminal: for readers, the shock of the arrest comes before the reason for it. In this case, O. Henry comes as close as a writer can to springing unsupported information on the reader, or pulling an unexpected detail out of thin air.

By comparison, the final plot twist is weak; it is somewhat unexpected, but just not very interesting. Readers find out in the last paragraph that the man Bob was waiting for, Jimmy Wells, was in fact the police officer he talked to earlier. Serious readers cannot be too surprised by this revelation. All along, the story is headed toward an explanation of what happened to Jimmy. Since he is not Bob or the arresting officer, it makes sense that he would be the only other character. Also, readers can look back from the end and see that the uniformed officer was the one who was at the appointed place at the appointed time with Bob. Of course he is Jimmy Wells.

The fact that Jimmy is the uniformed officer is somewhat ironic, given that Bob has become a criminal, but O. Henry is only able to add this irony by putting his story through some contortions that stretch credibility and empathy beyond the breaking point. The characters serve as broad symbols of their positions, not as representatives of people who might actually exist.

If any character in this story could be expected to show individual personality, it would be Bob.

He does most of the talking. He is the one who has traveled to see his old friend Jimmy for several reasons. On a basic level, he has arrived at his appointment because he is a man of his word, and he promised twenty years earlier that he would be back. On another level, he could be, like any person who attends a school reunion after becoming successful in the world, looking to show off. Later, when it is revealed that Bob is a wanted criminal, much more opportunity for psychological complexity arises. Readers cannot be too sure of what drives Bob: is it loyalty, pride, or even a psychological repression of his guilt that compels him to return to the last place of his innocence?

In a more artistic story, these issues would be acknowledged and explored, even if the author did not want to provide any simple answers. But O. Henry does not use "After Twenty Years" to indulge in curiosity about what could drive a man like Bob. There are no allusions to Adam losing his chance at peace in Eden, no references to wealth's inability to wash away the crimes that made a man rich. Bob's hands tremble when he reads Jimmy's note at the end, but O. Henry does not tell readers if that trembling is from anguish or rage.

At the end of the story, the focus shifts from the character who has been the center of attention all along to the character who has been absent throughout, Jimmy Wells. Instead of probing Bob's personality, readers are asked, in the last paragraph, to think about a new situation: the moral dilemma that faced Jimmy when he showed up to meet his old friend and ended up having to arrest him.

Jimmy's dilemma is only engaging in theory and lacks true emotional impact. It is introduced in the story after the difficult decision has already been made. Jimmy does not consider his actions within the story's narrative, but instead he explains them after he has acted. Readers are deprived of being participants in Jimmy's decision to have Bob arrested, as if there were no moral question involved. Yes, Bob is a criminal, but, judging by the nickname "Silky," he is probably not a violent criminal. In fact, O. Henry conspicuously omits telling readers what his crimes might be. He is a loyal friend, which is clear not only from the fact that he traveled so far to make a twenty-year-old appointment, but also in his unquestioning faith that Jimmy will show up, too. Aside from the basic rule that criminals belong in jail, there is no explanation for why Jimmy's betrayal of Bob's trust is the right thing to do. Artistic stories exist to question basic rules, while formulaic stories rely on them to establish guidelines that general audiences can recognize.

The readers who love O. Henry's stories love them for the same reasons that people like crossword puzzles and riddles: they are exercises in form. For these readers, there is no rule, written or unwritten, that says that literature must be deep. The critics who dismiss O. Henry's stories like "After Twenty Years," on the other hand, have particular expectations for fiction writers, and when they look at his stories, they are likely to find those expectations left unsatisfied.

Source: David Kelly, Critical Essay on "After Twenty Years," in *Short Stories for Students*, Gale, Cengage Learning, 2009.

B. M. Éjxenbaum

In the following excerpt, Russian literary scholar Éjxenbaum focuses on O. Henry's use of parody and irony in his short stories, contrasting the earlier stories of The Four Million *with his later stories.*

...O. Henry's literary beginnings were extremely characteristic for the nineties: the feuilleton, parody, anecdote—such were his first ventures published in the little humor magazine, the *Rolling Stone* (1894). Among these pieces, incidentally, there are parodies on Sherlock Holmes detective mysteries ("Tracked to Doom or the Mystery of the Rue de Peychaud,""The Adventures of Shamrock Jolnes" and "The Sleuths"). These stories are something like Bret Harte's "Condensed Novels"—detective mysteries carried to the absurd: instead of arresting the criminal whom he encounters in a saloon, the detective hastens to jot down in his note-book the details of the place, the time of the encounter, etc.; horrors come thick and fast; situations, surprises and transformations are of the most improbable sort—in short, all the stereotypes hyperbolized. Alongside these pieces we find an anecdote ("A Strange Story") about a father who went out to get some medicine for his sick child and returned home with the medicine after a lapse of so many years that he had since become a grandfather: he kept missing the streetcar.

Prison brought this newspaper work to an abrupt halt, cutting off O. Henry's contact with the literary world. However, as can be seen from

> "THE GENUINE, ORIGINAL O. HENRY IS FOUND IN HIS COMIC, PICARESQUE AND PARODIC STORIES, STORIES WITH SURPRISE ENDINGS, WITH CLEVER DIALOGUE AND IRONIC AUTHOR COMMENTARY."

Jennings' memoirs, he continued to write, using material collected during his stay in Austin, Texas, and in South America. One of his first stories written after prison was "A Retrieved Reformation" (about Jimmy Valentine), the details behind which were mentioned above. To this same period belong "The Duplicity of Hargraves,""Roads of Destiny" and others. In these O. Henry is far from parody; he is sometimes even serious, sentimental or emotional. Such is the general character of his first collection of stories, *The Four Million* (1906), which includes stories written between 1903 and 1905. Interestingly enough, O. Henry did not include in this collection certain stories written and published during this same period, considering them, evidently, unsuited to the collection as a whole. O. Henry apparently aimed at a certain cyclical organization when selecting stories for inclusion in collections. In certain instances, as will be seen later on, this cyclical organization is also supported by a unity of principal characters (Jeff and Andy in *The Gentle Grafter*), and sometimes the connection between the stories is underscored by their being called "chapters," as they are in the collections *Heart of the West* and *Whirligigs*. . . .

However consistent and homogeneous—and, in many people's opinion, even monotonous—O. Henry's work might appear, there are noticeable vacillations, transitions and a certain evolution to it. Sentimental stories—stories about New York shop girls or others of the type of "Georgia's Ruling"—predominate in the years immediately following his imprisonment (though they do also appear later). Generally speaking, the comic or satiric and the sentimental do very often go together in the poetics of one and the same writer in just their function of correlated contrasts; this is what we find in the work of Sterne, of Dickens and, to some extent, in the work of Gogol. In O. Henry this combination stands out with particular relief owing to the fact that his basic orientation toward the anecdote with its unexpected and comically resolved ending is so extremely well-defined. His sentimental slice-of-life pieces, therefore, give the impression of experiments—so much the more because they are all of them, in terms of technique and language, much weaker than the others. Usually they are drawn-out, wishy-washy, with endings which disappoint the reader and leave him feeling unsatisfied. The stories lack compactness, the language is without wit, the structure without dynamism. American critics, it is true, would seem ready to place these stories higher than all the others, but that is an evaluation with which we find it difficult to agree. An American, in his leisure time at home, readily gives himself over to sentimental and religious-moralistic reflections and likes to have appropriate reading. That is his custom, his tradition, a feature of national history conditioned by the peculiarities of his way of life and civilization. . . .

Working in the literary trade and tied down by the conditions of his contract and the need to make his writing "pay off," O. Henry was obliged to write stories to suit a variety of tastes, including those of newspaper editors and readers. Any story writer could have produced "Georgia's Ruling,""Blind Man's Holiday," "A Fog in Santone." The genuine, original O. Henry is found in his comic, picaresque and parodic stories, stories with surprise endings, with clever dialogue and ironic author commentary. They are the ones brimful of literary irony arising in consequence of his sensitivity to clichés both of language and of story structure. Unlike Mark Twain, O. Henry does not deal in straight humor; in his hands anecdote constantly turns into parody, into play on form, into material for literary irony—precisely the shape regeneration of a genre takes. O. Henry often stands on the brink of parodying the short story itself, reminding one of Sterne's devices in his novel-parody *Tristram Shandy*.

Let us start with his language, although for the Russian reader this aspect of O. Henry's stories is, of course, largely lost. Work on his language was about the most important thing for O. Henry. The stories, on being read, may appear to have been written swiftly and effortlessly, without any particular care taken to work them over or to revise them, without any special selection of words. Jennings, who remained on friendly terms with O. Henry after his imprisonment, recounts how O. Henry worked. A whole night was spent writing "The Halberdier of the Little Rheinschloss" and the story was finished by noon the next day:

> At about 10 minutes after 12 he called me up.
>
> "You're late. I'm waiting," he said.
>
> When I got to his room the big table where he did his writing was littered with sheets of paper. All over the floor were scraps of paper covered with writing in long hand.

In response to Jenning's question whether he always worked that way, O. Henry opened a desk drawer and said, "Look at those," pointing to "a crammed-down heap of papers covered with his long freehand." He did not usually make preliminary drafts; he would start writing only when the story was completely finished in his mind. But the work over his language was an involved process:

> O. Henry was a careful artist. He was a slave to the dictionary. He would pore over it, taking an infinite relish in the discovery of a new twist to a word.
>
> One day he was sitting at the table with his back to me. He had been writing with incredible rapidity, as though the words just ran themselves automatically from his pen. Suddenly he stopped. For half an hour he sat silent, and then he turned around, rather surprised to find me still there.
>
> "Thirsty, colonel? Let's get a drink."
>
> "Bill," my curiosity was up, "does your mind feel a blank when you sit there like that?" The question seemed to amuse him.
>
> "No. But I have to reason out the meaning of words."

Elsewhere Jennings recalls having spent several hours in O. Henry's room waiting for him to finish writing a story: "He was writing with lightning speed. Sometimes he would finish a page and immediately wrinkle it into a ball and throw it on the floor. Then he would write on, page after page, with hardly a pause, or he would sit silent and concentrate for half an hour at a stretch."

Thus, the construction of the story from beginning to end (rather, it would be better to say in this case—from end to beginning) had already formed in O. Henry's mind before he sat down to write, which is, of course, a very characteristic feature both for the short story . . . and for O. Henry. What he did at his desk was to work out the details of language and narration. What sort of work was that, what principles guided him, what procedures did he use? The basic principle was to get rid of stylistic clichés, to come to grips with "bookishness," with the slick "middle" style and to subject the "high" style to irony. This opened the way for his extensive use of slang in crime stories, his express avoidance of "artiness," his unfailingly downgrading images, their humor stemming from their oddity and unexpectedness, and so on. Frequently we find in O. Henry an attitude of outright irony toward one or another literary style, an irony which has the effect of bringing his own principles into the open. In "Let Me Feel Your Pulse," he even names names. After giving an account of the doctor's examination of his patients, O. Henry says: "I'll bet that if he had used the phrases: 'Gaze, as it were, unpreoccupied, outward—or rather laterally—in the direction of the horizon, underlaid, so to speak, with the adjacent fluid inlet,' and 'Now, returning—or rather, in a manner withdrawing your attention, bestow it upon my upraised digit'—I'll bet, I say, that Henry James himself could have passed the examination" (making reference to the complexity and ornateness of James' style); or in the same story, on description of mountains: "It was about twilight, and the mountains came up nobly to Miss Murfee's description of them."

At those points in his stories where the need to advance the narrative or tradition would have made a special description requisite, O. Henry turns the occasion to literary irony. Where another story writer would have used the opportunity to wax eloquent or to transmit detailed information about his characters—their personalities, outward appearances, dress, past history,—O. Henry is either exceedingly terse or ironic: "Old Jacob Spraggins came home at 9:30 p.m., in his motor car. The make of it you will have to surmise sorrowfully; I am giving you unsubsidized fiction; had it been a street car I could have told you its voltage and the number of flat wheels it had." ["A Night in New Arabia"] There you have a typical O. Henry twist. Another instance of the same kind—a description of the hero: "Overlooking your mild impertinence in feeling a curiosity about the personal appearance of a stranger, I will give you a modified description of him. Weight, 118; complexion, hair and brain, light; height, five feet six; age, about twenty-three; dressed in a $10 suit of greenish-blue serge; pockets containing two keys and sixty-three cents in change. But do not misconjecture because this description sounds like a General Alarm that James was either lost or a dead one." ["What You Want"] Sometimes the irony is underscored by parody. O. Henry simulates verbosity: "Ileen was a strictly vegetable compound, guaranteed under the Pure Ambrosia and Balm-of-Gilead Act of the year of the fall of Adam. She was a fruit-stand blond—strawberries, peaches, cherries, etc. Her eyes were wide apart, and she possessed the calm that precedes a storm that never comes. But it seems to me that words (at any rate per) are wasted in an effort to describe the beautiful. Like fancy, 'It is engendered in the eyes.' There are three kinds of beauties—I was foreordained to be homiletic; I can never stick to a story." ["A Poor Rule"]

The parodic device of substituting the language of an official report for literary description, such as in the example above, is systematically employed in the story "A Municipal Report." The story is, in the broad, a polemic—an answer to Frank Norris's assertion that only three cities in the United States were "story cities"—New York, New Orleans and San Francisco, whereas Chicago, Buffalo or Nashville held but nothing for a story writer. The story takes place, as a matter of fact, in Nashville, but instead of describing the city, O. Henry interpolates into the text quotations from a guidebook which clash with the style of the usual literary description. The very fact of inserting such quotations carries with it the character of parody. The narrator arrives in the city on a train: "All I could see through the streaming windows were two rows of dim houses. The city has an area of 10 square miles; 181 miles of streets, of which 137 miles are paved; a system of waterworks that cost $2,000,000, with 77 miles of mains." Further on, in a conversation between the narrator and one of the characters: "'Your town,' I said, as I began to make ready to depart (which is the time for smooth generalities), 'seems to be a quiet, sedate place. A home town, I should say, where few things out of the ordinary ever happen.' It carries on an extensive trade in stoves and hollow ware with the West and South, and its flouring mills have a daily capacity of more than 2,000 barrels."

It is an interesting fact that this parodic or playful use of quotation—one of O. Henry's most constant stylistic devices—was noted long ago by American critics. O. Henry quotes Tennyson, Spenser and others, informing their words with new meaning, inventing puns, deliberately misquoting parts, and so on. Russian readers unfortunately miss all of this as they also do, for the most part, those instances of play on words in O. Henry's crime stories which are motivated by the speaker's illiteracy (for example, confusion of scientific words as in the case of "hypodermical" instead of "hypothetical").

O. Henry's characters often behave in a way not usual in books, and this oddity of behavior is also sometimes underscored by the author himself. The hero of "A Technical Error," Sam Durkee, is preparing himself to commit an act of blood revenge ("feuding" is one of the traditional motifs in American fiction): "Sam took out and opened a bone-handled pocket-knife and scraped a dried piece of mud from his left boot. I thought at first he was going to swear vendetta on the blade of it, or recite 'The Gipsie's Curse.' The few feuds I had ever seen or read about usually opened that way. This one seemed to be presented with a new treatment. Thus offered on the stage, it would have been hissed off.... During the ride Sam talked of the prospect for rain, of the price of beef, and of the musical glasses. You would have thought he had never had a brother or a sweetheart or an enemy on earth. There are some subjects too big even for the words in the 'Unabridged.'" It is curious that this last notion, encountered constantly in the old romanticists (*cf.* the ending of *Dvorjanskoe gnezdo* [A Nest of Gentlefolk]) and used to motivate "ineffability" or reticence, serves in O. Henry's case to motivate the unexpectedness of what his characters say or do in an excited state—an unexpectedness of a literary nature.

The general observation should be made that O. Henry's basic stylistic device (shown both in his dialogues and in the plot construction itself) is the confrontation of very remote, seemingly unrelated and, for that reason, surprising words, ideas, subjects or feelings. Surprise, as a device of parody, thus serves as the organizing principle of the sentence itself. It is no accident that he goes out of his way to avoid orderly and scrupulous descriptions and that his heroes sometimes speak in a completely erratic way; the verbiage in these instances is motivated by a special set of circumstances or causes....

It is highly characteristic of O. Henry's general parodic bent that he frequently takes problems having to do with literary practice itself as themes for his stories, making theoretical and ironic comments on matters of style and now and again having his say about editors, publishers, reader demands and so on and so forth. Some of his stories remind one of the once very popular sonnet parodies where the subject matter was the process of composing a sonnet itself. These pieces disclose a very keen awareness on O. Henry's part of forms and traditions and confirm the view of his work as a sort of culmination point reached by the American short story of the nineteenth century. He was a writer of fiction no less than he was critic and theorist,—a feature very characteristic of our age which has completely dissociated itself from the naïve notion that writing is an "unconscious" process in which all depends on "inspiration" and "having it inside one." We haven't had a parodist with so subtle a knowledge of his craft, so inclined time and again to initiate the reader into its mysteries, probably since the time of Laurence Sterne.

However, first a few words more about O. Henry's style. His narration is invariably ironic or playful. His writing is studded with metaphors but only for the purpose of disconcerting or amusing the reader with the unexpectedness of the comparisons made—a surprise of a literary nature: their material is not traditional and usually runs counter to the "literary norm," downgrading the object of comparison and upsetting the stylistic inertia. This applies with particular frequency to descriptive passages about which, as we have seen above, O. Henry maintained an invariably ironic attitude. For instance, when describing a city, he says: "Though the dusk of twilight was hardly yet apparent, lights were beginning to spangle the city like pop-corn bursting in a deep skillet." ["Compliments of the Season"] There is no need to multiply examples—the reader of O. Henry cannot fail to notice them. A detailed and serious literary description of anything whatsoever is the height of absurdity in O. Henry's eyes. When putting a novice writer to the test (in "The Plutonian Fire"), O. Henry, who plays the role of his friend in the story, suggests: "'Suppose you try your hand at a descriptive article... giving your impressions of New York as seen from the Brooklyn Bridge. The fresh point of view, the———.' 'Don't be a fool,' said Pettit. 'Let's go have some beer.'" Naturally enough, in the narrative and descriptive passages of his stories, O. Henry more often than not enters into conversation with his reader, making no point of arousing in him an illusion of direct contact or of reality but rather forever emphasizing his role as the writer and, therefore, conducting the story not from the standpoint of an impersonal commentator but from that of his own person. He brings in an outside narrator (as in his crime stories) in those cases where there is occasion for using slang, for playing on words, or the like.

Given such a system of narration, dialogue stands out with particular relief and takes on a substantial share of the effect of plot and style. The terseness of the narrative and descriptive commentary is naturally compensated for by the dynamism and concreteness of speech in the dialogues. The conversations of the characters in O. Henry stories always have a direct connection with the plot and with the role the character in question plays in it; they are rich in intonations, fast-moving and often devious or ambiguous in some special way. Sometimes a whole dialogue will be built on an incomplete utterance or on mutual misunderstanding with implications, in certain cases, not only for style but for the plot, as well. In "The Third Ingredient," one girl talks about her trip and its unhappy outcome (she had thrown herself into the river in despair), while at the same time the other girl is preparing beef stew and lamenting the fact that she has no onion to put in it:

> "I came near drowning in that awful river," said Cecilia, shuddering.
>
> "It ought to have more water in it," said Hetty; "The stew, I mean. I'll go get some at the sink."
>
> "It smells good," said the artist.
>
> "That nasty old North River?" objected Hetty. "It smells to me like soap factories and wet setter-dogs—oh, you mean the stew. Well, I wish we had an onion for it." And so on.

A curious fact in this connection is that there is a kind of submerged analogy in the story between the role of the onion in the dish being prepared (meat and potatoes) and the role of the young man who appears at the end of the story (with onion in hand). The analogy comes out explicitly in Hetty's line with which the story ends. In another story ("The Ransom of Mack"), two friends carry on a conversation from which it is possible to conclude that Mack is getting married (a conclusion that Mack's friend does make). Taking his words in that meaning, the friend undertakes a whole complicated scheme designed to prevent the marriage from happening only to find out at the end of the story that Mack's words, "I'm going to marry the young lady who just passed tonight," plus his and the bride's subsequent words, meant only that Mack, no other suitable person being available, was going to perform the marriage rites himself.

Thus, in O. Henry's hands the short story undergoes regeneration, becoming a unique composite of literary feuilleton and comedy or vaudeville dialogue. . . .

Source: B. M. Éjxenbaum, Excerpts, in *O. Henry and the Theory of the Short Story*, translated by I. R. Titunik, University of Michigan Press, 1968, pp. 1–31.

Gerald Langford

In the following excerpt, Langford offers a summary of events surrounding the publication of The Four Million, *the collection including the story "After Twenty Years."*

. . . In April, 1906, Porter's second book was published: *The Four Million*, a collection of stories selected almost entirely from back numbers of the *World*. Approaching the editor for permission to republish the stories, Porter was so diffident that he offered to write the *World* a free story in return for the favor he was asking: an offer which was naturally declined by an editor accustomed to granting such permission as a matter of course. *The Four Million*, containing such favorites as "The Gift of the Magi," "Mammon and the Archer," "An Unfinished Story," and "The Furnished Room," was well received by the critics, though not so enthusiastically as the opinions expressed some years later would lead one to expect. "These sketches of New York life are among the best things put together in many a day," the *Critic* said. "The author," explained the *Independent*, "thinks that no cold 'Four Hundred' should limit our interest, as there are at least four million people in the metropolis who are worth writing about. . . . A bit like 'An Unfinished Story' is of more value than many long and labored books upon social conditions." The *Bookman*, although preferring *Cabbages and Kings*, agreed with the publishers' comparison of O. Henry with Maupassant: "Beyond this we need say nothing." The book even attracted the notice of the *Atlantic Monthly*, whose reviewer wrote:

> His stories are pervaded by gentleness. In symbolism and color his slang need not yield to that of Mr. George Ade; he knows his world as well, but he sees it with an eye for its beauty as well as its absurdity. There is imagination as well as vision, and beyond his expert knowledge of our colloquial tongue he possesses in the background, to be used when needed, a real style. . . .
>
> [By way of comparison with certain French writers:] Where their tendency is to forget that they are writing stories, to approximate as far as possible to a literal document, 'O. Henry' does not hesitate to round out, to fill in, to take advantage of coincidence, in short, to indulge his reader's weak-minded craving for a little human enjoyment. . . . And perhaps his picture with its glimmer of arc light and sunshine may be to the full as true as if it were altogether drawn in India ink and charcoal.

Looking through such reviews with Porter, his friend Hart MacArthur remarked: "You're a casual cuss. I would feel pretty happy if any work of mine should ever count for so much." To which Porter replied, "Train's late for any happiness, colonel."

It was after reviewing *The Four Million* for the Pittsburgh *Gazette* that George Seibel heard from one of his associates the story of the silver dollar which Porter had borrowed when he was preparing to move from Pittsburgh to New York. Seibel wrote up the story for the *Gazette*, and three months later, in July, Porter walked into the newspaper office to introduce himself while on one of his visits to see Margaret. Delighted at meeting the famous author, Seibel insisted on taking Porter home to lunch and afterward (since he was a member of the Board of Education) out to the auction of a run-down, discarded schoolhouse in one of the suburbs. "I've had a bit of experience in a land office," Porter told him. "I'll be an Eastern capitalist looking for investments, and maybe I can get you a better price by bidding up the property. I always felt I'd like to impersonate a plutocrat, and here's my chance at last." Porter's scheme worked, and the Board of Education was able to sell the property without incurring the loss which the members had feared was inevitable.

During the same summer, back in New York, Porter seems to have been sufficiently struck by a story called "Her That Danced," recently published in *McClure's*, to have expressed a wish to meet the author, a Mrs. Wilson Woodrow. A mutual friend, Archibald Sessions, then editor of *Ainslee's*, arranged a dinner for the three of them at the Café Francis, but Porter when he came was in one of his low moods. Mrs. Woodrow, who had been greatly flattered at the invitation, later wrote that her first impression of him was one of severe disappointment. For fully half of the evening Porter seemed "stolid" and so unresponsive that she "had the miserable feeling that I was a failure as a guest." Then, abruptly and unaccountably, Porter came alive, and in the light of the second half of the evening and of later meetings Mrs. Woodrow wrote: "I am sure that if his table-talk had ever been taken down in shorthand, it would have sounded very much like his written dialogue.... His wit was urban, sophisticated, individual.... It was packed with world-knowledge, designed to delight the woman of thirty, not of twenty, and yet I never heard him tell a story even faintly risqué. He was the most delightful of companions... and his wit never flagged; quite effortless, it bubbled up from an inexhaustible spring."

Porter's humor, Mrs. Woodrow suggested, was—like his formality of manner—a sort of protective armor worn by an extremely sensitive man. Of this hidden self she could only suggest the nature by describing two bare glimpses. At the time of their first meeting, Upton Sinclair's novel *The Jungle* had just been published, and Porter, like herself, was not eating meat after reading the book. On a later occasion they emerged from another restaurant to find rain pouring down to the accompaniment of lightning and thunder. In the cab that took them home the two of them crouched in apprehensive silence, for Porter had not outgrown his terrifying experience at the Halls' ranch in Texas.

Later in the same year or early in 1907 Porter met William Griffeth, who had succeeded Theodore Dreiser as editor of the *Broadway Magazine* and who tried to enlist Porter as a contributor. This proved a difficult undertaking because of Porter's chronic indebtedness to a small group of editors who had advanced him money for future stories. Griffeth, too, later commented on Porter's initial reserve. But after the ice was broken he found the man more interesting than his stories—a criticism which suggests what no one except Porter himself ever put so succinctly: that Porter was potentially a finer writer than he actually turned out to be, that his work never really did justice to his talent....

Source: Gerald Langford, "Chapter 11," in *Alias O. Henry: A Biography of William Sydney Porter*, The Macmillan Company, 1957, pp. 197–209.

Edward C. Echols

In the following essay, Echols identifies various classical allusions that O. Henry used in his short stories.

In addition to its contribution along humorous lines, the classical allusion is employed by O. Henry with serious and often significant intent. The 375 serious allusions in his short stories vary from the obvious and casual to references which assume a rather advanced classical knowledge for full comprehension. The average reader may have no difficulty with Cupid, Psyche, Jupiter, Juno, Mars, Minerva, *et al.*, but an appreciation of an "Autolycan adventure" and an "Autolycan adventurer" demands a better-than-average classical background.

The Classics find a broad range in O. Henry. Hotels have classical names: the Acropolis Hotel, the Hotel Lotus, the Hotel Thalia, the Hotel King Clovis. Parian and Carrara marbles are noted. Classical first names are frequent, often with symbolic meaning. Among the names are Septimius, Telemachus, Caligula, Artemisia, Aglaia, Calliope, Amaryllis, and the aptly-chosen Uncle Caesar of "A Municipal Report."*The Morning Mars* is a newspaper; there is a *Minerva Magazine*. There is a ship, the Ariadne, and a coal-black horse is named Erebus. Fifteen story-titles have classical overtones. It may be only coincidence that the premiere of O. Henry's one musical comedy was held in Aurora, Illinois.

The Classics stand as a convenient symbol of the educated man. In "Buried Treasure," a young man who had "all the attainments to be found in books—Latin, Greek ... " and who quoted "translations from the Greek at much length," poses the question: "Can there be anything higher than to dwell in the society of the classics ...?" By contrast, his unlettered rival says of himself that he never went "any further into Latin than simple references to *Orgetorix, Rex Helevetii.*"

Two snowbound Westeners find occasion for regret: "If we'd studied Homer or Greek ... we'd have some resources in the line of meditation and thought." Included in the description of a Westerner: "Any subject you brought up old Cal could give you an abundant synopsis of it from the Greek root.... " A cattleman says of his traditional enemy: "I never had believed in harming sheep men.... I see one, one day, reading a Latin grammar on hossback, and I never touched him." The whole West is classical; "I mean the modern Indian—the kind that takes Greek prizes in college.... "

A New York waiter-philosopher states the case for the educated man: "All the heroes on the bum carry the little book. It's either Tantalus or Liver or Horace, and it's printed in Latin...."

The Classics serve O. Henry most effectively in the many figurative comparisons. The more adequate similes include: as proud as Cicero; as proud as Julius Caesar; triumphant as Minerva; as simply as Homer sang; as big as the Iliad; quiet as a street in Pompeii; more like a dark horse than Pegasus; and crying like Niobe or Niagara.

Classical allusions add deft touches to personal descriptions. A face appeared as "clearly chiselled as a Roman emperor's on some old coin." An old negro had "a face that reminded me of Brutus." "Undisputed sway had molded him to the likeness of a fatted Roman emperor." "He wore a suit of dark cheviot that looked to have been draped upon him by an ancient Greek tailor...."

In "The Enchanted Profile," a girl who was "a holdover from the Greek classics" and "purely Paradisiac, not Olympian," turned "pink, perfect statue that she was—a miracle (shared) with Pygmalion only." Sunlight "burnished her heavy hair to the color of an ancient Tuscan's shield." "There were a thousand golden apples coming to her as Helen of the Troy laundries." "The bride wore a simple white dress as beautifully draped as the costumes of the ancient Greeks."

Sparta provides several references. "He was a lucky man... even though he were imitating the Spartan boy with an ice cream freezer beneath his doublet frapéeing the region of his heart." "It was the room of a Spartan or a soldier (!)." A Kentuckian, off to New York, "packed a carpet-sack with Spartan *lingerie*."

Still in the urban mode, "I can live as Nero lived while the city burns at ninety in the shade." The same city "seemed stretched on a boiler directly above the furnaces of Avernus." "'... New Yorkers, the most progressive and independent citizens of any country in the world,' I continued, with the fatuity of a provincial who has eaten the Broadway lotus." "But in New York you must either be a New Yorker or an invader of a modern Troy, concealed in the wooden horse of your own conceited provincialism."

The Classics point up the weather in "the January blasts (were) making an Aeolian trombone of the empty street" and "the Aeolian chorus of the wind in the house crannies." Markedly effective is: "At its worst... (snow) is the wand of Circe. When it corrals man in lonely ranches... the snow makes apes and tigers of the hardiest."

Latin makes a contribution. "*Omne mundus in duas partes divisum est*—men who wear rubbers and pay poll-taxes, and men who discover new continents." "You should know that *omnae* (*sic*) *personae in tres partes divisae sunt*. Namely: Barons, Troubadours, and Workers." Transients "carry their *lares et penates* in a bandbox." The weeks march along with "'Tempus fugit' on their banners" and two friends in the tropics help along "old tempus fugit with rum and ice and limes." An Unreconstructed Rebel, who asserts that "the Confederacy is running along as solid as the Roman empire," informs a Yankee in "Two Renegades" that "we sent a good many of ye over to old *mortuis nisi bonum*."

The following miscellaneous group will serve further to emphasize the range and subtlety of the allusions. The secrets of the ancients include "Etruscan inscriptions." An amateur night in vaudeville is an "illegal holiday of the Romans." A thug's "hand was itching to play the Roman and wrest the rag Sabine...." In "The Skylight Room," a girl climbs a "Stygian stairway" to an "Erebus of a Room." A tramp's "Odyssey would have been a limerick, had it been written," while a Westerner anticipates hearing an "Odyssey of the chaparral." In Mexico, "The mountains reached up their bulky shoulders to receive the level gallop of Apollo's homing steeds." "The bread of Gaul... (is) compounded after the formula for the recipe for the eternal hills." An editorial writer "lopped off the heads of the political hydra." In one of the best of the comparisons, a girl sees the disapproving congregation of her small village church as a "hundred-eyed Cerberus that watched the gates through which her sins were fast thrusting her."

O. Henry notes the decline in classical learning, apparently evident even in his day: "Where to go for wisdom has become a matter of serious import. The ancients are discredited...." Yet he falls back on the Classics as a frame of reference universally understood. It is doubtful that the writer of the present day can safely assume that marked degree of classical knowledge on the part of his theoretically better educated reader.

Source: Edward C. Echols, "O. Henry and the Classics," in *Classical Journal*, Vol. 44, No. 3, December 1948, pp. 209–211.

Hyder E. Rollins

In the following excerpt, Rollins analyzes O. Henry's mastery of the short story genre, claiming that although he does not consider O. Henry a great writer, he may be one of the best American writers of the short story.

. . . All critics, so far as I know, class O. Henry's stories as hyphenated, capitalized "Short-Stories"; but if they hold to the hidebound *a priori* rules which require a short-story to fulfil the three classic unities, to deal with one character only, and to show rigid compression and condensation of details, they are hoist with their own petard. For O. Henry gleefully breaks every rule and heartily enjoys the critics' discomfiture. The only thing that may be confidently postulated of his stories is that they usually produce a single effect on the mind of the reader. This alone, it would seem, is enough to make a short story a "short-story": most certainly it was the ideal that Poe had in mind. O. Henry recognized no rigid, unalterable laws of structure: the story was the thing, and there was a best method of telling each story. Indeed he declared: "Rule I of story-writing is to write stories that please yourself. There is no rule 2. In writing, forget the public. I get a story thoroughly in mind before I sit down at my table. Then I write it out quickly, and without revising it, send it to my publishers. In this way I am able to judge my work almost as the public judges it. I've seen stories in type that I didn't at first blush recognize as my own."

The elucidation was unnecessary, for his stories plainly evince such workmanship. That O. Henry was a technical artist, few will deny: even his mannerisms, such as his interpolative comments on plot-structure and his pseudo-moralizing divagations, cannot debar his narratives from the short-story class. Nevertheless, it is to be regretted that he took so many liberties, for his mannerisms may soon cease to amuse, and they are likely to lower his rank in literature.

It was quite usual for him to ramble carelessly afield, making sundry vague remarks about the attitude of the Columbia College professors towards grammar and the plagiarism he is contemplating, and then to lament that, in thus sparring for an opening, he has forgotten to follow Aristotle's directions! Or to open a story with the casual remark that "It was a day in March," and to advise: "Never, never begin a story this way when you write one. No opening could possibly be worse. It is unimaginative, flat, dry and likely to consist of mere wind." In later stories, such as "The Unprofitable Servant," he makes no 'bones' of confessing that he wrote thus in order "to swell the number of words" for which he was paid. Indisputably this is attractive, though one feels that it is unwarranted, that the author has taken an undue advantage to secure humor. The truth is O. Henry failed to take himself and his art seriously. He strove only to arrest the momentary attention of the rapidly moving mass of readers. And in his stories the first sentence, which is customarily some such remark as "No, bumptious reader, this is not a continuation of the Elsie series," invariably does this. Furthermore, since the preconceived effect that his stories attempt to produce is usually one of surprise or humor, his introductions always aid in producing this effect.

"THERE CAN BE LITTLE DOUBT THAT IT IS THE PRESENCE OF SLANG THAT MAKES O. HENRY APPEAL SO STRONGLY TO THE GENERAL READING PUBLIC TO-DAY; FOR THE PUBLIC IS DRAWN TO A WRITER WHO SCORNS ACADEMIC NICETIES OF SPEECH AND STRIKES OUT ON A NEW PATH, UNTRAMMELLED BY CONVENTION."

There is little skirmishing in the body of his stories: it progresses rapidly, and shows a rigid economy of words. O. Henry's mania for suppression of detail comes nearer to equalling that of "Guy de Mopassong" (as he calls him) and of other French writers than does that of any other American writer, not excepting Poe. He had a distinct aim, and he wrote every word with this aim in view. His stories are customarily short: not many run over three thousand words, and the majority contain about two thousand.

Yet, paradoxical as it may seem, nearly every one of his stories contains one or more digressions, which always seem necessary, and which remind one forcibly of Thackeray.

His conclusions—they are O. Henry's and no one else's. Children play "crack-the-whip," not for the fun of the long preliminary run, but for the excitement of the final sharp twist that throws them off their feet. So adults read O. Henry, impatiently glancing at the swiftly moving details in pleased expectancy of a surprising ending. The conclusion is an enigma: the author has your nerves all a-quiver until the last sentence. There are few explanations, the surprise comes quickly, and the story is finished. O. Henry is as much a master of the unexpected ending as Frank Stockton was of the insolvable ending, and one must admire his skill. For although these endings are unexpected, the author never makes any statement in the body that can be held against him. On the contrary, the body is a careful preparation for the dénouement, even if the most searching reader can seldom detect it.... But the continued use of the unexpected ending grows tiresome, and when one sits down and reads all or the greater part of the two hundred and forty-eight short stories, he feels that the biggest surprise O. Henry could have given him would have been a natural, expected ending. But it should be added that his surprise endings have none of the brutal cynicism which distinguishes de Maupassant's "Necklace" and Mérimée's "Mateo Falcone"; his endings, on the other hand, are genuinely humorous, genuinely sympathetic, and genuinely human.

For the sake of vividness the majority of the short stories are told in the first person. Either a character who participated in the action is the narrator; or an outsider tells the story as a participant told it to him; or the story is told apparently in the third person until the author intrudes with his own comments and makes it a first-person narrative. At other times the strict third-person narrative is used; but in whatever way the stories are told, O. Henry is always talking, always explaining his views.

Stages of plot as definite as those in the Shakesperean drama may be located in most of his stories, and they are well adapted for dramatization, as the recent success of *Alias Jimmy Valentine, A Double-Dyed Deceiver*, and others show. This goes to prove that even though O. Henry pokes fun at all rules, he obeys them in the fundamental particulars. He is a clever architectonist in spite of himself. While he prided himself upon his disregard of conventional rules and upon his originality, his technique (if one ignores his manneristic digressions) conforms closely to the very rules that he affected to despise.

Life is a mixture of smiles and sniffles and sobs, with the sniffles predominating, declared O. Henry in "The Gift of the Magi." The petty joys, the petty pretentions, the petty worries of his people confirm the statement; but he also has the idea that life is one constant surprise, that the unexpected continually happens. He is, then, a pure romanticist who strives earnestly for realistic effects.

[O. Henry's characters] are described by their actions, or by brief, trenchant sentences that are hurled at our heads, as "He wore heliotrope socks, but he looked like Napoleon." O. Henry uses rapid suggestive—never detailed circumstantial—description that is highly colored by bold figures of speech. Where many writers would waste three hundred words in a vain attempt to catalogue features so as to put an image of a character in one's mind, O. Henry can in twenty five words paint a clear, unforgettable picture. No other writer has excelled him in the use of suggestive description. Sometimes his characters are described by their unusual surroundings. But since he seldom assumes complete omniscience, it is rare that he attempts any psychological analysis.

Subjectivity of delineation makes our author's characters interesting chiefly as they reveal his views of life, and interest in characters is overshadowed by interest in plots. But for briskness, sympathy, and humor of characterization, O. Henry has few peers.

Just as his plots and his characters are humorous in conception and in treatment, so the most striking trait of O. Henry as a stylist is humor. In most instances his fun bubbles out spontaneously, but *The Gentle Grafter* bids somewhat too plainly for laughter. His stories show few pathetic-comic mixtures, for he recognizes no pathos save that of monotony, of degradation, of lost ambition, which is inherent in the lives of people; but they do show mixtures of sentiment and humor that verge on the ridiculous. Some of his means for securing humorous effects have already been noted: other and less satisfactory means used to attain this result are a continual juggling of words, execrable punning, and a superabundance of faulty literary allusions.

Humor lightens even the brief descriptions that are scattered through his stories. There is little more tendency to adjectivity in his descriptions of objects than there is in his descriptions of persons. The force and vividness of his descriptions are due rather to unusual words, to an abundance of verbs that suggest sound and movement, to numerous and striking similes and metaphors.

About O. Henry's diction let me explain in the apt words of one of his characters: "That man had a vocabulary of about 10,000 words and synonyms, which arrayed themselves into contraband sophistries and parables when they came out." His vocabulary, which is really very large, is a servant, not a master. He had absolutely no respect for conventional usage. Words must be coined to express his thought, or the usual meaning of words must be distorted; O. Henry did both without compunction. In addition to this maltreatment of words (and in the mouths of his low characters it becomes mere punning), his vocabulary was stretched by an appalling number of slang words and slang phrases. There can be little doubt that it is the presence of slang that makes O. Henry appeal so strongly to the general reading public to-day; for the public is drawn to a writer who scorns academic niceties of speech and strikes out on a new path, untrammelled by convention. There is no doubt, further, that in his unexcelled mastery of slang our author was quite effective. But taste changes and, what is more pertinent, slang itself changes, so that his constant use of slang will some day count heavily against him.

Henry Ward Beecher, who is reported to have said that when the English language got in his way it didn't stand a chance, had a worthy disciple in O. Henry. For the latter not only made a servant of words, but he also made a servant of grammar and rhetoric. It is amusing when he writes a sentence abounding in pronouns, becomes confused, and cries in parentheses, "Confound the English language," but it is also cheap. Like Mr. Kipling he affects the verbless and fragmentary sentence, often with good results; and his paragraphs often lack ease of movement, composed as they are of intentionally jerky sentences. That O. Henry's piquant audacities of style are attractive is indisputable, but they are certain to lose their piquancy and to lower his rank in literature.

On the other hand, his stories have the absolute harmony of tone so essential to the short-story writer. Harmony is felt even in "Let Me Feel Your Pulse," a short story that opens with broad burlesque and ends in the subtly allegorical. There is, also, a nice proportion, an artistic condensation of details, and a vividness of style that call to mind Poe in America, Mr. Kipling in England, and de Maupassant in France.

Many of his stories are marred by local and contemporaneous allusions that in a few years will be pointless and vague.... However pleasing such allusions may be when they are penned, they fail to interest succeeding generations. The slanginess of his style, too, is certain to render him distasteful, perhaps unintelligible, to future readers, just as it has already hindered the translation of his stories into foreign languages. Slang is ephemeral. It will make one a writer for the hour, not a writer for all time. Realizing this, O. Henry had planned a series of new stories. "I want to show the public," he said, "that I can write something new—new for me, I mean—a story without slang, a straightforward dramatic plot treated in a way that will come nearer my ideal of real story-writing." "The Dream," which was to be the first of the new series, was broken off in the middle of a sentence by his death. In its incomplete form it appeared in the September, 1910, *Cosmopolitan*,—a more pathetic "unfinished story" than that of Dulcie.

If necessary, O. Henry's claim to permanence in American literature could be based, like Poe's, on his mastery of the short-story form, for in this respect no other American writer has excelled him. But he has other admirable traits: his frank individuality, his genuine democracy, his whole-souled optimism, his perennial humor, his sympathetic treatment of characteristic American life are irresistible.

For several years O. Henry has been the most popular short-story writer in America, and the "four million" have cried for more stories. It would be absurd to say that the inherent value of his work was not primarily the cause of his popularity, for although slangy mannerisms might attract readers, the latter will not be held if there is not something worth while in the stories themselves; and it seems improbable that the public will soon change from an enthusiastic to a Laodicean temper. To judge O. Henry as if he were a novelist is unfair. He wrote only short stories. He should be judged only by the short-story standard. And although I cannot consider O. Henry great, because of the limitations previously mentioned, yet I do believe that he will always be counted as one of the best American writers of the short story. . . .

Source: Hyder E. Rollins, "O. Henry," in *Sewanee Review*, Vol. 22, No. 2, Spring 1914, pp. 213–32.

SOURCES

Fagin, N. Bryllion, "O. Henryism," in *O. Henry: A Study of the Short Fiction*, edited by Eugene Current-Garcia, Twayne Publishers, 1993, p. 168; originally published in *Short Story-Writing: An Art or a Trade?*, Thomas Seltzer, 1923.

Hansen, Henry, "Foreword," in *The Complete Works of O. Henry*, Doubleday, 1953, pp. v–x.

Henry, O., "After Twenty Years," in *The Complete Works of O. Henry*, Doubleday, 1953, pp. 88–91.

Luedtke, Luther S., and Keith Lawrence, "William Sydney Porter," in *Dictionary of Literary Biography*, Vol. 78: *American Short-Story Writers, 1880–1910*, edited by Bobby Ellen Kimbel and William E. Grant, Gale Research, 1989, pp. 288–307.

"Rise of Industrial America, 1876–1900: Frontier Justice," in *Library of Congress American Memory Timeline*, http://memory.loc.gov/ammem/ndlpedu/features/timeline/riseind/west/justice.html (accessed August 20, 2008).

Rollins, Hyder E., "O. Henry," in *O. Henry: A Study of the Short Fiction*, edited by Eugene Current-Garcia, Twayne Publishers, 1993, p. 158; originally published in *Sewanee Review*, Vol. 22, April 1914.

"Settling the West," Web site of the New York Public Library, http://www.nypl.org/west/hw_settl.shtml (accessed August 20, 2008).

U.S. Census Bureau, "Table 2—Increase in Population of States and Territories at Each Census, 1790 to 1890," in *Report on Population of the United States at the Eleventh Census: 1890*, Part 1, http://www2.census.gov/prod2/decennial/documents/1890a_v1-06.pdf (accessed August 20, 2008).

FURTHER READING

Courtney, Luther W., "O. Henry's Case Reconsidered," in *American Literature*, Vol. 14, No. 4, 1943, pp. 361–72.

Courtney gives a thorough examination of the case that sent O. Henry to prison, finding that the stories about his innocence are probably just the result of his fans' unwillingness to see their hero's flaws.

Gallegly, Joseph, *From Alamo Plaza to Jack Harris's Saloon: O. Henry and the Southwest He Knew*, Mouton, 1970.

Although "After Twenty Years" does not talk much about the West, the author's familiarity with life out on the frontier is implied throughout the story. This book shows how O. Henry was influenced by the time he spent there in his formative years.

Monkkonen, Eric H., *Police in Urban America, 1860–1920*, Cambridge University Press, 2004.

This book, part of the "Interdisciplinary Perspectives on Modern History" series, looks at how the rise of uniformed policemen during the named period helped shape the identities of the cities they patrolled.

O'Quinn, Trueman E., and Jenny Lind Porter, *Time to Write: How William Sydney Porter Became O. Henry*, Eakin Press, 1986.

This book combines biographical information about Porter's four years in prison with photos of places associated with his life around that time, and it includes twelve complete stories that he wrote while in prison.

Smith, Alonso, *O. Henry*, Martin and Hoyt, 1916.

This biography has the distinction of being written shortly after William Sydney Porter's death. Smith had access to original letters and manuscripts and to many people who knew O. Henry personally.

American History

JUDITH ORTIZ COFER

1993

Judith Ortiz Cofer's short story "American History" is a coming-of-age tale set in the early 1960s, when racism and segregation were still in full bloom. The story's fourteen-year-old protagonist, Elena, is a Puerto Rican immigrant living with her family in Paterson, New Jersey, when President John F. Kennedy is assassinated. Despite this tragic event, Elena is focused on Eugene, her new neighbor and the object of her daydreams. When Elena visits Eugene that evening, she experiences her own personal tragedy in the form of prejudice.

"American History" first appeared in Cofer's collection *The Latin Deli: Prose and Poetry* in 1993. This collection of poetry and prose won two honors: the Anisfield Wolf Book Award in 1994 and a placement on the Georgia Center for the Books Top 25 Reading List. Cofer's story has also been anthologized in the 2002 collection *Big City Cool: Short Stories about Urban Youth*, edited by M. Jerry Weiss and Helen S. Weiss.

AUTHOR BIOGRAPHY

Judith Ortiz Cofer is often referred to as a Latina writer because of her Puerto Rican heritage and her emphasis on the Hispanic experience in her writing. She was born in Hormigueros, Puerto Rico, in 1952. When she was three years old, her family left the island and moved to the United

States, finding a home in Paterson, New Jersey. Cofer's father was a member of the U.S. Navy and was stationed at the Brooklyn Navy Yard. Cofer's mother, who missed her homeland, often took Cofer back to Puerto Rico for extended visits. Sometimes Cofer stayed in Puerto Rico long enough to attend school there. This provided Cofer with the strong bicultural background that is reflected in her writing.

The family moved to Georgia when Cofer was a teen. After graduating from high school, Cofer was accepted at Georgia's Augusta College, where she earned an English degree in 1974. She then attended Florida Atlantic University in Boca Raton and received a master's degree in English in 1977. A few years later, Cofer took a teaching position at the University of Georgia at Athens in 1984 and, over twenty years later, was the Regents' and Franklin Professor of English and creative writing at the same university.

Cofer's first published works were poems. In 1986, she won the Riverstone International Chapbook Competition with her collection *Peregrina*. Though Cofer did not stop writing poetry, she tried her hand at writing fiction, which turned out to be a very successful form for her. Her 1989 novel *The Line of the Sun* received critical attention and was nominated for a Pulitzer Prize.

In addition to her poetry and novels, Cofer also has published short stories and essays. She writes for both adult and young adult audiences. In the course of her writing career, she has been honored with numerous awards. Her collection *The Latin Deli: Prose and Poetry* (1993), in which "American History" first appeared, was awarded the Anisfield Wolf Book Award. Her young adult book *An Island Like You: Stories of the Barrio* (1996) was named *Fanfare*'s Best Book of the Year and was given the American Library Association's Reforma Pura Belpre Medal. Furthermore, *The Year of Our Revolution: New and Selected Stories and Poems* won the Paterson Book Prize in 1998. Some of Cofer's more recent works include *Woman in Front of the Sun: On Becoming a Writer* (2000), a collection of essays; *The Meaning of Consuelo* (2003), a young adult novel; and a 2005 collection of poems, *A Love Story Beginning in Spanish*.

Cofer is married and lives with her husband, John (also an educator), and daughter, Tanya, in Athens and Louisville, Georgia.

PLOT SUMMARY

"American History" beings with a description of the narrator's neighborhood in Paterson, New Jersey, in 1963. The narrator, fourteen-year-old Elena, lives in what she refers to as a Puerto Rican tenement building called El Building. It is an old, rundown apartment building on a busy city corner. Because of the loud music that pours out of the windows, Elena refers to El Building as a "monstrous jukebox." Many of the people who live in this building are recent immigrants, who, according to the author, use the music to help drown out their worries.

Elena's narrative then describes a day when her class in the neighborhood school has been ordered to go outside. Though the students do not know it yet, President John F. Kennedy has just been shot. Shortly after they are sent outside, Mr. DePalma, the physical education and science teacher, as well as the school's disciplinarian, tells the students the shocking news. Some of the students respond with muffled laughter upon seeing DePalma shed some tears. This angers DePalma, and he calls them a bunch of losers. Then he yells at them and tells them to go home.

The students are delighted to be sent home early, especially Elena. She feels constantly humiliated at school, where her peers call her "Skinny Bones." They also make fun of her for her supposed Puerto Rican diet, teasing her about eating pork chops for breakfast. In addition to the jokes that are thrown her way, Elena hates the winter cold. She says she can never get warm no matter what she does. She wishes she were more like the African American girls who seem to have adjusted to the cold, icy winters.

At home, Elena spends a lot of time sitting on the windowsill in her bedroom reading. She likes her perch, which allows her to look down into the neighbor's yard. An elderly Jewish couple once lived in the house next door, and Elena watched them through their kitchen window. She could tell a lot about what was going on in their lives by the activities in their kitchen. When all was well, the husband and wife would eat their dinners together at the table. When one was sick, the other put food on a tray and carried it out of the kitchen. Elena also noticed when the husband and wife appeared to not be getting along well. The husband would leave the kitchen as soon as the meal was done, while his wife would remain at the table, staring into empty space.

There was a long time when Elena did not see the old man. One day, a crowd of people appeared in the kitchen. Later, a middle-aged woman assisted the elderly woman down the steps of the front porch, carrying suitcases out of the house. After that, the house was empty for several weeks. Elena guessed the old man had died.

Elena had watched as the small flower garden in the Jewish couple's backyard slowly wilted. She had thought about going over and watering the flowers. Then she had watched a new family move in: a man, a woman, and a boy who appeared to be Elena's age. She later learned that the boy's name is Eugene. Eugene is not in any of Elena's classes, but she makes a point of bumping into him in front of his locker and walking home from school.

Since Eugene's family has moved in, Elena has noted the changes. First, Eugene's father mows the backyard, which had turned into a mass of weeds. In the process, he has also mowed down all the remaining flowers in the garden. Elena also sees that the family never sits down at the kitchen table together. Eugene's mother, who comes home from work in a white uniform that Elena concludes is a nurse's outfit, sometimes eats at the kitchen table by herself. At other times, Elena sees Eugene sitting at the table alone, reading his books.

Elena and Eugene do not share any classes because Eugene is taking all honors classes. Although Elena gets straight As, she is not allowed to enroll in these advanced classes because English is not her first language. Elena is eager to talk to Eugene, so she nonetheless gathers up all her courage, catches up with him as they are walking home one day, and starts a conversation. She sees that Eugene is a bit shy from the way he looks at her, so she concludes that he, too, must have wanted to talk to her but was too embarrassed to speak up first. Since that day, they have walked home together. They also go to the library together. This makes Elena feel closer to Eugene. She has not told him that she watches him from her bedroom window, though. Now when she looks down and sees Eugene reading at the kitchen table, at least she knows what books he is reading.

One day, Elena's mother catches her staring out of her window. Her mom is concerned that Elena has become "stupidly infatuated." When Elena began puberty her mother became vigilant, afraid Elena might do something "crazy." Her mom constantly talks to her about virtue and morality, which Elena is not very interested in hearing.

Elena and her mother are quite different. Her mother is unhappy in Paterson and wants to move back to Puerto Rico. Elena, though sometimes tired of Paterson, has no fond memories of the island where she was born. All she remembers of her visits there is a bunch of strangers that crowded around her telling her that they were her aunts, uncles, and cousins. She has no dreams of ever moving back to Puerto Rico.

As Elena's relationship with Eugene grows, she longs for him to invite her inside his house. She wants to see all the other rooms of the house she had stared at from her bedroom window. She also wants to sit at the kitchen table with Eugene, just as she had watched the old Jewish couple do. She wants to talk with Eugene about the books they each read. Elena is reading *Gone with the Wind.* She is fascinated by the Southern culture and the way that the female protagonist lived. Eugene had told Elena that he was from Georgia, and she thinks he might be able to provide some insight into the story, which takes place during the Civil War.

Eugene is not having an easy time at the high school. Students make fun of him because of his Southern accent. They call him "the Hick." Elena is not disturbed by Eugene having difficulty making friends; this allows her to have Eugene all to herself.

On the day that President Kennedy is shot, Elena has an invitation to come to Eugene's house after school. Elena is, of course, very excited. She goes into her apartment to tell her mom she is going to study with a friend. Her mother is mortified. Elena's mother, as well as many of the families in the apartment building, love President Kennedy. They admire him so much that they have placed pictures of him on their walls and prayed to him. Elena's mother, in tears, tells Elena that she should go to church with her that night. Elena says she will go later because she has to first study for a test.

Elena walks out of her apartment building and heads for Eugene's house. The front door of his house is painted green. Elena remembers her mother saying that the color green represents hope. Upon knocking on the door, Elena hears footsteps inside the house. When the door opens, it is not Eugene. It is his mother. At first she is somewhat polite and asks what Elena wants. When Elena says that Eugene has invited her to study with him, the mother replies that Eugene needs no one to help him study. Then the mother points to Elena's apartment building. She asks if that is where Elena lives. Elena glances at the building. From the vantage point of Eugene's house, she notes that the building looks more like a prison than a place where families live. After Elena acknowledges that that is indeed where she lives, Eugene's mother tells her that there is not much sense in her wanting to be a friend to Eugene. The family will soon be moving away. The mother tells Elena not to take her remarks personally. Then she waits for Elena to leave. But Elena is shocked and feels frozen to the ground. The mother's tone becomes less friendly when she asks if Elena has heard what she had said. Finally Elena walks away and, as she does, she hears the green door closing behind her. After she returns home and goes to bed, Elena tries to think about the president but cries for herself instead. Late that night, a streetlight wakes her up. Through her bedroom window, she watches the snow fall.

CHARACTERS

Mr. DePalma

Mr. DePalma is the physical education and science teacher at Elena's school. Elena also describes him as the disciplinarian. It is to Mr. DePalma that students are sent when they get into trouble. So there appears to be some fear surrounding him, especially in Elena's eyes. When he openly weeps in front of students following President Kennedy's death, some students lose respect for DePalma. Although quietly, some students laugh at him.

DePalma is not very respectful of the students, either. He belittles them and tells them that they are all losers, which does not seem appropriate for a teacher. DePalma exhibits emotions at the death of President Kennedy, but he also crudely spits on the pavement while students are standing in front of him. When he dismisses them from school, he does so with anger and frustration.

Elena

Elena is the fourteen-year-old protagonist of Cofer's short story. Elena is in the ninth grade and lives in Paterson, New Jersey. Although she does not feel left out of her peer group at school, she does believe that she does not quite fit in. She mentions only the black girls from school with whom she plays at recess. She does not discuss other Puerto Rican or white friends, other than Eugene. Elena wishes she were more like the black girls, especially regarding their developing bodies, which are fuller than her own. She also wishes she were as agile as they are.

Though she claims she fears being rejected, she is determined enough to pursue Eugene, the new boy who has moved next door to her apartment building. It is not clear if she works hard to befriend Eugene for a relationship or for a chance to see the inside of his house. Elena, as narrator, says little about what Eugene is like. Instead the discussion about him revolves around Elena's fantasy of her and Eugene acting out a scene that parallels one Elena has previously watched—that of the elderly Jewish couple in their kitchen. From her bedroom window, Elena now watches Eugene in a similar way. Her next step is to get invited into his house so she can play out the role of the woman sitting opposite Eugene at that same table.

Although Elena is crushed when Eugene's mother does not allow her to enter the house, the story hints at the fact that Elena is resilient. The reader senses that she will bounce back. Her recovery is subtly conveyed by her watching the snow fall outside her window at the end of the story. She stares up toward the sky rather than looking down at the ground where everything automatically turns gray.

Elena's Mother

Elena's mother is presented as an adult who is trying to steer her daughter on a course that will avoid heartache. She is worried that Elena is acting rather strange, obsessively watching the house next door, and quickly realizes her daughter is infatuated. Elena's mother also represents the immigrant personality of the first generation. She is more attached to Puerto Rico and the practices of her culture than Elena is. Elena's mother does not want to stay in the United States. She misses her homeland and dreams of returning there upon her husband's retirement. Elena, in comparison, has adapted more to American culture and is working her way into a new kind of life.

In some ways, Elena's mother is similar to Eugene's. Both women do not want to be where they are presently living. They feel out of place and do not mingle with people who are not like them. They both restrict their children, although to different degrees. Elena's mother suggests what she wants Elena to do, whereas Eugene's mother insists on it.

Eugene

Eugene is Elena's age and has just moved into the house outside Elena's bedroom window. Eugene has no lines of dialogue in this story, and the author provides little exploration of his personality and none of his thoughts. Readers know Eugene only through Elena's observations of him, which are relatively superficial. Readers learn that he wears glasses, speaks with a Southern accent, comes from Georgia, and is somewhat shy. He apparently has no friends other than Elena.

Another characteristic that readers might question about Eugene is the fact that, at the end of the story, he does not come to the door to greet Elena. He is expecting her and probably hears his mother answer the door, but there is no sign of him in the closing section of the story when his mother is shooing Elena away. Of course, Eugene is still young. But his complete disappearance at the end imparts a sense of weakness or fearfulness in his personality. Unless, perhaps, his interest in Elena was only true in Elena's mind.

Eugene's Mother

When Elena describes Eugene's mother, she says that the woman is dressed all in white and somehow looks otherworldly. The woman uses polite words, but underneath these words, Elena senses coldness. Eugene's mother acts as if her life is caught in a sort of limbo. She is living in a place that she would rather forget. Her family will only be there for a short time, Eugene's mother tells Elena, so it makes no sense for Eugene to entertain any attachment to the people in the neighborhood or at school.

THEMES

Shame

Elena, the protagonist of this story, mentions several times that she feels shame—a sense of disgrace or a feeling of inadequacy. She is ashamed of her body, which she believes is too skinny. She is also ashamed of her body's movements, which are at times rigid, jerky, and awkward. Elena talks about her flat chest and wishes she had more feminine curves. She also wishes she had more meat and fat on her bones to keep her warm. Because she is often cold, she cannot keep up with the other girls in her class when they elegantly jump rope. Elena's body is almost frozen stiff, so her movements are anything but graceful. Later, when she is confronted by Eugene's mother and feels self-conscious, she juts her books forward toward Eugene's mother as if this were an accustomed form of salutation. She is nervous and feels ashamed for being so out of control.

Elena is also ashamed of the building that she lives in. The building is big, dark, and dilapidated. Her feelings of shame might also extend to her Puerto Rican culture, from which, at times, Elena tries to distance herself. She refers to the other Puerto Rican immigrants, at one point, as "these people," as if she did not identify herself with them. When she talks about visiting her relatives in Puerto Rico, she calls them strangers. She wants nothing to do with her parents' dream of returning to the tropical island and living in a home on the beach. Elena is not entirely comfortable in her new U.S. city, but she suggests that it is a lot better than living in the place where she was born.

Not only does Elena feel shame, she is shamed by others. She is humiliated by the girls at school who call her "Skinny Bones" and make stereotypical remarks about a Puerto Rican diet. They make jump-rope rhymes about eating pork chops and beans for breakfast. But Eugene's mother delivers the biggest blow when she denies Elena's dream. All Elena wants to do is sit with Eugene at his kitchen table and read or study with him. Eugene's mother bluntly denies Elena access to the house. She, in essence, tells Elena that the young girl is not the right type of person. She lets Elena know that she comes from the wrong kind of family, the wrong kind of ethnicity, and the wrong side of the street.

Although not as significant as the death of the president of the United States, shame can be debilitating. Shame can be self-generated, such as when Elena feels ashamed of her body type, or supplied by another person. Either way, shame eats away at a person's concept of self and can destroy confidence.

Religion and Death

Religion and death are minor themes in this story. Elena mentions going to church, praying,

TOPICS FOR FURTHER STUDY

- Why do you think the author chose the title of this story? What aspects of American history are brought into the story, and how do they affect the characters? Is the title literal or ironic? Direct a class discussion on this topic. Be prepared to introduce related issues and to ask pointed questions to keep the discussion lively.
- Investigate immigration to the United States from Puerto Rico. What are the main reasons for people from Puerto Rico to come to the United States? Are the reasons political, educational, or economic? How many Puerto Ricans immigrated to the United States each decade beginning with the 1930s? What cities and states are the major destinations? Organize your data in into charts and use this material to give a presentation to your class.
- Write an extension of Cofer's short story, creating a scene between Eugene and Elena a week after Eugene's mother has denied Elena access to the house. What would a conversation between Eugene and Elena be like? Would Eugene side with his mother? Would Elena still be Eugene's friend? Write the dialogue as if it were a scene from a play. Ask someone to take one of the roles, and then read your scene in front of your class.
- Interview adult family members or neighbors, asking them about President Kennedy's assassination. Do they remember how they heard about this tragic event? How did they feel? What did they do? How did they think his death would affect the country? What were their thoughts about Kennedy's widow and children? Choose your most interesting interview, and write a first-person narrative retelling the experience from that person's perspective.
- Draw or paint a picture of Elena's neighborhood as she describes it in this short story. Ask a partner to do the same. Then compare your different interpretations. Show the two pictures to your class. Ask your classmates how their impressions of Elena's neighborhood might be similar or different.

and having altars set up to honor saints and martyrs. The theme of religion is prominent in connection to President Kennedy's death. Death, in this story, brings out a sense of sacredness. Elena's mother is shocked, for example, when Elena thinks more about studying than she does about going to church to honor Kennedy's death and to pray for his family. The rest of the city, from Elena's point of view, is quiet, subdued, and respectful of Kennedy's passing. Although Elena also comes around to the practice of a memorial silence, she does so only after she has been rejected by Eugene's mother. Up until that time, all Elena thinks about is what she wants—to visit Eugene.

Religion and death bring some characters together. The adults turn to religion in their time of sorrow over the death of the president. Neighbors console one another. They meet at the church to pray together. Their problems are put to the side as they contemplate what this loss might mean to the president's family, to the nation, and to them. When contrasted with the death of Kennedy, the humiliation that Elena has endured because of Eugene's mother's prejudice seems minor, at least in the minds of the people around Elena. Of course, Elena might disagree.

Prejudice

Prejudice is a primary theme of the story and one that resonates with the historical setting of 1963, as the civil rights movement in the United States was then at its height. This theme is subtly applied throughout the narrative, culminating at the very end. Before her encounter with Eugene's mother, Elena encounters prejudice, but none severe enough to prepare her for that which she faces at the end of the story. For example, the black girls at school make fun of Elena but focus their taunts on her skinniness. Making a jump-rope song about pork chops and beans (what the black girls assume is a typical Puerto Rican breakfast) reveals some bias, but Elena is still included in the girls' game. Elena might be skinny, cold, and slow when it comes to jumping rope, but she is not sitting in a corner watching the other girls. She is not banned from joining them. So the prejudice does not appear to run very deep in this peer group.

Another hint of prejudice is demonstrated through the character of Mr. DePalma, the physical education and science teacher at Elena's school. He calls the students a bunch of losers when some of the students snicker at his sobs of grief. His outcry may indicate a hidden strain of prejudice that has bubbled up to the surface. DePalma's prejudice might not be based on race, although that is a possibility. It could be a prejudice based on age, though. It is possible that DePalma believes that young people are not very intelligent or feeling.

The most obvious prejudice is exhibited by Eugene's mother. Elena notes that Eugene's mother's attitude is not very friendly from the first moment the woman opens the door. She makes it clear to Elena that she considers herself and her family to be separate from the people who live in Elena's apartment complex. "I don't know how you people do it," she says. The words "you people" put Elena in a different social class, a class beneath Eugene and his family, in the mind of Eugene's mother.

STYLE

First-Person Narrator

Telling a story from a first-person point of view (using the pronoun "I") pulls the reader in to the story because it seems like the narrator is talking directly to the reader about a very personal experience. Another way of looking at it is that a first-person narration almost reads like someone's personal journal or diary entries.

Readers of first-person narratives are privileged to the intimate thoughts of the narrator. Often the narrator not only relates the actions that make up the story but also the emotions behind her or her own actions. For example, when someone in this story calls Elena "Skinny Bones," readers do not have to guess at how this affects the narrator. Since the story is written in first person, the narrator immediately conveys her reaction. The inner workings of a character's mind can be exposed in third-person narration (using the pronouns "he" and "she"), too, but in that case a narrator outside the story offers this information.

Readers have a tendency to believe that a first-person narration implies that the narrator and the author are one, which is not necessarily true. Although the author did grow up in Paterson, New Jersey, and does come from a Puerto Rican heritage, the story told in "American History" did not necessarily happen to the author. Cofer may have chosen the first-person point of view just to make the story sound more personal, something that may be appealing to teenage readers.

Use of Setting and Imagery

Authors often use setting, or the time and location of the story's events, and imagery, or descriptions of visual elements, to convey a mood or to reinforce a story's themes. The setting of Cofer's short story is rather bleak and dark. The imagery Cofer uses to describe the neighborhood, the school, and the apartment building create a sense of gloom. First, it is late November and very cold and uncomfortable outside. It is so cold that Elena has trouble moving. The skies are dark, and when it snows, the icy crystals change from white to gray because of the dirt and grime of the city. Buildings block the light and warmth of the sun and look like monstrous duplications of ugly prisons.

Through these images, Cofer uses the setting to relate the overall depressive tone of her story. Paterson, New Jersey, is not a friendly or nurturing environment. The winter has curbed all growth. The long shadows and neglect have killed the flowers in the backyard of the house next door. Loud noises from traffic as well as everyone's tape decks or radios blast out jarring sounds that prevent anyone from having peace and quiet in which to think.

The harsh setting is appropriate for this story. It complements the unkind words of the teacher Mr. DePalma and the cruel and unsympathetic comments by Eugene's mother. By combining the uncomfortable setting with the torment that Elena experiences, Elena's condition feels even more pathetic, adding a deeper dimension to her sadness.

In contrast to the dark, cold setting in which Elena spends most of her time is the house next door. When she watches the older couple in their kitchen, a place of warmth and good smells from cooking, she dreams of being married and having someone with whom to share her thoughts. When Eugene finally invites her to the house, one of the first things Elena notices is the green door at the front of the house, a sign, she believes, of hope. However, all hope is dashed when the door is closed to her.

Contrasting Perspectives

The author interweaves contrasting perspectives throughout her story to heighten the tension that the young protagonist Elena experiences. Teenagers, such as Elena, when passing from childhood into adulthood, often feel quite isolated. They are too old to remain children and must give up the childish comforts of their earlier years. Yet they are not yet old enough to fully grasp the adult world. This feeling of isolation is accentuated in Cofer's story by setting off the adult world from the world in which Elena lives. The author accomplishes this by contrasting the various perspectives of adults and teens.

Cofer separates the teen world from the adult world through Mr. DePalma. He is emotionally disturbed by the assassination of the president. His sobs indicate that he is feeling a deep loss. When a student giggles at his tears, DePalma seems to think the students are too thick-headed to understand what he is going through. DePalma then lashes out at the teens and attempts to put them in their place—a place beneath him. His angry words are an effort to remind the teens that he is the boss and that they have no right to make fun of him. They have crossed some imaginary boundary between the teen world and adulthood, which in DePalma's mind is an offense.

Elena's mother also makes a distinction between the worlds of adults and teens. In her adult world, due respect must be paid to the dead, and it must be paid according to adult rules. She can hardly fathom that Elena would do anything but go to church with her and pray after President Kennedy's death is announced. She believes her priorities are right and Elena's are wrong.

Eugene's mother believes that she has the right to choose her son's friends. She thinks that her discriminations are in her son's best interests. In some cases, this might be true. One could suggest that since adults have more experience, they may be better judges; however, Eugene's mother jumps to conclusions about Elena's worth based on where she lives and without consulting Eugene. She says her son is smart, implying that Elena is not. She attempts to narrow Eugene's world according to her own perceptions.

By presenting adult perspectives that contrast with Elena's, readers experience the sense of adult domination in the teenager's world. This helps them to empathize with Elena's frustrations.

Coming-of-Age Story

Coming-of-age fiction revolves around a teenager or adolescent on the cusp of adulthood. The protagonist might be naive about life and the world in the beginning, but as the story progresses, the character learns a lesson that helps her mature. In this story, Elena progresses from a young teen who is just beginning to learn about womanhood to a young woman who has experienced her first real heartbreak. She is fourteen and embarrassed of her flat chest. She wants to have a more womanly figure. In other words, she is ready to shed childhood. She thinks a lot about her future as she watches the older Jewish couple next door. When she fantasizes about her relationship with Eugene, she dreams about their friendship, but her first goal is to get inside that house where Eugene lives. She wants to sit down with Eugene at the kitchen table. She also wants to explore the other rooms of the house, rooms that she has not been able to see from her bedroom window. She has hope, symbolized by the green front door on Eugene's house, that she will become a woman one day, perhaps happily married and living in her own house.

The prejudice and bias she experiences teach her that dreams present challenges that must be overcome. Since her mother warned her that her way to Eugene's house may be blocked, Elena may also have learned that mothers sometimes have knowledge to share.

Elena may have learned a more subtle lesson, as demonstrated in the last few lines of the story. She watches the snow fall and she seems to indicate that she understands there are two ways to look at events in one's life. Elena stares at the snow as it floats high in the air, where it remains clean and white. She refuses to look at it as it touches the ground and turns gray. She does not want to look down where the dirt and other pollutants turn beautiful things into something ugly. This could mean that she is keeping her dreams, or even her dignity, intact, no matter how hard other people try to corrupt them.

COMPARE & CONTRAST

- **1960s:** The citizens of the United States are shocked by the assassination of President John F. Kennedy. The country mourns the loss of its leader.

  1990s: Several devastating events evoke national mourning: the bombing in Oklahoma City, the bombing during the summer Olympics in Atlanta, the bombing of U.S. military barracks in Saudi Arabia, and the shooting at Columbine High School in Colorado.

  Today: The citizens of the United States mourn the loss of thousands of victims of the terrorist attacks in New York City and Washington, D.C., on September 11, 2001. Other tragedies such as the 2007 shooting at Virginia Polytechnic Institute and State University unite the nation in mourning.

- **1960s:** The U.S. population reaches 200 million in the mid-1960s. According to the PEW Hispanic Research Center, of that number, 8.5 million are Hispanic.

  1990s: In the mid-1990s, the U.S. population reaches 260 million. More than 22 million people who claim a Hispanic heritage live in the United States.

  Today: In the mid-2000s, the U.S. population reaches 300 million. Of that number, 44.7 million are Hispanic.

- **1960s:** The Civil Rights Act of 1964, a bill introduced by President Kennedy in 1963, is passed, outlawing segregation in schools, public places, and employment. Prejudice is common in America, and numerous riots over civil rights take place.

  1990s: Affirmative action, a process by which formal steps are taken to represent women and minorities in employment and education in order to promote integration, is under attack, as some legislators claim these special considerations are unfair. While some racial prejudice still exists, it has become politically and culturally unacceptable.

  Today: The protections afforded by the Civil Rights Act of 1964 are applied on the basis of race and gender but not sexual orientation. Prejudice is a topic of public debate in relation to gay marriage and unauthorized immigration.

HISTORICAL CONTEXT

Assassination of President John F. Kennedy

On November 22, 1963, President John F. Kennedy was touring Dallas, Texas, in a convertible limousine. Although Lyndon B. Johnson, a native of Texas, was Kennedy's vice president, the Democratic pair had almost lost Texas in the 1960 presidential vote. Kennedy went to Texas to help gain support for the next election. The governor of Texas, John Connally, was sitting in front of the president as their car, which also carried Connally's wife, Nellie, and the First Lady, Jacqueline Kennedy, when shots rang out. It was a little past 12:30 p.m. The first shot hit President Kennedy in the back. The same bullet also hit Governor Connally. A few seconds later, another shot hit Kennedy in the head. Kennedy was rushed to the hospital. He was still technically alive, but he had no chance of survival, as the wound to his head was too great. He was officially pronounced dead at 1:00 p.m. Thirty minutes later, a public announcement was issued stating that the president of the United States had been assassinated. At 2:00 p.m., the president's body was taken to Air Force One, the official presidential plane. Vice President Johnson, who had also been in the motorcade but was unhurt, was also taken to the plane and at 2:38 p.m. was sworn into office as president.

The casket with the president's body was later placed in the Capitol Building in Washington,

D.C., for public viewing. Long lines of mourners wrapped around the building and into the streets. Hundreds of thousands of people wanted to pay their last respects to the young president. On November 25, government officials from ninety different countries came to Washington, D.C., to attend the president's funeral. Huge crowds formed on the sidewalks outside as the president's casket was pulled by a horse-drawn carriage from the church to Arlington National Cemetery, where Kennedy's body was laid to rest. As a monument to the president, an eternal flame was installed near his grave.

Lee Harvey Oswald was the presumed assassin of President Kennedy. He was arrested and was being transferred by the police two days later when Jack Ruby stepped out from the crowd and shot Oswald. Oswald claimed he was innocent but never went to trial. Although the government conducted investigations under the Warren Commission and concluded that Oswald was the assassin, controversies about Kennedy's death remain.

Paterson, New Jersey

Paterson, New Jersey, was once considered one of the major building blocks of the American industrial revolution. The city was specifically planned to be one of the greatest industrial centers in the United States. The Passaic River, upon whose banks the city was founded, has seventy-seven-foot-high waterfalls that provide the power to run many of the country's textile mills. At one point, the city was nicknamed Silk City because of its high production of silk. Later, other manufacturing plants, such as gun and railroad engine makers, built large plants in Paterson.

In 1792, Alexander Hamilton, the first secretary of the U.S. Department of Treasury, formed an investment group called the Society of Useful Manufactures. Money that was collected by this group was used to fund the planned industrial city. The city was named for William Paterson, an associate justice of the U.S. Supreme Court, who served as the second governor of New Jersey.

Paterson also became a center of labor unrest, a side effect of booming industry. Workers demanded safety in the workplace, a minimum wage, shorter working hours, and the end of child labor.

In the twentieth century, economic depression spread across the city. Many of the manufacturing factories were shut down as jobs were sent overseas to countries that could produce the goods less expensively. By the 1980s, Paterson was known as one of the most distressed cities in the United States. Unemployment rates soared. Even though Paterson had at one time been the central location for shopping for many northern New Jersey residents prior to the 1980s, new localized shopping malls were built in almost every little town, and people from outside of Paterson stopped coming. Many of the stores in Paterson thus were forced to close.

In the early twenty-first century, parts of Paterson have been experiencing a rebirth. In the Great Falls Historic District, artists have set up a thriving community. The changing character of the city is luring visitors and tourists back.

The 2006 U.S. Census estimated the city's population at just a little less than 149,000 people, which means that Paterson is New Jersey's third-largest city. Long known for its ethnic diversity, Paterson is home to large numbers of African Americans and Hispanic Americans. Of the Hispanic group, many have cultural roots in Peru, Colombia, the Dominican Republic, and Puerto Rico. Often, people immigrated because they suffered from poor economic opportunities in their homeland. Due to the expanding businesses, such as the booming industries in Paterson, many employers sent representatives specifically to Puerto Rico to recruit workers. Like other Puerto Rican immigrants, Cofer moved with her family from Puerto Rico to Paterson.

Paterson has many different pop culture distinctions. William Carlos Williams, the famous American poet, wrote an epic poem, "Paterson" about the city. Also, the 1989 movie *Lean on Me* was based on the life of Joe Clark, a principal at Paterson's Eastside High School.

Twentieth-Century Latina Writing

Along with the civil rights movement of the 1960s came increased awareness of ethnic groups other than the Caucasian culture that dominated much of the U.S. media. This spurred an interest in ethnic diversity in the world of literature. Publishers sought stories composed by African American, Asian American, Native American, and Hispanic American authors due to an increasing demand for such books. College campuses all over the United States began to offer courses in multicultural studies. In this atmosphere, writing by American authors with non-European backgrounds flourished. This trend has continued, and Latina literature has been one of the fastest-growing areas of U.S. literature in the early twenty-first century. Some of the prominent Latina authors aside from Cofer include Isabel Allende, Sandra Cisneros, Julia Alvarez, Cristina García, Rosario Ferré, and Magali García Ramis.

CRITICAL OVERVIEW

Although Cofer's writing has earned the author many awards, most of the critical attention on her work is focused on her novels. There are, however, a handful of reviews on her short story collection *The Latin Deli: Prose and Poetry* as well as the anthology *Big City Cool: Stories about Urban Youth*, both of which include "American History."

In 1994, shortly after Cofer's book *The Latin Deli* was published, Michael J. O'Shea, writing for *Studies in Short Fiction*, pointed out that other reviewers might have overlooked this collection because it contained not only short stories but also poems and essays. Other reviewers, O'Shea claimed, might also have dismissed the collection because it dealt with Puerto Rican themes. However, O'Shea argues that the poems and the essays inform the short stories, thus making the stories richer and the collection a cohesive unit. Furthermore, he states that even though the characters in the stories are Puerto Rican, the issues that they confront are challenges of human affairs. O'Shea comments that the book presents "profound, poignant, funny, universal and moving epiphanies." O'Shea adds that Cofer is "an author worth knowing."

Darren Crovitz, writing for the *Journal of Adolescent and Adult Literacy*, reviews the anthology *Big City Cool.* Although Crovitz does not single out "American History," he does distinguish the book as one that presents entries on a common theme: "the problems, challenges, and triumphs of urban youth." The young protagonists in these stories, Crovitz writes, discover "who they are." Crovitz described the stories in this anthology as "engaging," "colorful," "noisy," and "invigorating."

WHAT DO I READ NEXT?

- In her memoir *Silent Dancing: A Partial Remembrance of a Puerto Rican Childhood* (1990), Cofer writes that she learned her storytelling skills from her grandmother. In this collection of essays, the author recalls time spent listening to her grandmother telling stories as well remembering stories from her youth spent in Paterson, New Jersey.
- Esmeralda Santiago also has written a memoir of her childhood, which she shared with her seven siblings. In her book *When I Was Puerto Rican* (1993), Santiago recalls what it was like growing up both in both Puerto Rico and New York City.
- Julia Alvarez wrote *How the García Girls Lost Their Accents* (1991), a collection of stories about four sisters from the Dominican Republic, their immigration to the United States, and their rebellious natures.
- *House on Mango Street* (1984) by Sandra Cisneros contains stories about difficult times in a Hispanic community in Chicago.

CRITICISM

Joyce Hart

Hart is a freelance writer and author of literary essays and several books. In this essay, she examines the theme of isolation in "American History."

Isolation is a subtle but pervasive theme in Cofer's short story "American History." It is present when the teenage protagonist and narrator is at school and when she walks home in the afternoon. She seems to feel cut off from her surroundings no matter where she is. She is separated from the people in the street, from the people playing the music that streams out of her apartment building, from her peer group at school, and from her parents. This isolation has many different sources. Some of it is due to cultural differences, such as the ridicule she receives

"FOR ELENA, IT MIGHT BE EASIER TO DREAM WHILE STARING AT THE SNOW FALLING FROM THE CLOUDS RATHER THAN LOOKING DOWN AT THE GROUND WHERE HER ORDINARY, DAY-TO-DAY LIFE TAKES PLACE."

from the girls at school. Another source is the result of age difference, such as the gulf between Elena and her teacher, Mr. DePalma, and Elena and her parents. Yet another cause of this sense of isolation is prejudice, such as that displayed by Eugene's mother toward Puerto Ricans. But in some ways, the isolation is self-inflicted, as Elena seems to purposefully place herself in what could be called a protective blanket of seclusion. In this way, Elena has separated herself from the people and the world around her.

Elena lives in a new country, one in which she and her parents were not born. Whereas her parents lived in Puerto Rico until adulthood and therefore have developed roots in that country, Elena barely remembers anything about that island home. She is only fourteen, so she has not had enough time to truly define and understand herself, let alone this new environment. Since her parents are forever longing to go back to Puerto Rico, Elena has no one to help her adjust.

At school, Elena does not fare much better. She is uneasy and sometimes even ashamed because she is not like the other girls around her. She is too thin and not womanly enough, while the other girls have begun to develop. Neither is she one of the fancy-footed African American girls who far outshine her in jumping rope. Elena can barely even twirl the rope. She is often cold, whereas the other girls hardly seem fazed by the harsh winter weather. Although the girls invite her into their circle, they continue to tease her. They point out the differences between her and them. When Elena befriends Eugene, the taunting intensifies. Eugene is too Southern for the other students' taste. His Southern drawl, though it sounds melodious to Elena, irritates the other students. They make fun of him, too. They have nicknames for both of them, which crowns Elena's and Eugene's friendship with mockery.

Even when she is at home, Elena is disquieted and ill at ease. The building she lives in she likens to a monster and a jail. She refers to her neighbors as "the residents" or as "these people" as if she were not a part of them. She merely observes them and tolerates them as if she wished she lived somewhere else—perhaps in the house next door, where Eugene lives.

Inside her family's apartment, Elena isolates herself. She spends a lot of her time in her bedroom, where, at first, she watches the elderly Jewish couple. This Jewish couple has taken on the role of Elena's retreat from the world. She loses herself in imagining their story, just as she accuses her apartment neighbors of losing themselves in their loud music. Elena's withdrawal, though, is visual, like someone watching a silent television show. Not only does she watch them from a distance, but she does so completely concealed. She maintains only a one-sided relationship, watching them without their awareness. She not only observes them, she makes up her own stories about their lives. She speculates as to when the couple is having a disagreement by the way they treat each other at the kitchen table. She also guesses when one of them is sick in bed. She even guesses that one of the women who comes to visit is the older woman's daughter. She then guesses that the old man has died. None of these conjectures are proven by facts; they are all the fruit of Elena's fantasies, a world that she controls. She can imagine anything she wants. Since she does not interact with the real-life characters, she does not have to confront any contradictions that might exist between her imagined stories and the truth of this couple's life. The elderly couple does not know she exists. Elena seems to like it this way.

Elena's mother is one of only two characters for which the author creates dialogue with the protagonist, and this dialogue is brief. Throughout the story, the author interjects brief bits of conversations between Elena and her mother, but she does so to describe the divide between them. Elena's mother is a religious woman who dreams of returning to Puerto Rico. Elena keeps her distance from her mother's church and religious beliefs and will not even consider living in Puerto Rico again. Elena is determined to remain in the United States and go to school so she can become a teacher. No other relatives seem to live in the United States, so if her parents leave, Elena will have to stay behind, alone.

However, her college days are still a long time away. In the present moment of the story, Elena has another dream to fulfill. After Eugene moves into the house across the street, seeing him becomes, according to Elena, the "one source of beauty and light" in her life. As the story progresses, though, it does not seem that Eugene is the primary source of Elena's projected joy. Eugene is simply the key that unlocks the hidden treasure of Elena's long fantasy of the house next door.

Elena puts aside her anxieties of being rejected and pursues Eugene. She finds out what classes he is taking and locates his locker. She makes a point of making sure he sees and recognizes her. Then one day, she approaches him. To her surprise, Eugene seems to like her. They hang out together as they walk home from school. They go to the library together. But what kind of relationship do they have? Elena does not talk very much about him. There are no conversations between them that the readers are privy to.

Surprisingly, readers see Eugene only vaguely. Just as she had observed the elderly couple, Elena now observes Eugene and his family from a distance, unbeknownst to them. She notices Eugene's mother and father as they sit together in the backyard. She comments that the family never eats together in the kitchen, but Elena does see Eugene sit at the kitchen table to read. Elena's greatest desire is to be at that table next to him. She wants to sit with him just as the Jewish wife used to sit with her husband. This desire of hers makes Elena's relationship with Eugene seem distant and concealed, like her past fantasies. She does not mention wanting to hold his hand, nor do they share secrets or dream of going to a movie together. Her fantasy is born with a lot of space between them, from Elena's bedroom window looking down to Eugene's kitchen window. What is more telling about Elena's relationship with Eugene is that she hopes to finally see all the other rooms in the house through her friendship with him. All those rooms that have been hidden from her will finally be revealed, as if to complete the stories she's been watching through the kitchen window. It seems that the house, not Eugene, is the true the source of light in Elena's life. Eugene may be merely the means of entry to the house that Elena has been fantasizing about for so long. Elena may not be ready to unwrap the blanket of isolation that she has used as a cover to protect herself. Yet revealing oneself is what real friendships are all about. Is Elena merely pretending Eugene is her friend? Is she afraid of opening up to anyone?

"I LIKE TO THINK OF MYSELF AS SOMEONE WHO IS FULLY ENGAGED IN LIFE AND OCCASIONALLY FINDS REASONS TO WRITE EITHER A CELEBRATION OR AN ELEGY ABOUT WHAT HAPPENS AROUND ME."

The story ends with Elena back at her bedroom window. Once again she is alone. She appears to be more comfortable up in her room, detached from her surroundings and the people who inhabit them. She might feel safer staring up into the sky. For Elena, it might be easier to dream while staring at the snow falling from the clouds rather than looking down at the ground where her ordinary, day-to-day life takes place. Readers might wonder if the ground, or life, is too dirty, or difficult, for Elena to come in contact with it.

Source: Joyce M. Hart, Critical Essay on "American History," in *Short Stories for Students*, Gale, Cengage Learning, 2009.

Margaret Crumpton

In the following excerpt from an interview with Crumpton, Cofer asserts that stories provide for writers and readers alike a sense of who they are, arguing that she is driven by a "need for narrative."

... Margaret Crumpton: What was the first thing you ever wrote that made you think, "I can be a writer?"

Judith Ortiz Cofer: I don't recall having that response to my work. In fact the doubt that I face every day when I turn to the blank page makes me feel like what I'm about to say may be an exaggeration (laughs), but I think that the way that publication works for a literary artist is to reinforce the idea that the world may be willing to lend an ear. So I think that the first time that I considered myself as a real writer, as opposed to a closet writer or a potentially failed writer, was when my little poem "Latin Women

Pray" was accepted by a national journal. Before then my early poems had been published in college journals and other highly specialized short-lived publications, but this was accepted by the *New Mexico Humanities Review*, which was a nationally recognized literary journal. That gave me a feeling that my work had made it out into the world; it will actually exist beyond the moment. And so at that moment I think I said to myself "I can be a writer," and that lasted until I faced the next blank page. . . .

Crumpton: I am curious about your economy of language. You say in another interview that "poetry contains the essence of language. Every word weighs a ton," and I think this is especially true in your own poetry. It amazes me that there is so much meaning in poems that are really not very long at all. This is also true for your titles (like the story "American History" for example), which almost always mean two or more things at once. My question is, how do you get words to mean so much?

Cofer: That is a very difficult question, but frankly one of the obsessions that I work with—I always tell people that the older I get the more I realize that there are only, like, three or four obsessions, but I am going to get everything I can out of them. One of them is with the power of language. And words are, of course, the material of language. Language has the power to empower and to diminish, and as I examine each word I try to determine (perhaps not in a conscious way but in the way that the mind works when you are using words to construct art) "how much can a word contain?" I read constantly about language. I'm fascinated by the development of language. After all, even those of us who read only one book know that it begins with "in the beginning was the word." And from that word came story. And so it fascinates me to think that if all of creation can be encompassed in a narrative, surely we are wealthy if we possess a language. And so when I decide, particularly on a title, I ask myself "how much can three words carry?" so that after the person has read the poem or the story they can go back to the title and say "well I can see how that doesn't just mean American history—it can mean many things." I think that comes not only from my work as a writer but from my study of literature, where, as you know being a critic and a scholar, you examine each line for how much power it gives to the work of art. . . .

Crumpton: Your latest book, Woman in Front of the Sun: On Becoming a Writer, is a beautiful collection of essays that explores your development as an artist. This theme is present to a greater or lesser extent in almost all your books. Would you say that it is the most important story you have to tell?

Cofer: I choose to interpret this question as "what is the most important story I have to tell?" And I have decided that, really, all of my stories are about storytelling. Even the novel ends with an admission that it was just a story. And a story can always be changed and modified. I feel that "story," our sense of who we are and who we are to become, our story, is the single most important intellectual possession that we have. And I think that story is not just an individual thing. It has shaped the human race. We have a creation story from every group in the world. I am fascinated by the fact that most women that I meet have a birth story that was given to them by their mothers. They were always the smallest child, the biggest child, the child that almost died, the unexpected child, the child of my youth, the child of my old age. And that has shaped that person's perception of him or herself going through life. I think that my main theme is story. The stories that I have heard, the stories I made up, stories I will make up—what shape will they take? They may take shape as poems or essays or stories, but I realize that, at least for myself, without a sense that the story continues, I cannot see myself in the future. Other people don't think of story in such a conscious way. I think that writers are always thinking of their story. I always laugh when I hear the stories about how writers collected their stories. Like the great late Raymond Carver, who would get his friends to tell stories and then say "are you going to use that?"—like you say "are you going to eat that, can I take your french fries?" And he would take it home and make it his story. I think we are driven by our need for narrative. At least I am. If there is anything that I can say is the main topic for my stories, it's my need to tell stories.

Crumpton: Better answer than the question . . .

Cofer: No, no, I'm really thinking about your questions. Look at *The Latin Deli* story "Not for Sale," for example. That story's about the Scheherazade complex. And who was Scheherazade? Scheherazade is the woman who told stories to save herself and to save others. My mission is not quite so urgent; no human lives that I know of are dependent on my telling a story, except for one. Mine. It doesn't mean that I will physically die if I don't tell stories, but I know that I would cease to be interested in the shape of my days as much as when I'm telling a story.

Crumpton: Regarding your development as an artist, you have written about all the influences in your life—your grandmother's stories and women writers like Woolf and O'Connor, etc.—but now you are in the position to influence a new generation of writers through your work and through your role as a professor of creative writing. What would be the most crucial advice you would give to would-be writers?

Cofer: To would-be writers I would say, "don't do it unless you absolutely need to." (And they're not always young, by the way. One of my older graduate students pointed out that she really bristles when someone says, "this is dedicated to young writers"—she's in her forties and she just started to write. One of my best friends didn't publish her first poem until she was fifty, but then she published it in *The New Yorker*.) So I would say to a new writer, unless you want to be haunted by this phantom specter, by this thing that lets its presence be known in your life on a daily basis, unless you want to give your best hours to this, and the best years of your life, don't do it. And the best way to find out if you can do it is to treat it as a discipline. Books just don't get written as a hobby. Good books at least. Yes, I mean good books (laughs); some really bad books have been written as a hobby! I would tell them to think of it as if your doctor said that unless you do yoga and meditation every day, you're going to die in two years. Think of it in those terms, and give yourself the discipline of making writing a part of your life. If you cannot bear it, if you can always talk yourself out of it, if you find that you'd rather be doing almost anything else but working on that story or that poem, don't declare yourself a writer. Declare yourself something else. Something easier, an investment banker maybe, and you will lead an easier life. But if you find that need to write, then it will become the most satisfying, the most irritating, the most wonderful, and the most devastating thing that you have ever done. Because every time you write something and it's good, if you share it with the public, they'll expect you to write something better next time (laughs). It becomes then this daily struggle to keep up with your own standards, no one else's. And yet, my bad days begin when I don't have time to write.

Crumpton: I'd like to end this interview with a question about a particular poem. Your first poem in The Latin Deli *is called "The Latin Deli, an Ars Poetica." Could you discuss why this is your ars poetica?*

Cofer: As I was putting together *The Latin Deli*, I asked myself what my writing ought to do. I realized that my goal was very humble. It was basically to create work that found its center in the joyous things in life. And in the sadness too, in everything that allows us to believe that we are fully alive. That brings to mind what Robert Frost said: "the good poem always begins in delight and ends in wisdom." And I think delight meant an engagement, a full engagement, in life. If I am a poet at all, I am not a poet of the metaphysical. I'm not a philosopher. I like to think of myself as someone who is fully engaged in life and occasionally finds reasons to write either a celebration or an elegy about what happens around me. In this poem what I was trying to do was to celebrate the fact that we can find "home," that idealized concept of that place where you can always return. (Once again, misquoting the great Frost, "The place you haven't to deserve" is what he said home was.) And you can make that happen through your senses. For many of us who are from another place, that happens through food. And this poem was really a search for that place, that sacred place, where someone would come up and say to you "are you nostalgic? Do you need to be in touch with your mama and with your home? Let me show you what I have." And it will be the time machine, the vehicle that will take you back. I found such a place, really just a hole-in-the-wall bodega, in Atlanta, and the woman was a smooth operator, not a high priestess, but I decided this hole-in-the-wall temple and this good business woman/high priestess were going to have to do for my trip home. And so I wrote this poem in which I talk about this Latin bodega, a place where you went in and the smells of home assaulted you and took you back.

Source: Margaret Crumpton, "An Interview with Judith Ortiz Cofer," in *Meridians: Feminism, Race, Transnationalism*, Vol. 3, No. 2, Spring 2003, pp. 93–109.

"MY ART IS NOT REPRESENTATIONAL BUT IMPRESSIONISTIC. I LIKE FOR MY CANVASES TO COALESCE INTO MEANING RATHER THAN JUST TRY TO GET IT ALL PHOTOGRAPHICALLY CORRECT."

Bridget Kevane

In the following excerpt from an interview with Kevane, Cofer discusses her poetry and prose collection The Latin Deli, *describing the differences between the process of writing poetry and that of writing prose.*

. . . [BRIDGET KEVANE]: You once said that you don't believe in the muse. Why?

Although my writing gives me a spiritual life, I don't depend on anything extraordinary or supernatural or this thing called inspiration, which I believe is something other than what most people think it is. In my essay "5:00 A.M." in *The Latin Deli,* I said that for me the mysterious part is why I need to write. I need to write like some people need to run, like some people need to play a musical instrument, or like some people need to cook as a form of self-expression. Actually, I don't write for self-expression but for self-discovery. I started giving myself an assigned time, which was five to seven in the morning before my child got up and I had to prepare for my job and everything else. I found that I could will myself to be creative at that hour and that it was a process very similar to exercise. I don't like to exercise, but at a certain point in my day I say that I'm going to do an hour of exercise because I need to. If I don't, I'll regret it and my day will be less than it should be. So I found that it's a combination of the mystical and the practical.

I've always known that if I don't carve a little time for myself, then I won't write. And it's not inspiration. I always tell my students that if the muse does exist she's female and only goes to writers on the West Coast, male writers on the West Coast, who can make her famous in Hollywood. But seriously, I believe that inspiration is actually the culmination of a process of gestation. I believe that I start thinking about something I want to do and it obsesses me. I take notes on cards and put them in my purse, and at a certain point I need to sit down and work on it. For me, that's the point that most people call inspiration. But it's not a thunderbolt. It's been happening. You've been programming your brain, you've been getting ready for that moment. It's more of a natural than a supernatural process.

BK: Is writing a process you enjoy?

Who said I enjoyed writing?! [Laughs] I think that writing is one of the hardest, most painful of human endeavors. When I said that I experienced a moment of joy, the pain I have to go through for that moment of joy is only sometimes worth it. Because sometimes you go through the pain and the moment of joy doesn't come. What I'm saying is that I'm like that runner who is addicted to the high on reaching that third mile. Before then, of course, every bone hurts, every muscle hurts, and then there's that moment when those endorphins are released. But it's always a fearsome proposition to begin something new, and so the answer is no, I don't always enjoy writing. Some days I wish I could put my energies and intelligence into real estate! I'd be rich if I put into examining the stock market all the effort I put into writing a poem.

BK: But there must be some reward for all the effort in writing poetry?

For me, it's become like deep analysis. When I start thinking of a poem somehow my synapses connect and lead me to a place where I don't normally wander into. I know a poem works if it surprises me, if I discover something. The same thing happens over and over, and I always feel a sense of release and almost intense joy for a moment when that happens. Because I know that even if the poem never gets published, even if no one else ever reads it, it has shown me something. The discoveries are not earthshaking. They're discoveries that most people make if they lead examined lives over a long period of time. If you can make them into universal discoveries, then they become art.

BK: Is there a similar process in writing a novel?

It's a similar process but not as intense. I think that the poem is the hardest thing to write. That's why when people ask me to talk about writing I always talk about the poem. It's like comparing brain surgery to any other surgery. Both operations are difficult, but one requires

the skill of a diamond cutter. For me, writing a novel is a long commitment to a project and writing the poem is a rush of energy. Even though I revise the poem extensively and sometimes don't let it go for a year, it's still working with the minute. With a novel, you can delete a hundred pages and it can stand that. The patient won't die. With a poem, you can revise it into oblivion or you cannot revise it enough, and it's never quite clear to you whether you have or not.

BK: Which writers have served as models for you?

When I'm addressing a Latino audience and they ask me about models I pause because I know that they want me to say that my models were Puerto Rican writers. I can't say that. Because if you're talking about the models that formed me as an artist twenty years ago, well, there was no big multicultural drive in the United States, there were no Latino studies, nothing like it. In fact, when I was in graduate school, studying American and British literature was the only way that I could do what I wanted to do. Spanish literature from Spain did not represent my interests as closely as did American literature. My only model was Virginia Woolf, because she was the only woman who was allowed on the syllabus. But I didn't feel the shock of recognition until I happened to take a course in Southern literature where I encountered the work of Flannery O'Connor and Eudora Welty. I realized that these were women writing about ordinary lives that they had transformed through art. They weren't rich British women who could be counted among the world's Dead Englishman geniuses; these were women who were writing about family, land, religion. I would say Flannery O'Connor was the first one to give me that jolt, and years later, Alice Walker. Then followed Toni Morrison, because once you get into that era, then African-American and other people start publishing. But it wasn't until Gabriel García Márquez won the Nobel Prize and the so-called Latin American literary boom, when other Latin American writers were "discovered" by American publishers, that we then got Isabel Allende and other people in translation. It's been a long road. Now I do seek out and read the works of Puerto Rican women on the island.

I had one young person ask, "Was Sandra Cisneros your model?" I had to say, "She is a few years younger than I am!" We started publishing around the same time, she and Julia Alvarez and I. Esmeralda tells me that she used *Silent Dancing* as a model for when she began writing, so I'm already at that stage where my work is being used as a model! I have had the distinction, if one can call it that, of having been one of the original Puerto Rican writers writing in English, as opposed to being translated, or Latina writers in English. I had to make do, and it hasn't hurt me. I find that I can put into my work many things because I'm aware of the mainstream and have studied contemporary literature by all writers, not just limiting myself to Latino studies, because I think a writer needs to absorb everything.

JH: Your situation sounds like it's in harmony with Chicana writers like Cisneros and Viramontes who were reading a variety of authors as well.

Right, because we didn't have other people. And I think that it's wonderful to have African-American studies and Latino studies, but there's also an inherent danger in that if we're going to create a new generation of writers these studies need to be more interdisciplinary. These writers have to be aware of people like Cormac McCarthy and other fabulous writers who are changing the English language. How can we be innovators if we don't see what's being changed?

In my classes I teach American literature, which includes Cisneros and Gary Soto and Joy Harjo. The Library of Congress defines as an American writer a person writing in English within the boundaries of the United States who's an American citizen. So we're not minority writers, we are American writers who happen to belong to ethnic minorities. I've taught English for almost twenty years from instructor to professor now. My love is literature in all its forms by all its practitioners. But they always have to meet the criteria of excellence that I learned early to apply. I don't teach anyone because it's politically correct. I teach only those writers whose work I can justify to my students.

BK: Any examples you care to mention of what's politically correct that you refuse to teach?

No! I don't think I want to do that. I think that that would be very offensive to people out there. I would really just rather concentrate on the positive. The publishers are at fault in many ways because if a book becomes a best-seller or there's a popular trend to publish a particular kind of writer, then all of the sudden we have five books by five writers that are supposed to be like the other one. They'll say, "If you've read and

loved so and so, you will love so and so." I don't think, for example, that you can compare Alice Walker to [Terry] McMillan. You know what I mean? They're just completely different!

JH: Is there a difference for you between Maxine Hong Kingston and Amy Tan?

Well, those two I have a little more trouble with because I enjoy Amy Tan tremendously. But Maxine Hong Kingston was a crucial writer for me to read. She was an innovator, someone who did something completely new. Basically I really have to admire and love an artist's work and be able to justify it as literature before I teach it in my classes. But fortunately there are so many good writers out there representing so many different groups that I have no problem coming up with a very varied syllabus.

JH: Do you see yourself as a mentor for younger writers?

Yes, I do. Some of my graduate students spend four or five years under my tutelage. I end up spending a lot of personal time with them, and I don't mind it. These are extremely intelligent people, and some of them are very talented writers. Not all will have a successful future as writers, but I don't know that when I first meet them so they all get the same treatment. So, yes, I do see myself as a mentor, and as far as teaching, I knew I wanted to be a teacher before I knew I wanted to be a writer. I never thought of another career. Teaching is just what I always wanted to do ever since I was a child.

JH: What motivated you to publish poetry?

Actually there's never a great deal of encouragement to publish poetry. There's no money in it, you have to want to do it. At first, no one wanted to publish my poems for the same reason that they later wouldn't publish *The Line of the Sun*. A letter from a university press said that they liked my poems, but they used too much Spanish and their audience was not necessarily bilingual. I wondered if T. S. Eliot expected everyone to speak ancient Hindu when they read *The Wasteland*. Or whether Pound expected people to know Chinese. It didn't make sense. I sent it to Arte Público, and they took it and the next one to the Bilingual Press. At that time those were my only options because I was writing poems that contained a little Spanish, which I don't think interferes with understanding.

BK: Now the use of Spanish is more acceptable.

Exactly. It should always have been acceptable. If people care enough to read poetry, they care enough to look up a word. I went around with a bunch of dictionaries when I was reading American and British literature. Anyway, it's been a long road, and with me it hasn't exactly been like it has with Esmeralda and Sandra. My work, for whatever reason, has had to first find a home with the smaller university presses, and then, usually after it gets good reviews and awards, a big press like Penguin or Norton will pick it up. My agent just has one phrase that she uses about my work, "It is too literary." And I say, "What . . . does that mean?" It is not that it is hard to understand, it is just that it deals with subjects that are not easily translated into the mass media in some cases. I have been more fortunate recently in that my work has gotten into all the big anthologies, Norton, Oxford, that sort of thing. Now people seem a little more willing to take a chance. Norton published the paperback of the *Deli* and Penguin published the paperback of *An Island Like You*.

BK: Why do your works rely on oral histories? What's special about the oral quality of Puerto Rican literature for you?

I think that many cultures have that oral quality. In fact, my husband is a Southerner and comes from a storytelling family. But they tell their stories differently. There are certain stories that define a family and certain keywords that call them up and everyone knows that if you say something about someone or something in front of his grandmother, that she will immediately tell that story. And even though she usually tells it in the same way, it's expected and everyone enjoys it. What my grandmother liked to do that made her, at least I thought, different and unique was that she didn't mind changing the story for her audience. So I would hear her tell one story for my aunts in a particular way and assure us that it was absolutely true and then tell it to us in a different way to make a different point. What I learned about art from her was that it wasn't so much the facts as the poetic truth that was being made. I thought that was a great lesson to learn. She made an art out of stories that could've been just simple gossip. My mother and the women in the United States told stories to comfort themselves in their loneliness, to remember the island. I remember parties in the apartment in Paterson where people would actually start out telling a funny story and end up crying because the last time they heard it had been from their mothers. Storytelling is used in a culture to preserve its memories and to teach lessons for the same reason that artists write their stories. I give credit to the women in my family for giving me that lesson and some of the original stories that I used.

BK: It seems that you've also adopted your grandmother's view that when you tell a story it's for poetic truth.

Right. Absolutely. I have that little epigraph from Emily Dickinson that says, "Tell all the truth but tell it slant." I basically feel that unless I'm writing an essay where I am bound to stick to the genealogical and historical truth, I'm using my powers as a poet and an artist to compose a picture. My art is not representational but impressionistic. I like for my canvases to coalesce into meaning rather than just try to get it all photographically correct. In *Silent Dancing*, for example, I vowed to tell as much of the truth as I could. I think that book has meant a lot to some people because I think I captured the truth about what it was to be a Puerto Rican girl in the sixties. But I could not vouch that words that my grandmother had spoken back in 1960 were exactly what I had put down on the paper all these years later, so I told the poetic truth. I think that the contract with the reader is what matters as long as you let the reader know that you're working as a poet rather than a historian....

Source: Bridget Kevane, "The Poetic Truth: An Interview with Judith Ortiz Cofer," in *Latina Self-Portraits: Interviews with Contemporary Women Writers*, edited by Bridget Kevane and Juanita Heredia, University of New Mexico Press, 2000, pp. 107–123.

Kenneth Wishnia

In the following review, Wishnia comments on Cofer's first collection of short stories and poetry, "American History" among them, and notes that Cofer both "exposes and rejects common stereotypes" in her work.

Judith Ortiz Cofer's writing defies convenient classification, although she works with many themes that are common to ethnic-American literature, for example, the feeling of being in exile in a strange land, where the sound of Spoken Spanish is so comforting that even a grocery list reads "like poetry." The daily struggle to consolidate opposing identities is perhaps most clearly exemplified by the tradition which determines that a *latina* becomes a "woman" at age 15, which means, paradoxically, not more freedom but more restrictions, since womanhood is defined as sexual maturity, which must then be contained at all costs. This leaves one of her characters feeling "like an exile in the foreign country of my parents' house" because of "absurd" rules that do not apply to her present reality in Paterson, New Jersey.

Another striking example of such cultural clash occurs in the story, "Advanced Biology," in which a ninth grade Jewish boy tells the eighth grade narrator about both the Holocaust and reproductive biology. This leads her to doubt both God's "Mysterious Ways" and the Virgin Birth (and to have a screaming match with her mother on the topic), but concludes with her asking:

> Why not allow Evolution and Eve, Biology and the Virgin Birth? Why not take a vacation from logic? I will not be away for too long, I will not let myself be tempted to remain in the sealed garden of blind faith; I'll stay just long enough to rest myself from the exhausting enterprise of leading the examined life.

Indeed, Ortiz Cofer invites us to do the same when she presents the story of a young Puerto Rican girl's first disappointing attempt to date a non-*latino* Catholic. In "American History," we get a fictionalized account of the girl living in a tenement in Paterson, who takes a liking to a "white" boy from Georgia named Eugene, only to have her mother warn her, "You are heading for humiliation and pain." Soon Eugene's mother tells her in a "honey-drenched voice" that it's "nothing personal," but she should "run back home now" and never try to speak to the boy again. In "The Story of My Body," a similar situation occurs, and her mother tells her, "You better be ready for disappointment." The warning is followed by the boy's father saying, "Ortiz? That's Spanish, isn't it?", as he looks at her picture in the yearbook and shakes his head *No*. In the poem, "To a Daughter I Cannot Console," the narrator telephones her mother for advice on how to console her own lovesick sixteen-year-old daughter, and when her mother asks her "to remember the boy I had cried over for days. / I could not for several minutes / recall that face." The reader is left with the impression that such an event must have happened to Ortiz Cofer, or else why would she describe it three different ways in the same book? But it is precisely these "three different ways" that ask us—perhaps even compel us—to withdraw from "the exhausting enterprise" of examining too closely. Such events are common ethnic-American experiences, and thus all versions are in some way equally "true."

Other familiar themes treated in colorful and moving ways include the preparation of food (one character derives some fragment of solace after the death of her husband by entering her apartment building at dinnertime, and inhaling deeply "the aromas of her country"), . . . the untranslatability of certain culturally-bound concepts into English (*nada* can mean so much more than "nothing"), disappointment with fathers, men, and God, and the different standards of beauty between cultures. The essay, "The Paterson Public Library," should be required reading in all high schools and colleges.

One especially provocative issue will have to serve for discussion: "The Story of My Body" begins, "I was born a white girl in Puerto Rico but became a brown girl when I came to live in the United States." This essay, about how our identities are often dependent upon how others define us, is followed by a poem appropriately called, "The Chameleon," and another essay, "The Myth of the Latin Woman: I Just Met a Girl Named Maria," in which Ortiz Cofer exposes and rejects common stereotypes of *latinas* as "hot," "sizzling," etc., explaining that in Puerto Rico, women felt freer to dress and move "provocatively" because the climate demanded it, and they were more-or-less protected by "the traditions, mores and laws of a Spanish / Catholic system of morality and machismo whose main rule was *You may look at my sister, but if you touch her I will kill you.*"

Yet, at the opening of "The Myth of the Latin Woman," Ortiz Cofer writes about how she coveted "that British [self-] control," and in the poem, "Who Will Not Be Vanquished?" she writes:

> Morning suits us Spanish women.
> Tragedy turns us into Antigone—maybe we are bred for the part.

Perhaps an "insider" can write this, but does it not also suggest that we all have our own preferred stereotypes? . . .

In "5:00 A.M.: Writing as Ritual," Ortiz Cofer describes a period in her life when motherhood and adjunct teaching freshman composition at three different campuses somehow failed to fulfill her completely, and she writes that "There was something missing in my life that I came close to only when I turned to my writing." There is a bit of this sentiment in all of us.

Source: Kenneth Wishnia, Review of *The Latin Deli: Prose and Poetry* by Judith Ortiz Cofer, in *MELUS*, Vol. 22, No. 3, Fall 1997, pp. 206–208.

SOURCES

Central Intelligence Agency, *World Factbook*, s.v. "Puerto Rico," https://www.cia.gov/library/publications/the-world-factbook/geos/rq.html (accessed June 26, 2008).

Cofer, Judith Ortiz, "American History," in *Big City Cool: Short Stories about Urban Youth*, edited by M. Jerry Weiss and Helen S. Weiss, Persea Books, 2002, pp. 64–72.

Crovitz, Darren, Review of *Big City Cool*, in *Journal of Adolescent and Adult Literacy*, October 2003, Vol. 47, No. 2, p. 185.

"Great Falls Historic District Cultural Center," in *City of Paterson, New Jersey*, http://www.patcity.com/ (accessed August 19, 2008).

"Immigration . . . Puerto Rican/Cuban," in *American Memory from the Library of Congress*, http://memory.loc.gov/learn/features/immig/alt/cuban3.html (accessed June 26, 2008).

"Judith Ortiz Cofer," in *Voices from the Gap*, http://voices.cla.umn.edu/vg/Bios/entries/cofer_judith_ortiz.html (accessed August 19, 2008).

O'Shea, Michael J., Review of *The Latin Deli: Prose and Poetry*, in *Studies in Short Fiction*, Summer 1994, Vol. 31, No. 3, p. 502.

Pew Hispanic Center, s.v. "Immigration," http://pewhispanic.org/topics/index.php?TopicID = 16 (accessed June 26, 2008).

Rosales, F. Arturo, *Dictionary of Latino Civil Rights History*, Arte Publico Press, 2007.

Stockland, Patricia M., *The Assassination of John F. Kennedy*, Abdo, 2007.

U.S. Census Bureau, "Facts for Features," http://www.census.gov/Press-Release/www/releases/archives/facts_for_features_special_editions/010327.html (accessed August 19, 2008).

FURTHER READING

Acosta-Belen, Edna, *Puerto Ricans in the United States: A Contemporary Portrait*, Lynne Rienner Publishers, 2006.

Acosta-Belen provides an interesting look at Puerto Ricans who have migrated to the United States, exploring the reasons for their moves and their challenges in adjusting.

Dallek, Robert, *An Unfinished Life: John F. Kennedy, 1917–1963*, Back Bay Books, 2004.

This biography of Kennedy is written by a historian who provides not only the personal story but the background of one of the more famous U.S. presidents.

Gonzalez, Juan, *Harvest of Empire: A History of Latinos in America*, Penguin Books, 2001.

Gonzalez's popular book provides profiles of Latino immigrant families. In addition, the author offers historical background on the various political events that led these people to leave their homeland and seek refuge in the United States.

Hernandez, Carmen Delores, *Puerto Rican Voices in English: Interviews with Writers*, Praeger Paperback, 1997.

Hernandez, a literary critic, has collected interviews she conducted with fourteen prominent Puerto Rican writers living in the United States. The writers discuss their struggles in their new culture and their desire to communicate the results.

Pico, Fernando, *History of Puerto Rico: A Panorama of Its People*, Markus Wiener Publishers, 2006.

Professor Pico is considered an eminent authority on the history of Puerto Rico. His work is highly praised for its readability and his storytelling skills, which make reading history enjoyable.

Anxiety

GRACE PALEY

1985

Grace Paley's short story "Anxiety" was originally published in her third collection of short stories, *Later the Same Day*, in 1985. More recently, "Anxiety" was included in a compilation of her short stories, *Grace Paley: The Collected Stories*, published in 1994. Paley's short stories depict the lives and experiences of men and women living in New York City. Initially Paley's work captured the experiences of Russian- and Yiddish-speaking Jewish immigrants and the language of the community in which she was raised. Her later work was more feminist in tone and reflected Paley's commitment to the equal rights movement. As she became more feminist, Paley focused more on depicting the conflicts and trials of ordinary women trying to survive in a world designed for men's successes. The stories in *Later the Same Day* begin to move away from feminism and focus more clearly on Paley's antiwar interests, her pacifism, and her concerns for the future of the world. "Anxiety" fits well into Paley's later literary tradition of protest literature. The story's protagonist is a woman who worries so much about the possible destruction of the world that she accosts people walking on the street to warn them that the danger they face is so severe that they cannot ignore it even long enough to enjoy a moment of happiness. Paley's work, then, reflects the social shift from the 1950s ideal of women supporting a man's world to the women's movement of the

Grace Paley (© Getty Images)

1970s, and finally to the image of women as voices of caution and warning about the dangers that the world faces.

AUTHOR BIOGRAPHY

Grace Paley was born Grace Goodside on December 11, 1922, in New York City. Her father, Zenya Gutseit (later changed to Isaac Goodside), was a Russian Jew who immigrated to the United States in 1905 in the wave of Eastern European and Russian Jews who came to the United States at the turn of the century to escape the ethnic violence that plagued the Jews of that region. Paley's father attended medical school and became a doctor, while her mother, Manya (later changed to Mary), worked as a photography retoucher and managed her husband's medical practice on the first floor of the family home in the Bronx. Paley grew up in the same building that housed her father's medical office. She was part of an extended family of aunts and grandmothers, consisting of multiple generations, all under the same roof. She was also raised in the family tradition of socialists and anarchists, many of whom had died in Russia for their beliefs. Those who survived and came to the United States brought their willingness to protest. Paley was the youngest of three children, all of whom grew up speaking Russian, Yiddish, and English in a household with two cultures, the old and the new. Paley attended Hunter College (1938–39), and at age nineteen, she married Jess Paley, who was then sent overseas to fight in World War II. After he returned from the war, they had two children, Nora in 1949 and Daniel in 1951. Paley attended New York University briefly in the late 1940s but never completed a program of study. Paley also studied poetry with W. H. Auden in the early 1950s.

Paley began writing poetry and fragments of stories as a small child, but her first completed stories did not emerge until the 1950s. An initial three stories were shown to a family friend and editor, who asked Paley to write more stories, which he would later publish as her first collection of short stories, *The Little Disturbances of Man: Stories of Women and Men at Love* (1959). These first stories were considered significant enough that Paley was awarded a Guggenheim Fellowship in 1961 and a National Endowment for the Arts Award in 1966. After the publication of this first slim volume of stories, Paley turned her attention to the Vietnam War. As the youngest child by fourteen years, she had grown up in the company of adults. Paley absorbed her extended family's commitment to social concerns and was arrested several times as she protested on behalf of the antiwar organizations to which she belonged, including the War Resisters' League, Resist, the Women's Pentagon Action, and the Greenwich Village Peace Center. Paley and her husband divorced in 1971. In 1972, she married poet and playwright Robert Nichols.

A second collection of Paley's short stories, *Enormous Changes at the Last Minute*, was published in 1974. Her third collection of stories, *Later the Same Day* (1985), in which "Anxiety" first appeared, earned Paley the honor of being named the first State Author of New York in 1986. In addition to the three books of short stories, Paley was also writing poetry, and in 1985, her first collection of poems, *Leaning Forward*, was published.

Paley was honored with the Edith Wharton Award in 1983 and a National Endowment for the Arts Senior Fellowship in 1987. She was also elected to the American Academy of Arts and Letters. In 1989, Paley retired from Sarah Lawrence College, where she had been teaching writing since 1966. *Long Walks and Intimate Talks*, a collection of short stories and poetry, followed in 1991. In 1993, Paley received the Rea Award for the Short Story, considered to be the highest honor awarded to short story writers. Throughout her writing career, Paley frequently published short pieces in magazines, in newspapers, and in the occasional newsletter. A collection of these short essays and columns was published as *Just as I Thought* in 1998. Paley died August 22, 2007, at her home in Thetford Hills, Vermont, of breast cancer.

PLOT SUMMARY

"Anxiety" begins with a woman's observance of two fathers waiting for their children to emerge from school at the end of the day. The setting is spring, and the woman who watches the two fathers mentions that her window box contains greenhouse marigolds. The woman is so anxious for spring that she has planted the first hothouse blooms of the season at her window. It is also one of the first days nice enough to open a window and watch people walking along the streets. The window box partially hides her face, as she watches "through the ferny leaves."

When the bell rings the children rush through the doors to their waiting fathers. When one of the two fathers lifts his daughter to his shoulders, the watching woman notes that the child appears to be Chinese, or at least "a little" Chinese. The father was earlier described as having curly hair, which suggests that the little girl is of mixed heritage, since Asians do not often have curly hair. Paley uses this subtle piece of information to remind her readers that New York City is a mixture of different ethnicities. The second father also lifts his child, a son, onto his shoulders, but Paley has provided only a minimal description of this father, stating that he is physically similar to the first father. His child is not described at all.

As the two fathers and children begin walking away from the school, they pass under the window of the woman who has watched them walked from the school. She observes that the father of the little girl appears to be struggling with his daughter. He is slight and perhaps too frail to carry his daughter on his shoulders. The little girl wiggles and the father's discomfort leads him to tell the child to stop her wiggling. The child responds with "Oink oink." When challenged, she repeats the two words. The father, now clearly angry, grabs the child and sets her on the ground. The movement is hard enough that the little girl rubs her ankle, which now hurts. When she asks what she has done to anger him, he yells that she is to hold his hand.

At this point, the woman ceases to watch from between the leaves and now leans out the window and interjects herself into the tableau unfolding on the street. She echoes the man's agitation as she yells at him, "Stop! Stop!" It is not clear if the woman wants the man to stop yelling at his daughter or to stop walking. Perhaps she means for both to happen. The man quickly turns around to look up at the speaker and ask who she is. The suggested meaning of his words is to ask who she is to yell at a complete stranger. In response, she finally moves the flowers that have hidden her and emerges to be clearly seen by the walkers below.

Once the father can see her, the woman invokes the tradition of tenement women, who have lived in similar buildings in generations past. These women have leaned out their windows and supervised their children below. Her memories of this tradition make her brave enough to tell the young father that the history of mothers in this building enables her to lean out the window and give him the traditional wisdom of mothers, who have always leaned out their windows to advise and chastise. The young father is a bit embarrassed to be called out by this older woman, and he jokes with his friend about the old gray-haired woman leaning out the window.

She asks him his age, and he replies that he is thirty-three. In response she tells him that he is a generation ahead of his father in his relationship with his daughter. His father's generation is a generation of fathers who worked to provide for their families and did not walk to school to pick up their children. These fathers saw a clearer division of male and female spheres. In this earlier generation, mothers cared for their children, and fathers worked to support their family. The lines that defined parenting roles were more clearly drawn.

The narrator knows that complimenting the father is one way to begin the conversation and put him at ease. She has more that she wants to say to him, so she leans even farther out the window to caution him about the danger that all humankind face. The gravity of her words is first illustrated by her need to lean farther out the window. She wants to get as close to the young father as is possible when she tells him that "madmen intend to destroy this beautifully made planet." She warns him that the risk to his child and to other children needs to be a concern for all fathers. These words reflect a growing awareness that nuclear weapons, environmental pollution, and terrorism have the potential to destroy the world. At first, the father greets the woman's warnings with mockery, but he soon admits that he is also concerned about the future.

Now that she has the father's attention, the woman asks why he became so angry with his daughter that he slammed her to the ground. Once she is able to get the father to admit that it was the words "oink oink" that angered him, the old woman elicits the confession that hearing those two words reminded him of a time when he protested against the authority establishment and used those words. Now when those same words are directed toward him, he is reminded that he is over thirty and part of the establishment that he once held in derision. This realization defuses the young father's anger, as he recalls that, while he never wanted to be an authority figure, it has happened anyway. Fatherhood has made him a responsible member of society. The woman next suggests that the father should begin the walk again by returning to the school yard and pretending that he never lost his temper with his daughter.

Both fathers begin to pretend they are horses giving their children rides home. The little girl's father forgets his frailty, as his daughter cheerfully kicks his chest and screams, "giddap giddap." The fathers and children enjoy the moment of play as they gallop toward their homes. Only the old woman is not happy. She notices that they are galloping toward a very busy intersection and worries that they will not make it safely to their homes. After she closes the window, she sits and wonders how she can make sure that they will arrive home safely, with so many large cars, created as the "bulky dreams of automakers," putting their lives at risk. If they arrive home safely she would like to be certain that the children have a healthy snack of juice, milk, or cookies. The final brief paragraph of this short story serves to define the title "Anxiety." Readers finally grasp that this woman sees risk from her windows. She is like mothers everywhere who would like to protect all children from the risks they face in what has become an increasingly dangerous world.

CHARACTERS

Ken

Ken is one of only two characters whose names are mentioned in "Anxiety." His role is a minor one. He meets his son at school and carries the child on his shoulders until they are stopped by the woman's voice. Ken and his son accompany the other father and his daughter on the journey home. He has no important position in the story.

Rosie

Rosie is the child whose father is chastised by the woman watcher. Readers only learn of the child's name near the end of the story; for most of the story, she is identified as a giggling, playful child who wiggles too much. The first image of the child is one of happiness and joy, and thus the father's irritation that she is too playful is at first a bit surprising. His subsequent anger at the little girl's chanting "oink oink," which results in the child being forcibly set on the ground, is shocking. His anger seems to be an inappropriately severe reaction to the child's behavior. When the father finally admits that he was angry at the child because she was treating him as if he "was a figure of authority," his anger is defused and child's happiness is restored. The ease with which Rosie's mood is so quickly returned to joy suggests that the child's relationship with her father is filled with love. His momentary irritation is quickly forgotten, and Rosie easily and happily climbs back on her father's back to pretend that he is a horse giving her a ride home. At heart, she is a happy child, and the father's irritation with her seems to be nothing more than a momentary bad mood.

Woman Watcher

The woman who watches from the window is the narrator of "Anxiety." The only description given of her is that her hair is gray, so readers know that she is not a young woman and not as young as the father she accosts. She is at least a generation older. Readers know what is happening only from her perspective. She is also the voice of caution, of warning, and of fear. She worries that the young father is not patient with his child. She also worries that he is not appreciative of the present and does not cherish his daughter enough, since the future is so filled with risk. At the end of the story, she worries that he cannot get his daughter home safely past the busy intersection or beyond and "across other dangerous avenues."

She is like many mothers, who never stop worrying about their children, no matter how remote the danger. At first the woman seems to be only a concerned citizen who wants to stop a father from being short-tempered with his daughter, but at the end of the story, her worry extends to concern that the father might not be attentive enough to cross a busy intersection without calamity. Worry about busy intersections would seem justified if the small children were walking home on their own, but they are not. They are accompanied by their fathers, so when the woman worries about "how to make sure" that they will arrive home safely, she seems more inclined to worry than most mothers. She may also be lonely. Instead of being down on the street, she peeks out at the people on the street below, watching through the leaves of the plants in the window box. She is a watcher who observes life rather than participates in it.

The old woman is not given a name, although it is likely that she is Faith Darwin, who appears in many of Paley's stories. As she is unnamed, however, the woman becomes representative of a tradition of women who have leaned out of their tenement windows and watched their children at play on the streets below. From their windows, mothers could yell at their children to take care of a younger sibling or to come inside for dinner. Most important, these mothers could shout warnings to their children, just as the old woman now shouts at the young father who walks on the sidewalk below.

The streets used to be safer for children. There were fewer cars and the intersections were not so dangerous. There were also no threats from "the airy scary dreams of scientists," who create technologies that lead to environmental pollution or who create nuclear weapons and turn the world into a place where war threatens. Paley uses this woman's words as a way to remind readers that the world is not a safe place and that the future may be even more dangerous than the present.

Young Father

The young father is given no name, since he represents all fathers who need to be warned about the dangerous future their children face. This young father is described as being like other fathers. He and his friend are identified in the opening scene as identical. They both have curly hair and brown mustaches. They wait together, talking easily and eating pizza as they wait for their children to emerge from the school. He is like every other father who comes to the school to walk his child home. He assumes his own identity and individual characteristics on the journey home when he becomes upset with his daughter, who wiggles too much. At that point, Paley identifies him as frail. The wiggling child creates discomfort. He is uncomfortable enough with the child's weight on his shoulders that he becomes easily angered by the child's chanting "oink oink."

In response to being accosted by the woman in the window, the young father is a bit uncomfortable and embarrassed at having been caught being short-tempered with his daughter. Although he laughs at what the woman says, Paley describes him as doing so with a "little embarrassment." However, he quickly relaxes after the woman tells him that he is ahead of the previous generation in his treatment of his daughter. She is referring to the father's willingness to pick up his child from school. The previous generation of fathers did not do this; they worked at jobs all day, and mothers picked up the children.

The father's involvement with his daughter is a positive trait. By beginning with a compliment, the woman helps to diffuse the father's embarrassment and any anger he might feel at the woman interfering with his treatment of his child. The father does indicate that he is not completely accepting of what the woman tells him. He thinks the woman is being dogmatic and indicates this feeling when he tells her: "Speech, speech." However, he is interested enough in her remarks that he continues to stand and wait for her to continue speaking to him.

The young man's attentiveness validates the woman's concerns and indicates his own awareness of the precarious nature of the future of the world. He is clearly a concerned father who worries about his daughter's future. Paley makes the young man's concern evident when he turns a "serious face" to the woman and continues listening to her speak. The father also reveals a sense of

TOPICS FOR FURTHER STUDY

- In previous generations, mothers would have been the parents most often waiting outside the school to walk their children home. When Paley is writing, however, fathers also share their children's walk home. Research the changes in women's employment since 1965. Look for statistics that reveal the number of women who were been employed outside the home in 1965, 1975, 1985, 1995, and 2005. Prepare an oral presentation that discusses the information that you have discovered. Be prepared to ask your classmates about their own home experiences and how their mother's employment is reflected in parenting roles in their homes.
- Artists are often inspired by writers to create some of the most beautiful art imaginable. For instance, William Blake was inspired by John Milton's poetry to create illustrations of the poet's finest work. Spend some time looking through art books in the library and try to select a picture or illustration that you feel best illustrates Paley' short story. Then, in a carefully worded essay, compare the art that you have selected to the images that Paley creates in her story, noting the similarities and differences between art and prose.
- Paley mentioned in interviews that as a child she was told stories, and as an adult she became the writer of stories. What do you see as the difference between telling stories and writing stories? Research the history of the oral narrative. Look for information about when the oral narrative was replaced by the written narrative and prepare an oral report in which you discuss the history of both narratives, what you think was lost and gained by the transition from spoken stories to written stories, and what you see as the essential differences between these two narrative styles.
- One of Paley's concerns in this short story is the destruction of the planet. Research the role of the group Greenpeace and write an essay in which you analyze this group's work. What successes, if any, can attributed to their attempts to protect the planet from environmental destruction?
- The narrator refers to a tradition of women who watched over their children from the tenement windows. Research life in New York City in 1915 and 1985. How did people live during these two periods? Where did they work? What did they do when they were not working? What were families like? Create a poster in which you list the similarities and the differences that you have found between these two eras.

humor when the woman contrives to force an admission from him that he had used "oink oink" to address policemen during a demonstration years earlier, which is why he reacted so strongly to his daughter's use of the phrase. As soon as the young father realizes the source of his anger, he is quick to try to make amends and suggests that he be the horse and his daughter be the rider on the way home. The father's love for his child is evident in the final scene of the two of them together, as they gallop off toward their home.

THEMES

Anxiety

One important theme of Paley's short story "Anxiety" is taken directly from the title. Paley's protagonist is so anxious about the future that she sits and watches the world from her window. When she sees a father in need of a warning, she leans out of her window and speaks to him from the safety of her home. Initially it appears that the woman is only concerned about the father's harsh treatment of his daughter, but it quickly becomes apparent that the woman is mostly concerned about danger. The danger faced is not tangible or even defined. It is a vague danger in the future, with risks posed by madmen who "intend to destroy" the world. The woman warns the father that the risk for his child is sufficient that it should interfere with any pleasure that the father might be finding in his walk home with his daughter. Although her warning that they should not be finding any enjoyment in their lives seems excessive, even at this point of the narrative, the woman seems to be presenting reasonable fears about the dangers presented by war and the kinds of technology that creates weapons designed to destroy millions of people.

In the final two paragraphs, however, the true extent of her anxiety is revealed as a fear of the more vague possibilities of danger. As the children and their father leave to continue their journey home, she worries about the traffic at the intersection and then the intersections beyond the one at the corner. Finally, readers see that she even worries about the snack the children will eat when they return home, and she wishes that she could see that they are eating a healthy snack. Her anxiety about the world is severe enough that she needs to see that the children are safe and healthy. Of course, she cannot see them at their home, since like the hothouse marigolds, the woman is sheltered in her own home, safe from all the risks that lie outside her window.

Parental Love

Parental love is often described as unconditional and unlimited. Although children can occasionally test their parents' patience, most parents are able to quickly recover from momentary irritation, as the father in Paley's story does. Although the father becomes angry in the story, his love for his daughter is not in doubt. Because of his parental love, he seems to share the woman's concerns about the danger that children face when men try to "destroy this beautifully made planet." He also admits that he became angry because his child's words suggested that he was a figure of authority, which is not how he wants to be seen. Parental love is also about recognizing and acknowledging parental injustice. The brief conflict between the father and his child is resolved when he lifts her onto his back to continue their ride home. Both parent and child are enveloped in love as they alternate yelling "U-up" and "giddap" on their gallop home. In the face of an uncertain future, what this father can offer his child is evidence of his love for her.

Science and Technology

The warnings in "Anxiety" reflect the narrator's concern that humankind is not paying sufficient attention to the risks posed by science and technology. For example, the woman in the window warns the father that the futures of his child and of all children are in danger due to the actions of madmen, who are putting the world at risk. The exact risk is never defined. Making the risk vague allows Paley to encompass a wide variety of threats, such as pollution from too many large automobiles, ecological damage, weapons of war, or some as-yet-unknown technology. The woman warns that the risk of future destruction is so great that it should interfere with any pleasure that the father might experience as he walks with his child. The woman does not consider that her extreme warnings are excessive. Her fears for the future are so great that they propel her to warn strangers about the risks the world faces in a future where science and technology are not better controlled.

STYLE

First-Person Narrator

In a short story or novel, the term "narrator" is used to describe the person who tells the story, and a first-person narrator tells the story from his or her limited point of view. The woman is the first-person narrator in "Anxiety," and she is also the protagonist, the central character. She tells the story and interprets it for the reader. The reader learns something about the characters in "Anxiety" and almost nothing about their personal stories. This is because the other characters are filtered through the woman's eyes. The story is limited to the first-person narrator's experiences and observations. The woman lacks the omniscient view of a third-person narrator, in which the author serves as the narrator, offering all views. In some cases, authors use multiple narrators, in which several characters tell their stories. This gives the reader the opportunity to see the characters from multiple perspectives. Since Paley uses only one narrator, readers are limited in their understanding of characters' motivations and must simply interpret their actions. For example, when the father sets his daughter down on the ground so roughly that she rubs her ankle in pain, readers know that the man is angry at the child. This characterization through action is also clearly seen in the depiction of the woman's personality. She peeks out at the people on the street below, watching through the leaves of the plants in the window box, and readers understand that she is a watcher. Paley ultimately reveals to her readers the true nature of her narrator—she is so consumed with worry about the future that she does not participate in the present. She closes the window and sits and worries.

Protest Literature

Protest literature is writing that is designed to generate action. Authors who write protest literature hope to increase social awareness in their readers and thereby bring about change. Protest literature has a long history. Jonathan Swift, Charles Dickens, and Harriet Beecher Stowe used literature as a way to protest the treatment of the disenfranchised citizens of Ireland, England, and the United States, respectively. Paley embraces this tradition and uses her stories as a vehicle to promote her social activism. "Anxiety" reflects the author's concerns about war and the use of technology, which she worries might destroy the world. She refers to the "murder of our children by these men," who present an unnamed and undefined danger. This generalization provides a generic warning about the risk that children face in the future. At the end of the story, Paley labels "these men" as scientists and automakers. Most protest literature is more specific in its warnings, but Paley leaves room for interpretation.

HISTORICAL CONTEXT

Social Activism in the 1980s

Paley's writing was heavily influenced by her desire to create a better world. The early 1980s was a period in which wars were being fought in Afghanistan and in the Falkland Islands. The U.S. embassy in Iran was seized by terrorists, and the U.S. embassy in Lebanon was bombed. This was also a period in which scientists were trying to create more technologically advanced weapons, although there was briefly some hope that such weapons might never need to be used. By the mid-1980s, the Cold War between the Soviet Union and the United States was finally resolving, and it seemed that the long-time tension and threat of war that had existed between the two superpowers since the close of World War II would finally end. Although it appeared that President Ronald Reagan of the United States and General Secretary Mikhail Gorbachev of the U.S.S.R. might together bring peace to the world, Reagan continued to lobby for the creation of a Strategic Defense Initiative, nicknamed Star Wars, which would be capable of intercepting a missile launched by the Soviet Union. Work on the Star Wars program suggested that peace might not last, as so many people hoped.

The effects of industrial pollution led to worldwide acid rain that destroyed trees and plants. In response to worries about the destruction of the environment, a protest group called Greenpeace disrupted nuclear tests planned by the U.S. government. The success of these first protests led Greenpeace to begin working to save endangered animals. The accident at the Three Mile Island nuclear plant, the toxic waste contamination in the Niagra Falls neighborhood of Love Canal, several oil spills throughout the world, and increased activities by terrorist groups, such as the Red Brigades and militant factions of the Palestinian Liberation Organization, are all events that fed Paley's concerns about the state of the world and her worry—voiced in this short story—that children born in the 1980s would not have a world in which to grow if people did not become more involved in protecting the environment.

The Changing Role of Fathers

Although Paley never explicitly refers to a time in which her short story is set, it is reasonable to assume that the setting is the mid- to late 1970s or early 1980s, a time of tremendous social change, especially in the way that families were constructed. This is a period during which women demanded greater equality in the workplace and in the home. Women began to work outside the home in larger numbers, a trend acknowledged by the events in "Anxiety." Paley's female narrator stops a young father walking on the street below her window, tells him that he is "about a generation ahead" in his "attitude and behavior" toward his child. Since Paley's narrator does not know this father, she is basing this comment on

COMPARE & CONTRAST

- **1980s:** By the beginning of the 1980s, the effects of global pollution lead to warnings that the ice at the North and South poles will soon begin to melt. By the middle of this decade a hole in the ozone layer is discovered over Antarctica.

  Today: According to the *New York Times*, a 2007 United Nations study on global warming confirms that a warming trend is attributable to increased carbon dioxide levels created by humans. The study warns that sea levels could increase between 7 and 23 inches by the end of the twenty-first century due to the melting of the ice caps. Global warming is often considered to pose a significant risk to human life, especially for those who live near coastal areas.

- **1980s:** By the beginning of this decade, there are several terrorist groups well established in Spain (the Basque Fatherland and Liberty group), Italy (the Red Brigades), the Middle East (militant factions of the Palestinian Liberation Organization), and the United Kingdom (the Irish Republican Army). These groups claim responsibility for bombings, sniper attacks, and mass murder, all of which are designed to terrorize the inhabitants of these areas.

  Today: Terrorism remains a problem throughout the world. In addition to the terrorist attacks in New York City and Washington, D.C., on September 11, 2001, there are terrorist attacks in Istanbul, Turkey, in 2003; Madrid, Spain, in 2004; and London, England, in 2005. There are also multiple terrorist attacks in Thailand and Indonesia during the first years of the twenty-first century.

- **1980s:** The assassination or attempted assassination of political, religious, and cultural figures dominates the news during the first half of this decade. Egyptian president Anwar Sadat, Indian Prime Minister Indira Ghandi, and musician John Lennon are assassinated, while U.S. President Ronald Reagan and Pope John Paul II are wounded during assassination attempts.

  Today: The assassination of political figures has continued into the twenty-first century. Assassinated political figures include the prime minister of Serbia in 2003, the president of the Chechen Republic in 2004, a former prime minister of Lebanon in 2005, the mayor of Moscow in 2006, and the former prime minister of India in 2007. Numerous other minor dignitaries are also assassinated.

- **1980s:** An oil crisis at the end of the previous decade causes consumers to buy smaller foreign-made automobiles in the first part of the 1980s. U.S. automakers are unprepared for the increasing popularity of smaller cars and face serious economic problems with the decline in sales of large U.S.-made vehicles.

  Today: The increase in the price of oil in 2008 results in increases in food and transportation costs. The oil crisis also leads to an increased demand for hybrid cars that use less gasoline and a decreased demand for large vehicles, which in turn leads to economic problems for U.S. automakers, who have depended on the sale of large vehicles to make a profit.

- **1980s:** Soviet troops invade Afghanistan, beginning an occupation of that country that will last more than eleven years. The United States provides supplies, including weapons, to help the Afghan guerrilla troops resist the Soviet troops.

  Today: After the terrorist attacks in the United States in September 2001, U.S. troops invade Afghanistan in an effort to capture or kill the group funding and directing terrorist activities against the United States.

what she observes—two fathers who wait for school to end so that they can walk their children home. She has no other information about either the fathers or their children, but clearly her perception is that fathers in the 1980s are becoming more involved in their children's lives than were fathers in previous generations. Traditionally, fathers in earlier generations were the financial providers. Most women assumed responsibility for housekeeping and child care. According to Department of Labor reports, only 17 percent of women with children worked outside the home in 1948, but by 1985, the number of working mothers had climbed to 61 percent. By the end of the 1960s, women began to enter the workforce in larger numbers. Since many of these women were now providing economically for their families, it was expected that fathers would begin to fill the role of nurturer, rather than just provider. While "Anxiety" seems to suggest that this was occurring, some sociological studies challenge this perception. As reported by Ralph LaRossa in his study "Fatherhood and Social Change," a national survey conducted in 1981, just about the time that Paley was writing this story, fathers were spending only about five minutes more per day on average with their children than was reported in a 1975 study. The total time that fathers were spending with their children in 1981 was reported to be about 2.88 hours a week. Mothers reported spending 8.54 hours per week in child care. According to this national study, mothers were spending their time in caretaking, while fathers were spending their time primarily in play with their children. According to LaRossa, grandmothers and professional child care facilities began to fill the gap in child care. LaRossa argues that the perception that fathers were more involved in child care in the early 1980s, which Paley's narrator appears to share, was a folk myth. People wanted fathers to be more involved and simply chose to believe that they were.

Multigenerational Parenting

Paley's narrator is an older woman. The young father whom she accosts from her window refers to her as "that old gray head." In cautioning the father, she is fulfilling the traditional role of the mother, or in this case, the grandmother. The woman narrator even cites the tradition of women watching over the children below as her authority for yelling at him to stop and listen to her. Paley herself grew up in a multigenerational family and knows the importance of having more than two generations under one roof. The role of the grandmother in particular is one of augmenting child care and of passing along the wisdom of age. At the beginning of the twentieth century, new immigrants brought with them a tradition of housing extended families under one roof, just as Paley's family had done. With economic success, however, more families began to live in smaller units, without grandparents in the same household. A housing shortage after World War II led to a temporary increase in multigenerational families living together, but by the beginning of the 1950s, the typical residence once again consisted of parents and children, with only two generations in the same home.

Historian Steven Ruggles and Susan Brower point out that in 1850, 70 percent of the elderly lived with their children, where they were involved in family life and presumably in child care; by 1950, the percentage of elderly living with their children had dropped to 16 percent. Increasing mobility in the latter half of the twentieth century also meant that grandparents often lived a significant distance away from their grandchildren. By the 1960s more parents were divorcing, and by the 1980s, with the divorce rate reaching 50 percent, the family unit was no longer even defined as a father and mother living with their children. Sociologist Vern L. Bengtson suggests that multigenerational relations have once again become important in providing a more stable and nurturing family life for children. In a society with many divorces and the addition of stepparenting and sometimes multiple stepparenting, grandparents provide continuity in children's lives. They also serve as role models, as an economic resource and as a way to relieve the stress on overburdened parents.

Paley's narrator tries to assume the role of grandmotherly advisor and protector when a father is short-tempered and stressed. She cautions the father that he is being too hard on his daughter, and she warns him not to waste precious time with his child by scolding her so harshly. The narrator also worries whether the children are eating healthy foods. All of these concerns are in keeping with the role of the grandmother in a multigenerational family. By the early 1980s, when Paley was writing "Anxiety," the increasing divorce rate, combined with more women entering the workforce, meant that there was a greater need for volunteer help with child care. Paley's pseudo-grandmother suggests that older generations can provide extra help to parents who need guidance and assistance with child care.

CRITICAL OVERVIEW

When Paley died in August 2007, there were many tributes to her work and to the contributions that she had made to the literary world. These tributes did not suddenly appear with her death, as they so often do after a notable person has died. Instead, these tributes most often echoed what was written during her lifetime. When Paley's third collection of short stories, *Later the Same Day*, was published in 1985, it was reviewed in several publications. In the *New York Times Book Review* in April 1985, book critic Robert R. Harris states that Paley is "one of the best short-story writers . . . because of her uncanny ability to juxtapose life's serious and comic sides" in her work. He points out that Paley's stories remain fresh and do not become dated. Harris believes this is because Paley's work "has an honesty and guilelessness" that succeeds with readers because of her "artfully intricate prose style," which continues to surprise the reader and results in "fiction of consequence." In her 1985 review of *Later the Same Day*, novelist Anne Tyler writes in the *New Republic* that Paley is "unique, or very nearly unique, in her ability to fit large-scale political concerns both seamlessly and effectively onto very small canvases." Tyler celebrates Paley's talents with language and her ability to create characters whose activism is personal and authentic without displaying the "self-righteousness" that can be offensive to many readers.

In another 1985 review, published in the *Washington Post*, staff writer David Remnick moves beyond reviewing *Later the Same Day* and instead focuses on her body of work. Remnick claims that nearly all of Paley's forty-five published short stories are "remarkable for their clarity, their sense of place, their sympathies." Paley, suggests Remnick, is different from other short story writers, who try to be eccentric New York writers. Paley is the "genuine article, unpretentious, funny and wise." She is a writer, says Remnick, who captures the authentic experience of living in the city and of what it means to be a "New York type."

It is worth noting that not all reviewers were as enamored of Paley as Harris, Tyler, and Remnick. In her review for *Commentary*, Carol Iannone claims that once Paley became involved in protesting the Vietnam War, her stories began to "openly celebrate activism." Iannone does not see Paley's activism as a positive force in her writing. Instead, she asserts, after Paley became focused on antiwar activities, her stories became "skimpy throwaways, poorly thought out and obscure little fragments" that suggest that the writer has her mind focused on other things.

Iannone's analysis of Paley's work has proven to be the minority view. In her *Washington Post* obituary titled "Acclaimed Short-Story Writer," writer Adam Bernstein refers to Paley as "a master of the short story." In the obituary printed in the *Guardian*, writer Mark Krupnick states that Paley "was able to create in her fiction a world of voices and an ethnic style that was uniquely her own." Perhaps the most important measure of Paley's legacy as a short story writer is the tribute written by Pauline Watts, dean of Sarah Lawrence College, where Paley taught writing for more than twenty years. In the tribute, posted on the Web site of Sarah Lawrence College, Watts refers to Paley as an "iconoclastic writer" and notes the important role that Paley played in establishing the writing program at Sarah Lawrence. Paley, says Watts, thought that teaching writing was "a way to introduce young people to the difficult, life-long task of telling the truth." Her ability to influence young writers was one reason that her classes at Sarah Lawrence were so popular and suggests that her legacy as a writer is as much about teaching as it is about writing.

CRITICISM

Sheri Metzger Karmiol

Karmiol has a doctorate in English Renaissance literature and teaches literature and drama at the University of New Mexico. She is also a professional writer and the author of several reference texts on poetry and drama. In this essay, Karmiol discusses the depiction of the Jewish mother figure in "Anxiety."

In Grace Paley's three collections of short stories, she has frequently depicted the life of one central character, Faith Darwin, as she ages throughout the series of stories. Although Paley

WHAT DO I READ NEXT?

- *The Little Disturbances of Man: Stories of Women and Men at Love* (1959) was Paley's first collection of short stories. These first stories established Paley as a regional author whose characters were the people of her native New York City.
- Paley's second collection of short stories, *Enormous Changes at the Last Minute*, was published in 1974. This collection of stories reflects the author's activism and her concern about social issues. Several of these stories continue the story of Faith Darwin, who appeared in Paley's first collection of stories.
- Paley's *Long Walks and Intimate Talks* (1991) is a collection of short stories and poetry. Paley's character, Faith, is also present in the prose selections that appear in this book. The poems are more political than the stories, and both stories and poems are complemented by the paintings of artist Vera Williams.
- *Just as I Thought*, published in 1998, is a collection of Paley's essays, columns, and brief newsletter reflections. The pieces in this collection are autobiographical, so they provide information about Paley's life as well.
- *A Cynthia Ozick Reader* (1996), edited by Elaine M. Kauver, is a collection of Ozick's stories and poetry. Ozick is often compared to Paley. Like Paley, Ozick's stories focus on the lives of women, especially Jewish women.
- *The Woman Who Lost Her Names: Selected Writings by American Jewish Women* (1980), edited by Julia Wolf Mazow, is a collection of short stories that depict Jewish women in roles that move away from the stereotypes that portray Jewish women as either the Jewish American princess or the Jewish mother.
- *The Oxford Book of American Short Stories* (1992), edited by Joyce Carol Oats, is a collection of stories by some of the best-known American writers. What makes this collection interesting is that the editor has chosen to include a selection of stories that are less familiar to readers.

never mentions the name of the woman narrator in "Anxiety," it is likely that the narrator is Faith since, in a subsequent story in *Later the Same Day*, titled "The Story Hearer," Faith refers to an encounter with the young fathers earlier in the day. Faith is a mother, and more importantly, she is a Jewish mother, whom Paley uses as a vehicle to explore the people and places of her own life. The stereotype of the Jewish mother as a manipulating, guilt-inducing, nagging woman has been so prevalent in twentieth-century literature, film, and culture that she is a readily identifiable stock character for audiences of Jews and non-Jews alike. By the 1950s, when Paley began publishing the first of her short stories, the Jewish mother had become a caricature of motherhood. Paley uses her story "Anxiety" as a way to present a more positive depiction of motherhood that counters the negative stereotypes that the term "Jewish mother" presents. Paley does not simply refute this stereotype; she recasts her woman narrator in the image of the strong immigrant woman who first leaned out the windows fifty years earlier.

For Paley, a Jewish mother is a positive image of motherhood. Paley's mother figure is not the comic stereotype that became a standard of Jewish comedians, nor is she the overpowering emasculator depicted by Jewish male writers like Philip Roth, who in his novel *Portnoy's Complaint* creates a Jewish mother in control of every aspect of her son's behavior. In an interview with Ellen Rothman for *Mass Humanities* newsletter, Joyce Atler, the Samuel Lane Professor of American Jewish History at Brandeis University, says that Paley has given readers a very different portrait of the Jewish mother. Atler claims that for Paley, "mothering was a central

> **"THE STEREOTYPE OF THE JEWISH MOTHER IS A WOMAN WHO QUESTIONS MALE AUTHORITY, VOICES TOO MANY CONCERNS, AND DOES SO TOO LOUDLY AND TOO AGGRESSIVELY."**

artistic concern" in her work that provided "innovative, positive models of Jewish matriarchs." Atler's studies of Jewish mothers has revealed a tradition of mothers "who raised their children with moderate, flexible methods, passing on their own morals and values." The need to pass on wisdom and moral values is what motivates the actions of Paley's narrator, who feels compelled to offer advice and even some warnings to the parents who pass outside her window. When Paley's woman narrator sees a young father obviously annoyed with his daughter, she feels compelled to intervene. Her authority to do so, she tells readers, is the long tradition of Jewish mothers, women like the narrator, who leaned out of their windows, often as high up as the fifth floor, and yelled instructions and warnings to their children playing on the sidewalk or in the street outside.

Paley's woman narrator is cast in the tradition of these women whose strength and guidance helped their families survive and thrive after they arrived in the United States. In an essay written in the late 1970s called "Other Mothers," Paley begins with a familiar image from life in the city's tenement buildings: "The mother is at the open window." She is an observer of life who calls her children home and who, according to Paley, keeps her husband "from slipping" back down the rung of the ladder that he must climb if he will find success in this new country. The mother in Paley's short essay is cast in the image of that immigrant mother, the model for Paley's narrator in "Anxiety," who leans out the window and watches the world unfold beneath her. Atler claims that the stereotypes associated with the Jewish mother reflect the tension that immigrants felt when they first arrived in the United States at the beginning of the twentieth century. The anxieties that were created in leaving their homes for a new country, says Atler, "were often written onto the Jewish mother," whose dual personality was both "nurturant and encouraging" and "materialistic and manipulative." The Jewish mother was not given the opportunity to escape from her immigrant status, as her sons were. Instead, the Jewish mother was turned into a caricature—a mother, according to Martha Ravits, who must die before her son can become a man. In her essay "The Jewish Mother: Comedy and Controversy in American Popular Culture," Ravits traces the social, historical, and literary traditions that took Jewish women from a representation of a strong, independent immigrant woman, who capably helped her husband and children succeed, to a role of derision and an object of ridicule for Jewish comics. According to Ravits, the image of Jewish mothers evolved into a depiction of women who were unable to "observe the boundaries between proper parental concern and overprotection." The Jewish mother in film, literature, and popular culture was defined by a voice that "overflows with unsealed emotion and verbal excess." The Jewish mother loves too much and criticizes too much, and it is her son who bears the brunt of all this too-motherly love. By making the parents outside the narrator's window fathers, rather than mothers, Paley is able to counter this image of negative motherhood consuming and devouring the male progeny of Jewish mothers.

According to Ravits, there was a well-established tradition of making fun of mothers already in place before the Jewish mother became such an important part of American culture. The stereotype of the Jewish mother is a woman who questions male authority, voices too many concerns, and does so too loudly and too aggressively. Fortunately, with the passage of time, that depiction of the Jewish mother has become balanced with a more positive image, in large part because of writers such as Paley, whose works create a more positive image of Jewish mothers. Ravits claims that by the 1990s, the Jewish mother had become transformed into just another mother. Ravits credits this to a more secure place in American society for Jewish Americans, in which their ethnicity is less of a factor impacting their place in society. Ravits notes that during the cultural transition, where Jews were becoming assimilated into American life, "the stereotype of the Jewish mother was constructed to signify and mock Jews' concerns about the process of Americanization." Having the mother represent the old, pre-immigrant lifestyle allowed her children the opportunity to claim that they were more truly American than their parents. Ravits also suggests that the Jewish mother helped to diffuse anti-Semitism since both Jews and non-Jews could laugh together at the Jewish mother, who in truth was not much different from the Italian mother or the Irish mother.

For Paley, mothers, especially her own, have an important function in her work. In her essay "Other Mothers," Paley begins with the mother at the window, but she quickly moves to remembrances of mothers from her past, including her own mother. These were strong, wise women, women Paley remembers from fifty years ago. The past, though, continues to be a part of who she is: the "daughter of mothers." The connection to her mother is never far from Paley's writing. In "The Outsider Within: Women in Contemporary Jewish-American Fiction," Victoria Aarons says that it is "the figure of the mother [who] provides a deep connection to the past." It is the mother whose knowledge of the past is used to filter knowledge of the future. In Paley's world, mothers sit on the stoop outside their tenement buildings or lean out of their windows, and they talk to their neighbors and to those who pass by on the street. It is the mother, according to Aarons, who "because of her garrulity and penchant for participating actively in the lives of her neighbors," becomes a source of information for her family. This is the tradition of mother as a source of caution and information that Paley depicts in her women narrator. This is a woman who has something to say about the world she inhabits. Paley imbues her woman narrator with knowledge and a social and ecological awareness that needs to be voiced. From her window above the street, she can see farther, and as Paley's narrator makes clear, she can also see into the future clearly enough to warn those who pass below of the dangers that await them.

There is no hesitation for the woman narrator in "Anxiety." She is quick to stop the fathers, to yell, "Stop! Stop!" She knows that she is needed to offer advice and to stop this father, who seems not to recognize his daughter as one of the "lovely examples of what may well be the last generation of humankind." This narrator knows that what she has to tell the father is important. In her essay "To Aggravate the Conscience: Grace Paley's Loud Voice," Rose Kamel asserts that Paley's women narrators exhilarate readers "with a jaunty confidence that they have something vital to say" and that they have an "authority to which we cannot help but pay close attention." Certainly it is obvious that the young father in "Anxiety" is attentive to the woman's warnings, since he turns "a serious face" to the woman. Kamel also claims that Paley's narrators have "a creative sympathy for all children." This sympathy invigorates these narrators and makes them brave enough to accost strangers, especially when the goal is to protect a child. The narrator in "Anxiety" does not intrude on the father and child to be nosy or argumentative. She does so to offer wisdom and knowledge that she hopes will help protect the child. Although it appears that the narrator yells "Stop! Stop!" because she observes the father being too rough with his child, the woman yells at the father because she has a more serious warning to pass on. In a short essay titled "One Day I Made up a Story," first published in the *War Resisters Calendar* in 1985, Paley writes about the creation of the story "Anxiety." She explains that "I imagined a wild old woman leaning on her elbows at her open window, next door to the schoolyard, making a speech to the street." The old woman did not do this just the one time, as readers witness in reading "Anxiety"; she does it repeatedly. Paley states that after the woman closed the window, she played the piano for a while, but then "she opened the window and shouted again: Stop! Listen!" The old woman functions as a sort of town crier, warning those who come into her line of vision of the danger that lies in their future.

Paley uses her imagination and her memories of Jewish mothers from the tenements to create characters and situations that incorporate the traditions of her youth, while taking the text somewhere new and different. The street is dangerous, but so is the world. It is not just the busy traffic, with those huge cars that pollute the environment, that concerns Paley's narrator in "Anxiety." The world presents a danger that can best be viewed from the windows above, just as it always was in the past. Ravits claims that the Jewish mother, who emerged from the old stereotypes, remains "a cautionary figure" who still warns about the dangers that her listeners face. Paley's woman narrator is not concerned that she will be thought pushy or obnoxious, and she is unafraid of the Jewish mother stereotype

" A SHORT STORY, LIKE A POEM, IS SOMETHING THAT YOU ALMOST FEEL YOU COULD TAKE IN YOUR HAND AND LIFT UP TO THE AIR AND THE LIGHT—AND HAVE IT ALL IN ONE HAND."

that might silence her. Instead, this woman sees herself as fulfilling an important role. This Jewish mother is a woman of strength and endurance whose responsibility to protect the future is always taken seriously.

Source: Sheri Metzger Karmiol, Critical Essay on "Anxiety," in *Short Stories for Students*, Gale, Cengage Learning, 2009.

Kasia Boddy

In the following interview with Boddy, Paley shares her perspectives on being a Jewish woman writer.

...[KASIA BODDY]: This morning you said that you had been looking forward to a disagreement with Cynthia Ozick (who pulled out of the conference).

[Grace Paley]: We have political disagreements. She's a very strong Zionist. That's what she is, so, I'm not, and I never was. I wish Israel well. I have very good feelings towards it. I'm very upset now about [Ariel] Sharon and the way he's doing things—it really bothers me a lot: I think it's not only bad but stupid. Those would be our basic disagreements. I make a joke of it. She probably doesn't like that.

KB: Has she written anything about recent events?

GP: Well, I haven't read it. I haven't read a lot of stuff. I read a lot but I also miss a lot. I don't live in New York and a lot of things are happening that I miss. In a way it's good for me, but in a way. . . .

KB: Do you regret not living there?

GP: I do somewhat. I'm so used to being in on everything and so here I am not in on everything. But I'm in on enough, I guess, for my age, so it's okay! Shouldn't complain.

KB: You were talking about Isaac Babel this morning, and I recently read Antonia Pirizhkovova's memoir of Isaac Babel, At His Side, *and your foreword.*

GP: Oh you did?

KB: It's fascinating. And Babel's own writing is being reprinted.

GP: But the new translations are not good.

KB: Can I ask a little about what you say in the foreword to the memoir?

GP: Yes.

KB: You say of Babel that 'He didn't like literary talk. He didn't want to discuss his own work.'

GP: That's what he said: that's what she said he said!

KB: You've given, very generously, many interviews over the years. How do you feel about literary talk, about discussing your own work?

GP: I don't mind. I'm very much against mystification of anything. If people don't really know what's going on, I want them to know.

KB: How do you demystify the writing?

GP: I would be always glad to tell a class which little piece seems to me to have happened or that I heard and which piece is totally invented. People like to know that and I don't see why I shouldn't tell them.

KB: Do you get anything out of talking about your work, or is it always something you do for their sake?

GP: Sometimes talking about your work is very helpful, at a certain point in your life. I really don't need to talk about my work anymore. But sometimes you learn something—people ask you certain questions and you say, 'Oh, so that's what they think I'm doing'. Maybe those questions didn't help me write better but they made me think better about what I thought I was doing.

KB: In relation to that, I want to ask you about something you mentioned today, and talk about quite a lot elsewhere—the importance of generations and generational differences. I really like your poem 'People in My Family'—how different are the people born around 1914 from those born in 1905. How much do you think who you are, and what you believe, is determined by when, and where, you were born?

GP: That poem was really describing my sister and brother who are fourteen and sixteen years older than me and who were really born into the Depression. They have a slightly anxious feeling, which I never had. I was born into the War and so I was in a state of fury and so forth and so on. I became a pacifist, which they never did.

KB: Into fury and not fear?

GP: Well, I was in America and war was here; Europe was where people were suffering. I was married to a boy. I was very young then, and he went overseas. Before he went to the Pacific—both my husbands went to the Pacific—I lived on army camps. It was very interesting.

KB: Do you think that your writing is also shaped by your generation? By that moment?

GP: It must be. How could it not be?

KB: Your writing has had a big influence on several generations of writers (and critics) since you first published The Little Disturbances of Man in 1959. In the Sixties you were read as a metafictionist, in the Seventies as a feminist, now, within discussions of multiculturalism, perhaps the emphasis again is on Jewishness. Each generation picks out a different strand.

GP: What's interesting to me is that young people are interested in it, in such an old book! That's pretty thrilling! I'm sure some of them read me differently. The Women's Movement bloomed in the late Sixties and Seventies, but the women who made it were writing before that—not just me, Tillie Olsen, Muriel Rukeyser.

KB: Now though no one wants to talk about women's voices. They want to talk (here anyway) about Jewishness, about ethnicity.

GP: I'll tell you what happened at the Princeton conference a week ago. Similar discussions were being held. Morris Dickstein gave a talk that was about Jewish writers and power, and the power of the State. His point was that Bellow and Roth and even Malamud had held back from dealing with the power of the State and instead were dealing almost entirely with local affairs. But it was only about men. Suddenly a woman at the back got up and she asked what about Jewish women writers, and she mentioned my name and she mentioned two or three other names. And then Alice Hofstrucker got up very furious, and she said what about the poets, what about Adrienne Rich, and so on. He looked so appalled that I felt like comforting him later and saying there's still time for you, you're a young man, write your next chapter and put the ladies in! That's what Abigail Adams said when her husband was writing the Declaration of Independence; she said, 'Remember the ladies'. It is hard to hear about these guys all the time as if they are the only people writing. It doesn't bother me so much because I'm really past all that stuff, but it bothers me for young women that they're going to have to repeat the struggle.

KB: There wasn't much today about young Jewish writers, the current generation.

GP: That's absolutely right. At Princeton there were some younger writers but they were in such a state. They were the children of survivors and they were in rage that it wasn't paid enough attention to. It was quite . . . yet I understood how they felt.

KB: Have you noticed your own influence on young writers?

GP: I don't think about it.

KB: But do people tell you about it?

GP: Yes, people tell me that 'I couldn't have written this or that without you. . . .' It's nice, but there's a danger in leaning on that stuff and let[ting] it enter you. Too much work still to do.

KB: Gish Jen is one writer who's talked about your work, and who I've read you like.

GP: Yes, I like her. She was just at Dartmouth. She's a good friend of mine.

KB: I really like her. I teach her books.

GP: You do? I must tell her. She'll be so happy. She's such a doll.

KB: About four years ago she wrote an essay about being a judge for the PEN/Faulkner award in which she complained that multiculturalism had become both a 'pigeon-hole and an albatross'.

GP: She would say that she doesn't want to write as a Chinese woman. On the other hand, most of her experience is as a Chinese woman. Her father is Chinese, her mother is Chinese, her brothers are Chinese—they're all of course married to white Americans, including her! But still, if you asked Cynthia Ozick if she wanted to be considered as a Jewish writer she would say no; she would say I am a writer, and she would be right. I say, yes I'm Jewish so therefore I'm a Jewish writer. But writing in Jewish is a whole different scene which I tried to make clear this morning.

KB: What does Gish Jen write in?

GP: She writes a little bit in Chinese I think. She read a story that could have been in sheer dialect: that could have been her mother.

KB: Oh yes, 'Who's Irish?'

GP: Yes. It's very funny.

KB: Very funny story. So you don't think she had a genuine complaint about the literary world?

GP: She doesn't want to be pigeon-holed; I don't want to be pigeon-holed. Everybody wants to be in the mainstream. They don't realize that when you're not in the mainstream, it's glorious; you're free. The mainstream is just a sluggish river; it's got so many people in it already. Better to be in some river, stumbling over the rocks. It's better. That's how I feel.

KB: Is there as definite a sense of the mainstream now as when you started writing?

GP: That's funny. What they're talking about is exactly what was going on then. Roth's first book and my first book were published at the same moment practically and were reviewed together in a lot of magazines, and were equally praised. Then we were told to write novels. And he wrote novels. And I tried for two years to write a novel but I failed. So. It was so terrible, so pedestrian. I can't tell you.

KB: In your foreword to the Babel memoir you speak of his 'small production' and say that 'for some reason I feel this must be answered'.

GP: And then I pointed out that he really did lots of other writing, he wrote a screenplay, lots of shift work.

KB: Did you feel you wanted defend him partly because you face the same issue: that people are always urging you to write more, write longer?

GP: No, I didn't defend him for that reason. I defended him for his own reasons! One, I thought he had done great literary work and two, he had to go off for the party and visit farms and do agricultural reports and stuff like that.

KB: Although you haven't had to do that, you've also done a lot of non-literary work.

GP: Yeah.

KB: In Amy Bloom's latest book, A Blind Man Can See How Much I Love You, *she has a story ('Rowing to Eden') in which a character promises to help her friend get a girlfriend with 'Grace Paley's soul in Jennifer Lopez's body'.*

GP: I saw it. That was so funny. The soul of me. That was so touching.

KB: What do you think she means?

GP: I don't know. I don't know if she meant something bad or good, but I'm sort of touched by it—by my having a soul at all!

KB: Can I ask a little about your poetry?

GP: Oh yes, do!

KB: Partly about the relationship between writing poems and stories. In 'Two Ears, Three Lucks' in The Collected Stories you talk of suffering 'the storyteller's pain' that led you away from poetry. Yet you continued, you continue to write poetry.

GP: I just find myself writing poems and feeling good about it.

KB: What makes you want to write a poem rather than a story (and vice versa)?

GP: Sometimes I don't know. Sometimes I begin by writing a couple of sentences that might go one way or the other. But I think that I'm just in the mode for writing poems right now. Actually my intention when I get home is to get to work on two stories that I have in mind. I can't wait; I'm very eager to do it. I don't have enough poems for another book but I will probably by the end of next summer.

KB: You have 'A Poem About Storytelling' and many stories with poems in them, so in a way maybe they're not so separate after all.

GP: Well, I think that short stories are very close to poetry. If you write poetry and you write novels you're doing two different things. If you write short stories and you write poetry then you're doing things not so far apart from each other.

KB: Edgar Allan Poe said that a short story had all the beauty of a poem but some of the truth of prose.

GP: I didn't know that! That's nice!

KB: Is there less truth in poetry?

GP: No, I don't think so. What he really means is events. . . .

KB: Facts.

GP: Yes.

KB: The word you use, again about Babel's language, is density.

GP: A short story, like a poem, is something that you almost feel you could take in your hand

and lift up to the air and the light—and have it all in one hand. With a novel it's like you're scrambling around and picking this up and that up and you have all this stuff in your arms.

KB: You said of Babel's technique that he would start with longer, looser sentences and then condense and condense until he achieved the right density of language. Is that your method too?

GP: Not necessarily. Sometimes I increase and increase! It depends. But I do think that I'm a pretty good cutter of the unnecessary.

KB: So you go through lots of drafts?

GP: Oh yeah. Let me show you. [she produces a folder full of typewritten and pen-amended pages and starts leafing through them]... Here's something I can't even get back to because it's long and it's complex and I haven't [been] able to work on all this. Partly I can't because there's not enough pressure on me to do it.

KB: Do you rotate between different manuscripts?

GP: I suppose I do, but once I start really working on something I stay with it.

KB: As a definition of the short story Leonard Michaels once quoted a line from Kafka, 'A bird went flying in search of a cage.'

GP: That's really nice. And a definition of a long story might be 'A man went looking for a prison cell.'

KB: So at least the short story has some flight! Is ending a story like closing the door of the cage?

GP: Sometimes I like to tie things up; sometimes I like to open it up. I don't have an opinion on what's the best way to do it. I don't like writers who cut their characters off when if they'd let them live another half day it would have all been different. It's manipulative and I don't like it.

KB: Do you think your stories ever operate as Kafka-like parables or lessons? The word 'lesson' does come up sometimes; one character teaching another something about life.

GP: Right. The story I'll read tomorrow is 'My Father Teaches Me to Grow Old'.

KB: I read that in a magazine a long time ago.

GP: No, no, you must have read about two pages. It's now eleven.

KB: The Portable Lower East Side, *wasn't it?*

GP: Yeah, right. That's where it came from. I had it lying there until what? a half year ago. Now I finished it. I changed a lot of it, not an enormous amount, but I did a lot of cutting.

KB: I liked it a lot the old way!

GP: Well, I changed the title and added another nine pages.

KB: I look forward to hearing it. Other stories seem more arguments than lessons.

GP: Right. I do a lot of that, a lot of arguing. I write against things sometimes. Not in opposition so much, but leaning on the facts.

KB: Is writing in arguments a way of writing in Jewish?

GP: Very often, very often.

Source: Kasia Boddy, "An Interview with Grace Paley, 26 October 2001," in *European Journal of American Culture*, Vol. 21, No. 1, January 2002, pp. 26–33.

Vivian Gornick

In the following review, Gornick expresses admiration for Paley's voice in her stories, noting that this voice has become an important influence on the contemporary American short story.

I remember the first time I laid eyes on a Paley sentence. The year was 1960, the place a Berkeley bookstore, and I a depressed graduate student, leafing restlessly. I picked up a book of stories by a writer I'd never heard of and read: "I was popular in certain circles, says Aunt Rose. I wasn't no thinner then, only more stationary in the flesh. In time to come, Lillie, don't be surprised—change is a fact of God. From this no one is excused. Only a person like your mama stands on one foot, she don't notice how big her behind is getting and sings in the canary's ear for thirty years." The next time I looked up it was dark outside, the store was closing, and I had completed four stories, among them the incomparable "An Interest in Life" and "The Pale Pink Roast." I saw that the restlessness in me had abated. I felt warm and solid. More than warm: safe. I was feeling safe. Glad to be alive again.

There have been three story collections in 35 years. They have made Paley internationally famous. All over the world, in languages you never heard of, she is read as a master storyteller in the great tradition: people love life more because of her writing. In her own country Paley is beloved as well, but it's complicated. Familiarity is a corrective. Limitations are noted as well as virtues. The euphoria is harder-earned. For many

American readers, the third collection is weaker by far than the first. Scope, vision and delivery in a Paley story seem never to vary or to advance; the wisdom does not increase; the cheerful irony grows wearisome, begins to seem folksy. Oh Grace! the critically-minded reader berates a page of Paley prose, as though it were a relative. You've done this *before*. And besides, this, what you have written here, is not a story at all, this is a mere fragment, a little song and dance you have performed times without number.

Then suddenly, right there, in the middle of this same page refusing to get on with it, is a Paley sentence that arrests the eye and amazes the heart. The impatient reader quiets down, becomes calm, even wordless. She stares into the sentence. She feels its power. Everything Paley knows went into the making of that sentence. The way the sentence was made *is* what she knows: just as the right image is what the poet knows. The reader is reminded then of why—even though the stories don't "develop" and the collections don't get stronger—Paley goes on being read in languages you never heard of.

No matter how old Paley characters get they remain susceptible to the promise that someone or something is about to round the corner and make them feel again the crazy, wild, sexy excitement of life. Ordinary time in a Paley story passes like a dream, embracing the vividness of remembered feeling. Age, loss of appetite, growing children, economic despair, all mount up: "normalcy" surrounds the never-forgotten man, moment, Sunday morning when ah! one felt intensely.

Strictly speaking, women and men in Paley stories do not fall in love with each other, they fall in love with the desire to feel alive. They are, for each other, projections and provocations. Sooner or later, of course (mostly sooner), from such alliances human difficulty is bound to emerge, and when it does (more often than not), the sensation of love evaporates. The response to the evaporation is what interests Paley. She sees that people are either made melancholy by loss of love, or agitated by it. When agitated they generally take a hike, when melancholy they seem to get paralyzed. Historically speaking, it is the man who becomes agitated and the woman who becomes melancholy. In short, although each is trapped in behavior neither can resist and both will regret, men fly the coop and women stand bolted to the kitchen floor.

This sense of things is Paley's wisdom. The instrumental nature of sexual relations is mother's milk to the Paley narrator. She knows it so well it puts her beyond sentiment or anger, sends her into a Zen trance. From that trance has come writer's gold: the single insight made penetrating in those extraordinary sentences. Sentences brimming with the consequence of desire once tasted, now lost, and endlessly paid for.

Two examples will do: Faith Darwin—of "Faith in the Afternoon"—is swimming in misery over the defection of her husband Ricardo. When her mother tells her that Anita Franklin, a high-school classmate, has been left by *her* husband, Faith loses it:

> . . . At this very moment, the thumb of Ricardo's hovering shadow jabbed her in her left eye, revealing for all the world the shallowness of her water table. Rice could have been planted at that instant on the terraces of her flesh and sprouted in strength and beauty in the floods that overwhelmed her from that moment through all the afternoon. For herself and Anita Franklin, Faith bowed her head and wept.

Now, the obverse. In "Wants," the Paley narrator runs into her ex-husband and has an exchange with him that reminds her

> He had had a habit throughout the twenty-seven years of making a narrow remark which, like a plumber's snake, could work its ways through the ear down the throat, halfway to my heart. He would then disappear, leaving me choking with equipment.

These sentences are born of a concentration in the writer that runs so deep, is turned so far inward, it achieves the lucidity of the poet. The material is transformed in the sound of the sentence: the sound of the sentence *becomes* the material; the material is at one with the voice that is speaking. What Paley knows—that women and men remain longing, passive creatures most of their lives, always acted upon, rarely acting—is now inextricable from the way her sentences "talk" to us. She is famous for coming down against the fiction of plot and character because "everyone, real or invented, deserves the open destiny of life," but her women and her men, so far from having an open destiny, seem hopelessly mired in their unknowing middle-aged selves. It is the narrating Paley voice that is the open destiny. That voice is an unblinking stare, it is modern art, it fills the canvas. Its sentences are the equivalent of color in a Rothko painting. In Rothko, color *is* the painting, in Paley, voice *is* the story.

"PALEY'S CHARACTERS, WOMEN AND MEN WHO HAVE COMMITTED THEMSELVES TO TRYING TO ALLEVIATE SOME OF THE WORLD'S MYRIAD WOES, USUALLY APPEAR IN PRINT AS ACTIVISTS AT DEMONSTRATIONS, MARCHING WITH UPRAISED FISTS."

Like that of her friend Donald Barthelme, Grace Paley's voice has become an influential sound in contemporary American literature because it reminds us that although the story can no longer be told as it once was, it still needs to go on being told. The idiosyncratic intelligence hanging out in space is now the story: and indeed it is story enough. I felt safe in its presence in a Berkeley bookstore thirty years ago, it makes me feel safe today. As long as this voice is coming off the page I need not fear the loss of the narrative impulse. I need not, as Frank O'Hara says, regret life.

Source: Vivian Gornick, Review of *The Collected Stories* by Grace Paley, in *Women's Review of Books*, Vol. 11, No. 10/11, July 1994, pp. 29–30.

Wendy Smith

In the following essay, Smith discusses the political and social activism of Paley's short story characters.

Grace Paley has been a respected name in American letters for years. Her new book of short stories, *Later the Same Day*, confirms her as an utterly original American writer whose work combines personal, political and philosophical themes in a style quite unlike anyone else's.

Paley's characters, women and men who have committed themselves to trying to alleviate some of the world's myriad woes, usually appear in print as activists at demonstrations, marching with upraised fists. She has given them children, friends, lovers, aging parents, financial worries, shopping lists—in short, a private life to go with their public activities. Paley's work is political without being didactic, personal without being isolated from the real world.

This striking individuality accounts for the profound impact of Paley's writing, despite what is to her admirers a distressingly small body of work. Her first book, *The Little Disturbances of Man*, appeared in 1959; readers had to wait 15 years for the next one, *Enormous Changes at the Last Minute*, and just over a decade for *Later the Same Day*. "I do a lot of other things as well," explains the author. "I began to teach in the mid-'60s, and at the same time there was the Vietnam War, which really took up a lot of my time, especially since I had a boy growing towards draft age. And I'm just very distractable. My father used to say, 'You'll never be a writer, because you don't have any *sitzfleisch*,' which means sitting-down meat."

Her father's comment is hard to believe at the moment, as Paley sits tranquilly in a wooden rocking chair in the sunny living room of her Greenwich Village apartment. A small, plump woman in her early 60s, with short, white hair framing a round face, she resembles everyone's image of the ideal grandmother (so long as that image includes slacks, untucked shirttails and sneakers). As she does every Friday, she is simmering soup on the stove in her large, comfortable kitchen; she regrets that it's not ready yet, as she thinks it would be good for her interviewer's cold. She has to content herself with offering orange juice, vitamin C and antihistamines. Many of Paley's stories express her deep love of children; meeting her, one realizes almost immediately that her nurturing instincts extend beyond her own family to include friends and even a brand-new acquaintance. It's this pleasure in caring for others that makes her activism seem so undogmatic and natural, a logical extension of the kind of work women have always done. It's more complex than that, of course—lifelong political commitments like Paley's don't arise out of anything so simple as a strong maternal instinct—but it helps to explain the matter-of-fact way in which the author and her characters approach political activity as the only possible response to the world's perilous state.

The direction of Paley's work is guided by similarly concrete considerations. One of the reasons she switched from poetry, her first love, to short stories was that she couldn't satisfactorily connect her verse with real life. "I'd been writing poetry until about 1956," she remembers, "and then I just sort of made up my mind that I had to write stories. I loved the whole tradition of poetry, but I couldn't figure out a way to use my own Bronx English tongue in poems. I can now, better, but those early poems were all very literary; they picked up after whatever poet I was reading. They used what I think of as only one ear: you have two ears, one is for the sound of literature and the other is for your neighborhood, for your mother and father's house."

Her parents had a strong influence on Paley, imbuing her with a sense of radical tradition. "I'm always interested in generational things," she says. "I'm interested in history, I'm interested in change, I'm interested in the future; so therefore I'm interested in the past. As the youngest child by a great deal, I grew up among many adults talking about their lives. My parents were Russian immigrants. They'd been exiled to Siberia by the Czar when they were about 20, but when he had a son, he pardoned everyone under the age of 21, so they got out and came here right away. They didn't stay radical; they began to live the life of the immigrant—extremely patriotic, very hardworking—but they talked a lot about that period of their lives; they really made me feel it and see it, so there is that tradition. All of them were like that; my father's brothers and sister all belonged to different leftist political parties. My grandmother used to describe how they fought every night at the supper table and how hard it was on her!"

As Paley grew older, there were family tensions. "My parents didn't like the direction I was going politically," she recalls. "Although my father, who mistrusted a lot of my politics, came to agree with me about the Vietnam War; he was bitterly opposed to it." Her difficulties with her mother were more personal. "One of the stories in the new book, 'Lavinia,' was told to me by an old black woman, but it's also in a way *my* story," she says. "My mother, who couldn't do what she wanted because she had to help my father all the time, had great hopes for me. She was just disgusted, because all I wanted to do at a certain point was marry and have kids. I looked like a bust to my family, just like the girl Lavinia who I'm convinced will turn out very well.

"There's no question," she continues, "that children are distracting and that for some of the things women want to do, their sense is right: they shouldn't have children. And they shouldn't feel left out, because the children of the world are their children too. I just feel lucky that I didn't grow up in a generation where it was stylish not to. I only had two—I wish I'd had more."

The experience of her own children confirmed Paley's belief that each generation is shaped by the specific historical events of its time. "I often think of those kids in the Brinks case," she says, referring to the surviving fragments of the SDS, who were involved in the murder of a bank guard during an attempted robbery in the early 1980s, after they had spent years underground. "If they had been born four years later, five years earlier.... It really was that particular moment: they were called. In one of the new stories ["Friends"], I talk about that whole beloved generation of our children who were really wrecked. I mean, I lived through the Second World War, and I only knew one person in my generation who died. My children, who are in their early 30s, I can't tell you the number of people they know who have died or gone mad. They're a wonderful generation, though: thoughtful, idealistic, self-giving and honorable. They really gave.

"The idea that mothers and fathers raise their kids is ridiculous," Paley thinks. "You do a little bit—if you're rich, you raise a rich kid, okay—but the outside world is always there, waiting to declare war, to sell drugs, to invade another country, to raise the rents so you can't afford to live someplace—to really color your life. One of the nice things that happens when you have kids," Paley goes on, "is that you really get involved in the neighborhood institutions. If you don't become a local communitarian worker then, I don't know when you do. For instance, when my kids were very little, the city was trying to push a road through Washington Square Park to serve the real estate interests. We fought that and we won; in fact, having won, my friends and I had a kind of optimism for the next 20 years that we might win something else by luck." She laughs, as amused by her chronic optimism as she is convinced of its necessity. "It took a lot of worry, about the kids and buses going through the park at a terrific rate, to bring us together. You can call it politics or not; it becomes a common concern, and it can't be yours alone any more."

Paley believes such common concerns will shape future political activism. "One of the things that really runs through all the stories, because they're about groups of women, is the sense that what we need now is to bond; we need to say 'we' every now and then instead of 'I' every five minutes," she comments. "We've gone through this period of individualism and have sung that song, but it may not be the important song to sing in the times ahead. The Greenham women [antinuclear demonstrators who have set up a permanent camp outside the principal British missile base] are very powerful and interesting. When I went there the first time, I saw six women sitting on wet bales of hay wearing plastic raincoats and looking miserable. It was late November, and they said that on December 12 they were having this giant demonstration. I thought, 'Oh these poor women. Do they really believe this?' Well, three weeks later, on December 12, they had 30,000 women there. You really have to keep at it," she concludes. "It's vast; it's so huge you can hardly think about it. The power against us is so great and so foolish."

Yet Paley has never despaired—she notes in the story "Ruthy and Edie" that her characters are "ideologically, spiritually and on puritanical principle" against that particular emotion. "People accomplish things," she asserts. "You can't give up. And you can't retreat into personal, personal, personal life, because personal, personal, personal life is *hard:* to live in it without any common feelings for others around you is very disheartening, I would think. Some people just fool themselves, decide they have to make a lot of money and then go out and do it, but I can't feel like that." Her voice is low and passionate. "I think these are very rough times. I'm really sorry for people growing up right now, because they have some cockeyed idea that they can get by with their eyes closed; the cane they're tapping is money, and that won't take them in the right direction."

Despite the enormous amount of time and energy political matters absorb in Paley's life, they remain in the background of her fiction. "I feel I haven't written about certain things yet that I probably will at some point," she says. "I've written about the personal lives of these people; I haven't really seen them in political action, and I don't know if I need to especially, for what I'm trying to do. There has to be a way of writing about it that's right and interesting, but I haven't figured it out. I've mainly been interested in this personal political life. But I refer peripherally to things: in 'Living' in *Enormous Changes*, where [the protagonist] is bleeding to death, she remembers praying for peace on Eighth Street with her friend; in 'Zagrowsky Tells' in *Later the Same Day*, he's furious because they picketed his drugstore. That's the way a lot of politics gets in, as part of ordinary people's lives, and that's really the way I want to show it, it seems to me now. What I want is for these political people to really be *seen*."

The people who aren't seen much in *Later the Same Day* are men: Jack, the live-in lover of Faith (Paley's alter ego among her work's recurring characters), is a fairly well developed presence, but the book's focus is strongly female. "It wasn't that I didn't want to talk about men," Paley explains, "but there is so much female life that has so little to do with men and is *so* not-talked-about. Even though Faith tells Susan [in "Friends"], 'You still have him-itis, the dread disease of females, and they all have a little bit of that in them; much of their lives really does not, especially as they get older. I haven't even *begun* to write about really older women; I've only gotten them into their late 40s and early 50s."

Is Paley bringing her characters along to her own current stage of life? "I'm very pressed right now for time to write; I just feel peevish about it," she says. "But I've always felt that all these things have strong pulls: the politics takes from the writing, the children take from the politics, and the writing took from the children, you know. Someone once said, 'How did you manage to do all this with the kids around? and I made a joke; I said, 'Neglect!' But the truth is, all those things pull from each other, and it makes for a very interesting life. So I really have no complaints at all."

Source: Wendy Smith, "*Publishers Weekly* Interviews Grace Paley," in *Publishers Weekly*, April 5, 1985, pp. 71–72.

SOURCES

Aarons, Victoria, "The Outsider Within: Women in Contemporary Jewish-American Fiction," in *Contemporary Literature*, Vol. 28, No. 3, Autumn 1987, pp. 378–93.

Bengtson, Vern L., "Beyond the Nuclear Family: The Increasing Importance of Multigenerational Bonds," in the *Journal of Marriage and Family*, Vol. 63, February 2001, pp. 1–16.

Bernstein, Adam, "Grace Paley: Acclaimed Short-Story Writer," in the *Washington Post*, August 24, 2007, p. B7.

Cohany, Sharon R., and Emy Sok, "Trends in Labor Force Participation of Married Mothers of Infants,"

Monthly Labor Review, February 2007, Vol. 130, No. 2, pp. 9–16.

Courtenay-Thompson, Fiona, and Kate Phelps, eds., *The 20th Century Year by Year*, Barnes & Noble, 1998, pp. 268–89.

"Global Warming," in the *New York Times*, http://topics.nytimes.com/top/news/science/topics/globalwarming/index.html?inline = nyt-classifier# (accessed May 26, 2008).

Harris, Robert R., "Pacifists with Their Dukes Up," in the *New York Times Book Review*, April 14, 1985, p. 7.

Hollington, Kris, "Assassination in the 21st Century," in *Assassinology*, http://www.assassinology.org/id21.html (accessed May 26, 2008).

Iannone, Carol, "A Dissent on Grace Paley," in *Commentary*, Vol. 80, No. 2, August 1985, pp. 54–8.

International Union for Conservation of Nature and Natural Resources, "IUCN Red List of Threatened Species," http://www.iucnredlist.org (accessed May 26, 2008).

Kamel, Rose, "To Aggravate the Conscience: Grace Paley's Loud Voice," in the *Journal of Ethnic Studies*, Vol. 11, No. 3, Fall 1983, pp. 29–49.

Kaminsky, Ilya, and Katherine Towler, "An Interview with Poet and Fiction Writer Grace Paley," in *Poets & Writers* http://www.pw.org/content/interview_poet_and_fiction_writer_grace_paley (accessed April 16, 2008).

Krupnick, Mark, "Grace Paley: US Writer of Subtle and Discursive Short Stories, Poet, and 'Combative Pacificist,'" in the *Guardian*, August 24, 2007, p. 44.

LaRossa, Ralph, "Fatherhood and Social Change," in *Family Relations*, Vol. 37, No. 4, October 1988, pp. 451–57.

Paley, Grace, "Anxiety," in *Later the Same Day*, Penguin, 1986, pp. 99–103.

———, "One Day I Made up a Story," in *Just as I Thought*, Farrar, Straus and Giroux, 1998, pp. 196–98; originally published in *War Resisters Calendar*, 1985.

———, "Other Mothers," in *Feminist Studies*, Vol. 4, No. 2, June 1978, pp. 166–69.

Ravits, Martha A. "The Jewish Mother: Comedy and Controversy in American Popular Culture," in *MELUS*, Vol. 25, No. 1, Spring 2000, pp. 3–31.

Remnick, David, "Grace Paley, Voice from the Village: The Short Story Writer, Composing with the Sounds of the City," in the *Washington Post*, April 14, 1985, p. C1.

Rothman, Ellen K., and Joyce Antler, "Mothering Heights: An Interview with the Author of a Cultural History of Jewish Mothers," in *Mass Humanities*, Fall 2007, http://www.mfh.org/newsandevents/newsletter/MassHumanities/Fall2007/mothering.html (accessed May 30, 2008).

Ruggles, Steven, and Susan Brower, "Measurement of Household and Family Composition in the United States, 1850–2000," in *Population and Development Review*, Vol. 29, No. 1, March 2003, pp. 73–101.

"Special Report: Accident in Japan," in *Atomic Archive*, http://www.atomicarchive.com/Reports/Japan/Accidents.shtml (accessed May 26, 2008).

Tyler, Anne, "Mothers in the City," in the *New Republic*, Vol. 192, No. 18, April 29, 1985, pp. 38–9.

Watts, Pauline, "Remembering Grace Paley," Web site of Sarah Lawrence College, http://www.slc.edu/grace-paley/index.php (accessed May 24, 2008).

FURTHER READING

Antler, Joyce, *You Never Call! You Never Write! A History of the Jewish Mother*, Oxford University Press, 2007.

> This book uses humor and scholarship to dispel common stereotypes. Antler presents a study of the history of Jewish mothers, of women, and of Jewish life, and paints a picture of the culture that was so important to Paley's writing.

Arcana, Judith, *Grace Paley's Life Stories: A Literary Biography*, University of Illinois Press, 1993.

> Arcana uses conversations with Paley and with her family and friends as the basis for a biographical study that links Paley's life with her writings.

Bach, Gerhard, and Blaine H. Hall, eds., *Conversations with Grace Paley*, University Press of Mississippi, 1997.

> This text presents a collection of the many interviews that Paley gave during her long career, beginning in 1978 and continuing through 1995.

Cangro, Jacquelin, ed., *The Subway Chronicles: Scenes from Life in New York*, Plume, 2006.

> This book is a collection of twenty-seven essays and humorous stories about life under the streets of New York. Paley based her stories on the people she observed in New York, and this collection also attempts to reveal what life is like in the Big Apple.

Coltrane, Scott, *Family Man: Fatherhood, Housework, and Gender Equity*, Oxford University Press, 1997.

> This book presents an in-depth study of the role of the male in the family, as father and husband, and considers how parenting practices and the division of labor are divided in families.

Cosby, Bill, *Fatherhood*, Doubleday, 1986.

> Bill Cosby's television show The Cosby Show provided an example of involved fathering that led viewers to think that most fathers were taking an active role in parenting during the 1980s. This book is a humorous and semi-autobiographical account of Cosby's experiences as a father and includes common advice about parenting.

Dans, Peter E., and Suzanne Wasserman, *Life on the Lower East Side: Photographs by Rebecca Lepkoff, 1937–1950*, Princeton Architectural Press, 2006.

This book is a collection of photographs that depicts the changing street and community scene in New York during the period in which Paley was growing up.

Lopate, Phillip, ed., *Writing New York: A Literary Anthology*, Library of America, 1998.

This book is an anthology of stories, letters, poems, essays, memoirs, and diaries that celebrate living in New York City.

Lucke, Margaret, *Schaum's Quick Guide to Writing Great Short Stories*, McGraw-Hill, 1998.

This text provides an easy-to-follow guide for writing stories. There are many tips for where to find story ideas, how to develop a plot, and how to create memorable characters.

Newhouse, Alana, ed. *A Living Lens: Photographs of Jewish Life from the Pages of the Forward*, W. W. Norton, 2007.

The Forward was a daily Yiddish newspaper with a circulation in 1920 that was greater than that of the New York Times. This book provides a visual examination of the world in which Paley grew up, the area where Jewish immigrants settled when they arrived in the United States early in the twentieth century.

Charles

SHIRLEY JACKSON

1948

The American author Shirley Jackson's short story "Charles" was first published in the July 1948 issue of *Mademoiselle* magazine. The story subsequently appeared in Jackson's semiautobiographical collection of short stories titled *Life among the Savages* (1953). Jackson based this collection on her experiences of bringing up her four children. The child protagonist of "Charles," Laurie Hyman, has the nickname of Jackson's own son Laurence Hyman. According to Lenemaja Friedman in her biography *Shirley Jackson* (1975), the author based this story on the real-life Laurie's childhood tales of another boy at kindergarten.

"Charles" is the story of a young boy's first month at kindergarten. He returns home each day to recount the exploits of a naughty child called Charles who is repeatedly punished for being "fresh" to the teacher, injuring his fellow students, and indulging in other forbidden activities. Themes of the story are chiefly psychological and include the creation of self-identity, the fictionalization of the self, projection (the process whereby people locate undesirable or disapproved-of aspects of their own selves in others), and the ubiquity of evil. However, the treatment of this serious subject matter is humorous and ironic. The story never veers into the dark horror that typifies Jackson's stories and novels, though it does exemplify her interest in the workings of the human mind. "Charles" is Jackson's second-best-known short story, after "The

Shirley Jackson (AP Images)

Lottery" (1948), and it is widely taught in schools. It is often classified as domestic realism. "Charles" is currently available in Jackson's *The Lottery, and Other Stories* (2005).

AUTHOR BIOGRAPHY

Shirley Jackson was born Shirley Hardie Jackson on December 14, 1916, in San Francisco, California, to Leslie and Geraldine Jackson. Her father was an executive at a lithography company, and her mother was a housewife. While Jackson later claimed to have been born in 1919 to appear younger than her husband, her biographer Judy Oppenheimer, for *Private Demons: The Life of Shirley Jackson* (1988), determined that she was actually born three years earlier.

In 1923 the family moved to the affluent San Francisco suburb of Burlingame, where Jackson attended Burlingame High School. While there, she began to compose short fiction and poetry. In 1933 the family moved to Rochester, New York, and the following year Jackson enrolled in the liberal arts program at the University of Rochester. She withdrew in 1936 because of depression, a condition that was to recur in later years, and concentrated on writing, establishing strict work habits that she maintained throughout her life. In 1938 she decided to finish her schooling and attended Syracuse University, where she published pieces in campus magazines. She graduated in 1940 with a degree in English. In the same year she married her classmate Stanley Edgar Hyman, who became an author and critic, and the couple moved to New York City.

Jackson's first nationally published short story, "My Life With R. H. Macy," appeared in the *New Republic* in 1941. Over the next few years she continued to publish short stories. Her first child, Laurence, was born in 1942, and a daughter, Joanne, followed in 1945. In the same year the family moved to North Bennington, Vermont, where Jackson lived for the rest of her life. She and her husband had two more children, Sarah in 1948 and Barry in 1951.

Jackson's first novel, *The Road through the Wall*, was published in 1948. Its subject matter, the spitefulness and snobbery of affluent people in a respectable suburb, is characteristic of Jackson's bleak view of human nature. This disturbing element reached its peak in her best-known short story, "The Lottery," which was published in the June 28, 1948, issue of the *New Yorker*. The story features a modern version of an ancient scapegoat ritual in which a lottery held in small-town America culminates in the stoning to death of the winner. The story caused public outrage, and the publishers remarked that the story prompted more mail than anything the magazine had published before. It also cemented Jackson's reputation as a popular and critically acclaimed author. Her vision of the evil inherent in human nature is present even in the humorous story "Charles," which first appeared in the July 1948 issue of *Mademoiselle* magazine.

Jackson's second novel, *Hangsaman*, appeared in 1951. Its treatment of a young woman on the brink of mental breakdown shows Jackson's interest in the complexities of the human mind and in mental and emotional pathology, themes that are also evident in "Charles." Jackson wrote several novels influenced by the gothic genre, which combines horror and romance and reached its peak in the late eighteenth and early nineteenth centuries. Gothic novels typically involve an innocent young heroine who finds herself in danger at an old mansion, where she becomes involved with a mysterious but attractive man. Jackson's gothic-influenced novels include *The Sundial* (1958), *The Haunting of Hill House* (1959), and *We Have Always Lived in the Castle* (1962). Much of Jackson's fiction shows her lifelong interest in the supernatural, an interest reflected in her nonfiction book *The Witchcraft of Salem Village* (1956).

Jackson also published humorous books based on her life with her family. *Life among the Savages* (1953), in which "Charles" was incorporated, and *Raising Demons* (1957) are collections of short sketches originally published in women's magazines. In 1963 Jackson published a children's book, *9 Magic Wishes*. Her primary reputation as a novelist, however, was as a master of adult gothic fiction and the psychological thriller. Jackson was given the Edgar Allan Poe Award in 1961 for her story "Louisa, Please," and she won the Arents Pioneer Medal for Outstanding Achievement from Syracuse University in 1965.

On August 8, 1965, Jackson died suddenly of heart failure at her home in North Bennington, Vermont. At the time of her death she was working on a novel, which was published posthumously along with other stories and writings in *Come along with Me* (1968).

PLOT SUMMARY

In "Charles," the narrator, a mother who, it may be deduced, is called Mrs. Hyman, describes her son Laurie Hyman's first month at kindergarten. The story opens with Laurie abandoning his infant's clothes and walking off to kindergarten in a more grown-up outfit of jeans. He forgets to say goodbye to his mother.

Laurie returns home that day in an insolent mood. In the first of many daily reports about a naughty boy at kindergarten named Charles, Laurie tells his parents that today, the teacher spanked Charles for being "fresh." After Laurie's second day at kindergarten, he reports that Charles hit the teacher and was spanked again. Laurie behaves rudely to his father, Mr. Hyman. Then Laurie explains that after punishing Charles, the teacher told the other children not to play with him, but everyone did. On the third day, Laurie says that Charles hurt a little girl with a seesaw, and the teacher kept him in during the break. On the next two days, Charles is punished for pounding his feet on the floor and throwing chalk.

On Saturday, Mrs. Hyman asks Mr. Hyman if he thinks that kindergarten is suitable for Laurie, as Charles seems to be a bad influence. Mr. Hyman replies that there are people like Charles in the world, and Laurie may as well get used to dealing with them now as later.

On the following Monday, Laurie returns home late from kindergarten with another tale of Charles's bad behavior. This time, Charles yelled in class, and the teacher made him stay behind after school. All the other children stayed behind to watch him, as they find him interesting. Laurie greets his father disrespectfully, calling him an "old dust mop." Mr. Hyman asks Laurie what Charles looks like. Laurie replies that Charles is bigger than him, and he does not wear "rubbers" (overshoes) or a jacket.

On Monday evening, the first parent-teacher meeting since Laurie began kindergarten is held. Mrs. Hyman cannot attend as the baby has a cold. She is disappointed, as she very much wants to meet Charles's mother.

The next day, Tuesday, Laurie returns home with the news that the class had a visit from a friend of the teacher. The man had made the children do exercises, but Charles had not done them. Laurie demonstrates one of the exercises. Mrs. Hyman assumes that Charles had refused to do the exercises, but Laurie tells her that Charles had kicked the teacher's friend and so was not allowed to do the exercises. Mr. Hyman asks Laurie what will happen to Charles, and Laurie replies that Charles will probably be thrown out of school.

On Wednesday and Thursday, Charles yells during the story hour and hits a boy in the stomach, and on Friday he is kept behind after school. Once again, all the other children choose to stay with him.

Charles becomes a byword in the Hyman family for any kind of uncooperative, naughty, or even careless behavior. In Laurie's third and fourth weeks at kindergarten, however, Charles appears to be reforming. One day, Laurie announces that Charles was so good that the teacher gave him an apple and called him her "helper." Mr. and Mrs. Hyman can hardly believe this sudden reformation. Mr. Hyman thinks that Charles is merely plotting more wicked deeds. But for the next week, Charles continues to be helpful in class, and no one is kept behind after school.

Mr. and Mrs. Hyman are intrigued at this change in Charles, and Mrs. Hyman resolves to seek out Charles's mother at the next parent-teacher meeting, which will be held the following week, in order to investigate the reason for it. On the Friday of that week, however, Laurie reports that Charles is back to his usual naughty self. He told a little girl to say a bad word. The girl said it twice, and the teacher washed her mouth out with soap as a punishment, at which Charles laughed. Charles escaped punishment, as he was operating under the guise of teacher's little helper by handing out crayons. On Monday, Charles says the bad word himself and his own mouth is washed out with soap. He also throws chalk.

That evening, Mrs. Hyman sets out for the parent-teacher meeting. As she is leaving, Mr. Hyman asks her to invite Charles's mother over for a cup of tea, as he wants to meet her as well.

At the meeting, Mrs. Hyman scans the room for a woman who looks haggard enough to be Charles's mother, but there is no obvious candidate. No one there mentions Charles. After the meeting, Mrs. Hyman seeks out Laurie's teacher and asks her about her son. The teacher says that Laurie had some trouble adjusting to kindergarten for the first week or so but now is "a fine little helper" who has only "occasional lapses." Mrs. Hyman replies that Laurie usually adapts quickly and suggests that Charles's influence is unsettling him. The teacher, puzzled, replies that there is no child called Charles in the kindergarten.

CHARACTERS

Charles

Charles is an alter ego, or other self, that Laurie Hyman creates. In discussions with his parents, Laurie blames the fictional Charles for the mischief he himself creates at kindergarten: being "fresh" to the teacher and hitting her, throwing chalk, and injuring his classmates. In this respect, Charles becomes Laurie's scapegoat (a person unfairly blamed for a misfortune or unacceptable behavior).

If Laurie's claims are to be believed, Charles (in reality, the misbehaving Laurie) proves so interesting to the other children that when he is kept behind in detention after school, the others voluntarily stay behind with him. This shows that however annoying Charles is to the teacher, Laurie portrays him as having a magnetic attraction for his classmates. In fact, there is no objective evidence that the other children stay behind with Charles/Laurie, so this may be another of Laurie's fabrications. However, the reader is likely to find Charles the most interesting character in the story. When Charles is finally revealed to be a fiction, this adds a layer of complexity to the character of Laurie, who until that point is simply a rather rude child with little power to fascinate.

The Classmates

Laurie's classmates are foils to his identity as Charles. A foil is a person or thing that contrasts with the character under consideration, thus bringing his or her qualities into higher definition. Laurie variously portrays his classmates as the innocent victims of Charles's bad behavior, as his admiring audience (when they voluntarily stay behind to watch him in detention), and as his naive gulls (when he convinces a little girl to say a rude word and take the punishment that, morally, is due to him). The classmates are described only in relation to Charles, apparently having no individual identities of their own. This reflects the self-centeredness of Laurie's world, as he is utterly absorbed in creating his fictional other self.

Laurie Hyman

Laurie Hyman is the young son of Mr. and Mrs. Hyman and the protagonist of "Charles." At the outset of the story, he is beginning kindergarten, and the story covers his first month there. It is clear that this period is a rite of passage for Laurie and his mother. Laurie is no longer her baby, forgoing corduroy overalls with bibs. He walks off to kindergarten wearing the more adult outfit of jeans with a belt. His clothes are an outward sign that he has instantly grown up and begun to detach himself from his mother and to form his own identity. Overnight, he has become "a long-trousered, swaggering character who forgot to stop at the corner and wave good-bye to me."

When Laurie returns from kindergarten, he is often insolent to his father, on one occasion telling him, as part of a schoolboy's rhyme, "Gee, you're dumb." His growing disrespect toward his parents is another sign of his defining of his own identity and is indicative of the blooming of his alter ego, the obnoxious Charles. By blaming Charles for his bad behavior, Laurie is able to act out at school, tell his parents about it, and yet escape their wrath.

Laurie ultimately tries out two personas: the wicked and the good, the mischief maker and the teacher's helper. He begins with the first, then experiments with the second before returning to the first. Thus he develops throughout the story by channeling his behavioral impulses through his alter ego.

Mr. Hyman

Mr. Hyman is Laurie's father and the husband of Mrs. Hyman, the narrator. Mr. Hyman is not a fully developed character. His main role is to provide a focus for Laurie's disrespect and to provide a sounding board for Mrs. Hyman's thoughts about Laurie and Charles.

Mrs. Hyman

Mrs. Hyman is the narrator of the story, the mother of Laurie, and the wife of Mr. Hyman. Her main role is to inquire about Charles's exploits at kindergarten. In her unquestioning belief in Laurie's ruse in blaming Charles for his own bad behavior, Mrs. Hyman exemplifies two traits that Jackson frequently satirized in her fiction: first, a naive conformity in her readiness to embrace her son's fiction, and second, prejudice in her imagining the mother of a boy such as Charles to be a sight to behold. In Jackson's more serious fiction, conformity and prejudice often give rise to evil. In this story, Jackson's satire against these tendencies is much more gentle, giving rise to no consequences beyond a moral lesson for the Hyman parents. However, the story does raise implicit questions about the roles of these traits in allowing evil to grow and predominate in society.

The facts that Mrs. Hyman shares the same name as Jackson (whose married name was Mrs. Hyman) and that Laurie shares the same name as Jackson's own son are graceful touches that put forward the author herself and her family as the targets of the satire. Far from preaching to the rest of humanity, Jackson is aiming her psychological probings at herself and those closest to her.

The Teacher

Laurie's unnamed teacher appears in person only at the end of the story, but before then, Laurie frequently refers to her in his accounts to his parents of Charles's exploits. She seems to be a somewhat helpless butt of Charles's mischievous pranks. Although she punishes Laurie/Charles for his transgressions, this does nothing to prevent him from continuing his bad behavior.

THEMES

The Creative Imagination and the Fictionalization of the Self

In creating the imaginary Charles, Laurie is constructing an identity for himself. As Charles, he is first bad, then good, and finally bad again while masquerading as good. Thus, his self-fictionalization becomes increasingly sophisticated. At first, it enables him to escape the retribution of his parents. Later, when he persuades a little girl to say a bad word, such that she is given punishment that is morally due to him, it enables him to escape the retribution of his teacher, too.

Laurie's transformation of Charles from bad to good and then back to bad again shows that he has a sense of power over his creation as he experiments with different personas. His parents, up to the point when the teacher reveals that there is no Charles in her class, accept his fiction. They even use it as a reference point for unwanted or destructive behavior in the household: "the baby was being a Charles when she cried all afternoon." Thus they are taking as a moral standard the self-serving deception of their own small son.

Laurie's self-fictionalizing mirrors the act of the author in creating the story of "Charles." The parallel is reinforced by the author's naming Laurie after her own son and Mrs. Hyman after herself. The author appears to suggest that just as she creates fiction as a writer, all human beings can create themselves. The self that others see is to some extent a fiction. Often, even the people closest to the fiction maker, as in the case of Mr. and Mrs. Hyman, believe the fictions. In the same way, readers of a literary work of fiction temporarily suspend their disbelief.

TOPICS FOR FURTHER STUDY

- Jackson was interested in mental illness and imbalance and in the moral failings of ordinary people. Through researching the field of psychology, identify some of the mental pathologies and moral failings that are humorously exemplified in "Charles." Write a brief report on each trait, taking the story as your starting point and analyzing the trait in terms of psychological theory. Include in your answer an analysis of the most extreme forms of these behaviors from the point of view of psychology.
- Read Jackson's short story "The Lottery," which is available in *The Lottery, and Other Stories* (2005). Write an essay in which you compare and contrast the author's treatments of the theme of evil in "The Lottery" and in "Charles."
- Read one other literary work that may be said to contain the themes of dissociative identity disorder and/or the creative imagination. Possible works include the following novels: Mary Shelley's *Frankenstein* (1818), Robert Louis Stevenson's *Strange Case of Dr. Jekyll and Mr. Hyde* (1886), Shirley Jackson's *The Bird's Nest* (1955), and Patricia Highsmith's *The Talented Mr. Ripley* (1955). Write an essay on how these two themes are presented in the work you select. Include in your essay a section comparing the author's treatment of these themes in your chosen work and Jackson's treatment of these themes in "Charles."
- Write a short story, sketch, play, or poem in which you, or a fictional character, create a fictional alter ego (other self). Add a short analysis of what the creating character loses and gains through the invention of the alter ego.
- In psychology, psychological projection, or Freudian projection, is a defense mechanism in which one attributes to others one's own unacceptable or unwanted thoughts or emotions. In "Charles," both Laurie and his parents indulge in this behavior. Lead a class discussion in which people identify traits that they find unattractive or upsetting in other people and then examine the ways in which they themselves express or suppress that trait.

Prejudice

Prejudice means the act of pre-judging a person or thing, of forming an opinion without sufficient knowledge to back it up. Mr. and Mrs. Hyman are quick to accept Laurie's fiction to the effect that Charles is the wayward son of some other woman. Mrs. Hyman forms the view that Charles is a "bad influence" on her son, and, in a modern psychological version of an old circus-style freak show, both Hyman parents are fascinated by the prospect of meeting the mother of such a unique child. Their prejudice is turned back against themselves by the story's final ironic reversal, which reveals that the wicked Charles is none other than their own son Laurie.

Family Relationships

"Charles" reveals the problematic nature, as well as the comic potential, of family relationships. The first paragraph of the story reflects a common experience of mothers: the moment when the "sweet-voiced nursery-school tot" is "replaced by a long-trousered, swaggering character who forgot to stop at the corner and wave good-bye" to his mother. The incident shows the mystery and strangeness that can attach even to those we consider closest to us. Jackson shows that the minds of other people are essentially unknowable. Laurie exploits this fact, convincing his parents that his own actions are carried out by another person.

The story also conveys the helplessness that parents can feel when faced with the antics of their children. Mr. and Mrs. Hyman can do nothing except witness the unfolding of Laurie's drama. As Laurie becomes more independent, he moves to a great extent beyond the comprehension and control of his parents.

The Nature of Evil

The evil that can lurk beneath a veneer of respectability and ordinariness is a common theme in Jackson's fiction. In her story "The Lottery," small-town America becomes the scene of a brutal scapegoat ritual in which an innocent woman is stoned to death with the eager participation of her neighbors. The source of evil in this case is the very community that might be expected to support its individual members. Lenemaja Friedman, in her biography *Shirley Jackson*, comments that in "The Lottery" Jackson presents a view of humankind as "basically unenlightened, narrow, and evil."

Similarly, in "Charles," the source of evil turns out to lie disturbingly close to home. This is not apparent at the beginning, when the Hyman family seem to be the essence of respectability. They are concerned about their son being subjected to the "toughness," "bad grammar," and "bad influence" of Charles, and they even consider removing Laurie from school in order to avoid exposing him to these elements. But all along, the destructive traits they fear are located in their own son. Evil, Jackson seems to suggest, is not always conveniently located in some other place, in other people who are set apart from the decent majority. People must look for it within themselves and their own families and communities.

It is true that "Charles" is lighthearted in tone and subject matter, as nothing terrible happens or is likely to happen, at least within the time boundaries of the story. However, the plotline of Laurie's concealment of his own destructive traits in the persona of Charles could very easily have been transferred into one of Jackson's gothic suspense novels and given a much darker treatment.

STYLE

Situational Irony

"Charles" depends for its effect on situational irony, a literary device in which what transpires is different from what the reader and/or characters expect, lending a different level of meaning to everything that has previously occurred. The irony lies in the fact that the terrible Charles turns out to be the Hymans' own son, Laurie. The evil that they had comfortingly located in some other person is in their own family: they produced it. The "bad influence" on their son was not the fictional Charles, so the only possible candidates are themselves.

Dramatic Irony

In her encounter with Mrs. Hyman at the parent-teacher meeting, the teacher plays down Laurie's destructiveness. She says, "We had a little trouble adjusting, the first week or so . . . but now he's a fine little helper. With occasional lapses, of course." Readers are aware that this is an understatement that is possibly meant to salvage the teacher's or the school's professional reputation, as the full details of Charles/Laurie's bad behavior have already been disclosed. Readers also know that recently, Charles/Laurie escaped punishment that was due to him for persuading a girl to say a bad word. He escaped detection partly because at the time that the crime was committed, he was assuming the role of teacher's "fine little helper," by passing out crayons. The gap between what the teacher says and what the readers know creates dramatic irony (a literary device in which the reader or audience knows something that a character does not, lending a different meaning to what the character is saying or doing). A question then arises: if Laurie is already able to cause innocent people to be punished for his own misdeeds when he is outwardly helping the teacher, what evil might he accomplish were he to perfect his mask of respectability? Thus, readers may conclude that the teacher is deluding both herself and Mrs. Hyman in pronouncing her positive judgment of Charles's progress. The dramatic irony used in this episode also enables Jackson to satirize the euphemistic, politically correct, and less-than-honest manner in which authority figures often talk about troublesome people.

Domestic Realism

Jackson's "Charles" is often placed in the literary genre of domestic realism. Works of this genre attempt to examine the everyday customs and rules of society, particularly within the family and household, in a way that resists idealization. Domestic realism's first peak of popularity came in the form of nineteenth-century novels written mainly for and by middle-class women about the realities of daily life for women of their own class and the working class. Jane Austen's *Pride and Prejudice* (1813), George Eliot's *The Mill on the Floss* (1860), Louisa May Alcott's *Little Women* (1868), and Edith Wharton's *Ethan Frome* (1911) have all been cited as examples of domestic realism.

Toward the end of World War II and afterward, dramas of domestic realism dominated American theater. These included Tennessee Williams's plays *The Glass Menagerie* (1944) and *A Streetcar Named Desire* (1947), which centered on a tenuous model of family life, and Arthur Miller's *All My Sons* (1947), in which a crime against morality and society committed by a father splits apart his family.

In "Charles," Jackson simultaneously develops and undermines the notion of domestic harmony. Mr. and Mrs. Hyman are presented as a respectable suburban couple with a conventional life and strong views on right and wrong behavior. They are shocked and intrigued by the antics of Charles as recounted by Laurie. Charles represents a force of disobedience and anarchy that disturbs their comfortable world.

Jackson makes a strong satirical point of the fact that the Hyman parents duly locate the anarchist impulses outside their own world, placing the responsibility for the obnoxious Charles onto some haggard, worn-out mother who is fascinating by virtue of the fact that she must be different from them. When Charles and his mother are exposed as imaginary, the responsibility for evil, by default, rebounds upon the Hymans themselves. The disconnection between the outward appearance of respectability and harmony and the chaos that can lie beneath is a favorite theme of Jackson's. It disturbs the reader because it implies that evil is latent in the most bland and seemingly innocuous locations and situations.

Bildungsroman

A *bildungsroman* is a novel about the moral, psychological, and intellectual development of the protagonist, usually a young person. Generally, the character grows in moral stature and becomes wiser and more worthy of respect throughout the novel. The short story "Charles" subverts this tradition, as Laurie turns from an innocent tot to a "swaggering" character who causes chaos in kindergarten and deceives his parents into thinking the culprit is the fictional Charles. By the end of the story, Laurie has become able to hide his wickedness under the guise of being the teacher's "fine little helper." Laurie is perfecting not his moral character but his ability to get away with bad deeds. In this story, Jackson conveys through comedy a view of unregenerate humankind that is evident in darker hue in her more serious work.

HISTORICAL CONTEXT

World War II and the Growth of Psychology

In 1944 and 1945, the Allies (including Great Britain and the United States) discovered and liberated concentration and extermination camps in Europe. In these camps, the Nazis had exterminated around six million Jews, as well as unknown numbers of minority peoples such as Roma, homosexuals, and the disabled. Revelations about the extent of the Holocaust, as the genocide of Jews became known, prompted widespread shock and questioning about the existence of hidden evil within an apparently civilized society (Germany). Perhaps partly for this reason, the postwar years marked a massive growth of interest in the field of psychology, which examined and attempted to explain human mental pathologies and their characteristic behaviors.

Among the ideas that gained currency was that of psychological projection, or Freudian projection. The concept was originated by the psychologist Sigmund Freud (1856–1939) and developed by his daughter Anna Freud in her book *Das Ich und die Abwehrmechanismen* (1936; *The Ego and Mechanisms of Defense*, 1937). It was taken up and further developed by the psychologist Carl Jung (1875–1961). Psychological projection is a defense mechanism in which one attributes to others one's own unacceptable or unwanted thoughts or emotions. Laurie indulges in this mechanism in "Charles," locating his socially unacceptable behavior at kindergarten in his imaginary alter ego, Charles.

The Cold War

The cold war was a period of tension and rivalry between the United States and the Communist Soviet Union from the end of World War II in 1945 until 1991, when the Soviet Union

COMPARE & CONTRAST

- **1940s:** Domestic realism, a literary genre that focuses on the everyday customs of society, dominates American theater and is also found in fiction such as Jackson's. Frequently, the ideal of the stable and conventional family unit is subverted.

  Today: Literature reflects the wide variety of social customs and notions of family that have increasingly gained acceptance. These include same-sex marriages, mixed-race relationships, having children outside marriage, single-parent families, and other arrangements that were widely viewed as eccentric or unacceptable when Jackson wrote "Charles."

- **1940s:** The Holocaust and other events of World War II prompt a growth in the field of psychology, which attempts to explain the darker workings of the human mind.

  Today: Concepts from psychology such as projection, multiple personalities, and dissociative identity disorder influence literary works, particularly in the genres of psychological realism and crime and suspense fiction.

- **1940s:** The ongoing development of the atomic and hydrogen bombs after the end of World War II, along with the escalation of the cold war between the United States and the Soviet Union, creates widespread fear that humankind will destroy itself. The mood is reflected in literature by works expressing moral uncertainty and pessimism.

  Today: Governments and media reports focus on the likelihood that a terrorist group will obtain a nuclear weapon. While literature expressing a sense of doom for humankind abounds, some writers accuse governments of manufacturing or exaggerating the dangers for their own ends.

---

collapsed. The period was characterized by a nuclear and conventional arms race, massive military spending, and the involvement of both superpowers in proxy wars around the globe. The term *cold war* arose from the fact that no direct military action occurred between the superpowers. Nevertheless, many people in the United States and Europe lived in terror of nuclear devastation, and the period saw the growth of antinuclear "Ban the Bomb" demonstrations.

The horrors of World War II and the tension of the cold war combined to exercise a profound influence on the literature of the postwar years. In the case of Jackson's work, this influence is most explicit in her gothic novels. Her husband, Stanley Edgar Hyman, in his preface to *The Magic of Shirley Jackson* (1966), is unequivocal in drawing the connection between recent historical events and Jackson's work:

> Her fierce visions of dissociation and madness, of alienation and withdrawal, of cruelty and terror, have been taken to be personal, even neurotic, fantasies. Quite the reverse: they are a sensitive and faithful anatomy of our times, fitting symbols for our distressing world of the concentration camp and the Bomb.

It would be no exaggeration to note that some of these elements, namely dissociation, alienation, and cruelty, are present in implicit and embryonic form in the outwardly gentle comedy of "Charles."

Women, Domesticity, and Postwar Conservatism

The years following World War II in the United States marked a period of profound conservatism, in politics and in society. From the late 1940s to the late 1950s, a phenomenon known as McCarthyism took hold, characterized by intense anti-Communist suspicion. McCarthyism took its name from Senator Joseph McCarthy, who between 1947 and 1957 investigated politicians, artists, writers, actors, intellectuals, government employees, and other Americans for alleged Communist sympathies.

As any kind of progressive thinking came under suspicion, it was safest to lead a conventional and conservative life; many who were investigated saw their careers or lives destroyed. Mainstream films and advertising were dominated by a rigid vision of the family that from 1947 came to be known as the nuclear family (with the term springing not from associations with nuclear bombs or energy but from the Latin for *kernel* or *nut*). The nuclear family consisted of father, mother, and children. In the United States of the 1950s, convention dictated that the man, as head of the household, worked and was the breadwinner, while the mother looked after the home and had primary responsibility for bringing up the children.

This is the family model that is represented in "Charles" and the model that closely reflected Jackson's own situation, with the important qualification that Jackson combined her family duties with a successful writing career. Jackson exploits the convention of the nuclear family in order to subtly undermine it, showing the chaos and mystery that may lurk beneath the well-ordered veneer. The gap between the parents' expectations and what actually happens creates both unease and comedy.

CRITICAL OVERVIEW

Most critical writing on Jackson has focused on her gothic and psychological novels and on her best-known short story, "The Lottery." Lenemaja Friedman notes in her 1975 biography, *Shirley Jackson:* "Very little has been written about Shirley Jackson;... comments are often limited to a sentence or two." Friedman's bibliography lists just six short reviews of *Life among the Savages* (1953), the collection in which "Charles" was published. While all the reviews but one are favorable, they treat the collection as entertainment rather than a work of literary merit.

Critical appreciation of Jackson's fiction has increased over the decades. In parallel with this process has come a greater recognition of the darkness present even in her family chronicles, of which "Charles" is an example. Two early reviews of *Life among the Savages*, neither of which single out "Charles" for special mention, remark only on the upbeat aspects of the stories. Jane Cobb, in her 1953 review for the *New York Times*, contrasts the collection with the "creeping horrors" that she associates with Jackson's story "The Lottery," noting that it is "as warm as it is hilarious and believable." Marion West Stoer, in her review in the same year for the *Christian Science Monitor*, praises Jackson's "keen ear for dialogue," "quiet wit," and "resigned humor." In a comment that could apply to "Charles," Stoer remarks on the many "studies of amiable despair which parents everywhere will recognize," as well as on the "solid foundation of affectionate family relationship" and "wholesome aspect" that are evident in the collection.

Another critic who praises Jackson's ability to convey the trials of family life in a realistic and humorous manner is Anne LeCroy. In her *Studies in American Humor* essay, "The Different Humor of Shirley Jackson: *Life among the Savages* and *Raising Demons*" (1985), LeCroy comments that Jackson's humor most often stems from her understanding of the "everyday nuances and working of the average family," including "the helpless frustration mothers often feel at observing the inexplicable behavior of their children."

Judie Newman, writing in 1990, emphasizes the darker aspect of Jackson's chronicles of family life. In her essay in *American Horror Fiction: From Brockden Brown to Stephen King*, while not specifically mentioning "Charles," Newman notes that "the titles of these celebrations of maternal experience, *Raising Demons* and *Life among the Savages*, immediately suggest works of horror fiction." This theme is taken up by Roberta Rubenstein in her essay "House Mothers and Haunted Daughters: Shirley Jackson and Female Gothic," published in *Tulsa Studies in Women's Literature*. Rubenstein writes that the "droll tone" of *Life among the Savages* and *Raising Demons* is "belied by the title words, underscoring the 'savage' and 'demonic' elements that laced Jackson's vision of family."

Dale Hrebik, in his essay on Jackson for the *Dictionary of Literary Biography*, singles out "Charles" for special discussion. Unusually among critics, Hrebik directly confronts both the light and dark aspects of the story. He writes, "While it is a realistic and humorous family story, it also provides another instance of Jackson's interest in the evil within everyone, even the most familiar."

James Egan, in his essay in *Shirley Jackson: Essays on the Literary Legacy* (2005), argues that Jackson's fiction represents the comic, satiric, fantastic, and gothic literary modes alike. He notes that in her domestic tales, such as *Life among the Savages*, Jackson "simultaneously develops and undercuts, or at least qualifies, a normative environment." Egan adds that "the normative environment itself appears haphazard, topsy-turvy, on the verge of collision." This comment aptly describes "Charles."

Jackson's mastery of the gothic, horror, suspense, and comic genres has secured her place in the literary canon. "Charles" is the second-most frequently anthologized of Jackson's short stories, after "The Lottery," and is widely studied in schools.

CRITICISM

Claire Robinson

Robinson has an M.A. in English. She is a teacher of English literature and creative writing, and a freelance writer and editor. In the following essay, Robinson explores how Shirley Jackson's "Charles" operates on two levels: as a comic chronicle of the doings of a mischievous child and as a disturbing companion piece to her later horror fiction.

Comments by Stanley Edgar Hyman on the public's perception of his wife, Shirley Jackson, shed considerable light on her short story "Charles." In his preface to *The Magic of Shirley Jackson* (1966), Hyman notes that people often expressed surprise at the difference between Shirley Jackson's motherly appearance and gentle manner and "the violent and terrifying nature of her fiction." He adds that when she published "two light-hearted volumes about the spirited doings of our children, *Life among the Savages* and *Raising Demons*, it seemed to surprise people that the author of her grim and disturbing fiction should be a wife and mother at all, let alone a gay and apparently happy one."

These two aspects of Jackson—her comforting appearance and her discomfiting fictional creations—stand as a metaphor for possible reader responses to "Charles" (contained in *Life among the Savages*). On one level, "Charles" can be read as a chronicle of the mischievous but essentially harmless ways of a child. On another level, it is far more disturbing. This may be particularly true for those readers who, in common with Jackson, have some knowledge of psychology.

Many children and even teenagers create imaginary friends, and sometimes they use these imaginary friends to indulge in psychological projection, or Freudian projection. Psychological

WHAT DO I READ NEXT?

- Jackson's most famous short story, "The Lottery" (1948), is an interesting complement to "Charles." The two stories share the theme of the evil that lies latent under respectable appearances, but while "Charles" is at root a comedy, "The Lottery" is a dystopian horror story. *Dystopian* is the opposite of *utopian*; *utopian* describes an idealized society, whereas *dystopian* describes a nightmarish society.
- The Scottish author Robert Louis Stevenson's horror novel *Strange Case of Dr. Jekyll and Mr. Hyde* (1886) centers around the dual personality of the respectable Dr. Jekyll. Jekyll's alter ego, Mr. Hyde, is a violent, criminally minded man. Eventually, Jekyll is taken over by Hyde because of his moral weakness. Stevenson, like Jackson, was convinced of the inseparability of good from evil in humankind.
- The protagonist of Patricia Highsmith's novel *The Talented Mr. Ripley* (1957) is Tom Ripley, a man with a talent for mimicry who murders a rich young man and steals his identity, managing to build a successful life for himself as a result. The novel is a study in the manipulation of identity and psychopathic behavior.
- *The 1950s* (1999), by Stuart A. Kallen, gives an overview of 1950s America. The book is aimed at high school and college students and features sections on communism, racial injustice, the cold war, teen culture, science and technology, and other topics relevant to the era.

projection is a defense mechanism in which one attributes to others one's own unacceptable or unwanted thoughts or emotions. For example, the child or teenager may claim that while he does not disobey authority, engage in violence, or take drugs, his imaginary friend does. Some psychologists would interpret this claim to mean that the boy in question either does engage in these behaviors or would like to.

Most children grow out of their imaginary friends and the accompanying projections. But according to some psychologists, a more extreme form of projection can affect children and adults alike. Some psychologists claim the existence of a mental illness called dissociative identity disorder, in which the sufferer creates multiple identities or personalities with different characteristics and behaviors. (The condition was previously known as multiple personality disorder.) The degree of awareness of what is fantasy and what is reality varies between individuals and within the same individual from one time to another, as does the degree of control that the individual has over his or her other selves. The illness can become dangerous to society when one of the selves indulges in destructive or criminal actions that are not under the control of a self with moral awareness. These individuals may be unable to accept responsibility or to feel remorse for such actions because as far as they are concerned, they did not do them. Alternatively, they may be controlled by a self that feels detached from the laws and morals that govern most of society.

Is Laurie's behavior in "Charles," then, simply innocent childhood fantasy or a precursor to something darker? Readers may find something unsettling about Laurie's creation of Charles seemingly for the sole purpose of enabling himself to escape responsibility for his antisocial behavior. Jackson seems implicitly to ask what kind of adult such a child will grow up to be. This question is underlined by the visual image of Laurie setting off for his first day at kindergarten in the unaccustomed adult-style clothing of jeans and a belt. The fact that he forgets to say goodbye to his mother suggests that he is no longer under her benevolent control. He is becoming his own person, and the events that follow show how little anyone can know about the workings of another person's mind.

Laurie goes on to display insolence to his parents amid his stories of the wicked Charles. After his first day at kindergarten, he speaks rudely to his father and spills his baby sister's milk. Later, he calls his father "dumb" and an "old dust mop." Only once does he elicit the mildest of corrections from his parents, and they confine it to his grammar, replacing his use of the double negative, "I didn't learn nothing," with the grammatically correct "anything." On this occasion, in retrospect, the parents would have done better to pay attention to the new coldness with which he is addressing his father. But so focused are they on locating any disturbing behavior outside their own family, in the shape of Charles, that they utterly overlook the growing anarchy within their own household.

This is a compelling, psychologically nuanced situation presented by Jackson. The misplaced attention of the parents is eerily reminiscent of what happened in Germany during World War II, just a few years before Jackson wrote "Charles." While patriotic Germans focused on defeating their external enemies, the Allies, the evil of the Holocaust proceeded largely unnoticed and unopposed, as perpetrated by apparently civilized people like themselves.

It is true, as Stanley Edgar Hyman writes in his preface to *The Magic of Shirley Jackson*, that the tone of *Life among the Savages* in general and "Charles" in particular is "light-hearted." In spite of this, however, Hyman's comments on Jackson's last two gothic novels, *The Haunting of Hill House* and *We Have Always Lived in the Castle*, could also apply to the short story "Charles." Hyman calls these novels "a sensitive and faithful anatomy of our times, fitting symbols for our distressing world of the concentration camp and the Bomb." "Charles," too, contains the "dissociation" and "alienation" that Hyman identifies in the novels, though these themes are incongruously set against an outwardly normal and conventional family setting and are expressed in a comic tone.

Such is the dark subtext of this apparently innocent story. However, in an ironic and self-mocking twist through which she emphasizes the story's message that evil is not located externally but within, Jackson is effectively shining the spotlight on herself. The author, like Laurie, is a creator of fictions; and just as Laurie's parents have colluded in his fiction of Charles, so the author relies upon her readers colluding in the fictions she creates, including this story. Perhaps Laurie will grow up to suffer from dissociative identity disorder, or to be a cold-blooded murderer, or at the very least to be a troublemaker. But he could just as likely be a writer, like his real-life counterpart's mother. In fact, literature abounds with works that suggest that the line between destructive mental pathology and the writer's stance of detachment from the rest of society for the purposes of observation is a fine one. In her story, Jackson implicitly accepts that any diagnostic label that can apply to Laurie could also apply to her as a creator of fiction.

This graceful comic flourish is a fitting end to a story that, despite its dark aspects, is above all designed to entertain. It is also a gesture of humility from an author whose message in "Charles" is that evil is not "somewhere out there" but within every one of us.

Source: Claire Robinson, Critical Essay on "Charles," in *Short Stories for Students*, Gale, Cengage Learning, 2009.

Bernice M. Murphy

In the following excerpt, Murphy argues that although Jackson was "one of the most prominent female writers of the 1950s," her work has not received the critical attention it deserves.

During an episode of *The Simpsons* entitled "Dog of Death," Springfield's frequently fad-crazed citizenry succumb to a particularly virulent bout of gambling fever when the state lottery jackpot reaches an all-time high. The town's resident anchorman, Kent Brockman, begins the local news bulletin by announcing that people hoping to pick up tips on how to win the big prize have checked every copy of Shirley Jackson's *The Lottery* out of the local library. However, as Kent helpfully points out, "Of course, the book does not contain any hints on how to win the lottery. It is, rather, a chilling tale of conformity gone mad"—at which point a disgusted Homer Simpson tosses his copy into the fire.

I begin by referring to this witty scene not only because it is very funny, but also because I believe that it illustrates, in suitably ironic form, some of the most contradictory things about Jackson. It says a lot about the visibility of Jackson's most notorious tale that more than 50 years after its initial publication it is still famous enough to warrant mention in the world's most famous sitcom. The fact that Springfield's citizenry also miss the point of Jackson's story completely (after all, no one in their right mind would ever want to win *her* lottery) can perhaps be seen as an indication of a more general misrepresentation of Jackson and her work—a

> "JACKSON'S REFUSAL TO CONFORM TO CONVENTIONAL MORES WAS COMPLICATED BY THE MANNER IN WHICH SHE WAS POPULARLY DEPICTED DURING HER LIFETIME."

process that as we shall see, was well underway even before her death in August 1965.

A great early success, of the type that Jackson had with first "The Lottery" and later with the short-story collection of the same name, can be both a blessing and a curse for a writer. A blessing because of course every fledgling writer dreams of achieving the type of visibility that Jackson attained in the months following the story's publication in June 1948. However troubled Jackson was by the many disapproving letters she received following the tale's publication in *The New Yorker*, a part of her must have delighted in the fact that something she had written had provoked such strength of feeling—what writer of any real ambition would not . . . to some extent have relished this kind of attention? The downside to this type of early success is the danger that this early effort will overshadow the writer's every subsequent effort in the popular and critical mindset. It's a problem that Jackson was all too aware of: as she noted in her essay "Biography of a Story," her witty account of the genesis and aftermath of "The Lottery,"

> It was not my first published story, nor would it be my last, but I have been assured over and over that if it had been the only story I ever wrote or published, there would be people who would not forget my name.

There have long been those who have acted as though "The Lottery" was the only story Jackson ever wrote. Along with her classic novel of supernatural horror, *The Haunting of Hill House* (1959), it did in fact make her name and seal her reputation as a writer of elegant, allusive, literary horror fiction. But Jackson was much more, as this collection will illustrate. Long revered by enlightened readers of horror and the gothic, and fêted for her masterful contribution to the ranks of the classic ghost story, readers can be forgiven for not realizing that *Hill House* was actually among the very few supernatural stories that Jackson ever wrote. Even then, much of the allegedly "supernatural" incident in the novel is as likely to have a psychological as a ghostly cause: neurotic outsider Eleanor Vance is the focus of the novel and the likely catalyst for the many of the incidents that take place within its pages. Similarly, those expecting the rest of Jackson's many short stories to resemble "The Lottery" will be disappointed. While unmistakably Jackson both thematically and stylistically, the story is by no means typical of her *oeuvre*.

So who was Shirley Jackson? A conventional biographical summing-up would, as in the case of most writers, appear fairly unremarkable, save for her obvious literary talent, and, because of Jackson's sudden death in early middle age, poignantly brief. Born in San Francisco in 1916 (although some accounts erroneously state 1919) to comfortably middle-class parents, Jackson moved with her family to Rochester, New York, when she was in her teens. She attended college there for a while, but was unhappy and dropped out for a year, during which she worked on her writing and took on a number of temporary jobs. Jackson then enrolled in Syracuse University, with better results: she helped edit *The Spectre*, the college literary magazine, with her future husband, the academic and critic Stanley Edgar Hyman, graduated, got married, had four children in fairly rapid succession, and eventually settled in rural New England.

Like so many women of her class and generation, Jackson seemed absorbed in a life of apparently conventional domesticity: she raised her children, tolerated life as a faculty wife in a small, insular campus town, kept the family home running smoothly, and died at the age of 49 from heart failure. But of course, there was a great deal more going on in Jackson's life than the bare biographical facts would seem to suggest. Whatever she may have claimed in her family stories, Shirley Jackson was never just an "ordinary" housewife and mother: the importance of so much of her writing lies in the fact that she suggested so strongly that it was doubtful whether such a creature ever really existed at all.

It is no overstatement to say that Shirley Jackson was one of the most prominent female writers of the 1950s, so much so that one literary critic has even gone so far as to say that the "1950s became the decade of Jackson" (Wagner-Martin 107). Between 1948 and 1965 she published one best-selling short story collection, six novels, two popular volumes of her family chronicles, and many stories, which ranged from fairly conventional tales written for the women's magazine market to the ambiguous, allusive, delicately sinister and more obviously literary stories that were closest to Jackson's heart and were destined to end up in the more high brow end of the market. It is an impressive body of work for anyone to have produced in just over a decade and a half; when one considers that Jackson was also raising a family of four young children at the time it seems all the more notable.

Jackson was not alone in being able to find an audience for her work in both serious and popular outlets. As Joan Wylie Hall has observed, several of Jackson's contemporaries also published not only in *The New Yorker*, but also in mass market magazines—John Cheever featured in *Mademoiselle* and Ray Bradbury in *Charm*, while fellow writer of domestic humor Jean Kerr was a successful playwright whose work had been produced on Broadway. However, Jackson was "unusual for publishing so regularly in many of the magazines directed exclusively at a female readership . . . her name is the only one that is now at all familiar in issue after issue of *Good Housekeeping* and *Ladies' Home Journal*" (Hall xiii). Jackson's ability to prosper in both highbrow and popular markets was admired by none other than Sylvia Plath, who, as biographer Linda Wagner-Martin has noted, hoped to meet Jackson in June 1953 during her summer internship at *Mademoiselle*, and aspired towards a similar career.

By anyone's standards, Jackson's career was a successful one. After making her first national publication in 1941 with the semi-autobiographical story "My Life with R. H. Macy," Jackson's work began to appear regularly, with the first of her many appearances in *The New Yorker* occurring in 1943. She came to public prominence with the publication of "The Lottery" in 1948, and published *The Road Through the Wall* in the same year (it was generally liked by critics but not a great commercial success) and her first collection *The Lottery and Other Stories, or The Adventures of James Harris* in 1949. Her second novel, the unconventional Bildungsroman *Hangsaman* was published in 1951; like her follow-up, 1954's *The Bird's Nest*, it features a troubled young woman who suffers from a severe mental illness (schizophrenia and multiple personality disorder, respectively). The first (and most successful) of her so-called family chronicles, *Life Amongst the Savages* also appeared in 1954; the first of her "house" novels, *The Sundial*, appeared in 1956. The sequel to *Savages*, *Raising Demons*, was published in 1957, and Jackson's most famous novel, *The Haunting of Hill House*, appeared in 1959. Jackson's final completed novel, *We Have Always Lived in the Castle*, was published in 1962, though she was working on a new novel, *Come Along with Me*, at the time of her death three years later.

It is important to note that a surprising lack of critical work has been done on Jackson. I say surprising because at first glance, one would assume that she represents an obvious case for scholarship. In a revisionist academic climate in which some scholars have devoted entire careers to the rediscovery of marginalized writers—and from which a wealth of valuable feminist criticism has emerged—Jackson, a talented writer who focused on female anxieties and the contradictory pressures of domesticity and whose work has latterly been ignored, seems like a perfect choice for further study. And yet, an anecdotal biography, two book-length studies, around 40 or 50 critical papers and roughly the same number of dissertations represent the sum total of Jackson scholarship to date. Obviously, Jackson had not been entirely forgotten, but she has not been treated with the respect that her undeniable talent deserves....

Given Jackson's obvious talents, one might well ask why such a writer has until recently been denied the critical attention her writing would seem to warrant. Jackson's neglect can be attributed to a number of factors. Foremost among these is the fact that critics have not quite known what to make of her, a problem caused by the fact that she operated in two popular and yet frequently marginalized genres: those of horror and the gothic and the so-called domestic humor that appeared in women's magazines during the 1950s. As Lynette Carpenter has suggested in an important essay, Jackson's popularity, commercial success, and ability to simultaneously operate in two faintly disreputable genres has resulted in critical marginalization:

> Traditional male critics could not, in the end, reconcile genre with gender in Jackson's case: unable to understand how a serious writer of gothic fiction could also be, to all outward appearances, a typical housewife, much less how she could publish housewife humour in *Good Housekeeping*, they dismissed her [Carpenter 29].

Jackson's refusal to conform to conventional mores was complicated by the manner in which she was popularly depicted during her lifetime. Publicists and reviewers tended to focus upon two rather disparate but revealing representations of Jackson—either as "New England's only practicing amateur witch" or as matronly housewife. There was a grain of truth in each depiction, but ultimately neither revealed the true Jackson, and each would diminish the writer and her work. The polarization of Jackson's public personae began in 1948 with the publication of her first novel, the modestly successful *The Road Through the Wall.* The blurb on the dust jacket irreverently described Jackson as being "perhaps the only contemporary author who is a practicing amateur witch, specializing in small scale black magic and fortune telling with a tarot deck." As biographer Judy Oppenheimer notes, they were Jackson's husband Stanley's words and presumably it was also his idea to use this description—and, at "the time, since the book sold only moderately, it did no harm" (Oppenheimer 126). Stanley Hyman and Jackson had no way of knowing that in just over a year's time, this tongue-in-cheek publicity squib would come back to haunt them.

Jackson's relative anonymity ended on June 26, 1948, when *The New Yorker* published "The Lottery." Amidst the ensuing controversy, Jackson herself naturally became the object of much curiosity and speculation. Her stories were much in demand as a result of her newfound infamy, and now readers wanted to know more about the author of this all too memorable tale. With the hurried publication of the short-story collection of the same name in April of the following year, the publicity machine surrounding Jackson moved into high gear. It did not take long for publishing house Farrar Straus to rediscover Hyman's blurb for *Road*; and "Jackson herself had contributed biographical notes that could hardly have failed to pique interest" (Oppenheimer 139). The notes, which were perhaps just a little naive and revealing, outlined Jackson's unorthodox attitudes towards convention and the supernatural:

> My children and I believe wholeheartedly in magic. We do not any of us subscribe to the pat cause-and-effect rules which so many other people seem to use.... I have a fine library of magic and witchcraft and when I have nothing else to do I practice incantations [Oppenheimer 139].

There was an element of truth in Jackson's claims. As Oppenheimer notes, she did consider herself an expert on magic; she did have an extensive library of books on the subject; and she did make charms and mutter incantations to herself, as both family and friends testified (Oppenheimer 140); but it is also likely that Jackson was poking fun at the whole business of publicity and promotion, and most of all those who would be so gullible as to believe such a statement was said with an entirely straight face—no doubt the same rather impressionable section of the reading public who, a year earlier, had sent her angry letters demanding to know the name and location of the New England village whose arcane rites she had chronicled in "The Lottery."

However, there was something else there as well: deep-seated frustration towards the role she felt that a woman writer was supposed to adopt, and a genuine desire to evade conventional categorization. It was a desire that emerges strongly in the unpublished notes she made for that fateful biography:

> I am tired of writing dainty little biographical things that pretend I am a trim little housewife in a Mother Hubbard stirring up appetising messes over a wood stove.... I live in a dank old place with a ghost that storms around in the attic.... The first thing I did when we moved in was to make charms in black crayon on all the door sills and window ledges to keep out the demons [Oppenheimer 139].

This piece highlights the essential duality of Jackson's life and work—her consistent conflation of the domestic with the uncanny, the natural with the unnatural. What comes through most powerfully of all is Jackson's desire to resist imprisonment within the ideological norm, and a willful eccentricity and defiance that characterizes many of her finest fictional creations. The extract suggests that along with her faith in charms and incantations, Jackson had much in common with Merricat Blackwood, her most deeply felt character, of whom it could also be said, as it has been of Jackson, that "she would not be cubby holed, no matter how much easier it would make things for others" (Oppenheimer 139).

It did not take Jackson long, however, to realize that her mention of "witchlike" powers had badly backfired, for "rare was the interviewer who could resist asking her about black magic." At first, Jackson tended to respond to such questions truthfully. The result, as Oppenheimer puts it, "was the elbow nudging that surrounded her answers in print." Typical of such reports was one filed by Associated Press interviewer W.G. Rogers: "She says she can break a man's leg and throw a girl down an elevator shaft. Such things happen, she says! Miss Jackson tells you all this with a smile but she is not joking: she owns a library of two hundred books" (Oppenheimer 139)....

Source: Bernice M. Murphy, "Introduction: 'Do You Know Who I Am?': Reconsidering Shirley Jackson," in *Shirley Jackson: Essays on the Literary Legacy*, edited by Bernice M. Murphy, McFarland and Company, 2005, pp. 1–21.

SOURCES

Cobb, Jane, "Chaos Can Be Beautiful," Review of *Life among the Savages*, in the *New York Times*, June 21, 1953.

Egan, James, "Comic-Satiric-Fantastic-Gothic: Interactive Modes in Shirley Jackson's Narratives," in *Shirley Jackson: Essays on the Literary Legacy*, edited by Bernice M. Murphy, McFarland, 2005, pp. 34–51.

Friedman, Lenemaja, *Shirley Jackson*, Twayne Publishers, 1975, pp. 45, 147, 170.

Hrebik, Dale, "Shirley Jackson," in *Dictionary of Literary Biography*, Volume 234: *American Short-Story Writers since World War II, Third Series*, edited by Patrick Meanor and Richard E. Lee, The Gale Group, 2001, pp. 161–71.

Hyman, Stanley Edgar, Preface to *The Magic of Shirley Jackson*, edited by Stanley Edgar Hyman, Farrar, Straus and Giroux, 1966, pp. vii–ix.

Jackson, Shirley, "Charles," in *The Lottery, and Other Stories*, Farrar, Straus and Giroux, 1982, pp. 91–6.

LeCroy, Anne, "The Different Humor of Shirley Jackson: *Life among the Savages* and *Raising Demons*," in *Studies in American Humor*, Vol. 4, Nos. 1–2, Spring-Summer 1985, pp. 62–73.

Newman, Judie, "Shirley Jackson and the Reproduction of Mothering: *The Haunting of Hill House*," in *American Horror Fiction: From Brockden Brown to Stephen King*, edited by Brian Docherty, Macmillan, 1990, pp. 120–34.

Rubenstein, Roberta, "House Mothers and Haunted Daughters: Shirley Jackson and Female Gothic," in *Tulsa Studies in Women's Literature*, Vol. 15, No. 2, Fall 1996, pp. 309–31.

Stoer, Marion West, "Parental Recollections," Review of *Life among the Savages*, in *Christian Science Monitor*, July 9, 1953, p. 11.

FURTHER READING

Frazer, James, *The Golden Bough: A Study in Religion and Magic*, abridged edition, Dover Publications, 2002.

Frazer originally published his exploration of the origins of magical and religious thought in 1890. While some aspects of his work have been challenged in light of later scholarship, it has exercised a great influence on anthropology. Jackson studied the work during a course on folklore that she attended, and she used Frazer's findings on ancient scapegoat rituals in her story "The Lottery." The concept of the scapegoat is also explored in "Charles."

Haddock, Deborah Bray, *The Dissociative Identity Disorder Sourcebook*, McGraw-Hill, 2001.

This is a scholarly but easily readable introduction to dissociative identity disorder, written by a psychologist who specializes in the field. It is aimed at the general reader and offers helpful information for sufferers and their friends and relatives.

Hall, Joan Wylie, *Shirley Jackson: A Study of the Short Fiction*, Twayne Publishers, 1993.

This is a useful book for students that gives an overview of Jackson's short fiction and detailed analyses of her best-known stories, including "Charles." The book also contains interviews, essays, memoirs, biographical information, and critical responses.

Sewell, Mike, *The Cold War*, Cambridge University Press, 2001.

Sewell examines many aspects of the cold war, including its origins, its spread across the world through events in Europe and Asia, the Cuban Missile Crisis, and its conclusion in the 1980s. This accessible book offers an ideal overview for students.

Eleven

SANDRA CISNEROS

1991

Sandra Cisneros's short story "Eleven" first appeared in her 1991 collection *Woman Hollering Creek, and Other Stories.* In the twenty-two stories in that collection, Cisneros presents characters who live on the border between Mexico and the United States and who struggle with their identities, heritage, and circumstances. As a Chicana, a woman of Mexican heritage born or raised in the United States, Cisneros uses the language and images of her community. In many of the stories, Cisneros inserts Spanish words, phrases, and expressions without translation, thus emphasizing the dual linguistic lives of those who live in San Antonio, Texas, and other border towns. While the stories in the collection are not directly based on events in the author's own life, Cisneros drew on the emotional content of her experiences to create the stories.

Rachel, the first-person narrator of "Eleven," finds herself embarrassed and silenced by her teacher on her birthday, through no fault of her own. Any reader who has found himself or herself unjustly treated will identify with Rachel's pain. That the events of the story take place on Rachel's birthday adds a poignancy to the story. Thematically, Cisneros demonstrates the way that a majority-culture educational system reduces minority-culture girls to near invisibility. "Eleven" and the other stories in *Woman Hollering Creek* solidify Cisneros's reputation as a masterful, creative, and poetic writer. Her work continues to generate both popular and critical interest.

Sandra Cisneros (*AP Images. Reproduced by permission.*)

AUTHOR BIOGRAPHY

Sandra Cisneros was born in Chicago, Illinois, on December 20, 1954. Her father was a Spanish-speaking Mexican, while her mother was an English-speaking Chicana (a woman of Mexican descent either born or raised in the United States). Cisneros was one of seven children, but she was the only daughter in the family. They were poor and moved frequently. This fact of Cisneros's life, along with the extended trips to Mexico to visit her paternal grandmother, contributed to her sense of isolation as a child. In Mexico, she was an outsider because she spoke English and seemed American; in the United States, she was an outsider because she also spoke Spanish and seemed Mexican. Her sense of displacement influenced most of her later writings. In fact, in her loneliness, Cisneros turned to reading and writing as a source of comfort.

In 1966, the family moved to a small two-story house in Chicago's North Side, where Cisneros found some stability and community. The house later served as a model for the one in her first novel, *The House on Mango Street*. Cisneros graduated from high school in Chicago, having been the literary magazine editor. She attended Loyola University, graduating with a bachelor's degree in 1976. She next attended the University of Iowa Writers' Workshop, one of the most prestigious graduate writing programs in the United States, earning an M.F.A. in 1978. Her time there was very difficult, and again she found herself feeling like an outsider. Nonetheless, during her years at Iowa, she developed her voice and her subject matter, using her heritage and childhood memories as the basis for her early work. The poems that constituted her master's thesis were ultimately revised, expanded, and published as *My Wicked, Wicked Ways* in 1987.

Cisneros's first published work was a poetry chapbook called *Bad Boys* (1980). In the years immediately after graduate school, Cisneros taught at an alternative high school in Chicago, became active within the Chicano community, and worked briefly for Loyola. She also was the recipient of two National Endowment for the Arts fellowships, including one for fiction in 1982 and one for poetry in 1987. In 1984, Cisneros worked as the literature director of the Guadalupe Cultural Arts Center in San Antonio, Texas, the city she began calling home.

Meanwhile, during the late 1970s and early 1980s, Cisneros continued to work on a series of autobiographical vignettes that grew into her first novel, *The House on Mango Street*, published by Arte Publico in 1983. She finished the novel while serving as the artist in residence at the Foundation Michael Karolyi in Vence, France, in 1983. This book received strong critical acclamation, winning the Before Columbus Foundation's American Book Award in 1985. With the publication of *The House on Mango Street* and the 1987 publication of *My Wicked, Wicked Ways*, Cisneros found herself in demand as a visiting writer at many campuses, including California State University, Chico; the University of California, Berkeley; the University of California, Irvine; the University of Michigan; and the University of New Mexico.

In 1991, Cisneros published *Woman Hollering Creek, and Other Stories* through Random House, a large, mainstream publisher. The collection, in which "Eleven" first appeared, immediately received wide readership and strong critical support. The book garnered for Cisneros a host of awards, including the PEN Center West Award for Best Fiction of 1991; the Quality Paperback Book Club New Voices Award; the Anisfield-Wolf Book Award; and the Lannan Foundation Literary Award. The stories of *Woman Hollering*

MEDIA ADAPTATIONS

- *Woman Hollering Creek, and Other Stories*, including the short story "Eleven," was released on cassette tape along with the novel *The House on Mango Street* in 1992 by Random House Publishers.
- Books on Tape produced and released a compact disc set that includes *Loose Woman* and *Woman Hollering Creek, and Other Stories* in 2005.

Creek trace the lives of female narrators of all ages living in or near San Antonio, Texas.

An important event for Cisneros was her 1995 MacArthur Foundation Fellowship. Her commitment to her community was demonstrated by her establishment of the Latino MacArthur Fellows, a group that took as its mission community outreach. Cisneros is also the founder of the Macondo Foundation, dedicated to fostering creativity, generosity, and honor in Latino communities, and of the Alfredo Cisneros del Moral Foundation, an organization that gives grants to Texas writers.

After the publication of *Woman Hollering Creek, and Other Stories*, Cisneros published a collection of poetry, *Loose Woman* (1994), and a novel, *Caramelo* (2002). Cisneros's work continues to trace the journeys of those in the borderland between cultures. Groundbreaking in both subject matter and form, her writing speaks to new readers as well as to those who have followed her career closely. It is likely that Cisneros will long be considered one of the most influential writers of the late twentieth and early twenty-first centuries.

PLOT SUMMARY

"Eleven" is a brief narrative of only a few pages that is nonetheless a powerful statement on class and culture. Written in the first person, the story describes in the present tense the experience of a young Latina girl named Rachel in school on her eleventh birthday.

The story opens with Rachel's reflection on the nature of time as she contemplates her own birthday. She says that people contain all of the ages they have ever been, and that sometimes younger versions of oneself appear. For example, when someone is very hurt and wants to cry, it might be the three-year-old within him or her that does the crying. She even believes that sometimes an adult might need to feel like a three-year-old. She also astutely observes that the shift from one age to the next does not occur overnight; a person does not go to bed one night as a ten-year-old and wake up the next day eleven. Rather, it takes some getting used to, and it might take several months or almost a year before a person really feels like he or she is eleven years old.

The reason that Rachel contemplates age is because now, on her birthday, she wishes she were one hundred and two, not eleven. An incident with her teacher, Mrs. Price, has deeply wounded Rachel. In a recounting of the incident, when Mrs. Price holds up an ugly red sweater in front of the class and wants to know who owns it, she is clearly annoyed with the person who has left the sweater in the cloakroom for so long. After all the rest of the students deny ownership, Mrs. Price listens to a student say that it belongs to Rachel. Mrs. Price does not listen to Rachel, who is at first dumbfounded and then finally manages to deny ownership in "a little voice that was maybe me when I was four." The teacher overrules Rachel's protest and puts the sweater on her desk.

Rachel has a difficult time containing her inner three-year-old, who wants to cry, but she does so by remembering that her mother will have a birthday cake for her that evening to celebrate her eleventh birthday. She pushes the sweater slowly to the edge of her desk until it almost falls on the floor. Noticing this, Mrs. Price embarrasses Rachel again by interrupting the class and telling Rachel to put on the sweater. As earlier, she does not allow Rachel to speak, and she forces the girl to wear the offending piece of clothing. Rachel suddenly loses control and breaks down weeping, her head on her desk. "I wish I was invisible," she narrates, continuing to weep.

As if this humiliation is not enough, at lunchtime one of the other girls in the class remembers that the sweater belongs to her, and Mrs. Price neither comments nor offers an apology. Although Rachel no longer must wear the sweater, her birthday has been ruined. All she now wishes for is to be "far away like a runaway balloon."

CHARACTERS

Phyllis Lopez

Phyllis Lopez is a student in the elementary classroom. She is the rightful owner of the red sweater that is forced upon Rachel. Rachel says that Phyllis is "stupid." While this opinion cannot be considered objective, it is possible to state that Phyllis's lapse of memory is causative in spoiling Rachel's birthday.

Mrs. Price

Mrs. Price is the teacher of the elementary school classroom where Cisneros sets the story "Eleven." Her name suggests that she is an Anglo teacher, while her students' names are all Latino in origin. Mrs. Price does not appear to be at all sensitive to the feelings of her students. When she brings the old red sweater out from the cloakroom, she does not quietly try to find the sweater's owner. Rather, she holds it up in front of the whole classroom and complains that it has "been sitting in the coatroom for a month." Her attitude clearly demonstrates that the owner of the sweater is guilty of a transgression, and consequently, none of the students will claim the sweater. Mrs. Price does not consider that the condition of the sweater may reflect negatively on its owner. Furthermore, she does not consider the humiliation she causes Rachel by insisting that the child put on the sweater. She uses a loud voice and disciplines Rachel in front of the entire class, on the basis of dubious evidence. She calls Rachel's reluctance to wear the sweater "nonsense," another clue that she does not understand the values of her students. In addition, she does not respect her students enough to offer an apology to Rachel when it becomes obvious that she herself was in error. In "Eleven," Mrs. Price is the antagonist of the story, a character who represents the injustice of majority culture when dealing with minority students.

Rachel

Rachel is the protagonist in "Eleven." The entire story is told in a first-person, internal narrative, so the reader only understands events as they are filtered through Rachel's eyes. It is therefore possible to learn a great deal about her character from the details that she provides. Because the other students mentioned in the story have Latino names, and because Rachel calls her mother and father "mama" and "papa," and because all of the other stories in *Woman Hollering Creek, and Other Stories* feature female Latina protagonists, it is safe to assume that Rachel is a Latina herself.

Rachel is a kind and sympathetic character. Early on, she mentions trying to comfort her mother when her mother feels sad by telling her that it is okay to cry, even if she is an adult. In addition, Rachel also reveals that sometimes she feels the need to sit on her mother's lap, even though she is now eleven, because she feels scared. Moreover, it seems clear that Rachel is a very reflective child who thinks deeply about abstract matters such as the passage of time and the meaning of age. Her understanding that all people retain the childlike parts of themselves no matter how old they grow is both sensitive and mature.

Rachel is also a shy child, and she finds it difficult to answer her teacher when confronted with the ugly red sweater. Although it cannot be determined from the story, it is possible that Rachel is not a native English speaker, which would certainly contribute to her inability to stand up for herself when falsely accused. The reader also learns that Rachel is both "skinny" and disliked by Sylvia. These two details suggest that Rachel is an outsider in the classroom. It is possible that the other children pick on her, and it is likely that the teacher contributes to Rachel's isolation.

The events of the story take place on Rachel's eleventh birthday, and it is around this age that young women often become very self-conscious and easily embarrassed. In addition, young women at this age can be very cruel to those they see as outsiders. It is likely that Cisneros conceived of Rachel as eleven years old rather than younger because it places her at the tipping point between childhood and adolescence. The reader can imagine Rachel beginning her eleventh birthday as a child but, through the events of the day, returning to her home as a much older person, someone who understands at a very deep level that life is often unfair.

Sylvia Saldívar

Sylvia Saldívar is the student who suggests to Mrs. Price that the red sweater belongs to Rachel. The only description of Sylvia's motivation is in the following sentence: "Maybe because I'm skinny, maybe because she doesn't like me, that stupid Sylvia Saldívar says, 'I think it belongs to Rachel.'" It is difficult to analyze this character from these few words. On the one hand, Sylvia's remark to the teacher could be entirely innocent; she might have been trying simply to help establish the ownership of the sweater. On the other hand, Rachel feels that Sylvia does not like her. If this is the case, then Sylvia's remark could be interpreted as an attempt to both ingratiate herself with Mrs. Price and also deal Rachel a blow. Regardless of the class dynamics, however, Sylvia's remark is what sets the rest of the story in action.

THEMES

Culture Clash and the Immigrant Experience

Each of the stories in *Woman Hollering Creek*, including "Eleven," explores the experiences of girls and women who are members of a minority culture trying to navigate the waters of the majority culture in the United States. Rachel, like many young immigrants, finds herself spending most of her day in a public school setting. This is a place where she must learn not only the English language but also the values and customs of the majority culture. The names of the other students in the class suggest that they are of the same cultural background as Rachel. However, Rachel's depiction as an outsider in the class, someone the other children pick on and someone the teacher discounts, suggests that she may be a newcomer to the class, and most likely to the culture as well.

Rachel's thoughts of her family, her birthday cake, and the celebration that her family has planned for her at the end of the day serve as a contrast to the treatment she has received in the school. At home, as a fully integrated member of her family and its culture, she is an insider, someone who is valued and loved. She knows who she is, and she knows the conventions and values of her culture. Being a member of an immigrant family, at home her life is much the same as it would have been in the family's home country. At school, however, her life is very different. The public school classroom, as led by its majority-culture teacher, is an alien landscape for Rachel. It is a place where she learns important lessons about the authority structures of her new homeland. The teacher's disregard for Rachel's feelings allows the reader to experience firsthand what it is like to be a member of an immigrant community.

Justice and Injustice

In "Eleven," the narrator, Rachel, experiences injustice at the hands of her teacher and, to a lesser degree, her classmates. While the main event of the story, the mistaken attribution of a ratty red sweater to Rachel, might seem to be insignificant, for Rachel it proves a very important episode. To begin, everyone in the class, including Rachel, asserts that the sweater does not belong to him or her. Therefore, when one of the students tells the teacher that the sweater is actually Rachel's, it signals two possibilities to the others in the class: first, that Rachel is so poor that all her family can afford is a miserable looking red sweater, and second, that Rachel lied in denying that the sweater belonged to her.

To impose a legal metaphor on the scene, Sylvia plays the role of the prosecutor to Rachel's role of the accused. The teacher, of course, as the most powerful person in the classroom, fills the role of the judge, the dispenser of justice. In a place where justice is meted out fairly through a judicial system, there is an assumption that the accused is innocent until proven otherwise; an assumption that the judge will listen carefully to evidence before rendering a verdict; and an assumption that the judge will not punish the innocent, only the guilty. In addition, the accused is permitted to face his or her accuser and defend himself or herself.

The events of "Eleven" demonstrate a cruel perversion of justice. Mrs. Price listens only to Sylvia, who has no evidence that the sweater is Rachel's. Such hearsay evidence would not be permissible in a court of law attempting to serve justice. Further, Mrs. Price interrupts Rachel when she tries to defend herself and thus does not permit her to mount her own defense.

TOPICS FOR FURTHER STUDY

- Read *The House on Mango Street*, by Sandra Cisneros, and *How the García Girls Lost Their Accents*, by Julia Alvarez. Write a paper in which you compare and contrast the experiences of Esperanza and the García sisters as young Latina women living in American culture.
- Working with a small group, develop a multimedia presentation demonstrating the contributions of contemporary Latina writers living in the United States. Your presentation might include images of the writers; a world map identifying the writers' birthplaces; Latina music; appropriate artwork; audio files of the writers reading their works; images that represent themes in the writers' works; samples of food from the various cultures represented in your presentation; and video clips of the writers, among other items. Use your presentation to introduce your fellow students to your selected writers and their cultures.
- Read all of the stories of *Woman Hollering Creek, and Other Stories*. Identify Spanish phrases and words used in the stories and find translations for these words. Why do you think that Cisneros uses a combination of Spanish and English when writing her stories? What effect does the insertion of Spanish into her stories have on the reader? Is it necessary to be able to read both English and Spanish to enjoy the stories? Write a paper in which you discuss Cisneros's linguistic choices in *Woman Hollering Creek, and Other Stories*.
- Investigate the history of the American Southwest, particularly that of Texas. How did this area become a part of the United States? What happened to the people who were already living there? How do these historical circumstances inform your understanding of Chicano culture? How do these circumstances differ from the way Europeans immigrated to the United States? Write a paper discussing your findings. Be sure to cite your sources.
- Draw a map of where you lived when you were eleven. Make the map elaborate with details, including where you played, your friends' houses, places that were dangerous, and other such landmarks. Use the map as a tool for remembering stories about your childhood. Complete three ten-minute sessions of free writing on your three strongest memories, choose the one that you like best, and revise your free writing into a story. Display your map and story along with those of the other students in class.
- Imagine that your classroom is an art gallery and that you are responsible for mounting an exhibition of Chicano art. Find examples of Chicano art online or in books, and print or copy them, in color if possible. Write brief descriptions of each piece you select, noting information about the artist and the work. Develop a catalog of your exhibition for gallery visitors to read.

Mrs. Price also punishes Rachel unjustly by forcing her to wear a sweater that she finds embarrassing. According to Rachel, the sweater "smells like cottage cheese," its arms are pulled out of shape, it has cheap plastic buttons, and it is itchy. Because Mrs. Price condemns Rachel so, Rachel's status suffers in the eyes of her classmates, who now believe her a pitiable liar.

When the truth of the matter becomes apparent, Mrs. Price compounds the injustice she has perpetrated by ignoring it. Rachel receives no apology and no restitution. Although she is innocent, she has been treated as guilty, the victim of an egregious injustice at the hands of a person who should have been a trusted adult.

Various babushka dolls, close up, St. Petersburg, Russia (© Frans Lemmens / Getty Images)

STYLE

Coming-of-age Story

The coming-of-age story is one of the most popular in literature. In this type of fiction, a young protagonist, through adventures and misadventures, learns something important about life and grows from a child into an adult. In general, this growth signals a positive movement for the protagonist.

However, "Eleven" demonstrates that growth is not always happy, nor is it necessarily positive. When the story opens, Rachel is thinking about her birthday and about growing older. She demonstrates a keen understanding that growing older is difficult, because although one grows older birthday by birthday, all the characteristics of the younger self always remain. Thus, an adult who feels deeply sad might find herself behaving like a three-year-old and crying. This is precisely the situation Rachel finds herself in. Although she knows that on the day of the story she is eleven years old, her teacher makes her feel like a small child unable to control her tears or her feelings.

Rachel's growth can be charted by examining her early description of the birthday cake that awaits her at home where her family members will sing happy birthday to her. She uses this thought early in the story as a way of not thinking about her shame. However, after Mrs. Price fails to apologize or attempt to make restitution to her, even the thoughts of her birthday have changed: "There's a cake Mama's making for tonight, and when Papa comes home from work we'll eat it. There'll be candles and presents and everybody will sing Happy birthday, happy birthday to you, Rachel, only it's too late." The lessons that Rachel has learned are that her voice will not always be strong enough to be heard and that adults are not necessarily to be trusted to act fairly. It is now too late for her to enjoy her birthday the way a child should, with happy abandon. Rather, from this day on, the celebration of her birthday will be tinged with the memory of unjust shame and humiliation. No longer a child at eleven, Rachel has been confronted with a cruel reality of life as an adult.

First-person Point of View

In an interview with Bridget Kevane in the book *Latina Self-Portraits*, Cisneros asserts, "Living in San Antonio gives me so much. It's so rich. There is so much to tap in terms of voices." Recalling her frame of mind when working on her collection *Woman Hollering Creek*, she notes that the stories are "very much set on the border because I am living at the border. I was much more concerned with representing different types of Chicanos on paper." In the case of "Eleven," Cisneros assumes the voice of a particular child who is trying to celebrate her birthday in the face of shame and humiliation. In this story, Rachel represents one of the least powerful members of a family in America: she is a child, she is Latina, she is physically small, and she is temperamentally shy. Through the skillful use of point of view, Cisneros allows readers to understand and sympathize with Rachel without having to be told what to think.

Point of view serves as a narrative device. For example, a writer can choose to use a third-person omniscient point of view, meaning that the telling of the story is not embodied in a character but rather seems to come from some all-knowing consciousness that exists outside of the story itself. "Eleven" is told from the opposite perspective, in the first-person limited point of view. At its extreme, this point of view becomes an interior monologue. The entire story is told through Rachel's senses and thoughts. The reader is limited to what Rachel sees, hears, smells, touches, tastes, and thinks. Even the words of the other characters are not recorded in real time but rather are reported slightly later, filtered through the internal monologue of the protagonist.

The danger that a writer faces in using such a tightly controlled and narrow point of view is that the reader may begin to feel slightly claustrophobic. The internal monologues in "Eleven" and in other stories from *Woman Hollering Creek*, including "My Lucy Friend Who Smells Like Corn" and "Salvador, Late or Early," are successful in part because of their length; they are scarcely more than vignettes, extending only for a few pages. In addition, Cisneros draws on the reader's own memories of being a child, which certainly include being alternately happy, sad, embarrassed, and joyful. By using the limited first-person point of view, the author is able to capture the voice of a child, with all the abandon and linguistic creativity characteristic of a young person. In "Eleven," this is particularly crucial. Rachel must undergo a transformation from a happily innocent child to one who knows the true score of life. By telling the story in the girl's voice, Cisneros subtly draws the reader through that painful transformation along with Rachel.

Use of Imagery

While the word *image* is generally associated with the sense of sight, the word *imagery* is used more broadly in literature. It refers to language, often figurative rather than literal, that appeals to any of the senses. Thus, a poem or story could have auditory imagery, appealing to the sense of hearing; gustatory imagery, appealing to the sense of taste; tactile imagery, appealing to the sense of touch; kinesthetic imagery, appealing to the sense of movement; or olfactory imagery, appealing to the sense of smell. Because imagery is presented through very concentrated language, it is generally more common in poetry than in prose.

One of the most important images in "Eleven" is that of the red sweater: "It's an ugly sweater with red plastic buttons and a collar and sleeves all stretched out like you could use it for a jump rope." Readers can easily visualize the sweater through this image. Cisneros involves more of the senses each time she mentions the sweater. It sits on Rachel's desk "like a big red mountain." Rachel moves the sweater with her ruler, not even wanting to touch it, so as to distances herself as far from the offending sweater as she possibly can. Again, readers will have no difficulty picturing and feeling this movement through the images used by Cisneros to paint the scene. Perhaps the most effective use of imagery in the story is the moment when Rachel is forced to put the sweater on her own body: "I put one arm through one sleeve of the sweater that smells like cottage cheese, and then the other arm through the other and stand there with my arms apart like if the sweater hurts me and it does, all itchy and full of germs that aren't even mine." In this single sentence, Cisneros evokes the reader's olfactory, kinesthetic, visual, and tactile senses. By doing so, the reader experiences Rachel's humiliation from the inside out, not just from objective visualization. The feeling of the itchy sweater may linger on the reader's arms long after the pages of the book are closed.

COMPARE & CONTRAST

- **1990s:** Feminist Chicana writers such as Denise Chavez, Gloria Anzaldúa, and Sandra Cisneros, among others, find publishers for their work, followed by critical attention and wide readership.

  Today: Both Chicana and Chicano writers have grown in popularity among members of minority and majority cultures alike.

- **1990s:** A report prepared by the U.S. Department of Commerce in 1993 states that the Mexican population in the United States nearly doubled between 1970 and 1980 and nearly doubled again by 1990.

  Today: According to a 2008 report prepared for the Migration Policy Institute, more than 11.5 million Mexican immigrants are living in the United States as of 2006.

- **1990s:** The 1993 Department of Commerce report states that as of 1990, the primary language of about 14 percent of the population of the United States is a language other than English. Spanish is spoken by about 50 percent of all non-English speakers in the United States.

  Today: The U.S. Census Bureau reports that as of 2005, 32.2 million people in the United States speak Spanish as their primary language at home, constituting about 12 percent of the total population. Nearly one in eight U.S. residents speak Spanish.

HISTORICAL CONTEXT

Immigration from Mexico to the United States

Throughout the second half of the twentieth century, immigration from Mexico to the United States grew steadily. During the 1990s, the overall immigrant population of the United States from all countries grew by 11.3 million people, faster than at any other time in U.S. history. Meanwhile, a growing percentage of those immigrating to the United States were from Mexico. By 2006, 30 percent of all immigrants to the United States were coming from Mexico, according to a report prepared by Jeanne Batalova for the Migration Policy Institute in 2008.

In addition to those immigrants coming into the United States legally, from the 1990s onward, an increasing number of undocumented immigrants also entered the country. Mexico is the largest source of undocumented immigrants in the United States. Jennifer Van Hook, Frank D. Bean, and Jeffrey Passel estimate in a 2005 report for the Migration Policy Institute that 3.5 million unauthorized immigrants were living in the United States in 1990 and that the majority of those were from Mexico. By 2006, according to Batalova, "more than half of all unauthorized immigrants in the United States were from Mexico." She further estimates that 6.6 million unauthorized immigrants were from Mexico.

The implications of these changing immigration patterns have worked themselves throughout the social fabric of the United States. For example, beginning in the early 1990s, an increasing number of U.S. residents reported speaking Spanish in their homes as their primary language. As a result, in many communities, signs and public notices were printed in both English and Spanish. Further, many schools added aids and teachers who could speak Spanish and included English as a Second Language (ESL) classes in their curricula to accommodate the growing number of students who were not yet proficient in English. Additionally, "Spanglish," a form of speech that includes both Spanish and English words, came to be spoken and understood by a growing segment of the population. (Sandra Cisneros's linguistic choices in *Woman Hollering Creek, and Other Stories* mirror this trend.) Finally, a growing number of stores and businesses came to display signs indicating that they had the capability of conducting business in Spanish.

There has been negative backlash against these cultural shifts. Some Americans blamed Mexican immigrants for taking jobs from English-speaking U.S. residents, although this could not be documented statistically. In addition, some Americans did not want Spanish-speaking students to be taught in Spanish, nor did they want Spanish-speaking residents to be served in Spanish in businesses or in stores. They supported what was known as the "English only" movement, holding that if someone wanted to live in the United States, then that person should learn English.

The evidence actually suggests that immigrant groups arriving in the United States from 1990 onward have learned English at least one generation sooner than those immigrants who had arrived earlier. Young people in particular have learned English very quickly and have begun immediately assimilating themselves into mainstream culture. According to a 2005 survey, "among all those who speak Spanish at home, more than one-half say they speak English very well." At the same time, however, there has been fear among immigrant groups that they could lose their distinctive ethnic traditions and rituals through assimilation.

In many parts of the United States, Mexican traditions and rituals became well known beginning in the 1990s. For example, in many communities, Cinco de Mayo, the Mexican independence day celebrated on May 5, is marked with parades and celebrations. Likewise, the tradition of the *quinceañera*, the celebration of a girl's fifteenth birthday, serves as an important social event in many communities. Finally, Mexican food and drink became even more prevalent during the closing years of the twentieth century.

The Chicano Movement

The terms *Chicano* and *Chicana* are highly politicized words. *Chicano* refers to a person of Mexican descent either born or raised in the United States who chooses to identify with the term. During the 1960s and the 1970s, the Chicano movement strove (along with other civil rights movements of the same time period) to improve the educational and social status of Chicanos. Leaders such as César Chávez drew national attention to problems facing Latino farm workers. Through organizations such as the United Farm Workers, Chávez secured better working conditions and civil liberties for his people.

In the realm of the arts, the political activist and writer Roldolfo "Corky" Gonzales, with his 1967 epic poem "Yo Soy Joaquin" ("I Am Joaquin"), offered a new vision of what it means to be Chicano. As expressed by Gonzales in his poem, Chicanos are neither European nor indigenous but rather a combination of many identities, sometimes in conflict with each other. He also explores the myth of Aztlán, which he identifies as the legendary homeland of the Aztec people, located in the American Southwest. His work, as well as that of other activists, encouraged Chicanos throughout the country to value the strong cultural contributions they made to the American social fabric. Thus, one of the characteristics of the growing Chicano population in the United States in the last years of the twentieth century was the concomitant growth of cultural expression, as noted by Eva Fernández de Pinedo in her 2006 article "An Overview of Contemporary Chicano/a Literature." She writes: "The demographic rise in Chicanos/as during the last decades has been accompanied by the flowering of its cultural production, particularly literature."

Fernández de Pinedo accurately assesses the changing scene of Chicano literature during the 1980s and 1990s, the decades when Cisneros was writing *The House on Mango Street* and *Woman Hollering Creek, and Other Stories*: "After a period of male-dominated literary production, the 1980s and 1990s witnessed the emergence of Chicanas who dealt with gender and sexuality, issues largely ignored in previous Chicano writing." Indeed, the Chicana women who began writing in the 1980s and 1990s revitalized the movement through their inclusion of gender politics as an important consideration. The stories of women struggling with the twin yokes of patriarchy and racism struck a chord with both minority and majority readers.

Chicana writers seemed particularly well situated to comment on one of the most common themes in literature emerging during the 1990s, the borderlands. Chicana writers often found themselves straddling two worlds, one in English, the other in Spanish. Fernández de Pinedo notes that Chicano/a writers "express the need to combine two cultures and ways of life at the same time as they criticise the inability to be accepted by Mexico or the United States.... The idea of existing in a border state and not belonging, or being accepted by Mexico or the U.S. is a recurrent theme in this literature." Certainly, this is one of the primary issues that Cisneros addresses in *Woman Hollering Creek, and Other Stories.*

CRITICAL OVERVIEW

Although Sandra Cisneros received wide praise for both her poetry and her prose during the 1980s, she became much better known with the 1991 publication of *Woman Hollering Creek, and Other Stories.* Stories like "Eleven" earned her both critical respect and a cross-cultural readership. In fact, a number of critics have discussed the poetic qualities of Cisneros's prose. The novelist Barbara Kingsolver, for example, in the *Los Angeles Times Book Review* writes of *Woman Hollering Creek:* "Sandra Cisneros has added length and dialogue and a hint of plot to her poems and published them in a stunning collection." Kingsolver further notes that "nearly every sentence contains an explosive sensory image." Although she is talking about the stories in general, "Eleven" in particular demonstrates this stylistic characteristic of Cisneros's writing. Kingsolver asserts, "When you read this book, don't be fooled: It's poetry."

Many critics found growth in Cisneros's new collection of stories, noting that she had fleshed out her poetry and deepened her narrative sense. For example, in a 1991 review in the *Nation*, Patricia Hart notes that in *Woman Hollering Creek*, "Cisneros breathes narrative life into her adroit, poetic descriptions, making them mature, fully formed works of fiction." Carol Muske, writing in *Parnassus: Poetry in Review* in 1995, offers a similar assessment, calling the collection Cisneros's "most mature work."

The format of the stories has interested other critics; while the works are "fully formed," as Hart notes, it is sometimes difficult to easily place them within a genre. Are they poems? Are they vignettes? Or are they truly short stories? Mary Pat Brady argues in an article about *Woman Hollering Creek* in *American Literature*:

> Many of the stories (for example, "Eleven" and "Mexican Movies") defy, or at least ignore, the conventions of storytelling.... Without the soothing structure of a beginning, middle, or end, without a goal to tug a reader through the plot, these brief stories emphasize through contrast the predictability of conventional narratives.

Yet another group of critics has focused on these stories as statements of feminine and cultural identity. Michael Carroll and Susan Maher, in their *North Dakota Quarterly* article "'A Las Mujeres': Cultural Context and the Process of Maturity in Sandra Cisneros' *Woman Hollering Creek*," identify the author's terrain in noting that her "exploration of female maturation traverses within the rich yet conflicted cultural context of the Texas/Mexican borderlands." Certainly, the maturation process experienced by Rachel in "Eleven" is compounded and complicated by the cultural conflicts. Likewise, in a review of the collection by Peter S. Prescott and Karen Springen appearing in *Time*, the critics note: "Noisily, wittily, always compassionately, Cisneros surveys woman's condition—a condition that is both precisely Latina and general to women everywhere. Her characters... are without exception strong girls, strong women. The girls who tell their brief stories are so alert they seem almost to quiver." Finally, Jeff Thomson, writing in a 1994 article in *Studies in Short Fiction*, finds in the short story "Eleven" an expression of the way cultural conflicts can lead to the fragmentation of identity. Quoting the story, he argues that it "sets up a system of multiple selves like 'little wooden dolls that fit one inside the other' and the difficulty of maintaining a unity of self in the face of authority."

Perhaps Cynthia Tompkins, writing in the *Dictionary of Literary Biography* in 1995, best summarizes Cisneros's accomplishments in *Woman Hollering Creek, and Other Stories*, particularly in stories such as "Eleven": "By re-creating a Chicana child's perspective, Cisneros has already made a significant contribution to the development of the Chicano literary tradition. Moreover, by focusing on the socialization processes of the Chicana, she has criticized and challenged major stereotypes."

CRITICISM

Diane Andrews Henningfeld

Henningfeld is a professor of English who publishes widely on literary topics. In the following essay, she discusses the marginalization of the protagonist in "Eleven."

In the stories of *Woman Hollering Creek, and Other Stories*, Sandra Cisneros explores the lives of Chicana girls and women living in and around San Antonio, Texas. Her primary concern is with

WHAT DO I READ NEXT?

- *The House on Mango Street*, published in 1983, is Cisneros's first novel. The structure of the book is innovative, as it consists of short, poetic vignettes told through the voice of Esperanza, a poor Chicana girl.
- *Hairs/Pelitos*, a bilingual children's book by Cisneros, was published in 1994. Beautifully illustrated, the book lovingly describes the various heads of hair found in the family. Older English-speaking students will find that it offers an excellent opportunity to practice reading in Spanish.
- Cisneros's poetic skills are evident in several collections of poetry, including *My Wicked, Wicked Ways*, published in 1987, and *Loose Woman*, published in 1994.
- In her semi-autobiographical novel *How the García Girls Lost Their Accents* (1991), Julia Alvarez traces in reverse chronological order how a Spanish-speaking family who must leave the Dominican Republic due to political problems gradually becomes a part of the culture of the United States.
- Caryn Mirriam-Goldberg's biography *Sandra Cisneros: Latina Writer and Activist*, written for young adults and published in 1998, is a starting point for the study of Cisneros and her work.
- *Interviews with Writers of the Post-Colonial World*, edited by Feroza Jussawalla and Reed Way Dasenbrock and published in 1992, provides students with the means to compare and contrast writers from a variety of cultural backgrounds.

"IN THE STORY 'ELEVEN,' THE EDUCATION OF THE NARRATOR, RACHEL, INCLUDES SYSTEMATIC MARGINALIZATION BECAUSE OF HER STATUS AS A YOUNG PERSON, AS A GIRL, AND AS A CHICANA."

how these female characters locate their identity and personal authority in the midst of this cultural borderland. In many of the stories, women use the legends and mythology of their own heritage to define a strong identity. In the opening story, "My Lucy Friend Who Smells Like Corn," for example, the narrator celebrates her friend Lucy and the rich ethnicity of their lives together. Their identities are secure, and their joy is profound.

The second story of *Woman Hollering Creek*, to the contrary, features a narrator who does not become stronger as she recognizes her own identity but rather finds herself powerless in her interactions with her peers and her teacher. Tellingly, the transformation from strong and secure to weak and powerless takes place within a public school. In the story "Eleven," the education of the narrator, Rachel, includes systematic marginalization because of her status as a young person, as a girl, and as a Chicana.

Marginalization is a term often used by literary and social theorists to describe the way that an individual, group, or community is denied power. In the process of being marginalized, the individual or group is moved farther from the center of power in any structure, and as a consequence, the individual or group loses social or material status. Frequently, scholars discuss marginalization in terms of race or gender relations, demonstrating how those in power may wittingly or unwittingly secure their hold on power by lowering the status of individuals or groups who wish to access power. At times marginalization occurs when the powerful resort to stereotypical or biased thinking. Thus, culturally held assumptions about members of particular ethnic, gender, or socioeconomic groups end up contributing to the marginalization of those groups. As a result, those who are marginalized often find themselves both silenced and treated unjustly without recourse.

"Eleven" is instructional in laying bare some of the most insidious power structures in American culture. In the first place, while public school education is widely considered a standard of participatory democracy, the public school is also often a place where girls and ethnic minorities first taste the bitter fruits of marginalization. Mrs. Price, the teacher in the story, demonstrates how the power structures of schools assist in denying some students their rightful voice and justice.

There are a number of details that are easy to overlook when reading the story but that are essential in analyzing Rachel's marginalization. In the first place, Mrs. Price does not have a Latino name, indicating that she inhabits a social group different from that of her students. The name "Price" also carries with it symbolic resonance, as the teacher's approval can only be won at a terribly high price. Finally, in many, perhaps most elementary classrooms, a teacher will know when it is a student's birthday. Often the student will be singled out for special treatment or given special privileges. Mrs. Price apparently does not know that it is Rachel's birthday, or if she does know, she fails to mark the occasion in any special way. That none of the other students comment on the fact that it is Rachel's birthday can also be read as a clue that she is not a member of the inner group herself; she may have already been marginalized by teacher and fellow students alike before the story begins.

The events of the story begin with Mrs. Price holding up an ugly red sweater that no one in the class wants to claim. There are a number of reasons for the students to deny ownership. In the first place, Mrs. Price's words and gestures suggest that she is deeply annoyed by the offending sweater. Obviously, any student claiming the sweater could be subjected to the emotionally negative experience of a lecture or scolding. In addition, Mrs. Price is making a public announcement and is asking the culprit to publically claim the piece of clothing, a gesture that is likely to cause embarrassment and lead to a loss of stature for the student among the peer group.

A less obvious, but no less important, problem with Mrs. Price's request is that because the sweater is ugly, stretched out, and unclean, the owner of the sweater is likely to be a student whose family does not have enough money to provide nicer clothing. Thus, by claiming the sweater, the student will in effect be announcing his or her own membership in the lower class. Mrs. Price appears to be blind to this implication, a blindness that suggests her own membership in a social class that is higher than that of many of her students.

When one of the other students in the class, Sylvia, tells the teacher that the sweater belongs to Rachel, Mrs. Price immediately accepts the statement. By making the statement and seemingly assisting the teacher, Sylvia aligns herself with the power structure in the class, placing herself closer to the center of power while simultaneously participating in Rachel's marginalization. That Sylvia is believed suggests that she is part of an insiders' group, while in being put on trial Rachel is pushed farther outside the power structure.

Rachel does attempt to deny ownership of the sweater and thus reassert herself as a member of the class, but she finds that she cannot speak. When Rachel finally finds her voice, Mrs. Price interrupts her and contradicts her statement: "'Of course it's yours,' Mrs. Price says. 'I remember you wearing it once.'" In this brief statement, Mrs. Price takes away not only Rachel's voice but also her ability to speak her own past. Clearly, Mrs. Price's memory of past events is the only one that counts in the classroom. Rachel's memory is discounted; according to Mrs. Price, Rachel must have forgotten that she once wore the sweater. The implication is not lost on Rachel. She rightly notes, "Because she's older and the teacher, she's right and I'm not." This is a hard lesson to learn—that the correctness of a statement may have nothing to do with the facts of the matter and everything to do with the age and authority of the speaker.

The silencing of one small girl in a public school classroom has larger cultural implications as well. As Deborah L. Madsen argues in *Understanding Contemporary Chicana Literature*, "The denial of language and the enforcement of silence upon the women of the Chicano community are urgent issues for Chicana feminism." In this context, Rachel's being silenced is far more insidious than the teacher's mistreating a student. The episode is a graphic demonstration of how a dominant culture can systematically silence both women and minorities, beginning very early in the lives of girls.

Silencing is only the first step of Rachel's marginalization. Because of her powerlessness to speak on her own behalf, she is subjected to embarrassment and humiliation, a potent punishment for any eleven-year-old child. She also becomes the target for Mrs. Price's anger: "'Rachel,' Mrs. Price says. She says it like she's getting mad. 'You put that sweater on right now and no more nonsense.'"

Rachel's identity as a girl whose mother and father will be sharing her birthday cake with her at home that night crumbles as she assumes the identity of the red sweater. Wearing it identifies her visibly as a girl without power or voice. Rachel sits with her head on her desk, crying, with "little animal noises" coming out of her. The choice of words is significant: no longer a little girl on her eleventh birthday with choices, hopes, and dreams, Rachel has been reduced to a small, whimpering animal.

Rachel's marginalization is not complete, however, until Phyllis Lopez finally claims the sweater herself and Mrs. Price does not acknowledge her error. Rachel correctly identifies this moment as the worst part; that the teacher fails to publicly recognize her own error and also fails to apologize for the punishment she has unfairly placed on Rachel's shoulders reveals to the child that for the powerless, the world is not a fair place at all. Madsen argues that the world Cisneros portrays in "Eleven" is "a world that so often lacks the logic of justice and the closure of self-fulfillment." Just as Madsen suggests, "Eleven" closes without closure, ending in injustice. Through this story, then, Cisneros heart-wrenchingly reveals the ways that the majority culture, represented by Mrs. Price, can transform jubilant young Chicana girls, like the narrator of "My Lucy Friend Who Smells Like Corn," into silent, invisible, marginalized women who wish they were "far away like a runaway balloon."

Source: Diane Andrews Henningfeld, Critical Essay on "Eleven," in *Short Stories for Students*, Gale, Cengage Learning, 2009.

Deborah L. Madsen

In the following excerpt, Madsen provides biographical background on Cisneros and discusses the author's efforts to address cross-cultural identity in her stories.

In a 1990 interview Sandra Cisneros joked that after ten years of writing professionally she had finally earned enough money to buy a secondhand car. Her struggle for recognition as a Chicana writer earned her critical and popular acclaim with the publication of *The House on Mango Street* (1984), the success of which was followed by *Woman Hollering Creek and Other Stories* (1991). Her poetry collection *My Wicked, Wicked Ways* was published by the Berkeley-based Chicana Third Woman Press in 1987, and the outrageous themes of these poems continued in the poems collected in *Loose Woman*, which appeared in 1994. Cisneros's work is characterized by the celebratory breaking of sexual taboos and trespassing across the restrictions that limit the lives and experiences of Chicanas. These themes of trespass, transgression, and joyful abandon feature prominently in her poetry. The narrative techniques of her fiction demonstrate daring technical innovations, especially in her bold experimentation with literary voice and her development of a hybrid form that weaves poetry into prose to create a dense and evocative linguistic texture of symbolism and imagery that is both technically and aesthetically accomplished.

> "IN CISNEROS'S WORK THE EFFORT TO NEGOTIATE A CROSS-CULTURAL IDENTITY IS COMPLICATED BY THE NEED TO CHALLENGE THE DEEPLY ROOTED PATRIARCHAL VALUES OF BOTH MEXICAN AND AMERICAN CULTURES."

Sandra Cisneros was born in the Puerto Rican district of Chicago on 20 December 1954. Her parents' mixed ethnic background (Spanish-speaking Mexican father and English-speaking Mexican American mother) is reflected in the cultural hybridity that is one of Cisneros's recurring themes. She is the third child and only daughter in a family of seven children, a condition that Cisneros has described as leaving her marginalized as a consequence of her gender. During Cisneros's childhood her father's restless homesickness caused the family to move frequently between Chicago and her paternal grandparents' house in Mexico City, and always she lived in urban neighborhoods. Although her early years were spent in cramped urban apartments, Cisneros recalls her childhood as solitary. Cisneros ascribes to the loneliness of those formative years her impulse to create stories by re-creating in her imagination the dull routine of her life.

She graduated with a B.A. degree from Loyola University in 1976 and completed an M.F.A. in creative writing at the Iowa Writers Workshop in 1978. It was at Iowa that Cisneros discovered, first, a sense of her own ethnic "otherness" and, second, the unique literary voice that characterizes both her poetry and her fiction. She describes her early writing as inferior imitations of the work of mainstream writers; in the discovery of her difference came a rejection of this attempt to join the American literary orthodoxy. The voice she discovered, the voice she had unconsciously suppressed, is the voice of the barrio.

An ongoing commitment to those who grow up in the barrio has led Cisneros to become involved as a teacher in educational projects designed to assist the urban underprivileged, such as the Latino Youth Alternative High School in Chicago. She has worked variously as a teacher, a counselor, a college recruiter, a poet-in-the-schools, and an arts administrator in order to support her writing. Cisneros has taught creative writing at the University of California at Berkeley, the University of California at Irvine, and the University of Michigan in Ann Arbor. She is the recipient of a National Endowment for the Arts Fellowship; the Before Columbus Foundation's American Book Award; a Lannan Foundation Literary Award; the PEN Center West Award for the best fiction of 1991; the Quality Paperback Book Club New Voices Award; a MacArthur Foundation Fellowship; and the Frank Dobie Artists Fellowship, Austin, Texas. Sandra Cisneros moved to the Southwest in 1984; she now lives in San Antonio, Texas, and is currently working on a novel, *Caramelo.*

Cisneros describes writing as something she has done all her life from the time when, as a young girl, she began writing in spiral notebooks poems that only her mother read. Her first published book, *Bad Boys*, appeared as the Chicano Chapbook No. 8 (1980). Her novel *The House on Mango Street* was published by a small regional press in 1984 and the following year was awarded the Before Columbus Foundation's American Book Award. The novel draws heavily upon childhood memories and an unadorned childlike style of expression to depict life in the Chicano community. Issues of racial and sexual oppression, poverty, and violence are explored in a sequence of interconnected vignettes that together form a modified autobiographical structure. *Woman Hollering Creek and Other Stories* continues the exploration of ethnic identity within the patriarchal context of Chicano culture. The stories in this volume offer snapshots of Mexican American life: sights and smells recalled in childish memories, stories told by witches who see all of Chicano history from past to future, the hopes and aspirations of grandparents and grandchildren, friends and neighbors, Mexican movies, and "Merican" tourists. Her first volume of poetry, *My Wicked, Wicked Ways*, is described by Cherríe Moraga as "a kind of international graffiti, where the poet—bold and insistent—puts her mark on those travelled places on the map and in the heart." *Loose Woman* similarly invokes the cultural and the emotional in an intoxicating sequence of outrageously confessional moments. Cisneros has also published essays on writing and her role as a writer, most notably the selections titled "From a Writer's Notebook. Ghosts and Voices: Writing from Obsession" and "Notes to a Young(er) Writer," both of which appeared in the *Americas Review* (1987). Her books have been translated into ten languages.

In Cisneros's work the effort to negotiate a cross-cultural identity is complicated by the need to challenge the deeply rooted patriarchal values of both Mexican and American cultures. Cisneros writes, "There's always this balancing act, we've got to define what we think is fine for ourselves instead of what our culture says." Chicana feminism has arisen largely from this need to contest the feminine stereotypes that define machismo, while at the same time identifying and working against the shared class and racial oppression that all Chicanos/as—men, women and children—experience. To adopt models of femininity that are thought of as Anglo is, as Cisneros describes, to be "told you're a traitor to your culture. And it's a horrible life to live. We're always straddling two countries, and we're always living in that kind of schizophrenia that I call, being a Mexican woman living in an American society, but not belonging to either culture. In some sense we're not Mexican and in some sense we're not American."

Patriarchal definitions of feminine subjectivity, some Anglo but mostly Mexican, affect all of Cisneros's characters by creating the medium in which they live. The protagonist of *The House on Mango Street*, the girl Esperanza, compares herself with her great-grandmother with whom she shares her name and the coincidence of being born in the Chinese year of the horse, "which is supposed to be bad luck if you're born female—but I think this is a Chinese lie because the Chinese, like the Mexicans, don't like their women strong." This fiery ancestor, "a wild horse of a woman, so wild she wouldn't marry," is forcibly taken by Esperanza's great-grandfather, and her spirit broken, she lived out her days staring from her window. The narrator remarks, "I have inherited her name, but I don't want to inherit her place by the window." This woman is the first of many Esperanza encounters who are broken in body and spirit by the patriarchal society that defines the terms by which they live.

The primary effect of these prescriptive definitions is the experience of the self as marginal, as failing to belong in the culture in which one lives. Cisneros challenges marginality but in subtle ways and using the weapons at her disposal as an artist: imagery, symbolism, forms of narrative connectivity that are at odds with rational, discursive logic. Like so many Chicana writers, Sandra Cisneros rejects the logic of the patriarchy in favor of more provisional, personal, emotional, and intuitive forms of narrative. She creates stories, not explanations or analyses or arguments. The stories that comprise *The House on Mango Street* are linked according to a loose and associative logic. In this way the fragmented structure of the text embodies a quest for freedom, a genuine liberation that resolves rather than escapes the conflicts faced by the Chicana subject. María Elena de Valdés describes how Cisneros's narrative technique relates to the theme of feminist resistance: "The open-ended reflections are the narrator's search for an answer to the enigma: how can she be free of Mango Street and the house that is not hers and yet belong as she must to that house and that street. The open-ended entries come together only slowly as the tapestry takes shape, for each of the closed figures are also threads of the larger background figure which is the narrator herself." The threads with which the story is then woven are the complex image patterns Cisneros gradually develops and the imagistic connections she builds among the vignettes. The first story, which describes the houses in which Esperanza has lived, ends with her father's promise that their cramped and shabby house is temporary. The next story, "Hairs," begins with a description of her father's hair and goes on to contrast it with her mother's. The contrast between mother and father is continued and generalized in the third story, "Boys and Girls," which ends with Esperanza's hope that she will one day have the best friend for whom she yearns. The fourth story concerns the meaning of Esperanza's name, "Hope." In this way Cisneros creates vignettes that are self-contained, autonomous, yet link together in an emotionally logical fashion and build to create a picture of life in the barrio, seen through the experiences of the young Esperanza and her developing consciousness of herself as an artist.

The stories collected in *Woman Hollering Creek* are organized according to a similar associative logic. The volume is divided into three named sections: "My Lucy Friend Who Smells Like Corn," "One Holy Night," and "There Was a Man, There Was a Woman." Each section shares a loosely defined theme: the experience of Chicano/a children in "My Lucy Friend Who Smells Like Corn," "Eleven," "Salvador Early or Late," "Mexican Movies," "Barbie-Q," "Mericans," and "Tepeyac"; the betrayal of Chicana girl children in the stories "One Holy Night" and "My Tocaya"; and the limited choice of adult relationships available to women in patriarchal Chicano/a society in "Woman Hollering Creek," "The Marlboro Man," "La Fabulosa: A Texas Operetta," "Remember the Alamo," "Never Marry a Mexican," "Bread," "Eyes of Zapata," "Anguiano Religious Articles Rosaries Statues . . . ," "Little Miracles, Kept Promises," "Los Boxers," "There Was a Man, There Was a Woman," "Tin Tan Tan," and "*Bien* Pretty." Though many of these stories depict the lives of individuals who are comprehensively defeated by the sheer burden of work, worry, and care they are required to bear, in some of them Cisneros creates characters who are able to subvert oppressive definitions of gender identity in favor of marginal, hybrid selves. . . .

Source: Deborah L. Madsen, "Sandra Cisneros," in *Understanding Contemporary Chicana Literature*, University of South Carolina Press, 2000, pp. 105–34.

Jeff Thomson

In the following excerpt, Thomson explores gender and feminine adversity in the stories of Woman Hollering Creek, *arguing that "Eleven" is a story about "maintaining the unity of self in the face of authority."*

"The wars begin here, in our hearts and in our beds" says Inés, witch-woman and "sometime wife" to Emiliano Zapata in "Eyes of Zapata," the most ambitious story of Sandra Cisneros's second collection, *Woman Hollering Creek and Other Stories*. In Inés, Cisneros

"THIS IS A WORLD WITHOUT MEN, WHERE THE FATHERS ARE DRUNK OR ABSENT, THE MOTHERS ARE LEFT TO RAISE THE CHILDREN ALONE AND THE ONLY POSSIBLE SALVATION IS A SISTERHOOD THAT MORE OFTEN THAN NOT FAILS."

presents a narrator who is capable of seeing both at a distance and up close, who is able to encompass both the physically violent world of Zapata's revolution and the emotionally violent world of love. She is able to see both worlds and, more importantly, understands how the pain of both worlds is merely a manifestation of the same disease—a failure of love. Cisneros says in a voice that is Inés speaking to Zapata but also Cisneros speaking to the reader (the two are easily confused—even Cisneros claims to have woken from a dream believing she was Inés [Sagel 74]):

> We drag these bodies around with us, these bodies that have nothing at all to do with you, with me, with who we really are, these bodies that give us pleasure and pain. Though I've learned how to abandon mine at will, it seems to me we never free ourselves completely until we love, until we lose ourselves inside each other. Then we see a little of what is called heaven. When we can be that close we no longer are Inés and Emiliano, but something bigger than our lives. And we can forgive, finally.

When a writer claims to identify with a character to the extent that she wakes up unsure who is who, one can assume that that character is going to speak deeply and come as close to the truth as fiction can come to the truth of the human heart. This is true of Inés.

Inés is the fully aware feminine self, a woman who has seen her own reality—her people embroiled in a civil war and led by her deceitful, unfaithful husband—and does not flinch or look away. She takes the deepest pain inside herself and through it claims the power of her own identity. Ingesting the pain of her world by facing it head-on gives her strength and the will to persevere: "And I took to eating black things—*huitlacoche* the corn mushroom, coffee, dark chilies, the bruised part of the fruit, the darkest, blackest things to make me hard and strong." This is the power of Cisneros's women, to see and to remember, to master the pain of the past and understand the confluence of all things; women continue in a cycle of birth and blood; they become themselves through the honest acceptance of the world beyond the body. Cisneros believes women must overcome and change their worlds from the inside out. They must become the "authors" of their own fate.

Yet what sets Inés apart from most of the women in the collection is her acceptance of all pain, not just female pain. She sees the small boy inside Zapata, the boy thrust unprepared into leadership and war; she sees the bodies of the *federale* corpses hanging in the trees, drying like leather, dangling like earrings; she sees her father, who once turned his back on her, placed with his back against the wall, ready for the firing squad. What particularly defines this story is the acceptance of masculine suffering as well as feminine. "We are all widows," Inés says, "the men as well as the women, even the children. *All clinging to the tail of the horse of our* jefe *Zapata*. All of us scarred from these nine years of *aguantando*—enduring" (original italics). The image of every widow, male or female, clinging to the horse's tail doesn't absolve men from blame for beginning and continuing this war, but at the same time it doesn't exclude them from suffering.

The union of gender, and gender-based ideologies, is essential to the strong, feminine characters of the later stories of *Woman Hollering Creek*, because for Cisneros it is necessary to include masculine suffering to achieve a total synthesis. Each of the earlier pieces is independent of the others, yet as whole sections they define specific areas of adversity—specifically feminine adversity. The first section, "My Lucy Friend Who Smells like Corn," takes a form similar to that established by Cisneros in her earlier, applauded collection *The House on Mango Street*—childhood vignettes. The "Lucy Friend" story sets up the paradigm of the Cisneros's female world:

> There ain't no boys here. Only girls and one father who is never home hardly and one mother who says *Ay! I'm real tired* and so many sisters there's no time to count them.... I think it would be fun to sleep with sisters you could yell at one at a time or all together, instead of alone on the fold out chair in the living room.

This is a world without men, where the fathers are drunk or absent, the mothers are left to raise the children alone and the only possible salvation is a sisterhood that more often than not fails.

The stories continue in this vein, establishing aspects of an archetypal Chicana female identity. "Eleven" sets up a system of multiple selves like "little wooden dolls that fit one inside the other" and the difficulty of maintaining a unity of self in the face of authority. "Mexican Movies" and "Barbie-Q" are concerned with stereotypes and enforced identity. From her young girl's voice, Cisneros satirizes the portrayals of Mexicans in film by contrasting a Chicana family's daily life with the films of Pedro Infante (his name itself denotes a child-like, false identity) who "always sings riding a horse and wears a big sombrero and never tears the dresses off the ladies, and the ladies throw flowers from balconies and usually somebody dies, but not Pedro Infante because he has to sing the happy song at the end." Although the barrio life of Cisneros's families is usually far from wealthy, here at least she presents us with a world of safety and security, where the false happiness of women tossing flowers from balconies doesn't interfere with the games the sisters play in the aisles. And then

> The movie ends. The Lights go on. Somebody picks us up . . . carries us in the cold to the car that smells like ashtrays. . . . [B]y now we're awake but it's nice to go on pretending with our eyes shut because here's the best part. Mama and Papa carry us upstairs to the third-floor where we live, take off our shoes and cover us, so when we wake up it's Sunday already, and we're in our beds and happy.

The satire is so subtle that one is led to believe the girls and perhaps even her parents do not see the films as stereotypes that limit their ability to be accepted in the white world, but the reader is obviously meant to.

Similarly, in "Barbie-Q" Cisneros attacks artificial feminine stereotypes that are epitomized in every Barbie doll. The narrator and her companion play Barbies with two basic dolls and an invisible Ken (again a comment on the absence of male figures in the culture) until there's a sale on smoke damaged dolls. When the girls are able to buy an assortment of new dolls, Cisneros asks, in a bitingly satiric tone, "And if the prettiest doll, Barbie's MOD'ern cousin Francie . . . has a left foot that's melted a little—so? If you dress her in her new 'Prom Pinks' outfit, satin splendor with matching coat, gold belt, clutch and hair bow included, so long as you don't lift her dress, right—who's to know?" Cisneros is both attacking and acknowledging the depths our culture goes to in an attempt to hide women's assumed "faults" . . . . It is men whose theories and intellectual models have defined women as flawed, but it is also women who perpetuate that myth by buying Barbies for their daughters, in essence supporting male theory through their actions. The responsibility of both men and women for the system that keeps women confined in partial identity is a theme Cisneros will return to again and again. Ultimately, the female characters who escape this system are those who have assimilated characteristics of both sexes.

Perhaps exploring a similar situation from a different angle, "Salvador Late or Early" examines a social system that is not inherently feminine, but because of the absence of masculine figures one must assume its problems and their solutions are left to the resources of women. Like "Alice Who Sees Mice" from *Mango Street*, in which the title character must rise early and make her father's lunchbox tortillas after the death of her mother, "Salvador Late or Early" is a reworking of one of Cisneros's favorite tropes: children who have lost their childhood. Salvador is "a boy who is no one's friend"; he is a boy trying to be his father, trying to take care of the younger children while his mother "is busy with the business of the baby." Salvador "inside that wrinkled shirt, inside the throat that must clear itself and apologize each time it speaks, inside that forty-pound body of a boy with its geography of scars, its history of hurt . . . is a boy like any other." Cisneros's suggestion that the loss of childhood is normal and common is probably the most damning social criticism of all. She indicts everyone for the common failure of not protecting children from the horrors of the adult world.

The overall theme of these stories is the vulnerability of the mostly female narrators; their world is defined externally to them. The barrios and small towns are, as Barbara Harlow notes about *Mango Street*, filled with "stories which recount the short histories of the neighborhood's inhabitants embedded in the longer history of Hispanic immigration, relocation, and political displacement in the United States"

(161). The vignettes that Cisneros offers are not supposed to be read as isolated incidents, but rather emblematic of a social structure that allows little cultural movement and less possibility for the formation of an identity outside the boundaries of the barrio. Cisneros moves through a paradigm of feminine life—childhood, adolescence, adulthood—exploring avenues of possible escape, possible identity. . . .

Source: Jeff Thomson, "'What Is Called Heaven': Identity in Sandra Cisneros's *Woman Hollering Creek*," in *Studies in Short Fiction*, Vol. 31, No. 3, 1994, pp. 415–24.

"THE TASK OF BREAKING THE SILENCE, OF ARTICULATING THE UNPRONOUNCEABLE PAIN OF THE CHARACTERS THAT POPULATE *WOMAN HOLLERING CREEK*, WAS A VERY SERIOUS UNDERTAKING FOR CISNEROS."

Robin Ganz

In the following excerpt, Ganz examines the wide range of voices Cisneros used for the characters in the stories of Woman Hollering Creek.

. . . Sandra Cisneros's discovery of her poetic voice in Iowa was, up until that time, the single most important moment in her life as a writer and the result of that insight was both the personal accomplishment and critical success of *The House on Mango Street*. After she'd explored and mastered that territory, that is, writing from the point of view and in the voice of Esperanza (the young Sandra), moving on meant experimenting with many voices—voices as divergent and dissimilar as possible from her own. In *Woman Hollering Creek and Other Stories* she brilliantly realizes her intentions as she presents us, from one prose piece to the next, with a complex variety of voices and points of view. Her gamut of characters ranges from, for example, the disembodied spirit of Inés Zapata (Emiliano Zapata's wife), to Rudy Cantú, drag queen extraordinaire. Cisneros creates what she calls a "deluge of voices" (Campbell 6), "voices," she emphasized at the 1991 Poetry Conference in Santa Fe, "that weren't mine at all." They speak in language as rich and diverse as the expanse they embody—they are the expressions of her immediate family, of the Chicano-Riqueño community she grew up in, and the voices from her life both between and as a part of the two cultures in which she now dwells.

One particular prose piece, "Little Miracles, Kept Promises," is perhaps the most telling representation of the diversity of voices that make up *Woman Hollering Creek*. It is introduced by a prelude told in the voice of a young, working-class Chicana who, while shopping in a "religious store" for a statue or "holy picture" to give to a friend in the hospital, is told by the . . . storeowner, "I can see you're not going to buy anything." When the narrator protests and says that she will, she's just thinking, he replies, "Well, if it's thinking you want, you just go across the street to the church to think—you're just wasting my time and yours thinking here." She does go across the street, and inside the church she reads the little letters of supplication that the churchgoers leave for the Virgin and other saints. . . .

One of the unexpected reasons that Cisneros's stories resonate with such genuineness is that her indispensable source for names and other cultural information is the San Antonio phone book. When she's searching for just the right name for a character, she leafs through the listings for a last name then repeats the process for a first name, thereby coming up with a euphonious or suitable combination without appropriating anybody's *real* name. Cisneros also uses the Yellow Pages and mail-order catalogues in much the same way for the names of businesses and so forth. For inspiration, she reads the *Popul Vuh*, the Maya Bible.

About the experience of writing *Woman Hollering Creek* and giving voice to so many different characters, Cisneros said at the Santa Fe conference, "I felt like a ventriloquist." Her advice to the writers in attendance was to "transcribe voices of the people of a community you know," and confided that she keeps voluminous files of snippets of dialogue or monologue—records of conversations she hears wherever she goes. She emphasized that she'll mix and match to suit her purpose because, as she put it, "real life doesn't have shape. You have to snip and cut."

When Cisneros was at work on *Woman Hollering Creek*, she became so immersed in her characters that they began to penetrate her unconscious; once, while writing "Eyes of Zapata," she awakened in the middle of the night, convinced for the moment that she was Inés, the young bride of the Mexican revolutionary. Her dream conversation with Zapata then became those characters's dialogue in her story. The task of breaking the silence, of articulating the unpronounceable pain of the characters that populate *Woman Hollering Creek*, was a very serious undertaking for Cisneros. She said in a recent interview: "I'm trying to write the stories that haven't been written. I felt like a cartographer; I'm determined to fill a literary void" (Sagel 74). The pressure intensifies for her because of her bi-culturalism and bi-lingualism: She charts not only the big city barrio back alleyways, its mean streets and the dusty arroyos of the borderland, but also offers us a window into the experience of the educated, cosmopolitan Chicano/artist, writer and academic. While she revels in her bi-culturalism, enjoys her life in two worlds, and as a writer she's grateful to have "twice as many words to pick from . . . two ways of looking at the world," her wide range of experience is a double-edged sword. In the Sagel interview, she revealed another side of her motivation to tell many peoples's stories in their own voices—the responsibility and the anxiety which that task produces: "One of the most frightening pressures I faced as I wrote this book," she says, "was the fear that I would blow it. . . . I kept asking myself, What have I taken on here? That's why I was so obsessed with getting everybody's stories out" (74).

She feels under additional pressure as the first Chicana to enter the mainstream of literary culture. Until Random House published *Woman Hollering Creek* and *The House on Mango Street* was reissued by Vintage Press, the Chicano literature that had crossed over into the mainstream remained a male domain—Gary Soto, Luis Valdez, Richard Rodríguez, Jimmy Santiago Baca and Alberto Rios had all made the transition. Women, however, were unrepresented there until Cisneros's recent successes. On September 19, 1991 she said in a National Public Radio interview broadcast on *Morning Edition:*

> I think I can't be happy if I'm the only one that's getting published by Random House when I know there are such magnificent writers—both Latinos and Latinas, both Chicanos and Chicanas—in the U.S. whose books are not published by mainstream presses or whom the mainstream isn't even aware of. And, you know, if my success means that other presses will take a second look at these writers . . . and publish them in larger numbers then our ship will come in.

While it is undeniable that Sandra Cisneros has traversed the boundary dividing the small press market and the mainstream publishing establishment, a controversy continues about her writing among the critics over the issue of genre-crossing. In her review of *Woman Hollering Creek* in the *Los Angeles Times* titled "Poetic Fiction With A Tex-Mex Tilt," Barbara Kingsolver writes that "Sandra Cisneros has added length and dialogue and a hint of plot to her poems and published them in a stunning collection called *Woman Hollering Creek*." Later on in the review she elaborates:

> It's a practical thing for poets in the United States to turn to fiction. Elsewhere, poets have the cultural status of our rock stars and the income of our romance novelists. Here, a poet is something your mother probably didn't want you to grow up to be. . . . When you read this book, don't be fooled. It's poetry. Just don't tell your mother. (3–4)

In her review in *The Nation*, Patricia Hart writes, "In her new book, *Woman Hollering Creek and Other Stories*, Cisneros breathes narrative life into her adroit, poetic descriptions, making them mature, fully formed works of fiction" (598).

We might ask then, is *Woman Hollering Creek* poetry or is it prose? Ever since the publication of *The House on Mango Street*, critics have debated the degree to which Cisneros embraces both norms simultaneously. Gary Soto addresses the mirror image of the same issue in his review of her poetry collection, *My Wicked Wicked Ways:*

> I use the term "prosaic poetry" not in disapproval, but as a descriptive phrase. Cisneros, as she illustrated in *The House on Mango Street*, is foremost a storyteller. Except for the "Rodrigo Poems," which meditate on the themes of love and deceit, and perhaps a few of the travel poems, each of the poems in this collection is a little story, distilled to a few stanzas, yet with a beginning, middle, and end. (21)

It is unlikely that critics will ever reach a definitive agreement on the matter of whether Cisneros's writing is poetic prose or prose-like poetry. I predict, however, that this question will persist throughout her literary career, continuing to arise in subsequent criticism of her work. Cisneros herself is entitled to the final word (for the time being, at least) on the subject. At a reading in Albuquerque, New Mexico in October, 1991 she said that when she has the words to express her idea, it's a story. When she doesn't, it's a poem.

Sandra Cisneros is a relatively young writer, both chronologically and in the sense that she is a fresh voice, a new presence in the spectrum of contemporary literature. One is likely to forget her relative inexperience because of the wisdom and understanding that charge and permeate her stories and poems. From time to time I am reminded of it, however, when I come across a passage that verges on the cute—at times, whether in a poem or story, she veers dangerously toward the precious. A reviewer for *Booklist* wrote the following criticism about *The House on Mango Street*, but it could apply to her work in other instances as well:

> These vignettes of autobiographical fiction . . . written in a loose and deliberately simple style, halfway between a prose poem and the awkwardness of semiliteracy, convincingly represent the reflections of a young girl. Occasionally the method annoys by its cuteness. (281)

Far more often than it is coy or cloying however, Cisneros's work is affecting, charming and filled with the humor and the rich cultural offerings of Mexican America. Her style is as clear as water, as evinced in her unadorned syntax, her spare and elegant phrasing, and the entirely original Mexican-American inflected diction of her poetry and prose. Yet, as with the clearest water, beneath the surface, Cisneros's work is alive with complexity and depth of meaning. Cisneros's voice is the sound of many voices speaking—over the kitchen table, out on the street, across the borderlands, and through the years.

Source: Robin Ganz, "Sandra Cisneros: Border Crossings and Beyond," in *MELUS*, Vol. 19, No. 1, Spring 1994, pp. 19–29.

Jim Sagel

In the following interview with Sagel, Cisneros comments on her efforts to chart the "barrio ditches" and the "borderland arroyos" of the Latino landscape in her short stories.

Taped to her word processor is a prayer card to San Judas, a gift from a Mexico City cabdriver. Her two indispensable literary sources are mail order catalogues and the San Antonio (Tex.) phone book. She lights candles and reads

> "UNIVERSAL AS HER THEMES ARE, CISNEROS KNOWS HER CHARACTERS LIVE IN AN AMERICA VERY DIFFERENT FROM THAT OF HER POTENTIAL READERS."

the *Popul Vuh* before sitting down to write long into the night, becoming so immersed in her characters that she dreams their dialogue: once she awoke momentarily convinced she was Ines, bride of the Mexican revolutionary Emiliano Zapata.

Such identification with her characters and her culture is altogether natural for Sandra Cisneros, a writer who has always found her literary voice in the real voices of her people, her immediate family and the extended [families] of Latino society.

"I'm trying to write the stories that haven't been written. I feel like a cartographer; I'm determined to fill a literary void," Cisneros says. With the Random House publication of her new collection of stories, *Woman Hollering Creek* (Fiction Forecasts, Feb. 15), and the simultaneous reissuing of her earlier collection of short fiction, *The House on Mango Street*, in a Vintage edition, Cisneros finds herself in a position to chart those barrio ditches and borderland arroyos that have not appeared on most copies of the American literary map but which, nonetheless, also flow into the "mainstream."

The 36-year-old daughter of a Mexican father and a Chicana mother, Cisneros is well aware of the additional pressure to succeed with this pair of books that represent the opportunity for a wider readership, not only for herself but for scores of other Latina and Latino writers right behind the door that she is cracking open.

"One of the most frightening pressures I faced as I wrote this book was the fear that I would blow it," Cisneros says, sweeping a lock of her closely cropped black hair from her forehead as she sips a midmorning cup of coffee. "I kept asking myself, What have I taken on here? That's why I was so obsessed with getting everybody's stories out. I didn't have the luxury of doing my own."

Coupled with that "responsibility to do a collective good job," is Cisneros's anxiety about how her work will be perceived by the general reading public. Universal as her themes are, Cisneros knows her characters live in an America very different from that of her potential readers. From her friend Lucy, "who smells like corn," to Salvador, whose essence resides "inside that wrinkled shirt, inside the throat that must clear itself and apologize each time it speaks," Cisneros's literary landscape teems with characters who live, love and laugh in the flowing cadences of the Spanish language.

Yet, unlike her character Salvador, Cisneros offers no apologies when she speaks. Energetic and abounding with gusto—only the Spanish word will do to describe her engaging humor—Cisneros relishes the opportunity to startle the jaded reader and poetically unravel stereotypes, especially those that relate to Latinas.

"I'm the mouse who puts a thorn in the lion's paw," she says, with an arch smile reminiscent of the red-lipped sonrisa on the cover of *My Wicked Wicked Ways* (Third Woman Press, 1987), a collection of poetry celebrating the "bad girl" with her "lopsided symmetry of sin/and virtue."

"An unlucky fate is mine/to be born woman in a family of men," Cisneros writes in one of her "wicked" poems, yet it is that very "fate" that laid the groundwork for the literary career of this writer, whose name derives from the Spanish word for "swan."

Born in Chicago in 1954, Cisneros grew up in a family of six brothers and a father, or "seven fathers," as she puts it. She recalls spending much of her early childhood moving from place to place. Because her paternal grandmother was so attached to her favorite son, the Cisneros family returned to Mexico City "like the tides."

"The moving back and forth, the new schools, were very upsetting to me as a child. They caused me to be very introverted and shy. I do not remember making friends easily, and I was terribly self-conscious due to the cruelty of the nuns, who were majestic at making one feel little. Because we moved so much, and always in neighborhoods that appeared like France after World War II—empty lots and burned-out buildings—I retreated inside myself."

It was that "retreat" that transformed Cisneros into an observer, a role she feels she still plays today. "When I'm washing sheets at the laundromat, people still see me as just a girl. I take advantage of that idea. The little voice I used to hate I now see as an asset. It helps me get past the guards."

Among the first "guards" that Cisneros sneaked past were the literary sentinels at the University of Iowa's Writer's Workshop, which she attended in the late '70s. Her "breakthrough" occurred during a seminar discussion of archetypal memories in Bachelard's *Poetics of Space*. As her classmates spoke about the house of the imagination, the attics, stairways and cellars of childhood, Cisneros felt foreign and out of place.

"Everyone seemed to have some communal knowledge which I did not have—and then I realized that the metaphor of house was totally wrong for me. Suddenly I was homeless. There were no attics and cellars and crannies. I had no such house in my memories. As a child I had read of such things in books, and my family had promised such a house, but the best they could do was offer the miserable bungalow I was embarrassed with all my life. This caused me to question myself, to become defensive. What did I, Sandra Cisneros, know? What could I know? My classmates were from the best schools in the country. They had been bred as fine hothouse flowers. I was a yellow weed among the city's cracks.

"It was not until this moment when I separated myself, when I considered myself truly distinct, that my writing acquired a voice. I knew I was a Mexican woman, but I didn't think it had anything to do with why I felt so much imbalance in my life, whereas it had everything to do with it! My race, my gender, my class! That's when I decided I would write about something my classmates couldn't write about."

Thus it was that *The House on Mango Street* was born and Cisneros discovered what she terms her "first love," a fascination with speech and voices. Writing in the voice of the adolescent Esperanza, Cisneros created a series of interlocking stories, alternately classified as a novel and as a collection of prose poems because of the vivid and poignant nature of the language. Since its first publication in 1984 by Arte Publico Press, *Mango Street* has sold some 30,000 copies. The book is used in classes from junior high school through graduate school in subjects ranging from Chicano studies to psychology to culture, ideas and values at Stanford University, where it has been adopted as part of the "new curriculum."

Mango Street was also the catalyst that drew Cisneros to her literary agent or, to be more accurate, that led Susan Bergholz to Cisneros. Bergholz was so moved after reading the book that she did something she had never done before: she set out to track down the writer. "It was a delightful chase," Bergholz recalls, in spite of the fact that it took some three to four years to accomplish.

Ironically, even while Bergholz was enlisting the aid of Richard Bray of Guild Books to contact Cisneros, the writer was going through what she calls the worst year of her life, 1987. She had spent the previous year in Texas through the auspices of a Dobie-Paisano fellowship. Though the experience had convinced her to make Texas her permanent home, the writer found herself unable to make a living once the fellowship expired.

While her boyfriend waited tables, Cisneros handed out fliers in local supermarkets and laundromats, trying to scrape together enough students to teach a private writing workshop. At last, she was forced to leave her newly adopted home, her confidence shaken and her outlook on life darkened.

The depression she sank into followed her to California, where she accepted a guest lectureship at California State University in Chico. "I thought I couldn't teach. I found myself becoming suicidal. Richard Bray had told me Susan was looking for me, but I was drowning, beyond help. I had the number for months, but I didn't call. It was frightening because it was such a calm depression."

An NEA fellowship in fiction revitalized Cisneros and helped her get on her feet again, both financially and spiritually. Finally calling that Manhattan phone number stuffed in her pocket, Cisneros sent Bergholz a small group of new stories. With only 39 pages in hand, Bergholz sold *Woman Hollering Creek* to Joni Evans and Erroll McDonald at Random House/Vintage; Julie Grau became the book's enthusiastic editor.

Then, of course, the real work began for Cisneros, whose previous output had been about one story every six months. "There's nothing like a deadline to teach you discipline, especially when you've already spent your advance. Susto helps," Cisneros says, explaining that fear motivated her to put in eight-to-12-hour days. Though exhausting, the experience was genuinely empowering.

"Before, I'd be . . . waiting for inspiration. Now I know I can work this hard. I know I did the best I could."

That's not to say Cisneros believes she's done the best work of her career. "I'm looking forward to the books I'll write when I'm 60," she observes. She's also looking forward to the contributions other Latina and Latino writers will be making in the future. "There's a lot of good writing in the mainstream press that has nothing to say. Chicano writers have a lot to say. The influence of our two languages is profound. The Spanish language is going to contribute something very rich to American literature."

Meanwhile, this self-described "migrant professor" plans to continue her personal and literary search for the "home in the heart," as Elenita the Witch Woman describes it in *Mango Street*. As "nobody's mother and nobody's wife," Cisneros most resembles Ines Alfaro, the powerful central character in "Eyes of Zapata," the story Cisneros considers her finest achievement.

Small, but "bigger" than the general himself, Ines is the woman warrior, the *Soldadera* who understands what the men will never comprehend, that "the wars begin here, in our hearts and in our beds." She is the *bruja*, the *nagual* who flies through the night, the fierce and tender lover who risks all, the eater of black things that make her hard and strong.

She is, in short, a symbol of the Latina herself, the Mexican woman whose story is at last being told, a story of life and blood and grief and "all the flower colors of joy." It is a story at once intimate and universal, guaranteed to shove a bittersweet thorn into the paws of literary lions everywhere.

Source: Jim Sagel, "Sandra Cisneros: Conveying the Riches of the Latin American Culture Is the Author's Literary Goal," in *Publishers Weekly*, Vol. 238, No. 15, March 29, 1991, pp. 74–75.

Barbara Kingsolver

In the following review, well-known novelist Kingsolver offers a favorable impression of Woman Hollering Creek*, noting Cisneros's use of sensory images.*

From poetry to fiction and back doesn't seem too long a stretch for some writers. Linda Hogan's recently published *Mean Spirit* was a first novel, but the author's reputation runs long and deep in the tiny community of North Americans who buy and read poetry. Louise Erdrich is well known for her novels, but once upon a time she was (and surely still is) a poet. Joining their ranks, Sandra Cisneros has added length and dialogue and a hint of plot to her poems and published them in a stunning collection called *Woman Hollering Creek*.

The 22 stories mostly range from short to very short (six paragraphs), with a handful that are longer. All are set along the Tex-Mex border where people listen to Flaco Jimenez on Radio K-SUAVE and light candles in church to ward off the landlord and mean ex-lovers. Their language gets in your ear and hangs on like a love powder from the Preciado Sisters' Religious Articles Shop.

Nearly every sentence contains an explosive sensory image. A narrator says of her classmate, "A girl who wore rhinestone earrings and glitter high heels to school was destined for trouble that nobody—not God or correctional institutions—could mend." A child runs off in "that vague direction where homes are the color of bad weather." Emiliano Zapata's abandoned lover remembers: "It was the season of rain. *Plum... plum plum.* All night I listened to that broken string of pearls, bead upon bead upon bead rolling across the waxy leaves of my heart."

The subject of love, inseparable from babies, hope, poverty and escape, is everywhere in these characters' talk and dreams.... A girl explains that love is like "a big black piano being pushed off the top of a three-story building and you're waiting on the bottom to catch it." Her friend gives this account: "There was a man, a crazy who lived upstairs from us when we lived on South Loomis. He couldn't talk, just walked around all day with this harmonica in his mouth. Didn't play it. Just sort of breathed through it, all day long, wheezing, in and out, in and out.

"This is how it is with me. Love I mean."

In the face of all this fatal passion, though, women of grit keep fashioning surprising escapes out of radio lyrics and miracles. In the title story, a bride, whose knowledge of marriage comes from a Mexican soap opera, is taken by her new husband across the border to Texas, far from her family, where he beats her. The creek that runs past her house is called *La Gritona*—Woman Hollering Creek—and she's fascinated because she has heard women wail but never actually shout, an act requiring anger or joy. In the story's wonderful, non-soap-opera ending, she meets a woman who knows how to holler.

Another compelling heroine, in "*Bien* Pretty," is an educated Latina from San Francisco who's spent her life trying to nail down her ethnic identity. She moves to San Antonio for a job, where she falls into a lonely evening routine of chips and beer for dinner, falling asleep on the couch, and waking up in the middle of the night with "hair crooked as a broom, face creased into a mean origami, clothes wrinkled as the citizens of bus stations." She heads all her letters home with "Town of Dust and Despair," "until suddenly, disastrously, she falls in love with an exterminator from La Cucaracha Apachurrada who reminds her of an Aztec God. She loses her heart and learns what she can never be, but discovers what she is.

My favorite in the collection is "Little Miracles, Kept Promises," a sampling of letters of petition or thanks pinned onto the altar of the Virgin of Guadalupe. The Familia Arteaga thanks the Virgin in a businesslike manner for having saved them when their bus overturned near Robstown. Another note, more blunt, says, "Please send us clothes, furniture, shoes, dishes. We need anything that don't eat."...

It's a funny, caustic portrait of a society in transition that still pins its hopes on saints. The last of the letters begins, "Virgencita... I've cut off my hair just like I promised I would and pinned my braid here by your statue." This supplicant's family believes she is selfish and crazy for wanting to be an artist instead of a mother. She pours out her heart to a Virgin who traces her lineage not only to Guadalupe and Bethlehem but also to wild, snake-charming Aztec goddesses. It's a fine revelation of a cultural moment in which potent saints can hold a young woman back or send her on her way, depending on which traditions she opts to cherish.

Woman Hollering Creek is Cisneros' second collection of stories (following *The House on Mango Street*, which Random House is reissuing), and I hope there will be more. It's a practical thing for poets in the United States to turn to fiction. Elsewhere, poets have the cultural status of our rock stars and the income of our romance novelists. Here, a poet is something your mother probably didn't want you to grow up to be. Even the most acclaimed could scarcely dine out twice a year, let alone make a living, on the sales of their poetry collections. Fiction has a vastly larger audience that's hard not to covet.

So, if they're going to do it, all poets would do well to follow the example of Sandra Cisneros, who takes no prisoners and has not made a single compromise in her language. When you read this book, don't be fooled: It's poetry. Enjoy it, revel in it. Just don't tell your mother.

Source: Barbara Kingsolver, "Poetic Fiction with a Tex-Mex Tilt," in *Los Angeles Times Book Review*, April 28, 1991, pp. 3, 12.

Patricia Hart

In the following excerpt, Hart compares Cisneros's Woman Hollering Creek *to the work of Rosario Ferre and applauds Cisneros's characterizations and descriptions, calling them "fully formed works of fiction."*

. . . The wrenching pull of competing cultures and languages is just as important in Mexican-American Sandra Cisneros's art as it is in Rosario Ferre's. Anger repressed bursts the seams of life for Cisneros's female characters, who struggle valiantly to make something beautiful from the ugly fabric fate has given them to work with. Cisneros's first book of fiction, *The House on Mango Street* (1984), was a collection of prose-poem reflections on a girlhood in which creative talent fought to survive a hostile environment, sensitive memories set down as a graduate of the Iowa Writers' Workshop and winner of a National Endowment for the Arts fellowship. In her new book, *Woman Hollering Creek and Other Stories*, Cisneros breathes narrative life into her adroit, poetic descriptions, making them mature, fully formed works of fiction. Her range of characters is broad and lively, from Rudy Cantu, drag queen par excellence, in whose ears the crowd's applause sizzles like when "my ma added the rice to the hot oil"; to the disembodied spirit of Emiliano Zapata's wife; to a teenage girl who returns to the shrine of the Virgen de los Lagos to ask Mary to take back the boyfriend the girl previously prayed for.

Calques and puns are hidden throughout like toy surprises that double the pleasure of the bilingual reader. The title story, "Woman Hollering Creek," is an impish, literal translation of Arroyo la Gritona, a creek whose name sounds as though it may have been derived from La. Llorona, the weeping woman of Mexican folklore—part Circe, part Magdalene. The irony is that the main character, a young bride brought across the border from Mexico only to be abused, begins the tale crying over her plight, but in the end escapes the stereotyped role of tearful victim through the help of strong, independent Felice, who hollers in exhilaration like Tarzan as the pair cross the river to freedom.

In "*Bien* Pretty," the last story in the collection, Cisneros beautifully draws the struggle of a talented but underappreciated Chicana painter to connect culturally and sexually with men who circle and abandon her, a situation she survives nobly, "in my garage making art": The men who know her language and folklore may disappoint, but as painter she transforms one bug-exterminating lover into volcanic Prince Popocatepetl, and on her canvas, as in Cisneros's fiction, the results are at once dramatically specific and universal.

If superstition is the opiate of Latin America's desperate poor, it is no surprise that Ronfio Ferre's ire flowers into magic feminism. By contrast, the toughness that Sandra Cisneros's characters need to survive U.S. streets makes hard-eyed realism her ideal mode. The catalysts are remarkably similar for the two, but the resulting chain reactions of rage delight with a clear chemical difference.

Source: Patricia Hart, Review of *Woman Hollering Creek and Other Stories*, in the *Nation*, Vol. 252, No. 17, May 6, 1991, p. 598.

SOURCES

Batalova, Jeanne, "Mexican Immigrants in the United States," in *Migration Information Source*, April 2008, http://www.migrationinformation.org/USfocus/display.cfm?ID=679 (accessed June 21, 2008).

Brady, Mary Pat, "The Contrapuntal Geographies of *Woman Hollering Creek and Other Stories*," in *American Literature*, Vol. 71, No. 1, March 1999, pp. 117–50.

Carroll, Michael, and Susan Maher, "'A Las Mujeres': Cultural Context and the Process of Maturity in Sandra Cisneros' *Woman Hollering Creek*," in *North Dakota Quarterly*, Vol. 64, No. 1, Winter 1997, pp. 70–80.

Cisneros, Sandra, "Eleven," in *Woman Hollering Creek, and Other Stories*, Random House, 1991, pp. 6–9.

Fernández de Pinedo, Eva, "An Overview of Contemporary Chicano/a Literature," in *Literature Compass*, Vol. 3, No. 4, July 2006, pp. 658–75.

Hart, Patricia, "Babes in Boyland," in the *Nation*, Vol. 252, No. 17, May 6, 1991, pp. 597–98.

Kevane, Bridget, "A Home in the Heart: An Interview with Sandra Cisneros," in *Latina Self-Portraits: Interviews with Contemporary Women Writers*, edited by Bridget Kevane and Juanita Heredia, University of New Mexico Press, 2000, pp. 51–2.

Kingsolver, Barbara, "Poetic Fiction with a Tex-Mex Tilt," in *Los Angeles Times Book Review*, April 28, 1991, pp. 3, 12.

Madsen, Deborah L., *Understanding Contemporary Chicana Literature*, University of South Carolina Press, 2000, pp. 24, 40.

Muske, Carol, "Through the Ivory Gate," in *Parnassus: Poetry in Review*, Vol. 20, No. 1/2, 1995, pp. 409–23.

Prescott, Peter S., and Karen Springen, "Seven for Summer," in *Time*, Vol. 117, No. 22, June 3, 1991, p. 60.

Thomson, Jeff, "'What Is Called Heaven': Identity in Sandra Cisneros's *Woman Hollering Creek*," in *Studies in Short Fiction*, Vol. 31, No. 3, Summer 1994, pp. 415–24.

Tompkins, Cynthia, "Sandra Cisneros," in *Dictionary of Literary Biography*, Vol. 152, *American Novelists since World War II, Fourth Series*, edited by James Giles and Wanda Giles, Gale Research, 1995, pp. 35–41.

U.S. Census Bureau, "Facts for Features," July 16, 2007, http://www.census.gov/Press-Release/www/releases/archives/facts_for_features_special_editions/010327.html (accessed June 21, 2008).

U.S. Census Bureau, "We the American... Hispanics," September 1993, http://www.census.gov/apsd/wepeople/we-2r.pdf (accessed June 21, 2008).

Van Hook, Jennifer, Frank D. Bean, and Jeffrey Passel, "Unauthorized Migrants Living in the United States: A Mid-decade Portrait," in *Migration Information Source*, September 2005, http://www.migrationinformation.org/Usfocus/display.cfm?ID=329 (accessed June 21, 2008).

FURTHER READING

Augenbraum, Harold, and Margarite Fernández Olmos, eds., *U.S. Latino Literature: A Critical Guide for Students and Teachers*, Greenwood Press, 2000.

This book includes critical analyses of works by eighteen influential Latino writers, including Rudolfo Anaya, Sandra Cisneros, and Julia Alvarez.

Brackett, Virginia, *A Home in the Heart: The Story of Sandra Cisneros*, Morgan Reynolds Publishing, 2005.

Written for the young adult reader, this biography follows Cisneros's life from her childhood through the publication of Caramelo.

Herrera-Sobek, María, and Helena María Viramontes, eds., *Chicana Creativity and Criticism: New Frontiers in American Literature*, rev. ed., University of New Mexico Press, 1996.

This particularly interesting compilation of poetry, prose, criticism, and artwork demonstrates the range of themes in and growth of contemporary Chicana creativity, including work on female sexuality, social justice, and gender roles.

Hoobler, Dorothy, Thomas Hoobler, and Henry G. Cisneros, *The Mexican American Family Album*, Oxford University Press, 1998.

Structured like a family photo album, this book begins with the earliest Mexicans who suddenly found themselves living in the United States when the Americans annexed their property. It then traces the growth of Mexican Amerian culture in the United States through vintage photographs, text, and interviews.

Pollack, Harriet, ed., *Having Our Way: Women Rewriting Tradition in Twentieth-Century America*, Bucknell University Press, 1995.

Pollack provides a series of essays detailing the ways that contemporary women writers are expanding the canon of American literature through creative and innovative approaches to their own stories.

Rebolledo, Tey Diana, *The Chronicles of Panchita Villa and Other Guerrilleras: Essays on Chicana/Latina Literature and Criticism*, University of Texas Press, 2005.

This book contains twenty essays by Rebolledo on Chicana/Latina literature, including an overview called "Women Writers, New Disciplines, and the Canon."

A Horseman in the Sky

AMBROSE BIERCE

1889

Ambrose Bierce's short story "A Horseman in the Sky" was first published in the *San Francisco Examiner* on April 14, 1889. Bierce presented a slightly altered version in his anthology *Tales of Soldiers and Civilians* in 1891 (which was not sold until the first weeks of 1892). That version of the story also appeared in the edition of his complete works that Bierce oversaw in 1911, and it has been widely anthologized ever since. Recently it has appeared in *Phantoms of a Blood-Stained Period: The Complete Civil War Writings of Ambrose Bierce*, edited by Russell Duncan and David J. Klooster and published in 2002.

Bierce enlisted to fight in the Civil War in the first rush of patriotic fervor that swept through the country in the spring of 1861, and he became a heroic and then an experienced soldier and officer. After the war he became an important newspaper columnist and author, noted for his cynical attacks on the complacencies of American culture, which earned him the sobriquet "Bitter Bierce." In "A Horseman in the Sky," he mixes together the extreme realism of a veteran writing about the Civil War with fantastic religious and visionary elements that would later become characteristic of the literary style of magic realism. Bierce's purpose was to show through symbol and irony that the sentimental conception of the Civil War that was becoming prevalent in America in the Gilded Age amounted to a hypocritical betrayal of the real meaning that the war had in the lives of the soldiers who fought

Ambrose Bierce (© *Mary Evans Picture Library / Alamy*)

in it as well as an attempt to cover over the scars that were left on American life and history.

AUTHOR BIOGRAPHY

Ambrose Bierce was born Ambrose Gwinnett Bierce on June 4, 1842, in the Western Reserve, Ohio. His ancestors had been Puritans from Scotland who joined the colony of Connecticut. Ambrose was of a different temperament, however, and felt estranged and neglected by the patriarchal rule of his father, Marcus Aurelius Bierce, over the family. He looked on the coming of the Civil War as a deliverance, allowing him to set out on his own. He volunteered only three days after the outbreak of war on April 12, 1861; in fact, he went to the recruiting office for the Ninth Indiana Regiment the night before it opened and was the second man in line. He rose rapidly through the ranks and became an officer as a result of numerous citations for physical bravery in the face of the enemy. He eventually became a staff officer, but even then he put himself in the thick of the fighting; he was discharged as a major after being wounded in January 1865.

Bierce worked for a brief time in the military justice system (trying soldiers for cowardice and desertion) but finally spent much of the war as a topographer, or mapmaker. Bierce reenlisted soon after the war, joining a mapping expedition that covered much of the American West, and resigned his commission in San Francisco in 1866. He began to write for the *San Francisco Examiner*, a newspaper controlled by the publishing baron William Randolph Hearst, and it was this periodical that first published "A Horseman in the Sky," on April 14, 1889. While working for the *San Francisco Examiner*, Bierce became a nationally recognized reporter, columnist, and editor and was one of the most popular journalists in the country. Bierce was hated as much as he was loved by the public for the cynical and biting satire he used to expose hypocrisy and pretension in contemporary society. He might be described as a mean-spirited Mark Twain. Much of his most caustic writing was collected in the best-selling work *The Devil's Dictionary*.

By the late 1870s, Bierce had become one of the first writers to produce reminiscences and fictional accounts of his Civil War service. He is generally considered by critics to be the only literary figure of the first rank to have fought as a common soldier in the Civil War and used that experience as a basis for literary work. His other fiction consists mostly of stories of the supernatural. Bierce published hundreds of poems, essays, and short stories, such as "The Damned Thing," "Oil of Dog," and "Occurrence at Owl Creek Bridge," always initially in newspapers and occasionally afterward in collections, including *Black Beetles in Amber* and *Can Such Things Be?* In 1911, he reissued his entire collected works in a single set of eleven volumes. Bierce's death is something of a mystery. Although seventy-one years old, he traveled to Mexico in late 1913 to report on the uprising of Pancho Villa against the Mexican government. He disappeared without a trace sometime early in 1914.

PLOT SUMMARY

I

The first of the four sections of "A Horseman in the Sky" establish the action of the story during the opening months of the American

Civil War, in the early autumn of 1861. The location of the story is the countryside of West Virginia. The action of the story is described by an omniscient narrator who first calls attention to a single Federal (that is, Union or Northern) soldier who has been posted as a sentry. He is lying in hiding, as concealed by a grove of laurel trees, and has fallen asleep at his post. The narrator points out that this is a capital crime under military law, meriting the death penalty, and also offers the opinion that the man's execution, if he were to be found out and tried, would be just. Despite this notice, as Donald T. Blume points out in his book *Ambrose Bierce's Civilians and Soldiers in Context: A Critical Study*, a casual reader unfamiliar with military life might feel a natural sympathy for a soldier who is so exhausted that he falls asleep on duty. Once a reader has formed such an opinion of the matter, he or she may well fail to take to heart the later and more technical description of how the sentry is putting the lives of thousands of his comrades at risk. The sleeping sentry is meant to be guarding a Federal force of five regiments (about five to ten thousand men) hidden in a forest in a valley between two high ridges (approximately one thousand feet high). This force is waiting for nightfall to launch an ambush on a larger Confederate force atop one of the ridges. This plan has a good chance of success if the element of surprise can be maintained, but if the Federal force is discovered, its position in a valley with only a few outlets would doom it to complete destruction. Such a precise description of the relation of terrain and position to warfare would have been informed not only by Bierce's service in combat but also by his later experience during the war serving as a topographer.

II

At the beginning of the second section we learn that the sleeping sentry's name is Carter Druse. The narrator then explains Druse's backstory, telling how he came to be in the present situation. At the start of the Civil War, the state of Virginia was as split as the nation itself. When Virginia seceded from the Union, the western part of the state, in the Appalachian Mountains, in turn seceded from Virginia and remained in the Union as the new state of West Virginia. This split also happened to divide the Druse family. The reader is shown a scene in which Druse announces to his father over breakfast his intention to enlist in the Union army. His surprised father responds, "Well, go, sir, and whatever may occur do what you conceive to be your duty. Virginia, to which you are a traitor, must get on without you." The father's overtly formal tone and his dwelling on duty and treason show that he is thinking in terms of the code of honor that dominated antebellum genteel life. His ensuing comment, "Should we both live to the end of the war, we will speak further of the matter," might, in other circumstances, be taken as a challenge to a duel at that time; as the story shall go, the remark foreshadows the father's later service in the Confederate army and his encounter with his son. The father also suggests that Druse's mother, who is lying on her deathbed, does not need to hear of what he considers his son's treason. Blume points out an important fact to be considered in connection with the brief reference to Druse's dying mother: In the first days of the Civil War, young men on both sides believed that the war would quickly end in glorious victory for their own army. Accordingly, they were anxious to volunteer and have their share of adventure and honor before it was over. Many also saw the war as a means of escape from family authority, which was a far more domineering and controlling force in 1861 than it is today. This story perhaps reflects the circumstances of Bierce's own rapid enlistment. Druse's father's admonition to "do what you conceive to be your duty" may indicate that he considers his son to be selfishly seeking glory at the expense of his real duty to his dying mother.

Druse was given the important post of sentry because he was familiar with the local terrain, with his unit stationed in his native West Virginia. The narrator also mentions that Druse was selected because, "by conscience and courage, by deeds of devotion and daring, he soon commended himself to his fellows and his officers." However, as Blume points out, since no serious fighting had yet occurred in this theater of the war, this statement likely refers to acts of bravado rather than military competence, since neither Druse nor his superiors would have had actual combat experience useful for making judgments about his quality of soldiering. This statement, then, may reveal Bierce's love for subtle irony.

In a change from the heretofore realistic tone of the story, Druse is awakened from his sleep by an angel or demon; the narrative leaves this point purposefully obscure: "What good or bad angel came . . . , who shall say?" What Druse first sees on awakening is presented through ekphrasis, or a highly visual description: there is a colossal statue of a man mounted on a horse, sitting on a cliff before him looking down onto the valley. Druse immediately takes "a keen artistic delight" in the sight. The figure is described with technical artistic terms such as "foreshortened" and "cameo"; the very cliff it is sitting on is called a "pedestal," or statue base. The figure is the gray color of granite, with the form of the bearded rider compared to the form of a Greek god. Druse cannot help but feel that he is seeing in the statue a future monument to the war and its glories that will contrast to his own inglorious conduct of sleeping at his post.

Druse eventually realizes that the horseman is in fact a Confederate scout who has discovered the Federal troops laying in ambush. (Druse himself can see that some of them have left their hiding places in the valley to water their horses, so there is no doubt that the scout has seen them, too.) Just as clearly, he realizes that his duty is to kill the scout to prevent him from reporting what he has found out. Accordingly, he aims his rifle, intending to shoot the man. The narrative pauses for a moment to foreshadow later developments in the story by asserting that if Druse had fired at that instant, everything would have turned out well for him (probably indicating that he had not yet recognized the horseman). Instead, Druse waits a moment, and the scout happens to look directly toward him; Druse suddenly has the impression that the figure is looking not only at him (an impossibility due to his concealment) but through him, into him. The emotional effort needed to actually attempt to kill this other human being leaves Druse overcome with shock (a drop in blood pressure), turning him pale, making him shake, and nearly making him faint; his senses start to fail him. After a greater moral effort, Druse is able to refocus on his duty and again prepares to shoot, making certain the scout indeed saw the Federal troops. He seems to draw the strength needed to calm himself in recalling his father's admonition that, even as a traitor to Virginia, he must do what he believed to be his duty. Druse's soul then speaks to his own body, saying, "Peace, be still"—a quote of Jesus's command that calmed the storm on the Sea of Galilee prior to his walking on it. Druse aims and fires—yet not at the scout but at his horse.

III

After the abrupt and ambiguous ending to the preceding section, the point of view of the narrative switches to that of a Federal officer who is scouting on the valley floor along the base of the cliff. He suddenly sees a horse and rider falling together from the cliff above. The suddenness and strangeness of the sight unnerves him, and he imagines for a moment that he is having some sort of supernatural vision such as those described in the Apocalypse of St. John, in the New Testament. It seems to him at first as though the figures are flying rather than plummeting; he sees them fall as far as the treetops. He then sets out to search for them, but his impression of their flight is so strong that he searches a good distance away from the cliff, whereas in fact they would have fallen straight down to the foot of the cliff. He looks for a half hour but does not find them. He is so upset by what he has experienced that he thinks it better to omit all mention of the episode during his later report to his commanding officer.

IV

In the short final section, a sergeant, having heard Druse shoot, crawls to him through the underbrush, reaching him about ten minutes later. When he asks Druse for his report, the private at first says only that he shot a horse. The sergeant demands to know if there was anyone riding the horse. Druse says there was and reveals for the first time that he recognized him: the man was his own father. Most likely, after the death of Druse's mother, his father enlisted in the Confederate army and was made a scout for the same reason Druse was made a sentry, owing to his knowledge of the local terrain.

CHARACTERS

An Angel

An angel or fallen angel sets the plot of the story in motion by awakening Druse in time to encounter his father in the guise of the statuesque horseman. Bierce is purposely ambiguous in describing the angel as a supernatural entity but not clearly stating whether its awakening Druse is good or bad. This makes the reader consider the moral quality of the actions Druse consequently performs. The appearance of this angel is the first indication that on one level at least, the story will function as an allegory told in mythological terms.

The Commander

The commander hears the report of the officer who witnessed the fall of Carter Druse's father. While the officer omits his having seen the falling horseman at all, the commander is wise enough to infer that something was omitted from the report; yet he does not press the officer for the omitted details. The commander's objective distance from the events of the story—he receives his information only from the narrative of the officer—identify his viewpoint with that of the reader living twenty years (or more) after the events imagined in the story.

Carter Druse

The main character of the story, Druse, is a young recruit who felt bound by honor to join the Federal army and fight for the North. This causes a split with his father, who considers his decision to be treason to the state of Virginia. "By conscience and courage, by deeds of devotion and daring," Druse gains the recognition of his superiors. For this reason as well as for his knowledge of the local terrain, he is made a sentry protecting a Federal force that is preparing an ambush. The dreamlike character of the story derives from the fact that Druse has fallen asleep at his post as a sentry. The second section of the story justifies its mixed presentation of symbolic and realistic material from Druse's waking, rather than wakeful, state. The tension of the story is created by Druse's apparent dilemma in choosing between his duty to his family and to Virginia and his perceived duty to the United States, but his decision to enlist seems to be made not in response to any duty at all but rather as a means of avoiding duty. This is the flaw that ultimately dooms him when the climax of the story forces Druse to decide between the moral imperative of honoring his father and the military necessity of killing his father, whom he encounters as a Confederate soldier. While on the first reading Druse's character might seem sympathetic, faced as he is with the difficulties of war, deeper analysis concerning his abandonment of his family, his dereliction of duty, and his ultimate patricide (killing his father) may leave a different impression.

The Father

Carter Druse's father is a nearly godlike figure who serves many roles in the story. He initially is presented as a stern parent disapproving of Carter Druse's abandonment of his mother (perhaps even more so than of his political decision). His son's decision to kill him, in one sense to be viewed as an acceptance of military duty, perhaps has as much to do with the young man's chafing under strict patriarchal control. The father's decision to enlist may have had as much to do with the death of his wife and his abandonment by his son as with his obvious patriotism for Virginia. After his role in his son's backstory, he becomes more nearly a cipher, presented as the initially anonymous and in any case grandly symbolic figure of the horseman.

The Horseman

The figure that Carter Druse shoots is initially described simply as a horseman. His subsequent fall over a thousand-foot cliff is the source of the story's title. The entire tension and climax of the plot is created because the narrative voice of the story keeps the horseman's identity as Druse's father unrevealed until the last line of the story. The figure of the horseman is unusually fluid. He is initially presented as a sort of mythological revelation, and only slowly does he come to take on a more and more concrete reality, until his true human identity is fully established. Interestingly, once he has already been humanized in the eyes of Carter Druse, from Druse's initial epiphany to the point where Druse recognizes the horseman and shoots, he plays the same role in just such a sighting again, being initially perceived as a supernatural apparition by the anonymous officer, who only after some time realizes that what he saw was all too real. On one hand, the rapid fluctuation of meaning and interpretation attached to the figure of the horseman could stand for the sentimentalizing view of the war in the 1890s against which Bierce was writing. On the other hand, it may represent the contrast between the overwhelming immediate experience of war and the more comprehensible experience of memory. This fluidity allows the horseman to function at many levels of meaning. At one and the same time he is the embodiment of the Gilded Age's response to the war as much as he is Carter Druse's father.

The Mother

Druse's mother does not appear in the story, but her presence and situation shape her son's decisions and actions. She has a fatal but never clearly specified illness that is expected to soon end her life. Druse's father considers that his son would have done better to attend to his mother during what remains of her life.

The Officer

An unnamed Federal officer is the only witness to the death of Druse's father. Like Druse himself, he imagines the sight of the horseman, in this case as seen falling over a thousand foot vertical cliff, to be a supernatural apparition before adopting a more rational explanation of what he saw. After unsuccessfully searching for the horseman's body, he refuses to report on the matter to his superior. Perhaps this is a symbolic expression of the difficulties entailed when veterans consider describing their experience of combat.

The Sergeant

The sergeant hears Druse's sniping and prods from him the admission that he killed his own father. He is naturally astounded that the course of Druse's duty involved him in committing an act of patricide.

THEMES

Civil War

The Civil War (1861–1865) was one of the most significant events in American history. The Union victory against the rebellious secessionist states ensured that the United States would remain a unified nation and ended the institution of slavery. Manifold aspects of the war have been contemplated in American literature and film. The war forms the central thematic element in a number of Bierce's stories, and these works are generally considered the most important in the corpus of Civil War literature. Moreover, "A Horseman in the Sky" is acknowledged as among the best of Bierce's Civil War stories, in which the war is featured both literally and figuratively. By placing a father and son on opposing sides in "A Horseman in the Sky," Bierce presents a microcosm, a parallel situation on a reduced scale, of the rift that divided the nation.

Patricide

The killing of one's own father, or patricide, is a violation of the most basic strictures of all human cultures. Because of this, patricide has always been of keen literary interest. It forms the basis of the ancient Greek dramatist Sophocles' play *Oedipus Tyrannus*, in which it was prophesied that Oedipus would kill his father and marry his mother. Accordingly, Oedipus was abandoned as an infant, but he was later found and adopted. As an adult, he unknowingly fulfilled the prophecy, and the course of the drama concerns Oedipus's discovery of his own terrible crime. William Shakespeare's play *Hamlet* deals with the same theme but at a greater metaphorical distance: Hamlet kills his stepfather, Claudius, in revenge for Claudius's having killed his real father. Like Bierce, Roman poets

TOPICS FOR FURTHER STUDY

- Read Chapters 17 and 18 of Mark Twain's novel *The Adventures of Huckleberry Finn.* What attitudes toward honor and violence do the various characters demonstrate? The Grangerfords and the Shepherdsons? Huck Finn? What do you think Twain's opinion of these attitudes might have been? Write a paper comparing these views to those expressed by Bierce in "A Horseman in the Sky."
- Think of a facet of modern life that you find oppressive, hypocritical, or otherwise unacceptable. How can religious or magical symbolism make the issue clearer? Write a short story in which magic realism addresses the issue you chose.
- Read Bierce's short story "The Damned Thing." What fantastic element or elements are present in the story? What techniques does Bierce use to make the reader accept them as believable? Are they presented as magical or scientific? What contemporary scientific discoveries might they be based on? Give a class presentation comparing the fantastic elements in this story with those in "A Horseman in the Sky."
- Presented as a film, the material in "A Horseman in the Sky" would only run a few minutes. Research the lives of Civil War soldiers, gather some ideas from a few of Bierce's other Civil War stories, and write a treatment for a full-length screenplay based on the story.

such as Horace used the theme of relatives killing each other as metaphor for civil war. Bierce used this theme in several stories besides "A Horseman in the Sky" and collected them in *The Parenticide Club*. In "A Horseman in the Sky," Druse's act of patricide comes as the resolution to the conflict between two duties, to the family and to military discipline; it also seems to serve as a commentary on the divide between tradition and modernity.

Religion

Religion also figures prominently in "A Horseman in the Sky." Critic David M. Owens, in *The Devil's Topographer: Ambrose Bierce and the American War Story* (2006), draws attention to the remarkable amount of religious symbolism in the story. The officer who sees Druse's father fall over the cliff, thinking he is seeing some sort of supernatural apparition, wonders if he is seeing a new divine revelation such as John saw in the New Testament book of Apocalypse. More fundamentally but less obviously, Druse likens himself to Jesus by quoting him at a vital moment in the story. When Druse first recognizes his father, he is reluctant to kill him, and the strain causes him to shake and nearly faint. But then, "In his memory, as if they were a divine mandate, rang the words of his father at their parting: 'Whatever may occur, do what you conceive to be your duty.'" The recollection of these words allows Druse to impose order on his reluctant body, speaking to it as though his will were a separate force, "Peace, be still." This imperative is a quotation of Jesus's command in the Bible, at Mark 4:39, to calm a storm on the Sea of Galilee so that he and his disciples could walk on the water. (Of note, it seems to the officer that the falling horseman is walking on air.) It follows from this that Druse can be in some sense identified with Jesus, but the identification is an inversion of the Biblical myth. Druse acts in accord with his father's "divine mandate," but rather than suffering execution (as Bierce has already reminded us he deserved), he kills his father, sacrificing him to save the lives of his comrades. His father, rather than ascending to resurrection, descends into death.

STYLE

Magic Realism

The term *magic realism* was appropriated from art history in the 1950s by Latin American critics and writers to denote a particularly South American genre of literature in which elements that are magical are used to provide a revealing contrast to realism, especially in the work, for example, of Gabriel García Márquez and Jorge Luis Borges (who was strongly influenced by Bierce). *Magical* in this case means something that happens as governed by causes or a logic different from the physical laws known to science. Instances of magic are, in many cases, intrusions of traditional religious or folkloric beliefs into the modern world. *Realism* means that the whole of the story is presented in a highly realistic and plausible prose narrative. The magical elements, which are jarringly out of place in the modern world in which the narrative is anchored, are nevertheless presented in the same realistic style and detail and not treated by the narrative as incongruous or out of place. One feature that critics identify in magic realism is that the magical intrusion into the modern is a dialectical process, calling into question the validity of the post-Enlightenment conception of reality. This reflects a historical process. Traditional ways of viewing the world, such as in accord with magic or religion, often consist of superimpositions onto the world of elements of human consciousness and feelings. Since these older magical worldviews are based on human feeling, they can still have as much meaning to people as the scientific worldview that has disproven many of the reputed properties of such magic as physical facts. Magic realism is often used to criticize the underlying assumptions of the reality into which the magical elements intrude, for example, in terms of social justice by writers living under tyrannical regimes.

Writing before magic realism was defined as a literary style, Bierce prefigured some of its basic tenets. In "A Horseman in the Sky," Bierce presents a highly realistic narrative of the preparations for a Civil War battle in which reference is repeatedly made to the intrusion of angels, and the horseman appears in the epiphany of Druse to be some sort of god or apparition. The figure of the horseman bears the symbolic burden of Bierce's social criticism, but in narrative terms, it breaks into the story as a supernatural vision, only to become more and more concrete in Druse's view; and again, the figure is perceived as miraculous by the Federal officer, who also soon realizes his mistake. By the introduction of a perspective that allows for the magical, Bierce leads readers to explore the deeper meaning of the story for themselves. In the magical realism

U.S. Civil War Battle of Shiloh, 1862 (AP Images)

of Latin American authors, as the style evolved later in history, extremely improbable or even impossible events are more directly incorporated into the narrative. For example, in a situation that offers a fitting contrast to the magically oriented realism of the falling horseman in Bierce's story, in Márquez's *One Hundred Years of Solitude*, a character spontaneously floats away into the air and is never seen again.

Realism

Most American writers of the late nineteenth century, influenced for example by French authors such as Emile Zola, strove for an effect of realism in their work, drawing their subject matter out of everyday life rather than emulating the fantastic symbolism of Romantic writers of previous generations, such as in Mary Shelley's *Frankenstein.* Bierce, an experienced journalist, was a master of realistic writing, as exemplified in his Civil War stories, which were often closely based on his own experiences and observations during the war. Yet Bierce could rarely approach realism on its own terms, instead introducing ironic elements that largely undercut the realist effect of his prose. In "A Horseman in the Sky," Bierce begins with a detailed description of the effect of topography on warfare, a subject on which he was a considerable expert. This plausible discussion serves to engage the reader's belief in the narrative before the appearance of the apparition of the horseman calls on the reader to suspend disbelief and accept the fantastic, along with the symbolic value Bierce assigns to it.

Duality of Language and Meaning

Bierce was uncommonly concerned about language, even for a professional writer. Bierce was so particular about his style that he only either published his fiction with small presses owned by personal friends or self-published it, as he did not want to submit his writing to the final control of any other editor but himself. His *Devil's Dictionary* is a demonstration that language has as much power to deceive as to communicate, that words are often used to cover the truth rather than reveal it. Typical of his attitude is his definition of a Christian from *The Devil's Dictionary*: "One who believes that the New Testament is a divinely inspired book admirably suited to the spiritual needs of his neighbor. One who follows the teaching of Christ in so far as they are not inconsistent with a life of sin." Indeed, Bierce was obsessed in his own writing with precision and clarity of expression. As such, readers are often able to appreciate the true meaning of Bierce's fiction only when they discover for themselves the meaning that his language has purposefully covered over.

Classicism

Any serious efforts at education in mid-nineteenth century America entailed education in the Greek and Latin classics. Bierce's father seems to have taken a special interest in his son's learning, as he insisted that the youth supplement the normal high school curriculum with an even more intensive study of the ancient languages. Therefore, even the slightest classical reference in Bierce's work is liable to have an importance for its text that will become apparent only through careful consideration of its background and the qualities it evokes. For example, Carter Druse is first encountered in a grove of laurel trees. The mention of this plant, not native to West Virginia, is a foreshadowing of later events in the story at many levels; much of the rest of the story turns on demonic possession or inspired prophecy, both of which are within the province of the Greek god Apollo, whose symbol was the laurel. On the other hand, laurel wreaths were adopted to adorn the graves of "heroes" fallen in battle on Decoration Day (now Memorial Day) in the post-Civil War era in which Bierce was writing.

Omniscient Narrator

The action of the story is described by an omniscient narrator, that is, an unnamed authorial voice who sees things much more broadly than any particular character of the story does. This narrator supplies knowledge unknown to the characters as well as insights into their minds and thoughts to which no human observer could have access; the viewpoint is not limited by time or space.

Ekphrasis

An *ekphrasis* is a detailed narrative description of a work of art such as a painting or sculpture. Carter Druse's first sight of his father at the top of the cliff is presented as though it were an ekphrasis: "His first feeling was a keen artistic delight. On a colossal pedestal, the cliff,—motionless at the extreme edge of the capping rock and sharply outlined against the sky,—was an equestrian statue of impressive dignity." This is an instance of metaphor in which an actual person is described as a statue, but, since Druse is said to be in a dreamlike state and because no other context is given, the effect is to produce a sense of disorientation in the reader, who, though he knows no statue has suddenly appeared out of thin air, is unable at first to tell what plain sense the narrative is meant to convey.

In Medias Res

Many narratives, including those of the earliest Western literary texts, the *Iliad* and the *Odyssey*, begin at some dramatic moment of action that captures the reader's attention, even though the event is in the middle of the story (*in medias res*). Thus, the temporal sequence of the narrative is rearranged, with later material describing earlier parts of the story. Bierce does this in "A Horseman in the Sky." In the first section, a Federal sentry is asleep at his post, endangering his unit and its military operation; only in a later flashback in the second section is the reader told who the sentry is and how he came to be in that situation.

HISTORICAL CONTEXT

The Civil War in Retrospect

The American Civil War (1861–1865) was the defining event in the history of nineteenth-century America and in Ambrose Bierce's life. The country entered the war under the most romantic notions about honor, duty, and heroism, only to experience a reality of carnage that included the deaths of well over a million soldiers under conditions that eventually degenerated into almost industrial slaughter prophetic of World War I. Soldiers were expected to charge prepared positions under concentrated artillery and small arms fire many times greater than anything experienced before in human history.

Nevertheless, as time created distance from the devastating reality of the Civil War, the popular memory of the war began to take on a romantic character. By the 1870s, literature and art were beginning to be produced in which the Civil War was viewed in heroically ideal terms, replete with morally uplifting examples of personal heroism exemplifying medieval concepts of honor. Even many veterans acquiesced in a sentimental perception of the war that reinforced their heroism and worth, letting them turn away from the necessarily traumatic memories of battle. In the collective memory of the public, then, an abstract and fantastic "heroism" replaced the horrors of war.

COMPARE & CONTRAST

- **1860s:** Many Americans feel a greater sense of loyalty to their states than to the nation as a whole.

  1890s: The Pledge of Allegiance is introduced into public schools as a tribute to those who died in the Civil War fighting for the unity of the nation.

  Today: The Pledge of Allegiance is seen to have different significance among various groups. To some, it represents support for "traditional" American values; to others, national solidarity in the face of foreign aggression; to yet others, state–enforced political conformity.

- **1860s:** Most Americans live and work on farms.

  1890s: Americans are rapidly moving to cities and factory towns as the American economy becomes industrialized.

  Today: The population of the United States is overwhelmingly urban, with the economy in a transition to a basis in service and information technologies.

- **1860s:** Warfare in the Napoleonic model is believed to be an affair of honor that can quickly be decided by a few victories.

  1890s: In a series of essays on the growing arms industry, Bierce makes the point that the Civil War demonstrated the brutal industrial nature of modern warfare.

  Today: The industrialization of war has accelerated to the point that, thanks to high-tech weapons, warfare so efficiently leads to destruction that all-out war between nuclear powers is unthinkable, as it could result in the extinction of humanity.

- **1860s:** Dueling is an important part of public and political life. Previously, Andrew Jackson had gained national popularity by fighting a series of duels. Later, Abraham Lincoln had gained popularity by displaying his caustic wit in publically declining to duel.

  1890s: Though duels cease to be part of political culture, they continue to be common as part of a romantic reaction to modernity; one of Bierce's sons is killed in a duel in the early 1890s.

  Today: In view of the ease with which simple modern firearms can extinguish human life, dueling has become outdated and plays no part in American life.

- **1860s:** Freed slaves are initially integrated into the United States as full citizens under the civil rights amendments.

  1890s: *Plessy v. Ferguson*, an 1896 Supreme Court decision, legalizes the system of institutional segregation in the southern states.

  Today: After much social turmoil in the 1950s and 1960s, American citizens are equal under the law irrespective of race, although racist views among individual Americans remain common and many vestiges of racism remain in effect.

As Duncan and Klooster explain in their introduction to Bierce's Civil War writings, Bierce could not agree with this attitude. Though an exemplary soldier whose physical courage was exceptional, Bierce was keenly aware of the awful moral and physical dangers under which soldiers lived and fought during the war; he knew that many soldiers risked or gave their lives for vague principles, such as honor, virtue, and patriotism, that had little relationship to the underlying economic and political factors that led to the war, which ordinary soldiers did not, in general, understand. In fact, the disconnection that Bierce saw between the realities of the war and its later sentimentalization accounted for the essentially cynical and bitter tone that marked his whole literary output, with his main theme being the exposure of hypocrisy and pretense.

Indeed, it seems likely that Bierce's main motive in writing about the war, which he did copiously both in vignettes of memoir and in short stories, was precisely to present a more realistic view of the Civil War as an antidote to its sentimentalization.

The romantic view of the Civil War proliferated during what Mark Twain called, in a term worthy of Bierce, the "Gilded Age" (meaning that however much the postwar period appeared golden, that appearance was only a sham covering baser material). This period saw the institution of veterans' parades on Decoration Day (which Bierce never attended) and of the Pledge of Allegiance in American schoolrooms. But nowhere was the worship of idealized "heroes" more obvious than in the monuments erected during these years in town squares and parks in nearly every city and town in America, North and South. Many of the monuments were built to honor a locally raised regiment or some local notable who had risen to the rank of colonel or general. A few such monuments are of national importance, including General Ulysses S. Grant's tomb; the equestrian monument of General William Tecumseh Sherman in New York by Augustus Saint-Gaudens, a leading artist of the era; and the bas-relief sculpture at Stone Mountain, Georgia, completed at an enormous expense.

Almost invariably, monuments to individual officers took the form of equestrian statues, showing their subjects mounted on horseback, as if leading military operations. This was not a purely American phenomenon; Americans were influenced by taste in Europe, and this period saw a tremendous number of equestrian statues dedicated to historical figures who were becoming important in new national mythologies, including Joan of Arc and the medieval Holy Roman emperors Charlemagne and Frederick Barbarossa. The inspiration for all these equestrian statues came from the only surviving intact such statue of a Roman emperor. Although equestrian statues were common in antiquity, they were generally destroyed in the Middle Ages because the then-ruling Christian authorities considered them part of the idolatrous pagan worship of the Roman emperors as living gods. One example, in Rome, was spared because it was believed to represent Constantine, the first Roman emperor to become a Christian. In fact, however, as early as the Renaissance (sixteenth century), scholars realized that the statue depicted instead the earlier emperor Marcus Aurelius. Every artist and every wealthy young man making the grand tour of Europe would have seen this world-famous statue prominently displayed in Rome; the lithographic printing that was then becoming cheap and popular ensured that practically every literate person would have been familiar with it. It is not surprising, then, that this particular image became the archetype for the presentation of nationalist heroes in both Europe and America.

In "A Horseman in the Sky," Bierce seems to recall the days before the Civil War with great irony by claiming not to know whether his character Carter Druse is inspired by a "good or bad angel." This can be taken as a reference to perhaps the most famous political speech in American history, Lincoln's first inaugural address. In this speech, Lincoln expresses his hope that war can yet be avoided if Americans in both the North and the South can be touched "by the better angels of our nature." Given the failure of Lincoln's hope and the horror of the ensuing war, Bierce may be suggesting that America's inspiration for the war might instead have come from bad—that is, fallen—angels.

CRITICAL OVERVIEW

The first critical response to "A Horseman in the Sky" (from an anonymous 1892 review in the New York *Sun*, quoted in Duncan and Klooster) finds in it a failure of realism:

> 'A Horseman' in the sky [sic] is the worst in the book so far as illusion is concerned. We will venture to say that no such erroneous impression could have been produced in the Federal army, or in any portion of it, as the author here alleges. We are certain that the horseman in the sky was never mistaken for a repetition of the Apocalyptical vision, but was only regarded as a Confederate General and his horse descending a precipice in obedience to the laws of gravitation, as the facts warranted.

Bierce's friend and biographer Vincent Starrett, in his *Ambrose Bierce*, one of the first critical texts on Bierce, debates whether or not the patricide could have been closely based on actual events witnessed by Bierce during the war. Bierce's language is considered a failure of realism and a source of trivial humor and shock.

Cathy N. Davidson, in her 1984 study *The Experimental Fictions of Ambrose Bierce: Structuring the Ineffable*, approaches Bierce in modern critical terms for the first time. Though she does not cite his work as magic realism (preferring the critical terminology of Bierce's own era), she draws attention to the profound influence of Bierce on magic realist authors such as Borges. She locates the particular quality of Bierce's work in the disconnection between language and reality: "Bierce structures nearly all of his stories around breakdowns in perception and communication. These breakdowns are experienced by the characters in the text as well as by readers who recreate the text in the act of reading."

New historicist critics, who are interested in the historical context of literature as opposed to philosophical issues such as those raised by magic realism, show considerable interest in Bierce's Civil War stories. Donald T. Blume, in *Ambrose Bierce's Civilians and Soldiers in Context: A Critical Study*, concentrates on the textual history of "A Horseman in the Sky" and points out that Bierce made some significant changes in the text between its publication in the *Examiner* in 1889 and its inclusion in the 1891 anthology. The most important of these changes occur at the end of the story, when Druse is being interrogated by the sergeant. In the original version, in answer to the sergeant's question as to whether there was anyone on the horse that Druse shot, the soldier replies, "Do you mean the horse which had wings?" Blume believes that this single line means that Druse was driven mad by the moral conflict of shooting his father; the critic considers that the alteration to the text resulted in a completely new meaning and a lessening of the story's literary quality. David M. Owens, in *The Devil's Topographer: Ambrose Bierce and the American War Story*, demonstrates to a much higher degree than earlier critics how closely stories such as "A Horseman in the Sky" were based on Bierce's wartime experiences. He relates many of the events and places in the story to the real topography of the area of West Virginia where Bierce fought in the autumn of 1861, and he even discovered that a legend circulated around the Union army in West Virginia to the effect that a soldier fell off a spectacularly high cliff at Seneca Rocks.

Bierce has always been considered a master of the "plain style," or "pure English," because of the great concision and exactness of his use of language. For this reason, together with his critiques of conventional assumptions about morality, politics, and manifold other aspects of society, his short stories and essays had an important role in the English literature and composition curricula in the United States throughout most of the twentieth century, as the writings of the educators and *English Journal* contributors Bernice L. Caswell and Helen F. Olson attest. "A Horseman in the Sky" has always been among the most common of Bierce's stories to be used in the classroom. Owens points out that "A Horseman in the Sky" is frequently read in courses on military ethics at the American service academies.

CRITICISM

Bradley A. Skeen

Skeen is a classics professor. In this essay, he considers "A Horseman in the Sky" as an early example of magical realism and from the point of view of Freudian psychoanalysis.

The narrative of "A Horseman in the Sky" begins in a highly realistic manner, drawing on Bierce's own experience during the Civil War. A Federal sentry (Carter Druse) is neglecting his duty by sleeping on watch. The supernatural suddenly intrudes, however, as he awakens:

> What good or bad angel came in a dream to rouse him from his state of crime, who shall say? Without a movement, without a sound, in the profound silence and the languor of the late afternoon, some invisible messenger of fate touched with unsealing finger the eyes of his consciousness—whispered into the ear of his spirit the mysterious awakening word which no human lips ever have spoken, no human memory ever has recalled.

This passage may lead the reader to expect that what follows is the narration of a dream or vision. This impression is strengthened by the next sentence: "He quietly raised his forehead from his arm and looked between the masking stems of the laurels." In ancient Greek myth, the laurel was sacred to Apollo and his attendants, the Muses, who were responsible for inspiring prophets with visions and poets with verse. Indeed, the following paragraphs seem to describe the miraculous appearance of an equestrian statue atop the cliff Druse is guarding. The pose of the figure is likened to that of a Greek god, suggesting that Druse is seeing an epiphany or a vision of the appearance of a god on Earth. The reader is then just as suddenly brought back to reality as the movement of the supposed statue reveals it to be a mounted Confederate scout. The narrative then dwells on the horrible

WHAT DO I READ NEXT?

- In *Tales of Soldiers and Civilians*, published in 1891, Bierce edited and collected his Civil War stories together with a selection of stories of the uncanny.
- In *The Devil's Dictionary* (1911) Bierce collected his cynical newspaper columns criticizing Gilded Age culture through a series of definitions exposing the often hypocritical use of language.
- *The Adventures of Huckleberry Finn*, written by Mark Twain and published in 1884, is an exploration of the culture that existed in America before the Civil War from a viewpoint similar to Bierce's, as written in the rapidly changing nation of the 1880s.
- Shelby Foote's *The Civil War: A Narrative*, published in three volumes between 1958 and 1974, is a popular introduction to the Civil War.

"ON THE ONE HAND, THE CIVIL WAR COMMEMORATED BY THE STATUES, MEMORIALS, AND THE NEW HOLIDAY OF DECORATION DAY WAS A GLORIOUS TESTIMONY TO NATIONAL HONOR, BUT ON THE OTHER, THE WAR THAT VETERANS LIKE BIERCE REMEMBERED IN THE SECRET PLACES OF THEIR HEARTS WAS TERRIBLE AND DESTRUCTIVE."

psychological pressures on Druse in his having to act as a sniper and kill the scout suddenly and without warning.

The narrative next abruptly shifts to a description, still realistic, of a Federal officer in the valley below. He is placed so that he can see the falling Confederate horseman, and the reader is again plunged into a magical realm by his reaction: "Filled with amazement and terror by this apparition of a horseman in the sky—half believing himself the chosen scribe of some new Apocalypse, the officer was overcome by the intensity of his emotions; his legs failed him and he fell." Here, similarly, a natural event, the wounded horse and its rider falling from the cliff, is perceived by its viewer as a miracle and a sign of the biblical revelation of the end times.

In his brief response to a hostile review of "A Horseman in the Sky" (quoted following the story in Duncan and Klooster), Bierce is somewhat dismissive of this prophetic intrusion into the realistic narrative, pointing out that the Federal officer only "for that instant half believed" that he was experiencing something supernatural. Nevertheless, the descriptions of the two soldiers' flights of fancy constitute a large, and in many respects the most important, portion of the story. In "An Occurrence at Owl Creek Bridge," written the following year, Bierce makes the whole substantive action of the story an extended fantasy of escape in the mind of a Confederate spy during the instant it takes the rope to break his neck when he is hung by Federal troops; thus, the author was certainly well aware that the force of his fiction could rest in the detailed description of momentary fancies. Moreover, the singular intrusion of the mysterious or supernatural into an otherwise realistic narrative was a specialty of Bierce's. He had perfected this technique through his numerous horror stories. His formula was to keep the narrative as near to reality as possible and introduce only a single reality-breaking element that the reader must accept through the willing suspension of disbelief. In writing his Civil War stories, Bierce moved from the mere shock value of horror stories to attempts to inspire sober philosophical reflection in the reader.

The intrusion of the visionary into the realistic text of "A Horseman in the Sky" is certainly a key element in the meaning Bierce wished to convey through the story. The visionary aspects highlight the transformation of American culture in the crisis of the Civil War. This literary technique is known as magic realism, where the sudden intrusion of the dreamlike or miraculous into a realistic narrative is taken as a dialectic with reality, often establishing dissatisfaction with the existing nature of things and calling for change. Bierce, moreover, utilizes the symbolic nature of the fantastic elements to call into question the legitimacy of the American attitude to the Civil War, an attitude that was dramatically changing by the time of his writing in the late 1880s.

The horseman of Bierce's title first appears as a mysterious statue in Druse's vision. There can be no question that Bierce is calling to mind the typically equestrian statues of prominent Civil War officers that began to appear throughout America in the North and South in the 1870s: "For an instant Druse had a strange, half-defined feeling that he had slept to the end of the war and was looking upon a noble work of art reared upon that eminence to commemorate the deeds of an heroic past of which he had been an inglorious part." Such statues were eventually erected in almost every city and town in the nation. Druse's vision, then, serves to contrast the way the Civil War was coming to be viewed twenty-five years after it was over and the way Bierce and other soldiers had experienced it. On the one hand, the Civil War commemorated by the statues, memorials, and the new holiday of Decoration Day was a glorious testimony to national honor, but on the other, the war that veterans like Bierce remembered in the secret places of their hearts was terrible and destructive. The role of nearly every soldier, which was to kill, brutally if necessary, was inglorious compared to romantic ideals of virtue and honor. The contrast is developed through the hint of magic realism, by the intrusion of a vision of the future into the past. Bierce wished to demonstrate that the common idea that the Civil War was glorious was a dreamlike fantasy. From this perspective, the traditional association of laurel with prophecy and inspiration may be considered a masterful piece of misdirection by Bierce; given the retrospective context, the laurel grove in which Druse is hidden must refer to the laurel wreaths that became a stock symbol for graveside ceremonies held on Decoration Day (which officially became Memorial Day in 1967).

In the system of moral conduct viewed as the American ideal in the nineteenth century, one man settled an affair of honor with another by openly challenging him to a duel and fighting fairly before witnesses and referees. A man who simply killed with expediency was a criminal and a coward. But Carter Druse is forced by the circumstances of the war to lie in concealment and kill without warning any enemy he sees, thus honorably fulfilling his duty as a soldier. Indeed, the moral standards of traditional civilian life are inverted by the necessities of war. Druse's act of patricide, then, can be considered symbolic. The brutal realities of the war made the sentimental ideals of antebellum America obsolete; the death of Druse's father is the death of America's innocence. Bierce, cynic that he was, could only view as hypocrisy the nation's attempts to revive its state of innocence by covering over the reality of the war with a blanket of sentimentality. The realities of the war made any attempts to create heroes by erecting statues to veterans seem like acts of self-deception about the true character of life and how it had been changed by the war.

In the third chapter of the story, the Federal officer who sees Druse's father fall, "half believing himself the chosen scribe of some new Apocalypse," is introduced to reiterate the point. The biblical Apocalypse is a vision of the end of the world. The indiscriminate killing that transformed men in the crisis of the Civil War brought about the end of the civilized, traditional, and innocent world that had existed before. But such a truth is too awful for the officer to recount to his superior. "This officer was a wise man; he knew better than to tell an incredible truth. He said nothing of what he had seen." The commander, in turn, somehow seems to know the truth yet thinks it better to keep silent about it. His willful ignorance of the truth may be the hypocrisy that Bierce saw developing about the Civil War in his later years.

The murder of one's own relative is an apt symbol for Bierce's perception of the Civil War and its effects on American culture. The scenario of brother killing brother was one popular stereotype of the war, recalling the biblical story of Cain and Abel and the classical story of Romulus and Remus. Also a metaphor for citizens of the same state killing each other on the battlefield, this scenario heightens the drama and horror of the situation. Bierce returned to the same theme in another of his Civil War stories, "The Affair at Coulter's Notch," in which an artillery officer must bombard a town containing his wife and child and in fact kills them. On the one hand, no worse crime can be imagined, but on the other, the actions can be seen as entirely proper because they came about through a soldier honorably doing his duty. The point is that traditional morality was irreparably damaged by the war. The theme is highlighted in Druse's father's final admonition to him: "whatever may occur do what you conceive to be your duty." When his father says this, he means it as an ironic criticism of his son, who is abandoning his mother and betraying his biblically mandated duty to honor his parents. When Druse is forced to choose between the traditional duty of honoring his father and his military duty of killing his father, he resolves the paradox by recalling these very words and taking them as a warrant to do his military duty. The violence of the war exploded traditional morality.

Murder within the family seems to have had a special fascination for Bierce. A number of his comedic stories, such as "Oil of Dog," turn on this theme, and he reissued them in a separate collection titled *The Parenticide Club*. In his publication of *The Interpretation of Dreams* (1900), Freud popularized his discovery of the Oedipus complex. This identified psychological dynamics within a family according to which the infant first feels love in connection with the special relationship of dependency on his mother. The infant boy then experiences his father as a rival for the other parent's love and expresses this through unconditional hostility, since the infant's emotional range is still quite unrefined. To express this in adult terms, one would say that a baby boy loves his mother and wants to kill his father—events that actually occur in the ancient Greek myth of Oedipus. Although Freud was the first to articulate these psychological factors in scientific terms, he realized that writers going back to Sophocles, the playwright of *Oedipus Rex*, had nevertheless already approached the same psychological truth.

It is easy to explain the events of "A Horseman in the Sky" in psychological terms. One factor in Druse's initial abandonment of his mother by enlisting might well have been the overwhelming nature of the emotions he feels as a result of her impending death, making it easier for him to leave than to fully experience them. His decision to join the side that his father considers to be traitorous is unmistakably to be seen as an act of hostility against him. And then Druse indeed kills his own father. However, Druse's father looms largest in the story as an equestrian statue, a genre of art that is traced back to a single Roman equestrian statue of the emperor Marcus Aurelius. It is that statue, which he recognizes finally to be his father, that Druse must kill. It can hardly be a coincidence that Bierce's own father was named Marcus Aurelius. Part of the genesis of the story, underlying much of its emotional power, is Bierce's own patricidal fantasies, which naturally find an echo in the minds of his readers. In the same way, Roy Morris, Jr., has found the inspiration for the killing of the artilleryman's wife and child in "The Affair at Coulter's Notch" in events of Bierce's own life. At the time of writing, Bierce was in the process of divorcing his wife after discovering her in an affair, and his son had just been killed, ironically enough, in a duel arising over the honor of his fiancée.

Source: Bradley Skeen, Critical Essay on "A Horseman in the Sky," in *Short Stories for Students*, Gale, Cengage Learning, 2009.

Roy Morris Jr.

In the following excerpt, noted biographer and historian Morris describes Bierce's experiences in the West Virginia mountains during a Civil War campaign that formed the basis of the story "A Horseman in the Sky."

... Despite McClellan's earlier boast that "our success is complete & secession is killed in this country," Bierce and his regiment were soon back in Virginia, making sure that secession—or, at any rate, its stubbornly unburied ghost—remained dead. They found themselves again in the Cheat Mountain Valley, "holding a road that ran from Nowhere to the southeast." As veterans of the summer campaign, Bierce noticed that "we were regarded by the others with profound respect as 'old soldiers.' (Our ages, if equalized, would, I fancy, have given about twenty years to each man.) We gave ourselves, this aristocracy of service, no end of military airs; some of us even going to the extreme of keeping our jackets buttoned and our hair combed. We now 'brought to the task' of subduing the Rebellion a patriotism which never for a moment doubted that a rebel was a fiend accursed of God and the angels." Their burgeoning patriotism would soon be tested. Robert E. Lee, stung by the loss of western Virginia, personally led a new force into the valley, with the stated intention of retaking Cheat Mountain from the Union invaders.

Bierce's regiment, at Elkwater, was too far away to take part in the mishandled Confederate

> "THE STORY, LIKE THOSE IN *THE PARENTICIDE CLUB*, IS ANOTHER OF BIERCE'S COMPULSIVE ACTS OF PATRICIDE, AND THE IMAGE OF THE RIDER ON HORSEBACK SILENTLY PLUNGING THROUGH THE AIR TO HIS DEATH, HIS LONG HAIR STREAMING UPWARD LIKE A PLUME, IS GENUINELY EERIE AND AFFECTING."

attack on Cheat Mountain on September 12, but on October 3, it participated in a reconnaissance in force against rebel breastworks near the Greenbrier River. The subsequent skirmish there "has not got into history," wrote Bierce, "but it had a real objective existence. Its short and simple annals are that we marched a long way and lay down before a fortified camp of the enemy at the farther edge of a valley. Our commander had the forethought to see that we lay well out of range of the small-arms of the period. A disadvantage of this arrangement was that the enemy was out of reach of us as well, for our rifles were not better than his. Unfortunately—one might almost say unfairly—he had a few pieces of artillery very well protected, and with those he mauled us to the eminent satisfaction of his mind and heart. So we parted from him in anger and returned to our own place, leaving our dead—not many." One of the dead the regiment left behind was a fellow named Abbott, whose taking off, Bierce remembered with mordant irony, was distinctly unusual. "He was lying flat upon his stomach." Bierce wrote, "and was killed by being struck in the side by a nearly spent cannon-shot that came rolling in among us. The shot remained in him until removed. It was a solid round-shot, evidently cast in some private foundry, whose proprietor had put his 'imprint' upon it: it bore, in slightly sunken letters, the name 'Abbott'". The nineteen-year-old Bierce was quickly becoming a connoisseur of the grotesque.

Two months later, both his irony and his patriotism were severely challenged by a new engagement at Camp Allegheny, at the southern end of the Tygart Valley. Brig. Gen. Joseph J. Reynolds, the new brigade commander, had determined to probe the enemy defenses at Buffalo Mountain, a move that Bierce, as a rapidly seasoned veteran, justifiably considered one that was being made "more to keep up the appearance of doing something than with a hope of accomplishing a military result." What it accomplished was a stinging Union defeat. "Here," wrote Bierce, "the regiment had its hardest fight in Western Virginia, and was most gloriously thrashed." Revisiting the site decades after the war, Bierce found the rebel breastworks still standing, although so rotten that he could pick through the timber with his fingers for souvenir bullets (to his disappointment, he found none). The works had been admirably constructed to defend both front and rear, a wise choice, since Reynolds divided the attackers into two columns, each led by a guide who was a native of the parts. When the columns predictably failed to converge on the site for a simultaneous attack, the rebels found themselves enjoying "that inestimable military advantage known in civilian speech as being 'surrounded.'" Bierce's column, attacking from the rear, was pinned down behind an obstacle course of fallen timbers, an act that probably saved their lives, said Bierce, since it prevented them from forming into line for a frontal assault. "We took cover," he wrote, "and pot-shotted the fellows behind the parapet all day and then withdrew and began our long retreat in a frame of mind that would have done credit to an imp of Satan."

The regimental mind-set was scarcely improved by the sight that greeted them along their retreat. They had already passed "some things lying by the wayside" on their way to the front. These "things" turned out to be the corpses of Union scouts slain by "Allegheny Ed" Johnson's Confederate troops in earlier skirmish. Bierce, with his avid eye for the macabre, had already examined the bodies, "curiously lifting the blankets from their yellow-clay faces. How repulsive they looked with their blood-smears, their blank, staring eyes, their teeth uncovered by contraction of the lips!" The sight of their dead comrades left the men of the Ninth speechless—"for an hour afterward the injunction of silence in the ranks was needless." The troops were still as patriotic as ever, observed Bierce, "but we did not wish to be that way."

Repassing the site the next day, "feeble from fatigue and savage from defeat," Bierce and the others were surprised to see that the dead men seemed to have altered their positions and thrown off their covering. The reason—and its effect—was quickly seen. A herd of wild pigs had eaten the faces off the dead men. Years later, in his short story "The Coup de Grace," Bierce gives a graphic rendering of the hideous sight: "Fifty yards away, on the crest of a low, thinly wooded hill, he saw several dark objects moving about among the fallen men—a herd of swine. One stood with his back to him, its shoulders sharply elevated. Its forefeet were upon a human body, its head was depressed and invisible. The bristly ridge of its chine showed black against the red west. The swine, catching sight of him, threw up their crimson muzzles, regarding him suspiciously a second, and then with a gruff, concerted grunt, raced away out of sight." The real-life soldiers quickly shot the pigs—Bierce termed it "a military execution"—but they could not bring themselves to eat the repulsive animals. "The shooting of several kinds was good in the Cheat Mountain country, even in 1861," he noted dryly.

Bierce would make use of the mountainous West Virginia terrain in another postwar story, "A Horseman in the Sky." In it, the civilian guide who led Bierce's column up to the rebel camp at Buffalo Mountain is personified by a young, wellborn Virginian who has impulsively joined the Union army at Grafton. This traitor to Virginia, as his father sorrowfully calls him, finds himself posted as a sentry in a clump of laurel overlooking a sheer drop-off hundreds of feet below. The character's name, Carter Druse, bears a certain euphoric similarity to the author's, and it is perhaps something of a private joke that he is described as "the son of wealthy parents, an only child, [who] had known such ease and cultivation and high living as wealth and taste were able to command." Aware that his regiment is planning a surprise attack on the enemy camp that night, Druse is startled to see a Confederate scout suddenly appear on horseback on the ridge across the way. After a brief internal debate in which Druse struggles to reconcile himself with the act of shooting the horseman from ambush, he remembers his father's parting injunction to "do what you conceive to be your duty." He shoots the rider's horse, sending both man and beast plunging over the sheer precipice, and a Union officer coming up the mountainside witnesses "an astonishing sight—a man on horseback riding down into the valley through the air!" The horseman in the sky turns out to be Druse's own father, and the hardened sergeant to whom he later tells the story can scarcely stomach Druse's act. "Good God!" he says, walking away. The story, like those in *The Parenticide Club*, is another of Bierce's compulsive acts of patricide, and the image of the rider on horseback silently plunging through the air to his death, his long hair streaming upward like a plume, is genuinely eerie and affecting . . .

Source: Roy Morris Jr., "What I Saw of Shiloh," in *Ambrose Bierce: Alone in Bad Company*, Crown Publishers, 1995, pp. 21–39.

Giorgio Mariani

In the following essay, Mariani argues that while Bierce never glorified heroism or patriotism, he was nonetheless engaged by the martial spirit, as evidenced by his Civil War short stories.

No author would seem to be more resistant to the ritual celebrations of honor and military prowess that distinguished the work of many popular authors of the American 1890s than Ambrose Bierce. His well-known cynicism, corrosive irony, and predilection for the absurd appear resolutely antithetical to the patriotism, sentimentalism, and rhetorical embellishments characteristic of those texts which, whether explicitly or not, aimed at popularizing what T. J. Jackson Lears has aptly identified as the "martial spirit" of the age. Not surprisingly, critics have generally described Bierce's work, and especially his Civil War short stories, as the best anti-heroic war fiction to appear before Crane's *The Red Badge of Courage*. Eric Solomon, for example, has argued that Bierce's pieces are "vignettes of cosmic irony wherein man is brought to realize his insignificance in the face of the all-encompassing universe of war." Bierce consciously rejects "the glorious view of war" and is never sentimental about honor or glory; his business, Solomon insists, is to show "the irrationality of war." More recently Lawrence Berkove has proposed that both Bierce's fiction and his journalism are at the core "peace tracts." Bierce "truly and profoundly" believed that "war is both foolish and terrible, that its glamour is an illusion, and that the fine talk justifying it on the grounds of patriotism and idealism is all lies." Cathy Davidson has made a similar point in her interesting study of the dialectic of perception and misperception in his fiction. According to Davidson, Bierce shows that a military life grants no glory, that patriotism is dehumanizing, that the real meaning (or unmeaning) of war is to be found in its inevitable and chilling massacres.

"BIERCE'S IRONY, NO DOUBT, POINTS TO THE IRRATIONALITY AND MONSTROSITY OF WAR, AND YET HIS OWN IRONIC ASSAULTS ARE REGULATED BY AN ILL LOGIC THAT PARALLELS THE ONE RULING THE ARMY WORLD."

Yet, paradoxically, Bierce gained at least part of his reputation by writing for the San Francisco *Examiner*, a paper owned by William Randolph Hearst, one of the most distinguished and fanatical masterminds of war propaganda of the 1890s. Several explanations have been offered as to why Hearst continued to employ a writer like Bierce even during the Spanish-American war, when Bierce's attitude towards American involvement oscillated between qualified support and bitter opposition. One can, of course, wonder whether Hearst preferred to include a dissenter's views in his papers so that he could not be accused of ignoring positions different from his own, or whether he was simply eager to keep on the *Examiner's* staff a very popular journalist who attracted a wide readership. This, however, should not obscure the fact that Bierce's anti-war feelings—even in his Civil War tales, where they are supposedly expressed more strongly—are marked by structural and ideological limitations which prevented them from becoming objectionable to imperialists like Hearst.

As Berkove himself notes, though Bierce never glorified heroism and patriotism, "it is also true that he was ambivalent about war. His reason opposed it; his emotions were exhilarated by it." In sum, "Bierce was far from being a pacifist." Solomon appears to agree with this position because, in his view, if Bierce "was revolted, intellectually, by the harsh brutalities of a repellent, paradoxical world," he still "enjoyed the test of combat, the companionship and the excitement of war." The limit of such qualifications of Bierce's anti-war sentiments is two-fold. First, both Solomon and Berkove draw a clear-cut line between, on the one hand, Bierce's "intellect" and "reason," which would feed his anti-war position, and, on the other hand, his "emotions" and gut-feelings, which, in tune with the martial spirit of the times, would find war an exhilarating experience. One need not be an orthodox believer in psychoanalysis to find of dubious value such sharp distinctions between the rational and irrational spheres of the human mind. Moreover, by focusing on the author's personality, this way of approaching the issue moves attention away from the texts. On the contrary, the ambivalence of Bierce's anti-war views lies at the very heart of his best short stories of the Civil War. While he certainly subverts the stereotypes which dominated popular fiction through a constant juxtaposition of the idealistic view of war to the brutality and horror of the battlefield, Bierce does not try to expose the world of war as a cultural and historical reality serving specific interests, and which could be called into question by a different value-system. In the narrative machinery of his stories there is no slot free from the logic of war and aggression, so that any attempt at criticizing the martial universe becomes impossible. That world may be revolting and horrifying, but it is the only one the author knows, and the only one in which his characters can function.

"An Affair of Outposts" contains a characteristically Biercean anti-war tirade:

> In all this there was none of the pomp of war—no hint of glory. Even in his distress and peril the helpless civilian could not forbear to contrast it with the gorgeous parades and reviews held in honor of himself—with the brilliant uniforms, the music, the banners, and the marching. It was an ugly and sickening business: to all that was artistic in his nature, revolting, brutal, in bad taste.... "This is beastly! Where is the charm of it all? Where are the elevated sentiments, the devotion, the heroism, the—."

The "helpless civilian" is in fact the villain of the story. The Governor of the State, he grants a military commission to an Armisted, who wishes to enlist and die in battle since his wife has betrayed him. Even though Armisted later discovers that her secret lover was the Governor himself, he still gives up his life to save that of his personal enemy when the latter, during a visit to the battlefield, wanders too close to the enemy lines. The quoted passage, as is the entire story, is built on the contrast between the foppish and false world of the civilian and the tough, bloody, but real world of Captain Armisted. Though the first impression may be that the shocking violence of a real battle is meant to debunk the Governor's fantasies of "gorgeous parades" and "brilliant uniforms," a closer look at the events and structural opposition of the tale will reveal that the "revolting, brutal" war environment is constructed in fact as something of an ideal, a yardstick through which the "nobility" and courage of the captain, as well as the pettiness and cowardice of the Governor, can be measured.

The Governor is one of those "distinguished civilians" who like to catch a glimpse "of the horrors of war" as long as this can be done "safely." When his "showily horsed" staff visits the camp, "the bedraggled soldier looked up from his trench... leaned upon his spade and audibly damned them to signify his sense of their ornamental irrelevance to the austerities of his trade." Real soldiers, who can discern "expectancy and readiness" where the civilian can see only "carelessness, confusion, indifference," are better men, men with a first-hand knowledge of the ugly face of the world, and men who can distinguish between substance and appearance, between what is essential and what is "ornamental." Thus Bierce's satire invests what people like the Governor *think* of war; that is, the idealistic conception which undoubtedly many contemporary readers shared with the tale's villain. Yet to criticize the view of war that prevailed in the popular imagination is not the same thing as attacking the martial ideology itself.

By contrasting the "composure and precision of veterans" that characterizes "raw soldiers of less than a year's training" to the "pride and terror" of the frightened Governor, the author does not do away with the rather traditional notions of courage and heroism and the idealization of war as a "raw" experience. The story does have a "hero," and that hero is obviously Armisted, who sacrifices himself in order to be a truly honorable soldier. He is disgusted by the world of lies inhabited by the Governor and his wife, but what he turns to for purification, far from being a rejection of the Governor's world of "elevated sentiments... devotion... heroism," is an intensification of the latter. Armisted is a better man because he truly believes in the chivalric code of honor which for the Governor is a mere smoke screen. The "horrors of war" in the midst of which Armisted shows his valor and honesty turn out to be at least more "human" and real than the "horrors of peace," which characterize the Governor's everyday life. What happens in another story, "The Coup de Grace," where the only humane thing Captain Madwell can do for his horribly wounded and agonizing friend Sergeant Halcrow is to thrust his sword into the latter's breast and thus put an end to his suffering, typifies the inescapable logic of the martial universe in which "An Affair of Outpost" and *all* of Bierce's war tales take place. No matter how appalling and horrible war may be, Bierce's fiction shows that its logic cannot be transcended.

Of course Bierce's reputation as anti-war writer lies precisely in the uncompromising depiction of the most terrifying, disgusting details of the battlefield. In "The Coup de Grace," for example, Halcrow's mortal wound is described as "a wide, ragged opening in the abdomen. It was defiled with earth and dead leaves. Protruding from it was a loop of small intestine." The sergeant's stomach has been partly eaten away by pigs who have been feeding on dead or half-dead soldiers. The polemical, anti-sentimental content of such images is clear enough. Similarly, and even more explicitly, in "One Kind of Officer" Bierce contrasts the idealization of war to its reality. In this tale the dead soldiers lying on the battleground are depicted as "very repulsive... wrecks... not at all heroic, and nobody was accessible to the infection of their patriotic example. Dead upon the field of honor, yes; but the field of honor was so very wet! It makes a difference." Honor, here, is unmasked as an empty construct, a term that cannot contain and account for the tragedy and absurdity of war. It is also fitting that such an attack on the idea of honor and loyalty to a higher cause should be developed in a text where, in order to follow strictly the orders he has received, a captain ends up firing on his own men only to be eventually sentenced to death because the general who gave the order in the first place is killed in battle and no one can defend him.

Bierce's irony, no doubt, points to the irrationality and monstrosity of war, and yet his own ironic assaults are regulated by an ill logic that parallels the one ruling the army world. Captain Ransom, though aware all along that he is attacking his own troops, is too much of a soldier to question the orders received. He is chronically incapable of reasoning beyond the letter of military codes. Quite appropriately, when he himself becomes the victim of the rigidity of those iron laws, he does not even say a word to try to save his life. The execution that ends the tale—and which could also be seen as

Bierce's act of poetic justice against Ransom's total lack of common sense—duplicates the absurdity of the captain's own blind faith in discipline. He is, after all, only guilty of having carried out his orders; yet he must die. If Bierce's intention is to show his readers the absurdity of war and military life, one must note that his fictional world too is fed by a fascination for the absurd that mirrors the irrationality he seemingly wishes to unmask.

War, as Solomon argues, may well be "full of startling chances," but so is Bierce's fiction. Whether one finds his plots and situations forced or not, it would be hard to deny that their ironies have a certain "journalistic" flavor that would generally be associated with the sensationalist stories of crimes, scandals, and disaster that loomed very large in the yellow press of the day. Although it would be unfair to reduce Bierce's civil-war stories to their plot outlines, his tales too seem to exploit the popular demand for unusual, incredible, puzzling, irrational events. At the same time, they never point to any reality beyond that of the text itself. War, in his stories, is never treated as the result of larger social, political, or economic forces. War is a *given*, a second nature, an inescapable self-sufficient reality that provides Bierce's characters with all the knowledge they need to have.

More importantly, perhaps, like popular journalism of the day, Bierce's tales are programmed to evoke astonishment. Several of Bierce's war stories strive to perplex and shock the reader precisely by resorting to what Roland Barthes has called "disturbed causality." In "One Kind of Officer," for example, one would expect the captain to fire on his own men because he is a spy or a traitor. On the contrary, he does so because he is a supremely loyal soldier. In "An Affair of Outposts" one would think that Armisted would exploit the opportunity of taking revenge on the Governor. He does not: his "revenge" is to save his enemy's life. Similarly, in "A Coup de Grace" Madwell is brought to kill his friend Sergeant Halcrow in order to spare him further pain. In the strange, sensational world of Bierce's war stories, logic and normal causality are constantly subverted.

But Bierce makes an even more generous use of another type of disturbed causality, "the relation of coincidence." In "A Horseman in the Sky" Carter Druse, who, though from Virginia, has joined the Union Army, must fire on an enemy who has come too close to his camp and could report crucial strategic information to the Confederate Army. That man is his father. In "The Mocking Bird" Private Grayrock, while on duty as a night sentinel, fires at the "indistinct outlines of a human figure." Later he discovers he has killed his own twin brother, from whom he had been long separated. In "The Affair at Coulter's Notch" Captain Coulter, another southerner who has joined the Union, is ordered to engage the enemy encamped near his family house, and he bombs to death his own wife and child. In "One of the Missing" a recently shelled barn collapses on the scout, Jerome Searing, leaving him trapped by a timber and with his cocked rifle "protruding from a pile of debris . . . aimed at the exact centre of his head."

The sensationalist elements of Bierce's tales have not gone unnoticed among critics. Larzer Ziff, for example, has written that in the Civil War stories "grotesque coincidences abound, in contempt of the natural laws of probability." Cathy Davidson, on the other hand, has tried to answer the accusation that Bierce too often resorts to trick endings by arguing that his endings "are effectively designed to emphasize the author's narrative manipulations" (p. 4). For Davidson, the shocks generated by the text encourage the reader to reconsider the logic of the narration by calling for a second reading. As "open-ended and incomplete" texts, the best of Bierce's stories construct war episodes as "inescapably indeterminate" events: "The various perspectives, including the narrator's, give us different possible ways of looking at men at war—and, also, at peace—but no way of validating any particular vision." In other words, whereas some critics consider Bierce's plots strained and too sensational, Davidson points to the fact that they generate reading problems of impossible solution. The reader is not instructed as to whether Druse was right or wrong in firing on his father, nor given any counsel on how to interpret the unfailing obedience of people like Ransom and Coulter, or the final scene of "A Coup de Grace."

Davidson obviously believes that Bierce's texts call for "critical," "creative" readings, that they disclose new scenarios affording the reader a perspective from which war and the martial ideal can be condemned as dehumanizing and immoral. This point of view is far too optimistic. Davidson's reading model is obviously that of the contemporary post-structuralist moment, and she does not do much to show its applicability to the social and historical context in which Bierce operated. At any rate, the rhetorical and structural peculiarities she discerns in Bierce's tales are also common to texts (like those of the yellow press) which one would not normally call open-ended. Like several contemporary critics, Davidson tends to reify the category of indeterminacy by considering it as an automatic source of critical, open-minded, mature, responsible attitudes. The ambiguity and indeterminacy of Bierce's tales can be seen as generating effects rather different from the ones imagined by Davidson. No matter how nihilistic the general outlook of his texts may appear, and no matter how shockingly uncompromising their description of the horrors of war may be, the forces that dominate the world of war are those of a power *beyond* human control. In some sense Bierce allows his readers to have their cake and eat it too: they can morally condemn the perversity of war and at the same time blame it on the obscure design of a Destiny no one has really any ability to influence. Bierce's war universe is ahistorical not because it does not contain enough circumstantial details on the events presented but because the category of historical causality is replaced by Fate. Fate, as anyone knows, cannot be influenced by humans.

The main limit of Bierce's critique of war, therefore, is that nobody can really be held responsible for its horrors. In a piece he published some years after his Civil War tales, Bierce wrote:

> That is all the nonsense about "the horrors of war," in so far as the detestable phrase implies that they are worse than those of peace; they are more striking and impressive, that is all.... Wars are expensive, doubtless, but somebody gets the money; it is not thrown into the sea.... [Besides a] quarter-century of peace will make a nation of blockheads and scoundrels. Patriotism is a vice, but is a larger vice, and a nobler, than the million petty ones which it promotes in peace to swallow up in war. In the thunder of guns it becomes respectable.

The man upholding this philosophy of war is sarcastically labeled by Bierce a "superior intelligence." Yet his views are not refuted; they may not be Bierce's own, but they exemplify the deadlock into which his critique of war inevitably runs. Impermeable to his attacks on myths of military glory and heroic exploits, the martial spirit reemerges, phoenix-like, as a positive, cleansing force necessary to counter the corruption of modern society. Bierce's failure to position himself outside the martial discourse of his time shows that the war fever of the 1890s was hegemonic even in areas where it was contested. At the same time it also shows that while the causes that bring people to rationally and systematically plan ways to kill one another may be difficult, perhaps even impossible, to assess with scientific accuracy, to abdicate altogether all logical categories can only lead one to abandon the world of history and eventually blame every *man*-produced horror on Fate and Nature. Such an imperfect unmasking of the logic of war is very likely to bring one back, as in the case of the "superior intelligence," to a praise of the martial spirit since it does not supplement the criticism of weapons with any weapons of criticism.

Source: Giorgio Mariani, "Ambrose Bierce's Civil War Stories and the Critique of the Martial Spirit," in *Studies in American Fiction*, Vol. 19, No. 2, Autumn 1991, pp. 221–28.

Eric Solomon

In the following excerpt, Solomon identifies the source of Bierce's "bitter irony": the failure of reason, particularly amidst the madness of war.

In his brilliant study, *The Art of Satire* (1940), David Worcester defines cosmic irony as the satire of frustration which has a particular relevance for post-Copernican man, who is no longer the center of his universe. Ambrose Bierce's short stories of war, *Tales of Soldiers* (1891), are vignettes of cosmic irony wherein man is brought to realize his insignificance in the face of the all-encompassing universe of war as well as the futility of all "normal" acts and aspirations. Only Stephen Crane has written as powerfully as Bierce about the shock of recognition brought on by the Civil War.

The keynote of Bierce's war fiction is frustration. His soldiers are chagrined by their limits of knowledge and their lack of control. As Bierce states in his military memoirs, "Bits of Autobiography," "It is seldom indeed that a subordinate officer knows anything about the disposition of the enemy's forces... or precisely whom he is fighting. As for the rank and file, they can know nothing more of the matter than the arms they carry." Man in war, afflicted by the failure of reason and the impact of collective suffering, is also unable to live up to his preconceived ideals. Again in the memoirs, we find Bierce telling us of a gallant charge that has been beaten back by a heavy fire: "Lead had scored its old time victory over steel; the heroic had broken its great heart against the commonplace. There are those who say that it is sometimes otherwise." These two

"AMBROSE BIERCE'S SHORT STORIES OF WAR, *TALES OF SOLDIERS* (1891), ARE VIGNETTES OF COSMIC IRONY WHEREIN MAN IS BROUGHT TO REALIZE HIS INSIGNIFICANCE IN THE FACE OF THE ALL-ENCOMPASSING UNIVERSE OF WAR AS WELL AS THE FUTILITY OF ALL 'NORMAL' ACTS AND ASPIRATIONS."

concepts, unreason and failure, provide the basis for the bitter irony of Bierce's brief, rapid anecdotes, which silhouette the blackest side of war.

The fifteen extremely short "Tales of Soldiers" included in the collection, *In the Midst of Life*, strike a mean between violently contrived naturalism—replete with disgusting ugliness and shocking coincidence—and the accumulation of exact, realistic, and factual observations of combat life. There can be no doubt that the author loads the dice in each of his tales. The theme of every story is the death of the good, the honest, and the brave. A Northern soldier kills his rebel father; a young enlisted man on guard duty discovers his brother's corpse; a gunner destroys his own house, murdering his wife and children. All the gestures of heroism turn out to be empty. Certainly the coincidences are over-emphasized for added ironic effect in these war stories as in all of Bierce's work. The mordant cynicism of *The Devil's Dictionary* and *Fantastic Fables*, the misanthropic savagery of Bierce's treatment of insanity and the supernatural in *Can Such Things Be?* do not lead to an objective point of view. Life is terrible, and war is the epitome of its misery.

War fits Bierce's philosophy perfectly. The very nature of combat that involves a heightening, a tension, an absurdity of situation, an incongruity that calls for satire, suits his dark approach. In Bierce's "Tales of Civilians" which make up the second half of *In the Midst of Life*, his stories seem labored and contrived. The writer must spend much more time to build up the situation than in the war stories, where the background may be taken for granted simply because war is war. The later stories become discursive—an almost fatal flaw for an epigrammatic method—since Bierce must describe the mining camps or the San Francisco social hierarchy; within the war context everything is understood at once. The military situation, by its nature rapid and simple, supplies its own foreshortening. Wilson Follett, perhaps Bierce's most acute critic, points out that the chief artistic weakness in his fiction comes from the substitution of an external irony for the irony inherent in the nature of things. War, with its own frame of irony, is the finest subject for "Bitter Bierce's" corruscating, witty excursions into fiction.

Bierce had ample opportunity to learn about war first-hand. He enlisted in the Ohio Volunteers at the age of nineteen, young enough for the ironies of war to become an integral part of his education. Bierce later spoke of his six years of soldiering as spent under a magic spell, "something new under a new sun." He was a success as a soldier. He rose through the ranks to become a sergeant, then a lieutenant, and finally, as a topographical engineer, he became a member of the staff of General W. B. Hazen. Bierce sums up his war experiences with an old soldier's quiet modesty: " . . . although hardly more than a boy in years, I had served at the front from the beginning of the trouble, and had seen enough of war to give me a fair understanding of it."

He was at Shiloh, Stone's River (Murfreesboro), Chickamauga, Kenesaw Mountain, and Franklin, among other engagements. Like almost every veteran who lives long enough, Bierce is able in his memoirs to cast a gloss of sentiment over army life, but he is realistic enough to comprehend that this warm sentiment is not called for. "Is it not strange" he reminisced, "that the phantoms of a blood-stained period have so airy a grace and look with so tender eyes?—that I recall with difficulty the dangers and death and horrors of the time, and without effort all that was gracious and picturesque?" We must not be misled by his fine war record and vintage memories. Bierce's war recollections are also sprinkled with the materials that go into his stories—the irony of a man named Abbot being killed by a shell with the foundry mark "Abbot" on it, or the ghastly sight of his dead comrades after they had been trampled by a herd of swine. While Bierce enjoyed the test of combat, the companionship and the excitement of war, he was revolted, intellectually, by the harsh brutalities of a repellent, paradoxical world.

Moving from memoir to fiction, Bierce found the short, almost elliptical story to be his ideal form. As critics have been quick to point out, Bierce learned a great deal from Edgar Allan Poe's theories of fiction. Like Poe, Bierce is highly selective, fixing upon the decisive, revealing moment. For example, he catches the instant of an execution in his famous "An Occurrence at Owl Creek Bridge," the intense immediacy of the discovery of cowardice and courage in the two protagonist of "Parker Adderson, Philosopher," or the momentary stasis in "A Horseman in the Sky," where a boy quietly presses the trigger and his father's body slowly falls into space.

Unquestionably, Bierce's plots are forced. Consider the manipulation for effect in "An Affair of Outposts." Here a young man, Armisted, informs the governor of his state that he wants a commission in the army in order to die in battle because his wife has taken up with some unknown person. Much later, the governor visits the battlefield, wanders too far, is endangered by an enemy attack, and saved by Armisted, who dies in the attempt—but not until both men realize that they share the knowledge that the governor is the villain of the piece. The bare plot outline, as always, hardly does justice to the story, which gains its effect from the conjunction of the civilian and military frames of reference and the bitingly sarcastic tone of the narrative. Yet this example shows how Bierce uses a highly unusual military situation that focuses the whole history of his characters onto one remarkable event. Since war is full of startling chances, the author's controlling hand is less obtrusive than it might be.

Although Bierce's figures are flat (to use E. M. Forster's term), each story expresses a deep psychological trauma, one that ends in madness or loss. Again, war is the proper setting for the intensified emotion Bierce presents. In war character becomes automatized, part of the military machine. Relying on this firm military context, Bierce easily sketches as much or as little of his heroes' past lives as he desires. The immediate impression is important in the war construct. So the hero of "An Occurrence at Owl Creek Bridge" is a spy who is about to be hanged—that much is germane to the story. We take for granted the reason for his being in this situation and what his beliefs are.

Bierce provides the barest minimum of character description:

> Peyton Farquhar was a well-to-do planter of an old and highly respected Alabama family. Being a slave owner and like other slave owners a politician, he was naturally an original secessionist and ardently devoted to the Southern cause. Circumstances of an imperious nature, which it is unnecessary to relate here, had prevented him from taking service with the gallant army . . .

Who he is makes little difference. How he reacts to war is important. Bierce's attitude towards plot and character may be cursory, but his fictional treatment of war is, with the exception of the work of Crane (and possibly Rudyard Kipling), the most extensive in nineteenth century English and American fiction. Bierce's subject is man in war. He does not heighten his fiction with the details of war in the manner of John W. De Forest or John Esten Cooke; rather he steeps his stories in the aura, the meaning of battle. Bierce captures the principle that lies behind the facts. He catches war at its sources, and he makes it an intensification of personal experience. . . .

Source: Eric Solomon, "The Bitterness of Battle: Ambrose Bierce's War Fiction," in *Midwest Quarterly*, Vol. 4, No. 2, January 1964, pp. 147–65.

Stuart C. Woodruff

In the following excerpt, Woodruff argues that although Bierce was cynical about the possibility of meaning in human life, he nevertheless demonstrated "genuine concern" for the agony of his characters in his Civil War stories.

In his journalism and satiric verse, and especially in *The Devil's Dictionary*, Bierce is primarily concerned with castigating a flawed humanity, "a world of fools and rogues, blind with superstition, tormented with envy, consumed with vanity, selfish, false, cruel, cursed with illusions—frothing mad!" In his short stories, on the other hand, Bierce's characteristic theme is the inscrutable universe itself, whose mechanisms checkmate man's every attempt to assert his will or live his dreams. If the universe is not actively hostile or malevolent, as in many of his tales of the supernatural, it is at best always indifferent to human need. From birth, that "first and direst of all disasters," to death, life is but the "spiritual pickle preserving the body from decay." This dismal concept of the human situation is Bierce's central imaginative impulse in his short stories, the idea that gives shape to his fictional world. Repeatedly, his protagonists become enmeshed in some fatal trap or are destroyed by uncontrollable fears. They move in ignorance toward their

> "HIS CHARACTERS ARE CREDIBLE EVEN WHEN THEIR DILEMMAS ARE NOT, BECAUSE HE BELIEVED IN THE AGONY OF THEIR ORDEAL, EVEN IF HE BELIEVED IN LITTLE ELSE."

destiny, ground into oblivion by some spectacular ordering of events, or else unhinged by their encounter with the supernatural. To Bierce the picture was "infinitely pathetic and picturesque."

Although Bierce's expository writing was largely devoted to excoriating human folly, he would occasionally hold forth upon a universe whose Maker, as Stein tells Marlow in *Lord Jim*, was a "little mad." Like many nineteenth-century pessimists, Bierce was sensitive to the implications of scientific determinism and to the operation of vast impersonal forces in nature which reduced man to the status of a puppet jerked by the strings of chance. In *The Devil's Dictionary* he defines a calamity as "a more than commonly plain and unmistakable reminder that the affairs of this life are not of our own ordering," and in one of his newspaper columns he remarks: "I believe that in the word 'chance,' we have the human name of a malign and soulless intelligence bestirring himself in earthly affairs with the brute unrest of Enceladus underneath his mountain." Victim of what Bierce calls in one of his tales "the pitiless perfection of the divine, eternal plan," man vainly sends his prayers on high:

> From Earth to Heaven in unceasing ascension flows a stream of prayer for every blessing that man desires, yet man remains unblest, the victim of his own folly and passions, the sport of fire, flood, tempest and earthquake, afflicted with famine and disease, war, poverty and crime, his world an incredible welter of evil, his life a curse and his hope a lie.

As a scientific determinist, Bierce believed in evolution through natural selection, but to him it implied no march toward human perfection. Instead, he saw man caught in an eternal round of progress and disintegration. As a part of nature's principles of force and strife, man, innately selfish, engaged in an endless series of wars which destroyed the capable and strong while preserving the feeble and incompetent. Man's attempts at humanitarian and social reform, such as the rehabilitation of criminals, salvaged the very misfits and "incapables whom Nature is trying to 'weed out.'" Similarly, Bierce saw a strange irony in medical science, "which is mainly concerned in reversing the beneficent operation of natural laws and saving the inefficient to perpetuate their inefficiency." Scientific progress and discovery had managed to prolong man's life, but in so doing, had intensified the struggle for existence through overpopulation and increased competition. The basic paradox was that the very means by which man would save himself and improve his lot multiplied his problems instead of solving them. To Bierce, "the one goal of civilization is barbarism; to the condition whence it emerged a nation must return, and every invention, every discovery, every beneficent agency hastens the inevitable end." Consequently, "peace is more fatal than war, for all must die, and in peace more are born. The bullet forestalls the pestilence by proffering a cleaner and decenter death."

Perhaps Bierce's most violent diatribe against the inhospitable universe and the clearest expression of his attitude occurs in an essay sarcastically entitled "Natura Benigna." Despite the mannered and rhetorical flourishes, the violence of Bierce's assault suggests something of his own frustration and rage over a world in which "Howe'er your choice may chance to fall,/ You'll have no hand in it at all." Because Bierce always insisted, as did Poe, that a storyteller must remain detached and impersonal in his narrations, such personal concern is usually disguised in his fiction. Its deliberate concealment or distortion in the direction of macabre humor has caused several of Bierce's critics to call him "inhuman" or "without pity." As the following quotation from "Natura Benigna" indicates however, Bierce's frequent claim that "nothing matters" requires careful qualification:

> In all the world there is no city of refuge—no temple in which to take sanctuary, clinging to the horns of the altar—no "place apart" where, like hunted deer, we can hope to elude the baying pack of Nature's malevolences.... Dodge, turn and double how we can, there's no eluding them; soon or late some of them have him by the throat and his spirit returns to the God who gave it—and gave them.

Particularly evident in this essay is Bierce's compulsive desire to assault what disturbs him most profoundly. The thought of that "pack of Nature's malevolences" triggers a kind of frenzied despair:

> What a fine world it is, to be sure—a darling little world, "so suited to the needs of man." A globe of liquid fire, straining within a shell relatively no thicker than that of an egg—a shell constantly cracking and in momentary danger of going all to pieces! Three-fourths of this delectable field of human activity are covered with an element in which we cannot breathe, and which swallows us by myriads.... Of the other one-fourth more than one-half is uninhabitable by reason of climate. On the remaining one-eighth we pass a comfortless and precarious existence in disputed occupancy with countless ministers of death and pain—pass it in fighting for it, tooth and nail, a hopeless battle in which we are foredoomed to defeat. Everywhere death, terror, lamentation and the laughter that is more terrible than tears—the fury and despair of a race hanging on to life by the tips of its fingers! And the prize for which we strive, "to have and to hold"—what is it? A thing that is neither enjoyed while had, nor missed when lost. So worthless it is, so unsatisfying, so inadequate to purpose, so false to hope and at its best so brief, that for consolation and compensation we set up fantastic faiths of an aftertime in a better world from which no confirming whisper has ever reached us across the void. Heaven is a prophecy uttered by the lips of despair, but Hell is an inference from analogy.

Such a chilling vision, nourished by Bierce's own experiences in the Civil War, his incisive knowledge of "how it was," provides the main creative impulse for many of his stories, especially those contained in *Tales of Soldiers and Civilians.* The war became for Bierce a controlling metaphor of the world and its ways. Always irrationally destructive, war reduced life to its lowest common denominators; the war-world he depicted made a unifying dramatic action of the hopeless struggle for existence. Its elements of surprise, confusion, and the predatory instinct constituted that blind causality which struck with devastating and unpredictable finality. The common soldier, an expendable pawn ignorant of the larger strategies and issues, was shifted about at random, fighting his enemies in treacherous forest depths or dense fog. Shells leapt out at him from nowhere, stupid or depraved officers gave disastrous orders, irrational terror overwhelmed him. Under such pressures individual will or desire became not only impossible but irrelevant, or was converted into an obsessive longing to rush wildly into certain annihilation....

Bierce's fatalism is very similar to Thomas Hardy's, and both writers must necessarily rely on coincidence to enforce their particular vision. "One of the Missing," for example, is reminiscent of Hardy's poem "The Convergence of the Twain" in which the ship *Titanic* and the gigantic iceberg move relentlessly toward a collision that "jars two hemispheres." Both story and poem, moreover, point up the futility of any assertion of human will. But in a way "coincidence" is a misleading term, for Hardy and Bierce are careful to show at work an intricate pattern of causal connection, unseen by those involved but all too discernible to the detached gaze of an omniscient author. As Edmund Wilson once said of Dickens's novels, the mysterious connection events have with each other becomes the moral of the tale. And in Bierce, the plot becomes the trap that snaps shut on the helpless protagonist. Virtually all of Bierce's stories, in fact, have what has been called a "snap ending"; while the term is sometimes justly used in a pejorative sense, it is important to see how Bierce's conclusions derive from his ironic point of view....

Writing to a young female admirer in 1901, Bierce expressed the hope that she was "well and happy—as happy as it is consonant with the plans of God's universe for any of his helpless creatures to be—or believe themselves to be." This sense of man's helplessness, of the terrible inevitability of his fate, is the most persistent theme running through Bierce's stories, especially those dealing with war. For Bierce, war was the ideal metaphor to define the human predicament, not simply because he had known war intimately, but because it was the clearest demonstration of how the instinctive and the accidental combined to thwart human endeavor. But war's most important function was to represent what Bierce regarded as the central fact of existence: one's physical annihilation. Believing that the "mind or spirit or soul of man was the product of his physical being, the result of chemical combinations," Bierce looked upon death as the "awful mystery," awful because of its irreducible finality, its negation of all of man's hopes and creative impulses. As his friend David Jordan wrote: "Whether glory or conquest or commercial greed be war's purpose the ultimate result of war is death. Its essential feature is the slaughter of the young, the brave, the ambitious, the hopeful." Bierce's war stories are fables of life's essential movement toward disillusion, defeat, and death. They concentrate and accelerate the inexorable process of disintegration. Thus the demolished building in "One of the Missing" becomes Searing's "sole universe" as his "throbs tick off eternities," and the child in "Chickamauga" has "his little world swung half around" in a matter of hours.

For reasons that will be discussed in a subsequent chapter on Bierce's severe limitations as an artist, his stories always fall short of tragedy. Nevertheless, in the best of them, to be found among the tales of soldiers, there is a genuine pathos that arises from Bierce's intense awareness of a suffering humanity. . . .

The congealing sense of doom that permeates Bierce's war stories suggests a Calvinism from which all sense of grace or benevolent purpose has been removed. As one critic has put it:

> Bierce had rejected the God of his New England ancestors and his Puritan upbringing, but the code that he retained implied a metaphysic almost identical to the Calvinism that he denied. A harshly personal God was replaced by a harshly impersonal Fate. Every man's slightest action was preordained, and his duty was to submit to the mysterious workings of the supernatural.

One important effect of this rigid fatalism is to minimize or ignore the question of man as moral agent in favor of portraying the effects of a deterministic universe. This is not to say that Bierce was indifferent to moral values—the whole body of his journalism and satire shows how accountable he held man. But in the short stories his characters have no inner moral life in any decisive sense. What they do have is a kind of rudimentary psychology which reacts according to the stimulus they receive and their "constitutional tendency." Bierce's characters are really human types—types of susceptibility—rather than fully drawn individuals. They may have a history, but they lack an identity apart from the circumstances they are exposed to.

Since these circumstances are invariably destructive in one way or another, the story ends when the maximum pressure has been brought to bear on the protagonist. If he does not actually die, at the very least his private world collapses and death would even seem preferable—the "boon of oblivion" that Madwell accords his friend. He is a "humble, unheroic Prometheus" because his suffering serves no discernible purpose, and because his fate is not something consciously risked in defiance of the gods. Fate, like Major Halcrow concealed in the "haunted forest," simply comes upon him unaware. If the protagonist commits suicide, it is either because he realizes he is inextricably caught or because, like George Thurston, he has long recognized his fate as some inherent compulsion which makes life unbearable. In any event Bierce's characters are never responsible for what happens to them. Often, like Captain Madwell or Jerome Searing, they are good, brave men or, like the child in "Chickamauga," merely ignorant and naïve. Essentially passive, sometimes literally immobilized like Prometheus in his chains, they have an interior life of acute sensation. Because we can know them only through their feelings, which are usually very unpleasant or painful, we can only respond to them with pity. We do not really know *them*; we know their suffering.

Because it was the reality of their suffering and frustration that Bierce responded to, his war figures make a serious claim upon our attention. Only in the war stories does Bierce achieve the sense of genuine concern for human frailty endlessly cheated and baffled by life. His characters are credible even when their dilemmas are not, because he believed in the agony of their ordeal, even if he believed in little else.

Source: Stuart C. Woodruff, "'The Divine Eternal Plan,'" in *The Short Stories of Ambrose Bierce: A Study in Polarity*, University of Pittsburgh Press, 1964, pp. 19–53.

SOURCES

Bierce, Ambrose, *The Devil's Dictionary*, in *The Collected Works of Ambrose Bierce*, Gordian, 1966, p. 49.

———, "A Horseman in the Sky," in *Phantoms of a Blood-stained Period: The Complete Civil War Writings of Ambrose Bierce*, edited by Russell Duncan and David J. Klooster, University of Massachusetts Press, 2002, pp. 57–62.

Blume, Donald T., *Ambrose Bierce's Civilians and Soldiers in Context: A Critical Study*, Kent State University Press, 2004, pp. 145–60.

Caswell, Bernice L., "Character Education and the Short Story," in the *English Journal*, Vol. 23, No. 5, 1934, pp. 406–409.

Davidson, Cathy N., *The Experimental Fictions of Ambrose Bierce: Structuring the Ineffable*, University of Nebraska Press, 1984, pp. 1–5.

Duncan, Russell, and David J. Klooster, eds., *Phantoms of a Blood-stained Period: The Complete Civil War Writings of Ambrose Bierce*, University of Massachusetts Press, 2002, pp. 5–31, 64.

Freud, Sigmund, *The Interpretation of Dreams*, in *The Standard Edition of the Complete Psychological Works of Sigmund Freud*, Vol. V, edited by James Strachey, Hogarth, 1958, pp. 260–66.

Joshi, S. T., and David E. Schultz, *Ambrose Bierce: An Annotated Bibliography of Primary Sources*, Greenwood, 1999, p. 20.

"Lincoln's First Inaugural Address," in *American Treasures of the Library of Congress*, http://www.loc.gov/exhibits/treasures/trt039.html (accessed August 19, 2008).

Morris, Roy, Jr., *Ambrose Bierce: Alone in Bad Company*, Crown, 1995, pp. 31–2.

Olson, Helen F., "What Is Good Teaching of Written Composition?" in the *English Journal*, Vol. 50, No. 4, April 1961, pp. 238–45.

Owens, David M., *The Devil's Topographer: Ambrose Bierce and the American War Story*, University of Tennessee Press, 2006, pp. 28–36.

Starrett, Vincent, *Ambrose Bierce*, Walter M. Hill, 1920, pp. 27–33.

FURTHER READING

Calhoun, Charles W., ed., *The Gilded Age: Perspectives on the Origins of Modern America*, Rowman & Littlefield, 2d ed., 2006.

This collection of essays by contemporary historians covers a wide range of aspects of late-nineteenth-century American life.

Fuentes, Carlos, *The Old Gringo*, translated by Margaret Sayers Peden, Farrar, Straus and Giroux, 1985.

This magical realist novel is based on Bierce's final trip to Mexico and the mysterious circumstances surrounding his death; the title character of the novel, while not called by the same name, is based on Bierce. One section makes an extended reference to "A Horseman in the Sky."

O'Connor, Richard, *Ambrose Bierce: A Biography*, Little, Brown, 1967.

No full-scale scholarly biography of Bierce has yet appeared. However, the information provided in this older work has not in general been superseded and has been followed exceptionally closely by many later writers.

Stutler, Boyd B., *West Virginia in the Civil War*, Education Foundation, 1966.

This book provides the standard survey of the military actions that inspired "A Horseman in the Sky."

Jim Baker's Blue Jay Yarn

MARK TWAIN

1880

"Jim Baker's Blue Jay Yarn," by Mark Twain, first appeared in 1880 in *A Tramp Abroad*, a book about an American traveling in Europe. "Jim Baker's Blue Jay Yarn" is a fable of sorts, in that it features a talking blue jay, an unusual situation, and a comment about human nature. Yarns and tall tales were a popular form of humor writing in Twain's day, and many of his stories appeal to audiences who favor that genre.

The story centers on a determined blue jay who mistakenly believes that a hole in a roof is a hole he can fill with acorns. When a whole flock of blue jays arrive on the scene, they discover the first jay's folly and have a good laugh. The site becomes something of a tourist attraction in the blue jay community. Throughout the story, the narrator describes the language of blue jays and other animals in a matter-of-fact way that adds to the humor of the story.

"Jim Baker's Blue Jay Yarn" explores themes of determination and language. For readers in Twain's day, both themes were interesting and relevant. In the wake of the Civil War, two distinct cultures—those of the North and the South—struggled to unify into a single culture. Determination had led them into the war, and determination would have to bring them back together. Differing ways of expression and of handling conflict relate to the theme of language and communication as well.

Mark Twain *(AP Images. Reproduced by permission)*

Modern readers, who can find the story in a 1992 edition of the collection *The Celebrated Jumping Frog, and Other Stories*, may be unsettled by a simile that makes use of what is now a derogatory term for African Americans. In Twain's day, this was a common word that did not bear the offensive connotation it now carries. Just as in Twain's famous novel *Adventures of Huckleberry Finn*, readers must make their own decisions about their willingness to accept the story with the inclusion of this word. In some versions the word in question has been removed, but any version of the story in its original form will include it.

AUTHOR BIOGRAPHY

Samuel Langhorne Clemens, who would later take the pen name Mark Twain, was born on November 30, 1835, in Florida, Missouri. He was the sixth child of Jane Lampton and John Marshall Clemens (a lawyer). In 1839, John moved his family to the port town of Hannibal, Missouri. This move would shape the young Clemens in a deep way, giving rise to his unique voice in American literature. He loved the steamboats coming and going from such places as St. Louis and New Orleans, and his boyhood revolved around the trappings of life near the river, including homemade rafts, swimming, and exploring caves.

Twain ceased to attend private school at the age of twelve, when his father died of pneumonia. At thirteen, he secured a position as a printer's apprentice. Two years later, he became a printer and editorial assistant for his brother's newspaper. This was Twain's first taste of the writing life, and he liked it.

When he was seventeen, Twain began helping his brother manage several newspapers. Like their father, Twain and his brother lacked strong business skills, and the papers struggled. Twain spent three years traveling and writing before rejoining his brother in Keokuk, Iowa, to resume working on newspapers. In 1857, however, Twain left his brother's business with plans to travel to seek his fortune in South America. While traveling down the Mississippi, he became fascinated by life on the river, and he became a river pilot in 1859. It was here he heard the term "mark twain," which refers to a safe navigating depth of two fathoms. During his river travels, he submitted occasional pieces to various publications. More important, he drew inspiration for future novels and short stories. The Mississippi River and the lives of those on and around it inspired Twain in such a way that he would become one of the most important, and uniquely American, writers in English literature.

When the Civil War erupted, river trade slowed to a halt. Twain served briefly in the Confederate army and panned for gold in Nevada. When a fellow journalist challenged him to a duel, Twain fled to San Francisco, where he found newspaper work. He enjoyed his first taste of fame in 1865, when "The Celebrated Jumping Frog of Calavaras County" was published. This led to his first book of collected writings. More travel writing, short stories, novels, and essays followed as Twain's readership grew. *A Tramp Abroad*, in which "Jim Baker's Blue Jay Yarn" first appeared, was published in 1880, between *The Adventures of Tom Sawyer* (1876) and *Adventures of Huckleberry Finn* (1884).

In 1870, Twain married Olivia Langdon, whose father agreed to the marriage despite reservations about his son-in-law. Consequently, Olivia's father gave the couple a furnished home and gave Twain partial ownership of a newspaper in Buffalo. After Olivia's father died during the couple's first year of marriage, Twain and his pregnant wife moved to Hartford, Connecticut, where they stayed for twenty years. They had four children, although one died in infancy and two died in their twenties. Only Clara survived, and her only daughter had no children, ending the line of Twain's descendants.

Twain spent the rest of his career writing and traveling widely to lecture. By the 1890s, both he and his wife were in faltering health. After a trip to Florence, Italy, in 1903, Olivia died. In his final years, Twain was pessimistic and misanthropic. His wit became more malicious, but his admirers continued to buy his books and attend his lectures. In failing health, Twain died near Redding, Connecticut, on April 21, 1910.

PLOT SUMMARY

"Jim Baker's Blue Jay Yarn" is told in the first person by a speaker who matter-of-factly and conversationally tells the reader about a friend of his, Jim Baker, who is able to understand animal talk. The speaker relates secondhand information from Baker, especially about how different kinds of animals talk and how their language and expressions differ. The bulk of the story relates an incident ostensibly witnessed by Baker.

The speaker begins by reiterating something he assumes the reader already knows, which is that animals talk to each other despite the fact that very few people are capable of understanding what they say. His friend Baker, however, is very capable in this area. According to Baker (who is quoted from here to the end of the story), animals speak differently in much the same way people speak differently. Varying degrees of education, vocabulary, and talkativeness are evident in the animal kingdom. Baker asserts that blue jays are among the best of the animal talkers. This is partly because the blue jay himself is more complex and sophisticated, possessing a range of moods and ability to express them. Not only does the blue jay enhance his expression with metaphor, but he possesses an unusual command of language and rarely resorts to bad grammar. Baker contrasts the blue jay's even temper with a cat's excitability, claiming that a cat tends to get overly excited and lets his grammar go.

Describing the blue jay further, Baker claims that he is almost human in his emotional and intellectual complexity. However, he notes, a blue jay is unprincipled and will not hesitate to lie, steal, or break a promise. Blue jays are also skilled at profanity. Again, he contrasts the blue jay with a cat, saying that although a cat can swear, a blue jay is far more skilled in this area. Having introduced the reader to the blue jay, Baker proceeds with a "perfectly true" story about a blue jay.

Seven years ago, the area was all but abandoned, and empty houses were left behind. As Baker sat in front of his cabin, where he could see one of these houses, a blue jay landed on the roof of the empty house. The blue jay had an acorn in its mouth, but when he spoke, the acorn fell. Then the blue jay noticed a knothole in the roof. He looked into it with one eye and declared that it was in fact a hole, and with great delight, he picked up his acorn and dropped it into the hole. He was happy until he realized that he did not hear the acorn fall and strained to look into the hole to see the acorn. When he was unable to see it, he got another acorn to see if he could hear or see it fall. When he fails, he continues to get more acorns, eventually concluding that this must be some new kind of hole. He is determined to fill it up, regardless of how long it takes or how many acorns he must find.

Baker describes the exhaustion of the blue jay as he keeps bringing acorns to the hole and dropping them in, trying to hear or see them fall. For all his hard work, he sees no sign of any of the acorns, which confuses and frustrates the blue jay. Taking a break, the blue jay leans against the chimney to rest and swear like Baker had never heard before. During this time, another blue jay comes along, and the first blue jay tells him about his trouble with the hole. The second blue jay investigates the hole and, seeing nothing, calls for more blue jays. None of them could see a sign of any of the acorns that the first blue jay had dropped in the hole.

The blue jays launch into debates and discussions about the mysterious hole and the fate of the acorns, calling in more blue jays and more opinions. Baker claims that there must have been five thousand birds working on the problem. They examined the house until finally a blue jay landed on the partially opened door and looked inside. He realized what had happened and called all the other blue jays to see how the first blue jay had foolishly been trying to fill an entire house with acorns. They all looked into the house and laughed very hard. Baker says that after that, the blue jays stayed for about an hour to laugh and talk about the situation. Baker notes that not only do blue jays have a great sense of humor, they also have a great memory. For the next three years during the summer, blue jays came back to that house to look down the hole in the roof. In fact, other birds started to visit the site to enjoy the story of what happened there. Baker concludes the story by telling the reader that all of the birds enjoyed their visits, except an owl from Nova Scotia who failed to see the humor in it. But the same owl was also disappointed in his visit to Yosemite.

CHARACTERS

Another Jay

A second blue jay happens by while the first blue jay is working so hard to fill the mysterious hole with acorns. Overhearing the colorful frustrated language of the main blue jay, the second jay stops to ask what he is doing. When he hears the first blue jay's story, he asks for more details and then calls for three more jays to come hear and discuss the problem of the acorn-swallowing hole. This, of course, leads to more jays being called in to investigate the problem.

Jim Baker

Jim Baker is the one who tells the story of the blue jay. The narrator describes him as "a middle-aged, simple-hearted miner who had lived in a lonely corner of California." Before he tells the story, though, he discusses his ability to understand what animals say when they speak. He explains how different kinds of animals, and different kinds of birds in particular, have different ways of speaking. It is clear that Baker has put a lot of time into observing the speech patterns of animals, and he has put a lot of thought into analyzing those patterns. According to Baker, some birds use proper grammar, while others do not; some use plain speech, while some use figurative language and long speeches; some curse more than others; and some are more likely to express their moods in language than others. Baker is very matter-of-fact in these explanations, and the reader almost feels that he is talking about people instead of animals. Baker never qualifies his assertions or apologizes if they sound ridiculous. When he begins the story of the blue jay, he does not editorialize much, instead letting the blue jay's personality carry the story. Interestingly, Baker remains detached from the events he witnesses, rather than offering the misguided bird any kind of help or insight.

Blue Jay

The main character of the story is a blue jay, whose speech is understood by Jim Baker. The blue jay is very talkative and is usually talking to himself constantly. He is also impulsive, social, industrious, and persistent. He tends to focus completely on one thing at a time, whether it is filling the hole or laughing with his friends about it. When the reader meets him, the blue jay is carefree, has food in his mouth, and is looking for a place to alight. When he discovers a hole, he is stubborn and determined to fill it despite the fact that no matter how many acorns he drops in it, he can never see where the acorns go or determine in any way how long it will take him to fill the hole. This demonstrates that the blue jay is stubborn for the sake of being stubborn. His goals are arbitrary and silly, but he refuses to budge from his goal. He is diligent and tireless in his pursuit. When another blue jay discovers that the hole is actually in a roof, the first blue jay is able to laugh at himself for trying to fill a whole house and not even realizing it. He is a social creature who is happy to have all of the other blue jays around to perch and talk and laugh for hours. He is secure and not egotistical. He is gregarious and has a sense of humor.

Narrator

The narrator appears briefly at the beginning of the story, and his sole purpose is to make introductions. He establishes with the reader the fact that animals communicate with one another, and then he tells about his friend Jim Baker, who can actually understand what animals say. Though speaking in the first person, the narrator tells nothing about himself personally, and he exhibits no emotion about the story or Baker. Once he has brought the reader and Baker together, he exits the story entirely.

Old Jay

Baker tells the reader that finally, after a sizeable flock of blue jays had arrived at the house to figure out the mystery of the hole, one old jay happened to land on the door that was standing ajar. When he looked past the door, he realized that it was a door to an entire house, and he quickly realized what the foolish first blue jay had been trying to do. He responds by calling all the jays to see that the blue jay had been trying to fill up a house, not a regular hole. Readers should note that the old jay solves the mystery not through his wisdom or experience but by chance. And when he does realize the problem, he makes a big show of it rather than quietly telling the first jay in a way that might have preserved his dignity.

Owl

The humorless owl is the only bird mentioned specifically in the story that is not a blue jay. Baker says that other birds came to see the infamous hole, but only the owl is described. The owl, from Nova Scotia, came to America to visit Yosemite. He decided to stop by and see this hole he had heard about, but when he saw it, he failed to see the humor in it. Baker adds that the owl was also disappointed in Yosemite, which suggests that he has a grumpy, unimpressed nature.

THEMES

Determination

The fable about the blue jay is centered around his stubborn determination to fill a hole with acorns. It proves a silly exercise, but one that the blue jay is completely committed to seeing completed. He is not the least bit swayed by the fact that when he drops an acorn into the hole and tries desperately to see where it went, he never can. His solution is not to give up on the goal or even to investigate the hole but to keep doggedly dropping acorns in.

In the end, the blue jay's fierce determination adds to the humor of the situation when another blue jay alerts him to the fact that he is actually trying to fill up an entire house with acorns. The scope of the project coupled with the blue jay's blind determination to complete it makes the situation utterly ridiculous. The blue jay had set all reason aside in the pursuit of his goal. The reader cannot help but wonder what the blue jay would accomplish if he were to apply the same determination to something worthwhile.

TOPICS FOR FURTHER STUDY

- Fables have been around since ancient times. They are an effective way to illustrate a point and comment about life or human nature. Write your own fable that teaches a valuable lesson. Use the traditional characteristics of a fable in your work, and consider adding illustrations to bring your story to life.
- Blue jays are known for having strong personalities. Research blue jays and find out how they behave, why they behave the way they do, where they live, and how they impact communities where they live. Given what you have learned, is a blue jay a good choice for the main character of Twain's story? Using examples from the story, write an essay explaining why or why not.
- In the end, the blue jay realizes his own folly and is able to laugh at himself. What if he had a different attitude? Write an alternate ending to the story, keeping the blue jay's characterization consistent, in which the blue jay reacts differently.
- Choose one other work by Mark Twain (novel, short story, or essay) and compare and contrast it to "Jim Baker's Blue Jay Yarn." Prepare a short lecture on Twain's writing using your two examples. Conclude your lecture with other titles your audience might enjoy reading.
- Create a Web site about determination featuring the blue jay and a synopsis of his story on the home page. Using whatever organization and design you think is best, present other examples of determination to inform and inspire visitors to your site. Think about the purpose of your site and decide if you want to focus on the benefits of determination, the pitfalls of misguided determination, or both.

Cabin in forest *(© Richard Ross / Getty Images)*

As with any fable, the animals represent something about human experience or human nature, so the reader is left to question how wisely he applies his own determination to situations that arise.

Language

In this short story, Twain says a lot about the diversity and use of language. The story itself has three distinct speakers: the narrator, Jim Baker, and the blue jay. The narrator speaks briefly to introduce Jim Baker. The narrator's language is straightforward—he plainly states his purpose, and he connects with the reader by asserting that everyone (including the reader, presumably) knows that animals talk. He begins with, "Animals talk to each other, of course. There can be no question about that; but I suppose there are very few people who can understand them." In this way, the narrator uses language to draw the reader immediately into the suspension of disbelief necessary for Jim Baker's story.

Jim Baker's language is distinct from the narrator's and is characterized by exaggeration, storytelling, dialect, and humor. He is "spinning a yarn," which the reader understands from the title of the story. Baker's language is thus energized by his exaggeration and imagery. For example, when describing the way a blue jay talks, Baker says he uses "out-and-out book-talk—and bristling with metaphor, too—just bristling! And as for command of a language—why *you* never see a blue jay get stuck for a word. No man ever did. They just boil out of him!" And when he complains about the bad grammar that a cat uses when excited, Baker declares, "you'll hear grammar that will give you the lockjaw." Another example of hyperbole occurs when Baker is watching the frustrated blue jay and says that the jay "broke loose and cussed himself black in the face," and later he is depicted as "sweating like an ice pitcher." Although he tells the story as if it is true, the reader knows that there is a thin veil separating fiction from a farce of nonfiction.

Finally, there is the language of the blue jay. He is blustering, outspoken, and loud. He speaks his mind about his determination to fill that hole and see where the acorns are going, and he laughs loudly at himself when he realizes his foolishness.

One other way Twain comments on language is through the descriptions of how other animals speak. According to Baker, some animals speak directly, while others use an abundance of flowery words and metaphors; some curse, and others do not; some show their education in the way they speak, while others show their lack of education; and some use better grammar than others, although some animals' use of proper grammar is dependent on their emotional states. In these passages, Twain is illustrating a basic idea about language, which is that people adapt language to their individual needs, personalities, and moods. Language is a tool that is expressive and has an extremely wide range.

STYLE

Tall Tale/Yarn

Twain lets the reader know in the title that "Jim Baker's Blue Jay Yarn" is a far-fetched story. A yarn is just such an entertaining story, usually along the lines of a tall tale; tall tales were popular in frontier and folk literature as a way to present outlandish stories in humorous ways. Tall tales as a genre feature realistic detail and dialect or everyday speech, and they tell of wildly impossible events. Often, tall tales involve ordinary people with extraordinary abilities, such as Paul Bunyan and his extraordinary size and strength. Some tall tales arose around actual historical figures, such as Davy Crockett, Pecos Bill, and Johnny Appleseed. Although typically associated with American storytelling, examples of tall tales are also part of European (especially German) and Australian literature. Twain's story does not center on a person but instead involves an ordinary animal with the extraordinary abilities to reason, speak, and laugh at himself. Jim Baker's matter-of-fact explanations about how different animals use language differently also add to the tall-tale quality of the story. Twain invites the reader into the humor of accepting the story right from the beginning when he asserts that everyone knows animals talk to each other, but he knows only one man who can understand what they are saying. From here, the outlandish events unfold.

Frame Narrative

A frame narrative is a structure in which the author presents a story within a story. Well-known examples of this technique include Geoffrey Chaucer's *Canterbury Tales*, Nathaniel Hawthorne's *The Scarlet Letter*, and Mary Shelley's *Frankenstein*. Shakespeare used this technique for great dramatic purpose and to propel the storyline in *Hamlet*, when Hamlet arranges for an acting troupe to perform a play that acts out his uncle's murder of his father. In some cases, the outer story is the framework for multiple stories, while in other cases the outer story merely provides some context or pretense for the inner story. This is the case with "Jim Baker's Blue Jay Yarn"; the outer story is provided by the narrator as he introduces the reader to Jim Baker. In arranging the tale thus, Twain lends an air of credibility to the story because the narrator seems so reliable. This setup also adds to the humor of the story because the author has gone to the trouble to bring that credible voice to such an outlandish story. It is a tongue-in-cheek presentation of what is clearly identified as a yarn.

Use of Differing Voices

Twain separates the speaking styles of the narrator, Jim Baker, and the blue jay by giving them different voices. The narrator speaks in standard English and presents information in a straightforward way. He is there to introduce Jim Baker without bringing any emotion, humor, or doubt to the story. His main purpose is to give credibility to the idea that Jim Baker is genuinely able to understand what animals say. Once he has established this with the reader, he exits so that Baker can tell the story about the blue jay.

When Baker speaks, the voice is completely different. Although Twain uses quotation marks to designate when Baker is speaking, they are hardly necessary. Baker speaks in a southern vernacular, a nonstandard dialect particular to a region. His idioms and word choice tell about the man through his narrative voice. He is a common man with a knowledge of—if not a love for—hard work, and he has a sense of humor. He is also a keen student of the world around him, noticing the different personalities of different kinds of animals based on the way they speak and interact. Interestingly, the reader gets to know Baker in the same way. His manner of speaking puts the reader at ease and gives the feeling of sitting on a front porch telling stories. The blue jay has a voice similar to Baker's. Both use lively language and vernacular, which reflects their roots being in the same region.

HISTORICAL CONTEXT

Post–Civil War South

During the Civil War (1861–1865), almost 80 percent of healthy, young white Southern men went to fight. In the end, nearly one-third of them perished, while numerous others returned wounded, handicapped, or emotionally traumatized. Where the South had relied on strong patriarchs in families and society, it had to find new ways to move forward. Within families, the losses of fathers, uncles, grandfathers, and brothers meant that a generation grew up without the same strong sense of male leadership that prior generations had. Women assumed stronger roles in their families and also worked harder because the slaves were emancipated.

These issues surrounding the losses of healthy men created major problems for the South as it tried to lurch back into productivity and healing. As a result, the years following the war were uncertain, and poverty grew, with no solution seeming feasible. Problems were made worse by the toll the war exacted on the physical resources in the South. Land was damaged, homes were burned, railroads and manufacturing equipment were destroyed, and livestock were decimated.

The Reconstruction period (1865–1877) was difficult and tense. The North and South attempted to work together to rebuild the nation and set goals for its future. The tasks of punishing Confederate rebels, getting the Southern economy back on its feet without slaves, determining the proper status of African Americans, and neutralizing strong lingering feelings were daunting. The South experienced a basic social change, too, as the aristocratic strata diminished with the expansion of a middle class.

Prior to the Civil War, western expansion had kicked off in the late 1840s with the California gold rush and the end of Mexico's claim to American territories. By the end of the Civil War and Reconstruction, frontier literature was in full force. Tales of the Wild West and its colorful inhabitants captured the imaginations of readers across the nation, and a particular brand of humor emerged. Mark Twain, Artemus Ward, and Bret Harte were among the most important writers in the frontier tradition.

Realism in American Literature (1865–1900)

In the wake of the Civil War, the American economy faced tension between the industrialism of the North and the agrarianism of the South. This, in addition to lingering resentment, the overwhelming destruction of land and equipment, tremendous loss of life, and the South's being forced to remain in the Union, resulted in a nation that was anything but harmonious and unified. At the same time, progress was made in the areas of communication (with the invention of the telephone and the laying of the Atlantic cable) and transportation (with the completion of the transcontinental railroad in 1869 and automobile manufacturing in the 1890s). The strains and changes yielded an atmosphere of doubt and disillusionment, and the emerging works of Charles Darwin and Karl Marx added to this national intellectual mood. America after the Civil War was not the same America to which so many people had pinned their hopes for the future.

As the frontier opened ever wider and the circulation of newspapers and magazines spread, writers saw greater opportunity. While some poetry of this period recalled the English Romantic poets, other new voices emerged, including Walt Whitman and Emily Dickinson. James Whitcomb Riley's poetry spoke of patriotism in

COMPARE & CONTRAST

- **1880s:** Framework stories like "Jim Baker's Blue Jay Yarn," in which a story is told within the context of another story, are very popular. Other examples at the time include the Uncle Remus stories and Henry James's short novel *The Turn of the Screw*.

  Today: Framework stories continue to be popular among readers and moviegoers. Successful examples include Khaled Hosseini's *The Kite Runner*, which tells two stories from the point of view of a single narrator, and William P. Young's *The Shack*, which is told as if written by a ghostwriter who reveals his identity at the beginning as a close friend of the man whose story he is telling.

- **1880s:** Frontier literature captures the imaginations of readers all over the United States. Reading about people braving the American frontier, fighting Indians and each other, panning for gold, and living under rough circumstances provides excitement and intrigue. Writers such as Mark Twain, Artemus Ward, Bret Harte, and Caroline Kirkland gain popularity for their frontier writing.

  Today: Frontier literature has waned in popularity, as the genre was widely explored in previous generations. In the mid- to late twentieth century, television westerns, movie westerns, and novels by writers like Louis L'Amour and Larry McMurtry enjoyed popularity, but interest in this chapter of American history has considerably lessened.

- **1880s:** Stories involving talking animals are accepted forms of humor for children and adults alike. Hans Christian Andersen's fairy tales, first published in the mid-1830s, remain popular; Lewis Carroll's *Alice's Adventures in Wonderland* (1865) entertains its readers with such talking animals as the March Hare and the Cheshire Cat. The popularity and acceptability of such stories pave the way for Rudyard Kipling's *The Jungle Book*, to be released in 1894.

  Today: Stories involving talking animals are written primarily for children. Well-known modern examples include E. B. White's *Charlotte's Web* (first published in 1952 and adapted to film in 1973 and 2006) and high-budget films like Disney's *Finding Nemo*.

warm tones. Little happened in drama, as scripts tended to serve to support famous actors whose names alone could pack the seats. In fiction, uniquely American styles and subjects blossomed. Local-color writing enjoyed widespread popularity. Authors such as Mark Twain, William Dean Howells, Stephen Crane, Edith Wharton, and Henry James established careers that would produce classics of American fiction.

CRITICAL OVERVIEW

Twain's *A Tramp Abroad*, in which "Jim Baker's Blue Jay Yarn" appears, was published in 1880 and is often considered a companion or follow-up to his *Innocents Abroad* (1869). Both include Twain's travel writing, which is imbued with his humorous and often biting observations and commentary. *A Tramp Abroad* is about Twain's travels in Europe and also includes fictional tales such as the blue jay fable. Critics often remark on the loose structure of the book. In fact, the inclusion of the story about the blue jay (which took place in California) comes from a story about a raven in Europe that reminds Twain of the story about the blue jay. While some critics find the rambling course of the book to be hard to follow, others point to its merit. Jeffrey Alan Melton, in *Mark Twain, Travel Books, and Tourism: The Tide of a Great Popular Movement*, notes:

> Although for some readers the narrative suffers as a result of such floating, the rambling structure accurately captures the changing emphasis for American tourists at large, a move away from *seeing* the world as a set of pictures to *being* in the pictures themselves—more settled, more affluent, more experienced, more self-absorbed.

Carl Van Doren, in his book *The American Novel*, finds Twain to be somewhat restricted in employing this form. He remarks that *A Tramp Abroad* continues Twain's "now expected devices in humorous autobiography, without any important innovations. Certain episodes and certain descriptive passages emerge from the general level, but even they only emphasize the debt his imagination owed to memory. Writing too close to his facts he could never be at his richest." A contemporary of Twain's, William Ernest Henley, to the contrary, finds the book delightful and the story of the blue jay a highlight. He wrote in an 1880 edition of the *Athenaeum*, "Of uniform excellence *A Tramp Abroad* is not; but it is very vigorously and picturesquely written throughout; it contains some of the writer's happiest work." He adds that "Jim Baker's Blue Jay Yarn" is "a piece of work that is not only delightful as mere reading, but also of a high degree of merit as literature. It is the best thing in the book though the book is full of good things."

WHAT DO I READ NEXT?

- Translated by Laura Gibbs as part of the "Oxford World's Classics" series, *Aesop's Fables* (2003) contains six hundred fables translated from Latin and Greek. Many of them had never before been translated into English.
- *Riches for All: The California Gold Rush and the World* (2002), edited by Kenneth N. Owens, explains how the gold rush affected California in the mid-nineteenth century and how its impact reached the world. Considering history, economy, and culture, this book provides a comprehensive context that allows students to understand the sweeping nature of the event.
- Mary Ellen Snodgrass's *Encyclopedia of Frontier Literature* (1999) offers more than 500 pages of works spanning genres, authors, regions, time periods, cultures, and characters. The result gives a strong sense of what the American frontier was like and how the themes of frontier literature strongly conveyed the experiences of the people who lived it.
- Any serious student of Twain's work will want to read *The Adventures of Huckleberry Finn* (1885). The book draws heavily on Twain's love of and experience with river life and is considered a classic of American literature.

CRITICISM

Jennifer Bussey

Bussey is a freelance writer specializing in literature. In the following essay, she considers the theme of determination in mid- to late-nineteenth-century American fiction, comparing the brand of American determination depicted in Mark Twain's "Jim Baker's Blue Jay Yarn" with that in Herman Melville's Moby Dick *and Theodore Dreiser's* Sister Carrie.

There are few themes that Americans identify with more than the theme of determination. America's very genesis and the birth of its independence tell of determination in the face of overwhelming odds. Attendant themes include sacrifice, purpose, fate, and the American dream. In American fiction, the theme of determination is well represented and explored from various perspectives. This can be demonstrated by considering three very different works by three very different authors writing in the nineteenth century—Herman Melville's 1851 novel *Moby Dick*, Theodore Dreiser's 1900 novel *Sister Carrie*, and Mark Twain's oft-overlooked 1880 short story *Jim Baker's Blue Jay Yarn*. All three feature stubborn main characters whose lives and fates are shaped by their intense focus and determination. Each character's motives and outcomes distinguish his or her individual story and reveal much about the character's true self. While Ahab and Carrie allow their determination to rule their lives in very pervasive and intense ways, the blue

"THE BLUE JAY DIFFERS FROM AHAB AND CARRIE IN THAT HIS BLIND DETERMINATION COSTS HIM LITTLE MORE THAN TIME AND DIGNITY, NEITHER OF WHICH SEEM TO BE ALL THAT IMPORTANT TO HIM."

jay's fierce determination does not change the course of his life.

Melville's famous *Moby Dick* protagonist, Captain Ahab, is singularly focused on finding and destroying the elusive white whale that claimed his leg. He is motivated by hatred and vengeance. He is blind to his own arrogance as he seeks to punish nature for being itself. The story of *Moby Dick* is told by Ishmael, who has found work aboard Ahab's ship. He soon finds that his one-legged captain is eccentric and unpredictable. Ahab is obsessed with finding this particular white whale, called "Moby Dick," even admitting that the sole purpose of their voyage is to find him. When another captain begs Ahab to help him find a lost crew that includes his son, Ahab refuses because he knows that Moby Dick (who claimed the crew) is nearby. This episode speaks to the essential self-centeredness of Ahab's obsession with revenge; he is willing to allow another man's son to perish (a greater loss suffered because of Moby Dick than the loss of his leg) in order to pursue his wild-eyed fixation on revenge. Had Ahab chosen to be reasonable and redirected his determination on finding the man's son, his intensity would have been pointed toward a worthwhile goal and used for good. But Ahab is too narrowly focused to put his own drive into perspective. Ultimately, Ahab and his crew find Moby Dick and try for three days to kill him, until the whale finally rams and sinks the ship. The only survivor is Ishmael.

Ahab is bent on finding Moby Dick, no matter the risk or cost. He is even willing to trick skilled men into joining his crew for the sole purpose of seeking revenge. This selfishness on Ahab's part ultimately costs those tricked men their lives; Ahab effectively hijacks their rights to determine their own destinies and decide what is worth dying for. Compassion for other men is inconsequential to Ahab, as are warnings about the whale that he is so fiercely determined to destroy. In the end, his determination brings about his own destruction—and the deaths of innocent crew members. Thus, Ahab's willingness to take risks costs him his ship and his life, and he never achieves the one thing that mattered to him. He does not destroy Moby Dick; rather, Moby Dick destroys him. The tragedy is in the deaths of the crew members who, by the time they knew the real purpose of the voyage, were trapped aboard the ill-fated ship. They did not die for something that was important to them but for the dangerous obsession of one man. Ishmael alone survives to tell the story of Ahab, and the reader understands it to be a cautionary tale. Determination in the right context and with the right objective is healthy and inspiring, but misguided determination brings ruin. If Ahab had redirected his determination to something productive for himself or society, he might have been a hero instead of a foolish and tragic figure. Instead, he died—and essentially killed other men—to chase after a whale that had simply been provoked to kill him and had never thought or felt anything about it.

Dreiser, in turn, writing fifty years later, gives readers the example of Caroline Meeber in *Sister Carrie*. In the character of Carrie, Dreiser gives readers an early example of a woman pursuing her version of the American dream. Carrie begins her journey by going to live with her sister and her family in Chicago. Carrie takes a job in a shoe factory but soon becomes dismayed at the working conditions and the rough people with whom she works. After being fired from her job, she decides to leave her sister's home and live with a dashing salesman she met on the train coming to Chicago. This relationship begins to change her; she becomes more sophisticated and bends her previous moral standards while pursuing her dream of security and a comfortable life. She ends up going to Canada with a married man who has embezzled money from the bar he manages. Forced to return the money, he agrees to return to America, where he and Carrie marry and move to New York. Although he finds work, the life he offers Carrie does not come close to the sort of life she dreamed of. Up to this point in her life, Carrie's determination to live a better life led her to rely on others—first her sister and then two different men. When her husband fails to support or romance her as she desires, she finds work in the theater, where her heart has always been drawn. Once she is independent, she abandons her husband, who ultimately ends up impoverished and commits suicide. Carrie, on the other hand, becomes a star of the stage. She achieves her dreams through determination and willingness to change her identity and character along the way.

When Carrie has the life she always wanted, however, she discovers that fame, adoration, and wealth do not fulfill her. Happiness continues to elude her, and with it, her belief that happiness is possible. Carrie's determination was as flawed as Ahab's, but with a different focus. Where Ahab was single-mindedly focused on Moby Dick, such that everything he did, every choice he made, and every man he manipulated was in service of that focus, Carrie had the same intense focus on living a lavish lifestyle and feeling important. Like Ahab, she uses people along the way with no regard for their sacrifices or personal goals. She is always on the lookout for something that will get her where she wants to go faster, and in the end, the goal does not deliver. Where Ahab was actually killed by his pursuit, Carrie is left empty and disillusioned at the end of her pursuit, and her character and morality have perished along the way. Her motivation was finding happiness and security in the big city. She sought the American dream, and she was so focused on reaching it that she was willing to sacrifice her manners, morality, relationships, and self-understanding. Once she achieved this dream, she discovered that her determination had led her astray. Having become jaded along the way, she stopped believing that she could achieve happiness. Had she embraced a different attitude, her determination surely would have taken her to a better American dream.

Twain's short story "Jim Baker's Blue Jay Yarn" features a man named Jim Baker who can understand what animals say when they speak. He tells the story of a blue jay who lands on the roof of an abandoned house and notices a hole. Not knowing he is on a roof, he is perplexed by the hole because when he drops an acorn into it, he cannot see where the acorn goes. He works diligently to fill the hole with acorns despite the fact that he keeps looking in the hole and seeing nothing. Still, he is stubbornly determined to fill that hole. When other blue jays come to see what he is doing, one of them eventually discovers that the hole is atop a house. He tells the first blue jay that he is trying to fill a whole house with acorns, and they all have a good laugh at his foolishness. The blue jay is able to laugh at himself and realizes that his determination was misguided. Had he taken the time to find out more about the hole, rather than being so stubborn, he would have realized that his exercise was futile. But the reader also sees that even if it had been an ordinary hole in a tree or the ground, the goal of filling it at any cost would still have been silly. Although many animals (and birds in particular) have an innate drive to hoard food, the blue jay in the story is not trying to be practical and forward-thinking. He is not preparing for a time when food might not be so abundant; he is filling the hole simply for the purpose of filling the hole. He could just as well have been filling it with rocks because the food was beside the point. The blue jay is very focused and determined, and if he were to direct his drive at something worthwhile, he could accomplish something meaningful for himself or his community. He seems content, however, to have provided his fellow blue jays with a good laugh and a local legend. The blue jay differs from Ahab and Carrie in that his blind determination costs him little more than time and dignity, neither of which seem to be all that important to him. He is not destroyed as a result of his dogged pursuit of a goal, nor is he changed in any way. Readers can safely assume that the blue jay enjoyed a good laugh with his fellow blue jays, enjoyed a little bit of fame, and continued on just as he had before the roof hole incident.

Taking these three examples of determination from American literature within a fifty-year period, and in light of many others, one can conclude that this theme was meaningful to American readers at the time. Given that the nation endured the Civil War and underwent tremendous change during this period, this theme reflects a basic element of American culture and nationhood and how Americans were then seeing themselves as a nation. Ahab, Carrie, and the blue jay represent different manifestations of determination, and they all demonstrate different outcomes of being singly driven toward something. What is missing among these three characters and their literary circumstances is the positive side of determination. While their characters, settings, situations, and motives are entirely different, the lesson is ultimately that misguided determination brings only negative consequences. Ahab, Carrie, and the blue jay have in common a faulty sense of determination, and that lack of insight shapes them to some degree; in Ahab's and Carrie's cases, the degree is extreme, while in the blue jay's case, it is less extreme in the consequences but equally telling about his character. Ahab's determination led only to destruction. He was killed, and he took other innocent men with him, while the whale lived. His stubbornness brought devastation, loss, and disappointment. Carrie's determination resulted in her getting what she thought she wanted, but it left her changed and disillusioned. It was a hollow achievement that left her with hopelessness. The blue jay's determination resulted in meaninglessness and mockery. His goal was ultimately revealed to be misunderstood and insignificant. He thought he was working on one thing, but he was spending his time and energy doing something considerably different.

These three examples, then, feature different characters (man, woman, animal), from different backgrounds and walks of life, with different goals, and different outcomes—one character dies, another is left feeling empty and hopeless, and another feels foolish. All three stories are cautionary tales, serving to warn the reader about the potential dangers of unchecked determination. It is a universal sentiment, and in these literary characters, we have the opportunity to learn from the mistakes of others. The overall lesson is one of balance; a single pursuit should not define an entire life. Dogged determination let loose without wisdom or direction will take a person somewhere other than where he or she wanted to go; at best, it could result in wasted time and embarrassment, but at worst, it could lead to utter disaster.

Though written within fifty years of one another, these three stories actually represent three different movements in American literature: romantic (Melville), realist (Twain), and naturalist (Dreiser). This is significant because none of the three examples explored concludes with a happy ending. Although determination was a foundational value in America, Americans no longer held an innocent or naive view of it by this era. While they still valued it, a fact reflected in the literature they favored, Americans did not believe that determination alone was enough to build a life on. A more mature understanding was being sought in American thought and letters.

Source: Jennifer A. Bussey, Critical Essay on "Jim Baker's Blue Jay Yarn," in *Short Stories for Students*, Gale, Cengage Learning, 2009.

"THE IMMEDIATE SOURCE FOR 'JIM BAKER'S BLUE JAY YARN' IS A TALE MARK TWAIN HEARD JIM GILLIS TELL WHILE THE AUTHOR LIVED WITH GILLIS AT JACKASS HILL IN CALAVERAS COUNTY, CALIFORNIA, DURING THE WINTER 1864–65."

James D. Wilson

In the following excerpt, Wilson provides an overview of "Jim Baker's Blue Jay Yarn," including the publication history, the context of composition, and the relationship of the story to Twain's other works.

PUBLICATION HISTORY

"Jim Baker's Blue Jay Yarn" first appeared in chapter 3 of *A Tramp Abroad*, published in March 1880. Among the "separatable stuff" of *A Tramp Abroad*—as Mark Twain wrote to William Dean Howells—the anecdote is a narrative digression, self-contained, and frequently reprinted in anthologies of southwestern humor and collections of Mark Twain's short fiction (DeVoto 247–53; *Humor of the Old Southwest* 402–5). It is sometimes given the title, "What Stumped the Bluejays."

Most anthologists and editors reprint the story as a self-contained unit. Gibson, however, argues that the yarn must be seen in its original context. In *A Tramp Abroad* Mark Twain introduces the tale in the second chapter as he describes his walk through the Black Forest. Evoking an atmosphere of "German legends and fairy tales" in a manner reminiscent of Washington Irving, Mark Twain encounters some ravens who seem to caw insults at him. Gradually he transforms the ravens from adversaries who "bandy words in raven" to masters of the western American art of the insult. He slips into the vernacular voice of Jim Baker, who tells the story of the American jay. Gibson contends that in reading the yarn out of context we overlook Mark Twain's masterful control of narrative technique: the story's "seamless narrative development, its easy passage through formal opening into a vernacular tale of real elegance, and its transmuting the atmosphere of German legend into the air of Western myth" (67–71).

"Jim Baker's Blue Jay Yarn" is the high point of a book that continually frustrated Mark Twain during its composition and, as Blair contends, was "not worth all the trouble it took to write it" (168; Paine 665). For all its aesthetic problems, however, *A Tramp Abroad* proved a commercial success: it sold sixty-two-thousand copies during the first year, far outstripping sales of Mark Twain's previous three books; in England, *A Tramp Abroad* achieved the best sales record of all Mark Twain's books during the author's lifetime (Kaplan, *Mr. Clemens* 350; Emerson 105).

CIRCUMSTANCES OF COMPOSITION, SOURCES, AND INFLUENCES

In early March 1878 Mark Twain signed a contract with Elisha Bliss to write for the American Publishing Company a subscription book about travel through Europe. The original idea was to produce another book like the enormously successful *Innocents Abroad* (1869). The contract with Bliss may have been the impetus for an extended trip to Germany, but more probably Mark Twain used the contract to justify a trip he had already decided was necessary to revitalize his sagging creative spirit. His humiliation at the Whittier birthday dinner in Boston 17 December 1877 had left him uncertain of his role in American letters. Acutely self-conscious, he had written to Howells a week after the dinner: "I feel that my misfortune has injured me all over the country; therefore it will be best that I retire from before the public at present" (*Mark Twain-Howells Letters* 212). Emerson hence suggests that Mark Twain left for Germany in mid-April 1878 largely to escape his embarrassment and the lethargy it engendered (98). In any event, upon his arrival in Germany, he began immediately writing material for *A Tramp Abroad.* But quickly a fundamental aesthetic problem arose: there was no focus to the project, no "narrative plank" to provide unity to the miscellaneous tales, sketches, short stories, and anecdotes he prepared. He wrote to Frank Bliss in July 1878: "I have written 800 pages of ms.... but it is in disconnected form & cannot be used until joined together by the writing of at least a dozen intermediate chapters" (Hill 133). A visit from his close friend Joe Twichell triggered an idea for a unifying thread. Mark Twain decided his book would be a burlesque account of a walking tour through Europe, undertaken by two American tramps—Mark Twain and a companion named Mr. Harris—who manage to do no walking at all. The strategy, however, proved unsuccessful. By this time Mark Twain was too sick of travel—of hotels, trains, museums, etc.—to bring the same freshness and ironic vision that had informed *Innocents Abroad. A Tramp Abroad* does indeed offer a series of chapters describing Mark Twain's adventures while traveling with Mr. Harris through Germany, Switzerland, and Italy—but there are frequent digressions, most of which, like the "Blue Jay Yarn," have nothing to do with Europe or the tour. What he could not fit even as a digression, Mark Twain stuffed into six appendices (Emerson 105; Rogers 80). The result is a disjointed work with occasionally brilliant digressions, the whole characterized by what Blair calls the "labored pursuit of humorous effects" (Mark Twain 168).

Throughout the composition of *A Tramp Abroad* Mark Twain knew he was having trouble and, in fact, looked for a pretext to abandon the project altogether (Kaplan, *Mr. Clemens*, 336). He wrote to Howells on 8 January 1880 that he had "been fighting a life-&-death battle with this infernal book & *hoping* to get it done some day.... A book which required 2600 pages of ms, & I have written nearer four thousand, first & last" (*Mark Twain-Howells Letters* 286–87). Hill points out that in writing *A Tramp Abroad* Mark Twain reversed the process he had followed in *Innocents Abroad.* In the earlier book, the *Alta* letters had at the outset furnished a rudimentary structure, a "narrative plank"; in revising the letters for book publication he had only to flesh out his series of letters with appropriate anecdotes. In *A Tramp Abroad*, however, the digression became the basic structural unit, preceeding the flimsy unifying principle of the burlesque walking tour to which it bore scant resemblance (139).

The immediate source for "Jim Baker's Blue Jay Yarn" is a tale Mark Twain heard Jim Gillis tell while the author lived with Gillis at Jackass Hill in Calaveras County, California, during the winter 1864–65. Inclement weather forced Mark Twain to pass his time indoors, around the fire in Gillis's cabin or in the hotel saloon at nearby Angel's Camp. Here he heard Gillis and Ben Coon spin yarns from a vast storehouse of western American lore. Mark Twain remembered these tall tales, even jotted down notes about some of them, and used them later as the basis of such classic pieces as "Jim Smiley and His Jumping Frog" (1865) and the "Blue Jay Yarn." But he was struck as deeply by the tellers themselves and their deadpan manner of delivery (Bellamy 146; Benson 124). Long argues that behind Jim Baker or Simon Wheeler lies the narrator of the western tall tale—a real, vital person like Gillis or Coon who spins his fantastic yarn in an authentic idiom (133, 321).

The story belongs to the tradition of the bestiary, dating back to before Chaucer but surfacing in the antebellum South of Mark Twain's youth in the Negro slave narrative (DeVoto 251; Long 321). Mark Twain remembered fondly the stories he heard in childhood from the old Negro slave Uncle Dan'l and, as Lynn points out, later tended to conflate his memories of Uncle Dan'l with his response to Joel Chandler Harris's Uncle Remus tales (240). Harris supplied Mark Twain not an analogue for this particular story but the example of a method; as Arnold points out, the birds in the "Blue Jay Yarn" portray "frontier society just as Harris' creatures allegorize antebellum plantation life" (206). Mark Twain's 1881 correspondence with Harris reveals also that in the Uncle Remus tales Mark Twain found confirmation of his theory that the frame that encloses a story—the character of the narrator and his interaction with the auditor—rather than the actual yarn itself, is of paramount importance (Bellamy 149–50).

Like "Jim Smiley and His Jumping Frog," the "Blue Jay Yarn" bears strong affinities to the tradition of southwestern humor (Cohen and Dillingham 387–88). This genre, Arnold contends, involves two divergent strains of development, both of which leave their mark on Mark Twain's fiction. The first strain appears in the work of such ironic humorists as George Washington Harris, A. B. Longstreet, and Johnson Jones Hooper—essentially conservative satirists who use animals or metaphors featuring animals to expose the boorishness and cruelty of simple frontier people and hence assure an educated eastern audience of its inherent moral and cultural superiority. In the tales of Sut Luvingood or Simon Suggs, animals rarely achieve any autonomous personality for their function is either to illuminate human inadequacies or to provide occasion for slapstick humor at the expense of the country bumpkin. From Longstreet, Arnold contends, Mark Twain "learned his descriptive techniques," and the episode of the poodle and the pinch bug in *Tom Sawyer* (1876) testifies to his use of the slapstick tradition for humorous and satiric effect.

The second strain comes to Mark Twain from such "animal-admiring humorists" as Alexander McNutt and T. B. Thorpe. In McNutt's "Chunkey's Fight with the Panthers" the panther proves an awesome beast, a worthy and respected adversary in what becomes an epic conflict; in "The Big Bear of Arkansas," Thorpe creates a mythical bear, a creature he loves "like a brother," and in doing so demonstrates an affinity with what Arnold labels "the deeper rhythms of unity with the animal world which is central to Twain." Mark Twain, Arnold contends, fuses the two traditions of animal portraiture in southwestern humor, moving in the "Blue Jay Yarn" and later stories about the Indian crow to complete empathy with the animals and the natural realm they represent (196–202).

RELATIONSHIP TO OTHER MARK TWAIN WORKS

"Jim Baker's Blue Jay Yarn" shares much in common with "Jim Smiley and His Jumping Frog." Both are based on tall tales Mark Twain heard while living in Calaveras County, California, during the winter 1864–65, and both are rooted in regional folklore. Moreover, both tales are told in a frontier idiom by folk narrators who, as Hansen writes, "seem never to leave their rocking chairs" (420). Blair points out that the "Blue Jay Yarn" exploits the humorous effects resulting from the juxtaposition of realistic and fantastic passages, a technique that governs the "Jumping Frog" story and works well in Huck's account of the exploits of the duke and the dauphin in *Huckleberry Finn* (1885) ("Mark Twain's Other Masterpiece" 134–38).

The "Blue Jay Yarn" belongs to a long series of stories, sketches, and fragments about animals, virtually all of which are collected by Brashear and Rodney in *The Birds and Beasts of Mark Twain*. Animals of course play a significant role in Simon Wheeler's tale about Jim Smiley's gambling adventures and in *Tom Sawyer*, where their antics serve the purposes of burlesque humor. In Jim Baker's yarn, however, the jay becomes what Arnold calls a "full-fledged protagonist." Mercifully, Mark Twain here does not treat the jay in a vein of maudlin sentimentality, as he later treats the animal protagonists of "A Dog's Tale" (1903) and "A Horse's Tale" (1906). But he does identify with his animal protagonist, for like Jim Baker's frustrated jay

Mark Twain knew well what it was like "to dump money, or the manuscript pages for a book, into holes which seemed too huge ever to fill" (Blair, *Mark Twain*, 176). Arnold contends that the jays manifest those qualities that made Mark Twain the celebrated spokesman for and chronicler of the American West: "his virtuosity at the profanity, bragging, posturing, exaggerating, and lying that constituted conversation in the frontier towns" (208)....

Source: James D. Wilson, "'Jim Baker's Blue Jay Yarn,'" in *A Reader's Guide to the Short Stories of Mark Twain*, G. K. Hall, 1996, pp. 153–61.

Ronald J. Gervais

In the following article, Gervais traces the meaning of the central joke in "Jim Baker's Blue Jay Yarn" by placing it in the context of A Tramp Abroad *and suggesting that the empty spaces in the American landscape engender the need for both language and humor.*

Mark Twain's fable of the bluejay, the acorns, and an unfillable knot-hole in a cabin roof has been called "the high point of *A Tramp Abroad*," "the most perfect example of the genuine Western tall tale" in all of Mark Twain's works, and even the greatest of Twain's shorter comic works. But it has been praised almost exclusively for its technical virtuosity and management of material, for its "harmonious blending of the material of fantasy and the framework of realism," and not for any point it might be making. Even the central action of the tale has had little meaning for critics. "Baker's bluejay . . . dumped acorns into his knot-hole for reasons that never were clarified," writes Walter Blair. This essay will attempt to clarify those reasons.

The American "yarn" should be seen in relation to the carefully established atmosphere of "German legends and fairy tales" that prepares for it in Chapter 3 of *A Tramp Abroad* (1880). The practice followed by most anthologists of printing the yarn without this context is to ignore the European-American contrast that Twain sets up. The tall tale can stand by itself as skillful entertainment, but it makes more serious sense when seen as the recollection by an American in Europe of a faraway friend's story. The Neckar hills above Heidelberg where Twain the tourist strolls are peopled "with gnomes, and dwarfs, and all sorts of mysterious and uncanny creatures" (this and all following citations of

> "'BAKER'S BLUE-JAY YARN' SHOWS A CHARACTERISTIC AND CONTINUING AMERICAN CONCERN FOR FILLING IN WITH APPROPRIATE LANGUAGE THE HUGE SPACES OF A NEWLY-SETTLED CONTINENT."

"Baker's Blue-Jay Yarn" are from *A Tramp Abroad*, Ch. 3). With enough reading and "dreamy thoughts," he even gets to imagining that he glimpses "kobolds and enchanted folk" flitting "down the columned aisles of the forest." This mood is broken by some ravens, whose croaks have "a distinctly insulting expression," as if to say "in raven, 'Well, what do *you* want here?'" These European ravens turn out to be experts in the art of Western American slangy insult: "What a hat!" "Oh, pull down your vest!" they croak at the humiliated intruder. In his self-conscious working up of legendary European atmosphere, Mark Twain suddenly feels "as foolish as if he had been caught in some mean act," and is driven imaginatively back to the American scene.

Having established an imaginative world where animals can talk, Twain makes it a bridge between the forests of Germany and the "lonely corner of California," where lives the man who can understand animal talk, and who will narrate the blue-jay yarn—Jim Baker. The difference between the two places is that the former is thickly peopled with ancient imagined-beings, while the latter must create its dramas out of the rawest materials. The tourist frame of *A Tramp Abroad* and the frontier fable of "Baker's Blue-Jay Yarn" posit a contrast between the richly enculturated landscape of Europe and the culturally empty landscape of the American West. Along the Neckar hills, Twain has "the huge ruin of Heidelberg Castle, with empty window arches, ivy-mailed battlements, moldering towers—the Lear of inanimate nature,—deserted, discrowned, beaten by the storms, but royal still, and beautiful." In the Sierra foothills, he has the house of the last man but Baker to have moved away from the region. "There stands his house,—been empty ever since; a log house, with a plank roof—just one big room, and no more; no ceiling—nothing between the rafters and the floor." This very poverty of human culture stimulates the comic possibilities within language itself. Twain transmutes German legend into Western myth through the vernacular language of the frontier, the language of American humor.

Jim Baker's preamble to his tale establishes the language ability of jays, from the impressive propriety of their grammar to the equally impressive impropriety of their profanity. Baker asserts that a bluejay is unsurpassed in putting his moods and feelings into language: language variegated, faultless in grammar, and "bristling with metaphor, just bristling." The tale then provides what was promised—a gaudy display of language. The display begins when a bluejay lights on the empty house "with an acorn in his mouth," perhaps symbolic of his oral gifts.

This hole in the roof is the most "bristling" of the yarn's metaphors. It becomes an empty silence that mocks and provokes the jay's outraged eloquence. An entire "congress" of jays convenes to peer into it and deliver themselves of thoroughly human opinions, "jawing and disputing and ripping and cussing." One old jay finally peers into the half-open cabin door and dispels the mystery: "Come here! . . . Come here, everybody; hanged if this fool hasn't been trying to fill up a house with acorns!" In revealing counterpoint, the bluejay who tries to fill up an empty frontier house with acorns suffers the same humiliation as the "Mark Twain" who had tried to work up a romantic atmosphere in the German forest, suggesting the truth of Baker's claim that "a jay knows when he is an ass just as well as you do—maybe better."

The compensation for man and beast is humor, specifically a humorous manner of talking and telling. The jays "guffawed over that thing like human beings. It ain't any use to tell me a bluejay hasn't got a sense of humor, because I know better." And in counterpoint to such European tourist attractions as the Heidelberg Castle described earlier by Train, the California jays bring birds "from all over the United States to look down that hole, every summer for three years." Only that symbol of conventional wisdom—the owl from Nova Scotia, who rounds off the tale as a tourist in the West just as Twain had opened it as a tourist in Europe—only he is bound to be disappointed and not to "see anything funny in it." For he comes expecting to see *something*, when the point is what remains when everything is left out.

"Baker's Blue-Jay Yarn" shows a characteristic and continuing American concern for filling in with appropriate language the huge spaces of a newly-settled continent. In the absence of such traditional European materials for creating literature as a complex social structure, a native accumulation of legend and myth, and an already extant literary tradition, there evolved in America a literary strategy that might be called negative description. From de Crèvecoeur to Robert Frost, lists of what is missing define "the land vaguely realizing westward, /but still unstoried, artless, unenhanced." Coming to imaginative terms with this negative state, this emptiness, seemed a capital "joke" to sensibilities as different as Henry James and Mark Twain.

De Crèvecoeur's rhetorical negation sets the tone for the next century in delimiting the empty spaces between the old and the new, between European preconceptions and unmanageable American facts.

> He is arrived on a new continent; a modern society offers itself to his contemplation, different from what he had hitherto seen. It is not composed, as in Europe, of great lords who possess everything, and of a herd of people who have nothing. Here are no aristocratical families, no courts, no kings, no bishops, no ecclesiastical dominion, no invisible power giving to a few a very visible one; no great manufacturers employing thousands, no great refinements of luxury. The rich and the poor are not so far removed from each other as they are in Europe.

Cooper adopts the negative mode without the same exuberance when he cites glumly in *Notions of the Americans* the worst obstacle against which American literature has to contend—the poverty of materials.

> There are no annals for the historian; no follies (beyond the most vulgar and commonplace) for the satirist; no manners for the dramatist; no obscure fictions for the writer of romance; no gross and hardy offenses against decorum for the moralist; nor any of the rich artificial auxiliaries of poetry.

In his preface to *The Marble Faun*, Hawthorne pities himself for the difficulties this impoverishment causes him as a writer, yet sees it as a condition of American innocence. The author's well-known ambiguity makes the now familiar list of "no's" both complaint and thanksgiving.

> No author, without a trial, can conceive of the difficulty of writing a romance about a country where there is no shadow, no antiquity, no mystery, no picturesque and gloomy wrong, nor anything but a commonplace prosperity, in broad and simple daylight, as is happily the case with my dear native land.

This whole practice of negative description achieves a grand climax in James's *Hawthorne*, where he uses a provocative slyness in combining a string of reservations, deliberately comic in their tedious enumeration. The secret "joke" that remains, as James knows, after everything is left out, will shortly be sprung by Mark Twain.

> No sovereign, no court, no personal loyalty, no aristocracy, no church, no clergy, no army, no diplomatic service, no country gentlemen, no palaces, no castles, nor manors, nor old country houses, nor parsonages, nor thatched cottages, nor ivied ruins; no cathedrals, nor abbeys, nor little Norman churches; no great universities nor public schools—No Oxford, nor Eton, nor Harrow; no literature, no novels, no museums, no pictures, no political society, no sporting class—no Epsom nor Ascot! . . .The natural remark, in the almost lurid light of such an indictment, would be that if those things are left out, everything is left out. The American knows that a good deal remains; what it is that remains—that is his secret, his joke, as one may say. It would be cruel, in this terrible denudation, to deny him the conciliation of his national gift, that 'American humor' of which of late years we have heard so much.

The burden of that American humor which remains after everything is left out is to create a language to express a landscape lacking nearly all the appurtenances of civilization. All of that unhumanized, unlanguaged space—an empty house that Americans could not even begin to fill. When we realized our problem, we could only laugh, and our laughter began to fill the house.

> Under the almost savage conditions of a wild new land, laughter was one of the means by which the frontiersman could for a time forget his hardship, preserve his courage, and retain his balance and his humanity. Through his tall tales and his exaggerated, at times almost bestial, behavior, he could laugh at himself and know at the same time that he was playing a role, that his civilized self remained intact.

Jim Baker, the frontiersman, seems to project his own loneliness and need for language and humor unto the birds. He begins to understand their language just when the last man in the region but himself has moved away, and the action begins as he contemplates this last man's empty "house," and thinks of his own "home" away yonder in the states that he has not heard from in thirteen years. The distinction between house and home, the sense of abandonment hinted at in "hadn't heard from," the pathetic fallacy of "lonely" leaves, and the emphatic negativity in the description of the empty house—"just one big room, and no more; no ceiling—nothing between the rafters and the floor"—all imply an integral relation between domestic space and language. Without a language to fill it, the American house is not yet a home. Lacking "the pleasant legendary stuff" of Europe, Baker fills the house with the "jay language" of tall tale humor. His comic insistence on standards of correctness, on "good grammar," in the face of his own demonstrated ignorance of it, shows him overcoming a possible sense of inferiority through bravado. His faith that whatever a jay feels he can put into language, is the faith that American speech can deal with the "terrible denudation" cited by James, faith that American humor does know the joke of what remains when everything is left out—the power of inventive language and cathartic laughter over the empty places.

Contemporary evidence suggests that we have come to appreciate what remains. Of growing up in Michigan, Theodore Roethke declares in his "Open Letter" to John Ciardi, "sometimes one gets the feeling that not even the animals have been there before, but the marsh, the mire, the Void is always there . . . It is America." And Robert M. Pirsig seeks the same vision on the Great Plains:

> In my mind, when I look at these fields, I say to her, 'See? . . . See?' and I think she does. I hope later she will see and feel a thing about these prairies I have given up talking to others about; a thing that exists here because everything else does not and can be noticed because other things are absent.
>
> I thought maybe in this endless grass and wind she would see a thing that sometimes comes when monotony and boredom are accepted. It's here, but I have no names for it.

There are no names for it because the condition unnamed is a preter-linguistic consciousness that permits an exhilarating and scarifying glimpse into nature's empty house, where our few words lie scattered about like acorns. When we realize, as we do in "Baker's Blue-Jay Yarn," that our cultural and language universe is not coincident with the larger universe, as has been especially true in the American experience as compared with the European, then we no longer lament the hollow spaces or strain anxiously to fill them, but perceive them as filled with the humorous and human latencies of what remains when everything is left out.

Source: Ronald J. Gervais, "What Remains When Everything Is Left Out: The Joke of 'Baker's Blue-Jay Yarn,'" in *Mark Twain Journal*, Vol. 21, No. 4, Fall 1983, pp. 12–14.

SOURCES

American Journey Online, s.v. "The Civil War," http://www.wadsworth.com/history_d/special_features/amjourney.html (accessed August 19, 2008).

Covici, Pascal, Jr., "Mark Twain" in *Dictionary of Literary Biography*, Vol. 11, *American Humorists, 1800–1950*, edited by Stanley Trachtenberg, Gale, 1982, pp. 526–55.

Gribben, Alan, "Samuel Langhorne Clemens" in *Dictionary of Literary Biography*, Vol. 74: *American Short-Story Writers before 1880*, edited by Bobby Ellen Kimbel and William E. Grant, Gale, 1988, pp. 54–83.

Harmon, William, and C. Hugh Holman, "Realistic Period in American Literature," in *A Handbook to Literature*, Prentice Hall, 2003, pp. 422–23.

Henley, William Ernest, Review of *A Tramp Abroad*, in *Athenaeum*, No. 2739, April 24, 1880, pp. 529–30.

Melton, Jeffrey Alan, "Touring the Old World: Faith and Leisure in *The Innocents Abroad* and *A Tramp Abroad*," in *Mark Twain, Travel Books, and Tourism: The Tide of a Great Popular Movement*, University of Alabama Press, 2002, pp. 59–94.

Twain, Mark, "Jim Baker's Blue Jay Yarn," in *The Celebrated Jumping Frog, and Other Stories*, Reader's Digest Association, 1992, pp. 95–99.

Van Doren, Carl, *The American Novel*, Macmillan, 1921, pp. 157–87.

FURTHER READING

Audubon, John James, *Birds of America*, edited by Colin Harrison and Cyril Walker, Wordsworth Editions, 1997.

> This book combines facts with Audubon's renowned lavish illustrations of American birds.

Blair, Walter, *Tall Tale America: A Legendary History of Our Humorous Heroes*, University of Chicago Press, 1987.

> Blair revisits folk history to uncover tall tales that include completely fictional figures as well as historical figures such as Davy Crockett and Johnny Appleseed. The style is fun, as Blair writes about these events and people as if they were real.

Powers, Ron, *Mark Twain: A Life*, Free Press, 2005.

> Powers offers readers a thoroughly researched, insightful look into the life of Mark Twain. Rich with facts, this biography seeks to show readers the real Twain and how he became a unique voice in American literature.

Twain, Mark, *Collected Tales, Sketches, Speeches, and Essays*, Vol. 1, edited by Louis J. Budd, Library of America, 1992.

> This collection of Twain's writing includes fiction and nonfiction from the first part of his career. The anthology gives readers a sense of his humor and American perspective through a full range of fiction as well as through travel writing, opinion pieces, and reporting.

Liberty

JULIA ALVAREZ

1996

"Liberty" is a story by Julia Alvarez, an American writer of Dominican origin. It is set during Alvarez's childhood in the Dominican Republic in the late 1950s and early 1960s. The story was first published in 1996 in *Writers Harvest 2: A Collection of New Fiction*, which remains in print. It is also available in *Elements of Literature: Fourth Course* (Holt Rinehart Winston, 2000) and in *Literature & Language Arts: Third Course* (Holt Rinehart Winston, 2003). The story is told from the point of view of an unnamed child of about ten who is one of four young girls living in their family home with their parents. Her parents are worried about the political situation in the country and are planning to emigrate from their native country to the United States to secure their freedom. The story centers on a pet dog named Liberty who must be left behind when the family leaves their home. During the course of the story the young narrator is presented with some difficult and cruel situations that she does her best to understand and learn from. In style and subject matter, "Liberty" is typical of Alvarez's work and shows why she is one of the most acclaimed contemporary writers in the United States.

AUTHOR BIOGRAPHY

Julia Alvarez was born in New York City on March 27, 1950, to parents from the Dominican Republic who were staying in the United States

Julia Alvarez *(AP Images)*

at the time. When Alvarez was three months old, her parents returned with their family to the Dominican Republic, where Alvarez remained until she was ten years old; in 1960, the family fled political oppression in their homeland and returned to the United States, settling in New York City. As a new immigrant in an unfamiliar world, Alvarez felt insecure, and she turned to writing as a way of understanding herself and her life. Encouraged by her teachers, she decided when she was in high school that she wanted to be a writer.

In 1967, Alvarez enrolled in Connecticut College, transferring to Middlebury College in 1969. In 1971 she received her bachelor of arts degree summa cum laude. Pursuing her goal of becoming a writer, Alvarez entered a creative writing program at Syracuse University in 1973, receiving her master of fine arts degree in 1975.

Alvarez then held various positions teaching creative writing. From 1975 to 1978, she taught in the poetry-in-the-schools programs in Kentucky and Delaware. From 1979 to 1981, she taught English and creative writing to grades nine to twelve at Phillips Andover Academy in Massachusetts. During the 1980s, she taught creative writing at the University of Vermont (1981–1983), and the University of Illinois at Urbana-Champaign (1985–1988). In 1991, she became a professor in the English department at Middlebury College.

In the 1970s and 1980s, Alvarez published numerous poems and short stories in literary magazines. In 1991, she published her first novel, *How the García Girls Lost Their Accents*, about four sisters who immigrate from the Dominican Republic to the United States and face the challenge of becoming integrated into American culture. This novel was Alvarez's breakthrough as a writer, winning her favorable reviews and a national reputation. It was selected as a notable book by the American Library Association in 1992. Alvarez followed this with another novel, *In the Time of the Butterflies* (1994), based on the true story of the murder of three sisters in the Dominican Republic in 1960 and the resistance in that country to the repressive dictatorship of Rafael Leónidas Trujillo.

Alvarez's short story "Liberty" was published in *Writers Harvest 2: A Collection of New Fiction* in 1996. The following year her novel *¡Yo!*, about a Latina girl named Yolanda, appeared. Another novel, *In the Name of Salomé*, was published in 2000, followed by *Finding Miracles* (2004), a novel about a fifteen-year-old girl who was born in the Dominican Republic but was adopted by American parents and came to live in Vermont. Alvarez's sixth novel, *Saving the World*, was published in 2006.

Alvarez has also published volumes of poetry, including *Homecoming: New and Selected Poems* (1996) and *The Woman I Kept to Myself* (2004). She has also written nonfiction, including a collection of autobiographical essays called *Something to Declare* (1998) and *Once upon a Quinceañera: Coming of Age in the USA* (2007), about the Latin American tradition, which is continued in Latino communities in the United States, of celebrating a girl's passage into womanhood at the age of fifteen. Alvarez has also written a number of books for young readers. As of 2008, Alvarez was writer-in-residence at Middlebury College.

PLOT SUMMARY

Section 1

"Liberty," which is divided into five short sections, is narrated by a young girl of about ten who witnesses events at her family home that she does not fully understand. The story is set in an unnamed Latin or Central American country that is likely the Dominican Republic.

In Section 1, the narrator's father brings home a puppy, but his wife, the narrator's mother, does not like the look of the dog and tells her husband to return it. He protests that the dog is a gift from the American consul, a man he calls Mister Victor, in gratitude for all that Papi and his family have done for him since he was appointed as the U.S. representative to their country.

Mami complains that what she really wants is not a dog but visas, so that they can leave the country and enter the United States. The narrator does not understand what is going on and is puzzled by the fact that when Mami and Papi discuss leaving the country, they look frightened. Papi tries to reassure his wife that the visas will arrive soon. He also says that they will keep the dog in a pen in the yard. The dog will not be allowed in the house, and Papi is certain that it will be well behaved. In deciding what to call the rambunctious puppy, Mami suggests the name Trouble, but Papi says the dog will be called Liberty, and he quotes the U.S. Constitution about the importance of liberty. He thinks the dog will bring them luck.

Section 2

Mami proves to be right about the dog being troublesome. He eats the flowers, knocks things off tables, and tears up the yard. Mami yells at him to no avail. Mami grows frustrated with the dog and angry with her husband's attempts at humor. It transpires that she has changed her mind and no longer wants to emigrate to the United States. She does not like it when the American consul visits their house and talks with her husband about serious matters. She does not want any bad things to happen, she says. She does not go into any details because she does not want her daughter to hear.

The narrator tells the reader more about herself. She enjoys playing with Liberty. She had always been more adventurous and more likely to get into trouble than her three sisters. She offers to take Liberty back to his pen to get him out of her mother's way. As she takes Liberty away, she notices that her mother, who had been talking to her father, has started to cry.

The narrator describes Liberty's fenced-in pen, in the middle of which stands a doghouse, which her father painted green. Liberty does not like going in the pen, and on this occasion he heads for a shady tree in the front yard that cannot be seen from the house. The narrator follows him but is shocked when she sees two men she does not know behind the hedge. One of the men has grabbed Liberty's collar and is pulling on it. The girl begins to back away but one of the men grabs her arm.

The men give the dog back to her and tell her not to tell anyone that she has seen them. The girl does not understand what is going on but is grateful to get Liberty back. She comforts the dog and leads him back to his pen. Then she goes back to the house, planning on telling her parents what has just happened.

Section 3

The narrator tells of how Mister Victor spends large amounts of time at their house. He and Papi, as well as any visiting relatives, go to the back of the property to talk, presumably so that they can be assured of privacy. The narrator reports that her mother found some wires in the study behind a portrait. The wires connect to a little box outside, suggesting that the house is being spied on electronically. The girl's mother says it is not safe to talk in the house about certain topics. But she does not explain to the puzzled girl what the situation is.

The girl's mother refuses to say what is wrong, but the girl observes that she is always crying. In spite of this, the narrator seems to be enjoying herself, eating foods normally forbidden. One day Mister Victor talks to her about the dog. She gets Liberty to show Victor some of the tricks she has taught him, and he laughs.

The narrator listens to the men of the house, including some visiting uncles, as they talk about an upcoming hunting expedition, but a lot of what they are saying makes no sense to her. They are in fact talking in a coded language to veil their meaning, but she does not understand this. She feels that life is about to change dramatically, and she puts her arm around her dog for comfort.

Section 4

The girl learns that their visas have arrived and that they are to depart for the United States that night. Her mother tries to pretend that she is happy with this news and gives each child a job to do to prepare for their departure. The narrator says she wants to take Liberty with her to America, but her mother says this is not possible. The girl begs her to change her mind, to no avail. The distressed girl then begins to cry, and soon her mother is crying, too. One of the girl's aunts tries to comfort her by telling her that she will find liberty in America. The girl does not understand what she means; the aunt does not explain but tells the girl that they must go and pack.

Section 5

Late that night someone comes and tells the family it is time to leave. The four sisters leave their bedrooms and sit on a bench and wait while the adults rush around. Mister Victor comes and tells them that they must wait a little longer. The narrator then slips away and goes to the backyard. She is afraid that the two scary men she encountered earlier will return after the family has gone, smash the place up, and find Liberty in his pen. She opens the pen for the dog and urges him to run away, but instead the dog follows her. She kicks him until he runs away from the house. At first the girl thinks she will meet Liberty again in the United States, but she then realizes that this will not happen. She hopes he will be there when she and the family return home, since her mother has promised that they will return.

CHARACTERS

Liberty

Liberty is the black and white puppy that Mister Victor gives to Papi and the family. He is a purebred dog, although his breed is not stated. Papi expects the dog to be well behaved, but he has not yet been trained, so he tends to make a nuisance of himself, to the annoyance of Mami. However, the narrator loves Liberty, and from the time of his arrival she plays with him rather than with her sisters. It is as if they are two of a kind, both being adventurous and often getting into trouble.

Mami

Mami is the narrator's mother. She is a tense, nervous, sometimes angry woman who is under a lot of strain because of the uncertainty of the family situation. It is enough for her to have to look after her four daughters without having a dog to worry about as well. She and Liberty do not get along. The dog is troublesome and does not obey Mami's commands, which only increases her frustration. Mami is also confused about what she wants. Initially she wants to emigrate to the United States, but she later changes her mind. It seems that the danger the family appears to be facing weighs heavily upon her mind. She no doubt wants the best for her daughters, but she is in a difficult position. The men wield the power in this family, and she is not in a position to question what they decide, so her frustration and anxiety continue to build. Her habit of punishing the children for their misdeeds appears not to be the best way to make them behave, as Aunt Mimi has apparently pointed out to her. The narrator likes to argue with her mother and try to get her own way, and Mami's frustration with her daughter is obvious from her impatient reply to the narrator's impossible request to take Liberty to the United States.

Tía Mimi

Tía Mimi is the narrator's aunt. Unlike anyone else in the family, she has been educated in the United States. She is intelligent and sophisticated and reads a lot. She takes an interest in the narrator, buying her a book on the Arabian Nights and promising her that she will "find liberty" in the United States. The narrator is fond of her and likes to listen to the intelligent way she talks. Tía Mimi obviously has a way with children, in contrast to the heavy-handed approach of Mami.

The Narrator

The narrator is a girl of about ten. She is one of the four daughters of Mami and Papi, and she is in fifth grade in school. She is an adventurous, inquisitive girl who tries hard to understand the world around her, although she is frequently mystified by the words and actions of the adults in her life. She seems to be a high-spirited girl who frequently gets into trouble, to the exasperation of her mother. The narrator describes herself as "the tomboy, the live wire, the troublemaker, the one who was going to drive Mami to drink, the one she was going to give away to the Haitians." In this sense she is rather different from her more conventional, feminine sisters, and she finds her ideal companion in Liberty, the puppy, with whom she forms a close bond. She plays with him as often as she can and wants to take him to the United States. When this proves impossible, she does everything she can to ensure that after she is gone Liberty does not fall into the hands of the two frightening strangers.

During the course of the story, the narrator grows in the sense that she discovers that there are bad people in the world, that life is not simple, and that one cannot always have everything one wants. She also shows great ingenuity and determination in making sure that her beloved dog Liberty has every chance of survival after they leave him behind on their journey to the United States. The difficult circumstances in which she finds herself force her to achieve a level of maturity beyond her years.

Papi

Papi is the narrator's father. He wants to emigrate to the United States so that he can return to school there. It appears that he is an admirer of the United States and the freedom it offers. There are certainly other reasons for his desire to leave his home country, since it appears that he and his family are under surveillance by the government. However, no details are given about why this is so. Papi befriends Mister Victor, the American consul, who helps him obtain visas for himself and his family, as well as having given them the gift of the puppy. Papi does not want to offend Mister Victor by refusing the puppy, even though his wife is not pleased with the addition to the family. Papi appears to be a good husband and father who wants the best for his family. He is an optimistic man who looks on the bright side of things.

The Two Intruders

The intruders are two men, perhaps government agents of some kind, who may be spying on the activities of the narrator's family. The narrator encounters them crouched behind a hedge. They are both wearing sunglasses, and one of them, who is fat, is pulling hard on Liberty's leash. The other man grabs the narrator's arm. She is frightened by them and does not know who they are or what they want. It is her first encounter with "mean and scary people."

Mister Victor

Mister Victor is the American consul; he gives the puppy to Papi. It appears that Victor has only recently been appointed as consul and that Papi and his family have done much to make him welcome in their country. Mister Victor in turn has befriended the family and is frequently over at their house, talking seriously, perhaps about the political situation in the country, with Papi and the narrator's uncles. It is Mister Victor who facilitates the granting of visas so that the family can leave the country. Mister Victor appears to be a kind man, speaking gently to the children. From the childlike point of view of the narrator, Mister Victor "had a funny accent that sounded like someone making fun of Spanish when he spoke it." The narrator likes Mister Victor because of his laugh and the fact that his freckled face makes him look as if he and Liberty are somehow related.

THEMES

Liberty

The theme of liberty is associated with the United States. *Liberty* means freedom from oppressive control by others; to live in liberty

TOPICS FOR FURTHER STUDY

- Write a story in the first person, with a child of about ten as the narrator. Show the child observing the adult world and understanding it as best he or she can, and make it clear that the child does not grasp many things. End the story by showing how the child has in some way grown or matured in his or her understanding of life through the events he or she has narrated.
- Read one of two other works by Alvarez, either *In the Time of the Butterflies* or *How the García Girls Lost Their Accents.* Give a class presentation in which you summarize what the novel is about and describe how it sheds light on either life in the Dominican Republic in the late 1950s and early 1960s or on the experiences encountered by Spanish-speaking immigrants in the United States.
- Interview several students or other people in your community who are first-generation or second-generation immigrants, from a Spanish-speaking country if possible. Ask them about their experiences in adjusting to life in the United States. Mention such things as language, culture, and education. Write an essay based on your interviews in which you examine the lives of immigrants in your community.
- Research the history of U.S. policy toward the Dominican Republic throughout the twentieth century. What were the principles that governed U.S. policy? How did it change over the years? Write an essay in which you discuss your findings.

means to have individual rights and freedoms protected under constitutional rule. The concept of liberty is most famously referred to in the Declaration of Independence, written in 1776, which proclaims that all men are endowed by God with "unalienable rights," including "life, liberty, and the pursuit of happiness"—the words quoted by Papi in the story as he explains why he would like the puppy to be named Liberty. (The narrator makes a small error when she says that her father was quoting the U.S. Constitution, since the words he used are from the Declaration of Independence.) He and his family look to the United States as a land of freedom, where their liberties will be preserved, in contrast to their own country, in which they appear to be under hostile surveillance by the government.

The narrator's entire family appears to share this view of the United States as a land of freedom. The girl's aunt, for example, tells her that she will find liberty in the United States. However, the narrator is too young to have any idea of political concepts such as liberty and thinks at first that she will find Liberty, her dog, in the United States. For her, liberty means the freedom from the usual restraints imposed on her by her parents, as when she enjoys a "heyday of liberty" when her mother and father are too preoccupied with their difficult situation to pay as much attention to her. Liberty for this ten-year-old means such trivia as getting away with "having one of Mister Victor's Coca-Colas for breakfast instead of my boiled milk with a beaten egg." At the end of the story she does guess that with regard to finding liberty in the United States, her aunt means something other than finding her dog, but she is not yet old enough to understand what that meaning might be. For the reader, however, the last line in the story does disclose a wider meaning. The girl says that when she returns to her native land she hopes that "my Liberty will be waiting for me here." She is referring of course to her dog, but the words also convey the need for political freedom in her country of origin, which appears to be suffering under an oppressive government.

Loss of Innocence

The fifth-grade child who narrates the story knows little about the harshness of life. She is one of four children in a close-knit, loving, extended family. But during the course of the story she is exposed to some of the cruelty and danger that exists in the world. Her first shock comes when she encounters the two intimidating strangers on the family property. One of them pulls hard on Liberty's leash, almost breaking the dog's neck (at least as the narrator views the incident), and the other one grips her arm hard enough to leave fingerprint marks on her flesh after releasing her. This is a glimpse for the girl of

Dalmatian dog (© age fotostock / SuperStock)

the brutal world that exists beyond the security of her own home; indeed, it has invaded her previously invulnerable home. As she says, it was the first time she had "come across mean and scary people."

The girl must also face the fact that sometimes events proceed out of her control and against her wishes; she must leave her beloved dog behind when the family emigrates to the United States. Another important lesson she learns, and a sign of the maturity that is forced early upon her, is that in certain circumstances she may need to appear cruel in order to ensure the best interests of a creature she loves, in this case her dog. This happens at the end of the story when she is anxious to ensure that the two men will not be able to ill-treat Liberty when they return to the property after the family has gone. She kicks the dog, gently at first, in order to stop him from following her and to encourage him to escape. When the dog continues to follow her, she kicks him harder, until he whimpers and then runs off. She has learned to act decisively and courageously when a loved one is threatened. As her father has said to her, "All liberty involves sacrifice," and as she absorbs this lesson she necessarily loses some of her childish innocence about life.

STYLE

Child's Point of View

Alvarez's story is told in the first person by a young girl. This means that all the events are described from the point of view of the child. Much of the effectiveness of the story consists in the fact that the girl does not understand the events that are going on around her. No one tells her the real situation. This is cleverly dramatized when she overhears the men talking in a kind of code about their plans. Not aware of the code, she has no idea of what they are discussing. Also, she does not understand that the discovery of the wires in the house shows that the family is being spied upon. Her lack of understanding gives the story a sense of mystery. The reader has to put together the pieces that the child misses. However, while the child may not understand everything that is going on, she is fully responsive to people's moods and to the atmosphere in the home. She has the ability to feel, and that is another factor that allows the reader to become emotionally engaged in the story.

Past Tense and Present Tense

Almost the entire story is told in the past tense. But in the last section, beginning with "Late in the night someone comes in and shakes us awake," the narrator switches to the present tense, and this continues for the remainder of the story. This is an unusual device, since an author would normally be consistent in use of tense in a short story. However, changing to the present tense for the final section creates a greater sense of immediacy and urgency for the reader, who has the illusion of being there as the story reaches its climax.

Liberty as Symbol

It is significant that the dog is named Liberty. Living up to his name, he shows how much he likes to be free. He does not obey the rules that the humans, especially the girl's mother, make for him, and he does not like being confined in his pen. It is entirely appropriate that after being given some prods by the narrator, Liberty escapes to freedom at the end. He may be taking his chances in the outside world, but that will be better than being at the mercy of the two thugs who may return. The dog as a symbol of liberty therefore supports the theme of the importance of liberty: It is better to take risks and remain free than to allow others to dictate the course of one's life.

COMPARE & CONTRAST

- **1950s–1960s:** The Dominican Republic suffers under the repressive dictatorship of President Rafael Leónidas Trujillo. Opposition groups backed by the United States plot Trujillo's assassination, which occurs in 1961.

  Today: The Dominican Republic has a democratic system of government and holds regular competitive elections. In May 2008, President Leonel Fernández, head of the centrist Dominican Liberation Party, wins election to a third four-year term. His success largely stems from his ability to keep the nation's economy prosperous. However, many people in the Dominican Republic remain poor and unable to meet their basic needs.

- **1950s–1960s:** During the repressive atmosphere of the Trujillo dictatorship, high-quality fiction writing does not flourish in the Dominican Republic. One of the nation's most talented writers, Juan Bosch, goes into exile rather than live under Trujillo's regime. After Trujillo's assassination and the civil war of 1965, a new generation of writers emerges to make major contributions to the literature of the nation.

  Today: Dominican writers, including José Alcántara Almánzar, Manuel de Jesús Galván, Manuel del Cabral, Juan Bosch, and Julia Alvarez, have international reputations for their work. Many of these writers cover the Dominican diaspora experience. A novel by Viriato Sención, originally written in Spanish and translated into English as *They Forged the Signature of God* (1995), includes reference to the difficulties experienced by Dominican immigrants in New York City.

- **1950s–1960s:** In response to the political and economic turbulence in their country, a large number of Dominicans immigrate to the United States, with the majority settling in New York City; Paterson, New Jersey; southern Florida, especially Miami and Fort Lauderdale; and Lawrence and Boston, Massachusetts.

  Today: According to the U.S. Census Bureau, in 2006, there are approximately 1.2 million people of Dominican descent in the United States. This figure includes those born in the United States as well as those born elsewhere. The states that contain the largest Dominican populations are New York, New Jersey, Florida, Massachusetts, Pennsylvania, Rhode Island, and Connecticut.

HISTORICAL CONTEXT

Political Oppression in the Dominican Republic

The Dominican Republic occupies the eastern two-thirds of the island of Hispaniola, between the Caribbean Sea and the North Atlantic Ocean. "Liberty" is set during a particularly difficult time in the history of the Dominican Republic, when unrest and opposition to the brutal regime of the dictator Rafael Leónidas Trujillo was on the rise. Trujillo first came to power in 1930. He was a military man who had risen to the rank of brigadier general in the national armed forces. After waging a campaign consisting of intimidation and terror in the national presidential election of 1930, Trujillo declared himself the winner and became the country's president. He proved himself to be a corrupt leader, amassing a personal fortune through the ownership of many of the country's industries. He ruthlessly eliminated any political opposition, using torture and murder to accomplish his goals and setting up a feared secret police, known as the SIM. (It is likely that the two men whom the narrator in "Liberty" finds hiding on the family property are members of the SIM.) In 1937, Trujillo ordered the mass killing of Haitians who lived on the border between Haiti, on the western third of the island, and the Dominican Republic. Many of the Haitians were unemployed, having crossed the border looking for work. Between fifteen thousand and twenty-five thousand Haitians were massacred.

During this period of the 1930s and 1940s, the United States supported the Trujillo dictatorship, which preserved the appearance of democracy, holding regular elections and granting women the right to vote. The economy also grew, with large investments in public works. Many schools were built during these decades. The national foreign debt was eliminated. The United States therefore overlooked the tyrannous and brutal nature of Trujillo's rule. However, after World War II, opposition to Trujillo began to grow in the Dominican Republic, and U.S. support for the dictator began to wane. A visit to Washington, D.C., in 1952 improved Trujillo's standing in the United States, but five years later the Dominican economy went into decline as a result of excessive borrowing. In the late 1950s and early 1960s, the era in which "Liberty" is set, opposition to his rule grew. Julia Alvarez's father was involved in a failed plot to overthrow Trujillo. Before he was implicated in the plot, some Americans friends helped him to acquire a visa that allowed him and his family to emigrate from the Dominican Republic to the United States.

Trujillo responded to the growing opposition to his regime with more brutal repression. One of the most notorious of the regime's crimes was the killing of the three Mirabal sisters, Patria, Minerva, and María Teresa, in 1960. These three sisters were members of an underground revolutionary group known as J14 that was dedicated to the overthrow of the Trujillo dictatorship. The murders created an international outcry and effectively ensured Trujillo's overthrow, which was made more certain by the continuing deterioration of the nation's economy. Trujillo was assassinated in May 1961 by a group of conspirators who had received arms from the U.S. Central Intelligence Agency (CIA). The U.S. government was fully aware of the assassination plot.

Latino Literature in the United States

Latino American literature refers to works written by those of Spanish-speaking heritage, including Mexican Americans, Cuban Americans, Puerto Rican Americans, and many other groups. When Alvarez first began to write, in the late 1960s and early 1970s, there were few opportunities for women of her ethnic heritage to be published by major publishers or be accepted into the canon of American literature. This applied to most nonwhite writers, including African Americans, Native Americans, and Latinos. However, during the 1970s the situation began to change. One of the first Latino novels to gain wide mainstream readership was *Bless Me, Ultima*, by Rudolfo Anya, which was published in 1972 and by the end of the 1980s had become an established classic. The success of *The House on Mango Street*, by the Mexican American Sandra Cisneros, was a breakthrough for Latina literature in 1983, as was the 1985 English language publication of *The House of the Spirits*, a novel by the Chilean American Isabel Allende that became a best seller. In 1989, the Cuban American writer Oscar Hijuelos won the Pulitzer Prize for his novel *The Mambo Kings Play Songs of Love*. In this late-1980s publishing environment that was becoming favorable to minority writers, several Latina writers emerged, including the Mexican Americans Ana Castillo and Denise Chávez, the Puerto Rican Americans Judith Ortiz Cofer and Esmeralda Santiago, and the Cuban Americans Cristina García and Himilce Novas. Alvarez's own breakthrough novel, published in 1991, was *How the García Girls Lost Their Accents*. She was the first Dominican American female writer to publish a novel that enjoyed mainstream success. Another Dominican American writer, Junot Díaz, who like Alvarez spent much of his childhood in the Dominican Republic before immigrating to the United States in 1974, published his acclaimed short story collection *Drown* in 1996, the same year that Alvarez's story "Liberty" appeared.

CRITICAL OVERVIEW

Alvarez is known primarily for her novels and her poetry; she has not published many short stories, and since "Liberty" was published as a single story in an anthology that also contains stories by other writers, it has not received attention from reviewers. However, the story is typical of her work in that it concentrates on a female protagonist and draws on Alvarez's own background as a child in the Dominican Republic. The story exhibits much of the style that has won critical praise from reviewers of Alvarez's other works published during the same decade. Perhaps most relevant is *How the García Girls Lost Their Accents*, a novel that can also be seen as fifteen interrelated short stories, some of which take place in the Dominican Republic during the same period in which "Liberty" is set. In a comment on this novel that might also apply to "Liberty," Ilan Stavans, in *Commonweal*, states, "Alvarez has an acute eye for the secret complexities that permeate family life. Although once in a while she steps into melodrama, her descriptions are full of pathos." Similarly, Kay Pritchett, writing in *World Literature Today*, praises Alvarez's novel *In the Time of the Butterflies*, about the Mirabal sisters: "She masterfully orchestrates the four voices, using throughout a simple prose that is pleasantly fresh and feminine." The same could well be said of Alvarez's use of the child's voice in "Liberty."

CRITICISM

Bryan Aubrey

Aubrey has a Ph.D. in English. In this essay on "Liberty," he discusses the autobiographical elements in the story, as well as some of its political implications.

Although "Liberty" is an isolated short story published in an anthology, it fits neatly into the main body of Julia Alvarez's fiction. Much of the inspiration for Alvarez's fiction has come from her own life. Her first novel, *How the García Girls Lost Their Accents* (1991), is semi-autobiographical, as she fictionalizes some actual events in order to tell a good story. Likewise, "Liberty" is clearly based on Alvarez's own childhood experience just before she and her family left their homeland to immigrate to the United States, but the main element of the plot, centered around the dog called Liberty, is fictional (although the family did own a pet dog).

"Liberty," published in 1996, and the novel published five years earlier almost overlap at one point. This occurs in the novel chapter "The Blood of the Conquistadores," which takes place in the Dominican Republic during the time when Alvarez was a child there. Even more so than does "Liberty," that chapter gives a picture of what it was like living in a police state under the Trujillo dictatorship. Two armed agents of the SIM, the dictator's secret police,

WHAT DO I READ NEXT?

- *The Dew Breaker* (2004), by Edwidge Danticat, is a novel about the legacy of torture in Haiti during the Duvalier dictatorship, which lasted from 1957 to 1986. Haiti occupies the western third of the island of Hispaniola, bordering the Dominican Republic. The author was born in Haiti and now lives in the United States. The novel focuses on the life of one man in particular who tortured people in Haiti and then moved to New York City, where he lives an outwardly stable and placid life. However, the author shows how the legacy of torture lives on, affecting not only the man himself but also his family and the entire Haitian American community.
- Amy Tan's best-selling novel *The Joy Luck Club* (1989) focuses on four Chinese American families and the generational conflicts within them. The younger, American-born women rebel against their mothers, who were raised in China and still cling to the traditional values of their culture. Tan's book has much in common with Alvarez's *How the García Girls Lost Their Accents.*
- *Why the Cocks Fight: Dominicans, Haitians, and the Struggle for Hispaniola* (1999), by Michele Wucker, is an American journalist's examination of the troubled relations between Haiti and the Dominican Republic. Wucker provides a lively portrayal of the cultures of both countries, their relationships to the United States, and the experiences of Haitian and Dominican immigrants in the United States.
- Alavarez's historical novel *In the Time of the Butterflies* (1994) takes place in the Dominican Republic in 1960. It is about the murder of the three Mirabal sisters, who had been working to overthrow the Trujillo dictatorship. The novel paints a vivid picture of life under Trujillo's rule and was nominated for the 1995 National Critics Circle Award.

> "IN 1960, AS ALVAREZ RECORDS IN 'OUR PAPERS,' HER ENTIRE FAMILY WAS UNDER VIRTUAL HOUSE ARREST. BECAUSE HER FATHER WAS A MEMBER OF THE UNDERGROUND OPPOSITION TO TRUJILLO, THE FAMILY KNEW THAT IT WAS ONLY A MATTER OF TIME BEFORE HE WOULD BE TAKEN AWAY."

arrive at the family home to interrogate the mother and father. Like the two strangers in "Liberty," they wear dark glasses, which give them an intimidating appearance. The father hides in a closet in the bedroom.

The chapter in the novel gives a clue to the coded talk between the men that the child in "Liberty" overhears. In that story, the men talk of hunting goats, but the father cannot accompany them because "his tennis shoes were missing." In the chapter in the novel, the mother gives instructions to call Victor Hubbard, the American consul (who appears to be the same Mister Victor present in "Liberty"), and tell him to come over straightaway to pick up his tennis shoes. It is clear from the context that the talk of tennis shoes is a coded reference to the gun that Papi has, which was smuggled to him by Victor, who in addition to being the American consul is the CIA chief in the Dominican Republic who has helped to organize the plot against Trujillo. Also, Trujillo is nicknamed "The Goat," which explains the reference to hunting goats. It is also revealed in this chapter that one of the family, a cousin of the girls, was arrested and tortured in prison but chose to commit suicide rather than betray his friends. This chapter therefore makes explicit what "Liberty" only implies: the great danger the family was living in and the fear that they, too, might soon be arrested.

Alvarez sheds more light on "Liberty" in her book of essays, *Something to Declare*, published in 1998. When she was only about five or six, as she relates in "Our Papers," the SIM arrested her grandfather and kept him in jail for two days. He was not subjected to torture, as so many people were, but was forced to sell some of his land at a very low price to the dictator's daughter. This was typical of how Trujillo and his family built up their immense private wealth, by forcing people to essentially give up what was rightfully theirs so that Trujillo and his associates could build their business empire. It is estimated that by 1939, within a decade of his taking power, Trujillo and his family owned more than half of all the industries in the Dominican Republic.

In 1960, as Alvarez records in "Our Papers," her entire family was under virtual house arrest. Because her father was a member of the underground opposition to Trujillo, the family knew that it was only a matter of time before he would be taken away. Her uncles were also involved in the plot to overthrow Trujillo. At night, a black car with SIM agents inside would be parked in their driveway, preventing them from going anywhere. "The men talked in low, worried voices behind closed doors," reports Alvarez, exactly as the men do in "Liberty." Her mother wore a worried expression all the time, and the parents shielded the children from the truth, again as happens in "Liberty." Her father was fortunate in that he had friends in the United States who helped him apply for a two-year visa to train as a heart surgeon. The Dominican Republic had no heart surgeons at the time, a fact that persuaded the regime to grant him the visa. Just as the child in "Liberty" is told that they will at some point be returning to the Dominican Republic, so the young Julia was told that the visit to the United States would be temporary. Alvarez writes that, according to her aunt, had they announced that they were leaving for good, they would all have been killed.

Other details in "Liberty" also turn out to be autobiographical. As Alvarez writes in "First Muse," another essay in *Something to Declare*, she was a badly behaved, unruly child who hated going to school. She thought that their living under a dictatorship was the reason why she was forced to spend such long, boring days at school, and she would refuse to do her homework. But she did discover the pleasures of reading, thanks to a gift from her maiden aunt Tití, who like the narrator's aunt in "Liberty," gives her a copy of *The Thousand and One Nights* (sometimes known as *Arabian Nights*). Through reading of the adventures of the fictional heroine, Scheherazade, the young Alvarez learned the power of stories. In "Family Matters," another essay in *Something to Declare*, Alvarez directly states that her fiction has been inspired by events that happened to her and by the stories told by her family, but she adds a caveat:

> I don't mean that my fiction slavishly recounts "what really happened," but that my sense of the world, and therefore of the world I re-create in language, comes from that first encompassing experience of familia [family] with its large cast of colorful characters, its elaborate branchings hither and yon to connect everyone together.

What really matters to the reader, of course, is not the extent to which a story is autobiographical but the themes and meanings that it conveys as a work of literature standing on its own merits. In this sense, one very noticeable element in "Liberty" is the highly positive presentation of the United States and everything it stands for. Every reference to the United States is a favorable one. Papi approvingly quotes the Declaration of Independence, hailing "life, liberty, and the pursuit of happiness," to explain his naming of the dog. He even promises that Liberty will be well behaved, like "an American dog." The dog symbolizes the great virtue of liberty for which the United States is renowned. This message is reinforced for the narrator by her aunt, who assures her, even though she does not grasp the meaning, that she will find liberty in America. The positive impression of the United States is further reinforced by the family's friendship with Mister Victor, the American consul, who gives them a dog "for all we'd done for him since he'd been assigned to our country." At one point, Victor practically lives at their house. Although this character is only briefly sketched, he is presented in an attractive light. He speaks kindly to the narrator about Liberty, and he laughs when she shows him the tricks she has taught the dog. Victor has a freckled face, and his coloring even resembles that of Liberty, prompting the narrator to comment that she "had the impression that God had spilled a lot of his colors when he was making American things," another fairly idealistic portrayal of the United States.

These aspects of "Liberty" offer a marked contrast to how the character of Victor Hubbard the American is portrayed in *How the García Girls Lost Their Accents*. Hubbard is overtly described as a CIA agent whose title as consul is only a front. He was sent to the Dominican Republic solely for the purpose of organizing the plot to overthrow the dictator, and he is presented as an amoral man who simply follows his orders, whatever they might be (and he gets contradictory messages from his superiors in Washington), without identifying with the cause of the Dominican people. Tellingly, when he receives the summons to rescue the family from the interrogations of the two SIM agents, he is in a bordello where he is indulging his interest in young adolescent girls. Thus, through the character of Victor Hubbard, the United States is presented in a much more critical light than it is through Mister Victor in "Liberty." This accords with comments made by Alvarez in "First Muse," one of the personal essays in *Something to Declare*, about the ambivalence of the United States toward the Dominican Republic, as American involvement was dictated by considerations that were not always related to the real needs of the Dominicans: "The powerful country to the north . . . had set our dictator in place and kept him there for thirty-one years." The comment is accurate; the United States had indeed been a supporter of the Trujillo regime for decades. As Bernard Diederich states in *Trujillo: The Death of the Goat*:

> Ironically, some of the weapons used to destroy Trujillo had been provided by the same Americans who had helped him to power thirty-one years before, who had forged the political support system to maintain him and who had turned a blind eye when his excesses drew public censure abroad.

Such an understanding of the role of the United States in the politics of the Dominican Republic is of course beyond the capacity of the young girl who narrates "Liberty." She knows nothing of the Cold War, the post–World War II struggle between the United States and its Western European allies against the Soviet Union and its allies, a struggle that led the United States to embrace all kinds of unsavory third-world dictators as long as they were strongly anti-Communist. All the narrator knows at the time is that "a world without Liberty"—that is, her dog—"would break my heart"; only later, with the coming of maturity, will she be able to grasp the deeper meaning of her words and the complexities that such a sentiment involves.

Source: Bryan Aubrey, Critical Essay on "Liberty," in *Short Stories for Students*, Gale, Cengage Learning, 2009.

Elizabeth Coonrod Martinez

In the following excerpt, Martinez argues that Alvarez will be remembered as one of the "initiators of Latina literature."

"'YOU KNOW, YOU MOVE INTUITIVELY AS A WRITER, USING CRAFT. THEN LATER PEOPLE WILL SEE OR POINT OUT, OR YOU YOURSELF WILL SEE A COUPLE OR MORE BASIC THEMES RUNNING THROUGH THERE, BUT YOU DIDN'T KNOW YOU WERE SPINNING IT, EVEN INTENTIONALLY.'"

History demonstrates that literary periods are launched by daring, intrepid writers or poets who appear to have suddenly sprouted from nowhere. Later these writers are acclaimed as initiators of movements, but the many years they barely subsisted while writing tomes that languished in wait for a publisher are rarely remembered.

Think of Gabriel Garcia Marquez, now recognized as one of the "fathers" of the so-called Latin American Boom of the late 1960s, when (mostly male) writers erupted onto the international stage with their novels dubbed as magical realism. Or the two Mexicans—Laura Esquivel and Angeles Mastretta—recognized for launching a "boom" of women writers in the 1980s, when women's novels finally began to be published in greater numbers. Just as Garcia Marquez and the writers of his generation were not the first to create a great Latin American novel, Esquivel and Mastretta are not the only significant women writers of the 20th century. But in each case they will forever be remembered as those who launched a literary period.

Julia Alvarez occupies a similar place in U.S. literature as one of the initiators of Latina literature, principally novels written in English by women of Latin American heritage. While members of the largest minority population in the U.S. had been producing novels and poetry throughout the 20th century, few who published before Sandra Cisneros' *The House on Mango Street* or before the beginning of the now-recognized Chicano/Latino era are famously remembered.

"I feel very lucky to happen to have been a writer at the watershed time when Latino literature became a literature that was not just relegated to the province of sociology," Alvarez says. "But I still feel there is a certain kind of condescension toward ethnic literature, even though it is a literature that is feeding and enriching the mainstream American literature . . . [And], definitely, still, there is a glass ceiling in terms of the female novelists. If we have a female character, she might be engaging in something monumental but she's also changing the diapers and doing the cooking, still doing things which get it called a woman's novel. You know, a man's novel is universal; a woman's novel is for women."

The content of novels written by women may be different, but Alvarez feels that all stories come from the same source: "The great lesson of storytelling is that there is this great river that we all are flowing on of being a human being and a human family. So, when the market comes up and says 'Latina writers,' and this is for this or that market, it is [simply] part of how things are broadcast out there, but really, that's not what the writing is about. It's about interconnectedness. And sure, Faulkner is from the south, or such and such poet has an Irish background and you can hear it in the lines; that is a way to get a handle on this mysterious current of narrative that is so important to us."

In Alvarez's case, she is the ubiquitous Dominican-American writer. Her novel *In the Time of the Butterflies*, based on the heroic Mirabal sisters who lived in the time of the Trujillo dictatorship in the Dominican Republic, is now a staple of college literature classes. Her first novel, *How the Garcia Girls Lost Their Accents*, published in 1991—along with Cisneros' *The House on Mango Street* in 1984 and Cristina Garcia's *Dreaming in Cuban* in 1992—officially launched the new movement of Latina writers. Their "hyphen" experience, straddling borders or cultures in the U.S. as people of Latin American or Caribbean descent, foments new critical ideas. The current generation of Dominican-American New York writers (Angie Cruz, Loida Maritza Perez, Nelly Rosario, and Junot Diaz) now hopes to achieve the success Alvarez has had.

A certain element of luck, and very precise publicity, played a role in the now easy recognition of Julia Alvarez and Sandra Cisneros. In 1990 they and two other writers—Denise Chavez and Ana Castillo—posed for a group photo arranged by their New York agent Susan Bergholz to promote their forthcoming novels. The one-page photo article ran in the magazine *Vanity Fair* under the title, "The Four Amigas," a publicity stunt that helped usher in a Latino literary generation.

"That was a shock to me," Alvarez says, "One of the things that surprised me was the publicity machine that happens around books, and that people take pictures. I only knew how to love a book and go to the library and get the next book by the writer. You don't think of all the publicity stuff.

"I was just so happy that I had this novel coming out because I was up for tenure, and my chairman basically said, 'you know if you don't have a book, it's not going to be a pretty story.' So when I heard that *Garcia Girls* was taken and would be published, I just thought of it as the book that would get me tenure. But then it did so well that seven years later, I gave up tenure to become a full-time writer."

Her first novel was followed by *Butterflies* in 1994, a sequel to *Garcia Girls* called *¡Yo!* in 1997, and another historical novel, *In the Name of Salome*, in 2000. In a period of fifteen years Alvarez has released fifteen books: four books of poetry, a collection of essays titled *Something to Declare*, four children's books, and *A Cafecito Story*, which counters global capitalism and demonstrates the need for a slow process of growing and preparing excellent coffee beans. Last April, she embarked on a multi-city book tour to promote her latest novel, *Saving the World*. It was a grueling schedule, with 24 stops in five weeks, but she appeared radiant late in the tour, sparkling with enthusiasm during her readings.

The slender woman with dark, curly hair and hazel eyes is a vegetarian, which may account for her physical stamina, but she also possesses a vibrancy of spirit that draws people in. Her ophthalmologist husband, Bill Eichner, accompanied her on the tour. At each juncture, they presented a gift of organic coffee, brewed and served to those who turned out to hear her. She explained how she was researching a new historical novel when the September 11 tragedy occurred in 2001 and that that occurrence had influenced her to create a second story, alternating a contemporary character's angst with the historical journey of a small expedition that transported the smallpox vaccine across the world. She quotes from Dante, stating that her modern character is experiencing a "dark night of the soul, which we now pathologize and call depression." Alvarez's voice is soft but her words are very clearly enunciated: "It is about being a human being. With stories we have these ways of deeply connecting as human beings."

After the reading, she takes questions, and responds candidly to each. Does her story have a moral or a message? "Sometimes things happen to us, and [since] we humans have created narrative, at times like this we bring it to bear on what has happened. I do think narratives are important and powerful, but novels don't answer questions, they're not solutions."

Someone asks whether she first writes in English or Spanish. When Alvarez responds, "I am not truly bilingual, I am English-dominant," there is silence in the room, as though the audience is surprised by that revelation. Her works, like those of many other Latino writers, are translated to Spanish by other individuals.

Despite the fact that she and her husband purchased farmland in the Dominican Republic in 1996 to help foment a cooperative of independent coffee-growers, they do not visit the island regularly. In 2004, they sold some of the tracts to others who wanted to help in the project, and Alvarez spends most of her time at her permanent residence for nearly two decades in Weybridge, Vermont. It is quite near the Canadian border, and there are many more residents of French and German heritage than Latinos; her reality is more of a snowy setting than a tropical one. She frequently states, "I live in sleepy Vermont. I live on a dirt road." The surrounding community consists mostly of farms and the nearest town is Middlebury, where Alvarez holds the position of Writer-in-Residence at Middlebury College. She describes her routine as time spent in the college library or in her home office. "I go to work every day and I do the work, the same way that my neighbor goes and takes care of his sheep, and Bill goes to the office. That's just what I do, and what I am focused on."...

Like other well-known writers at the inception of a literary period, Alvarez will forever be remembered as the first Dominican-American writer and one of the first Latinas in a decade of a great deal of attention for this group. What is her impression of the critical reception of her work?

"You know, you move intuitively as a writer, using craft. Then later people will see or point out, or you yourself will see a couple or more basic themes running through there, but you didn't know you were spinning it, even intentionally."

It is the reader that matters most to her. In fact, she feels that no story is "alive" until the reader has absorbed it. "What you hope for with a story is that it opens up some little insights, some knowledge of character and of self that wasn't there before, that it nurtures the human spirit and gets passed on, so that we're able to make different choices and be a little more aware of each other, of the human experience.

"Why does Whitman say, 'Look for me under your boot soles' at the end of *Leaves of Grass?* He doesn't mean that literally. He is dead, he is under our boot soles, or our shoes, but he is alive while we are reading this poem, he's inside us. At the end of *The Woman I Kept to Myself*, there's a poem entitled 'Did I redeem myself?' and the last two lines are: 'And you, my readers, what will you decide when all that's left of me will be these lines?'"

Source: Elizabeth Coonrod Martinez, "Julia Alvarez: Progenitor of a Movement: This Dominican-American Writer Weaves Passionate Sensibilities through Her Works with the Gift of Seeing through Others' Eyes," in *Americas* (English Edition), Vol. 59, No. 2, March–April 2007, pp. 6–14.

Jonathan Bing

In the following interview, Alvarez discusses her family's flight from the Dominican Republic, an experience that informed "Liberty," and her status as an immigrant writer.

In 1991, Julia Alvarez made a resounding splash on the literary scene with her first novel, *How the Garcia Girls Lost Their Accents*, whose narrators, the four vibrant and distinctive Garcia siblings, captivated readers and critics. Like their author, the characters emigrated to middle-class Queens, N.Y., from the Dominican Republic, and the novel provided a keen look at the island social structure they wistfully remember and the political turmoil they escaped.

The second-oldest sister, Yolanda, now a well-known author, is the protagonist of Alvarez's third novel, *¡Yo!*, out next month from Algonquin (Forecasts, Oct. 14). Alvarez brings to Yo's portrait an empathy of shared experiences, anxieties and hopes.

In 1960 at the age of 10, Alvarez fled the Dominican Republic with her parents and three sisters (her father was involved in the underground against the dictator Raphael Trujillo). She has since roamed this country, teaching writing in far-flung schools and communities, before finally putting down roots in Middlebury, Vt., and writing two books of poetry and three novels, including 1994's *In the Time of the Butterflies* (Algonquin).

> "LIKE MANY POLITICAL REFUGEES, ALVAREZ SOON FOUND THE DISPLACEMENTS OF LANGUAGE AND GEOGRAPHY TO BE THE STUFF OF ART. AS AN ADOLESCENT, SHE SAYS, THE ACT OF WRITING HELPED TO ALLAY THE PAIN OF ACCULTURATION AND THE STIGMA OF BEING AN OUTSIDER."

A current exhibit at the New York Public Library, "The Hand of the Poet from John Donne to Julia Alvarez," displays snapshots of the author in the Dominican Republic (she travels there at least once a year), riding horseback, dancing the merengue and obstreperously bartering for plantains. When *PW* catches up with Alvarez, it is in the rare-book room of the Middlebury College library, where a standing-room-only audience has gathered to hear her read from the new novel. Brushing unruly, dark bangs from her lively face, her voice inflected by a faint Latin twang, she shows few signs of the butterflies fluttering in her stomach, induced by the prospect of reciting her work on her own turf.

"I couldn't sleep last night before this reading," she confesses, later ushering *PW* into the living room of her secluded ranch house, which is brimming with plants, cacti and photographs of her extended family. Alvarez, who first came to Middlebury to attend the Breadloaf Writers' Conference as an undergraduate in the late 1960s and is now a tenured professor of English, has lived here permanently since 1988, and it is here that she met her husband, an ophthalmologist. Yet she expresses ambivalence at the thought of becoming something of a local fixture.

"I see myself marginally in the academic community, which I think in part is good for a writer, because it keeps you on your toes," she says. "When I first moved here, people would come up to me and say things that I hadn't told them. Or remark upon things that I didn't know they knew. I didn't realize that everything's connected. There's no anonymity. The good part of that is, as a friend said, 'Julia, you've always wanted roots. But now you realize that once there are roots, there are worms in the soil.'"

In conversation, Alvarez is an ebullient blend of insecurities, tart anecdotes and spitfire judgments, often punctuated by a deep, chesty laugh. Scooping up an obese marmalade cat named Lucia, she babbles half in English and half in Spanish into its fur, then offers us a glass of wine and sits cross-legged on a leather ottoman, recalling the tumult of a childhood bifurcated by conflicting cultural milieus.

"I grew up in that generation of women thinking I would keep house. Especially with my Latino background, I wasn't even expected to go to college," she says. "I had never been raised to have a public voice."

Herself the second-oldest, Alvarez was sent to boarding school in her early teens under the protective wing of her older sister. "My parents were afraid of public school. I think they were just afraid in general of this country. So I went away to school and was on the move and not living at home since I was 13 years old."

Like many political refugees, Alvarez soon found the displacements of language and geography to be the stuff of art. As an adolescent, she says, the act of writing helped to allay the pain of acculturation and the stigma of being an outsider. "I came late into the language but I came early into the profession. In high school, I fell in love with how words can make you feel complete in a way that I hadn't felt complete since leaving the island. Early on, I fell in love with books, which I didn't have at all growing up. In the Dominican Republic, I was a non-reader in what was basically an oral culture and I hated books, school, anything that had to do with work."

Alvarez went to Connecticut College, but after winning the school's poetry prize, she departed for Breadloaf and Middlebury, where she earned her B.A. in 1971. After an M.F.A at Syracuse University, she lit out for the heartland, taking a job with the Kentucky Arts Commission as a traveling poet-in-residence. For two years, Alvarez traversed the back roads of the Bluegrass State, with *Leaves of Grass* as her Baedeker. "I would just pack up my car. I had a little Volkswagen. My whole car was a file system. Everything I owned was in there.

"In some communities I'd give workshops or talk at night in the local church. I loved it. I felt like the Whitman poem where he travels throughout the country and now will do nothing but listen. I was listening. I was seeing the inside of so many places and so many people, from the Mennonites of Southern Kentucky to the people of Appalachia who thought I had come to do something with poultry."

When that job ended, other teaching jobs beckoned, and Alvarez careened around the country for more than a decade. "I was a migrant poet," she laughs. "I would go anywhere."

With no fixed address, Alvarez gradually assembled her first collection of poetry, which Breadloaf director Bob Pack placed with Grove. Aptly called *Homecomings*, it featured a 33-sonnet sequence called "33," which portrays the emotional vertigo Alvarez suffered on her 33rd birthday, facing middle age without a secure job, a family of her own or a career blueprint to sustain her. Alvarez nevertheless greeted the book's publication, in 1984, with great trepidation. "It was scary," she says. "I thought 'Oh, my God, what if my parents read this? There are love affairs in here. Maybe I can go out and buy all the copies.'"

She has since reprinted *Homecomings* and issued another book of verse with Dutton (*The Other Side*, 1995). Now, however, she writes poetry less frequently than fiction. "I think what's hard for me about writing poetry is that it is so naked," Alvarez explains. In retrospect, it's not surprising that her emergence as a novelist coincided with her first tenure-track job at Middlebury. *How the Garcia Girls Lost Their Accents*, a novel displaying a historical sweep and mobility of voice not found in her poetry, was a natural next step after years of rootlessness.

"It used to turn me off, the idea of writing something bigger than a poem," she reflects. "But you grow as a writer and you start to imagine other possibilities."

Susan Bergholz, certainly the most influential agent of Latino fiction, whose clients include Ana Castillo, Sandra Cisneros and Denise Chávez, has represented Alvarez since placing *Garcia Girls* with Shannon Ravenel at Algonquin. As Alvarez remembers, Bergholz approached her at a reading she gave in New York after winning a 1986 G.E. Foundation Award for Younger Writers. "She was interested in my work, so I sent her a bunch of things. She really plugged away at that stuff, sending it around and talking to people and finally she landed Shannon. I'm very grateful to Susan as the person who really fought that battle for me, which—because of my background and because of my self-doubt—I probably would not have fought for myself."

Yet when *Garcia Girls* first reached Ravenel, "there was no book there," Alvarez says. "I sent portions of it to Shannon and she said: 'There's a bigger story here you're trying to tell.'"

Today Alvarez can't imagine publishing with a larger house at any price, provided that Ravenel stays put. "Shannon helped form me as a writer. She often helps me to think of how to put my books together. Sometimes, I'll say, 'our book' and she'll say, 'Julia, it's your book.' Maybe a place could initially offer you more money or more razzmatazz. But I was 41 when *Garcia Girls* came out. If I were writing to make a whole lot of money, I would have given this craft up a long time ago. I'm doing the writing because it's the way I understand my life. It's what I do and I want a place that is sympatico to that."

THE BUTTERFLIES INTERVENE

Alvarez's trajectory as a novelist has hardly followed a predictable scheme. Her second novel revisits the last days of the Trujillo regime and retells the story of the three Mirabal sisters, Patricia, Minerva and Maria Teresa—actual political dissidents called Las Mariposas (the Butterflies)—who in 1960 were murdered by Trujillo's henchmen. The event galvanized the political insurrection that led to Trujillo's assassination in 1961. "It's always been a story I wanted to tell. But I didn't know how to do it. They seemed to me such enormous, mythical figures. I didn't know how to touch them and make them real. I thought it would be a sacrilege even to do that in some people's eyes. But I knew it was a story I wanted to tell."

Alvarez had previously tackled the subject in an essay in a small press book on heroic women, but in returning to the island to research the novel, she made an astonishing discovery: there were, in fact, four sisters, and the eldest, Dédé, had survived and was still living in the Dominican Republic. Alvarez interviewed Dédé and began to piece together the minutiae of the sisters' lives. "I understand the politics of a four-daughter family with no boys in a Latino culture," she notes.

All of Alvarez's novels are constructed from multiple viewpoints, ranging freely from sassy gossip to animated autobiography, but always concealing a forceful political undercurrent. She attributes her interest in voice to the storytelling traditions of Dominican life. "We didn't have TV, we didn't have books. It was just what people did. That was our newspaper."

Yo, of course, means "I" in Spanish, but Alvarez has shrewdly left the self at the center of the novel absent. Yolanda isn't granted a voice in the novel. Instead, Alvarez builds the book around the memories of those who have suffered the manipulations of the budding author. The liberty a writer takes with her family and background is a subject of increasing importance to Alvarez as her books grow more popular. "My sisters had a hard time with *Garcia Girls*. But I think they're proud of me, and I think the books have helped them understand their lives better. Sometimes they will remember something that I think I invented. Now it's almost like the stories in that book are part of the memory pool."

In 1993, *Vanity Fair* ran a splashy profile of Alvarez, Castillo, Cisneros and Chávez (all are indeed friends) under the rubric "Los Girlfriends," portraying a cliquish set of Latina writers sharing the same literary concerns and themes. It's precisely such hype and labeling that *¡Yo!* set out to interrogate. "One thing I didn't like about it from the beginning, which didn't have to do with the people involved, is I thought how I would feel if I was a Latino writer and I saw *the* Girlfriends and these are the [only] Latino writers. I felt there should have been 100 writers on either side of us. Not that I think it was a terrible thing. I just wonder and worry about what all of this publicity and labeling comes to."

Discussing the extravagant antics of book marketing, the 22-city tour she is about to embark on and the persistent film interest in her work (*Butterflies* has been optioned to Phoenix Pictures), Alvarez grows antsy. "As you talk, I realize I am always that immigrant. This, too, I am experiencing and watching. But I don't put faith in it. In a minute, it can be swept away." She needn't worry. Once an author without an address, a language or a homeland to call her own, Alvarez now has a loyal readership that in years to come will undoubtedly only grow larger.

Source: Jonathan Bing, "Julia Alvarez: Books That Cross Borders," in *Publishers Weekly*, Vol. 243, No. 51, December 16, 1996, pp. 38–39.

SOURCES

Alvarez, Julia, *How the García Girls Lost Their Accents*, Plume/Penguin, 1992, pp. 195–224.

———, Julia Alvarez Web site, http://www.juliaalvarez.com (accessed August 20, 2008).

———, "Liberty," in *Writers Harvest 2*, edited by Ethan Canin, Harcourt Brace, 1996, pp. 192–200.

———, *Something to Declare*, Algonquin Books of Chapel Hill, 1998, pp. 16, 125–26, 135.

"Ancestry Maps," *ePodunk*, http://www.epodunk.com/ancestry/Dominican-Republic.html (accessed August 20, 2008).

Central Intelligence Agency, *World Factbook*, s.v. "Dominican Republic," https://www.cia.gov/library/publications/the-world-factbook/geos/dr.html (accessed August 20, 2008).

Diederich, Bernard, *Trujillo: The Death of the Goat*, Little, Brown, 1978, p. 5.

Pritchett, Kay, Review of *In the Time of the Butterflies*, in *World Literature Today*, Vol. 69, No. 4, Autumn 1995, p. 789.

Sirias, Silvio, *Julia Alvarez: A Critical Companion*, Greenwood Press, 2001.

Stavans, Ilan, Review of *How the García Girls Lost Their Accents*, in *Commonweal*, Vol. 119, No. 7, April 10, 1992, pp. 23–25.

U.S. Census Bureau, "Selected Population Profile in the United States," http://factfinder.census.gov.

Varnes, Kathrine, "Julia Alvarez," in *Dictionary of Literary Biography*, Vol. 282, *New Formalist Poets*, edited by Jonathan N. Barron, Thomson Gale, 2003, pp. 16–23.

FURTHER READING

Brown, Isabel Zakrzewski, *Culture and Customs of the Dominican Republic*, Greenwood Press, 1999.

In addition to providing a historical survey that extends from colonial times to the end of the twentieth century, this book covers religion, social customs, media, cinema, literature, the performing arts, architecture, art, sculpture, and photography. It includes many illustrations, a map, and a chronology.

Callin, Anne, Ruth Glasser, and Jocelyn Santana, editors, *Caribbean Connections: The Dominican Republic*, Teaching for Change, 2006.

This work presents an overview of the history, politics, and culture of the Dominican American community. It includes essays, oral histories, poetry, fiction, timelines, and maps. Featured authors include Julia Alvarez, Edwidge Danticat, Junot Díaz, and Pedro Mir.

Johnson, Kelli Lyon, *Julia Alvarez: Writing a New Place on the Map*, University of New Mexico Press, 2005.

This book offers an extended analysis of Alvarez's oeuvre in terms of her journey to establish an identity for herself as a writer who is both Dominican and American.

Kevane, Bridget, *Latino Literature in America*, Greenwood Press, 2003.

Kevane discusses works by eight major Latino writers in the United States: Alvarez, Rodolfo Anaya, Sandra Cisneros, Junot Díaz, Christina García, Oscar Hijuelos, Judith Ortiz Cofer, and Ernesto Quinonez. Topics covered include acculturation, generational conflicts, immigration, assimilation, and exile. Kevane also discusses issues of language, religion, and gender.

Race at Morning

WILLIAM FAULKNER

1955

William Faulkner's 1955 short story "Race at Morning" is one of several of the author's well-known hunting stories. It was in fact Faulkner's last published hunting story. This is notable because the story ends in a way that indicates the end of an era, one in which it was once enough for a man to live off of the land, and when there were such things in the world as real wilderness and mystery. Often compared to Faulkner's famous long story "The Bear" (1942), "Race at Morning" reflects Faulkner's growing unease with the changing world around him. Written in a southern vernacular or slang, the story is a challenging read that is simultaneously a deceptively simple story about a deer hunt. The narrative predominantly takes place over the course of one day on which an unnamed boy and his guardian attempt, often comically, to chase a deer. In that time, the story explores themes of innocence and innocence lost.

"Race at Morning" was first published in the *Saturday Evening Post* on March 5, 1955, and it was published later that same year in Faulkner's collection *Big Woods*. A more recent edition of the collection was published in 1994 as *Big Woods: The Hunting Stories*.

AUTHOR BIOGRAPHY

William Faulkner was born William Cuthbert Falkner on September 25, 1897, in New Albany, Mississippi. Faulkner was the eldest of the four

William Faulkner (© Pictorial Press Ltd. / Alamy)

sons of Murry and Maud Falkner. The family settled in Oxford, in Lafayette County, Mississippi, when Faulkner was nearly five years old, and he spent the bulk of his life there. Oxford was the model for Jefferson, the fictional town that appears throughout Faulkner's writing, with Lafayette County in turn represented throughout his work as Yoknapatawpha County. Faulkner began to write poetry at a young age, but he did not begin writing fiction until his late twenties, when the famed author Sherwood Anderson persuaded him to do so.

Too short to join the U.S. forces during World War I, Faulkner joined the Royal Air Force, and it is likely that he changed the original spelling of his name during this time period in order to sound more British. Regardless, by the time Faulkner finished his military training, World War I had ended, although the stories he would tell about his time in the service did not reflect this fact. Upon completing his service, and without having received a high school degree, Faulkner returned to Oxford and enrolled in the University of Mississippi in 1919. He began writing for the school paper, and it was during this time that he experienced his first publication, a poem in the *New Republic*. Faulkner left the university in 1920 without graduating, moving briefly to New York City before returning to Oxford. His first book of poetry, *The Marble Faun* (1924), was not a success, and Faulkner moved to New Orleans soon after its publication in 1925. In New Orleans, Faulkner was advised by Anderson to send a draft of his first novel to a publisher, and *Soldier's Pay* was duly published in 1926.

In 1929 Faulkner published the novel *Sartoris*, the first of his many works set in Yoknapatawpha County. Indeed, 1929 was an important year for Faulkner; his first master work, *The Sound and the Fury*, was published, and Faulkner married his childhood sweetheart, Estelle Oldham Franklin, in Oxford. Estelle divorced her first husband in order to marry Faulkner, and she brought two stepchildren, Victoria and Malcolm, to the marriage. Faulkner and Estelle would themselves have two daughters, Alabama, who died in infancy, and Jill. The following year, while he worked the night shift at the local power station, Faulkner published his second master work, *As I Lay Dying*. Also in 1930, Faulkner purchased the traditional southern estate he called Rowan Oak, and the Faulkner family lived there until the house was sold to the University of Mississippi in 1972. It remains as it was when Faulkner lived there, preserved as a museum for his life and work.

In 1931, the same year in which Alabama was born and died, Faulkner published his first collection of short stories, *These 13*. The book contains some of Faulkner's best-known stories, including "A Rose for Emily," and it was dedicated to Estelle and Alabama. In 1932, while still actively publishing novels and short stories, Faulkner began to write screenplays, traveling between Oxford and Hollywood, California. His best known screenplays are *Gunga Din* (1939), and *The Big Sleep*, a 1946 film adaptation of Raymond Chandler's novel of the same title.

Some of Faulkner's other notable books are *Absalom, Absalom!* (1936) and *Go Down, Moses* (1942). Through the early 1940s, Faulkner's career flagged somewhat, and many of his earlier books were already out of print. Faulkner next regained critical attention upon the 1946 publication of *The Portable Faulkner*, and three years later he was awarded the Nobel Prize for Literature. Faulkner used much of the prize money to fund a prize for aspiring writers, now the well-known PEN/Faulkner Award.

Although Faulkner was hospitalized throughout his life for chronic back pain and alcoholic binges, he remained a prolific writer well into his late career. In 1951 Faulkner's *Collected Stories* (1950) won the National Book Award, and his novel *A Fable* (1954) won both the National Book Award and a Pulitzer Prize in 1955. Also in 1955, "Race at Morning" was first published in the *Saturday Evening Post* on March 5. The story was then published shortly afterward in Faulkner's 1955 collection *Big Woods*. It was also during this period that Faulkner acted as a cultural delegate for the U.S. State Department.

By the end of his career, Faulkner was splitting his time between Oxford and Charlottesville, Virginia, where he was writer in residence at the state university there. Faulkner died of a heart attack on July 6, 1962, in Byhalia, Mississippi. He was buried the following day in Oxford.

MEDIA ADAPTATIONS

- An audiobook of *Big Woods: The Hunting Stories* was recorded by the National Library Service and Potomac Talking Book Services in 1995. The collection is narrated by Barrett Whitener.

PLOT SUMMARY

"Race at Morning" is narrated by an unnamed twelve-year-old boy who speaks in southern vernacular. Set just outside of Yoknapatawpha County, the story opens as the boy claims, "I was in the boat when I seen him." It is unclear who the boy sees, but his head is out of the water and there is a "rocking chair" on it. This odd description does not make what is going on any more clear to the reader. Then the boy notes that it is dusk and discusses "the season" that will be ending the next day. The boy also makes a passing reference to "game wardens." From these combined statements the reader can deduce that it is hunting season and that the strange thing with a "rocking chair" on his head is a deer, a buck with antlers. Given the way the boy speaks about the deer, it is apparent that he has been trying to hunt this particular buck for some time. The boy is excited, as he plans to lay in wait for the buck with Mister Ernest the next morning.

The boy returns to the camp from the woods and tells Mister Ernest about what he saw, and they "et supper and fed the dogs." The boy then helps Mister Ernest play poker. The narration indicates that Mister Ernest is likely very old—he is nearly deaf and has lost some of his sight—and that the boy is meant to help Mister Ernest get around. One of the poker players, Roth Edmonds, asks the boy to go to bed as it gets late. Another player, Willy Legate, first suggests that the boy study if he is not going to bed and then pokes fun at him for being illiterate. The boy replies that he does not need to know how to write his name because "I can remember in my mind who I am." Walter Ewell asks the boy, "Man to man now, how many days in your life did you ever spend in school?" Willy replies for the boy, sarcastically implying that there is no "use in going to school" when the boy will just have to quit to help Mister Ernest during the brief hunting season. Willy then asks the boy why he never calls anyone "mister," and this is really a comment about the boy's lack of respect for his elders. The boy replies that he calls Mister Ernest "mister." Unaware of this exchange, Mister Ernest tells the boy to go to bed.

A little while later, Mister Ernest comes to bed, and although the boy wants to talk to him about the buck, he does not want to scream at the near-deaf man to do so. The boy falls asleep and is awoken by Simon at 4 a.m. for coffee, and everyone gets ready for the hunt. The boy feeds Dan (Mister Ernest's horse) and Roth Edmonds's horse, which the boy calls "Edmondziz." The boy comments that it will be "a fine day, cold and bright." This, according to the boy as he refers to the buck, is "jest exactly the kind of day that big old son of a gun . . . would like to run." After the camp eats breakfast, the boy gets the stand-holders for Uncle Ike McCaslin; stand-holders are used to reserve a hunting stand. A hunting stand (often a platform in a tree) is used to simultaneously hide from game and have a good vantage point from which to shoot at it. The boy reports that Uncle Ike is the oldest and most experienced hunter, so he will likely know the best places to wait for the buck to pass by. The boy also notes that the buck is very old, aged to a point that "would amount to a hundred years in a deer's life." Then the boy excitedly comments that he and Mister Ernest are "going to git him."

The boy, Mister Ernest, and Roth Edmonds send the dogs to Simon, who holds the lead dog, Eagle. Then Roth gets on his horse and Mister Ernest gets on Dan. Dan bucks until Mister Ernest hits him on the head with his shotgun, which he has already loaded. The boy climbs up on Dan, too, sitting behind Mister Ernest. They set off for the bayou with Simon and the dogs leading the way. Again, the boy mentions the fine weather, anticipating the way the sun will rise, causing the frosted landscape to sparkle and making the boy feel "light and strong as a balloon." Thinking about the fine day, the boy notes that even if the buck waited "another ten years" to be caught, "he couldn't 'a' picked a better one."

When the hunting party gets to the bayou, they see the buck's footprint, which is described as being "big as a cow's, big as a mule's." The dogs get so excited as they pick up the buck's scent that Mister Ernest tells the boy to dismount and give Simon a hand. The boy says that the buck usually lays in the canebrake (a dense patch of reeds) and waits for the dogs to run off after a different doe or other young deer before swimming out into the bayou and leaving the area. The boy notes that they are not going to let that happen this time. Roth leaves the group in order to cut off the buck and send him toward Uncle Ike's stands. Then the group continues on without him until they are near enough to the brake to let the dogs loose. The horse takes off after the dogs, and the boy hangs on to Mister Ernest's belt to avoid falling off of Dan.

The dogs find the buck, and the boy can hear it crashing through the canebrake. Mister Ernest maneuvers Dan as the boy points the way. The boy hangs on for dear life, commenting that "when the jump come, Dan never cared who else was there neither; I believe to my soul he could 'a' cast and run them dogs by hisself." The dogs and buck are now out of sight, though the boy thinks that they must be getting close to Uncle Ike's stands. Mister Ernest must think so too, as he reigns in Dan so that they can listen for any gunshots. When none are forthcoming, they start up again, but given how long they have waited, Mister Ernest and the boy know that the buck has somehow gotten past the stands without being shot at. The boy comments that the buck must be "a hant," or a ghost. As soon as he and Mister Ernest leave the thicket, they find Uncle Ike, who confirms what they believe had happened. Uncle Ike urges them to continue the chase before the buck makes it to a neighboring camp.

As the boy and Mister Ernest continue their chase, the boy observes that the sun has now fully risen and that the wind is picking up. Now and then the boy can hear the dogs when the wind blows in his direction. The boy imagines that the buck must be surprised to come upon yet another camp filled with people. He imagines the buck thinking, "Is this whole durn country full of folks this morning?" The boy imagines the buck caught between the dogs and the camp, wondering "how much time he had to decide what to do next." The boy then states that this time the buck "almost shaved it too fine," because he and Mister Ernest can hear gunfire now. They hear so much gunfire it sounds "like a war." The boy is very upset by this, as he and Mister Ernest want to get the buck "because he was ourn." The boy notes that the buck has been living on their land and eating their food and that they have been watching for him every hunting season.

Mister Ernest tells the boy to be quiet and listen, and the boy realizes that the buck must still be running because he can still hear the dogs chasing it. Sure enough, he and Mister Ernest pass by the group of men who had shot at the buck "looking at the ground and the bushes, like maybe if they looked hard enough, spots of blood would bloom out on the stalks and leaves." One of the men tells Mister Ernest that they think they hit him, and Mister Ernest promises to bring them the buck if this turns out to be true. As the boy and Mister Ernest continue their chase, they end up in unfamiliar country, having never had to run after a deer for so long. When they come to the bayou, they try to find a crossing, but rather than lose time, Mister Ernest decides to jump Dan. The boy sees a grapevine hanging in the way, but Mister Ernest does not see it, and the vine snags on the saddle, which slides off of Dan with Mister Ernest and the boy still on it. Both of them sit on saddle, hanging in mid-air until the vine snaps under their weight. Mister Ernest is knocked out by the fall, and the boy gets some water to throw on him. When Mister Ernest comes to, he yells at the boy for not warning him about the vine and for crushing him in the fall. He tells the boy to make sure he jumps out of the way if something like that ever happens again. The boy and Mister Ernest get Dan, who is waiting nearby, and they improvise a makeshift saddle tie before continuing the chase.

The boy notices that it is now afternoon. He can no longer hear the dogs, but he does hear more gunshots. The only other camp in the area is about thirty miles from their camp, so he realizes how far they have traveled. When the boy and Mister Ernest arrive at the camp, "it was jest like before—two or three men squatting and creeping among the bushes, looking for blood." This time, however, Mister Ernest and the boy do not stop to talk to the men. Mister Ernest instead turns the horse north, away from the chase. When the boy protests, Mister Ernest, looking "tired," tells him that the buck has "done done his part, give everybody a fair open shot at him, and now he's going home." Thus, the boy and Mister Ernest begin making their way back to the canebrake. The boy envisions the buck, Dan, Mister Ernest, and himself, as they make their way to their beds, in a sort of camaraderie. The boy observes,

> "All three of us was still what we was—that old buck that had to run, not because he was skeered, but because running was what he done the best and was proudest at . . . and me and Mister Ernest and Dan, that run him not because we wanted his meat, which would be too tough to eat anyhow, or his head to hang on a wall, but because now we could go back and work hard for eleven months making a crop, so we would have the right to come back here next November."

Then, for the first time all day, the boy and Mister Ernest finally catch a glimpse of the buck. As the sun is setting, while the dogs lay all around panting, the buck rises up slowly, "big as a mule." He turns and walks into the thicket. "It might 'a' been a signal, a good-bye, a farewell," the boy thinks. Eagle stands before them with his legs splayed, looking defeated, and Mister Ernest stops Dan and tells the boy to look at the dog's feet. The boy knows the dog is tired and that nothing is wrong with Eagle's feet, but Mister Ernest insists. As the boy obeys, he can hear Mister Ernest's shotgun pumping, and he figures that Mister Ernest is checking the gun in case they get a clear shot at the buck.

The boy and Mister Ernest continue and indeed come upon the buck once more, the setting "sun sparking on the tips of his horns . . . so that he looked like he had twelve lighted candles branched around his head." Mister Ernest aims and fires: It is a perfect shot, but the gun is empty, and the buck turns and disappears into the thicket once and for all. Mister Ernest sits quietly, mumbling "God dawg." The boy promises not to tell anyone that Mister Ernest forgot to load his gun or even to mention that they saw the buck at all. Mister Ernest replies, "Much oblige."

The boy and Mister Ernest make their way back toward their camp in the dark, walking beside Dan. After some time, Mister Ernest tells the boy to "get on the horse" lest they "spoil him." In reality, Mister Ernest is just being kind to the now tired boy, and the boy relates that Mister Ernest was once his parents' landlord. Two years ago, the boy's mother ran off with another man, and the next day his father also abandoned him. After the boy was left alone, Mister Ernest came to retrieve him, and the boy has been with Mister Ernest ever since. Finally, the boy and Mister Ernest make it back to the camp, and the boy imagines the buck resting in its canebrake.

The next morning, hunting season is over, and the rest of the camp goes back up the river, leaving Mister Ernest and the boy alone. The boy says that Mister Ernest is not just a landowner but "a farmer, he worked as hard as ara one of his hands and tenants." This, the boy claims, is how he knew he would get along with Mister Ernest, implying that Mister Ernest is a good man. Mister Ernest is a widower, so living with him was "jest fine . . . without no women to worry us." The boy says that they will be leaving the camp soon, though they like to stay for one day longer than everyone else, enjoying the leftover food and whiskey. After this day, they will return to their home to plant next year's crop. The boy thinks that he and Mister Ernest work hard all year to "have the right" to go hunting for two weeks and that the buck had to run for those two weeks to "have the right" not to be bothered the rest of the year. Because of this, the boy thinks that "the hunting and the farming wasn't two different things atall—they was jest the other side of each other." The boy says that once they put in the new crop, it will be November again before they know it.

Hearing this, Mister Ernest tells the boy that he will not be planting this year, and that he will be going to school instead. The boy protests because he wants to be a farmer, but Mister

Ernest says, "That ain't enough any more," and he tells the boy that he must "belong to the business of mankind." The boy protests again, but Mister Ernest continues, saying that it "used to be enough—just to do right. But not now. You got to know why it's right and why it's wrong, and be able to tell the folks that never had no chance to learn it." The boy tells Mister Ernest he has been listening to Willy Legate and Walter Ewell too much and suggests that this is why Mister Ernest did not shoot the buck, emptying his gun on "purpose." Mister Ernest denies the first accusation but concedes the second, asking the boy whether he would prefer to have the buck's "bloody" carcass now or to have him alive and waiting to be caught next year.

The boy says that they will definitely "git him" next year, but Mister Ernest only replies, "Maybe." The boy scoffs at this, and Mister Ernest says that "maybe" is "the best word in our language, the best of all. That's what mankind keeps going on: Maybe." Mister Ernest then asks the boy to make him a drink, and the boy asks if he wants Uncle Ike's homemade whiskey or "Roth Edmondziz" store-bought whiskey. Echoing Willy's earlier chastisement, Mister Ernest chides the boy for not using the word "mister" when referring to Roth Edmonds. The boy replies, "Yes sir," continuing defiantly, "Well, which do you want? Uncle Ike's corn or that ere stuff of Roth Edmondziz?"

CHARACTERS

The Boy

The boy is the unnamed protagonist and narrator of "Race at Morning." He is twelve years old; his parents abandoned him when he was ten, at which point he went to live with his landlord, Mister Ernest. The boy helps Mister Ernest farm and also acts as the aging man's eyes and ears. Mister Ernest is the only person the boy will call "mister," indicating that Mister Ernest is the only person that the boy respects. Indeed, both Mister Ernest and Willy Legate scold the boy for this, but the boy ignores them. The boy is the first person to spot the buck, sparking the hunt that takes up the bulk of the story's narration. The boy is happy farming and hunting and does not want to go to school; he thinks it is better to "remember in my mind who I am" than to be able to spell his name. Unfortunately, by the end of the story, he finds out that Mister Ernest intends to send him to school.

Over the course of the hunt, the boy imagines what the dogs and the buck are thinking and doing. He even imagines what the horse thinks, stating, "When the jump come, Dan never cared who else was there neither." While chasing the buck, the boy imagines that the buck must be surprised to come upon yet another camp, perhaps thinking, "Is this whole durn country full of folks this morning?" Toward the end of the hunt, the boy describes Eagle as standing with his legs "spraddled and his head . . . down; maybe jest waiting until we was out of sight of his shame, his eyes saying plain as talk when we passed, 'I'm sorry, boys, but this here is all.'" Through his empathy with the animals around him, the boy also respects them or holds them in awe, especially the buck. The "fine" weather is something of an omen during the hunt, and the boy describes the buck in awesome terms, calling him as "big as a mule." As the buck stands in the setting sun, the boy describes the buck with the "sun sparking on the tips of his horns . . . so that he looked like he had twelve lighted candles branched around his head."

Where Mister Ernest is wise enough to understand that the buck's value lies in the chase and not the kill, the boy shows his youth in his enthusiasm for the kill, his eagerness to "git him," and his dread that any other camp might beat them to it. Despite this single-mindedness, the boy seems to respect Mister Ernest's decision to remove the shells from his shotgun, promising Mister Ernest that he will not tell anyone about it and pretending that Mister Ernest had made a mistake rather than a purposeful decision to spare the buck. The boy also comes to a realization stemming from the hunt itself:

> "All three of us was still what we was—that old buck that had to run, not because he was skeered, but because running was what he done the best and was proudest at . . . and me and Mister Ernest and Dan, that run him not because we wanted his meat, which would be too tough to eat anyhow, or his head to hang on a wall, but because now we could go back and work hard for eleven months making a crop, so we would have the right to come back here next November."

The boy comes to believe that he and Mister Ernest work hard all year to "have the right" to go hunting for two weeks and that the buck had to run for those two weeks to "have the right" not to be bothered the rest of the year. Because of this, the boy thinks that "the hunting and the farming wasn't two different things atall—they was jest the other side of each other." The boy says that once they put in the new crop, it will be November again before they know it.

Soon after, when Mister Ernest tells the boy that he must go to school to "make something" of himself, the boy protests that he is already doing so. He tells Mister Ernest, "I'm doing it now. I'm going to be a hunter and a farmer like you." To the boy, becoming like the only man he respects is the definition of "making something" of himself. The boy appears unimpressed by Mister Ernest's arguments about school. Indeed, echoing Willy's earlier chastisement, Mister Ernest chides the boy for not using the word "mister" when referring to Roth Edmonds. The boy replies obediently but then continues defiantly: "Well, which do you want? Uncle Ike's corn or that ere stuff of Roth Edmondziz?" Although he is unmoved by Mister Ernest's reasoning, it seems inevitable that the boy will be sent to school.

The Buck

The buck is a major figure in the story, representing perseverance, desire, and wildness, among other things. The buck must be smart, as it usually disappears from the area on the first day of hunting season and only reappears after the season has closed. The boy says that it is almost as if the "game wardens had give him a calendar." This year, however, the buck appears a day early, almost as if he's accidentally "mixed up" the dates. Indeed, there is something almost fateful about the buck's appearance. On the day of the hunt, the boy comments that it will be "a fine day, cold and bright." This, according to the boy as he refers to the buck, is "jest exactly the kind of day that big old son of a gun . . .would like to run." Later, referring to the good weather, the boy says that even if the buck waited "another ten years" to be caught, "he couldn't 'a' picked a better one."

The buck is old and big, living to what "would amount to a hundred years in a deer's life." Interestingly, it was once thought that the number of antlers on a buck indicated its age, and under this belief the buck would be twelve years old, just like the boy. The buck's footprint is described as being "big as a cow's, big as a mule's." Despite his size, though, the buck is able to evade the first set of hunting stands almost as if he is "a hant." Throughout the hunt, the boy imagines the buck's thoughts and movements. At one point, he imagines the buck thinking, "Is this whole durn country full of folks this morning?"

Despite wanting to hunt down the buck, Mister Ernest, the boy, and the rest of the hunting party respect the very animal they are trying to kill. At the end of the day when Mister Ernest turns toward home, he says the buck has "done done his part, give everybody a fair open shot at him, and now he's going home."

When Mister Ernest and the boy first come face to face with the buck, it is described in terms that are magnificent and respectful, almost awesome. The sun is setting as the buck rises up slowly, "big as a mule." When they next catch sight of him, he stands magnificently with the setting "sun sparking on the tips of his horns . . . so that he looked like he had twelve lighted candles branched around his head." Mister Ernest aims and fires. It is a perfect shot, but the gun is empty. Mister Ernest has gained so much respect for the animal that he has emptied his shotgun of its ammunition on purpose, understanding that it is more important for the buck to be waiting for him and the boy next year than lying dead in the camp. The boy, too, comes to his own understanding of the buck, believing that he and Mister Ernest work hard all year to "have the right" to go hunting for two weeks and that the buck had to run for those two weeks to "have the right" not to be bothered the rest of the year.

Dan

Dan is Mister Ernest's horse. He runs in the hunt with Mister Ernest and the boy riding him. Dan provides much of the comic relief in the story. The horse regularly tries to buck his riders and only stops when he is hit in the shoulders with the butt of Mister Ernest's gun. Dan jumps obstacles with little regard for his riders, ultimately leaving Mister Ernest and the boy hanging in midair on an empty saddle like cartoon characters. When Dan cannot jump an obstacle, he crawls under it, with the boy describing Dan as "crawling on his knees like a mole or a big coon." The boy also says of Dan that, "when the jump come, Dan never cared who else was there neither; I believe to my soul he could 'a' cast and run them dogs by hisself."

Eagle

Eagle is the lead dog in the chase, and he strains at the leash to go after the buck before Simon releases him. All of the other dogs follow Eagle. As the chase progresses, the boy can hear Eagle barking and imagines that Eagle is saying, "There he goes." The boy also knows what the other hunters do not: he knows that they could not have shot the buck because Eagle would have bayed to alert them to any blood. The dogs chase the buck from dawn to dusk before finally giving up. When the boy comes across the tired pack, he describes Eagle as standing with his legs "spraddled and his head . . .down; maybe jest waiting until we was out of sight of his shame, his eyes saying plain as talk when we passed, 'I'm sorry, boys, but this here is all.'"

Roth Edmonds

Roth Edmonds is one of the hunters in the camp. When it gets late, he jokingly tells the boy to go to bed while he and the other men play poker. Aside from Mister Ernest, Roth is the only other hunter with a horse. He starts the hunt with Simon, the dogs, Mister Ernest, the boy, and Dan. After the chase begins, Roth leaves the little group to herd the buck toward Uncle Ike's hunting stands. After he has done his part in the hunt, Roth goes back to the camp and prepares to return to town, leaving some of his store-bought whiskey behind. The boy often refers to Roth disrespectfully and in vernacular, calling the man's horse and whiskey "Roth Edmondziz."

Mister Ernest

Mister Ernest is the boy's guardian, having been so for the past two years. He is older and slightly hard of hearing and has poor eyesight. Because of these handicaps, the boy acts as Mister Ernest's eyes and ears during the hunt, sitting behind him on the horse and telling him which way to go. Mister Ernest is a landowner. The boy and his family were Mister Ernest's tenants, but after the boy's parents abandoned him, Mister Ernest took him in. Mister Ernest is described as a good man who works "as hard as ara one of his hands and tenants." At the end of the hunt, when the boy is tired, Mister Ernest tells the boy to get on the horse since they do not want to "spoil him," but he is really giving the boy a chance to rest. Mister Ernest also shows his true nature by surreptitiously removing the ammunition from his gun before coming upon the buck. Mister Ernest understands that the buck is worth more alive than dead, that the point of chasing the buck is the chase itself. He also recognizes a degree of morality in the buck, declaring that the buck is returning to its territory after having "done his part, give everybody a fair open shot at him."

Mister Ernest is the only man in the story whom the boy respects. The boy calls him, and only him, "mister," even after Mister Ernest asks the boy to refer to others with the same respect. Mister Ernest understands that as the boy grows older, he must go to school, stating that the world has changed and that being a farmer "ain't enough any more." He tells the boy that he must "belong to the business of mankind," claiming that it "used to be enough—just to do right. But not now. You got to know why it's right and why it's wrong, and be able to tell the folks that never had no chance to learn it." Yet, even in a world where one must know what is right and what is wrong and why, Mister Ernest asserts that "maybe" is "the best word in our language, the best of all. That's what mankind keeps going on: Maybe." This is a complex juxtaposition of ideas, one that reveals that Mister Ernest is not only a good man but also something of a philosopher. Mister Ernest acts as a catalyst, or agent of change, in the story, determining the outcome of the hunt and the course of the boy's life.

Walter Ewell

Walter Ewell is one of the hunters in the camp. While he plays poker with the other men, he, like Willy Legate, makes fun of the boy for being illiterate and for never going to school or studying. It is fair to assume that Walter is one of the hunters at Uncle Ike's stands, waiting to shoot the buck when he runs by. After he has done his part in the hunt, Walter returns to the camp and prepares to return to town. The boy holds Walter's and Willy's talk responsible for leading Mister Ernest to unload his gun before shooting at the buck and also for persuading Mister Ernest to send him to school.

Willy Legate

Willy Legate is one of the hunters in the camp. While he plays poker with the other men, he makes fun of the boy, along with Walter Ewell, for being illiterate and for never going to school or studying. Willy also asks the boy why he never calls anyone "mister," commenting on the boy's lack of respect for his elders. It is fair to assume that Willy is one of the hunters at Uncle Ike's stands, waiting to shoot the buck when he runs by. After doing his part in the hunt, Willy, like Walter, returns to the camp and prepares to return to town. The boy holds Willy's and Walter's talk responsible for leading Mister Ernest to unload his gun before shooting at the buck and also for persuading Mister Ernest to send him to school.

Uncle Ike McCaslin

Uncle Ike McCaslin is the oldest and most experienced hunter in the camp, and because of this, he is in charge of reserving the hunting stands that he thinks the buck is most likely to run by. When the buck gets past the stands, Uncle Ike is shocked, and he urges the boy and Mister Ernest to go after the buck before he enters a neighboring camp. Like many of the other hunters, Uncle Ike returns to the camp after he has done his part in the hunt, preparing to return to town. Uncle Ike leaves some of his homemade whiskey behind.

Simon

Simon appears to be the camp's helper or servant. He is the one who cooks the meals, and he comes out in the dark to help Mister Ernest and the boy back to camp following the hunt. He is also the person who takes the rest of the hunting party back to town. Simon is in charge of the hunting dogs, and he releases the lead dog, Eagle, on Mister Ernest's command.

THEMES

Respect

Much is made of respect in "Race at Morning." The boy deeply respects Mister Ernest, and this is evidenced by the fact that he uses the term "mister" when referring to him. Indeed, he exclusively uses the term to refer to his guardian. The boy remains steadfast in this practice despite Willy Legate's comments and even despite the request of the very man he respects. The boy admires Mister Ernest not only because he adopted him in all but name but also because Mister Ernest is a landowner who is also "a farmer," a man who "works as hard as ara one of his hands and tenants." Furthermore, though the boy may not agree with Mister Ernest's decision to spare the buck's life, he respects and honors that decision by promising not to tell anyone about the incident.

The boy also shows respect for the buck. Though he may want to kill the animal, he also shows empathy for it, imagining what the buck is thinking and doing at given moments. The boy holds the buck in awe, describing it often in magnificent terms. He even comes to respect the animal more over the course of the story, becoming aware of the symbiotic, or closely joined, relationship he shares with the buck. The boy realizes that the buck has to run for those two weeks to "have the right" not to be bothered the rest of the year, and that he and Mister Ernest work hard all year to "have the right" to go hunting for two weeks. The boy understands that the buck does not run from them "because he was skeered, but because running was what he done the best and was proudest at."

Mister Ernest also shows respect for the buck, so much so that he refuses to kill it. It is enough for Mister Ernest to chase the buck, to aim and fire his empty gun at it. Mister Ernest understands the buck on a deeper level than does the boy. The

TOPICS FOR FURTHER STUDY

- "Race at Morning" is written in a way that attempts to accurately capture the way people speak; that is, in vernacular. Write a brief story in standard English and then rewrite it in vernacular. How does the tone, or feeling, of the story change between the two versions?
- Research education and literacy rates in Mississippi during the 1950s. Was school attendance mandatory? How many children, like the boy in Faulkner's story, did not go to school? Summarize your findings in a report.
- Choose another southern writer, such as Mark Twain, Eudora Welty, or Tennessee Williams, and read some of his or her work. In an essay, compare and contrast your selection with Faulkner's work. Are the themes and language similar or different? How so?
- There are no female characters in "Race at Morning." In fact, the only passing mention of women in the story portrays them in a derogatory light. Research social attitudes toward women in the 1950s, focusing especially on attitudes in the South. How are these attitudes reflected, or not reflected, in the story? Give a class presentation on the topic.

Male mule deer with rack (© Joe McDonald / Corbis)

boy protests when Mister Ernest turns the horse away from the chase, but Mister Ernest asserts that the buck has "done done his part, give everybody a fair open shot at him, and now he's going home." Also unlike the boy, Mister Ernest respects the value of education, especially its growing value in a changing world—which the boy is unable, or unwilling, to recognize.

Loss of Innocence

The story is ultimately a chronicle of lost innocence, and this is reflected by the shrinking forest, both a literal and metaphorical symbol of the increasing pressure to "belong to the business of mankind." Indeed, the last passages in "Race at Morning," in which Mister Ernest tells the boy why he will indeed be going to school, are perhaps the most important part of the story. In a sense, it is almost as if the comical and fruitless, yet poetic, hunt that takes place for the main part of the narration exists only as a foil, or contrast, for the final passages. Indeed, the hunt is a portrait of a dying lifestyle. Unaware of this, the boy is a true innocent. He does not know how to read, write, or spell his name. He respects the man who saved him from abandonment and is blindly loyal to him. He exists in a world that is entirely free of women. He lives to farm and hunt, and he wants no more and no less from his life than what he already has. A life like the boy's was once more common than not, though at the time this story takes place (sometime in the early to middle twentieth century), it was becoming less and less common.

Mister Ernest is painfully aware of the changing world, which is why he has decided to send the boy to school. The boy protests because he wants to be a farmer, but Mister Ernest says, "that ain't enough any more," and he tells the boy that he must "belong to the business of mankind." The boy protests again, scoffing, "Mankind?" But Mister Ernest continues undaunted, saying that it "used to be enough—just to do right. But not now. You got to know why it's right and why it's wrong, and be able to tell the folks that never had no chance to learn it." Mister Ernest knows that the boy will not be able to avoid taking part in society, that he will be compelled to "belong to the business of mankind."

In his innocence, the boy lives in a morally black-and-white world, but Mister Ernest tells him that "maybe" is "the best word in our language, the best of all. That's what mankind keeps going on: Maybe." This statement indicates Mister Ernest's knowledge that the world—especially for those who remain dependent on and in harmony with nature—is an uncertain place, that no one can be sure of what will happen. He tells the boy that "the best days of [a man's] life ain't the ones when he said 'Yes' beforehand: they're the ones when all he knew to say was 'Maybe.'" It is this acknowledgment of the uncertain and changing world that nearly closes the story, contrasting with the boy's final and staunch persistence in acting as if his life is not about to be forever changed.

STYLE

Vernacular

"Race at Morning" is told in southern vernacular, or a slang dialect spoken in the South. Examples of this are when the boy says "ara one" instead of "every one" and "skeered" instead of "scared." This stylistic choice gives the story a great deal of character and immediacy. It is impossible to overlook that the story is taking place in the South and is being told by a young southerner. Indeed, the story may be as much about the South as it is about the boy telling it.

The vernacular emphasizes the narrator's illiteracy and general lack of formal education, which is an important aspect of the overall story. Following the hunt, the boy is told that he will be sent to school. All of the other characters in the book speak in the same manner as the boy, so the reader understands that the people in the boy's immediate society are also relatively uneducated. Furthermore, the use of vernacular emphasizes some of the comical aspects in the story, such as when Mister Ernest and the boy are thrown from their horse. As Mister Ernest and the boy sit in the saddle that is now only supported by the vine that snagged them, the boy says that the vine is like "the drawed-back loop of a big rubber-banded slingshot." As they fall, the boy makes sure that he lands on Mister Ernest and not vice versa, and when Mister Ernest complains about this, the boy says, "You would 'a' mashed me flat!" Mister Ernest replies, "What do you think you done to me?"

First-person, Unreliable Narrator

The first-person narrator, the unnamed boy, dominates the story with his point of view. Part of the value of the narration lies in the boy's imagination; he tells the reader what must be occurring during the parts of the hunt that he cannot see. The boy also imagines what the animals in the hunt are thinking, from Dan the horse and the buck to Eagle and the other dogs. The boy's tone is very conversational, with a casual reference to an unspecific other being made in the first sentence of the story: "I was in the boat when I seen him." It is unclear who the boy sees, but his head is out of the water and there is a "rocking chair" on it, which is a rather confusing image. When the boy discusses "the season" and makes a passing reference to "game wardens," the reader can deduce that it is hunting season and that the strange other with a "rocking chair" on his head is a deer. Thus, with such a first-person narrator, the reader must infer what is going on in spite of any details being left out or construed in colloquial ways. This stylistic characterization is sometimes referred to as the unreliable narrator.

Symbolism of the Buck

The buck is a symbol for many things. When Mister Ernest decides not to kill the buck, it is almost as if he is making a conscious choice to turn away from the life of farming and hunting that has sustained him. This choice becomes clear when he informs the boy that he must take part in "the business of mankind," noting that hunting and farming "ain't enough any more." The buck is also a symbol of desire. The boy wants to capture the buck; yet, that which is desired can only be desired if it is not possessed. In other words, the boy cannot desire the buck once it is captured and killed, he can only desire the buck while it is being chased. Mister Ernest makes this clear when he asks the boy, "Which would you rather have? His bloody head and hide. . .in a pickup truck on the way to Yoknapatawpha County, or him with his head and hide and meat still together. . .waiting for next November for us to run him again?" The buck's power in part lies in the possibility of his being captured. Once killed, that possibility and power would be no more.

HISTORICAL CONTEXT

Southern Literature

A subset of American literature, southern literature is written by and/or about southerners. William Faulkner and his work are a part of this tradition, if not one of the definitive aspects of it. The American South is a region with a

COMPARE & CONTRAST

- **1950s:** In the South, racial segregation is enforced via the so-called Jim Crow laws. African Americans are not allowed to eat at the same restaurants, drink at the same water fountains, sit in the same movie theaters, or go to the same schools as white people.

  Today: The Civil Rights Act of 1964 legally ended segregation, yet segregation still exists in economic terms. Residents of inner-city ghettos, where most live below the poverty level, are predominantly African American.

- **1950s:** A 1959 U.S. census report on education notes that the illiteracy rate in the South is 4.3 percent, the highest of all regions. The next highest illiteracy rate is in the Northeast, a mere 1.5 percent.

  Today: The U.S. census report on education no longer tracks literacy rates in 2000, instead tracking education levels, such as high school, college, and advanced degrees. This indicates that illiteracy in the United States is no longer common.

- **1950s:** Female and African American writers producing work at this time, such as Carson McCullers, Eudora Welty, Flannery O'Connor, and Zora Neale Hurston, are ultimately accepted as part of the canon of southern literature. Their work reflects the themes commonly found in the genre.

  Today: Southern literature is no longer as clearly defined as it once was, largely due to the culture's increasing homogenization, or uniformity, with the rest of the nation. Nevertheless, the works of contemporary southern authors like Cormac McCarthy and Edward P. Jones still reflect traditional southern themes.

distinct culture and dialect, largely owing to the fact that the South was built as an agrarian (farming) society with legalized slavery, leaving it vastly different from the rest of the nation. This is the heritage of the South, and its distinct culture gave rise to a singular style of literature. Much of Faulkner's work is about southerners, and furthermore the stories and situations portrayed are such that could only occur within the confines of the South. Some themes and devices common to southern literature are racial tensions, class disparity, regional dialect (vernacular), emphasis on place, and man's relationship with the land. Other well-known writers whose work falls into this category are Mark Twain, Carson McCullers, Eudora Welty, Flannery O'Connor, Tennessee Williams, and Harper Lee.

There are several notable periods of southern literature, stretching from the eighteenth century to the mid-twentieth century. The stages are largely defined by historical changes in the South, such as the Civil War, Reconstruction, and the civil rights movement, for instance. One of the last defined periods of southern literature, known as the Southern Renaissance, is the period in which Faulkner wrote. This period reached its peak in the 1920s and 1930s, and many of the works produced in this time, much like "Race at Morning," mourn the death of the South's rural culture as it gave way to industrialism.

The 1950s and the Changing South

Faulkner first published "Race at Morning" in 1955, on the cusp of the civil rights movement that was about to sweep through the South and change it irrevocably. Faulkner himself was a staunch advocate of civil rights. These particulars shed much light on the closing passages of the story. Mister Ernest tells the boy that it is no longer sufficient to know right from wrong, as one must know "why it's right and why it's wrong." Mister Ernest then goes one step beyond this, informing the boy that it will be his responsibility to impart this knowledge to "the folks that never had no chance to learn it." For a young man living on the cusp of desegregation, this edict is very powerful indeed.

The South at this time was also in the final throes of its transition from a primarily agrarian economy to a primarily industrialized one. Given this, one can take the meaning of Mister Ernest's claim that farming "ain't enough anymore" quite literally. In order to make a good living, more and more southerners entered into the burgeoning industrialized economy, working in factories and moving toward city centers, a process that had already taken place in the North a century earlier. Industrialized societies depend more upon educated citizens than do agrarian societies; for instance, it is not necessary to know how to read in order to farm corn, but it is necessary to know how to read in order to sign business contracts or review a machine's operating manual. Where individual farms can be relatively isolated, cities and factories are sustained by large populations of people living and working closely with one another. This is the "business of mankind" that Mister Ernest refers to. By the 1950s, in the wake of growing cities and shrinking rural areas, it became increasingly impossible to avoid modernized life.

CRITICAL OVERVIEW

William Faulkner is one of the most-studied and best-known American writers. *The Sound and the Fury* and *As I Lay Dying* forever changed the face of American literature. Another of Faulkner's critically acclaimed master works is *Go Down, Moses* (1942), which can be classified as either a novel or a collection of related short stories. Set in Yoknapatawpha County, the book largely focuses on racial themes. The *Mississippi Quarterly* critic Barbara L. Pittman points out that "over half" of the text in *Big Woods*, the collection in which "Race at Morning" first appeared, is derived from *Go Down, Moses*. Faulkner, however, changes the focus of the material from race to what Pittman calls "the minor theme of the decline of the American wilderness and the simultaneous rise of the white man's civilization." Pittman also implies that because of this shift, *Big Woods* did not receive the acclaim that was lavished upon *Go Down, Moses*.

Nevertheless, there is much scholarly criticism of *Big Woods* and of "Race at Morning" in particular. The *Booklist* contributor David Wright says that the collection contains some of Faulkner's "most accessible and enjoyable writing." Hans H. Skei, writing in the *Dictionary of Literary Biography*, asserts that "Race at Morning" is "Faulkner's most successful story from his later years." However, this success may be due to the fact that "Race at Morning" can be seen as "closely resembling the earlier hunting stories," as James Ferguson posits in *Faulkner's Short Fiction*. Ferguson, however, calls the story "didactic," stating that it has "turgid, flabby qualities." Commenting on the conspicuous absence of women in the story, Ferguson states, "Like Hemingway, Faulkner cannot portray an idyll involving women."

Countering these statements in a *Herald Tribune* article (reprinted in *William Faulkner: The Contemporary Reviews*), Coleman Rosenberger calls "Race at Morning" "a delightful story." Rosenberger notes, "The world has changed. But to the boy...the 'pageant-rite' [of the hunt] has its old power." The *New York Herald Tribune* contributor Lewis Gannett, in an article reprinted in *William Faulkner: The Contemporary Reviews*, does not feel that *Big Woods* suffers on account of its recycled content. Indeed, he states that "put together with new connective tissue—story, legend, poetry and memory—it is something new. It is Mr. Faulkner's fabulous Old Testament."

CRITICISM

Leah Tieger

Tieger is a freelance writer and editor. In the following essay, she explores the disappearing wilderness as it is overtaken by civilization in "Race at Morning." Tieger also discusses whether or not "Race at Morning" can be considered a coming-of-age story.

William Faulkner's work was often set in the fictional Yoknapatawpha County. Adjacent to this setting was the Big Woods, where Faulkner's most famous story, "The Bear," takes place. The collection *Big Woods*, in which "Race at Morning" first appeared in book form, brings together "The Bear" and other stories that are set in the Big Woods. The stories often feature recurring characters at different times in their lives; for instance, the main character of "The Bear" is sixteen-year-old Ike McCaslin, the same person who appears as the old man Uncle Ike in "Race at Morning." By bringing these stories together in one collection and setting them so that they can be traced chronologically according to the progressive ages of

WHAT DO I READ NEXT?

- One of Faulkner's definitive and best-loved works is *As I Lay Dying*, published in 1930. Like much of Faulkner's work, the story takes place in Yoknapatawpha County and is written in southern dialect.
- Mark Twain is arguably the father of southern literature. His most famous work, *The Adventures of Huckleberry Finn* (1884), explores racial issues and the immorality of slavery. The book is likewise written in southern vernacular.
- *The Making of the American South: A Short History, 1500–1877* (2006), by J. William Harris, provides a comprehensive overview of the history of the region and culture that gave rise to southern literature.
- Tennessee Williams's Pulitzer Prize–winning play, *A Streetcar Named Desire* (1947), is another fine example of southern literature at its best. Where "Race at Morning" lightly touches upon the clash between the old South and the new South, this play takes the theme as its main motif.

"WHERE ADAM AND EVE ARE EXPELLED FROM PARADISE BECAUSE THEY HAVE EATEN FROM THE TREE OF KNOWLEDGE, THE BOY IS EXPELLED FROM HIS PARADISE BECAUSE HE MUST ACQUIRE KNOWLEDGE."

the characters, Faulkner presents an epic picture of the Big Woods—of what they were and of what they have become. Indeed, *Big Woods*, in stories such as "Race at Morning," reveals that the wilderness is being quickly usurped by civilization.

In "Race at Morning," it is not so much the loss of the wilderness that is mourned as the loss of its attendant lifestyle. The time when it was enough to know wrong from right, to be a "hunter and a farmer," is no more. Although one could once choose to avoid "the business of mankind," that choice is not available to the boy, a fact Mister Ernest is well aware of. In light of this and other Faulkner works with similar themes, critics have commented that there is a parallel between "Race at Morning" and the biblical story of the Garden of Eden. Indeed, some interesting similarities and congruities exist. Where Adam and Eve are expelled from paradise because they have eaten from the tree of knowledge, the boy is expelled from his paradise because he must acquire knowledge.

This interpretation becomes even more compelling when one considers the absence of women in the story. Writing in *Faulkner's Short Fiction*, James Ferguson points out that in many of Faulkner's stories, "Eve has yet to make her appearance." Ferguson goes on to state that "in the case of 'Race at Morning,' it is her defection that has created the paradise." Mister Ernest is a widower, and the boy's mother abandoned him two years before the story begins, ensuring that, as the boy says, "it was jest fine...without no women to worry us or take off in the middle of the night."

Comparing the differences in "The Bear" and "Race at Morning," the *Mississippi Quarterly* critic Barbara L. Pittman notes that the hunt in the latter story is "fast and frantic," unlike the "still, quiet hunting" in "The Bear." Pittman concludes that the essential difference between the hunts is not their pace but the fact that the boy is not learning "the lessons Ike learned: patience, respect for the life taken, man's relationship to nature." Pittman even goes so far as to say that the reason Mister Ernest does not kill the buck is because of the diminished forest: "The loss of space and game in the dwindling wilderness forces the hunters to replace the hunt with a race." Pittman concludes that because of this, "the hunters are wise enough to see that [the hunt] is an activity empty of life-lessons." Based on this reasoning, it would seem that Mister Ernest hopes that education; that knowing what is wrong, what is right, and why; and that taking part in "the business of mankind" will teach the boy the lessons that can no longer be learned in the vanquished woods.

Another compelling argument regarding the wilderness considers the civil rights movement, which was beginning when "Race at Morning" was first published. Indeed, it is impossible to be unaware that the story is taking place in the South and is being told by a southerner. The story is as much about the South as it is about the boy telling it. If the story can be said to be a portrait of the South, then it is both a literal and metaphorical portrait. The shrinking woods are a literal reflection of the shrinking rural areas of the South, but they are also a metaphorical representation of the immense social upheaval taking place in the region. Based on these considerations, one could also interpret the forest simply as a metaphor for change and for the need to embrace change.

By pushing the boy to abandon what "ain't enough any more," Mister Ernest forces the boy to embrace change. The boy will be expelled from his Edenic life into a new world, one filled with more possibility than the now-vanquished wilderness. Mister Ernest even attempts to explain the value of possibility to the boy, stating that "maybe" is "the best word in our language, the best of all. That's what mankind keeps going on: Maybe." He tells the boy that "the best days of [a man's] life ain't the ones when he said 'Yes' beforehand: they're the ones when all he knew to say was 'Maybe.'"

The boy's world is morally black and white. He respects Mister Ernest because the man works as hard as his tenants and because he has become the boy's guardian. The boy shows this respect in simple, yet certain, terms, referring to Mister Ernest alone as "mister" and ignoring all requests to refer to others in the same manner. This moral simplicity can also be seen in other aspects of the boy's life. For instance, the boy respects the buck but wants to kill him, believing that "he was ourn" simply because the buck has been living on their land and eating their food and because they have been watching and waiting for him every hunting season.

This moral simplicity, as sustained by the boy's unwillingness to change, is why "Race at Morning" cannot be classified as a coming-of-age story. In fact, critics never discuss the story in such terms. This would at first seem odd, given that "Race at Morning" does contain some elements essential to the coming-of-age story. For instance, the boy is on the cusp of adolescence; he participates in a ritualistic hunt; he comes to an understanding of his relationship to the buck and vice versa; and he is, as this essay has established, about to be expelled from his Eden. However, while "Race at Morning" contains some attributes that are common to coming-of-age narratives, it is missing the elements that are the most essential.

In "Race at Morning" the boy does not change, learn, or grow in any real, quantifiable way. Simply put, the boy goes on a hunt, fails to kill his prey, and looks forward to returning to try again next year. The only epiphany that the boy can be said to have is the realization that he and the buck exist in a symbiotic, or intertwined, relationship; the boy farms throughout the year to have the "right" to hunt, and the buck runs during the hunt to have the "right" to not be bothered the rest of the year. Yet this epiphany, unlike those in traditional coming-of-age stories, also called bildungsromans, does not reveal to the boy his place in society. Indeed, it almost reveals the opposite.

Perhaps, then, one could call "Race at Morning" a pre-bildungsroman, a portrait of the boy during his last moments in the primordial forest, just on the cusp of learning to take part in "the business of mankind." Regardless, the epiphany that will ultimately lead to the boy's enlightenment does not come from within. Instead, it comes from without, via Mister Ernest's decision to send the boy to school. This decision, then, does reinforce Pittman's statement that, on account of the diminished forest, "the hunters are wise enough to see that "the hunt" is an activity empty of life-lessons." Still, it is Mister Ernest, and not the boy, who comes to understand this.

Source: Leah Tieger, Critical Essay on "Race at Morning," in *Short Stories for Students*, Gale, Cengage Learning, 2009.

Wiley C. Prewitt Jr.

In the following essay, Prewitt examines Faulkner's hunting stories, including "Race at Morning," arguing that the "natural cycle in his hunting fiction makes Faulkner's work peculiarly appropriate for an inquiry into long-term environmental change."

As an activity that brings humanity into contact with the natural world, hunting has become a vital issue in contemporary ecological debate. Some environmentally orientated writers believe that hunting can lead to a positive relationship between humans and the land. Such writing echoes the work of philosophers like

> "IT WAS IN THIS ENVIRONMENTAL MIX OF DIMINISHED WILDERNESS, DISAPPEARING LARGE GAME, AND THE PURSUIT OF PREDOMINANTLY SMALL GAME THAT FAULKNER DEVELOPED HIS IDEAS ABOUT HUNTING AND THE HUMAN CONNECTION WITH NATURE."

Ortega Y. Gassett and Aldo Leopold who saw hunting as a positive and abiding factor in the cultural evolution of humanity and the thought of Paul Shepard who argued that hunting and gathering societies maintained the highest expression of human physical, social, and mental health. In contrast, some thinkers describe hunting as a dark anachronism that humans must strive to overcome. One of the best of these scholars, Matt Cartmill, offers the idea that hunters justify their killing in part by a perverse and false philosophical boundary between the values of human and animal lives. Thoughtful, ecologically concerned people remain divided with regard to the hunt wherever it occurs.

And few places contain a more abundant and diverse hunting legacy than the South. Scholars have often acknowledged the importance of hunting in the South. Social and cultural historians have characterized the Southern fascination with hunting as manifestations of innate violence, regional ideals of manhood, the need for indulgent recreation, or simply the subsistence needs of an often impoverished populace. Environmental historians interested in the South have only begun to use hunting as a point of inquiry for describing human interaction with the natural world. In one of the few environmental histories devoted to the chase, Stuart Marks created an intimate portrait of hunters in a North Carolina county by relying heavily on the oral traditions and hunting literature of the region. Hunting and its literature have been largely ignored as sources, as two critics recently complained: "our writers and poets have paid more attention to American hunting than have our academic environmental historians." Of writers who have used hunting in their work, William Faulkner has portrayed the chase with the most striking combination of realism and spirituality. His rich descriptions of the separate worlds of farm and wilderness in turn-of-the-century Mississippi invite a specific examination of the ways people lived with the land. At the same time, his hunting stories imply a mystical cycle of regeneration in which such large game as deer and bear are not only flesh and blood but spiritual representations of the natural world.

Faulkner wrote his hunting stories during a time of widespread environmental upheaval within Mississippi and the South. During his lifetime, habitat types and their accompanying game species prospered and declined in relation to the agricultural systems and socioeconomic interworkings of humans. As a hunter he encountered the effects of environmental change in habitats and game populations. As a hunter who was also a writer, the local environmental background must have influenced his fiction as much as did his region's history, culture, and society. My paper places Faulkner's hunting stories within the changing environmental context of his locale and his lifetime. It also shows that the idea of a natural cycle in his hunting fiction makes Faulkner's work peculiarly appropriate for an inquiry into long-term environmental change.

The land of North Mississippi in the late nineteenth century was a place of distinct dichotomy between the wild and the domesticated. Until the 1880s, land clearing and the establishment of farms proceeded in the upland areas and a in few well-drained bottomlands. The overwhelming majority of people engaged in agriculture to some degree, and that farming population was broadly distributed over the arable land. Large expanses of bottomland hardwoods stretched along the alluvial plains of rivers throughout the state where frequent floods and the costs of land clearing discouraged farms. Bottomlands were the wilderness counterpoint to settled areas all over Mississippi, located along rivers and streams both large and small like the Big Black in the central counties, the Pascagoula in the south and the Tombigbee in the east, in addition to Faulkner's *Tallahatchie*. Faulkner's imagery of a "tall and endless wall of dense November woods" juxtaposed with "skeleton stalks of cotton and corn in the last of open country" offer excellent illustrations that typified much of the land in Mississippi.

By the 1880s, however, Northern timber speculators began purchasing the timberlands of the

South, sometimes for as little as one dollar per acre. Attracted first by the vast longleaf pine forests of the coastal plain, timber buyers soon moved to acquire the bottomland hardwoods. The timberland of the upper Yazoo and its tributaries, including the Tallahatchie, changed hands in their turns. Lumbering interests from the exhausted cutovers of the Great Lakes region bought the lands or timber rights from speculators as railroads subsequently crept into the bottoms, making it feasible to remove the timber in quantity. Timber cutting pushed back the Big Woods along rivers all over the state. The dynamic of clearing land, with the moving boundary of the virgin timber and the approach of the cotton farm, runs throughout Faulkner's hunting stories. Ike McCaslin remembered that in just some twenty years the logging train grew from an ineffectual example of human technology to an ominous portent of inevitable changes in the land. Across Mississippi the felling of the virgin forests took only about fifty years. From 1880 to 1930 sawmills reduced the vast stands of timber to only scattered remnants surrounded by farmland.

Wildlife populations responded to the land clearing and to what one scholar called "live at home semisubsistence farming." Until the years of intensive logging, the dichotomy between wilderness and farmland was reflected in the distribution of game in Mississippi. Large game like deer, turkeys, and bear occurred in wild unsettled areas while such small game as quail, rabbits, and foxes lived in the brushy margin habitats created by premechanized agriculture. Farming itself did not repel large game; the raiding of cornfields and the killing of shoats by Old Ben has some basis in fact. Rather, large game could not withstand the intensive hunting pressure from the hungry and well-armed rural population. The agricultural cycle allowed ample time for hunting and trapping both large and small animals by a farm population almost uniformly interested in taking a share of the game. Farm life encouraged a very direct and often subsistence-oriented relationship between people and local wildlife. Hunting and trapping were both recreation and important sources of protein for the farm family. Small game adapted to this constant pressure with high reproductive rates and by benefiting from the ideal habitat that smallfield agriculture provided. Settled areas sustained frequent and long-term hunting of species like quail and rabbits that thrived in close communion with humans while larger, less prolific species like deer and bear simply could not make up their losses and were confined to nonfarm habitats.

As timber cutting advanced, the cotton culture followed, bringing with it the habitat that favored small game and exposing the last refuges of larger animals. In 1928, more than a decade before Faulkner's hunting stories appeared, Aldo Leopold, one of the pioneers of modern wildlife biology and environmental ethics, conducted a historic survey of game in Mississippi and estimated that only a few thousand deer and turkeys survived statewide. Bears were so scarce that he ignored them as a viable game specie in the very state where Teddy Roosevelt's bear hunting exploit had led to the creation of that most familiar of toy animals. Compared with the near total devastation of large game he found adequate numbers of small creatures, particularly quail, that helped make possible what Leopold called a "widespread and intense popular interest in game and hunting."

It was in this environmental mix of diminished wilderness, disappearing large game, and the pursuit of predominantly small game that Faulkner developed his ideas about hunting and the human connection with nature. Scholars offer a multitude of interpretations that deal with "The Bear" and to a lesser extent Faulkner's other hunting stories. A common theme in interpretations is that the activity of hunting provides humans with a connection to the natural world that critics have seen variously as positive, negative, or both. However, not just any hunting will do. For Faulkner's hunters, only the pursuit of large game reaffirmed a bond between humans and the natural world. In his fiction, Faulkner made much of the distinction between hunting small game in the farmland and hunting large game in the Big Woods. Animals that coexisted with humans were somehow less worthy as game and Faulkner's hunters pursued them only as training or when nothing else was available.

Large game hunting, and particularly deer hunting, was in Ike McCaslin's eyes the hunter's reason for being. Deer hunting took place in the Big Bottom, away from the farm and the human dominated landscape. The chase for large game outside the boundary of the settled land gave a balance to the life of the young deer hunter in "Race at Morning" so that he could say, "the hunting and the farming wasn't two different things at all—they was jest the other side of each other." Deer were rare enough for a kill to be an event, and a proper first kill could become a rite that would initiate a novice into a group of hunters. Conversely, hunting the farmland became to young Ike McCaslin "the child's pursuit of rabbits and 'possums." And one can sense the disdain in Sam Father's voice when during a fox hunt he tells young Isaac, "I done taught you all there is of this settled country . . .you can hunt it good as I can now. You are ready for the Big Bottom now, for bear and deer. Hunter's meat." Years later, the elderly McCaslin surveyed the changes in the land he had known and mused that "now a man has to drive a hundred miles to find enough woods to harbor game worth hunting." The settled land was too understandable, its mysteries too easily found out. Sam Fathers taught Isaac before he reached ten years of age all there was to know about hunting the animals of the settled country while the boy dedicated his entire life to hunting the Big Woods. In Faulkner's work, small game assumed part of the less-than-noble character of civilization. Just as Isaac attempted to repudiate his family's land because of his perception of its taint of slavery, miscegenation, and incest, he also disavowed small game hunting because of its symbiotic relation to agriculture.

Faulkner rejected small game hunting in his fiction when rabbits, raccoons, 'possums, squirrels, birds, and especially quail constituted the most available game for Southern hunters, including himself. J. M. Faulkner remembered that Mr. Bill himself was an avid quail hunter and had a great appreciation for a fine dog and a good shotgun. Also, Faulkner's endorsement of wilderness and the pursuit of large game was significant because it emerged during a time when hunting writers were creating a vast body of literature surrounding that most typical of Southern small game creatures, the bobwhite quail. If, as some scholars suggest, Faulkner described hunting as a quasi religious activity of mythic and spiritual meaning connected to the wilderness, then other Southern writers recorded the parameters of a parallel cult of quail hunting in the settled country. Stuart Marks in *Southern Hunting in Black and White* found that as quail became more common after the 1880s hunting writers began explaining the practice of upper-class quail hunting and praising its virtues in a voluminous body of work that involved much of the South. The association of quail hunting with the upper class is due largely to the enthusiasm of wealthy Northerners who bought large estates in the South where quail hunting became a highly ritualized winter pastime. The editor of an 1980 anthology of quail hunting literature lists works by over fifteen different authors that cover over one hundred years. In the midSouth few writers were more closely associated with the rituals of quail hunting than was Nash Buckingham. A native of Memphis, born in 1880, educated at Harvard, Buckingham came of age during the same era of environmental change as Faulkner. The child of a wealthy banker, Buckingham hunted at some of the finest duck clubs in the Arkansas and Mississippi Deltas and could afford considerable quail hunting time in the uplands of north Mississippi. In books and articles from the '20s through the '50s Buckingham reinforced some of the connections between the pursuit of quail and the upper class that Stuart Marks found.

In his 1936 collection of stories called *Mark Right!*, Buckingham portrays quail hunting as an extension of upper-class views and expectations for society. For Buckingham, one's social position translates into one's position in the hunt. In the story "Buried Treasure Hill" he reminisces over the quail hunts he and three friends took over the years on a large plantation. Only the upperclass whites hunt in the story, assisted by fawning black servants. They pass over a landscape radically different from the Big Woods, following well-trained bird dogs through "meadows," "old orchards," "ragweed flats," and the ruins of an antebellum plantation house. Their access to the game is associated with their agricultural dominion over nature and their social position, as opposed to any spiritual connection to the earth.

Nash Buckingham's quail hunts reflected the order the upper class wanted in society. In other stories Buckingham elaborated on the themes of good breeding in dogs, fairness to the birds, and an understood system of courtesy and respect between hunters. Poor whites appear in Buckingham's work, and they sometimes hunt, but generally only for food; the complexities of ritual are lost on them, like the rural blacksmith Mr. Fenley in the story "Carry Me Back." Buckingham and his friend accepted a challenge from Fenley that his pointer bitch Belle was a bird dog comparable to one of their animals. The hunt proceeded, Belle proved exceptional, and several days later as if to affirm that a dog of her caliber was out of place with a blacksmith, Buckingham purchased her and two of her pups, giving them what he termed a "Cinderella start in life." Fenley kept one pup, saying he could "kill over her all the birds he needed to eat."

Even though hunting literature associated the bird with the upper class, there were a great many Mississippi quail hunters and they more closely resembled Mr. Fenley than Nash Buckingham. Bobwhite quail, which Southern hunters invariably called simply "birds," were immensely popular as game and were generally available to people in farming areas. Almost every rural family had a shotgun and a dog with some level of ability for quail hunting. For those without guns or the money for shells, the birds could be trapped easily. Rural folk frequently sold or bartered quail in local communities, and wild birds were occasionally on the menu of Mississippi restaurants until game law enforcement discouraged the practice in the '30s and '40s.

A fascination with quail did not quell all regrets for the passing of the bottomland forests among hunting writers in Mississippi and the region. Even Buckingham himself, a devoted wingshooter, mourned the loss of the "unlogged wilderness" where he and his companions might happen upon a deer or turkey to add to their game bag. Hunting writers frequently depict specific places or times that give their stories meaning simply through inaccessibility and distance associated with the hunts they describe. Stories about the "Good Old Days" abound in hunting literature. Mississippi writer Reuben Davis left a poignant memory of the bottomland in his novel *Shim*. The novel turns on the hunting and early life of young Shim Govan, heir to a remote Delta plantation around the turn of the century against a backdrop of timber cutting and the expansion of cotton culture. Davis began writing *Shim* in the late '40s and his story lines parallel some of those in Faulkner's hunting fiction, particularly the role of Sam Fathers as a hunting mentor and the use of Old Ben as a symbol of the wilderness. Young Shim received his instruction in hunting and woods lore from Henry, his father's black plantation foreman. During a hunt at the end of the story, Shim's brother Dave kills a black wolf that symbolizes the old indomitable Delta wilderness before the arrival of the logging crews. With the death of the wolf, the spell of the free hunting life in the wilderness is broken. The next day Henry departes for a refuge deeper in the woods and Shim is left alone to ponder the enormous sawmill equipment that slowly approaches the forest he knew.

Nash Buckingham and Reuben Davis crafted a lament for the passing of the wilderness that combined a sense of regret and nostalgia with a belief in the positive progress of civilization. In their stories, hunters have the most to lose from the destruction of the wilderness, but they are unable and probably unwilling to save it. Ike McCaslin accepts a sad and inevitable end to the wilderness but simply continues hunting in the ever dwindling remnant of the Delta forest. Indeed there seemed little reason for optimism about the Big Woods of Mississippi and its complement of large game. Yet, within Faulkner's fiction, scholars have noticed a cycle of destruction and renewal among humans and the natural world. That cycle implies a chance for a future hunt absent in the work of most other hunting writers.

The idea of a cycle owes much to the reflection of Native American belief systems in Faulkner's work. Francis Lee Utley and other scholars have compared some of the rituals in the hunting of Old Ben to the ceremonial bear hunts of certain eastern Native American tribes. Further similarities exist in the commitment to the spirit of the deer that elderly Ike McCaslin finally articulates in the reminiscence of his first kill. In his memory he comes close to apologizing to the deer and dedicates himself to hunt thoughtfully thereafter in such a way as to honor the life the deer had given. Many Native American tribes believed that animals gave themselves to hunters who had shown the proper respect and had fulfilled various rituals in the preparation and the carrying out of the hunt. After the hunt, more ceremony followed in the butchery, division, and consumption of the animal, often concluding with a symbolic return of some part of the body to the earth. With the fulfillment of the rituals a hunter appeased the spirit of the animal, which then assumed another body. Sam Fathers had "taught the boy the woods, to hunt, when to shoot and when not to shoot, when to kill and when not to kill and better, what to do with it afterward." Thus, the deer that revealed itself to Sam Fathers and young Ike after the boy had made his first kill was both flesh and spirit, able to leave physical tracks, yet it was also the spirit of a deer that emerged from Walter Ewell's kill.

The system of reincarnation among game and the appearance of animals like old Ben, the large deer, and even the large rattlesnake as creatures of symbolic significance owe more to Native American belief systems than to a Judeo-Christian oriented interpretation of wilderness in Faulkner's hunting stories. While critics caution against attributing too much anthropological background to Faulkner's work, the idea of a cycle of renewal that is reminiscent of Native American ideology exists within the stories. Many critics interpret the snake that Ike encountered at the end of "The Bear" as a symbol of fundamental evil in the wilderness garden of Eden. Some connect the snake to the entrance of human evil into the forest, and certainly Ike McCaslin's comparison of the logging train to "a small dingy snake" reinforces that idea. In the light of Native American ideology, however, the snake suggests power, and certainly danger, but not pure evil in the Judeo-Christian sense of Lucifer in the garden. For many tribes in the Southeast, snakes represented an underworld, a terrifying place inhabited by strange monsters, but also according to one anthropologist, "the source of water, fertility, and a means of coping with evil." Since Ike's experience occurred in North Mississippi, we can assume that this serpent is Crotalus horridus whose local name of timber or canebrake rattlesnake closely links it to the forested bottomland. The rattlesnake was a particularly potent creature in Southern and Southwestern Native American belief systems. Rattlesnake motifs were common enough among the artifacts of the Southeastern Native Americans that in 1906 an anthropologist described the artwork on a sandstone disk from a mound in Issaquena county as "the conventional, mythical, feathered rattlesnakes of the South." Thus Ike's reverential meeting with the rattlesnake immediately after he comes from the graves on the knoll may be an affirmation of the ultimate cycle of renewal that signified, in his words, "There was no death, not Lion and not Sam: not held fast in earth but free in earth."

The visions that young Ike experiences expose him to a mythical world in which he maintains a faith until the end of his life. After the spirit/deer reveals itself to young Ike, his cousin suggests that they participate in an economy of souls and bodies; as he tells Ike of living and hunting, he says "and all that must be somewhere; all that could not have been invented and created just to be thrown away. And the earth is shallow; there is not a great deal of it before you come to the rock. And the earth dont want to just to keep things, horde them; it wants to use them again." It was in that hope that Ike buries Sam, Ben, and Lion and it is in that hope that he approaches death and another dimension when toward the end of his life he dreams "the wild strong immortal game ran forever before the tireless belling immortal hounds, falling and rising phoenix-like to the soundless guns." If Faulkner's use of reincarnation imagery reflected some elements of Native American ideology, then that spiritual dimension must have a physical component that was possibly suspended with the death of Sam, Ben, and Lion but was not destroyed. If the deer that young Ike saw was both flesh and spirit, then we can expect that the spirits of the dead game have not utterly vanished and may some day assume bodies.

Even if one only accepts the implication of a natural cycle of renewal in Faulkner's work, it makes his view of the hunt vastly different from standard hunting literature and from straightforward laments for lost wilderness. The hint that the mysteries of nature might still be alive urges us to look beyond the decline of the traditional wilderness, and the high point of the premechanized small farm way of life. During the forties, forces emerged that would alter the habitat of Mississippi as drastically as had the lumbering boom and the cotton culture of the earlier decades. While a deepening agricultural depression began displacing the rural poor after the turn of the century, and rural exodus occurred between 1900 and 1940, the decades stand out more for the increasing density of the rural population in Mississippi. Farm acreage increased and the average acreage in farms decreased as the number of people actually living on the land grew. As agricultural historians have shown in their studies of the fragmentation of cotton production in the postbellum South, cotton culture and its share and tenant systems resisted change until government subsidy programs made it profitable to limit cotton acreage and technology allowed planters to produce with less labor. During the forties, agricultural herbicides, pesticides, tractors, and (by the end of WWII) a few cotton pickers appeared on Mississippi farmland. As farmers mechanized their operations, the need for tenant labor disappeared and agricultural employment began a sharp decline. From around 420,000 directly involved in farming in 1940, farmers numbered only 41,000 in 1980. In Mississippi, as across the South, the number of farms decreased and the size of individual farms increased.

Faulkner personally experienced the last gasp of small-scale farming during what Joel Williamson called his "Greenfield years." After Faulkner purchased the 320 acres he called Greenfield, he brought in several tenant families and in testimony to the times lost a good deal of money, subsidizing the operation with his writing income. Williamson sets the dates for Faulkner's interest in his farm from 1938 to the early 1950s, coinciding with the time of transformation in Mississippi agriculture. The fact that Faulkner was a writer and not a farmer certainly contributed to the failure of Greenfield as a viable operation; however, his experience followed the pattern of most small farms throughout the state. As the position of the small farmer grew more untenable, many families joined the migration from the state or simply commuted to work in the towns. Mechanized agriculture concentrated in the flat expanses of blackland prairie and in the Delta, while the long-farmed upland began losing its rural population. And more importantly for the habitat of the uplands, the decline of premechanized farming took people out of a direct relationship with the land. With agriculture in the hands of a small cadre of professional farmers, what rural life there was became simply living outside the city rather than a personal struggle with nature on a day to day basis.

Abandoned farmland in north Mississippi returned to various forest types, sometimes regenerating on its own to a mix of oak, hickory, and shortleaf pine and sometimes through the planting of loblolly pine seedlings. Lafayette County followed a pattern of reforestation typical of north Mississippi with the addition that Oxford was the headquarters of the forestry division of the YazooLittle Tallahatchie Flood Control Project. The Y-L T, as it is known in Forest Service literature, grew out of the 1928 Flood Control Act. Its environmental impact on the upland areas included dams on the tributaries of the Yazoo constructed by the Corps of Engineers, including the Tallahatchie in 1940 and the Yocona in 1953. The Forest Service planted over 600,000 acres to trees, primarily loblolly pine, in parts of nineteen counties after 1948. From 1949 to 1959 Forest Service personnel helped plant some 39,000,000 young pines in Lafayette County alone. Joel Williamson argued that Faulkner recognized the end of the small farm and the move to town in his Snopes trilogy and that he had abandoned his own plain farmer persona by 1959. Significantly, in September of that same year the Oxford Eagle published an eight-page section praising the "growth and advancement made in the field of forestry in this county" and Oxford's mayor Pete McElreath issued a proclamation anointing the town the "Reforestation Capital of the World."

The abandoned farms of the uplands and the general depopulation of the countryside brought back a wealth of opportunities for the large game that Faulkner's hunters had found so important. The Mississippi Game and Fish Commission had created refuges, purchased deer from other states, and attempted deer restocking on a small scale since its inception in 1932. After WWII, with Federal money and more manpower, the Commission began an aggressive restocking program with deer trapped on Mississippi refuges that targeted suitably depopulated areas. Deer responded well to the releases, and the population showed steady growth to an estimate of around 20,000 in 1947. That year the Commission estimated the deer kill at around 1500 statewide with most still concentrated in the last of the Delta bottoms that had escaped the saw and the plow in the counties of Warren, Sharkey, Issaquena, and Yazoo, those lowest parts of the Delta that Faulkner called "the notch where the hills and the Big River met." Hunters in Lafayette, Marshall, and Benton counties killed around ninety deer in 1947 primarily out of the Holly Springs National Forest areas. Sixteen years later, whitetails numbered about 160,000 statewide and the Lafayette County kill was over 300. Turkey restocking also proved successful after biologists perfected capture techniques for the wild birds, and by 1960 the population stood close to 35,000. The Bottomlands of the Delta, once the richest environment of the state, had become in biological terms, a howling wasteland of monocultural agribusiness. Nonmigratory game species in the Delta retreated to the batture forest between the Mississippi river levees and the isolated patches of forest on either public land or hunting clubs. And in a further exercise in irony, much of the small game regime of the state began collapsing as the upland forest returned. Today, the memories of the quail hunting tradition can generate as much nostalgia among north Mississippi hunters as the vestiges of deer hunting fostered in 1940. Across Mississippi, counties that had not held deer and turkey for generations now supported hunting seasons. Through a cycle of wilderness destruction, a wrenching dislocation of the rural poor, and the rise of agribusiness, large game found refuge in a new forest on the Mississippi upland where the hunt continues; sometimes in that familiar "gray and constant light of the late November dawn."

The new upland forest is not as majestic as the virgin bottomland timber, and modern forestry's emphasis on loblolly pine monoculture sometimes inhibits its potential biological diversity. Yet the withdrawal of a large human population from an intimate daily contact with the countryside and its wildlife has renewed the possibility of if not wilderness, then at least an alternative to the city and the cotton field that Faulkner would have appreciated. As people have withdrawn further from the daily facts of sustaining life, the counterpoint to a human dominated environment can be just beyond the air conditioning and the mowed lawn. And in parts of the forest where deer and turkey returned some biologists believe the bear can follow. Possibly fifty black bear inhabit the timberland of extreme southwestern Mississippi in addition to an undetermined number in the batture lands between the levees of the Mississippi River. The Mississippi survivors along with larger numbers of bears in the Tensas and Atchafalaya basins of Louisiana are slowly increasing and, though anything like a restoration of the bear to its historic range may be impossible, the fact of a small growing population is a miraculous testimony to the regeneration of wild places in Mississippi. The regeneration of game populations can astound us even today. Not due to any one factor or group of people and not without its own set of environmental problems, the recovery of large game must be seen as a part of ongoing changes in the land. Through his hunting stories, Faulkner left us a faith in the resilience of the natural world and the chance to see ourselves as only parts of a broad cycle of life and death. If we can truly recognize our place in the land with the creatures we hunt, we will have gone a long way toward the humility young Ike McCaslin sought.

Source: Wiley C. Prewitt Jr., "Return of the Big Woods: Hunting and Habitat in Yoknapatawpha," in *Faulkner and the Natural World: Faulkner and Yoknapatawpha, 1996*, edited by Donald M. Kartinganer and Ann J. Abadie, University Press of Mississippi, 1999, pp. 198–221.

Barbara L. Pittman

In the following excerpt, Pittman considers "Race at Morning" in the larger context of Big Woods, *arguing that the four stories point to the "apocalypse of the wilderness" and a turn to a new way of life.*

...*Big Woods* contains more than just a desire to retrieve the lost wilderness. Embodied in the idea of wilderness is the "wild"—a quality both feared and desired, and a quality frequently attributed to the African and Native Americans who are a part of both narratives in *Big Woods*. When the wilderness was a dominant landscape, whites enjoyed the position of dominance in America. Thus, the lament for the loss of a dominating wilderness masks a lament for the lost of white domination. This narrative of domination in *Big Woods* is even more important in the historical context of post-*Brown v. Board of Education* 1955, when racial segregation in America is being openly challenged, particularly in Faulkner's South. For Faulkner to refigure his earlier text about racial injustice into this "nice book" that laments the loss of that condition, not only reveals some of the frustration and tension that moderate Southern whites were feeling as their society was daily dissected by the national media, but also speaks the unspeakable desire to dominate. My analysis begins with a lengthy discussion of how *Big Woods* instructs the formation of myth as the deconstruction of its "apocalyptic discourse. The four rifled stories represent a narrative "reality" beginning when the wilderness was still dominant, and illustrate the actual physical decline of the wilderness along with the loss of hunting ethics; the italicized narrative utilizes an oracular narrative voice, and exemplifies the myth that will survive physical extinction; the drawings, in collaboration with the written text, reinforce the idea of myth in their interpretation of the text. Finally, I will return to Morrison and to the historical circumstances that motivate Faulkner to excise race, to represent the loss of an empowering wilderness, and to preserve the past in a static myth. I hope to show how Faulkner creates a complex narrative structure that both masks and maintains the power of domination.

The first task of an apocalyptic text is "revelation of the apocalypse" (Derrida, p. 87). Faulkner makes the revelation in the four titled stories that focus on Isaac (Ike) McCaslin and progress in time from his boyhood initiation into hunting to his position as the elder, experienced

THERE IS AN ACTUAL HUNT IN THIS STORY, WITH THE TWIST JOHNSON NOTES THAT THE HUNTERS DO NOT KILL ANY GAME BUT ONLY CHASE IT, AND THE LESSON IS ONE THAT MOVES 'TOWARD LIFE.'"

hunter. The episodic selection of stories reveals to the reader not only the end of the wilderness but also the end of the hunting ethics learned there. The order of the first two stories—"The Bear" and "The Old People"—is reversed from the *Go Down, Moses* order. This reversal helps to illustrate the types of values that like Ike learns in the wilderness, and how those values become part of his identity, a movement that parallels the larger movement from history to myth. Thus, when we see in the second pair of stories—"A Bear Hunt" and "Race at Morning"—the decline of such values, we sense the ending of the environment that produced them.

The first titled story, "The Bear," preaches the end of the wilderness as near at hand—a "doomed" environment "whose edges were being constantly and punily gnawed at by men with plows and axes"; already the bear is "an anachronism," an "apotheosis of the old wild life." Thus, Isaac is initiated into a way of life in its last stages; in *Big Woods*, Isaac is the last man, a role he senses even in his youth:

> It seemed to him that something, he didn't know what, was beginning; had already begun. It was like the last act on a set stage. It was the beginning of the end of something, he didn't know what except that he would not grieve. He would be humble and proud that he had been found worthy to be a part of it too or even just to see it too.

As the last man of this wilderness, the last one to inherit the teachings of Sam Fathers, Isaac appropriately becomes "as competent in the woods as many grown men with the same experience," a "better woodsman" than either General Compson or McCaslin Edmonds. The older hunters recognize his position and so permit him to assume such privileges as riding the "one-eyed mule" Katie into the hunt, and skipping school that merely teaches "what some hired pedagogue put between the covers of a book." The values Isaac learns from Sam Fathers are grounded in respect for nature and wildlife, and in the development of man's right relationship to the natural world. He is not there to return to some primitive brutality, but to learn "humility" and "patience." As a child too young to go on the hunt, Isaac "would watch the wagon . . .depart for the Big Bottom" not even expecting the hunters to return with a trophy. To him, they were going not to hunt bear and deer but to keep a yearly rendezvous with the bear which they did not even intend to kill. The hunt is more of a "yearly pageant-rite" that enables the hunters to renew their perspectives. When Isaac finally enters the wilderness, he joins a race that is "dwarfed . . . into an almost ridiculous diminishment" by the sheer size and indifference of nature.

By the last section of "The Bear," civilization is bringing the end of the wilderness at a more rapid rate. A "lumber company [has] moved in and [begun] to cut the timber." Isaac's mentor, Sam Fathers, has died and Major de Spain, we learn, never returns to the camp. The last hunt in the story is the actual last hunt for General Compson. When Isaac arrives for the hunt, he is "shocked and grieved" at the sight of "a new planing-mill" cutting miles into the woods. Even more insidious is the threat of the locomotive, once "harmless" and "carrying to no destination or purpose sticks which left nowhere any scar. . . . But it was different now. . . .this time it was as though the train . . .had brought with it into the doomed wilderness even before the actual axe the shadow and portent of the new mill not even finished yet and the rails and ties which were not even laid." The locomotive reveals its true power in the speed with which it can permit deforestation.

"The Bear" completes the apocalypse of the wilderness in the "civilized" intrusion of Boon Hogganbeck banging on the pieces of his faulty gun and greedily yelling, "They're mine!" The deaths of Sam and Old Ben signal the end of the wilderness, and Hogganbeck's civilization of machinery and greed that replaces it will be a poor substitute. The scope of this story depicts the broad cycle of decline, and with its primary position in the work firmly sets the tone of despair.

"The Old People" returns to the moment in section two of "The Bear" which mentions that Isaac has already "killed his buck," and fills in the entire episode. This story perpetuates the ritual of initiation, and reveals the origin of the ritual saluting of wild game that appears in "The Bear."

Even this tale, however, which goes back in time, preaches the end through the genealogies of Isaac and Sam Fathers—the two of them are the last of their lines. Isaac has no descendants, and Sam's blood is "now drawing toward the end of its alien and irrevocable course." Sam's genealogy begins with the story of his father, a Chicksaw appropriately named Doom, a phonetic perversion of the French "Du Homme" that tragically foretells the future of his people. The genealogy also includes his "quadroon slave" mother, and suggests that African-Americans are always already defeated by the history of enslavement in their blood, and that this defeat is visible, at times, in Sam's eyes, reflecting a "knowledge that for a while that part of his blood had been the blood of slaves." Thus, the idea of the doomed environment, including the doomed races, is seen to have existed at least since Isaac was about ten. By returning to events before those in "The Bear," Faulkner predicts and fulfills the decline evidenced in it.

The last two stories propel us more than forty years into the future, when Ike is one of the older experienced hunters. Instead of predicting the doom of the wilderness, these stories illustrate its decline. "A Bear Hunt" is not a tale about a bear hunt, although the narrator tells us incidentally that "'two days before Major had killed a bear.'" The hunt itself is no longer of central importance to the hunters; the ritual of going to the hunting camp and telling stories replaces it. The "participants" of this hunt, with the exception of Uncle Ike, are descendants of the hunting party of "The Bear." Luke Hogganbeck is the forty-year-old son of Boon; the Major is Major de Spain's son (the title is honorary); Ash is the son of Ash Wylie. These "hunters" have gathered at the camp for their annual ritual, but Luke's continuous hiccuping interrupts their supposed hunt. Luke "has acquired his hiccups by overeating, a fact indicative of his lessened stature" (Ragan, p. 312). Unlike the hunters of old, these men exploit the wildlife by killing more than they need. Luke is stuffed with "venison... coons and squirls...bear meat and whisky."

That storytelling assumes a greater role than the hunt is evidence by the use of two narrators. Faulkner divides "A Bear Hunt" into two sections; the first is "narrated apparently by Quentin Compson" (Ragan, p. 312) and introduces the second narrator, V.K. Ratliff. The two narrations signal in their own ways the changes in the *Big Woods*. Quentin notes that Ratliff now "uses model T Ford" instead of the "light, strong buckboard" of the past. And it is this first narration that gives the genealogies of the hunting-party members, that provides a sense of continuity while at the same time reminding readers that these are not the same men. Ratliff's story is a rousing one full of burlesque antics, but in the context of Big Woods, the absence of the hunt itself is ominous. Ragan notes that the characters display a "selfishness" that "underlines what the loss of the wilderness...really means. (p. 312). They are more interested in playing tricks, the effectiveness of which depends on superstition instead of on knowledge of the wilderness.

Glen M. Johnson points out that "the structure of *Big Woods* literally surrounds...hope with...despair," and sees "Race at Morning" as a story of hope. There is an actual hunt in this story, with the twist Johnson notes that the hunters do not kill any game but only chase it, and the lesson is one that moves "toward life." (pp. 257, 250). But, to believe that, one must believe that life is in civilization and that it can teach the same lessons and values that the wilderness previously taught, that civilization will teach the "business of mankind." This shift of focus away from the wilderness represents a clear departure from "The Bear." The business of mankind in "Race At Morning" is reading and writing, and knowing not just "what's right and what's wrong" but "why it's right and why it's wrong." In "The Bear," the hunters put little hope in "what some hired pedagogue put between the covers of a book" when regarding Ike's education. So, in this story there is no still, quiet hunting as when Sam led young Ike on his hunts, and there are no ritual salutes. There is a fast and frantic chase on horseback, in which the main hunter, Mr. Ernest, relies on the horse and the dogs and a boy to hear the dogs. Although Mr. Ernest is a skilled hunter, there is little need for him to rely on his skills in this situation. What is the boy learning as Mr. Ernest's ears? Certainly not the lessons Ike learned: patience, respect for the life taken, man's relationship to nature. Mr. Ernest would save the buck for next year's hunt rather than have "half his meat in a pickup truck." The loss of space and game in the dwindling wilderness forces the hunters to replace the hunt with a race; the hunters are wise enough to see that it is an activity empty of life-lessons.

The four rifled stories complete a circle of "a boy's education in the wilderness" (Ragan, p. 314).

They also show that with the decline of the wilderness, civilization becomes the focus of man's attention. Mister Ernest encourages the unnamed boy of "Race at Morning" to turn toward civilization and away from the Big Woods, which are physically and spiritually diminished. Despite Johnson's and Ragan's persuasive readings of hope, the stories clearly predict the apocalypse of the wilderness—no matter what avenues Faulkner leaves open for the human characters. . . .

Source: Barbara L. Pittman, "Faulkner's *Big Woods* and the Historical Necessity of Revision," in *Mississippi Quarterly*, Vol. 49, No. 3, Summer 1996, pp. 475–97.

David Paul Ragan

In the following excerpt, Ragan examines the revisions Faulkner made to the story "Race at Morning" between its initial publication in The Saturday Evening Post *and its subsequent inclusion in* Big Woods, *concluding that the changes make the story more symbolic, "add to the humor," and "emphasize the beauty of the wilderness."*

Despite the fact that it has been largely ignored by students of his work, Faulkner's *Big Woods* extended the author's lifelong habit of not repeating himself and of providing new challenges for his readers. Following his practice in novels such as *The Unvanquished*, *The Hamlet*, and *Go Down, Moses*, which incorporated previously published short stories, Faulkner drew together materials which had appeared as early as 1930 for this collection of hunting stories. And though he departed from that earlier practice as well—typically in *Big Woods* he limited the implications of the material, shortened and condensed, rather than enlarging and expanding, as he had usually done for earlier works—Faulkner obviously considered the volume a serious artistic project, one in which he advanced some of the most important and moving themes he dealt with in the final decade of his career.

When the collection appeared in October 1955, most reviewers criticized it as a lesser effort, one which lacked the power and range of earlier Faulkner works from which parts of it were drawn. As Malcolm Cowley put it, its strengths had "been achieved too much at the cost of other books from which the material was taken by right of eminent domain." Other reviewers labelled the volume a mismatched group of previously published selections designed only to make money. Even so perceptive a critic as Warren Beck suggested that "a fragmented and even denatured Faulkner is being peddled." Such comments fail to consider the author's craftsmanship, signalled in the fact that much of the material, such as the prose introductions to several of the stories, was almost completely rewritten. And even when a piece was incorporated essentially unchanged, its context within the new volume forces the reader to interpret it differently, for he finds his expectations significantly altered by the surrounding material. The collection consists of four hunting stories: "The Bear," "The Old People," "A Bear Hunt," and "Race at Morning," all previously published. A narrative selection serves as a prelude to the entire book, and another one serves as a sort of postlude, or epilogue; other passages provide transitional links or interludes between the stories. Each of these pieces was drawn from work already published, but each has been carefully adapted for its thematic and structural purpose within the collection.

"IT CONDEMNS THOSE WHO DESTROY THE LAND, THE WILDERNESS, FOR THEIR OWN PROFIT, BUT IT ALSO CONDEMNS THOSE LIKE ISAAC MCCASLIN, WHO WISH TO KEEP THE LAND INTACT FOR EQUALLY SELFISH REASONS."

That Faulkner took the project seriously is indicated by the changes he made in the material. With the exception of "The Old People," each of the four stories comprising the volume has been revised: "The Bear," as Faulkner explained at the University of Virginia, appears in its story version without section 4; changes in "A Bear Hunt" and "Race at Morning" help to bring them into greater conformity with other stories in the collection by altering characters, chronology, and emphasis. Even the function of "The Old People" is very much different since it follows "The Bear" in *Big Woods*, instead of preceding it as in *Go Down, Moses*.

The author's concern with the artistic integrity of the book is even more evident in the careful orchestration of the prologue, the interludes between the stories, and the epilogue. In an interview with Harvey Breit before the publication of

Big Woods, Faulkner referred to these "remarks" which he had written for the stories as "interrupted catalysts." Though this term is quite possibly only the result of Faulkner's disagreement when Breit inquired if they were "commentaries" on the stories, his statements emphasize the extent to which he conceived of these sections as independent of their sources. The reader already acquainted with Faulkner's fiction will quickly recognize that they have been extensively revised from their original forms. Within the context of *Big Woods*, such alterations are completely justified, and criticism that the extractions violate the original versions fails to comprehend their function within the collection. They provide transitions between the stories, set the tone for each individual piece, underline themes of the collection as a whole, and create a sense of progression in both space and time. These special purposes are indicated by the fact that all the passages are printed in italics on unnumbered pages; the fact that their right margins are not justified gives them, as Glen Johnson has suggested, the appearance of blank verse.

The great interest Faulkner took in the preparation of *Big Woods* is also clearly demonstrated in his concern over the "decorations," pen-and-ink drawings by Edward Shenton, who had provided the illustrations for *The Unvanquished.* In an unsigned letter to his editor, Saxe Commins, in February 1955, Faulkner made careful suggestions about the dummy prepared by Shenton. The letter implies detailed prior discussions with the artist about the nature of the illustrations. Although Faulkner requested certain alterations, the letter reveals that he was generally delighted with Shenton's work. The importance of the drawings to the total design of the book is expressed in Faulkner's comments about the sketch of Isaac and Sam saluting the buck, intended to precede "The Old People":

> The drawing is splendid. To Mr Shenton: would you risk suggesting Sam Fathers is an Indian to this extent? He is bare-headed, his hair a little long, a narrow band of cloth bound or twisted around his head? or maybe definitely long hair showing below a battered hat? Since you are not illustrating, but illuminating (in the old sense) you could have any liberty you like.

In a closing addition to the letter, possibly written the following day, Faulkner reconsidered some of his suggestions and decided that "Mr Shenton is doing so well, I am extremely timid about getting in the way." The final drawings conform closely to Faulkner's suggestions and play an important role in the book's celebration of the wilderness and the hunt.

Clearly, then, Faulkner approached the task of assembling *Big Woods* with a dedicated craftsmanship similar to that he had employed throughout his career. By examining each section individually, we can appreciate both the extent of his imaginative commitment and the measure of his success....

This emphasis upon life looks forward to the themes of the final story in *Big Woods*, "Race at Morning." Like "A Bear Hunt," the story is set in modern times, but both the humor and the themes are of another order entirely. Unlike the preceding tale, "Race at Morning" describes a genuine hunt for game. Yet the chase is different from that depicted in "The Bear" as well. A clue to this difference is provided in the interlude which introduces it; the goal of the hunt is now *"not to slay the game but to pursue it, touch and let go, never satiety."* Although the chase itself is comic, it is heightened by powerful description of the beauty of the woods and the nobility of the deer, magnifying the tragedy inherent in their destruction for selfish economic gain.

Most of the additions Faulkner made to "Race at Morning" serve one of three functions: they place the action on a more symbolic level; they add to the humor; they emphasize the beauty of the wilderness. The longest addition concerns the horse, Dan, which becomes a beast of almost mythical ability, linking him with both Lion and Old Ben. Another added passage describes the deer himself in supernatural terms, "like that old son of a gun actually was a hant, like Simon and the other field hands said he was," reminding the reader of the tremendous buck at the end of "The Old People." The descriptions which Faulkner included as part of the narrator's perception are also reminiscent of Isaac's reverent attitude toward the Big Woods; the boy describes the sun as "bright and strong and level through the woods, shining and sparkling like a rainbow on the frosted leaves." Such additions place "Race at Morning," like the first two stories in the book, on the level of symbolic ritual.

Other parallels between "The Old People" and "Race at Morning" point toward the latter's purpose in the collection. Like the earlier story, "Race at Morning" concerns a boy's education in the wilderness; and once again the significance of his experience is verbalized by an older man, in this case Mister Ernest. Further, the lesson itself has close ties with Cass's speech concerning the value of life. The event under consideration is Mister Ernest's allowing the great buck to go free after he and the boy had chased it all day. When the narrator confronts him about it, Mister Ernest explains his reasons: "'Which would you rather have? His bloody head and hide on the kitchen floor yonder and half his meat in a pickup truck on the way to Yoknapatawpha County, or him with his head and hide and meat still together over yonder in that brake, waiting for next November for us to run him again?'" The significance of the hunt has been altered in light of changes in the environment. A similar alteration is required on a larger scale, as Mister Ernest had stated earlier; when the boy declares that he would be a hunter and farmer too, Mister Ernest says:

> "That ain't enough any more. Time was when all a man had to do was just farm eleven and a half months, and hunt the other half. But not now. Now just to belong to the farming business and the hunting business ain't enough. You got to belong to the business of mankind."

This statement, appearing near the end of the final story in *Big Woods*, is central to understanding the themes of the book as a whole. It condemns those who destroy the land, the wilderness, for their own profit, but it also condemns those like Isaac McCaslin, who wish to keep the land intact for equally selfish reasons. Both ignore the "business of mankind" for more limited interests; both disregard responsibilities to the larger human community. . . .

Source: David Paul Ragan, "'Belonging to the Business of Mankind': The Achievement of Faulkner's *Big Woods*," in *Mississippi Quarterly*, Vol. 36, No. 3, Summer 1983, pp. 301–17.

Charles S. Aiken

In the following excerpt, geographer Aiken provides a detailed description of the geography of Faulkner's mythic Yoknapatawpha County, the setting of "Race at Morning."

William Faulkner (1897–1962), an outstanding twentieth-century American author, was a prolific writer who explored unique styles and literary devices. He set the best of his novels and short stories in Yoknapatawpha County, Mississippi, which has become one of the famous fictional places in literature. Beginning with "Sartoris" in 1929 and ending with "The Reivers" in 1962, bit by bit, Faulkner unfolded so much concerning the people, the history, and the geography of Yoknapatawpha with such consistency that to many readers it seems to be an actual county. Robert Penn Warren has observed that geography is "scrupulously though effortlessly presented in Faulkner's work," and its "significance for his work is very great."

> **"FAULKNER, A PRIVATE PERSON, WOULD HAVE CRINGED AT CARNAL ESTABLISHMENT AND COMMERCIAL EXPLOITATION OF HIS WORLD, BECAUSE HE BELIEVED THERE IS A BETTER WAY FOR IT TO LIVE."**

Faulkner's prominence has resulted in a voluminous outpouring of criticism, none of which has been produced by geographers despite a growing awareness by them that fiction profoundly influences the images that people hold concerning places. This lack of evaluation is even more curious in light of the author's overt sense of geography. But lack of criticism of Faulkner's works by geographers has not resulted in lack of geographical evaluation. For more than two decades literary critics have written about the parallels between fictional Yoknapatawpha and real Lafayette County, Mississippi, and they have produced some material concerning Faulkner's geography. Many aspects, however, have not previously been considered, and the process by which he converted geographical fact into fiction has not until now been synthesized. The following assessment, in part, incorporates recognized aspects of his use of geographical reality. In part, it goes beyond into the unrecorded, legendary history and the minute, ordinary geography of northern Mississippi, Faulkner's obscure source material which only a few persons can invoke.

FACT, BASIS OF FICTION

Vital to interpretation of much of Faulkner's work is the realization that he was raised in an atmosphere in which the past was considered a better time than the present. Faulkner was born in 1897 in New Albany, Mississippi, but in 1902 his family moved to Oxford, political seat of Lafayette County, where he lived almost all the remainder of his life. Oxford was less than seventy years old in 1902, but, like a person whose difficult life has accelerated the aging process, so the tragedies of the Civil War and Reconstruction had made history seem ancient. The poverty of the postwar period contributed to the development of a backward-looking people who, by the turn of the century, had begun to romanticize both the antebellum era and the war itself....

Throughout his fiction Faulkner leaves no doubt as to the exact location of Yoknapatawpha County. Like Lafayette, it is in the loess region of northwestern Mississippi east of the Yazoo Delta and approximately eighty miles south of Memphis. The most vivid description of the small-scale geographical context of the county is in "Intruder in the Dust" where, from a vantage point at the eastern edge of Yoknapatawpha, Charles Mallison sees

> his whole native land, his home...unfolding beneath him like a map in one slow soundless explosion: to the east ridge on green ridge tumbling away toward Alabama and to the west and south the checkered fields and the woods flowing on into the blue and gauzed horizon beyond which lay at last like a cloud the long wall of the levee and the great River itself flowing not merely from the north but out of the North.

The setting of Yoknapatawpha is accurate even to concepts of perception. In "The Hamlet" the Pine Hills are characterized as "a region which topographically was the final blue and dying echo of the Appalachian mountains." Of course, Lafayette County is on the coastal plain, far removed from the Appalachian Highlands. Superficially, it appears that Faulkner is attempting to conceal the location of his county by such a statement or has simply found "dying echo of the Appalachian mountains" a pleasing phrase. Actually he is merely reiterating a commonly held belief in northern Mississippi—that the prominent hills are the end-remnants of Appalachia....

Today, people who visit Oxford and Lafayette County to experience the flavor of Jefferson and Yoknapatawpha County are probably disappointed. During the past twenty-five years sweeping social, economic, and spatial changes have come to Mississippi and the entire South. Much of the basic geographical framework of the Lafayette County that Faulkner knew, including some roads and place names, remains, but almost all of the color of his time is gone. Forests dominate the landscape that as recently as 1950 was pasture and cropland. Cotton remains important, but machines have replaced the legions of mules and humans that once toiled in the fields from sunup to sundown from April through October.

Oxford is now a progressive small city of 12,000, not the agricultural town that Faulkner knew. Tobacco-chewing farmers in bib overalls no longer flock to the square on Saturdays, and with them have vanished the dust-covered wagons and pickup trucks loaded with watermelons parked around the courthouse on hot summer days. Most of the stores on the square that served an agrarian society are gone, replaced by businesses that cater to an Ole Miss student population that, since 1940, has grown from 1,400 to almost 10,000. Faulkner's characters would have difficulty moving among businesses that include the New World Bicycle Shop, the New Orleans Oyster Bar, and Good Earth Natural Foods. The courthouse remains largely unchanged, from the peeling white paint on the exterior to the musty land records vault in the Chancery Clerk's office, but the old jail was razed and replaced by a modern one in the early 1960's. Because of a recent attitude toward preservation among Oxford's leaders, there is little danger that the courthouse will be destroyed. With the university, with new shopping centers, and with proximity to Sardis Lake and metropolitan Memphis, Oxford has the potential to become the type of rural city that many Americans of the 1970's perceive as ideal.

To the visitor, almost nothing indicates that Oxford-Lafayette County was the home of William Faulkner. Even after he won the 1949 Nobel Prize for literature, Faulkner continued to live simply among his fellow Mississippians. A decade and a half after his death, no signs advertise New Albany as the birthplace of William Faulkner or Oxford as the home of a noted writer. The historical marker for Saint Peter's Cemetery indicates that it is the burial place of Supreme Court Justice L. Q. C. Lamar and other prominent early settlers, but the location of Faulkner's simple monument is unknown to all but local people. Faulkner's home, Rowan Oak, is now owned by the university and, still secluded from the street, is maintained much as he left it.

Although many residents of Oxford largely ignored Faulkner during his lifetime, today they freely discuss him and pride themselves in having known the eccentric man some once called "Curious Bill." A few have even read his books.

Among the factors in this new openness are the widespread changes that have come to Mississippi in a short time. Faulkner and his world, with many of its peculiar characters burlesqued from reality, belong to the past. A person who may recognize in Faulkner's works himself or members of his family as models can rationally dissociate himself from such characters. Also, the saga of Temple Drake and other Faulkner episodes that shocked and outraged Mississippians several decades ago seem bland in a more permissive age.

As the years pass the historical Oxford–Lafayette County and Jefferson–Yoknapatawpha County will gradually blend and become one. This process, the exact reverse of what Faulkner performed, is a prime example of how the fictional becomes the real. Faulkner buffs, both local and foreign, scout Oxford and the countryside in increasing numbers, trying to identify sites and buildings. Approximately 15,000 of the people who visit Oxford each year are drawn by Faulkner, and entrepreneurs are beginning to realize that the tourist potential is much greater. One factor in Oxford's movement to preserve buildings is recognition of their relationship to Jefferson. In the not-too-distant future, transformation of Jefferson–Yoknapatawpha County into the historic Oxford–Lafayette County will be accelerated by commercialization of Faulkner. If this sad time does come, then one will be able to lodge at the Holston House, eat at the Blue Goose Cafe, and tour the rebuilt jail. On a grander scale I can envision on the outskirts of the city recreations of the McCaslin Plantation and Varner's Crossroads complete to its Littlejohn's Hotel.

Faulkner, a private person, would have cringed at carnal establishment and commercial exploitation of his world, because he believed there is a better way for it to live. He thought that a primary goal for any artist is "to arrest motion, which is life, by artificial means and hold it fixed so that a hundred years later, when a stranger looks at it, it moves again." Faulkner is dead and the reality from which he created the fictional world of Yoknapatawpha County has all but vanished. But that world, almost as complete as any fictional place can be, from its origin in "Sartoris" to the final, romantic backward glance in "The Reivers," comes to life—with a bittersweet fragrance of nostalgia that stimulates no desire to return in those who intimately knew the reality—each time Faulkner is read.

Source: Charles S. Aiken, "Faulkner's Yoknapatawpha County: Geographical Fact into Fiction," in *Geographical Review*, Vol. 67, No. 1, January 1977, pp. 1–21.

SOURCES

Faulkner, William, "Race at Morning," in *Selected Short Stories of William Faulkner*, Random House, 1970, pp. 285–306.

Ferguson, James, "The Theme of Solipsism," in *Faulkner's Short Fiction*, University of Tennessee Press, 1991, pp. 50–83.

Gannett, Lewis, "*Big Woods*," in *William Faulkner: The Contemporary Reviews*, edited by M. Thomas Inge, Cambridge University Press, 1995, pp. 421–23; originally published in *New York Herald Tribune*, October 14, 1955.

Padgett, John B., "William Faulkner," in the *Mississippi Writers Page*, http://www.olemiss.edu/mwp/dir/faulkner_william/index.html (accessed May 7, 2008).

Pittman, Barbara L., "Faulkner's *Big Woods* and the Historical Necessity of Revision," in *Mississippi Quarterly*, Vol. 49, No. 3, Summer 1996, p. 475.

Rosenberger, Coleman, "Four Faulkner Hunting Stories, Rich in Narrative and Symbol," in *William Faulkner: The Contemporary Reviews*, edited by M. Thomas Inge, Cambridge University Press, 1995, pp. 423–24; originally published in the *New York Herald Tribune*, October 16, 1955.

Skei, Hans H., "William Faulkner," in *Dictionary of Literary Biography*, Vol. 102, *American Short-Story Writers, 1910–1945, Second Series*, edited by Bobby Ellen Kimbel, Gale Research, 1991, pp. 75–102.

U.S. Census Bureau, *Educational Attainment: 2000*, http://www.census.gov/prod/2003pubs/c2kbr-24.pdf (accessed May 7, 2008).

U.S. Census Bureau, "Illiteracy of Persons 14 Years Old and Over, by Color and Sex, by Age, Residence, and Region, for the United States: Civilian Noninstitutional Population, March 1959," http://www.census.gov/population/socdemo/education/p20-099/tab-06.pdf (accessed May 7, 2008).

Wright, David, "Blood Sports," in *Booklist*, Vol. 101, No. 1, September 1, 2004, p. 52.

FURTHER READING

Bryant, J. A., Jr., *Twentieth-Century Southern Literature*, University Press of Kentucky, 1997.

Bryant's academic overview of southern literature is an informative mix of history and literary criticism. The fourth and sixth chapters of the book are largely devoted to Faulkner and his work.

Morris, Willie, *Faulkner's Mississippi*, photographs by William Eggleston, Oxmoor House, 1990.

This collection of Faulkner's writing, complemented by photographs of Mississippi and Morris's commentary, sheds further insight on the areas upon which Faulkner's Yoknapatawpha County is based.

Parini, Jay, *One Matchless Time: A Life of William Faulkner*, HarperCollins, 2004.

The novelist and critic Parini presents a literary biography that traces Faulkner's life and work in an attempt to draw connections between the two. The book is based upon Faulkner's memoirs and letters as well as on interviews with the people who knew him.

Williams, Juan, *Eyes on the Prize: America's Civil Rights Years, 1954–1965*, introduction by Julian Bond, Viking, 1987.

This volume traces the history surrounding the civil rights movement, to which "Race at Morning" briefly alludes.

This Blessed House

JHUMPA LAHIRI

1999

"This Blessed House" by Jhumpa Lahiri was first published in *Epoch* literary magazine in 1999 and then published in Lahiri's collection of short stories, *Interpreter of Maladies*, later that year. The collection was Lahiri's first book, and it won the Pulitzer Prize. Reviewers praised Lahiri's lucid, distinctive style, as well as her mature insight into the emotional lives of her characters, and these qualities of her work continue to resonate with readers and students.

The characters in Lahiri's stories are mostly Indian, often people who have immigrated to the United States and are trying to find their place in a new culture. Some of the stories deal with feelings of dislocation, exile, and loss. In "This Blessed House," however, the young, newlywed Indian couple Sanjeev and Twinkle have adjusted well to life in America. Sanjeev is successful in business, and he and Twinkle have just moved into a new house. However, they do not know each other all that well, and tensions between them surface when Twinkle finds a number of Christian devotional items left behind by the former owners. She likes them and displays them on the mantel, but Sanjeev wants to get rid of them. This sets the stage for a struggle between Sanjeev and Twinkle over who is going to control their relationship. Sanjeev, from whose point of view the story is mostly told, learns a great deal about his new wife and what it will take for them to have a harmonious marriage.

Jhumpa Lahiri (Photograph by Suzanne Plunkett. AP Images)

AUTHOR BIOGRAPHY

Jhumpa Lahiri was born in London, England, in 1967. She was raised from the age of three in South Kingston, Rhode Island. Her parents were immigrants to the United States from Calcutta, India. Her father was a librarian at the University of Rhode Island, and her mother was a teacher's aide at an elementary school.

In spite of the fact that they lived in the United States, Lahiri's parents considered themselves Indian, and every few years they made trips to Calcutta, accompanied by their two daughters. Lahiri would stay in India for periods lasting up to six months, although she did not feel at home there. Nor did she feel quite at home in Rhode Island, where she was conscious of her different ethnic background and often felt like an outsider.

Lahiri became an avid reader when she was a child, and she also began to write stories. At the age of seven, she would coauthor with her classmates stories of up to ten pages in length.

After graduating from South Kingstown High School, Lahiri attended Barnard College, from which she graduated with a bachelor of arts degree in English literature. Continuing her studies, she received three master of arts degrees from Boston University, in English, creative writing, and comparative studies in literature and the arts. She also obtained a doctoral degree from Boston University in Renaissance Studies. Her dissertation was on the representations of Italian architecture in early seventeenth-century English theater.

In the summer of 1997, while working on her dissertation, Lahiri worked as an intern for *Boston* magazine. She had already begun writing short stories and had won the Henfield Prize from *Transatlantic Review* in 1993 and the *Louisville Review* fiction prize in 1997. Her work at *Boston* magazine, however, was limited to writing blurbs for consumer products.

Lahiri taught creative writing at Boston University and the Rhode Island School of Design, but her real ambition was to write fiction, a goal that received a major boost when the *New Yorker* published three of her stories and named her one of the twenty best young writers in the United States. Her collection of nine short stories, *Interpreter of Maladies*, including "This Blessed House," was published by Houghton Mifflin in 1999. It was an immediate success, winning the Pulitzer Price for Fiction in 2000, an impressive achievement for a young writer with her first book. The title story was awarded the O. Henry Award in 1999.

Three years later, Houghton Mifflin published Lahiri's first novel, *The Namesake*, which she had begun working on in 1997. The novel is about a family that moves from Calcutta to New York. One of the main characters is a second-generation Indian American named Gogol who struggles to find his place in the world. The novel received critical acclaim and was nominated for the 2003 *Los Angeles Times* book award for fiction. It was made into a movie directed by Mira Nair.

Lahiri married Alberto Vourvoulias, an American-born journalist, in 2001, at a ceremony in Calcutta. They have two children. In 2002, Lahiri received a Guggenheim fellowship. Since 2005, Lahiri has served as vice president of the PEN American Center.

PLOT SUMMARY

"This Blessed House" is set in present-day Connecticut. A young Indian couple, Sanjeev and Twinkle, are recently married and have just moved into their new house. As they go about investigating and fixing up the house, they begin to find small Christian knickknacks, left behind by the previous owners. Twinkle first finds a porcelain effigy of Christ. Sanjeev does not like it and tells Twinkle to get rid of it, but she thinks it is pretty and might even be worth something. Sanjeev reminds her that they are not Christians. No, she confirms, they are Hindus. She puts the statue of Christ on the fireplace mantel.

Over the next few days, more Christian items turn up: a 3-D postcard of Saint Francis, which had been taped to the back of a medicine cabinet; a wooden cross key chain; a framed paint-by-number painting of the three wise men, which had been hiding in a linen closet; a tile trivet showing Jesus delivering a sermon on a mountaintop; and a snow-filled dome containing a miniature Nativity scene. Twinkle arranges them all on the mantel. Sanjeev thinks they are all silly and wonders why Twinkle is so charmed by them. He wants her to throw them all away, but Twinkle says it would feel sacrilegious to do so. She hopes to find more.

A week later, Twinkle finds a watercolor poster of Christ, weeping and with a crown of thorns on his head. She wants to display it, but Sanjeev refuses. Twinkle says she will put it in her study, so he will not have to look at it.

When Sanjeev has a moment to himself, he recalls a dinner he and Twinkle had in Manhattan a couple of days before. Twinkle drank four glasses of whiskey in a bar, then dragged him into in a bookstore for an hour, and then insisted that they dance a tango on the sidewalk.

A few days later, Sanjeev returns from the office to find Twinkle on the phone to her girlfriend in California, talking enthusiastically about the "Christian paraphernalia." Each day is like a treasure hunt, she says. As Sanjeev observes her, he is aware that certain things about her irritate him. The way she sometimes spits a little as she speaks, for example. They have not yet been married two months, and they only met four months before. The meeting, which took place in Palo Alto, California, had been arranged by their parents. Twinkle's parents live in California, and Sanjeev's parents live in Calcutta, India. They married in India after a brief long-distance courtship punctuated by weekends together.

They are preparing for a housewarming party at the end of October, to which they have invited thirty people, all of them Sanjeev's acquaintances. Twinkle, who is still a student at Stanford University, knows no one in the area. The weekend before the party, Twinkle finds a plaster Virgin Mary in the yard, behind an overgrown bush. Twinkle wants to keep it but Sanjeev says the neighbors will think they are insane. As they argue about it, Sanjeev begins to realize that he does not know Twinkle very well, and he is not sure whether he loves her. Nor is he sure that she loves him.

That evening, when Twinkle is lying in a bubble bath, Sanjeev says he is going to remove the statue of the Virgin from the front lawn and take it to the dump. Twinkle stands up and says she hates him. She gets out of the bath, wraps a towel around her waist, and follows him down the staircase. She says she will not let him throw the statue away. He notices that she is crying, and his heart softens. They agree on a compromise. The statue will be placed in a recess at the side of the house so passersby will not see it, although it will still be visible to anyone who comes to the house.

They make extensive preparations for the party, cooking and cleaning. The first guests to arrive are Douglas and Nora. Having seen the statue of the Virgin, Douglas inquires whether Sanjeev and Twinkle are Christians. Sanjeev replies that they are not.

Soon all the guests have arrived. Everyone is elegantly dressed. They congratulate Sanjeev and admire the house. They admire Twinkle even more, and gather around her, laughing at her anecdotes and observations. Twinkle takes them on a tour of the house, and she tells Sanjeev that they all loved the poster of Christ in the study.

After Twinkle explains about how they found all the Christian items, everyone starts to search around the house to see if they can find any more. They climb up a ladder to get to the attic, although Sanjeev has no desire to join them. He hears a shriek, followed by waves of laughter. When Twinkle descends from the attic, she is carrying a large silver bust of Christ. Sanjeev takes it from her and finds it is heavy, weighing about thirty pounds. Twinkle asks if she can display it on the mantel just for the evening. After that, she says, she will keep it in her study. But Sanjeev knows this will never happen. Twinkle will keep the bust of Christ on the center of the mantel along with all the other items he dislikes. But he does not argue with her. Instead, he follows her into the living room, carrying the statue.

CHARACTERS

Douglas

Douglas is one of the guests at the housewarming party. Tall and blond, he is a consultant at the firm at which Sanjeev works.

Nora

Nora is the girlfriend of Douglas. Like him, she is tall and blond.

Prabal

Prabal is a guest at the housewarming party. He is an unmarried professor of physics at Yale University. He admires Twinkle and tells Sanjeev: "Your wife's wow."

Sanjeev

Sanjeev is a thirty-three-year-old Indian immigrant to the United States, married to Twinkle. His parents still live in India. Sanjeev is a successful man, with an engineering degree from the Massachusetts Institute of Technology (MIT). After graduating, he moved from Boston to Connecticut to work for a firm near Hartford. He excels at his work, in which he supervises a dozen people, and is being considered for vice president of the company. He is efficient, tidy, and methodical in his habits, perhaps excessively so. He arranges his engineering books in alphabetical order on his bookshelf, even though he almost never consults them. He expects Twinkle to be neat and tidy around the house and is exasperated when he discovers that she is not.

Sanjeev also has a touch of vanity about him, since he is given to looking at himself in the mirror and convincing himself that he has a distinguished profile. Also, he is of average height but he wants to be an inch taller than he is. Sanjeev is therefore a man who is conscious of appearances, which is also revealed when he worries about what people will think if they see the "Christian paraphernalia" in the house.

Before he married Twinkle, Sanjeev lived a rather lonely bachelor life, conscious at social gatherings of his single status in the midst of apparently happy couples. He had never been in love. Eventually, he got tired of coming home to an empty condominium and listened to the advice of his mother, who told him he needed a wife to love and take care of. He was quite smitten with Twinkle from the beginning, and after she visited him for the weekend he would save in an ashtray the cigarettes she had smoked while she was there. He married her after a brief courtship and is now getting used to living with her. He discovers that he is a better cook than she is, and she irritates him with some of her sloppy habits. When they have their disagreements over the Christian knickknacks that Twinkle finds in the house, Sanjeev realizes that he does not know whether he loves his wife or not. He does not really know what love is. But he seems sufficiently charmed by Twinkle's beauty and her feminine ways to let her have her way, and at the end of the story his attachment to her has deepened.

Sunil

Sunil is a guest at the housewarming party. He is an anesthesiologist.

Twinkle

Twinkle is an Indian immigrant who lives in the United States and is recently married to Sanjeev. Twinkle's parents live in California, but it is not stated whether she is a first- or second-generation immigrant. It is likely that she has lived in the United States for some while, since she is very attuned to American values and has none of the angst of the immigrant. Any anguish she has suffered in life appears to have stemmed from failed romance, not the difficulties of being an immigrant, since Sanjeev learns when he first meets her that she has recently been abandoned by a failed American actor.

The name Twinkle is a childhood nickname, taken from the nursery rhyme "Twinkle, Twinkle, Little Star," but she has not yet outgrown it. Her full name is Tanima, but this is rarely used. When Sanjeev introduces her as Tanima to one of the guests, Twinkle immediately says, "Call me Twinkle." The name gives a clue to Twinkle's childlike nature. Sanjeev notes that she is "excited and delighted by little things, crossing her fingers before any remotely unpredictable event, like tasting a new flavor of ice cream or dropping a letter in a mailbox." He also observes that her face still looks girlish. Although she is twenty-seven years old, well educated and intelligent—she is completing her master of arts degree from Stanford University, writing about an Irish poet—Twinkle has not lost her childlike playfulness. This is shown, for example, when she insists that Sanjeev dance a tango with her on the streets of Manhattan. She appears to be impulsive and has a wild streak, as when she drinks four whiskeys in a bar and then forgets all about it. In the house that she and Sanjeev have just bought, she is more interested in going on a treasure hunt for more Christian items than in doing the practical tasks that Sanjeev suggests are necessary to spruce up the place. Sanjeev also notes that she talks for a long time on the telephone to her friend in California at a time when the telephone charges are at their most expensive, which suggests that she is careless of such practical matters as the need to economize and not spend money unnecessarily. Twinkle has an alert, lively, curious nature that makes her attractive to others. She is strikingly attractive; Prabal thinks she is "wow," and all the guests admire her. At the housewarming party, Twinkle completely outshines Sanjeev and gathers around her a little circle of guests who appear to hang on her every word.

THEMES

The Struggle for Dominance

Twinkle and Sanjeev, although they are married, do not know each other very well. They have only been together for a few months, so their relationship is still in the formative stage. Sanjeev in particular is finding out that dating someone on weekends is quite a different matter from living with her. It may be that Sanjeev is inexperienced with women (he has never been in love before). When he bought the house that he and Twinkle are to live in, he had a romantic and perhaps naïve belief that they would "live there together, forever." Now he is discovering that living together is not always a bed of roses, however sweet and beautiful his new wife might be. He discovers that he is having to adapt to the way Twinkle does things, and he is still trying to puzzle her out. In fact, his life with her seems to become a series of surprises, none of them especially pleasant. There is more than a hint of frustration at the beginning, when he points out to Twinkle—whose fascination with the Christian items she finds baffles him—that they are not Christians. The narrator comments: "Lately he had begun noticing the need to state the obvious to Twinkle." Since they are both Hindus, Sanjeev wonders why his wife should care about such Christian trinkets, which in his eyes, are vulgar and express no religious sentiment at all.

TOPICS FOR FURTHER STUDY

- Interview some immigrants in your school or community. Find out why they came to the United States and how they have adjusted to life in America. What has been their experience here? Do they try to maintain the customs and practices of their countries of origin or are they adapting to American ways? Do they think of themselves as Americans or as Asian Americans, Mexican Americans, etc.? Record your interviews and write an essay in which you summarize your findings.
- What are the traditional roles ascribed to women in Western societies? Why are women given these roles? In what ways are women in the United States presented with more choices about their lives than women from other countries? Can you make a case for the continuance of traditional roles for women in the United States, or are these roles falling out of favor? Lead a class debate on the topic.
- What is the position of Indian Americans today? As Asian Americans, do they face discrimination? Are they successful, in terms of educational and income levels? What sort of occupations do Indians take up in America, and what geographical areas do they tend to live in? How does their experience in the United States resemble or differ from that of other immigrants groups such as Chinese Americans or Mexican Americans? Present your findings to the class.
- Read Lahiri's story "The Treatment of Bibi Haldar," and write an essay in which you describe what the story shows you about Indian culture and how it differs from American culture, particularly regarding customs of courtship and marriage. Conduct further research on Indian practices such as the giving of dowries. What is the dowry system? What purpose does it serve?

Sanjeev is surprised again by some of Twinkle's habits, like the day he came home one afternoon and found her in bed, reading. He wonders why she should be in bed in the middle of the day, and she replies merely that she is bored. What follows is a key moment. Sanjeev wants to tell her that there are plenty of things to do around the house; she could unpack some boxes or sweep the attic. But he says nothing, only reflecting on the fact that such unfinished matters around the house did not bother her at all. This is the developing pattern of their relationship; she is getting the upper hand, doing what she likes, while he is more passive, trying to understand her and get along with her. She seems in many ways to be the stronger personality, and he tries to accommodate her, as when he lets her browse in a bookstore for an hour even when he has no interest in the place. In some respects Twinkle is a mystery to him. For example, he does not understand the excitement she shows at little insignificant things: "It made him feel stupid, as if the world contained hidden wonders he could not anticipate, or see."

Being so recently formed, there is an uncertainty to their relationship, in terms of who is going to adapt to whom, and whether there are going to be arguments and quarrels or harmony and peace. If it is to be the latter, what price will be paid for it, and who will do the paying? How things will eventually be between these newlyweds is suggested in two key scenes. The first is the dispute over the statue of the Virgin. Sanjeev is determined to get rid of it, and plucks up the courage to speak his mind. But after they speak sharply to each other, Twinkle cries, and her tears melt his heart. In this battle of wills, she uses what are sometimes called "women's weapons," and the result is that they agree on a compromise which is far more favorable to her than it is to him.

The second key scene comes right at the end. While Twinkle and the guests rummage around in the attic, the frustrated Sanjeev has visions of himself taking charge of the household. He will take "Twinkle's menagerie"—the Christian items—to the dump, and while he is at it, he will smash the statue of the Virgin with a hammer. Then he will come home, make himself a gin and tonic, and listen to some Bach music. But when Twinkle descends from the attic carrying the large bust of Christ, he says nothing of this. He has a feeling of warmth toward her, although the fact that he hates the statue mostly because Twinkle loves it suggests an underlying hostility in his emotions regarding his wife. But he knows that Twinkle will have her way: the bust will be displayed on the mantel whether he likes it or not. As he carries it into the living room, it is his arms that ache from the weight of it, not hers. It is he who follows, while she leads. He must merely go along with the will of his pretty, unpredictable, mysterious wife, and he knows that he is just going to have to get used to it.

The Dual Cultural Life of the Immigrant

Twinkle and Sanjeev are both Indians living in the United States. As such, they participate in two cultures, that of their native India and that of their adopted home. Twinkle's parents live in California, and it may be that she is a second-generation immigrant, although when her parents immigrated to the United States is not mentioned. Sanjeev's parents, on the other hand, still live in India; he immigrated to the United States as a single man, not with the rest of his family.

In many ways, both Twinkle and Sanjeev have assimilated with the dominant culture. Twinkle studies the work of a Western poet; Sanjeev has an interest in Western classical music, listening to Mahler and Bach. But they remain Hindus, which is the religion of the majority of people in India, and the fact that they discover Christian items all over the house is a reminder that they do not adhere to the dominant religion in the United States. Twinkle, of course, is not in the least bothered by this, but Sanjeev is, not wanting anyone to think that they are Christians. At the housewarming party, he finds that he has to explain again and again that they are not Christians. However, this seems more of a symbolic issue for him than anything else, since neither he nor Twinkle show any sign of being religious or of following the teachings and practices of Hinduism. Indeed, Twinkle's ironic comment that they are "good little Hindus" suggests her lack of genuine interest in religion.

It appears, then, that Sanjeev is more aware of his Indian heritage than is Twinkle, and this is apparent in other ways. Before he was married, Sanjeev was influenced by his mother's desire for him to make a traditional Indian marriage. She would send him photographs of prospective brides from Calcutta "who could sing and sew and season lentils without consulting a cookbook." However, in the end, Sanjeev chooses not a traditional bride who lives merely to serve her husband, but the feisty Twinkle, who soon shows that she will please herself as often as she pleases him.

The fact that Sanjeev and Twinkle married and honeymooned in India shows that in some ways they are still attached to their country of origin. Another sign of their identification with India and the Indian immigrant community in their area is the fact that at the housewarming party, many of the guests are Indians. Some of the women arrive wearing "their finest saris, made with gold filigree that draped in elegant pleats over their shoulders." It is also notable that these Indian immigrants appear not to be facing any hostility or discrimination based on their ethnicity. They are part of an upwardly mobile class of young Indian professionals, able to succeed in their adopted country because the American dream is open to all.

STYLE

Third-person Point of View

The story is told in the third person by what is known as a limited narrator. This means that the narrator tells only of what is felt or thought by a single character, in this case Sanjeev. The reader is given almost no direct insight into Twinkle's mind; she must be assessed by what she says and does, and what Sanjeev thinks, observes, and reveals about her. The effect is that for the reader, Twinkle becomes as enigmatic as she is for Sanjeev. Since the reader is experiencing Twinkle through Sanjeev's eyes, he or she shares in Sanjeev's attempts to understand Twinkle and shares in the range of emotions Sanjeev goes through, including bewilderment, surprise, irritation, frustration, defiance, and finally acceptance. Had the story been told from Twinkle's point of view, it might have created a very different impression. The choice made by the author to tell the story through the narrator's insight into Sanjeev's mind is appropriate, because he is a more reflective, aware character than Twinkle, and it is he who for the most part has to adjust to her, rather than the other way around. It is Sanjeev, for example, who shows change and development during the course of the story, whereas Twinkle stays the same.

Religious Imagery

Two key images in the story are the watercolor poster of Christ weeping and the plaster Virgin Mary that Twinkle discovers in their yard, with "a blue painted hood draped over her head in the manner of an Indian bride." Twinkle loves both items; Sanjeev cannot stand either of them. When their dispute over the statue of the Virgin comes to a head, Twinkle is taking a bubble bath and has also coated her face with "a bright blue mask." By the time she has got out of the bath and is arguing with Sanjeev, the mask has dried and taken on an ashen quality. Some water from her wet hair drips onto her face, but then Sanjeev notices "that some of the water dripping down her hard blue face was tears." Twinkle does not try to stop the tears; she looks "strangely at peace. For a moment she closed her lids, pale and unprotected compared to the blue that caked the rest of her face." Twinkle thus takes on something of the appearance of a religious icon—a combination of the weeping Christ and the calm, compassionate Virgin. Her appearance touches Sanjeev's heart and he immediately seeks a reconciliation with her. He may have been repelled by the poster of Christ and the statue of the Virgin, but here he finds a living icon to which he is compelled to offer his devotion.

HISTORICAL CONTEXT

Indian Immigration to the United States

Lahiri was raised in the United States by Indian immigrant parents who still identified with their country of origin. She therefore knows firsthand about the milieu of the Indian immigrant in America. The Indian American community has grown considerably over the last forty years, following the 1965 Immigration and Naturalization Act, which removed the national origins quota system in favor of criteria that emphasized possession of desirable skills.

During the 1970s, sizable Indian American populations grew up in the United States, concentrated in four states, California (where in "This Blessed House" Twinkle's parents live), New York, New Jersey, and Illinois. Indian immigrants adjusted well to being in the United States and became one of the most prosperous of immigrant groups, many of them becoming highly paid professionals such as doctors or businessmen and women (like Sanjeev, Prabal, and Sunil in the story). During the 1980s, the Indian American community became more diverse, as those who were already in the United States sponsored their relatives to join them. This second wave of Indian immigrants was, in general, not as highly educated as the first wave.

In the 1990s, Indian immigrants made a significant impact on the booming information technology industry. Many Indian entrepreneurs settled in California's Silicon Valley and established their own highly successful companies there.

The Indian community in the United States became the second-largest Asian community after the Chinese. During the twenty-first century, the Indian community in the United States has continued to grow.

Indian Literature in English

Coinciding with the rapid increase of Indian immigration to the United States has been the growth of literature written by Indians in English. Some Indian writers who have made their homes in the United States or Canada, including Bharati Mukherjee, Ved Mehta, Michael Ondaatji, and the poet A. K. Ramanujan, have written about the collective experience of Indian immigrants in North America. Therefore, when she began writing her stories in the 1990s, Lahiri was contributing to an existing body of work by Indians or those of Indian heritage living in the West.

During the 1990s and early 2000s, many new writers of Indian origin made their mark on the American literary scene. Vikram Seth is known for his novel *A Suitable Boy* (1994). Kiran Desai, who was born in India and is now a permanent resident of the United States, published her first novel, *Hullabaloo in the Guava Orchard*, in 1998, to critical acclaim. She is the daughter of Anita Desai, also a noted Indian author. Vikram Chandra, also born in India, received widespread recognition when he published his first novel, *Red Earth and Pouring Rain: A Novel*, in 1995, and the five stories that make up his collection *Love and Longing in Bombay* (1997). Pankaj Mishra's novel, *The Romantics* (2000), about people struggling to lead fulfilling lives in cultures not their own, won the Los Angeles Times Art Seidenbaum award for first fiction. Even more recently, Raj Kamal Jha and Indra Sinha have made their mark with their first novels, *The Blue Bedspread* (2001) and *The Death of Mr. Love: A Novel* (2004), respectively.

Nativity scene *(Photograph by Kelly A. Quin. Gale, a part of Cengage Learning)*

CRITICAL OVERVIEW

Lahiri's collection of stories, *Interpreter of Maladies*, was enthusiastically received by reviewers. Laura Shapiro's comment in *Newsweek* is typical of the kind of praise Lahiri received: "Jhumpa Lahiri writes such direct, translucent prose you almost forget you're reading, so to look up from the page and see your own living room is startling." In the *New York Times*, Michiko Kakutani describes Lahiri as "a wonderfully distinctive new voice." Kakutani singles out "This Blessed House" for comment, noting that the newlyweds "uncover the fault lines in their partnership as a silly tiff over some Christian knickknacks... [which] escalates into a fight not only about religion but also about autonomy and control."

Kakutani concludes with a general comment about Lahiri's stories that could certainly apply directly to "This Blessed House": "Ms. Lahiri chronicles her characters' lives with both objectivity and compassion while charting the emotional temperature of their lives with tactile precision. She is a writer of uncommon elegance and poise." In the *New York Times Book Review*, Caleb Crain discusses the collection in terms of "marriages that have been arranged, rushed into, betrayed, invaded and exhausted." He reports that "This Blessed House" (one of the stories in which marriage is rushed into) is his favorite story in the collection, and he devotes over one-third of his review to discussing it. In particular, he discusses the important scene in which Sanjeev and Twinkle quarrel over the statue of the Virgin Mary. The weeping Twinkle, with her blue face mask, has become "the Madonna statuette that she is so taken with. She has breathed her own life into the Christian icon's plaster, not deliberately and not ironically but humanely, and she demands that her husband respond to this achievement with mercy and respect."

CRITICISM

Bryan Aubrey

Aubrey holds a Ph.D. in English. In this essay on "This Blessed House," he discusses the story in terms of changing gender roles.

As an American writer of Indian heritage, Lahiri in her stories gives much insight and food for thought about the interactions between American and Indian culture, the challenges faced by immigrants to the United States, and the different strategies they develop for living in their adopted country. One focus of interest is gender roles. Under the influence of the feminist movement that began in the 1960s, women's roles in work and marriage in the United States have changed dramatically over the last forty years. The traditional marriage, in which the man was responsible for earning a living and providing for his family and in which the woman stayed at home cooking, cleaning, and looking after the children, is no longer the cultural norm. Most women are now part of the workforce, and many earn as much as, or even more than, their husbands. Household and child-rearing tasks are now more evenly divided than they used to be; it is no longer a universal

WHAT DO I READ NEXT?

- Like many of her stories, Lahiri's highly praised first novel, *The Namesake* (2003), deals with the immigrant experience. The main character, Gogol Ganguli, who was born in the United States to Indian parents, feels that he is an outsider, belonging neither to Indian nor American culture. The novel follows his attempts to define himself until he finally learns to accept both the American and the Indian aspects of his heritage.
- *The Middleman and Other Stories* (1988), by Bharati Mukherjee, explores the immigrant experience in America, including not only the experience of Indians but also of Italians, Filipinos, West Indians, and even an Iraqi Jew. Her stories document the changing ethnic composition of the United States and the challenges faced by those who find themselves living in an unfamiliar culture in which they are not always welcome.
- In *Becoming American, Being Indian: An Immigrant Community in New York City* (2002), Madhulika S. Khandelwal describes the Indian immigrant community in New York City and how it has grown rapidly and become more diverse since its inception in the 1960s. Drawing extensively on interviews, Khandelwal examines the ways in which immigrants have preserved their culture, and also the ways in which they have been absorbed into and changed by the American experience.
- Gish Jen, a Chinese American, is a highly acclaimed writer whose work focuses on the different ethnic groups in America, including Jews and African Americans as well as Asian Americans. Her collection of eight stories, *Who's Irish?* (2000), presents the immigrant experience in all its colorful range, including the tension between the desire to assimilate with the mainstream and the need to uphold a cultural heritage.

"IT SEEMS, THEN, THAT SANJEEV AND TWINKLE FORM A MARRIAGE THAT, IN TERMS OF GENDER ROLES, REFLECTS SOME OF THE CHANGES THAT HAVE TAKEN PLACE IN AMERICAN SOCIETY AND CULTURE."

assumption that the wife is responsible for looking after the home. American couples, now lacking a cultural norm on which to model their marriage, have to work out for themselves how to make their marriage work in terms of who does what and who is responsible for what. Greater equality and less fixedness in gender roles have become the new norm.

In India, the worldwide feminist movement has also had an effect on attitudes toward marriage and gender roles, but not to the same extent as it has in Western societies. Women in India marry much younger than they do in the United States. The median age of Indian women when they marry is just under nineteen (compared to twenty-five in the United States), and nearly half the women in India are married between the ages of fifteen and nineteen. The majority of marriages in India are arranged by the parents and other relatives of the couple. Marriage is considered an alliance between families rather than simply a union of two individuals. It is the task of the man's family to arrange the marriage, and professional matchmakers are used to find suitable matches. Lahiri's story "The Treatment of Bibi Haldar," which takes place in India, gives a somewhat satirical picture of what might happen when an Indian family selects a woman as a possible bride. Bibi's friends prepare her for the interview that will follow:

> Most likely the groom will arrive with one parent, a grandparent, and either an uncle or an aunt. They will stare, ask several questions. They will examine the bottoms of your feet, the thickness of your braid. They will ask you to name the prime minister, recite poetry, feed a dozen hungry people on half a dozen eggs.

An important part of Indian marriage custom is the payment of a dowry by the bride's family. Dowry payments can be considerable, and may include specific items (a luxury car, for example) as well as cash.

Such practices are of course quite foreign to American customs, and when Indians immigrate to the United States, they may find themselves caught in a clash of cultures and values. The usual pattern, not only for Indians but also immigrants from other non-Western countries, is that first-generation immigrants maintain their ties to their homelands, think of themselves as Indian (for example) rather than American, and try to uphold the traditional practices of their cultures. Second-generation immigrants, however, who are born in the United States, tend to be more naturally adapted to American culture, and this can lead to intergenerational conflict within immigrant families.

Sanjeev and Twinkle in "The Blessed House" make an interesting couple in this respect. There is just a trace of the arranged marriage in their story. Before he met Twinkle, Sanjeev would receive photographs from his mother in Calcutta of possible, and very traditional, brides, ladies who "could sing and sew and season lentils without consulting a cookbook." At one point Sanjeev started to rank these prospects in order of preference, but he never followed through on it. When Twinkle emerged as a prospect, it was their parents who set up the couple's first meeting, and it appears that matchmakers were also employed. But Sanjeev and Twinkle had a typical American rather than Indian courtship, even down to eating popcorn at the movies.

Now, as young married Indians living in the United States, Sanjeev and Twinkle maintain their links with India—they were married in India and honeymooned there—but their marriage does not conform to the traditional Indian type. To begin with, twenty-seven-year-old Twinkle, whose Indian parents live in California, married late by Indian standards, although not by American ones. In addition, like many American women, Twinkle is rather independent-minded and does not confine herself to a traditional gender role. While the marriage is traditional in the sense that Sanjeev is the sole wage earner, in other respects there is almost a reversal of gender roles.

This reversal can be seen in the different attitudes Sanjeev and Twinkle have to cooking, cleaning, and keeping the house tidy, traditionally the responsibilities of the wife. But in this marriage, it is the man who is more concerned with maintaining a neat, orderly, and clean environment. At the beginning of the story, Sanjeev points out to Twinkle that the mantel needs dusting, but a few days later, it still has not been dusted; Twinkle has been too busy using it as a display shelf for her newly discovered Christian trinkets. As far as household tasks are concerned, Sanjeev appears to have expectations of Twinkle that she seems unwilling to fulfill. He wants her to pull her weight in getting the house they have just moved into in good order, but she is unresponsive to his requests, preferring to read, talk on the telephone with her friends, or pursue her "treasure hunt" for Christian devotional items. Her casualness about such important matters annoys Sanjeev, but as a concession to commonly held attitudes in the culture he finds himself in—in which women reserve the right to refuse traditional roles ascribed to them—he does not seem to expend much energy in trying to impose his way on her. He is learning to be resigned, to cede to his wife a certain degree of control that would be unthinkable in a traditional marriage. He begins to realize that if he wants to satisfy his desire for neatness and cleanliness, he had better take care of these things himself. Twinkle will continue to drop her underwear on the floor at night instead of putting it in the hamper, whatever he says about it. There is a hint of irony in this last little source of tension, since in America the cultural stereotype is of the woman who has to clean up after the untidy man. But in this household, things are a little different.

It is the same with cooking. Sanjeev likes to cook Indian food, taking the time on weekends to prepare a decent curry with mustard oil, cinnamon sticks, and cloves, while Twinkle, more adjusted to the American preference that food be prepared quickly and easily, thinks cooking Indian food is too much bother. She does not even know how to use a blender, and seems to have no desire to learn. As the narrator puts it rather gently: "She was not terribly ambitious in the kitchen."

The different attitudes to cooking also hint at another difference between this couple: Sanjeev, although in many ways at home in American society and culture, is more attached to Indian ways and thought than is his wife. Sanjeev is far more concerned than she is, for example, that because of the "Christian paraphernalia" in the house, people might think they are Christians. Although he does not seem to be especially religious, he still identifies with being a Hindu, which is the majority religion in India. In another telling detail, Sanjeev is pleased that his new wife is "from a suitably high caste," caste being a term used in India to refer to the hereditary class system.

It seems, then, that Sanjeev and Twinkle form a marriage that, in terms of gender roles, reflects some of the changes that have taken place in American society and culture. But even as they adapt to American ways, they remain conscious of their connections to their country of origin. Even Twinkle, who seems very fashion conscious and wears "three-inch leopard-print pumps" when the couple goes out to dinner in Manhattan, wears a salwar kameez, a traditional Indian garment consisting of loose trousers with a long shirt or tunic, at the housewarming party. In fact, the party presents an interesting picture of the mingling of two radically different cultures. Twinkle wears her traditional salwar kameez, and there are silk paintings from Jaipur, India, on the walls. Many of the guests are Indian. But the music that Twinkle selects to play on the stereo is jazz, that quintessential American musical form. And at the end of the party the focus of interest is not on anything Indian but on a bust of Christ, the embodiment of the divine in the Christian religion.

The picture the author presents of Sanjeev and Twinkle is therefore of two Indian immigrants who are able to function well in American society by fitting in fairly easily with the majority culture, although their Indianness is never in doubt either. Twinkle is quite a contrast to another character in a Lahiri story, Mrs. Sen, in the story "Mrs. Sen's," which is included in *Interpreter of Maladies*. Mrs. Sen, an Indian immigrant of about thirty (only three years older than Twinkle) is married to a taciturn professor who is out all day at the university. Mrs. Sen is far more conservative in her Indianness than Twinkle. She wears saris and also puts vermilion on the center of her forehead in the red dot, known as a bindi, that Indian women wear to show they are married. Mrs. Sen has not adapted well to American life, and this failure is symbolized by the painful struggle she goes through trying to learn how to drive a car. (She eventually crashes it into a telephone pole.) Mrs. Sen's only pleasures are receiving aerograms from her relatives in India and shopping for fresh fish, which reminds her of her home in Calcutta, where, she says, people eat fish twice a day. Mrs. Sen lives a sad, lonely life, unable to

WHAT HAS NOT BEEN SUFFICIENTLY NOTICED IS THAT CAREFULLY EXECUTED RITUALS MARK THE RELATIONSHIPS IN *INTERPRETER OF MALADIES*."

flourish in her new environment, in sharp contrast to the vivacious, inquisitive Twinkle. In these two stories, "The Blessed House" and "Mrs. Sen's," Lahiri presents both sides of the experience of the Indian immigrant in the United States—those who adapt to living in America and those who do not. It is clear that the former lead the happier lives.

Source: Bryan Aubrey, Critical Essay on "This Blessed House," in *Short Stories for Students*, Gale, Cengage Learning, 2009.

Noelle Brada-Williams

In the following excerpt, Brada-Williams claims that the stories in Interpreter of Maladies, *including "This Blessed House," are not individual stories. Instead, she defines them as parts of a story cycle.*

...The popularity and critical success of Lahiri's *Interpreter of Maladies* in both the United States and India could in part be due to the delicate balancing of representations she provides through the cycle as a whole. For example, the cheating husbands of "Sexy" are balanced by the depiction of the unfaithful Mrs. Das of "Interpreter of Maladies." The relative ease with which Lilia of "When Mr. Pirzada Came to Dine" participates in an American childhood is contrasted with the separation and stigmatization that the Dixit children experience in the story "Sexy." Mrs. Sen's severe homesickness and separation from US culture is contrasted with the adaptability of Lilia's mother and Mala in "The Third and Final Continent." The balancing of the generally negative depiction of an Indian community in "A Real Durwan" with the generally positive portrayal in "The Treatment of Bibi Haldar" is yet another example not only of the resulting balanced representations that the genre affords Lahiri but is itself one of many ways through which Lahiri constructs a conversation among her pieces.

The first and last stories in the cycle most clearly evoke a balancing dialogue through a careful mirroring of their basic plots. "The Third and Final Continent" both reflects and reverses the plot of the first story, "A Temporary Matter." While the first story of the cycle relates the tale of the death of a son and the possible destruction of a marriage, the concluding story provides a tale of the survival and resilience of both the parents' marriage and their son. The plot of the final story emphasizes the "ordinary" heroism of the narrator and his wife through the trials of migrating across continents and coming to care for a stranger by contrasting the pair to the narrator's fragile mother and their life in the United States to the short stay of the astronauts on the moon. They are also connected to the elderly Mrs. Croft and her near-miraculous ability to survive; she seems to have traveled as far in time as the main characters have in space. By placing Shoba and Shukumar's story in her readers' minds first, Lahiri is able to inform readers of the final story of the ways Mala and her husband could have failed as a couple and as parents, thus emphasizing their experiences as achievements rather than mere norms. The placement of these two stories at the beginning and end of the collection also helps to signal readers of the cyclical nature of the collection.

Susan Mann notes that titles are key "generic signals" and that "collections that are not cycles have traditionally been named after a single story to which the phrase 'and other stories' is appended....Generally placed first or last in the volume, the title story represents what the author feels is the best work or, in some cases, the best-known work" (14). Mann cites Faulkner's insistence on having "and Other Stories" removed from *Go Down, Moses* as support for the absence of the phrase as a conscious signaling device, as can be seen in Lahiri's text. Other critics have described the title of Lahiri's cycle as descriptive of her talents and her subject matter in all of the stories, rather than just a naming of the third story in the collection.

Scholars have noted many common themes among the stories, often focusing on the sense of displacement attached to the immigrant experience. In their analysis of "A Temporary Matter," Basudeb and Angana Chakrabarti make several claims regarding common themes in Lahiri's stories, for example, that "this sense of belonging to a particular place and culture and yet at the same time being an outsider to another creates a tension in individuals which happens to be a distinguishing feature of Lahiri's characters" and that Lahiri deals "with broken marriages" (24–25). Ashutosh Dubey looks at the immigrant experience in three of the nine stories and notes that three more stories dealing with second generation Indian immigrants focus on the "themes of emotional struggles of love, relationships, communication against the backdrop of immigrant experience" (25). In "Food Metaphor in Jhumpa Lahiri's *Interpreter of Maladies*," Asha Choubey traces her theme through five of the nine stories, analyzing their representation of Indian food and the use of food as metaphors for home and the connection between people. She also asserts that Lahiri's "protagonists—all Indians—settled abroad are afflicted with a 'sense of exile'" (par. 4). A sense of exile and the potential for—and frequent denial of—human communication can be found in all of Lahiri's short stories and indeed are the defining, structuring elements of her short story cycle. Yet despite their insights, many of the critics cited above ignore the two stories set wholly in India and without any American characters, "A Real Durwan" and "The Treatment of Bibi Haldar." Choubey's statement also ignores the non-Indian protagonists of Miranda ("Sexy") and Eliot ("Mrs. Sen's"). Common themes are important to defining a story cycle; but to distinguish between a collection containing stories merely characteristic of a writer's dominant interests and a true short story cycle, a single theme tying every story together is needed.

Many critics have suggested marriage as the unifying theme for the collection, and marriage is indeed a key element of most of the stories. Even "A Real Durwan" has the subplot of Mr. and Mrs. Dalal's bickering and reconciliation. Mrs. Sen's marriage to Mr. Sen may not be the main focus of her story, but it does create an important backdrop for her homesickness and several of her more pertinent observations to Eliot. The one story that breaks with the theme of marriage or marital problems is "When Mr. Pirzada Came to Dine." Although it depicts a married couple and their friend Mr. Pirzada, who is himself a married man, the relationships at the focus of the text are those between Lilia and Mr. Pirzada and the trio that Mr. Pirzada and Lilia's parents temporarily create during East Pakistan's war of independence. As Lilia notes, "Most of all I remember the three of them operating during that time as if they were a single person, sharing a single meal, a single body, a single silence, and a single fear." Ironically they achieve this unity as their nations enter into the war that will eventually allow East Pakistan to become the independent nation of Bangladesh. Not only human connection but human communication is yet another important theme for the cycle which runs through this story as Mr. Pirzada learns to interpret the American "thank you" just as Miranda in "Sexy" gradually comes to interpret the title of her story.

What has not been sufficiently noticed is that carefully executed rituals mark the relationships in *Interpreter of Maladies*. For instance, "When Mr. Pirzada Came to Dine": Lilia takes care to save up the candy Mr. Pirzada gives her, treating it like an offering in her prayers for Mr. Pirzada's family. Each evening at dinner Mr. Pirzada carefully winds and sets out the pocket watch he keeps set to the time of his homeland, which is one of the things Lilia notices after she begins "to study him with extra care." These details evoke the most important theme running throughout the cycle: all nine stories are woven together with the frequent representations of extreme care and neglect. Repetitions of this dichotomy occur in a variety of communities including whole neighborhoods, marital and extramarital relationships, and relationships between children and adults. Sometimes carelessness as a trait in *Interpreter of Maladies* defines a period of significant tension or even mourning as Lilia's parents shift from carefully prepared meals to simple boiled eggs and rice as the crisis in East Pakistan deepens. At other moments in the collection, a lack of care signifies fundamental differences between peoples or is represented as a permanent flaw, a human failing central to an individual character or even a whole community. The needs for "care" are linked to love, duty or responsibility, and homesickness. Images of neglect range from a dress that has slipped off its hanger to a car accident. Such images serve as augurs of the characters' emotional states and processes. "A Temporary Matter" opens with a description of a woman arriving home: Shoba "let the strap of her leather satchel...slip from her shoulders, and left it in the hallway." We are then told that she looks "like the type of woman she'd once claimed she would never resemble," namely, one who came home in gym clothes and with her makeup either rubbed off or smeared. Readers quickly come to realize that a dramatic change has come over the woman once marked not only by her physical beauty but her careful and meticulous manner in all things. We learn these details indirectly through a third-person narration that is filtered through Shoba's husband's point of view, the husband who will later put her things away but who is himself marked by personal neglect. He has not yet brushed his teeth by the evening of the day on which the story begins and has taken to lying in bed and avoiding work on his dissertation or even leaving his home.

Lahiri uses a variety of such small details to evoke not only the vast change that has come over the couple since the stillbirth of their son, but to reveal the great neglect in which their own relationship as a couple has fallen since that tragedy. One small image of neglect and decay is particularly resonant with the state of their marriage: When Shukumar, the husband, picks up a potted ivy in order to use it as a makeshift candle holder while the electricity will be turned off, he finds that "Even though the plant was inches from the tap, the soil was so dry that he had to water it first before the candles would stand straight." Thus, Lahiri subtly evokes the couple's common state of shock and lack of interest in their shared environment as both have failed to water a plant even when doing so would have taken almost no effort at all. Taken together, the sheer number of these small failures to provide care helps to define the depths of Shoba and Shukumar's common yet isolated experience of grief for their lost child as well as their waning care and love for each other.

"Interpreter of Maladies" similarly focuses on a young couple with severe marital problems, but their carelessness is most often evoked in their treatment of their three children. "Interpreter of Maladies" is a third-person narrative filtered through the point of view of Mr. Kapasi, the family's driver while sightseeing in India. The story opens with the parents bickering over who will take their daughter to the restroom. Mr. Kapasi will later think that the family is "all like siblings...it was hard to believe [Mr. and Mrs. Das] were regularly responsible for anything other than themselves." The first paragraph of the story notes that the mother "did not hold the little girl's hand as they walked to the restroom." As in "A Temporary Matter," small signs of negligence add up to reveal deeper emotional difficulties and detachments. This otherwise unremarkable scene acts as foreshadowing for what may be called the twin climaxes of the story: the attack on one of the boys by monkeys and the revelation of his illegitimate birth. Notably it is the popcorn that his mother has carelessly dropped that draws the monkeys to her son as well as the fact that he is left unsupervised that leads to the attack.

Mr. and Mrs. Das's lack of carefulness in raising their children extends to their carelessness in maintaining their marriage vows, at least on Mrs. Das's part. Although their driver, Mr. Kapasi, recognizes similarities between the Das's marriage and his own, he himself functions as a stark contrast to Mr. and Mrs. Das's lack of care. Not unlike Mr. Pirzada, Mr. Kapasi is characterized by his carefully tailored clothing and meticulous manners. Simon Lewis has read this story as a rewriting and updating of the trip to the Marabar Caves in E.M. Forster's *A Passage to India*, this time from the perspective of an Indian national, Mr. Kapasi in the role formerly held by Dr. Aziz (219). Lewis's argument can be supported by Mr. Kapasi's dream "of serving as an interpreter between nations," which he fantasizes fulfilling through a future correspondence with Mrs. Das. The way in which Mr. Kapasi gives Mrs. Das his contact information is illustrative of their essential differences as characters: she hands "him a scrap of paper which she had hastily ripped from a page of her film magazine" upon which he writes "his address in clear, careful letters." She then tosses "it into the jumble of her bag." The clear differences in these two characters in their relationship to care or lack of care, specifically in relation to responsibility, makes their final disconnect inevitable. While they both can be seen longing for communication with others, Mrs. Das is a woman with a life of relative comfort and ease who yearns to be freed of the responsibilities of marriage and children, and Mr. Karpasi is a man who has given up his dreams to support his family and who only yearns for some recognition and interest in his life. By the time his address falls out of Mrs. Das's bag and is borne off by the wind, Mr. Kapasi has already let go of his fantasy of communicating across continents and between individuals.

In "Mrs. Sen's" the title character takes excellent care of the eleven-year-old Eliot, the filter of the third-person narrative, for most of the story. One period when she acts differently is when she learns of her grandfather's death. As in "A Temporary Matter," images of carelessness and the cessation of past routines are used to evoke characters in mourning. Mrs. Sen's caregiving activities include not only feeding Eliot as well as his mother when she arrives to pick him up but in preparing elaborate meals for her and Mr. Sen's evening meal. During her hour-long daily ritual of chopping up ingredients, Mrs. Sen has Eliot stay on the couch, far from her chopping blade: "She would have roped off the area if she could. Once, though, she broke her own rule; in need of additional supplies . . .she asked Eliot to fetch something from the kitchen . . .'Careful, oh dear, be careful,' she cautioned as he approached." This same daily ritual or routine connects Mrs. Sen with India. Describing the scene before a wedding when the neighborhood women would gather to prepare food with blades such as hers, she states, "It is impossible to fall asleep those nights, listening to their chatter. [. . .] Here in this place where Mr. Sen has brought me, I cannot sometimes sleep in so much silence." She also asks Eliot, "if I began to scream right now at the top of my lungs, would someone come?" Drawing on his own experience, Eliot can only answer, "Maybe. . . . They might call you, . . .But they might complain that you were making too much noise."

Mrs. Sen is homesick for the kind of community she had in India, a community defined by a responsibility to participate in the lives of others rather than a responsibility not to interfere or be in any way intrusive in the lives of others. Mrs. Sen's statement when she is contemplating the fearful task of driving is ironically applicable to both the other drivers and herself: "'Everyone, this people, too much in their world.'" The American model of polite behavior depicted in Lahiri's work is to be wholly in one's own world and to maintain the smells, sounds, and emotions of that world so that they do not encroach upon another individual's life. Mrs. Sen's notion of community is the opposite. Yet her ability to become distracted while driving marks her as someone lost in her own world and oblivious to the needs and safety of other drivers. While Eliot's mom views the other cars as mere scenery, as inanimate objects, and is able to negotiate the road to the beach with ease, Mrs. Sen is hyper-conscious of the existence of other beings on the street but unable to perform in such a way as not to intrude in the lives of other drivers. This otherwise careful person becomes an extremely careless driver, and an accident results. Although the accident causes very little physical damage to Eliot or Mrs. Sen, it puts an end even to the limited form of community that the two had come to share with each other.

Lahiri represents examples of Indian community in two stories that are set off from the other seven stories not only by being set wholly in India and with all Indian nationals as characters but in their distinctive narrative style. "A Real Durwan" and "The Treatment of Bibi Haldar" continue to focus on a central dichotomy of carelessness and carefulness. Both stories shift from Lahiri's usual practice of using a filtered third-person or first-person narrative. While elsewhere this technique provides a detailed look into the interior life of most of Lahiri's characters, the lives and unspoken thoughts of Boori Ma and Bibi Haldar are left unknown to the reader. Each story resembles a legend as it depicts characters who manage to suffer through and survive extreme adversity. The lack of representation of their individual thoughts, memories, and motivations also lends the title characters a mythic or allegorical quality. In these two stories the community surrounding the character referred to in the title is as much the focus of the tale as any single character.

Boori Ma is a refugee who, although a woman, performs the duties of "A Real Durwan" or doorman in a Calcutta apartment building. We are told that she "maintained a vigil no less punctilious than if she were the gatekeeper of a house on Lower Circular Road, or Jodphur Park, or any other fancy neighborhood." When we first meet her, she is inspecting her tattered bedding for insects. A sympathetic resident of the building asks, "Do you think it's beyond us to provide you with clean quilts?" As this statement reveals, the neighbor's good intentions are mixed with her sensitivity to her own limited social status. The same day will bring a change in the neighbor's status and will propel the entire building into a fury of building renovations aimed at increasing each resident's relative status in the world. Boori Ma, who had previously swept the stairs twice a day and kept suspicious characters away from the building, is pushed out of her routine and even her post by the renovation efforts. The residents seem to forget to be hospitable in the rush to be genteel. Boori Ma begins wandering the neighborhood and spending her life savings on snacks. Eventually the keys and savings that she had so carefully saved despite partition, dislocation, and the loss of her family, are stolen from her. In the meantime, the sink that began the renovation craze is stolen and Boori Ma is blamed for carelessness and literally thrown out onto the street. In the focus on and care for material status and the material repair of the building that physically defines the community, the apartment community has failed to care for its members, including Boori Ma who for years had been the primary caretaker of the building.

"The Treatment of Bibi Haldar" provides a depiction of community in opposition to that described in "A Real Durwan." Lahiri's technique in this story is similar to Faulkner's method in "A Rose For Emily," even down to the use of a first person plural narrator, a communal "we." Lahiri acknowledges her debt to Faulkner in an interview with *Pif Magazine*, where she states it "was an experiment for" herself to replicate the nonspecific collective narrative voice of Faulkner's tale. She describes the narrator of her story as "a group of women [with] no particular identity." The first person plural inevitably emphasizes the role of the community in the story. In contrast to the neighbors in "A Real Durwan," the community represented in "The Treatment of Bibi Haldar" take their responsibility to a fellow community member very seriously.

In "The Treatment of Bibi Haldar," set in an unnamed small town outside Calcutta, the narrative "we" take turns feeding, clothing, teaching, chaperoning, and generally looking out for Bibi. The care given to Bibi, first by her father and then by an army of "family, friends, priests, palmists, spinsters, gem therapists, prophets, and fools"—as well as other "concerned members of our town," at least in treating her epilepsy-like illness, is so great that it is burdensome. But after she loses her father and is left in the neglectful care of her only remaining family, her cousin Haldar and his wife, she begins to yearn for marriage. As much as they do for her, the neighbors admit "she was not our responsibility, and in our private moments we were thankful for it." Incensed by her family's ill treatment of Bibi, the neighbors boycott the cousin's cosmetics shop and succeed in driving him out of business and out of town. The neighbors "At every opportunity [...] reminded her that we surrounded her, that she could come to us if she ever needed advice or aid of any kind." But they leave her to herself at night and eventually Bibi is found to be pregnant. This pregnancy leads to an amazing transformation in which she is almost miraculously healed and becomes a capable, self-supporting businesswoman who now takes great care not only of her business but, as newly trained by the community of women around her, of her son as well. Bibi's desire for marriage and seemingly magical cure by motherhood balances and contrasts the depiction of Mrs. Das, who is seeking a remedy for the responsibility of marriage and motherhood. The mystery of Bibi's pregnancy is never solved. Although several possibilities are suggested, it is ultimately unclear not only who the father of her child is but even whether the birth arose out of an unreported crime or through Bibi's own choice and willing consent. Lahiri leaves it up to the reader to decide.

We see Lahiri's characteristic refusal of definite closure in many other stories as well, including "This Blessed House" which is similar to "The Treatment of Bibi Haldar" in that both stories offer a more nuanced depiction of the collection's general valuing of carefulness. Bibi flourishes only once she is without the continual care of others and yet is herself given the responsibility for caring for another. The carefulness of Sanjeev in "This Blessed House" seems more related to his own worries about what other people think and the rituals he had established as a bachelor than anything positive for his marriage. His wife Twinkle's carelessness is ultimately connected with creativity and joie de vivre as much as it is with selfishness. While ever-practical Sanjeev can recognize, via the opinions of his friends, his wife's objective value, he seems unable to appreciate it. The silver bust of Jesus that they find in the attic becomes symbolic of Twinkle herself:

> He hated its immensity, and its flawless, polished surface, and its undeniable value. He hated that it was in his house, and that he owned it. Unlike the other things they'd found, this contained dignity, solemnity, beauty even. But to his surprise these qualities made him hate it all the more. Most of all he hated it because he knew that Twinkle loved it.

The story closes with Sanjeev carrying the silver bust to the living room where Twinkle has asked it to be placed on the mantel, against Sanjeev's wishes. Our last image is of Sanjeev in a balancing act, being "careful not to let the feather hat slip" from the statue and following his wife. Readers can interpret this as one of Sanjeev's last acts to please his wife or, in stark contrast, as indicative of an eventual balancing of their character differences and Sanjeev's following of Twinkle into a more spontaneous and playful approach to life.

We are given the freedom to create our own closure, and in many cases our own judgments as to the outcomes suggested by Lahiri's narratives. But with this freedom comes our responsibility to read with care. Reading the text as a short story cycle and not just a collection reveals Lahiri's careful balancing of a range of representations and her intricate use of pattern and motif. By reading the stories as a cycle, readers not only receive the additional layers of meaning produced by the dialogue between stories but a more diverse and nuanced interpretation of members of the South Asian diaspora.

Source: Noelle Brada-Williams, "Reading Jhumpa Lahiri's *Interpreter of Maladies* as a Short Story Cycle," in *MELUS*, Vol. 29, Nos. 3/4, Fall–Winter 2004, 8 pp.

> "WHILE SANJEEV PURSUES HAPPINESS IN THE FORM OF THE AMERICAN DREAM THROUGH HIS JOB, HIS PRETTY BRIDE, AND HIS HOME, TWINKLE PURSUES HER OWN WHIMS, FINDING HAPPINESS IN THE SEARCH FOR TRINKETS."

Jennifer Bess

In the following article, Bess analyzes several aspects of the short stories in Lahiri's Interpreter of Maladies, *including "This Blessed House."*

A plate of peanut butter crackers and a Jesus trivet become, in Jhumpa Lahiri's *Interpreter of Maladies*, icons of alienation and loneliness. In the Pulitzer Prize winning collection of short stories, everyday items and events expose the liminal situation unique to the first- and second-generation immigrant characters, but also embody the author's timely lament over the failure of global living to bridge the gaps between cultures and between individuals (cf. Dubey 23; Lewis 219). In fact, although firmly grounded in the concrete and in the present, Lahiri's collection weaves together universal themes of alienation, connection, and loss as her characters embark on unique quests to find the union between understanding the human experience and finding satisfaction in their individual lives. Moving between values of collectivist and individualist cultures, they are perfectly suited to navigate the relationship between the universal and the unique, but they find that the homogenizing forces of globalization, the chaos of mechanized living, and the silence of loneliness threaten cultural identity instead of fostering a sense of community and that they threaten individual identity instead of nurturing self-knowledge. It is, ironically, only in the most transient of relationships that the sought-after union between understanding humanity and understanding self is found, creating in the collection a dialectic between the failure to understand the human condition and the hope of embracing its richness.

In "Mrs. Sen's," the title character attempts to become a global citizen by maintaining her Indian identity at the same time she adapts to American culture. Newly arrived from Calcutta with her husband, she struggles to maintain the traditional role of the wife to Mr. Sen through her careful attention in preparing Indian cuisine. Although she laments the fact that bhetki is not available, she finds that fresh halibut will suffice. Collected from a seaside fishmonger, the fish is prepared with a special blade from India. This blade, Mrs. Sen explains to the young boy she baby-sits, recalls to her the community of women she has left behind: "'Whenever there is a wedding in the family [. . .] my mother sends out word in the evening for all the neighborhood women to bring blades just like this one, and then they sit in an enormous circle on the roof of our building, laughing and gossiping.'" In India the women's "chatter" extends into the night, filling the silence with meaningful companionship and common purpose. In the United States, however, Mrs. Sen is assaulted sometimes by a cacophony of voices and street noises and other times by an unbearable "silence" that keeps her awake at night. Longing for her home, where anyone who raised her voice to "'express grief or joy of any kind'" would find the "'whole neighborhood'" at her doorstep, Mrs. Sen has lost her sense of belonging, her sense of shared human experience. Likewise, she loses her own uniqueness as she must make a traditional meal without green bananas, an essential ingredient, thereby failing to fulfill the role she finds most satisfying. Finally, when the chaos of the city street causes her to get into an accident, she becomes a victim of the noisy flow of machinery with which she cannot merge. If the commonality she found in communal cooking fostered her identification with others and her own sense of purpose, then the despair with which she abandons her cutting blade in favor of peanut butter and crackers after the accident exposes the fact that she has lost the only identity she has ever known—nurturer, homemaker, wife of Mr. Sen. In her effort to adapt, Mrs. Sen has lost herself to the silence of loneliness and the noise of modern life.

If Mrs. Sen, a recent immigrant, loses both her sense of community and her sense of identity to the forces of the global market that called her husband to work at an American university, Sanjeev and Twinkle of "This Blessed House" suffer a similar fate as they are overwhelmed after settling into a lovely suburban home, which they find hides "a sizeable collection of Christian paraphernalia" in its corners and closets. Whereas Twinkle delights in uncovering and displaying trinkets, including a Jesus trivet and a paint-by-number portrait of the three wise men, Sanjeev feels only irritation and repeatedly reminds his bride that they are not Christian, but Hindu. To him the objects lack "a sense of sacredness," a spiritual value and meaning, but to her, they bring joy. Like the din of the traffic in "Mrs. Sen's," the trinkets in "This Blessed House" expose the relationship between the characters and the modern, global world they inhabit: While Sanjeev pursues happiness in the form of the American Dream through his job, his pretty bride, and his home, Twinkle pursues her own whims, finding happiness in the search for trinkets. In a sense, they are both seeking meaningless tokens and avoiding the complexities of communication with each other, thereby distancing themselves from their humanity. By the end of the story, when Twinkle descends the stairway carrying a huge silver bust of Christ (a scene that fills Sanjeev with hatred), an object which emanates "dignity, solemnity, beauty" yields in him the same silence, the same lack of meaning and intimacy, that haunts Mrs. Sen. Although Sanjeev knows Twinkle will display the bust proudly on their mantle, he says nothing. Her joy remains unknown to him and his animosity is unknown to her. The invasion of the Christian tokens into the Hindu household has created a personal and spiritual vacuum; the clutter—in this case the visual cacophony compared to the aural assault Mrs. Sen experiences on the roadway—overcomes any opportunity for a meaningful exchange of religious or cultural experience and any opportunity for two people to understand each other or themselves.

Although the married characters in the collection tend to suffer silently and separately, the most transient of relationships are the ones that offer a hope of fostering individual and universal understanding, an understanding of what it is to be unique and of what it is to be part of the human collective. The silence suffered by Mrs. Sen, Sanjeev, and Twinkle is finally shattered in "The Third and Final Continent," in which a single word, "splendid," punctuates the story like a refrain. Significantly, the first-person narrator is unnamed. Although the use of the first person emphasizes his individuality, his namelessness simultaneously celebrates his universality, thus creating a glimpse of a unity that the other characters have not experienced. In this final story in the collection, the narrator seeks temporary housing with a centenarian, Mrs. Croft, when he first moves to America. She welcomes him into her boarding house in her own idiosyncratic way, insisting that he say "splendid" after she tells him of the recent moon-landing. This brief conversation becomes a nightly routine for them, one which he first finds awkward. But after time passes, the seemingly trivial exchange becomes the foundation of something more intimate than the feelings revealed between the two married couples. Through their brief exchange, the narrator pleases Mrs. Croft and, in doing so, satisfies himself. He discovers that if he was unable to care properly for his own mother when she went insane, he can care for his landlady in this exchange and in handing her his weekly rent money. In "these simple gestures," the unnamed narrator finds his humanity and confirms hers. As a result, he evolves from the groom who could not console his weeping bride on their wedding night to a husband who prepares thoughtfully for her arrival to America. Thirty years later, the narrator has described what Mrs. Sen, Sanjeev, and Twinkle cannot: "As ordinary as it all appears," he says, referring to his own life, "there are times when it is beyond the imagination." He mourned, he loved, and he raised a child; he has, in other words, lived a life that is rich with the universal feelings that bind men and women together across continents and across time. But at the same time that his life has been "ordinary," universally human, it has also been unique, unimaginable, for he has lived on three continents, he has been profoundly touched by Mrs. Croft, and he has loved a woman named Mala. The universal and the individual have converged.

Source: Jennifer Bess, "Lahiri's *Interpreter of Maladies*," in *Explicator*, Vol. 62, No. 2, Winter 2004, 4 pp.

SOURCES

Crain, Caleb, "Subcontinental Drift," in the *New York Times Book Review*, July 11, 1999, p. 11–12.

Kakutani, Michiko, "Liking America, but Longing for India," in the *New York Times*, August 6, 1999, Vol. 148, p. B46.

Lahiri, Jhumpa, "This Blessed House," in *Interpreter of Maladies*, Houghton Mifflin, 1999, pp. 136–57.

———, "The Treatment of Bibi Haldar," in *Interpreter of Maladies*, Houghton Mifflin, 1999, p. 165.

Shapiro, Laura, "The Diaspora's New Star," in *Newsweek*, Vol. 134, No. 3, July 19, 1999, p. 67.

FURTHER READING

Bala, Suman, ed. *Jhumpa Lahiri, the Master Storyteller: A Critical Response to Interpreter of Maladies*, Khosla Publishing House, 2002.

> This collection of essays offers a wide range of critical response to Lahiri's stories.

Brians, Paul, *Modern South Asian Literature in English*, Greenwood Press, 2003.

> This book presents an introduction to the varied world of South Asian literature in English. Each of the fifteen chapters covers a significant Indian, Pakistani, or Sri Lankan writer. Discussion of Lahiri's work is also included.

Kalita, S. Mitra, *Suburban Sahibs: Three Immigrant Families and Their Passage from India to America*, Rutgers University Press, 2003.

> Kalita, who is the daughter of Indian immigrants, examines the struggles and successes of three Indian-American families from Middlesex County, New Jersey, who together represent a new factor in American society—the growth of ethnic enclaves in the suburbs.

Rothstein, Mervyn, "India's Post-Rushdie Generation; Young Writers Leave Magic Realism and Look at Reality," in the *New York Times*, July 3, 2000, p. E1.

> This article is about the new generation of Indian and Indian-American writers whose work, in English, has earned much acclaim in the West. Rothstein comments that the phenomenon stems from the success of Salman Rushdie's Midnight's Children. The young writers discussed include Lahiri, Raj Kamal Jha, Arundhati Roy, Pankaj Mishra, Amit Chaudhuri, and Kiran Desai.

The Use of Force

WILLIAM CARLOS WILLIAMS

1938

William Carlos Williams's short story "The Use of Force" is about a country doctor who is summoned to the home of some poor people to examine a sick little girl. When he suspects that her persistent fever might be caused by diphtheria, a particularly deadly disease that was rampant when this story was published in the 1930s, he asks to examine her throat. The girl refuses, and what follows is an escalating battle of wills, in which the doctor loses his professionalism and reverts to a state of rage not much less savage than the girl's own fury.

If this story seems to be particularly realistic, that is because Williams knew his subject matter well. In addition to being an author, he was a practicing pediatrician in rural New Jersey for decades. The story, told from the doctor's point of view, captures the ways in which even the most calm, objective professional can fail when faced with the horrors of disease and the unthinking emotionalism of youth.

Williams was known primarily as a poet, and he is most often associated with the Imagist movement, which was a movement to write with concise imagery and language. His terse, objective poetic writing style is evident in this story, which was originally published in his 1938 short story collection *Life along the Passaic River*. It is available in *The Doctor Stories*, a 1984 collection of Williams's fiction that is still in print.

William Carlos Williams (Alfred Eisenstaedt / Time and Life Pictures / Getty Images)

AUTHOR BIOGRAPHY

William Carlos Williams was born September 17, 1883, in Rutherford, New Jersey. His father, a businessman, was of English descent, while his mother, an amateur painter, came from a mix of French, Dutch, Spanish, and Jewish heritage. The household that Williams grew up in was morally strict, giving him the intellectual rigor and discipline needed to study medicine. In 1906, he received his M.D. degree from the University of Pennsylvania. He interned in Leipzig, Germany, from 1906 to 1909, then moved to Bergen, New Jersey, where he ran a private medical practice for more than forty years, until 1951.

Williams was interested in writing early in his life. Originally, he wrote poetry, and it is for his work in that genre that he is best known today. In 1909, he paid for the publication of his first collection, called *Poems*. He did not draw attention as a poet, though, until 1912, when the magazine *Poetry Review* printed a few of his poems with an introduction by the poet Ezra Pound. Pound, who by then was one of the most famous poets alive, had recently read some of Williams's poems, and a correspondence ensued that became the basis of a long friendship. Through Pound, he became acquainted with the greatest poets of his generation, including Hilda Doolittle (who wrote under the name "H.D."), Wallace Stevens, and Marianne Moore. His first commercial poetry collection, *The Tempers*, published in 1913, established Williams as an important voice in American poetry.

In his professional life as a physician, Williams maintained a quiet, stable demeanor. As a poet, however, he was on the cutting edge of the avant-garde. He followed the principle that Pound and others of his generation laid out, struggling to write a kind of poetry that the world had never seen before. Despite his renown as one of the cutting-edge artists of his day, however, most people who knew him in Bergen, New Jersey, knew him only as a local doctor, and had no idea that he was regularly published as one of the country's preeminent poets and fiction writers. Most of his stories were about people and situations that he encountered in his own life. Such is the case with "The Use of Force," which was included in his 1938 collection *Life along the Passaic River*, and which has been frequently included in anthologies since then.

Health problems slowed Williams down in the late 1940s, starting with the first of a series of strokes he was to suffer for the rest of his life. It was around then that he started his master work, the epic poem "Paterson," which was published in five volumes between 1946 and 1958. At the same time, he was befriended by the young writers of the time. Just when his poetic style was starting to seem dated, the publication of *The Autobiography of William Carlos Williams* made him interesting to members of the Beat Generation, who sought him out for artistic advice, which he gave happily. Until the end of his life on March 4, 1963 (following a series of strokes), he was active as a writer and as a member of the American poetic community. The winner of many smaller awards throughout his lifetime that gave him status among poets, Williams was recognized in the final year of his life with the Pulitzer Prize for Poetry (for *Pictures from Brueghel*) and the American Academy of Arts and Letters gold medal for poetry from the National Institute of Arts and Letters.

PLOT SUMMARY

"The Use of Force" begins with the doctor arriving at the Olson house, reflecting on the fact that he has not heard much about the child that he is going to examine other than that she is "very sick."

He is met at the door by a woman, Mrs. Olson, who leads him to the kitchen: the sick child is being kept in the kitchen by the stove, where it is warm. There, he meets Mr. Olson and the child. He finds the little girl, Mathilda, to be extraordinarily pretty, like the young models in magazine spreads in the Sunday newspaper. No one from the family talks to the doctor much.

The father tells the doctor that his daughter has had a fever for three days. There is no clear cause for her fever, but the doctor, knowing that several children from the child's school have come down with diphtheria lately, suspects that it would be a good place to start the investigation. A diagnosis of diphtheria, however, relies on knowing whether the child has had a sore throat.

Mathilda views the doctor as an enemy, and refuses to talk to him. The parents say that they have asked her and she has said that her throat does not hurt, but the doctor does not believe that they have been told the truth. He decides to examine her throat for himself.

When he asks the girl to open her mouth for an examination, she refuses. Her suspicion of the doctor is made even stronger when her mother tells her that the nice doctor will not hurt her: the doctor, who understands how children think, knows that the child will focus on the word "hurt" above all others. In response, Mathilda jumps out of her chair and tries to claw the doctor's eyes with her fingernails. Though she is not successful, she does knock his glasses off, and they land on the floor a few feet from him.

When the mother, in her embarrassment, chides Mathilda and tells her to apologize, the doctor takes the child's side, telling her mother that he understands why she would not want to cooperate with a strange man who wants to put something in her mouth. He also does not, however, want to leave without taking a throat culture: the dangers of diphtheria are too great. He explains to the parents that he will go ahead with the examination, even against their daughter's will, but only if they agree to it. Making sure that they understand that the child could die if she is actually suffering from diphtheria, he nonetheless concedes that he is willing to leave Mathilda alone if they want him to. What he does not say aloud to them is that he feels great love for the child, due to her wild temperament, and that he is disgusted with the parents' attempts to suppress her natural feelings. The child is not moved by her parents' stern talk: she does not apologize, nor open her mouth for the doctor.

The father, though he is big and strong enough to hold onto his daughter, lets her squirm out of his hands before the doctor can pry her mouth open with a wooden tongue depressor because he is afraid of hurting her. He is near fainting when the doctor, angry, tells him to put Mathilda on his lap and hold her wrists. When the father does, the girl tries a new tactic: instead of keeping her mouth shut, she opens it and screams out that she is in pain, that the force her father is exerting is killing her. The doctor tries to ignore her words and go on with his examination.

He is finally able to pry a wooden tongue depressor into her mouth, and is about to use it to pry her jaw open so that he can look at her throat when she brings her teeth together with enough ferocity to shatter the wooden tool into splinters. Once again, her mother tries to embarrass the girl, telling her that she ought to be ashamed to behave in such a way in front of the doctor.

In a swirl of emotions that include anger, frustration, and fear that this child whom he admires so much might be dying with diphtheria, the doctor sends the mother to bring a metal spoon with a smooth handle. Though he realizes that he might be better able to perform the required task if he were to come back later, after his temper has cooled, he lets his rage get the better of him, and he throws himself into the task of taking a throat culture with no willingness to accept failure.

He makes a final attack, lunging at Mathilda with the silver spoon, forcing her jaws open and shoving the utensil down her throat, making her gag. When her mouth opens, he can see her tonsils, and they are covered with mucus, a sign that she does indeed have diphtheria. He knows that she has had a sore throat all of the times that her fever has risen, and that she has been lying to her parents about it, keeping it a secret, even though it could have potentially fatal results.

Having had her secret forced out into the open, the child tries to pounce at the doctor, though her father is still holding her. In her eyes, the doctor can see tears of defeat. The doctor's own feelings are a complex mixture of admiration and concern, love and hatred, tenderness and aggression, but he ends his story without telling the reader how he feels.

CHARACTERS

Doctor

The doctor is the narrator of this story. His name is not given because he thinks very little about himself, instead focusing his thoughts on his reactions to the other characters.

It is clear that this doctor knows his business. He understands the sorts of people who would call on him, interpreting the silence of Mr. and Mrs. Olson as a sign that, poor as they are, they want him to work for his money and come up with a diagnosis on his own. He knows enough about disease, and about children, to realize that Mathilda's claim that her throat is not sore does not fit with her other symptoms, and to conclude that she is probably lying. He also knows that he cannot give in to her refusal to have her throat examined because doing so, though it might seem kind, could kill her.

Though the doctor knows that he must examine the child against her will, his job is complicated by the fact that he likes her. He finds her to be a beautiful child when he first meets her, but that does not affect his formal approach to her. He becomes truly interested in her after she strikes out at him: her spirit and unwillingness to bend to her parents' pleas or threats make her admirable.

The doctor is professional enough to know that he must continue with his examination even though the child is against it, but then he runs into an even deeper emotional conflict. Because he likes her, he becomes emotionally involved in the struggle against her. Under other circumstances, he would not be too insistent that Mathilda give in to his demand to see her throat. At one point, he even admits, after the fact, that it might have been better to walk away until all tempers were given time to cool. But his fondness for the girl stirs up his concern for her health, and the fact that he acknowledges emotions at all opens the possibility for his own anger. By the end of the examination, the doctor is as unreasonable as the child, acting out of anger rather than reason.

Mathilda Olson

This story is centered around the stubbornness of a little girl, Mathilda. She has had a fever for three days, and her parents do not know the cause of it. She has told them that she does not have a sore throat, but the doctor who has been called to examine her is not sure that she has told the truth. When he asks to examine her, she refuses to cooperate, and when he tries to force her to let him look at her throat she struggles against him. In the end, when she is overcome and the examination reveals that her throat really was covered with secretions after all, the girl is not grateful that her life has been saved: instead, she becomes even more enraged than before, lunging at the doctor who has violated her sanctity and revealed her secret.

Mathilda's actions are dangerous, possibly even life-threatening, but the doctor admires her fierce independence. He understands her unwillingness to be examined, but, unlike her parents, he is not willing to let her have her way simply because she is unhappy. As a result, Mathilda takes a two-step approach to stopping the examination. When she cries in pain, her parents become uncertain of themselves, and instinctually act to calm her: this tactic accelerates until Mathilda shouts out hysterically: "You're killing me!" Even though he is fond of her, the doctor does not allow himself to be moved by her cries. Seeing this makes Mathilda even more upset, and she strikes out at him. The first time she does this, she catches him by surprise, knocking his glasses off his face, but after that her father knows enough to hold tight to her. In the end, when her jaw has been forced open against her will, she is still struggling against her father's grip to strike out at the doctor, even though he poses no threat to her anymore. The shame of her defeat leaves Mathilda angrier than ever, and her fury displays the savage liveliness that the doctor finds admirable.

Mr. Olson

Mr. Olson is the father of the sick girl. He is described as a large, awkward man, uncertain of how to handle himself in this situation. He does not talk much, and when he does talk, his poor grammar indicates a lack of formal education.

Throughout the story, the girl, Mathilda, sits on her father's lap. When the father first arrives, she is there, presumably for comfort. Once the doctor realizes that he needs to examine her, and that she is not willing to be examined, he enlists Mr. Olson's help, telling him to hold his daughter still. Although Mr. Olson realizes the importance of this examination and takes the child's hands, his fear of hurting her and his shame at the way that she is behaving cause him to use a grip that proves too light, and she is able to pull herself away. He does, however, recognize the serious consequences that would befall her if she has diphtheria that is not treated, and so he tells the doctor to continue with the examination, humbly accepting the doctor's command about how to hold his daughter still.

When his wife shows concern for the daughter, as she is screaming about the pain of being held too tightly, Mr. Olson impresses on her the gravity of the situation. Though the husband and wife are similar in their skeptical view of the doctor, Mr. Olson understands the practical need for having Mathilda examined. He is somewhat emotional about his daughter, but he forces himself to put his emotions aside and be pragmatic.

In the story's last paragraph, after the examination is over and the evidence of diphtheria has been uncovered, Mr. Olson keeps a tight hold on his daughter. Here, the force that he uses on her is not meant to ensure her health, but to protect the doctor who has possibly saved her life.

Mrs. Olson

If there is an antagonist in this story, it is Mathilda's mother: with her well-meaning but softhearted expressions of concern for her daughter, she unwittingly encourages the child to rebel while displaying a personality type that the doctor finds irritating. From the first, when she answers the door with the remote phrasing "Is this the doctor," Mrs. Olson shows her skepticism about the coming examination. When Mathilda proves to be resistant to the doctor, her mother tries to give her comfort, but the things that she tells the child to comfort her are, in the doctor's opinion, just wrong. For instance, telling her that the doctor will not hurt her is less likely to make Mathilda think she will not be hurt than it is to make her focus on the word "hurt," reminding her of the pain that might be forthcoming. When her mother calls the doctor a "nice man," he tells her to not use that phrase, since Mathilda obviously does not think that he is nice. He is offended by the mother's willingness to lie to her daughter in this life-or-death situation.

The doctor's demeanor, and his exasperation with Mrs. Olson, spreads to the girl's father in the course of the examination, and eventually he, too, becomes impatient with Mrs. Olson, directly telling her to stop worrying because he knows how serious the results of the examination can be. After that, Mrs. Olson stops talking, cooperating with the doctor's request for a spoon silently, so that she will not say anything that will cause trouble.

THEMES

Violence as a Useful Function

Violence is generally associated with destruction and is therefore avoided in our society. In this story, Williams regretfully acknowledges that violence does serve a useful function. One of the most obvious themes in this story is its examination of how violence, though regrettable, might be used in selective circumstances to serve a greater good.

When the doctor arrives at the Olson house, he surveys the situation and finds it tense. The parents are country people, suspicious of outsiders like him, and the child who needs medical help is suspicious of him and of her own parents. When he hears that the child claims to not have a sore throat, her claim does not make sense with his diagnosis of her prolonged fever. His decision that examining her throat is more important than her refusal to be examined gives him no other recourse than to use violence to get the examination done.

The parents' initial skepticism about the doctor gives Mathilda a chance to divide the adults against each other: when she acts as if the force the doctor is using is causing her unbearable pain, her parents consider stopping the exam. Her father is the first one to think through to the results that could occur if she had diphtheria and left it undiagnosed, and so he reluctantly holds her steady, even though it means repressing his natural level of concern for his daughter's cries. Her mother continues to worry about the violence being done to Mathilda until her husband and the doctor convince her of the urgency of the situation.

TOPICS FOR FURTHER STUDY

- When this story was published, there was an antitoxin available to treat diphtheria, but no vaccine to prevent it. Research how antitoxins and vaccines work, particularly on this disease, and show your class a presentation explaining the science behind them.
- Research the history and theories of the Imagist movement. Take a poem published in a current publication and write an essay in which you explain what you think might be examples of the Imagists' influence on the poem.
- Research the Depression and today's economic climate. Based on your findings, write a dialog between the doctor and Mr. and Mrs. Olsen as it might occur if this story took place today, instead of during the Depression. How do these vastly different economies change the story?
- William Carlos Williams was a doctor in poor rural areas, just like the doctor in the story. Read *The Autobiography of William Carlos Williams* and other biographies about the author. Based on what you've learned, can "The Use of Force" be said to be autobiographical or no? Why or why not? Explain your thesis in an essay.

Even though he knows that it is the best course of action, given the circumstances, the doctor is not able to use violence and remain dispassionate about it. Halfway through the forced examination, after Mathilda counters his violence with her own violent act of biting his tongue depressor in half, the doctor finds himself ablaze with anger. He later acknowledges that continuing with the examination when everyone's emotions were so high was probably not the wisest course of action, but at the time, caught up in the moment, he can only think of countering Mathilda's violent action with one of his own. It is in this way that Williams shows that, even when undertaken for a noble cause, violence begets violence and takes on a life of its own.

Compassion

Though the doctor comes into the Olson house with a cold professional demeanor and conducts his examination as if he has no personal concern for the sick girl, his narration lets readers know that he feels compassion that grows from the moment that he meets Mathilda. His first impression is positive, as he is struck by what a beautiful child she is, likening her looks to those of children featured in photo spreads in the Sunday newspaper. His empathy for her grows when he hears her mother tell Mathilda that the doctor will not hurt her, because he knows that the only thing she will take from that claim is the idea of being hurt, and not her mother's denial that it would happen. By this point, the doctor sees the situation from Mathilda's perspective more clearly than he sees it from the adult perspective.

Of course, even though he feels great compassion for the girl, the doctor does not allow that compassion to keep him from examining her throat. If he were to allow his fondness for her to stop him, the result might be much, much worse for Mathilda than the short-term discomfort she would undergo during a throat exam. The message for readers is that compassion does not always mean the same thing as gentleness, and that force is not necessarily the same thing as the anger with which it is so often associated.

Humiliation

In the last line of this story, Mathilda is crying over the defeat that she has suffered because of the forced examination. By that point, readers can see clearly that the main driving force behind her struggle has been nothing more than a power struggle against her parents and the doctor. Since there is no good reason for her opposition to the exam, and plenty of reasons for her to have cooperated with it, her ultimate humiliation could seem a minor detail. The doctor understands her so well, though, that readers are moved to feel pity when they see her taking defeat so seriously.

The humiliation of Mathilda is not the same thing as a victory for her doctor, who could be seen as her opponent in this struggle. Because he empathizes with her, the doctor feels her humiliation, even though he is the one who has forced her, against her will, to open her mouth. Although

The doctor in the story, like the doctor pictured here, makes house calls *(W. Eugene Smith / Time and Life Pictures / Getty Images)*

the doctor does admit at one point that he finds pleasure in attacking her, in overcoming her obstinacy, her humiliation in the end is presented as an unfortunate turn of events for everyone.

Professional and Personal Contempt

While the doctor's attitude toward Mathilda changes throughout the course of their struggle, he feels a steady sense of contempt for her parents from the start of the story to the end. At first, he does not admit any dislike, noting their suspicion of him without commenting on it: he views them with a professional detachment, expecting no more from them than help in the examination at hand. His dislike for them becomes personal, however, when he observes how their attitude toward their daughter encourages her in the dangerous refusal to have her throat examined. Because he understands how the girl feels, he knows what she must think when her mother says that he is a nice man who will not hurt her, and he knows that it will have the exact opposite effect on her than her mother intended.

As they go on with the exam, his contempt wears off on the father, who adapts the doctor's attitude somewhat when he shouts at the mother while she is trying to comfort their daughter. At first, the father is only concerned with making the fragile little girl feel more comfortable, as his wife is, but the doctor's contempt for their softness moves him to see how grave the situation is, and his new insight into what is going on makes him lash out at the mother, blaming her just as the doctor has blamed the parents for what is happening.

STYLE

The Absence of Quotation Marks

Like most works of fiction, "The Use of Force" alternates between narrative description of the action and direct quotation. Williams breaks with standard of style, however, by presenting direct quotations from characters without using quotation marks to indicate that these are things that were actually said out loud.

By leaving out the quotation marks, Williams takes a chance that he will confuse his readers. He does indicate that the words presented are spoken by using the word "said" before and after quotes, but readers who are accustomed to seeing quotes set off in quotation marks might wonder, at least until they catch on to Williams's style, whether these are actually the exact words the character is supposed to have said.

That ambiguity in the mind of the reader creates an effect that fits with the tone of the story. Throughout the story, the doctor speaks in an objective, impersonal voice, in an attempt to relate the events with as little emotion as possible. By leaving the quotation marks off of dialog that was spoken out loud, Williams removes some of the drama from the situation, flattening the tone so that readers can focus on the complex relationships rather than the style of speaking that each individual has. Although the story is made of both narrative and quotations, the tone of the entire story remains consistent.

Use of Symbolism

Williams tells this story with very little comment, and so readers are left to find the impact of the story through careful reading. In order to steer readers to the conclusions that he wants them to reach, he uses strong symbols, or physical objects that can be used to emphasize the points he is making.

The most striking images used here are the two items that the doctor inserts into Mathilda's mouth to pry her jaws open. The first is a wooden tongue depressor, a standard tool of doctors who are conducting a throat exam. When she bites down on it, it becomes a symbol of her rage. The fact that her bite is powerful enough to break it to splinters is a symbol that she has in her a level of ferocity beyond what one would expect of a little girl. The fact that the splinters of what is left cause her mouth to bleed provides readers with a visual image of Mathilda as a savage animal, as blood drips from her teeth.

When the tongue depressor is shattered, the doctor is given a silver spoon to conduct his examination. Generally, the phrase "silver spoon" is used in American culture to indicate a childhood of wealth and privilege, which is certainly not the case with the Olson family. What it does represent, however, is the rise of overpowering technological force. If the child's jaws have an equal chance with the naturally grown wood probe, they have no chance against a metal instrument, which is as overwhelmingly powerful as the adults' hands that hold her. The change of tools is as important as the change from empathy to force.

HISTORICAL CONTEXT

The Depression

When Williams wrote this story, America was in the middle of the Depression. Historians generally identify the start of the Depression as October 24, 1929, when the U.S. stock market was hit with a massive sell-off. That day, commonly referred to as "Black Thursday," U.S. stock values took an unprecedented drop in value. The ensuing panic, as people tried to cash in their stocks, created an even worse crisis, so that by November, stock prices were down 40 percent from where they had been in September. The lack of money caused a chain reaction: businesses were wiped out and unable to pay their bills, which ruined other businesses, putting people out of jobs, which glutted the employment market with skilled workers. The Depression spread to other countries and become a worldwide event.

The New Deal policies of Franklin Delano Roosevelt, elected first in 1932, helped to ease the economic pressure on some of the country's poorest citizens. The New Deal was a mixture of policies involving dozens of agencies that were started to employ citizens for diverse jobs such as construction work and social programs. Though employment did help individuals, the U.S. economy stayed weak throughout the 1930s and only began to thrive again when the country entered World War II in 1941.

Diphtheria

Diphtheria is a disease that attacks the respiratory tract. It is characterized by a sore throat, low-grade fever, and the formation of a membrane around the tonsils. The membrane grows until it blocks the breathing passages, causing the infected person to eventually suffocate.

Throughout human history, diphtheria has been feared as one of the most dreaded and potentially devastating diseases to attack humankind. It is very contagious, and outbreaks of the disease spread quickly through communities that had practically no defense against it. In colonial New England, for example, a diphtheria epidemic was estimated to have killed 80 percent of the population of children under 10 in some towns in the five years between 1735 and 1740. In the 1920s, when William Carlos Williams was a practicing physician, there were an estimated 100,000 to 200,000 cases of diphtheria in the United States each year, resulting in an average annual death toll close to 15,000. The 1925 outbreak that threatened to decimate the population of children in Nome, Alaska, led to a convoy of dog sled teams moving diphtheria serum from Anchorage, an event that is commemorated every year with the famous Iditarod sled dog race.

A cure for diphtheria was slow in coming. Early treatments in the 1800s entailed inserting a tube down through the respiratory tract, to hold off the development of the membrane and allow the patient to continue breathing. An antitoxin against the disease won the first Nobel Prize in the 1890s, but it only neutralized the poisons that the disease caused in the patient and it did not stop diphtheria itself. A vaccine to prevent the drug was developed in 1923, but it was not until the post-war years of the 1950s that there came

COMPARE & CONTRAST

- **1930s:** The United States is mired in the Depression. People struggle to find jobs; money and resources are scarce.

  Today: The economy continues to fluctuate and reaches a Depression-like low in the early 2000s, with banks and auto companies asking for federal assistance.

- **1930s:** Diphtheria is a common fatal illness, killing thousands of people, particularly children, each year.

  Today: With vaccines and modern antibiotics, diphtheria has practically been eliminated.

- **1930s:** A doctor making the decision that force is necessary to conduct an examination on a child would feel free to do so.

  Today: A doctor, or any other professional for that matter, would have to consider whether he or she might be taken to court later or be professionally disciplined for actions that cause harm, even unintentionally.

an antibiotic that could effectively treat patients who already had diphtheria.

Today, thanks to inoculation and early treatment, diphtheria is very uncommon. Between 2000 and 2007, for example, only five people in the United States died of the disease.

Imagism

William Carlos Williams is remembered first as a poet and second as a short story writer. His fiction reflects his poetic style. Williams was one of the earliest writers associated with a style called Imagism.

The Imagist movement came into being around 1909, just as Williams was starting his career in poetry. It was spearheaded by Williams's friend and mentor, Ezra Pound, and Chicago poet Harriet Moore, who, after lengthy discussions with other poets and critics about the problems faced by modern poets, published an anthology in 1914 called *Des Imagistes: An Anthology*, featuring poetry that they felt represented their artistic views.

Pound, who was living in Paris during the early 1900s, met regularly with other poets to discuss what they felt to be a pressing problem of modern poetry; namely, how words could be used to capture the vagaries of existence. To them, the poetry of previous generations, most notably the Victorian writing that evolved out of the Romantic style, was too rigid, too stiff, too focused on emotion and morality. Pound, Moore, and the others, including Pound's ex-lover Hilda Doolittle (who wrote under the name "H.D.") and her new fiancé, Richard Aldington, looked to the French Symbolist poets and Japanese haiku for models of how poetry could convey its meaning without ever discussing intangible emotions, if the right imagery was chosen. From their discussions, critic T. E. Hulme developed the artistic philosophy called Imagism. The word became familiar to readers when *Poetry* magazine, which Moore edited, published H.D.'s first poems in 1913, and then through Pound's anthology in 1914.

Williams was one of the dozens of young poets who began publishing in the 1910s and was strongly influenced by the Imagist philosophy. Though he was never a member of the core Parisian group, he was very involved in the poetry scene in New York City in the 1920s, with which Pound was also frequently active. Williams's poem "The Red Wheelbarrow" is considered to be not only a prime example of Imagist theory in practice, but also one of the greatest American poems ever published. It presents one single image without comment, just as "The Use of Force" presents a situation but leaves readers to determine the moral implications for themselves.

The Imagist movement was short-lived: poet Amy Lowell published a few more anthologies under the names *Some Imagist Poetry* in 1915, 1916, and 1917, but the founders of the movement

In "The Use of Force," the doctor's tool—a spoon—becomes a weapon (© vario images GmbH & Co.KG / Alamy)

disagreed about each other's artistic principles, so that by the time of the final book there was little agreement among even its adherents as to what exactly Imagism was. Still, its impact reaches to today, as the movement and its stated philosophy altered the course of poetry and the idea of what a poem should and could accomplish.

CRITICAL OVERVIEW

While William Carlos Williams is often considered one of the great literary figures of the twentieth century, it is usually his poetry that earns him praise: critics mention his fiction, and no in-depth study of his career would be complete without an analysis of his novels and short stories, but they are seldom discussed on their own, without some mention of how they are related to his poetry. In the 1920s and 1930s, when he wrote it, Williams's fiction was generally viewed as a welcome diversion between poetic works. His novels were more studied for their experimental qualities than appreciated as works of art unto themselves. An example of this can be seen in *William Carlos Williams: An American Artist* by James E. Breslin. Breslin praises the novel *White Mule*, published in 1937, for creating "an immaculate surface, swiftly recording domestic events in all their casualness... to bring through fundamental qualities of character." Breslin contrasts this with Williams's 1923 experimental book *The Great American Novel*, which was considered more of an exercise than a novel and was all but forgotten not long after its publication.

Williams's shorter fiction has always been more widely respected, though it was not commercially successful in its time. In particular, critics have applauded the authenticity in his stories about doctors in rural New Jersey. As Cid Corman says in an essay in *William Carlos Williams: A Collection of Critical Essays*, "The Use of Force" is "for all its anthologizing, a beautiful clean thing, prose, direct in its attack, sure in its sense of when to leave off, its language crisp and true, touching." This success when dealing with autobiographical material also crosses over into Williams's poetry, such as Williams's long, multi-volume poem *Paterson*, about the town in New Jersey where Williams spent most of his life. Robert Lowell, one of the twentieth century's best-known poets, says of *Paterson* in *Profile of William Carlos Williams*: "By personifying Paterson and by 'Patersonizing' himself, he [Williams] is in possession of all the materials that he can use." This statement speaks for most critics over the years, many of whom have appreciated Williams's fiction, its short, controlled bursts and its intimate connection between Williams's life and work—of which "The Use of Force" is a prime example.

CRITICISM

David Kelly

Kelly is an instructor of creative writing and literature. In this essay on "The Use of Force," he explores the idea that the central conflict in this story is not between the doctor and the child, and that they are instead kindred spirits in their opposition to the girl's parents.

People who read William Carlos Williams's short story "The Use of Force" are inclined to describe it as a struggle of wills between the two main characters: an adult doctor, who finds himself increasingly unable to maintain his professional demeanor, and a sick girl who fights throughout her examination. As the narrator of the story, the doctor is the character whom readers watch most closely. In a classic short story arc, the doctor starts as one thing, a man of reason, and by the final paragraph is convincingly transformed into its opposite, a mindless savage. It would be difficult to refute that this is the story's main point. But it is scarcely the only point. Williams packs the corners of this very short work with depth and nuance, so that elements that might be missed in the first reading prove to carry an importance that was not originally clear.

Of all of the elements, the most easy to overlook is the importance of the girl's parents. Readers tend to pay the parents little attention because the doctor gives them little attention, dismissing them quickly as nuisances rather than as an integral part of their child's life. Williams has his narrator treat them decently, even as his patience with the whole situation wears thin, but he thinks of them with disdain throughout. He tries to forget them while he is locked in a combat with the little girl, Mathilda. And that, to some extent, is the point: as the doctor's focus on the child drags him further and further from the balance and compromise that the adult world requires, the girl's parents seem more and more ridiculous to him and to the reader. In fact, though, they are not that ridiculous at all.

The relationship between the doctor and Mathilda, and in particular the change in his personality that she elicits, is so clear and powerful that readers are not likely to focus on anything else in the story. For one thing, it a physical, violent relationship, carrying the "force" referred to in the story's title. He grips her roughly; she

WHAT DO I READ NEXT?

- Anton Chekhov is recognized as a great short story writer, and, like Williams, he was a practicing doctor. Readers can get a sense of Chekhov's tone and themes from "Gooseberries," one of his most popular stories, published in 1898. It is often anthologized and is included in *Anton Chekhov's Short Stories* (1979).
- For a sense of how prevalent diphtheria once was, and how it came to be controlled, read *Epidemics Laid Low: A History of What Happened in Rich Countries* (2006), by Patrick Bourdelais. It examines the responses to epidemics from Bubonic Plague to AIDS, and how these diseases have affected societies.
- Much of Williams's work, both fiction and poetry, was drawn from his life. *The Autobiography of William Carlos Williams* (1949) is considered one of the great literary biographies, full of insight and self-awareness, showing the author to be quite the same kind of man as the stoic characters he wrote about.
- Robert Coles's 1975 analysis of Williams's fiction, *William Carlos Williams: The Knack of Survival in America*, devotes a long section to explaining the themes and biographical background of the stories in *Life along the Passaic River*.

> "THE DOCTOR DOES NOT NECESSARILY DISLIKE MRS. OLSON BECAUSE SHE IS A WOMAN, BUT BECAUSE SHE TALKS TOO MUCH. AS HE LOSES HIS CALM BEARING, HE SEES NOTHING BUT THE FALSENESS OF SOOTHING WORDS, AND THE HONESTY OF PHYSICAL ACTION."

tries to scratch his eyes; he forces a piece of wood in her mouth and she counters by crushing it with her jaws, even though the resulting splinters cause her pain; he overcomes her in the end by forcing a metal spoon into her mouth, and then she loses any semblance of self-control. Their struggle against each other is magnified by the differences between them. They could not be any less alike: the doctor, a grown man with a medical degree, a professional who has clearly dealt with reluctant children before, is brought down to the same emotional level as an unreasoning, helpless child. Williams clearly understands how such a change in the doctor's personality is possible, and he renders it convincingly in a short space. The intensity of this central relationship relegates all other aspects of the story—most notably, the girl's parents—to the corners.

But the parents, slow and superficial as they may be, still provide an effective counterbalance against Mathilda and the doctor. While the doctor is Mathilda's opponent in the physical struggle to examine her throat, he is also, in the struggle against her parents' stifling ways, the little girl's partner. The whole conflict with Mathilda is the result of his attraction to her. He finds her to be a strikingly beautiful child when they first meet, and he understands and respects her fear of being examined by a stranger. His fondness for her clouds his judgment, filling him with a degree of anxiety that makes it difficult for him to maintain a professional demeanor, which then leaves him with little recourse against her tantrum but force, which in turn makes her even more loud and violent—and on and on in a self-perpetuating spiral. They hate each other, they love each other, but the most obvious point is that together they have little use for Mathilda's parents.

The easiest way to interpret this would be to take the doctor at his word and write the parents off as despicable. But Williams gives the parents each just enough character traits to dignify and humanize them, which he would not do if they were merely meant to be despicable foils to the story's central figures. The fact that they have individual personalities makes it possible to explore what each one means to this story's overall message.

Mathilda's parents, in fact, represent the two elements of the doctor's personality that are central to the emotional conflict in this story. He comes into the Olson household as a man of reason and compassion and ends up letting his forceful side take control. The same struggle that goes on within the doctor's mind manifests itself externally within the Olson family.

When the doctor arrives, the parents are treated as one. The story does not differentiate between them in their silence and suspicion. They do not have much personality to him, but he does not have much individuality to them, either. Mrs. Olson meets him at the door with "Is this the doctor?" as if she is talking to a third party, and not to him. She does not ask his name, but he does not introduce himself, either.

The main distinction separating the doctor from the other two adults in the story seems to be one of social class. He is an educated professional, and, though there is no explicit indication of what they might do, it is clear from their stilted and informal diction that they are uneducated people. The class distinction is made clear by the way the mother apologizes to the doctor for making him go through the inconvenience of walking to the back of their house to see the little girl, as if making him look at their humble possessions might be asking too much of him. From his perspective, the doctor writes off the Olsons as a certain type of people he has encountered before, and assumes the ability to read their thoughts about him.

During the troublesome examination of Mathilda, the girl's father becomes more acceptable to the doctor. He is quiet and functional, exerting force against the girl when the doctor needs help holding her still. He is somewhat hesitant to do what the doctor feels must be done, but he does seem to be trying, and the doctor gives him credit for that. "The father tried his best," he narrates at one point, empathizing with the man's natural hesitancy to see harm come to his daughter, even though he still, by the time that sentence comes to an end, states that "I wanted to kill him." The father's hesitance toward forcing an examination on his daughter is exasperating, but understandable.

The narrator is less charitable about the girl's mother. To the doctor, the mother is meddling, making an already difficult job even more difficult with her attempts to calm the child. She tells Mathilda that the doctor is a good man, that his examination will not hurt; the doctor, who understands the child so well, knows that Mathilda will hear in her mother's words only insincerity and vulnerability that she can exploit. It is the mother who drives the narrator to raise his voice and speak harshly. He finds her offensive for the same reason that he finds the child admirable: there is a level of phoniness about what she says, it is the inverse of the raw honesty of Mathilda's shrill tantrum.

The doctor's greater level of disdain for the girl's mother could be a result of the sexist times the story takes place in, but it also can be caused just by social understandings that, while related to sexism, are more pronounced. During the exam, Mr. Olson starts out being fairly quiet, and he becomes even quieter still: like the doctor, he becomes drawn more and more toward the perspective that what is called for in this situation is silent force. Mrs. Olson, on the other hand, tries to comfort her daughter by talking to her, then tries to shame her for embarrassing them in front of the doctor. Even though these two approaches, force versus reasoning, may correspond to traditional gender roles in Western society, the more important aspect is that they correspond to the change that the doctor undergoes in this story. The doctor does not necessarily dislike Mrs. Olson because she is a woman, but because she talks too much. As he loses his calm bearing, he sees nothing but the falseness of soothing words, and the honesty of physical action.

When the girl's mother voices her concern for Mathilda, who is crying out and exaggerating her pain, Mr. Olson tells her: "You get out." Williams leaves this expression intentionally vague. The words themselves command the woman to leave, to go somewhere else and let the men handle this situation with force. Still, the rural dialects that the Olsons use, and the fact that the mother does not in fact leave the room, indicate that the real meaning is more along the line of "be quiet." When she does talk again, it is not to comfort the girl, but to chastise her for embarrassing them in front of the doctor: she lines up on the doctor's side and submissively fetches a spoon when he requests one, no longer questioning his judgment.

In the course of this story, the doctor never does make Mathilda agree to his examination. He does overpower her, but his ability to do so is never really in question. The story of a man engaged in a battle of wills with a child and losing his professional detachment is an interesting one, but even more interesting is watching how the same dynamics that can bring a stranger to use force against a little girl can eventually convince her parents that sympathy and compassion will not work.

Source: David Kelly, Critical Essay on "The Use of Force," in *Short Stories for Students*, Gale, Cengage Learning, 2009.

William Baker

In the following article, Baker analyzes common interpretations of "The Use of Force" and presents his own view of the story's primary conflicts.

Note the urgency and immediacy of the opening paragraph: "They were new patients to me, all I had was the name, Olson. Please come down as soon as you can, my daughter is very sick." The two sentences might have been punctuated as four, but William Carlos Williams, anxious to get to his point, uses commas to keep us flowing with him. Here and throughout he omits quotation marks for the direct address, another device to convey urgency. From the first rushing sentences Williams comes on like the Ancient Mariner, grabbing our lapels to tell of the doctor's compulsion. At first we think we might have a classic rescued-from-death tale, since early on we read, "As it happens we had been having a number of cases of diptheria in the school to which this child went during the month." The last two thirds of the story, though, is not about death but about the strange problem of getting to see the girl's throat.

On his first try, the doctor almost gets his face clawed. On his second, the girl bites through the wooden tongue depressor. On his third he is successful, but he is ashamed of overpowering the little girl. He hates her parents who collaborated in his "unreasoning assault," and, finding the girl "an unusually attractive little thing," he says, "I had already fallen in love with the savage brat." Her tonsils were covered with membrane, but if we anticipate that the girl was diagnosed, treated, and then recovered, we are disappointed, for still urgently, almost obsessively, getting the story off his chest, the doctor ends by saying, "Now truly she was furious. She had been on the defensive before but now she attacked. Tried to get off her father's lap and fly at me while tears of defeat blinded her eyes." Initially, we are puzzled that the story ends here.

What does this compulsively told narrative mean? On the surface, it is the story of a doctor overpowering a girl, but we sense immediately that such a "meaning" is too superficial, and that the story is too short.

The pseudo-Freudians move in and suggest the symbolic story of sexual conquest (or a rape), for the invasion is made against the girl's will and the sanctity of her privateness is violated. They point out the suggestiveness of the line, "Will you open it now by yourself or shall we have to open it for you?" And they try to clinch their case by noting the doctor's lines, "It was a pleasure to attack her. My face was burning with it."

A more reasonable Freudian analysis was made by Fergal Gallagher in the May, 1972, *CEA Critic*. He suggested that the parents represent the super-ego (conventions of society), the girl the id (instinct), and the doctor the ego (reason), with the doctor surprised to discover his id taking over when he resorts to force. An interpretation that depends on identifying characters as symbols seems to me to be a little too neat.

There are two conflicts: one within the girl and the other within the doctor. The girl feels, I believe, that if evil is not discovered it does not exist. As long as we keep evil to ourselves, it is containable and controllable. When others discover our secret, we are no longer in control and all is lost. Thus, the little girl hid her sore throat for the same reason that some of us avoid a dentist who will find cavities in our teeth. We know we are acting unreasonably, but we don't go to the same lengths, nor is our fear as strong as the girl's, for she fought with supreme effort, crying bitterly when she lost.

The second conflict, more interesting to Williams the writer rather than Williams the medical doctor, is about an adult's anger at himself when he is required to use force to accomplish his aim—even if the aim is noble in itself. Force is alien to a mature and cultivated mind, though learning about its psychological effect is part of growing up. When all else fails, reason tells us we must resort to force, but we are disgusted with ourselves when we give in. The anger and disgust rob the occasion of any sense of satisfaction: we win the physical battle but lose the war within our psyche.

A common-sense analysis would point out that it is natural to feel anger and disgust when using violent force, as in rape. The doctor says, "Perhaps I should have desisted and come back in an hour or more. No doubt it would have been better." The solution then is patience and a sensible and safe relief of frustration, but that's a story with a moral.

The power of the story is its sense of urgency and its brevity. The author doesn't have time to fill in the blanks. His intention is not character-development nor plot-exposition in the usual sense. His intention is to get in and get out quickly, focusing on what he has discovered about the use of force.

Source: William Baker, "Williams' 'The Use of Force,'" in *Explicator*, Vol. 37, No. 1, Fall 1978, 2 pp.

Fergal Gallagher

In the following article, Gallagher aligns the characters in "The Use of Force" with the components of the human psyche as defined by psychologist Sigmund Freud.

In his interesting article on *William Carlos Williams'* "The Use of Force," R. F. Dietrich points out the sexual connotations of the story that "are there because they express the savagery in human nature that, lying so close to the surface, can erupt at any moment in a flow of irrational behavior..." (*Studies in Short Fiction*, Summer 1966). The interpretation of the doctor-child conflict in terms of a sexual encounter does indeed appear to be valid when one considers the sexual overtones of the language of the story as Dietrich does. However, I would like to suggest a further interpretation based upon Freudian theory. I believe that the three sets of characters in "The Use of Force"—the doctor, the parents, and the child—are motivated by the three zones of the human psyche, the ego, the super-ego, and the id, respectively, and I also believe that the doctor, at first governed by the ego, permits his id to dominate him during his encounter with the child.

It is evident that the child, in her unrestrained passion and aggression, is acting entirely according

"NO CHANGE OCCURS IN THE BEHAVIOR OF THE PARENTS OR THE CHILD. THROUGHOUT THE STORY THE PARENTS REMAIN DOMINATED BY THE SUPER-EGO, AND MATHILDA IS GOVERNED BY THE ID. BUT THERE IS A REMARKABLE CHANGE IN THE BEHAVIOR OF THE PHYSICIAN. HE LOSES CONTROL OF HIMSELF, OR, IN FREUDIAN TERMS, HE PERMITS HIS ID TO DOMINATE THE EGO."

to the dictates of the id, which Freud describes in his *New Introductory Lectures on Psychoanalysis* as "striving to bring about the satisfaction of the instinctual needs subject to the observance of the pleasure principle." The aim of the id is to seek pleasure and to avoid pain, functioning without regard for the conventional restraints of society or morality, and even without regard for self-preservation. The id, as Freud remarks, "knows no judgements of value: no good and evil, no morality." Mathilda's blind fury and her instinctual, hysterical attack on the doctor, when he moves closer to examine her, indicate that she is completely unconcerned about the doctor either as someone capable of helping her or in his role in society as someone to be respected. Describing her as lunging at him with "one catlike movement" while "both her hands clawed instinctively" for his eyes, the doctor emphasizes Mathilda's instinctual, animal-like aggressiveness, characteristic of an individual governed by the id. In other words, the child appears to be dominated by the id, and reason or conventional morality (the ego and the super-ego) form little part of her psyche.

According to Freud, the instinctual aggressions and passions of the normal adult psyche are regulated and repressed by the reason (the ego) and the conventions of society and morality (the super-ego). As Mathilda's behavior would seem to indicate that she is dominated by the id, the control and repression of her untamed aggression must be supplied from some external source. Freud points out that "young children are amoral and possess no internal inhibitions against their impulses striving for pleasure. The part which is later taken on by the super-ego is played to begin with by an external power, by parental authority." In their physical attempt to hold their daughter still so that the doctor can examine her throat, the parents are, in effect, attempting to repress her passion and aggression. In Freudian terms the super-ego is attempting to repress the id. In regarding the parents as the super-ego, I think it is worth noting that their reaction to Mathilda's behavior is not one of anger, but rather one of extreme embarrassment and mortification. At the child's first attack on the doctor, "both the mother and father almost turned themselves inside out in embarrassment and apology." The father releases her at the critical moment because of his "shame at her behavior and his dread of hurting her." When Mathilda reduces the wooden spatula to splinters, her mother asks her: "Aren't you ashamed to act like that in front of the doctor?" Rather than considering the doctor as one who can help their child, the parents seem to regard him as one socially superior to them because of his professional status. This is why they are embarrassed rather than angered at their child's behavior. And this display of embarrassment on the part of the parents is indicative of the feelings of guilt associated with the super-ego.

Whereas the parents are governed by the super-ego, the doctor, understanding the practical nature of the problem, is governed by the ego, which, Freud says, "stands for reason and good sense." The physician realizes that he "had to have a throat culture for her own protection." He is annoyed with the mother when she refers to him as a nice man. He realizes he has a job to do: "For heaven's sake, I broke in. Don't call me a nice man to her. I'm here to look at her throat on the chance that she might have diphtheria and possibly die of it." This is the reasonableness of the ego opposing the super-ego's concern with social convention.

No change occurs in the behavior of the parents or the child. Throughout the story the parents remain dominated by the super-ego, and Mathilda is governed by the id. But there is a remarkable change in the behavior of the physician. He loses control of himself, or, in Freudian terms, he permits his id to dominate the ego. As he first encounters the patient he behaves with reason and circumspection. He is annoyed at the stupidity of the parents and is determined to obtain the necessary throat culture. After the second fruitless assault, the doctor reasons with himself whether he should continue or try again later. But he realizes the urgency of the situation and tries again to force open the patient's mouth. Up to this point the doctor is controlled by the ego, and even in the motivation for his final forceful attempt to obtain the throat culture he is behaving rationally, for he realizes the necessity of force under the circumstances. But, in the use of force, he loses his ability to reason as he attacks the girl with the same blind fury with which she resists him: "But the worst of it was that I too had got beyond reason. I could have torn the child apart in my own fury and enjoyed it. It was a pleasure to attack her." So in a "final unreasoning assault" the doctor manages to force open Mathilda's mouth and examine her throat. But, in so doing, he loses his ability to reason and permits his passions and aggressions to govern him. The doctor's ego submits to the id as he enjoys the momentary release of instinctual aggression. It should be noticed here, however, that this is not a total domination of the ego. For if the doctor were totally governed by the id, he would have probably merely struck the girl in blind fury. Perhaps it was Williams' intention here to demonstrate the *usefulness* of force in such a crisis. Without the use of force, it would not have been possible for the doctor to obtain the necessary throat culture. Nevertheless, there is no doubt that the doctor derives pleasure from his attack, even if only for a moment.

According to Freud, in the normal individual the ego acts as a mediator between the id and the super-ego. At the beginning of "The Use of Force" the doctor, governed by the ego, serves as the intermediary between the parents dominated by the super-ego and the child controlled by the id. Thus, as we should expect, the physician is the one who acts with reason and circumspection. But in the process of examining his patient he, too, becomes momentarily unbalanced. Therefore, "The Use of Force" deals not only with the conflict between doctor and patient, but also with the inner conflict between the psychic forces of reason and aggressive passion, between the ego and the id.

Source: Fergal Gallagher, "Further Freudian Implications in William Carlos Williams' 'The Use of Force,'" in *CEA Critic*, Vol. 34, No. 4, May 1972, pp. 20–21.

SOURCES

Breslin, James E., *William Carlos Williams: An American Artist*, Oxford University Press, 1970, pp. 163, 165.

Corman, Cid, "*The Farmer's Daughters*: A True Story about People," in *William Carlos Williams: A Collection of Critical Essays*, edited by J. Hillis Miller, Prentice-Hall, 1966, p. 164.

Lowell, Robert, "Paterson I and II," in *Profile of William Carlos Williams*, compiled by Jerome Mazzaro, Charles E. Merrill Publishing, 1971, p. 72.

Williams, William Carlos, "The Use of Force," in *The Doctor Stories*, New Directions, 1984, pp. 56–60.

FURTHER READING

Dietrich, R. F., "Connotations of Rape in 'The Use of Force,'" in *Studies in Short Fiction*, Vol. 3, No. 4, Summer 1966, pp. 446–50.

Dietrich's essay does not imply that the doctor's actions in this story constitute actual sexual abuse, but it looks at ways in which the doctor's actions can be seen to have sexual overtones.

Engel, Jonathan, *Poor People's Medicine: Medicaid and American Charity Care since 1965*, Duke University Press, 2006.

Told in a series of anecdotes, this book offers an opportunity to compare and contrast the doctor's visit that Williams describes with the way rural health care for the poor is handled in today's post-Medicaid world.

Guimond, James Williams, *The Art of William Carlos Williams: The Discovery and Possession of America*, University of Illinois Press, 1968.

Though this book, like many literary overviews, focuses mainly on Williams's career as a poet, its insights into his uniquely American style apply to his fiction as well.

Mariani, Paul, *William Carlos Williams: A New World Naked*, W. W. Norton, 1990.

One of the most detailed and extensive biographies of Williams available, this massive book is presented in a compelling style.

A Wagner Matinee

WILLA CATHER

1904

First published in *Everybody's Magazine* in 1904, Willa Cather's "A Wagner Matinee" was written early in the author's career and provides a preview of the tone and style that would later become hallmarks of Cather's fiction. In this short story, Cather explores with stark realism the physically and emotionally damaging effects of pioneer life in rural Nebraska. The story is narrated by Clark, who hosts his Aunt Georgiana when she comes to Boston after leaving her Nebraskan homestead for the first time in many years. Just as "A Wagner Matinee" features a male character's point of view, Cather's later works similarly employ male characters from whose points of view the stories are told. Perhaps most notably, Cather uses this approach in her well-known novel *My Ántonia* (1918), a work that is set in rural Nebraska. Her first book-length exploration of the frontier setting was the highly acclaimed *O Pioneers!* (1913).

While "A Wagner Matinee" is set in Boston, it is a frontier story at its core, in its focus on Aunt Georgiana and her transformation from a music teacher in Boston to a woman worn and wounded in both body and spirit after decades on a Nebraskan homestead. The story traces the emotional response of Aunt Georgiana to a concert of the music of the German composer Richard Wagner, a concert that Aunt Georgiana attends with her nephew. Clark's observations of his aunt's behavior and appearance are interspersed with recollections of the harsh years of

Willa Cather (*AP Images. Reproduced by permission*)

his own youth, which he spent with Georgiana on her farm. Georgiana's tearful reaction to Wagner's music suggests a longing for her former, perhaps fuller life in the city.

"A Wagner Matinee" is available in *The Troll Garden*, a short story collection by Willa Cather. Originally published in 1905, this collection is available in a 1983 volume edited by James Woodress and published by the University of Nebraska Press. Cather revised the story slightly between its magazine publication in 1904 and its appearance in *The Troll Garden* in 1905; for example, she eliminated some of the harsher details about Georgiana's appearance in the later version, changing a description of her figure as misshapen to one of her being stooped in posture. An online version of the 1904 *Everybody's Magazine* printing of "A Wagner Matinee" is available at the Willa Cather Archive, sponsored by the University of Nebraska.

AUTHOR BIOGRAPHY

Born in 1873 near Winchester, Virginia, Willa Cather was the first of seven children born to Charles F. Cather and Mary Virginia Boak Cather. The family moved to Nebraska in 1883 to join Charles Cather's brother and parents, who had already established a ranch on the plains. After a challenging year on the homestead that they had struggled to establish, the Cathers opted to sell their land and settle themselves in the town of Red Cloud. Cather would move again several years later, to begin her college preparatory studies in 1890 in Lincoln, followed by four years at the University of Nebraska. Upon graduation in 1895, she returned home to Red Cloud for a year before departing for Pittsburgh, Pennsylvania, to begin a job as a magazine editor in 1896. Cather soon landed a job as a newspaper editor and drama reviewer for the *Daily Leader*, a position she held for several years before turning to teaching, first at Pittsburgh's Central High School and later at Allegheny High School.

Cather's first volume of poetry, *April Twilights*, was published in 1903. In 1904, her short story "A Wagner Matinee" appeared in *Everybody's Magazine*. The following year Cather included the story in her collection of short stories *The Troll Garden*. Shortly after, in 1906, Cather moved to New York City to accept a position on the editorial staff of *McClure's* magazine. In 1908, she moved into an apartment with Edith Lewis, who would become her lifelong companion. After leaving the magazine in 1912, Cather began writing and publishing in earnest. Her first novel, *Alexander's Bridge*, appeared in 1912, and it was soon followed by the two highly acclaimed novels *O Pioneers!* (1913) and *My Ántonia* (1918). While she focused on writing novels, producing twelve in the course of her career, Cather also published several volumes of short stories and essays. Her last novel, *Sapphira and the Slave Girl*, was published in 1940. Cather died in her New York City home from a massive cerebral hemorrhage on April 24, 1947.

PLOT SUMMARY

Cather's "A Wagner Matinee" opens with the narrator, Clark, receiving a letter from Nebraska, which the reader soon learns is from Clark's Uncle Howard. The letter informs Clark that his Aunt Georgiana will be visiting him in Boston when she comes to attend to the estate of a deceased relative. Uncle Howard's letter asks Clark to meet Georgiana at the station and aid her in whatever way is necessary during her stay

MEDIA ADAPTATIONS

- "A Wagner Matinee" is included in the Audio Bookshelf's 1997 cassette recording titled *Willa Cather: Stories*, read by Melissa Hughes.
- Sponsored by the Public Media Foundation at Northeastern University's College of Arts and Sciences, the "Scribbling Women" Web site at http://www.scribblingwomen.org/wcwagner.htm maintains a 2007 audio recording of a play version of "A Wagner Matinee." The story was dramatized by Sara Baker and directed by Martin Jenkins.

in Boston. Upon reading his uncle's letter, Clark recalls details of his youth spent on his aunt and uncle's farm in Nebraska. He remembers playing Aunt Georgiana's piano with fingers sore and raw from husking corn.

At the train station, Clark experiences some challenges in collecting Georgiana. Not only is she the last of the passengers to disembark, but she is covered with soot and dust from her journey. Clark's landlady, Mrs. Springer, settles Georgiana into her quarters for the evening upon her arrival in Clark's home, and Clark does not see his aunt again until the following morning. Reflecting on Georgiana's haggard appearance, Clark notes how much the woman has changed since she worked as a music teacher in Boston some three decades ago. The reader learns from Clark's recollections that Aunt Georgiana had fallen in love with a young man from the country, wed him, and followed him to the Nebraskan frontier. Clark mentally enumerates the facts of Georgiana and Howard's primitive existence and the tolls his aunt's hard life has exacted on her appearance. He realizes also how much he owes his aunt, as she sacrificed much of her time to teach him. She would, he recalls, help him with Latin verb conjugations and listen to him read Shakespeare after she had tucked six children into bed.

On the day following Georgiana's arrival, Clark takes her to a concert given by the Boston Symphony Orchestra, which would be performing the works of the German composer Richard Wagner. Clark wonders whether Georgiana will, after her years of hardship and deprivation, be able to enjoy or appreciate the music. She seems reluctant to be out in the city and distracted by tasks left undone back home in Nebraska. As the musicians are seated in the concert hall, Clark studies his aunt's reaction closely, noting that she seems to stir with anticipation and finally begins to become tuned in to her surroundings. The concert begins, and Aunt Georgiana grasps Clark's sleeve; he thinks that these first strains of music are breaking thirty years of silence inflicted upon his aunt by the Nebraskan plains. Images of Georgiana's bleak homestead appear in Clark's mind. Wondering what his aunt is gleaning from the music, he recalls what a good pianist she had once been and remembers the breadth of her musical education.

During the intermission, Clark questions his aunt about one of the songs they heard, and she informs him that she has actually heard it before, as sung by a German immigrant back in Red Willow County. Aunt and nephew briefly discuss the music and its structure. During the second half of the concert, Aunt Georgiana weeps repeatedly. Again Clark wonders how much of the music's complexities his aunt can comprehend, how much of her ability to process the music has been dissolved through the hard labor and isolation she has endured for so many years.

The concert concludes, and the spectators depart the concert hall, yet Clark and his aunt remain behind. When Clark addresses Aunt Georgiana, who has made no move to leave, she bursts into tears, telling him that she does not wish to leave. Clark interprets his aunt's response as an indication not simply of her unwillingness to leave the music behind but also of her extreme reluctance to return to the harshness of her life in Nebraska.

CHARACTERS

Georgiana Carpenter

Georgiana Carpenter is the wife of Howard Carpenter and the maternal aunt of the narrator, Clark. From the beginning, the reader is offered a startling physical portrait of Georgiana, whom

Clark initially describes as "pathetic and grotesque" in her appearance. Filthy from her travels, Georgiana seems disoriented and fatigued, and Clark comments that only after a little while does she seem to recognize him. Commenting on her meeting of and subsequent marriage to Howard, Clark states that at thirty, Georgiana had been "angular" and "spectacled." Apparently unable to comprehend his aunt's ability to live the kind of life Howard took her to in Nebraska, Clark remarks that, having measured off their homestead, the couple proceeded to build "a dugout in the red hillside, one of those cave dwellings whose inmates so often reverted to primitive conditions." From then on, through Clark, Georgiana is continually presented as a reduced version of her former self, a foreign oddity. He regards her in the same way that explorers are viewed when they return to civilization with missing limbs. He observes that the wind and alkaline water have yellowed her skin so that it is like that of a "Mongolian's." Her teeth are false and do not fit well in her mouth, and her posture is stooped, her chest sunken.

At the same time, Clark remembers warmly the way Georgiana tutored him when he lived with her as a youth. She was knowledgeable not only in music but in Latin, mythology, and Shakespeare as well. When Clark struggled with difficult piano pieces, she implored him to not love music too much, because if it were ever to be taken from him, as it was from her, the sacrifice might seem too great. Georgiana does indeed seem to resist her response to the music when Clark takes her to the concert; she attempts to not "love it so well," as she had once cautioned her nephew. She seems saddened by listening to the second half of the program, and Clark wonders about her ability to comprehend the structure of the music. Nevertheless, she appears to ascertain enough about the music to feel moved by it, for she weeps during much of the second half of the concert. Georgiana does not rise to leave when the music finishes, instead sobbing to Clark that she does want to go.

Howard Carpenter

Howard Carpenter is the husband of Georgiana and the uncle of Clark. He sends Clark a letter informing him that Georgiana will be coming to Boston to attend to the estate of a bachelor relative who has died. Howard requests in his letter that Clark meet Georgiana at the train station and assist her in whatever way he can. Clark notes that, "characteristically," Howard put off writing the letter for so long that Clark would have missed his aunt entirely if he had been away from home for the day. Clark additionally reveals a little of Howard's character as the story progresses, describing him as having been "the most idle and shiftless of all the village lads" in one of the mountain towns to which Georgiana had gone to teach music. The reader is additionally informed that Howard was twenty-one when he met the thirty-year-old Georgiana, whom he followed back to Boston when she returned. The pair eloped, and Howard took his new bride to the frontier in Nebraska. According to Clark, Georgiana's friends and family were critical of her decision to wed Howard, whom Clark points out "of course" had no financial security to offer Georgiana.

Clark

Clark is the narrator of "A Wagner Matinee." The reader does not learn his last name, only that he is the nephew of Georgiana, his maternal aunt, and her husband Howard Carpenter. Clark does not reveal much about himself directly throughout the course of the story. His reflections pertain primarily to his aunt, although he does comment about the years he spent on Georgiana and Howard's Nebraskan homestead. Much of what the reader knows about Clark's character is gleaned from his views about his aunt. He seems to revere her for the sacrifices she has made and is, at the same time, somewhat repulsed by the woman into which she has degenerated. Pity and revulsion are the first emotions that rise up when he recalls her appearance, and reading her name in his uncle's letter dredges up in Clark powerful memories from his youth when he was a shy, "gangling farmer-boy," with hands "cracked and sore from the corn husking." He recalls practicing musical scales on Georgiana's organ with his painful fingers.

After seeing his aunt disembark from the train and escorting her home, Clark's response to her is again a combination of positive and negative feelings. He remarks upon her disfigured appearance just prior to discussing the respect he has for her. Clark then, in a somewhat condescending tone, describes the absurdity of Georgiana's attraction to Howard when the couple first met and remarks that "of course" Howard was penniless when the pair left for Nebraska.

Clark's continued fascination with the flaws in his aunt's physical appearance is revealed when he describes her drab clothing, sallow skin, and poor posture. These exterior flaws Clark juxtaposes with the "reverential affection" he possesses for Georgiana. He fondly recalls all she taught him despite her personal fatigue and suffering, admitting how much he owes her.

During the course of the Wagner concert, to which Clark takes his aunt in an effort to entertain her with the music that so inspired her life years ago, Clark's attitude is a mixture of pity and concern. He wonders on more than one occasion if she is able to understand the intricacies of the music's structure and composition. He worries that perhaps he should have left her memories undisturbed, so as to have let her remain in what he perceives to be a numbed state. When at the end of the concert Georgiana sobs and blurts that she does not want to go, Clark claims to understand her despair. For her, he states, just beyond the door of the concert hall lies the rough frontier life that she has temporarily left behind. Having tasted her former life once again, Georgiana is desperate to forestall her return to Nebraska, Clark assumes.

Mrs. Springer

Mrs. Springer is the landlady at the boarding house where Clark, the narrator of the story, lives. She shows Georgiana to her room, and Clark observes the consideration Mrs. Springer shows Georgiana by hiding any surprise she might have had at Georgiana's bedraggled appearance.

THEMES

Frontier Life

Although "A Wagner Matinee" is set in Boston, the story is at its core about life on the western frontier. In particular, the harshness of frontier living is contrasted with the pleasantness of urban society in the Northeast. Through the observations of her narrator, Clark, Cather takes pains to demonstrate the brutal effects of frontier living on the former Boston music teacher, Georgiana. Her appearance is regarded as horrifying and alien. Whereas Georgiana was once an ordinary, if "angular" woman of thirty, after thirty years on the prairie she is now viewed as "grotesque," her figure "stooped," her skin sallow in pallor and leathery in texture. Clark attributes these developments to Georgiana's isolation from civilization, to the monotony of her daily routine, and to the intense physical suffering resulting from the labor necessary to make one's living on a Nebraskan homestead. Clark did not return unscathed from his own youthful years spent on his aunt and uncle's homestead, during which he was "riding herd" for his uncle. The mere mention of his aunt's name conjures in him potent memories of husking corn until his hands were red, raw, and cracked. Clark recalls that his aunt's duties included cooking breakfast at six o'clock in the morning and working until midnight, long after she had put six children to bed.

Once she has arrived in Boston, Georgiana remains distracted by the chores awaiting her back home—by the calf who needs special care, or by the food in the cellar that needs to be eaten before it spoils. All of these details, from Clark's recollections of his youth to Georgiana's current itemization of pending chores and concerns, serve to emphasize the all-consuming nature of frontier life. Through Clark's characterization of his aunt's appearance and preoccupations, Cather underscores the notion that life on the Nebraskan prairie is devouring Georgiana spiritually and mentally. Clark is quite convinced that his aunt can no longer appreciate or comprehend the elements of the music she used to love so passionately. He views her as having been numbed into some sort of stupor by her harsh life, and he even wonders whether it would have been best to send her back home "without waking her." The story closes with a fresh reminder of the toll frontier life has taken on Georgiana. Sobbing, she pleads to her nephew as the concert ends, "I don't want to go, Clark, I don't want to go!" That she is crying and that she repeats the sentiment serve to indicate that she is not merely reluctant to leave the music hall because she has enjoyed the program so much. Rather, the reader is intended to take her reaction, as Clark does, as an indictment of frontier life. Clark suggests that for Georgiana, the act of leaving the concert hall will be a symbolic one, whereby she will again turn her back on who she once was, to return once more to a lonely life devoid of civilized pleasures and comforts.

Regret

The theme of regret in "A Wagner Matinee" is voiced through Clark, who contrasts his notions of who his aunt used to be with who she has

TOPICS FOR FURTHER STUDY

- "A Wagner Matinee" deals in part with the hardships of homestead life, but Cather tells the story from the point of view of Clark, whose time on his aunt's homestead was rather limited. Research what homestead life on the Nebraskan frontier was like during the late 1800s and write a short story from Georgiana's point of view. What is her typical day like? Does she regret having left the comforts of civilized society? What types of activities did homesteaders partake in for entertainment? What might Georgiana have enjoyed about her life as a homesteader?
- Nebraskan farmers often faced harsh conditions, such as droughts, that hampered their abilities to produce the crops that they sold for profit and with which they fed their families. Research the types of food crops that Nebraskan frontier farmers produced and the types of family meals that would have been prepared from such crops. Was the diet fruit and vegetable based? What kinds of meat products did the farmers produce? Which grains thrived? Prepare a typical recipe, such as a bread made from wheat and cornmeal, and share the food with your class.
- In Cather's story, Clark and his aunt visit the Boston Symphony Orchestra to listen to a concert featuring the music of the German composer Richard Wagner. Research the music of Wagner and its impact on classical music in the late 1800s and early 1900s. How popular was Wagner's music in Europe and in America? For which musical form is Wagner best known? Write a report based on your findings. Consider playing a recording of Wagner's compositions, perhaps one of those mentioned in Cather's story, for your class.
- The settlement of the American frontier, which expanded the borders of the United States and provided the nation with valuable natural resources, led to the death or displacement of countless Native Americans from many tribes. Research the short- and long-term effects of the passage of such acts as the Kansas-Nebraska Act (1854) and the Homestead Act (1862) on Native American communities. How many individuals were relocated? How many were killed? What did the federal government gain by passing such acts? How did Native Americans and homesteaders react to one another? Could or did they coexist? Write an argumentative/persuasive paper, supported by facts, that demonstrates your opinion on the federal government's treatment of Native Americans during this time period.

become after thirty years of frontier living. He cannot help but see her as irreversibly diminished by her experiences. Personally, he appears to pity her, while he projects the notion of regret onto her. This is indicated in several ways. As Clark and his aunt listen to what Clark describes as "Siegfried's funeral march," he intuits from the "trembling of her face" that Georgiana is responding to the death of hopes and dreams that the music conveys. The music explores the extinguishing of hope, and Clark assumes that if his aunt is able to respond to anything in the composition, it will be to this theme in particular. As Clark extrapolates from his aunt's reluctance to leave the concert hall that she fervently wishes to avoid returning to her life in Nebraska, it is suggested that Georgiana regrets ever having gone to Nebraska at all. The reader views Georgiana's likely regret through the filter of Clark's observations. His personal experience of life on the frontier adds weight to his interpretation. Clark is not simply guessing how taxing the work of maintaining a homestead is; he experienced it firsthand and was an eye witness

Model state set for Wagner's Tannhauser, *which looks like a cave interior* *(© Arthur Thevenart / Corbis)*

to the toll it took on Georgiana. Seeing her again after so many years reinforces his understanding of the burden of such a hard life, and it is no great leap of Clark's imagination to assume that his quiet, uncomplaining aunt feels at least some regret over her decision to leave her city life as a music instructor to follow a man to the frontier.

STYLE

Realism

Cather's style in "A Wagner Matinee" is characterized by the realism with which she describes the events of the story and the narrator's recollections of Nebraska. Cather does not make many generalizations or exaggerations during her narrative, nor are any aspects of the characters' lives idealized. Rather, the author exploits the details of harsh frontier life to make accessible and apparent to the reader the pain and suffering Georgiana lives with on a daily basis. Additionally, Clark's observations, while arguably condescending in tone at times, do come across as precise assessments of Georgiana's current debilitated condition. The details he chooses to convey are both stark and suggestive of Georgiana's suffering, as when Clark itemizes, for example, the deficiencies in Georgiana's physical appearance. As the story concludes, Clark comments on the dishcloths hanging on the "crook-backed ash seedlings" to dry, and the "gaunt, moulting turkeys picking up refuse about the kitchen door." Such specific details recall Clark's earlier description of his aunt's own crooked, thin posture and also serve to imply the ever-present chores that await Georgiana back home.

First-person Narrator

Cather elected to tell this story in the first person, but from Clark's point of view rather than from Georgiana's. This allows the reader to glean not only information about Georgiana and her life but also Clark's opinion of it. Given that Clark provides a firsthand account of his own experiences on the frontier, of his aunt's life there, and of her response to her current visit to Boston, the reader must determine the extent to which

Clark's opinion of his aunt's life is a biased one. Cather's usage of the first person for this story allows the reader only Clark's viewpoint, and the actual dialogue between Clark and Georgiana is quite limited, so she has very little opportunity to express her own opinions. When she does voice her thoughts, they seem to support Clark's notions about the suffering she has endured as well as about her reluctance to return to frontier life. The extent to which Clark's ideas regarding the Nebraskan frontier reflect the author's own views is a subject of critical discussion. As Clark is the point-of-view character, and as his experiences mirror Cather's own in some ways, it has been suggested that the author uses Clark to express her personal opinions regarding frontier living and the sacrifices it requires.

HISTORICAL CONTEXT

The Politics of Homesteading

In Cather's "A Wagner Matinee," the narrator reflects on the series of events that led his aunt to the Nebraskan frontier, and he notes that Georgiana has lived on her homestead there for roughly thirty years. Clark also mentions the way his aunt and her husband measured off their eighty-acre parcel of land: by counting the revolutions of the wheel of their covered wagon. Through the usage of such details, Cather underscores the ways in which the fictional Georgiana and her husband Howard represent the many would-be homesteaders who were drawn westward following the 1862 passage of the Homestead Act. This act, passed by Congress and President Abraham Lincoln, gave up to 160 acres of "public" land to any head of household who had lived on the land and farmed it for five years. The availability of land offered for little financial cost appealed to poor Americans and European immigrants seeking new lives. The so-called public land, however, was available due to the federal government's reversal of prior agreements with Native American tribes. In 1854, several years before the Homestead Act enticed new settlers to western regions of the country, the Kansas-Nebraska Act was passed. This act reopened vast tracts of land for settlement, land that had previously been vouchsafed for independent Native American nations. Other territories throughout the West that had been protected by agreements between Native Americans and the federal government were similarly opened for settlement.

American Politics at the Turn of the Twentieth Century

When Cather published "A Wagner Matinee" in 1904, Theodore Roosevelt was serving as president. He had served under William McKinley as vice president and succeeded to the presidency after McKinley's assassination in 1901. A naturalist, an outdoorsman, and an explorer, Roosevelt wrote books on the American frontier, outdoor life, and natural history. In addition to his efforts to steer the United States into the arena of world politics, to break up monopolies in business, and to ensure the creation of the Panama Canal, Roosevelt was known for his efforts in the area of conservation. A love of the American frontier was instilled in Roosevelt during the late 1800s. Following the death of his first wife, he set off to roam the Dakota Territory, eventually establishing his own ranch. Such experiences influenced his causes after he became president.

With the power his office bestowed, Roosevelt advocated the efficient use of the nation's natural resources. He was responsible for the creation of numerous national forests as well as federal bird reservations, national game preserves, and national parks. Roosevelt was moved to protect at least some of what was once the great American frontier from oversettlement, but he was aware that land that could actually be called "frontier" in the truest, wildest, unsettled sense of the word was becoming quite rare. In fact, following the U.S. census taken in 1890, many believed that the frontier was "closed," that there was no longer a clear demarcation between settled and unsettled territory. Life in newly settled territories was harsh and uncivilized in many aspects, but the land was being developed by increasingly large numbers of homesteaders. Such acts of settlement—the building of homes, the cultivation of farms—were becoming common enough by the close of the nineteenth century that Roosevelt and others began to look to the rest of the world (since America's own frontier had disappeared) for places with the potential to be influenced by the type of American ideals that had "tamed" the wilderness.

Classical Music

Although the German composer Richard Wagner, to whom Cather refers in "A Wagner Matinee," died in 1883, his orchestral pieces and operas were still being enjoyed by many

COMPARE & CONTRAST

- **Late 1800s and early 1900s:** Land in America's central region and in the West that had previously been designated as frontier is becoming increasingly populated after years of homesteaders being enticed to settle on public land. These parcels of land are made available for purchase at low cost after five years of habitation and development. Population densities remain heaviest along the East Coast of the United States.

  Today: Virtually no land is seen as frontier any longer in the United States, as has been the case since the years after Alaska gained statehood, along with Hawaii, in 1959. Population density remains heaviest in the eastern half of the country, with the exception of select regions along the West Coast and in southwestern portions of the United States.

- **Late 1800s and early 1900s:** America's land and natural resources are becoming jeopardized by increased settlement. The longtime outdoorsman, naturalist, and conservationist Theodore Roosevelt addresses this issue in his writings and in the political arena, particularly after he becomes president in 1901. Roosevelt protects America's natural resources through the creation of numerous national forests, wildlife preserves and reservations, and national parks.

  Today: The conservation of America's natural resources is threatened by the efforts of some businesses and politicians to exploit protected public land in order to draw on potential oil reserves, particularly in Alaska's Arctic National Wildlife Refuge.

- **Late 1800s and early 1900s:** Women are just gaining regular employment in occupations other than those related to domestic chores. With the industrialization of America, factories offer a variety of new opportunities to women, although the cost on their health from long hours, hard labor, and dangerous conditions is high. Other women with access to higher education are able to seek employment as nurses, as writers (like Cather), or in the field of education (like Cather's character Georgiana). Most female workers earn substantially less than their male counterparts.

  Today: Women make up a large percentage of the educators and health-care professionals in the United States but are also employed in virtually every field imaginable. Despite the advancements made in the range of opportunities for employment for women, a wage discrepancy between men and women remains.

- **Late 1800s and early 1900s:** Boston, the setting of Cather's "A Wagner Matinee," is a city known for its culture. It is a thriving venue that supports writers, artists, and musicians. The Boston Symphony Orchestra, which plays a prominent role in Cather's story, is established in 1881.

  Today: Boston maintains its historic reputation as one of America's premier cultural cities, attracting lovers of music, theater, art, and dance. The Boston Symphony Orchestra is world renowned.

Americans in the early twentieth century, the time Cather's story was published. Wagner was known for exploring the limits of the traditional boundaries of musical performance in terms of musical forms, instruments and performers used, and the utilization of performance spaces. Performances of classical music by European and American composers were heard by audiences in the orchestral halls of cities recognized as the cultural centers of America at that time. Such cities included Boston and New York. American composers of classical music were influenced by and studied with European composers, but they would soon begin to establish a reputation for having their own unique style and sound.

CRITICAL OVERVIEW

Despite the fact that "A Wagner Matinee" is one of Cather's earliest works of fiction of any length, the work is generally agreed to be a well-constructed story. In it, many critics find intimations of Cather's later, more accomplished style as well as early treatments of themes that Cather continued to explore throughout her many published works of fiction. The literary scholar James Woodress, in his introduction to the 1983 edition of *The Troll Garden*, states that "A Wagner Matinee" is "an excellent story, lean and compact." Woodress observes that Cather uses the same point of view—that of a young man—to great effect in her later novel *My Ántonia*. Other critics have focused instead on Cather's employment of autobiographical details in "A Wagner Matinee." David Daiches, in his 1951 book *Willa Cather: A Critical Introduction*, finds that Cather's usage of details drawn from her own life is subtle. Daiches notes that with a few such observations, Cather is able to contrast the isolation of the Nebraskan farm with the cultural sophistication of Boston. While Daiches contends that the structure of the story "is simple and the point rather obvious," he nevertheless identifies in the work the development of Cather's original style and emotional tone.

Another critical approach to "A Wagner Matinee" explores the story's characterization. Often critics focus on the character of Georgiana, the subject of the narrator's thoughts and the embodiment of the suffering wrought by frontier life. Susan J. Rosowski, in the 1986 volume *The Voyage Perilous: Willa Cather's Romanticism*, concentrates instead on Clark, Georgiana's nephew. Rosowski studies Clark's own transformation in the story, arguing that Clark changes from a cold observer to an empathetic friend. Marilyn Arnold, in an essay in *Willa Cather*, edited by Harold Bloom and published in 1985, finds that Clark's assessment of and behavior toward his aunt is consistently loving, respectful, and warm. Clark's harsh descriptions of his aunt, for example, are "mellowed by his loving regard for her."

Although "A Wagner Matinee" is often found to be among the best stories in the volume in which it was published in 1905, *The Troll Garden*, it is often slighted when compared with Cather's later fiction. Some scholars assert that Cather's style became richer and more effective over time, claiming that her later works create deeper emotional responses in the reader or that her realistic style grew to be more precise and subtle. Rosowski maintains, rather, regarding *The Troll Garden*, that "Cather's technique in these stories is often quite good." She argues, though, that what the stories lack is the conviction in the reassuring powers of artistic creation that her later works possess.

CRITICISM

Catherine Dominic

Dominic is a novelist and a freelance writer and editor. In this essay, Dominic examines Cather's characterization of Clark and Georgiana in "A Wagner Matinee," arguing that through Clark's often negative assessments of his aunt, Cather expresses her own views regarding the painful realities of frontier life as well as her opinions regarding the virtues and pleasures of life in a cultured society.

Through Clark, the narrator of "A Wagner Matinee," Cather offers the reader a cool and somewhat distant assessment of the character of Georgiana; all the reader is able to ascertain about Georgiana is captured through the filter of Clark's observations. Yet through Clark's observations of, comments about, and attitude toward Georgiana, his own character is revealed. Cather employs a youthful male character, one who appears perfectly at home and content with life in the city, to present a portrait of an elderly female character, one who, having transplanted herself from an eastern city, has resided on the western frontier for three decades. By presenting Georgiana in this manner, as a contrast to Clark and to the culture that seems vital to his character, Cather challenges the reader to uncover Clark's biases and perhaps the author's own as well. Ultimately, Cather's characterization of Georgiana and Clark suggests the author's bias in favor of the American East and its culture and sophistication over the raw and unruly American West.

Upon discovering that his aunt will soon be visiting him in Boston, Clark begins to reminisce about his aunt and the Nebraskan homestead where she lives and where he himself spent some time as a youth. Clark does not withhold his judgments of Nebraska, his aunt, or her choices in life. Her physical appearance is

WHAT DO I READ NEXT?

- *O Pioneers!*, Cather's second novel, published in 1913, is considered her first great work and is acknowledged by many to be her masterpiece. In it she treats themes that would remain integral to her work throughout her career, particularly the challenges and suffering attendant to frontier living. The work is available in a 2007 Echo Library edition.
- Cather's *My Ántonia*, first published in 1918 and available in a 1995 edition by Mariner Books, explores the lives of an immigrant family, including a young girl named Ántonia, who have settled in rural Nebraska in the late 1800s. The beauty of the land is contrasted with the hardships endured by the family, and the beauty and pain are further juxtaposed with the opportunities offered back east.
- A portion of the nineteenth-century English poet Christina Rossetti's poem "Goblin Market" was selected by Cather to introduce her volume of short stories *The Troll Garden*, in which "A Wagner Matinee" appears. A poem that explores a variety of subversive temptations, "Goblin Market" was published in 1862 and is available in a 1994 edition by Dover Publications.
- Frederick Jackson Turner's influential 1893 essay "The Significance of the Frontier in American History" discusses the way the frontier shaped America's history and identity. The essay is available in the volume *Rereading Frederick Jackson Turner: "The Significance of the Frontier in American History," and Other Essays*, edited by John Mack Faragher and published by Yale University Press in 1999.
- Theodore Roosevelt was inspired in his conservationist efforts as president by his life on the frontier, which he describes in *Hunting Trips of a Ranchman.* In this volume, Roosevelt extols the virtues of frontier life and portrays the challenges of such a life as well. The book was originally published in 1885 and is available in a 2004 edition by Pavilion Press.

recollected in the most pejorative of terms, and upon seeing his aunt, Clark does not soften the adjectives he uses to describe her. In memory she is "pathetic and grotesque," and at first sight at the train station he comments on her disheveled appearance, covered as she is in soot and the grime of travel. The 1904 version of the story, in contrast with the 1905 version, compares Georgiana's appearance when getting off the train to that of a burned body. In recalling how Georgiana came to reside in Nebraska, Clark recounts the meeting between Georgiana and Howard. She was an "angular, spectacled woman of thirty," a teacher of music employed by the Boston Conservatory, he explains. Her soon-to-be husband, Howard, was a young "country boy" possessing an "extravagant" attraction for Georgiana. The pair eloped after Howard followed Georgiana back to Boston, and Clark is certain that his aunt sought to escape "the reproaches of her family and the criticisms of her friends" by accompanying Howard to the Nebraskan frontier. In these recollections, Clark's disapproval and condescension is plain, and he continues to view his aunt in this light for the remainder of her stay in Boston. Her choice to leave in the first place clearly left Clark feeling slightly disgusted, and this negativity was compounded by his disapproval of the man Georgiana married, the couple's destination, and the fact that Howard was in fact poor.

Following Clark's discussion of Georgiana's marriage and departure for Nebraska, he provides an almost clinical assessment of her appearance. Her skin is yellow and leathery; she wears false teeth; her posture is poor. Clark

> "THROUGH CLARK AND HIS ASSESSMENT OF GEORGIANA, CATHER PAINTS A LARGELY NEGATIVE PICTURE OF THE WESTERN FRONTIER AND A GLOWING PORTRAIT OF THE EASTERN AMERICAN CITY."

claims that as a youth, he possessed a "reverential affection" for Georgiana. Yet his memories of his youth with her indicate that the suffering she endured from the back-breaking, unending physical labor as well as from the isolation from her former society are tainted by his understanding that she willingly sacrificed the society and culture she had once held so dear. Clark states that "she had the consolations of religion and, to her at least, her martyrdom was not wholly sordid." The implication here, emphasized by the phrase "to her at least," is that while to Georgiana the sacrifices that she has made for things she believes in are not contemptible, to Clark, the sacrifices Georgiana made are indeed contemptible or ignoble in some way. Clark then conveys an anecdote in which Georgiana expresses her fear that if he loves music too well, it will be taken from him, and that this is the worst type of sacrifice one can make—losing something that one loves so dearly. Georgiana appears to feel that there is some reason for her suffering, in that she seems to feel her martyrdom was not "sordid." Yet this comment is almost immediately followed by Georgiana's prayer that Clark's sacrifice will not be having to give up something he loves so well as music. The juxtaposition of these two anecdotes underscores Clark's general disapproval of his aunt's outlook: he appears discomforted by the fact that she alternately seems to take responsibility for her choices and then appears to feel that she was the victim of circumstances, that sacrifices have been inflicted upon her.

The views Clark possesses fuel an attitude that borders on scornful, or at least pitying, as when he describes taking his aunt about the city. To his eyes, she appears to be sleepwalking, unable to understand that she now has returned to the city where she had lived when she was much younger, "the place longed for hungrily half a lifetime." After mentioning the way Georgiana had confided with him years ago about a musical performance she enjoyed in Paris, Clark begins to doubt his aunt's ability to enjoy the Wagner program to which he is planning on taking her. He hopes even that her taste for such music has died, maintaining that it would be merciful if she had forgotten entirely the things that used to give her pleasure. Presumably, Clark believes that hearing the musical performance might make Georgiana long for her past life, or for aspects of it that are no longer available to her.

At the concert hall, Clark describes the beautiful finery that all the women in attendance are wearing. He has previously noted Georgiana's own dull, ill-fitting black clothing. Clark's pleasure in the lovely women dressed properly for the concert is obvious; he describes the colors as those one might find in a sun-drenched painting by an impressionist. To Georgiana, meanwhile, he ascribes no ability whatsoever to appreciate the scene before her. The lavishly dressed women, Clark states, were viewed by Georgiana "as though they had been so many daubs of tube-paint on a palette." While Clark appreciates the beauty of the clothes and compares the women's fashions to a scene from a work of art, he believes that Georgiana is only able to see the women in such outfits as blotches of color. Similarly, Clark recalls the transformation he felt within himself upon viewing the musicians at the concert hall for the first time after returning from Georgiana's homestead: he was dazzled by the details of the musicians' garments, the shapes of their instruments, the light playing on the cellos, the first strokes and strains of orchestra. Such an account of Clark's fully articulated memories of a deeply felt response is contrasted with the "little stir of anticipation" Georgiana demonstrates upon seeing the musicians enter the concert hall. While Clark does identify this small response in his aunt, his own ability to respond to his rich surroundings and to be intensely moved by the music is clearly given more weight by Cather within the text.

Georgiana's response to the music is muted. She clutches Clark's sleeve, she weeps quietly, she mentions having heard one of the songs before. Clark wonders about her ability to comprehend the music's structure, yet we know that in the past she was a music instructor; it had been her job not only to understand the formal structure of such pieces of music but also to enable others to appreciate it as well. When at the end of the concert Georgiana expresses her unwillingness to leave, Clark presumes to understand her feelings. He imagines that for her, departure from the music hall posits her squarely back on the homestead, with all the isolation and suffering it represents to her. Indeed, very little of what Georgiana has said or done contradicts Clark's assumptions.

Thus, Cather appears to encourage her readers to share Clark's views about his aunt. The fact that life on the western frontier has in so many ways debilitated Georgiana is a central thrust of the story. Cather grew up on the Nebraskan frontier, only to go on to college and later move back east, where she supported herself through various jobs and eventually through her writing. In portraying Clark and Georgiana as she has, Cather appears to be accomplishing a variety of ends. Georgiana, while perhaps a sympathetic figure in that she seems to have been motivated in her choices by love—love of Howard, love of Clark—nevertheless is depicted as diminished by her choice to leave Boston, her career, and her life as an independent woman employed in a field that she loved. Her path is the opposite of the one Cather chose for herself. Clark, on the other hand, appears to serve as a mouthpiece, to a certain degree, for Cather's views on frontier life and the apparent superiority of city living. Frontier homesteading has deprived Georgiana of many things—her vitality, her youth, and her ability to appreciate art and culture. Clark, however, thrives in a city environment and is deeply appreciative of most things his senses perceive, from the color of a woman's dress to the sounds of a Wagner matinee. Cather's characterization of the two main characters is wrought primarily through the details Clark fixates on throughout the course of the story. Through Clark and his assessment of Georgiana, Cather paints a largely negative picture of the western frontier and a glowing portrait of the eastern American city. As Philip Gerber observes in his critical biography *Willa Cather* (1995), in "A Wagner Matinee" Cather "comes as close as she ever did to rejecting the West."

Source: Catherine Dominic, Critical Essay on "A Wagner Matinee," in *Short Stories for Students*, Gale, Cengage Learning, 2009.

Janis P. Stout

In the following excerpt, Stout tracks Cather's writing career and the events surrounding the publishing of The Troll Garden, *pointing out that "A Wagner Matinee" brought on "a storm of public protest."*

"CONTRARY TO THE DEEP LOVE FOR THE NEBRASKA SOIL THAT WOULD CHARACTERIZE *O PIONEERS!*—LONG TAKEN AS THE DEFINITIVE EXPRESSION OF CATHER'S OWN FEELINGS—SEVERAL OF THE EARLY STORIES CONVEY A SENSE OF DEADNESS, HARSHNESS, OR HOSTILITY IN THE PRAIRIE ENVIRONMENT."

. . . The figure of the female leader had appeared full-blown, of course, a full decade before "Macon Prairie" in *O Pioneers!*, the novel in which Cather said (in an inscription in the copy she sent Carrie Miner) that she "hit the home pasture."

It is often said that until she did hit that home pasture she had been writing poor imitations of Henry James. But she did not begin her overtly Jamesian period until perhaps a decade after she began to publish stories. Her period of most obvious influence by James was 1903 to 1912, the year of *Alexander's Bridge*. Her very first stories, "Peter" and "Lou, the Prophet," drew on Nebraska materials, as did several others written during the 1890s. In those early works, however, she was not yet ready to write with assurance. Until *O Pioneers!* or perhaps "The Bohemian Girl," written in late 1911 when she was revising *Alexander's Bridge*, everything she wrote was, as she inscribed Carrie Miner's book, "half real and half an imitation." She was, after all, just learning to manage narrative, dialogue, and the challenge of igniting emotional power, and she could be forgiven the excesses of emotional coloring or the biblical intonations by which she tried to approximate Old World speech. Like her poems, her apprentice stories bounce about among styles and subjects so much that they are difficult to discuss in any coherent way. But until about 1903, when S. S. McClure took an interest in her, and later when she began editorial work at *McClure's* and became more sharply aware of both literary fashion and the ways in which fiction got itself published, that variability did not tend toward a Jamesian mode.

Thirteen of the stories before *Troll Garden* are set on the prairies. Even so, not all are the "home pasture." "The Clemency of the Court" (1893) was based on newspaper reports of prison atrocities, and "The Affair at Grover Station" (1990) used knowledge of railroading gleaned from her brother Douglass, then working as a Burlington agent in Cheyenne, Wyoming. The home pasture is not just a matter of setting, but of attitude and language as well. Yet characteristic ways of thinking, such as attention to the power of the unstated and the dignity of reticence, appear even in some of the most amateurish and artificial of them. For all its clumsy exoticism, for example, "A Tale of the White Pyramid" (1892) develops motifs of secrecy and concealment that would recur throughout Cather's creative life (O'Brien, *Emerging* 199–200). "The Sentimentality of William Tavener" (1900) demonstrates the power of emotions held in reserve. "The Count of Crow's Nest" (1896), laborious and uneven but a story in which a manuscript reader for *Cosmopolitan* showed an encouraging interest, elevates both the value of "the indefinite" in "the domain of pure art" and the dignity of conducting oneself with reserve—a principle Cather would later carry to the point of a kind of habitual secrecy.

Several of the early stories demonstrate the speciousness of rigid gender roles and give favorable treatment to characters who undermine conventions. The vigorous heroine of "Tommy the Unsentimental" (1896), a girl with a boy's name, a face "like a clever wholesome boy's," "the lank figure of an active half grown lad," and a "peculiarly unfeminine mind that could not escape meeting and acknowledging a logical conclusion," prevents a run on a bank by riding some twenty-five miles uphill on her "wheel." A set of "old speculators and men of business" undermines gender roles by "rather tak[ing] her mother's place." In "The Sentimentality of William Tavernor" Hester can "talk in prayer meeting as fluently as a man" and shows that it "takes a strong woman to make any sort of success of living in the West." The stalwart Margie of "A Resurrection" (1897) has eyes "serious and frank like a man's" (426), and another Margie, in "The Treasure of Far Island" (1902), has "preserved that strength of arm and freedom of limb that had made her so fine a playfellow" (278). In "The Professor's Commencement" (1902), a revelation of Cather's own fear that her "best tools [will] have rusted" if she spends her life teaching high school, the professor has hands "white as a girl's" while his sister is "the more alert and masculine character of the two" but also his "protecting angel." At the end, after he has again forgotten the memorized lines he meant to speak, the professor confesses with shame that he "was not made to shine, for they put a woman's heart in me," but it is clear that we are not to accept that pronouncement at surface value. Even if the professor has not lived up to his own expectations, he *has* shone, for his colleagues see him, only half facetiously, as a Horatius who has "kept the bridge these thirty years." Like others of the early stories, "The Professor's Commencement" is not well resolved, but even so one wonders why critics have found the professor's love for literature "almost unnatural" (Meyering 204, summarizing Joan Wylie Hall, 142–50) and Cather's acceptance of his "emasculation" (a term that betrays the conventionalism of the critic's own definitions) a "dangerous" sign (Thurin 115).

The artist figures in these stories are vaguely androgynous. Given the common stereotype, of course, the yearning for beauty can itself be seen as a kind of feminizing touch, and since Cather certainly identifies with the characters who have that yearning, we can assume that she also identifies with their evasion of conventional notions of gender. In most of the stories before 1906 she centered her narrative attention on male protagonists or masculine activities, even football (in "The Fear That Walks by Noonday," written at the suggestion of Dorothy Canfield), though not literally the sea or battle. In several ("The Count of Crow's Nest," "The Treasure of Far Island," "A Night at Greenway Court"), she views events from a male perspective, a practice that Sarah Orne Jewett would label "a masquerade" (246). Again we see Cather moving between genders, reluctant to be typecast by conventions.

Contrary to the deep love for the Nebraska soil that would characterize *O Pioneers!*—long taken as the definitive expression of Cather's own feelings—several of the early stories convey a sense of deadness, harshness, or hostility in the prairie environment. Lou, the Prophet, in an 1892 story, is essentially driven insane by prairie drought. The "scorching dusty winds" in "On the Divide" (1896) "seem to dry up the blood in men's veins as they do the sap in the corn leaves," so that it "causes no great sensation there when a Dane is found swinging to his own windmill tower, and most of the Poles after they have become too careless and discouraged to shave themselves keep their razors to cut their throats with." Her tone here may be grimly humorous, but the prevalence of suicide in her fiction of Nebraska is evidence that she was basically serious. When she speaks of the "awful loneliness" of the Divide, a country "as flat and gray and as naked as the sea," one hears an implicit contrast with the green hills and settled social relationships of Back Creek, Virginia. In "El Dorado: A Kansas Recessional," where Kansas is surely (as Woodress indicates of "The Sculptor's Funeral") another name for Nebraska, a man from Virginia thinks "it would have been better for us if we'd never left it" (Woodress, introduction to *TG* xxi). In "A Resurrection" (1897) the town of Brownville, which Cather wrote about directly and dismally in an 1894 *Journal* article, is a place "without aim or purpose." Although she would sometimes insist that Nebraska was the only place she could live and be happy (while she continued to live elsewhere), it appears in these stories as a place to be escaped. The narrator of "The Joy of Nelly Deane" (1911) recalls hearing the "faraway world . . . calling to us," as it called to Cather.

Naturally, Cather offended people in the state by writing in this way. A storm of public protest was evoked by "A Wagner Matinée" (1904), which shows Nebraska not merely as flat, empty, and harsh but as a trashed wasteland that shatters the spirit of the sensitive. Aunt Georgiana, a close portrait of Cather's own Aunt Franc, seems worn out and positively starved for beauty. Taken to an afternoon concert during a visit to Boston, she is overcome by the music, begins to cry, and pleads at the end, if the male narrator is right, not to go back to the "tall, unpainted house, with weather-curled boards; naked as a tower, the crook-backed ash seedlings where the dish-cloths hung to dry; the gaunt, moulting turkeys picking up refuse about the kitchen door." Cather told Dorothy Canfield that she had been barraged with angry letters and that her family felt disgraced. When her old mentor Will Owen Jones rebuked her in print she replied that she had not had the slightest intention of disparaging the state.

By aligning the harshness of prairie life with its effect on a person of artistic sensibility, as she does with devastating force in "A Wagner Matinée" and "The Sculptor's Funeral" as well as such early stories as "Peter" and "Eric Hermannson's Soul," she sharpens the opposition of East (or Europe) and West running through much of her fiction and poetry and links it to the opposition between art and a philistine world. This dual opposition is customarily seen as the central structuring theme of *The Troll Garden.* Hermione Lee, for example, points to an opposition between "mid-western philistinism" and the world of art as the principle of the whole.

Many critics have located that pervasive opposition in the two epigraphs to the volume. The first (with ellipses as shown here) is from Charles Kingsley's introduction to *The Roman and the Teuton:*

> A fairy palace, with a fairy garden; . . . inside the trolls dwell, . . . working at their magic forges, making and making always things rare and strange.

The second comes from Christina Rossetti's "The Goblin Market":

> We must not look at Goblin men,
> We must not buy their fruits;
> Who knows upon what soil they fed
> Their hungry thirsty roots?

The two epigraphs set up, in Brown's words (113–14), a conflict between artists (the "industrious" trolls) and the enemies of art (the goblins). But even if we accept that art is the central theme, its import is by no means so simple. *Neither* goblins nor trolls, after all, are figures that usually evoke trust, and the trolls of Kingsley's parable are in fact considerably more sinister than Cather's elided quotation would indicate. When the ellipses are restored, we see that Kingsley labeled them "evil" and their garden a "fair foul place," that is, a place reminiscent of Klingsor's garden in *Parsifal*, a story whose importance for Cather would be manifest in *One of Ours*. Klingsor's garden is mentioned, in fact, in "The Garden Lodge," where it denotes the artistic workshop, so to speak, the world of opera productions and concerts, in contrast to the "quiet nature" behind the walls of a real garden. It is alluded to, as well, in "The Marriage of Phaedra," where the walls of a garden have glass embedded in the top. Another problem with interpreting the epigraphs so rigidly is that *both* trolls and goblins produce, or at least possess, things "rare and strange." And if we read Kingsley's parable in full we see that the trolls' "rare and strange" products entice the "forest children" to corruption as surely as the fruits of the goblin men entrap Rossetti's Laura in an incessant hunger for more.

The epigraphs, then, as well as the stories themselves, show art as being dangerous. Yet its absence, in "The Sculptor's Funeral" and "A Wagner Matinée," is a kind of death. What *The Troll Garden* proposes is not a clear alternative in which one choice (art) is good and the other (a philistine existence) is not, but a duality expressing great personal ambivalence—as Cather's dualities generally do. That ambivalence is compounded not only when one story is compared with another, but when other pairs of dualities—East/West (or as Rosowski defines it, prairie/garden), male/female—are layered onto the opposition of art and philistinism.

The volume opens with "Flavia and Her Artists," an unmistakably Jamesian story about a woman who feeds upon art, and ends with two stories about sensitive souls who hunger for art, "A Wagner Matinée" and "Paul's Case." In only one of the seven stories, "The Sculptor's Funeral," is the contrast between art and small-town philistinism clearly drawn. In the others, human values do not follow such a dichotomy. The sequence moves back and forth between East (New York, Boston, London) and West (Kansas, Wyoming, Nebraska). A linkage of the East with art or a specious appetite for art is established at the outset by the fact that Flavia has insisted on moving from a house on Prairie Avenue in Chicago to the Hudson Valley to establish her temple to art, which proves instead to be a temple to artificiality. The opposite, the West's artistic void, appears in the benighted narrowness of the Kansas town in "The Sculptor's Funeral," the sense of exile of the dying singer in "A Death in the Desert," the littered and barren Nebraska home where Aunt Georgiana longs for the musical joy of her Boston youth in "A Wagner Matinée." The sequence also moves back and forth between focus on male and on female characters, as well as focus *through* male and female observers. As O'Brien points out (275–80), a subtext of concern about "gender and vocation" runs throughout. Vocation, in the sense of career, was still Cather's great problem, inseparably tied to both her sense of the artist's vocation (literally, calling) and her misgivings about the marketplace for art. But it is not so clear as O'Brien claims that she develops a theme of male suppression of female creativity.

Flavia, in the first story, is one of the consumers in the artistic marketplace; indeed, she is a consumer in the predatory sense, the celebrities she attracts to her country-house salon being her "prey." A woman of no aesthetic or intellectual discernment, she is responsive only to whether a given celebrity's stock is rising. From the artist's point of view, then, to be boosted by publicity is to make oneself vulnerable to a predator like Flavia—again, evidence of Cather's concern for privacy. But if the desire for art can become a feeding frenzy, the opposite, an indifference to art, is even more deadening—as shown in the contrasting "The Sculptor's Funeral." Illustrating the artfulness of Cather's structuring of the volume, "The Sculptor's Funeral," second in order, is counterbalanced by "A Wagner Matinée," also about deprivation, second to the end, while "Paul's Case," where an appetite for the trappings of glamour that surround the world of the arts again lapses into an orgy of effete consumption, comes last, balancing "Flavia and Her Artists." Paul is more poignant than Flavia because of his youth, but his hunger for art has an equal speciousness. It is really a hunger for lifestyle.

In the three central stories of the volume the interplay of artistic creation and artistic consumption is more complex, though the stories may be less successful. In "The Garden Lodge," Caroline, the central character, has been reared in a household in which she and her mother were virtual servants of the husband-father, a composer and sometime piano teacher, while both parents carried on "a sort of mystic worship of things distant, intangible, and unattainable" that rendered them personally ineffectual. Caroline herself has narrowly escaped enslavement to the paternal taskmaster, not by suppressing her creativity, as O'Brien asserts, but rather by rebelling against his plan to make her a concert pianist. When she "came into the control of herself," she broke off her training for the concert hall and chose to build a career as an accompanist and teacher, further defying her father by refusing to have her pupils study his compositions. Since she is already well established in this career when she marries, the choice that O'Brien attributes to her of an "orderly controlled marriage rather than an artistic career" (275) is actually never posed. The conventionally feminine role of accompanist does not so much frustrate her creativity as afford her the satisfaction of doing something well and making her own way, just as a woman journalist might who successfully "accompanied" male publishers and editors-in-chief. Indeed, two other good accompanists in *Troll Garden* are male—only one of the many ways in which Cather undermines conventions of gender in these stories. One is the "lovable"

Everett Hilgard, in "A Death in the Desert"; the other is Flavia's apparently inartistic businessman husband.

It is generally acknowledged that the husband in "Flavia and Her Artists" was modeled on Flavia Canfield's husband, Dorothy's father, but he is not presented as being *only* the husband of a foolish wife, as commentary on the story usually insists. It is he rather than Flavia who is sought out for conversation by the truest artist in the group of guests, and it is he who is sensitive to the feelings of the narrator, Imogen Willard (a name borrowed from Cather's Pittsburgh friends May and Mary Willard). Cather did feel that Dorothy's mother dragged her about to museums without consideration of her feelings and seems to have preferred Dorothy's father, Professor Canfield. It is the apparent philistine, then, rather than the supposed lover of art, who becomes "magnificent" at the end of the story, by defending Flavia in a way she does not even understand. The figure of Imogen, the Jamesian *ficelle*, is a sketch of Dorothy herself, who had recently completed a doctorate in Romance languages at Columbia after conducting research at the Sorbonne. Imogen "had shown rather marked capacity in certain esoteric lines of scholarship, and had decided to specialize in a well-sounding branch of philology at the Ecole des Chartes." But her scholarship is regarded with mild amusement (she is "brim full of dates and formulae and other positivisms"), and the third story in the volume, "The Garden Lodge," makes gratuitous reference to "withered women who had taken doctorate degrees." One wonders whether these barbs were added as revenge for Dorothy's interference with "The Profile" and whether she was offended. Her interference was actually beneficial to the volume, however, since the substitution of "Flavia and Her Artists" provided its strongest structuring element.

All but one of the artists in "Flavia" are boring egoists who hang about and flatter Flavia because they need a place to stay or plan to expose her foolishness in (presumably well-paid) print. Similarly, the artist in "The Garden Lodge," an opera singer named d'Esquerré, is a . . . parasitic egoist. In "A Death in the Desert" the artist is so utterly preoccupied with self that he uses his twin brother for errands and can be kind only when it costs little effort, and one gathers that his sponsoring of the career of his former pupil, now dying in the cultural desert of Wyoming, involved some element of . . . vampirism that drained her of her vitality. She is actually dying of tuberculosis—perhaps a pun on "consumption," since she is both consumed by her obsession with Adriance and eager to consume news of the New York art scene. Such is the insatiability of her hunger—like Laura's for the enticing fruits in "Goblin Market"—that she takes no interest in the actual life remaining to her, but only in the life she might have had. The life of the artist has unfitted her for any other. Similarly, when Caroline falls under the spell of d'Esquerré in "The Garden Lodge," she can think of nothing else and wishes to maintain the cottage as a shrine to his creativity. . . . In resisting that urge, she opts for a dry kind of existence, but a balanced one in which she can remain a free agent, within the limits of her marriage. The conclusion seems to indicate that for a woman, at least, there are no perfect answers, but she has steered as satisfying a course as circumstances allowed. For a schoolteacher trying to write fiction in her spare time, that was probably a reassuring conclusion.

In posing such unlikable artist figures as Adriance Hilgard, d'Esquerré, the backbiting Roux in "Flavia and Her Artists," and the overweening Hugh Treffinger of "The Marriage of Phaedra" (a story bearing the marks of James's "The Real Thing"), Cather was continuing to ponder an issue on which she had touched in her newspaper columns, the connection between private character and artistic performance, the mystery of whether art can be genuine when it emerges from personal shallowness. The question of genuineness, both in the artistic creation itself and in what Slote refers to as "the real desire versus the false," is recurrent. Also recurrent and familiar to us from Cather's newspaper columns is a motif of gender-role fluidity. Some of these blurrings of gender boundaries—the women who speak in baritone voices in "Flavia and Her Artists" and "The Marriage of Phaedra," the diminutive Italian tenor with red lips, Paul's sybaritic unmanliness, the curious suggestion that Flavia's exploits might have "unmanned" her—are faintly disturbing, but others are accepted or affirmed. An actress who looks like a boy and is called Jimmy is one of the few likable characters of "Flavia"; in "The Sculptor's Funeral" the old father is feminized by his tenderness for his "gentle" son while the mother only feigns the conventionalized woman's role. The attentive reader is being asked to question assumptions about male and female. . . .

Source: Janis P. Stout, "Finding a Voice, Making a Living," in *Willa Cather: The Writer and Her World*, University Press of Virginia, 2000, pp. 71–104.

Bruce P. Baker

In the following essay, Baker argues that in many of Cather's early short stories, including "A Wagner Matinee," the author portrays Nebraska "as a cultural desert, a setting antagonistic to the inherent artistic needs of the human spirit."

For many years Willa Cather's novels set in Nebraska have been praised for their evocation of the era of the pioneers, a time of splendid heroism and achievement symbolized by the famous plow against the sun in *My Ántonia.* On the plains of the great Midwest, sturdy and creative men and women joined themselves with the fertile soil and brought forth a kind of new Eden wherein fallen man seemed to be able once again to unite with the raw material of the earth and create something beautiful and enduring. For example, in Cather's rhapsodic tribute to the pioneer spirit in *O Pioneers!*, Alexandra Bergson transforms "The Wild Land" in part one into the rich, fruitful fields of part two. It is important to note that Cather does not seem to portray Alexandra's success as merely an Horatio Alger rags-to-riches *exemplum.* Rather, her triumph is not so much a material as an artistic one; in a very real and significant way, Alexandra is a creator, an artist who has shaped out of often unwieldly material an orderly and beautiful work.

But Cather had not always viewed the Nebraska of her formulative years as a place wherein the artist, be it a Thea Kronberg or an Alexandra Bergson, could work out their destinies of creative artistry. Quite the contrary, for in much of Cather's early written response to the Great Plains, Nebraska is portrayed as a cultural desert, a setting often hostile to those of artistic bent, a place indifferent if not actively hostile to man's creative spirit.

Cather's first published story, "Peter," which appeared in a Boston literary magazine, *The Mahogany Tree*, on May 31, 1892, portrays exactly that situation: old Peter Sadelack, a sensitive, artistic immigrant to the "dreariest part of southwestern Nebraska" finds himself unable to endure his new life on the plains. The piece is often very explicit; much is said, little is suggested. Cather comments: "[Peter] drank whenever he could get out of [his son] Antone's sight long enough to pawn his hat or coat for whisky. He was a lazy, absent-minded old fellow, who liked to fiddle better than to plow." Peter is desperately homesick for his native Bohemia and particularly for the opportunities he had had there for artistic expression.

> "OF ALL CATHER'S EARLY STORIES, PERHAPS IT IS IN 'A WAGNER MATINEE,' ONE OF THE SEVEN STORIES IN *THE TROLL GARDEN* (1905), THAT CATHER MOST DRAMATICALLY EXPLORES THE PLIGHT OF THE SENSITIVE AND ARTISTIC PERSON WHO FINDS HIMSELF IN A RESTRICTIVE IF NOT OPPRESSIVE ENVIRONMENT."

Cather uses the symbol of Peter's violin in order to enhance the story's theme and intensify the emotion: that beautiful instrument represents not only his dearest possession but also those values to which Peter has always been dedicated. The first two sentences in the story point up the conflict between father and son and characterize their respective points of view: "'No, Antone, I have told thee many times, no thou shalt not sell it until I am gone.' [His son Antone replies,] 'But I need money; what good is that old fiddle to thee? Thy hand trembles so thou canst scarce hold the bow.'" In a flashback we learn that Peter was once a second violinist in Prague until partial paralysis of his arm brought those days to a close. Then come the last two paragraphs in which Peter "pulled off his old boot, held the gun between his knees with the muzzle against his forehead, and pressed the trigger with his toe."

Before going to the old sod stable, however, Peter had attempted to play his violin for the last time: "His hand shook more than ever before, and at last refused to work the bow at all." Peter's decision is irrevocable, Cather thus suggests rather obviously, for his "life," his playing of the beloved fiddle, is already over. Hence immediately before pulling the trigger, Peter breaks his violin over his knee and comments: "[Anton] shall not sell thee, my fiddle; I can play thee no more, but they shall not part us. We have seen it all together, and we will forget it together."

Peter himself thus personifies the violin in a speech which makes explicit the symbolic function of that instrument: Peter and his violin are one, both are broken, and the music which they have made together is now over. The style of "Peter" is, of course, rather heavy-handed by Cather's later standards, but in this first story Cather not only anticipates the suicide of Mr. Shimerda in *My Ántonia* but also deals symbolically for the first time with a motif which appears in many of her other stories: the plight of the sensitive immigrant in an environment which does not yet value beauty and creativity.

Mildred Bennett calls "Eric Hermannson's Soul," which appeared in *Cosmopolitan* magazine for April 1900, Cather's "first important story." As the title indicates, this narrative is concerned with Eric Hermannson, "the wildest lad on all the Divide," his "conversion" during a prayer meeting, and his reaction some two years later to the visit to the Divide of beautiful Margaret Elliot. Cather divides the story into three sections, the first dealing with Eric's conversion during a prayer meeting led by Asa Skinner, a "converted train gambler" who is now "servant of God and Free Gospeller." Asa feels that "the Lord had this night a special work for him to do" and directs his "impassioned pleading" to handsome Eric. Section one is at once a remarkable transcription of a frontier revival meeting and an introduction to the central symbol in the story, Eric's violin.

Like the violin of Peter Sadelack, Eric's instrument represents his love of beauty and the importance of music to this passionate, young immigrant who has tried to capture some joy in life in spite of the barrenness of life on the Nebraska plains. The symbolic function of Eric's violin is fully explicated in this first section of the story; Cather again leaves little to the imagination and even less to suggestion. "In the great world beauty comes to men in many guises, and art in a hundred forms, but for Eric there was only his violin. It stood, to him, for all the manifestations of art; it was his only bridge into the kingdom of the soul."

For Asa Skinner and the Free Gospellers, however, the violin is clearly an abomination to the Lord and the symbol of Eric's sinful ways; again Cather explains rather than suggests: "Tonight Eric Hermannson ... sat in [the] audience with a fiddle on his knee, just as he had dropped in on his way to play for some dance. The violin is an object of particular abhorrence to the Free Gospellers. Their antagonism to the church organ is bitter enough, but the fiddle they regard as a very incarnation of evil desires, singing forever of worldly pleasures and inseparably associated with all forbidden things."

By the end of section one, however, Cather succeeds in suggesting through these established symbols much more than is merely said. In the final sentence of this section Eric Hermannson is "saved" as he symbolically destroys what has been for him "his only bridge into the kingdom of the soul": "He took his violin by the neck and crushed it to splinters across his knee, and to Asa Skinner the sound was like the shackles of sin broken audibly asunder." Thus Cather suggests through the symbolism of the broken violin and the final simile in this sentence that the "saving" of Eric Hermannson's soul has in fact been a *losing* of it. The irony is clear: Eric has lost the only thing which helped make life worth while; his "soul" is destroyed at the very moment when Asa Skinner feels that it has been saved. Thus, like the harshness of the Nebraska land and climate itself, the narrow fundamentalist religions of the frontier have further intensified the spiritual and cultural sterility of early life on the plains.

Of all Cather's early stories, perhaps it is in "A Wagner Matinee," one of the seven stories in *The Troll Garden* (1905), that Cather most dramatically explores the plight of the sensitive and artistic person who finds himself in a restrictive if not oppressive environment. In the first paragraphs Clark, the narrator, awaits the arrival of his Aunt Georgiana, a woman whose early life as a music teacher in Boston had been drastically changed by her elopement with Howard Carpenter and their subsequent life on the Nebraska frontier. After their marriage, the Carpenters had homesteaded, "built a dugout in the red hillside," and struggled for some thirty years in their effort to survive; during that time, Georgiana "had not been further than fifty miles from the homestead." But now she is coming to Boston to attend to the settling of a small estate left her by a bachelor relative, and Clark dreads seeing "what was left of my kinswoman." Her "misshappened figure" and stooped bearing are, it would seem, outward symbols of what Clark refers to as her "martyrdom." He observes that his aunt appears to be in a "semisomnambulant state" and wonders if his plan to take her to the Wagner matinee was ill conceived: "I began to think it would have been best to get her back to Red Willow County without waking her."

But they make their way to the first balcony, and as the orchestra plays the *Tannhauser* overture, "Aunt Georgiana clutched my coat sleeve. Then it was I first realized that for her this broke a silence of thirty years; the inconceivable silence of the plains." As the program proceeds, Cather skillfully juxtaposes Aunt Georgiana's imaginative return to the world of the arts and Clark's return to the prairie on which he has been reared. Clark reminisces: "... I saw again the tall, naked house on the prairie, black and grim as a wooden fortress; the black pond where I had learned to swim, its margin pitted with sundried cattle tracks; their rain-gullied clay banks about the naked house...." The repeated words are "naked" and "black," adjectives which summarize Clark's attitude toward the Nebraska of his youth.

The ultimate questions which this story ask are ones which, no doubt, emerged from Cather's knowledge of life on the plains of Nebraska: what does the frontier do to the innately sensitive, artistic personality? Is it possible for such a person to survive in the nakedness of such an environment? Clark finds his answer: "Soon after the tenor began in 'Prize Song,' I heard a quick drawn breath and turned to my aunt. Her eyes were closed, but the tears were glistening on her cheeks, and I think, in a moment more, they were in my eyes as well. It never really died, then—the soul that can suffer so excruciatingly and so interminably; it withers to the outward eye only; like that strange moss which can lie on a dusty shelf half a century and yet, if placed in water, grows green again."

As the concert comes to a close, Cather uses an image derived from the plains to suggest Aunt Georgiana's inevitable return to Red Willow County: "the men of the orchestra went out one by one, leaving the stage to the chairs and music stands, empty as a winter cornfield." Georgiana's cry expresses her emotion: "'I don't want to go, Clark, I don't want to go!'" The story closes with Clark's perceptive observation: "I understood. For her, just outside the door of the concert hall, lay the black pond with the cattle-tracked bluffs; the tall, unpainted house, with weather-curled boards; naked as a tower, the crookbacked ash seedlings where the dishcloths hung to dry; the gaunt, molting turkeys picking up refuse about the kitchen door." Aunt Georgiana must return to all this—and to her martyrdom. Thus in the last paragraph of the story, Cather uses setting as symbol in order to convey the sterility and bleakness of the scene. The unforgettable picture of the "unpainted house," the "black pond," the "crookbacked ash seedlings," and finally the "gaunt, molting turkeys picking up refuse about the kitchen door," suggest powerfully the toll which life in Nebraska has taken upon the innately sensitive, artistic person who finds himself there.

Thus Cather's later reputation may well have been based in part on her ability to gain more perspective about the Nebraska of her youth, but in many of her early short stories, and especially in "Peter," in "Eric Hermannson's Soul" and in "A Wagner Matinee," Nebraska is portrayed as a cultural desert, a setting antagonistic to the inherent artistic needs of the human spirit.

Source: Bruce P. Baker, "Nebraska's Cultural Desert: Willa Cather's Early Short Stories," in *Midamerica*, Vol. 14, 1987, pp. 12–17.

Curtis Bradford

In the following excerpt, Bradford argues that Cather carefully controlled which of her early stories appeared in later collections, including "A Wagner Matinee" but excluding others, suggesting that she was attempting to "contrive and set before us a picture both prettier and simpler than the actuality."

Between 1896 and 1930 Miss Cather published some twenty-five short stories in magazines of national circulation. Most of these were never included in the three collections of her shorter fiction made during her lifetime, and testamentary restrictions prevent reprinting them. In addition, four stories included in *The Troll Garden* (1905) were dropped from subsequent collections. When this extensive and widely scattered body of work is read and fitted into the sequence of the canonical works, certain new insights into Miss Cather's development as a writer emerge.

Miss Cather's undergraduate stories began appearing in 1892; her posthumous stories appeared in 1948. The material is so extensive and appeared over so long a time that some sort of classification of it is necessary. Her work, both collected and uncollected, for the most part falls into three main groups: stories of pioneers, of artists, and of her particular type of passionate woman. The order among these groups is the order of Miss Cather's developing interests. She wrote about pioneers before she wrote about artists, and about artists before she turned to lost ladies. The arrangement of the groups is unclimactic because the most interesting material comes first, and not all the stories Miss Cather wrote fit into these groups. But the problem is to shed such light as we can on Miss Cather's development as a writer, and a study of these materials in the order of her developing interests seems to do this best. . . .

Miss Edith Lewis has written that Willa Cather believed that every writer should have the right of supervision over his own published work. The world would not, I think, agree, but there can be no doubt that Miss Cather exercised this right extensively and is in fact still exercising it through a series of unprecedented testamentary restrictions. The uncollected stories we have been discussing are not to be reprinted so long as they remain in copyright. We cannot be certain why Miss Cather rejected from her accepted canon so much mature work that she had once been glad to have printed under her name, but no serious student of her art can avoid speculating about the problem.

One's first assumption would be that Miss Cather rejected so much of her short fiction from her collected work on aesthetic grounds alone, including the good stories and excluding the poorer ones. I believe this assumption untenable. While it is true that no stories as good as her best—as good as "Paul's Case" or "Old Mrs. Harris"—have been rejected, there is both competent and interesting fiction among the rejects. Certainly stories such as "The Bohemian Girl" and "Behind the Singer Tower" represent a serious handling at length of material that was at one time more important to Miss Cather than that handled in slight works such as "A Wagner Matinée" or "Scandal," each hardly more than a sketch. No doubt accident was on occasion responsible for the omission of a story from the canon. The two Pittsburgh stories published in the twenties—"Uncle Valentine" and "Double Birthday"—would not have fitted very well into *Obscure Destinies* (1932) either in tone or subject matter. They may have been put aside for that reason.

A more tenable assumption is that Miss Cather exercised the control over her work which she challenged for the writer to shape its total impact, to form the final impression which she wished it to leave. For instance, if one judged from the canonical work alone, one would assume that Miss Cather was primarily an affirmer of America's pioneer past and a critic of the later America which has replaced it. A reading of the total body of her work will not sustain such an assumption. For twenty years, from 1892 to 1912, she had little good to say of Nebraska. Only two stories, "The Sculptor's Funeral" and "A Wagner Matinée," remain in the canon from the large body of critical work written during those years. This gives the erroneous impression that what had really been a prevailing attitude was more or less incidental. There can be no doubt that the later exploitation of these materials was the more successful, and Miss Cather seems in time to have assumed that her attitude had always been what it eventually came to be.

A perusal of the rejected works shows, too, that Miss Cather explored nearly every mode of popular fiction practiced during the long years of her apprenticeship. This hesitation between the "kitsch" and serious forms of fiction can hardly be paralleled in the careers of other good writers. Up at least through *The Song of the Lark*, artistic success seems to have been for her a form of worldly success, a way of making money and thereby gaining respect in banks and the better hotels, but especially in Red Cloud, Nebraska. *My Ántonia* marks the first emergence of a richer concept of success. There is a pleasant irony involved in the fact that Miss Cather became a popular writer when she quit trying to be one, when she no longer consciously tried to adapt her work to public taste.

There is a good deal of evidence to indicate that Miss Cather regretted nearly all her early work. Twenty-one of the twenty-three rejected stories appeared before the publication of *My Ántonia.* The Library Edition of her works begins with *O Pioneers!* rather than *Alexander's Bridge. The Song of the Lark* was provided with a rather apologetic preface which reminds one of the "Preface" to the 1922 edition of *Alexander's Bridge*. A comparison of texts will show that in this same edition she "unfurnished" the last two sections of *The Song of the Lark* quite ruthlessly, changing early Cather into late Cather much in the manner that Yeats operated on his early poems. We noted earlier that a retrospective writer will be a long time getting under way. Once Miss Cather had fully achieved her characteristic nostalgic tone in *My Ántonia*, she seemed to wish to forget—perhaps even to conceal in so far as she could—the many experimental ventures that were stations on the way to it.

It must be admitted that Miss Cather's manipulation of her work, her attempt to establish a canon, has its unattractive side. Her early life, like her early work, was the subject of a good deal of manipulation—her birth date moved forward three years; the events of the decade spent in Pittsburgh were upgraded a good deal. These manipulations are disappointing to us for rather obscure reasons having to do with our ideal impressions of the artist who should have existed behind such candid books as *My Ántonia* and *Death Comes for the Archbishop*. Granted that of necessity Miss Cather had to reject the mass of journalistic writing she had done up to the time she left *McClure's*, which bulks much larger than her total serious work and which is only very indirectly related to it, there is in her treatment of her short fiction further evidence of an effort to contrive and set before us a picture both prettier and simpler than the actuality. And, more important, a picture much less interesting than the actuality.

Source: Curtis Bradford, "Willa Cather's Uncollected Short Stories," in *American Literature*, Vol. 26, No. 4, January 1955, pp. 537–51.

SOURCES

Arnold, Marilyn, "Two of the Lost," in *Willa Cather*, edited by Harold Bloom, Chelsea House Publishers, 1985, pp. 177–83.

Bennett, Mildred R., Introduction to *Willa Cather's Collected Short Fiction, 1892–1912*, edited by Virginia Faulkner, University of Nebraska Press, 1965, pp. xiii–xli.

"Biography of Richard Wagner," Web site of the Kennedy Center, http://www.kennedy-center.org,

Cather, Willa, "A Wagner Matinee," in *The Troll Garden*, edited by James Woodress, University of Nebraska Press, 1983, pp. 94–101.

———, "A Wagner Matinee," in *Everybody's Magazine*, Vol. 10, March 1904, pp. 325–28, http://libtextcenter.unl.edu/cather/writings/cat.ss011.php (accessed June 19, 2008).

Daiches, David, "The Short Stories," in *Willa Cather: A Critical Introduction*, Cornell University Press, 1951, pp. 141–74.

Gerber, Philip. "Cather's Shorter Fiction, 1892–1948," in *Willa Cather*, rev. ed., Twayne Publishers, 1995, pp. 75–87.

Rosowski, Susan J., "*The Troll Garden* and the Dangers of Art," in *The Voyage Perilous: Willa Cather's Romanticism*, University of Nebraska Press, 1986, pp. 19–31.

Theodore Roosevelt Association Web site, http://theodoreroosevelt.org (accessed on May 8, 2008).

Woodress, James, "Willa Cather," in *Dictionary of Literary Biography*, Vol. 9, *American Novelists, 1910–1945*, edited by James J. Martine, Gale Research, 1981, pp. 140–54.

———, Introduction to *The Troll Garden*, by Willa Cather, edited by James Woodress, University of Nebraska Press, 1983, pp. xi–xxx.

FURTHER READING

Giannone, Richard, *Music in Willa Cather's Fiction*, University of Nebraska Press, 1968.

Giannone explores Cather's intense interest in and extensive knowledge about music and the theater and discusses the way these factors informed Cather's fiction.

Hine, Robert V., and John Mack Faragher, *Frontiers: A Short History of the American West*, Yale University Press, 2007.

The authors explore the impacts of events such as the Gold Rush, the purchase of Alaska, and the U.S.-Mexican War on the cultural and socioeconomic development of the American western frontier.

Luebke, Frederick C., *Nebraska: An Illustrated History*, Bison Books, 2005.

Historian Luebke offers an overview, illuminated by photographs, of the early frontier history of Nebraska, its settlement, and its development.

Magee, Bryan, *Aspects of Wagner*, Oxford University Press, 1988.

This highly acclaimed book provides an analysis of the music of Richard Wagner. Magee treats some of the controversial aspects of Wagner's life but focuses more intently on the form, structure, and influence of Wagner's music.

Meltzer, Milton, *Willa Cather: A Biography*, Twenty-First Century Books, 2008.

Acclaimed biographer Meltzer provides a detailed biography of Cather that is geared toward students. Meltzer explores the ways in which Cather's childhood and adolescence on the Nebraskan frontier informed her fiction throughout her lifetime.

The Writer in the Family

E. L. DOCTOROW

1984

In "The Writer in the Family," E. L. Doctorow condenses a narrative that resonates with the amplitude of a full-scale novel of family conflict and individual growth into a short story of less than fifteen pages. With a concision whose effectiveness comes from the author's inside-out knowledge of the personalities and family dynamics he is dramatizing, Doctorow not only tells a story of longstanding family animosity and its resolution but also presents the coming-of-age story of a young writer who learns the meaning of art by learning the meaning of self-assertion and artistic integrity. As the opening tale in a collection of six stories and a novella bound in a volume called, after the novella, *Lives of the Poets*, "The Writer in the Family" is ostensibly the first of six stories written by the narrator and subject of the novella, Jonathan; in the novella, he is a man of fifty, a New York Jewish writer, while in the first story, he is of high-school age. Thus, "The Writer in the Family" is presented not only as a freestanding short story but also as an example of the work of a fictional writer of fiction whose story Doctorow presents directly in the novella and variously and indirectly in the six short stories that precede it. *Lives of the Poets* was published by Random House in 1984. A 1997 reprint is available from Plume.

E. L. Doctorow (AP Images)

AUTHOR BIOGRAPHY

Edgar Lawrence Doctorow, the son of well-educated second-generation Russian-Jewish parents—his father was a musicologist, his mother a pianist—was born Edgar Lawrence Doctorow on January 6, 1931, in New York City, in the Bronx. He attended the Bronx High School of Science, where he concentrated more on the arts. After graduating from Kenyon College in 1952, Doctorow did graduate work at Columbia University. Drafted into the U.S. Army, he was stationed in Germany. In 1954, during his time in the army, Doctorow married Helen Setzer. The couple has three children. After being discharged from the army, Doctorow began his career as an editor reading scripts at Columbia Pictures in 1955. He did not continue a career in the movie industry but became a senior editor at New American Library in 1959. In 1964 he moved to the Dial Press, where he became editor in chief.

Although Doctorow wrote his first novel, *Welcome to Hard Times*, in 1960, he first achieved success and recognition in 1971 with *The Book of Daniel*. A fictionalized account of the life and trial of Julius and Ethel Rosenberg, who were electrocuted by the U.S. government in 1953 on the charge of having passed atomic secrets to the Soviet Union, the novel is ostensibly written by their son. "The Writer in the Family," which first appeared in 1984 in *Lives of the Poets*, is an anomaly in Doctorow's body of work since he usually writes novels rather than short connected stories, as he did in that book. As in much of his work, the political subtext in the novel reflects Doctorow's concern with matters of social and economic justice and civil liberties. These concerns are expressed not only in his fiction but also in a collection of essays, *Jack London, Hemingway, and the Constitution: Selected Essays, 1977–1992*, and in his active opposition to the Vietnam War, the invasion of Iraq, and violations of the U.S. Constitution and international accords like the Geneva Conventions, which were attempted or accomplished by the government of George W. Bush.

Doctorow has received the National Book Award, two National Book Critics Circle Awards, the PEN/Faulkner Award, the Edith Wharton Citation for Fiction, the William Dean Howell Medal of the American Academy of Arts and Letters, and the National Humanities Medal. Several of his books, including *Ragtime*, *Billy Bathgate*, and *The Book of Daniel*, have been made into movies. Doctorow has taught at Yale, Princeton, Sarah Lawrence College, the University of California, and New York University.

PLOT SUMMARY

Section 1

The year is 1955. The narrator of the story is Jonathan. His father, Jack, has just died, preceding Jack's ninety-year-old mother, who is living in a nursing home. Afraid of the effect the news of her son's death will have on the old woman's precarious health, her daughters (Jonathan's aunts) tell her that he has moved to Arizona for his bronchitis. Jack was throughout his life financially unsuccessful. His purported retirement to Arizona makes his mother think that he has finally achieved financial success.

Because it is assumed that Jack has taken his entire family with him to Arizona, none of the family can visit his mother. This does not bother Jonathan, his brother, Harold, or his mother, Ruth. The boys never enjoyed their visits, and their mother never liked Jack's mother or any of Jack's family. That the sisters did not consult

MEDIA ADAPTATIONS

- An audio cassette recording of "The Writer in the Family" and "The Leatherman," read by author Doctorow, is available through American Audio Prose Library (1990).

Ruth about their story gave her one more piece of evidence of their sense of superiority and their contempt.

The lie Jack's sisters tell their mother does not give closure to the situation. After a few weeks, Jonathan's grandmother begins to wonder why her retired son does not write to her from Arizona. Frances, the wealthier aunt, who lives in affluent Larchmont and is married to a lawyer, and both of whose sons go to the prestigious Amherst College, telephones Jonathan and requests that he write a letter, pretending to be his own father in Arizona, and send it to her so that she can read it to Jack's mother.

As Jonathan begins to compose the letter, he recalls his father, remembering, first, his failure to rise from the working class to the professional class. He also recalls the pleasure his father took, as he traveled through New York City on his rounds as an appliance salesman, in going to the old part of the city, below Canal Street, to pick up exotic cheeses, spices, vegetables, teas, and nautical devices like barometers or "an antique ship's telescope in a wooden case with a brass snap." The letter Jonathan then writes captures his father's voice and spirit, the voice and spirit his worldly failure may have tended to obscure. Jonathan writes about his father's sense of well-being and of the beauty of Arizona, capturing the serenity and vigor of the landscape. His aunt calls to tell him how touching the letter was and how strongly it made her feel a sense of loss regarding his father.

Section 2

Jack's death has left his family in straitened economic circumstances. Jack had borrowed money against his insurance policy, so there is little left when he dies. His firm is withholding some commissions it still owes him, and Jonathan's mother is unable to withdraw any of the few thousand dollars from their savings account before the estate is settled. The lawyer handling the estate is Aunt Frances's husband, whose dedication to following legal niceties is stronger than his concern for Jack's family's welfare. Jonathan's mother takes a job in the admissions office of the hospital where her husband died.

As they are clearing out their cramped apartment, Jonathan tries on the jacket of one of his father's suits. It is too big for him, and he feels an uncomfortable sense of his father's presence. His brother simply refuses to try on any of his father's clothing.

Section 3

Aunt Frances calls after a few weeks and tells Ruth that she wants Jonathan to write another letter from Jack to his grandmother, especially since the old woman is depressed after having bruised herself in a fall. Frances's presumption annoys Ruth. She complains that even her husband's death is controlled by his family; she says that knowing her son is dead will not kill his mother.

Though uncomfortable doing it, Jonathan writes another letter. His brother, Harold, who switched from day classes at college to night school when their father became ill in order to help support the family, tells Jonathan, "You don't have to do something just because someone wants you to." In the letter, Jonathan tells his grandmother that Jack dresses casually and has opened an electric appliance shop. When Frances calls again, she tells Jonathan that he is very talented and advises him to continue to write more about the electrical appliance shop. Jonathan says that he would rather not continue, as to write the letters is dishonest, and Frances becomes annoyed. She tells him to tell his mother "not to worry," that his grandmother only wishes the best for his mother and that she will die soon anyway. Jonathan does not report the conversation to his mother. He does feel torn, being in the center of a family conflict; he feels like his father, unable to take a side. Jonathan recalls an ongoing family argument, once it became clear that Jack was a failure in business, concerning who was responsible for that failure. Jack's family blamed his wife, Ruth.

In the spring, Jonathan, Harold, and Ruth go to the cemetery to visit Jack's grave. Jonathan notes that his father does not seem to be "honorably dead" or "properly buried" because his grave is missing a headstone. Although one had been chosen and paid for, the stonecutters had gone on strike. Ruth remembers how Jack's family thought they were better than other people, better even than Jack, who, according to Ruth, was good only to get things for them at wholesale prices. As Ruth cries and complains, Harold wanders away to look at tombstones. Jonathan joins him and tells him their mother is crying. Harold tells him that that is what she came to the cemetery to do. When Jonathan says that he feels like crying, too, Harold puts his arm around him and, noting the way carving monuments has changed, points out that everything changes.

Section 4

Jonathan has troubling dreams. He is taking his father home from the hospital after his death, but he is alive. Jack is unwieldy, impatient with everyone, and angry. They have trouble getting him home: the car changes shape; it will not start; Jack's bandages get stuck in the spokes of his wheelchair; his clothes are too big and get stuck in the door; a suitcase will not stay closed. Jonathan feels guilty because his father senses in the dream that his family does not want to live with him. When Jonathan wakes with a scream, he does not tell his brother about the dream, saying he forgot what it was. His dreaming becomes so disturbing that he tries not to fall asleep. He tries to remember the good things about his father, the bounce in his walk, his eagerness to see what was ahead of him.

Section 5

Frances calls again to ask Jonathan to write a letter on the same evening that Harold brings Susan, a girl he has begun to see, home for dinner. The family is in good spirits. Jonathan fools around, setting the table as if he were a high-class waiter. His mother likes Susan. Just as they are toasting, Frances calls requesting another letter. Jonathan tells his mother the call was from a school friend checking on the pages for their math homework.

Section 6

Harold notes that there is really no need for the elaborate letter charade. Their grandmother is nearly entirely blind and half deaf. Frances could write the letters herself or ask one of her own sons to. Jonathan asks, then, why Frances has asked him to write the letters; Harold reminds Jonathan that Frances and her sister used Jack to do them favors continually, with no consideration for him. They wanted to be served. Jonathan responds that "it was a matter of pride" for his father "to be able to do things for them," and Harold wonders why that was. Jonathan realizes that the question about what gratification can be gained in serving Frances applies to him.

Section 7

When Jonathan gets home from school one afternoon, he sees his aunt's impressive Buick in front of his house. He notes that he had always liked his aunt and that she had always seemed to like him, as well as that she is quite pretty. She refuses to go into his house when he invites her, instead telling him to get into the car. Upset by the last letter he wrote, she tells him that it was cruel and that he has been poisoned by his mother's bitter feelings. She proceeds to say that Ruth ruined Jack's life with her constant demands for material things and that he sacrificed himself for her because he loved her. Frances then exculpates herself, saying that she does not like speaking ill of others and that she would invite him and his mother and brother to her house for the Passover holiday if she thought Ruth would accept the invitation. She gives Jonathan back the letter and tells him that she hopes he will think about what he has done by writing the letter.

Section 8

Jonathan watches his mother that evening, noticing that she is not as pretty as his aunt. She is heavy, and her hair is plain. She asks him why he is looking at her, and he says he is not. She says she learned that they may be eligible for a small pension because of the time Jack spent in the navy. This comes as a surprise to Jonathan. They search through Jack's closet to discover a document proving his service and a picture of him as a young man aboard a ship with other sailors. Jonathan puts the picture by his bedside and connects it to the series of books about the sea that his father had given him and to the nautical instruments his father collected. Jonathan regrets that he had never seen his father for the person he really was or "understood while he was alive what my father's dream for his life had been." Yet Jonathan takes some comfort in the last letter, the one his aunt returned without reading to his grandmother, which he wrote before knowing of his father's dream of the sea. In it, Jonathan, as his father, states that it will be his last letter because the doctors say he is dying. He tells his mother he has sold his store and is sending her a check for five thousand dollars. He says that the desert was not the place for him and that he is "simply dying of the wrong life." He says that his body will be cremated and the ashes "scattered in the ocean."

CHARACTERS

Essie

See Grandma

Frances

Jack's sister Frances, who asks her nephew Jonathan to write letters to Jack's mother in his name after his death in order to conceal the death from the old woman, is a complex person. She is wealthy and appears to be condescending and even exploitative in her relations with Jonathan and his mother. Yet the reader does not have enough background information to judge whether her impatience with Ruth is warranted or not. She seems to enjoy being in control of situations. According to Harold, she is accustomed to telling others what to do and to being obeyed. She apparently used Jack when he was alive, but she felt it was Ruth's fault that he did not achieve what she considered to be his potential. When she becomes angry, characteristically, she becomes self-righteous and insinuates character faults to those who do not behave as she wishes. She exercises self-control when angry as well as control over others. She sits in her Buick holding on tightly to the wheel as she reproaches Jonathan. She remains in the driver's seat and pictures herself, as she pictures her mother, as the victim of other people's pettiness.

Grandma

Essie, called Grandma throughout the story, is Jack's ninety-year-old mother, now living in a nursing home. Although she is often the center of each character's attention, she never appears in the story in person. According to Ruth, Jack's widow, Grandma was a tyrannical mother who kept her son tied to her apron strings all her life and did everything she could to thwart Ruth's wishes. According to Frances, she is a kind woman who never wished her daughter-in-law ill. Jonathan's aunts believe that the news of Jack's death would be fatal to his mother. In the nursing home, she boasts of her son's belated good fortune, and it seems she wants letters from him in order to show them to the other women. Since Grandma is never shown, it is impossible for the reader to resolve the ambiguities of her character, which might just accurately reflect her complexity as a person and the ambiguities of her motives.

Harold

Harold is Jonathan's older brother. He is a solid, responsible, and serious young man. When his father became sick, he switched to night school so that he could work in a record shop during the day. He comforts Jonathan at the cemetery and gives him character advice, as when he tells him he does not have to do something just because someone tells him to. He considers the complexity of situations, as when he wonders why Frances needs to set up the elaborate charade of the letters. He treats his mother with regard but without sentimentality, as when he lets her cry at the cemetery. He is confident and outgoing. He has a lovely girlfriend who is fond of him. He is comfortable in his own skin and does not like to have others encroach on him, as is shown when he will not try on his dead father's clothing.

Jack

Jack, Ruth's husband and the father of Jonathan and Harold, is dead when the story begins. He had been an appliance salesman who never achieved real success or financial security in business. According to his wife, he was ever tied to his mother's apron strings. According to his sister, he was hobbled by a demanding wife. According to his son Harold, he was used by his sisters and his mother. According to Jonathan, he did not live the life he ought to have lived. Jack had once been in the navy and had an abiding love for the sea that showed itself in his collection of novels about sailing and the sea and in his scattered purchases of antique nautical instruments and exotic foods. From Jonathan's description he was also a friendly, lively, generous, and outgoing person.

Jonathan

Jonathan is the narrator of the story, a high school student who writes letters to his grandmother as if they are written by his deceased father, at the request of his aunt, who wants to keep the news of Jack's death from her. In the course of writing the letters, Jonathan comes to have a better understanding of his father and of his own would-be vocation as a writer. He is polite and tries to satisfy his aunt. He feels guilty about usurping his father's identity for his aunt's sake, but he is thoughtful and overcomes his difficulties because of a good sense of human empathy that reveals itself in his letters. Jonathan is imaginative and actually does get a sense of the lost side of his father's life, causing the reader to feel that he expresses an aspect of his father that his father would have but could not. Jonathan is actually haunted by his father in his dreams, in which his father gets entangled with him and Jonathan cannot free himself. His sense of guilt at his desire to be free of his father seems to be displaced onto the deceased man in his dreams when his father feels he is not wanted. Jonathan finally frees himself from his father by entering into his consciousness in the letters and by symbolically allowing him to die in his last letter.

Ruth

Ruth is Jack's widow and the mother of Jonathan and Harold. According to Frances, she hobbled Jack and held him back from becoming a success with her nagging, demanding disposition. Ruth resents Jack's family, blaming his mother for his lack of success because she hampered his independence. She complains that his family do not even allow him to be dead when he is dead. Ruth is resourceful and responsible. When the family is in financial difficulty after Jack's death, she takes a job in the admissions office of the hospital where he died. Rather than avoiding the past and its grief, she stoically confronts it. But she is not entirely stoical. At the cemetery she weeps at Jack's grave; the reader may feel that she weeps as much for the loss that was present in her relationship with her husband as for his death. She mourns her own lost life. She is troubled by Jack's sisters' deception, and old animosity between her and them and Jack's mother is once again brought to life because of that deception. At times Jonathan avoids telling her about his aunt's phone calls in order not to disturb her.

Susan

Susan is the girl Harold brings home to dinner. She is thin, has straight hair, and is impressed by the number of books in his house. Ruth thinks that she is "adorable." She serves the function of showing that Harold is a young man who has a healthy life in the world.

THEMES

Integrity

In the course of writing the letters to his grandmother that are supposed to be from his father, Jonathan develops a sense of his own integrity as a person and as a writer, and he achieves insight into his father as a man who failed to realize his integrity. Moreover, by asserting his own integrity, Jonathan confers integrity upon his father. In the final letter he writes, the one his aunt will not accept, he presents a picture of the true man, the self his father had buried deep inside. By doing so, Jonathan symbolically confers upon his father the life his father had never achieved. Jonathan understands that his father was not a failure but a man who led "the wrong life." By having his fictional father say that, Jonathan redeems his actual father.

With the help of his brother, Jonathan comes to understand that he does not have to do something to please others, especially if it violates his integrity as a person and, in his case, as a writer. In consequence, he writes the last letter not to please his aunt or to win her praise but to honor his father's memory by extricating himself and his deceased father from his aunt's schemes, as well as extricating himself from the need to serve others by compromising his own values. In the process, he actually penetrates his father's reality, realizing in his imagination his father's never-realized dream of being a seaman. Jonathan's last letter, though a pretense, presents the fundamental truth of his father's life.

Family Conflict

The long-standing conflict between Ruth and her husband's family, rather than being laid to rest with Jack's death, is actually reconstituted when Jack's sisters decide, without consulting Ruth, to withhold the news of his death from his aged and infirm mother. For Ruth, their behavior is one more manifestation of their contempt both for her and for Jack. She is bitter over the way they exploited him when he was alive, demanding favors of him and disdaining her. She resents the hold Jack's mother had on

TOPICS FOR FURTHER STUDY

- The revelation that his father had been in the navy makes Jonathan view him differently from how he had seen him during his father's lifetime. Recall something you learned about a family member or friend that caused you to see her or him in a new light. Write an essay describing the person as you knew him or her before the revelation and after. How did the new information affect your regard for, understanding of, or relationship with that person?
- Jonathan and his family live in the Bronx, a borough of New York City, while his Aunt Frances lives in Larchmont, a rural suburb of the city. Compose a series of letters between two high school students, one living in the city and the other in the suburbs, in which they describe their lives, their schools, their homes, their pastimes, their wishes, and their regrets. Focus on how the two different environments affect the two students' outlooks.
- In "The Writer in the Family," Jonathan is faced with a problem of divided loyalties, caught in the middle of a conflict between his mother and his aunt. In a story or expository essay, describe a situation in which you faced a similar problem. Who were the people involved? What was the conflict? How were you drawn into it? What pressures were put on you? How did you handle the situation? How did the episode affect you?
- Jonathan seems to be ambivalent about the task of letter writing that Frances imposes on him. In part he seems to write the letters under a sense of obligation, but he also seems to be engaged in the task and to enjoy the praise his first efforts earn. Interview perhaps half a dozen people, including friends and relatives of varying ages, asking about what motivates them to act—a sense of obligation to others or an internal drive, or perhaps a combination of both. Compile the responses in a report, analyze them, and outline your conclusions in an oral presentation to the class.
- Although what he is doing is ostensibly done to spare his grandmother pain, Jonathan feels that writing the letters is dishonest, and it is. In an essay of a thousand words, consider the morality of "little white lies." Think of works of fiction or drama in which such fibs play a significant role in the development of the plot, and incorporate references to these works into your essay.

him and her influence; Ruth complains that Jack's mother, Essie, kept her son tied to her apron strings and continually thwarted any of Ruth's wishes. Ruth's perceptions are confirmed by her older son, Harold. On the other hand, Frances, Jack's wealthy and self-satisfied sister, rather than being able to understand Ruth's point of view, describes Ruth as a bitter person who begrudges her mother-in-law a little pleasure. Frances puts Jonathan in the middle of the family conflict when she commandeers him into writing the letters purportedly from his father in Arizona to his grandmother.

The Nature of Fiction

Aunt Frances tells Jonathan that when she read his first letter to his grandmother, supposedly from his father, "the full effect of Jack's death came over her" and she wept. She was so greatly moved because Jonathan's letter gave her a sense of Jack. Thus, Jonathan's rendition of Jack has the power to represent Jack more thoroughly than Frances's memory of the actual Jack. Fiction is not merely false representation but a means of approaching what is essential—a way of conveying the depths of reality. Through his acts of literary ventriloquism, Jonathan does not make

Elderly woman watching TV (© Pinto / zefa / Corbis)

his father into a puppet or dummy but reveals his truest, deepest self. He also elicits the truth about Frances, who demonstrates that she uses people for her own ends and expects them to cooperate. In the last letter, Jonathan not only frees himself from his aunt's demands but also asserts his father's independence. He accomplishes this through the act of writing fiction after he discovers that the fiction about his father can be a means of expressing truth, especially unwanted truth, rather than a vehicle for promulgating socially constructed lies that may be deemed useful or convenient by some. The writer, Jonathan discovers, can be a champion of truth and a rebel against the established order that thwarts human actuality.

STYLE

First-person Narrator

Jonathan, the central character in "The Writer in the Family," also tells the story. This technique allows Doctorow to relay the story from Jonathan's point of view and give the reader a sense of closeness and connection to Jonathan. His personality is not only depicted in the story but also demonstrated through his manner of telling the story and presenting himself to other characters and the reader.

Characterization through Physicality

A sense of character is often created in "The Writer in the Family" through a gesture a character makes or a rendering of a characteristic pose. Frances sits behind the wheel of her parked Buick looking straight ahead, with her white gloved hands on the steering wheel, as if she were keeping her eye on the road while driving. She is actually talking to Jonathan, but she uses the same affect that she might have if she were negotiating traffic. The physicality of the interaction shows that she is the one who is in control, in the driver's seat. Elsewhere, the happy family excitement that arises when Harold brings Susan to dinner is conveyed by Jonathan's comical assumption of the role of a high-class waiter as he sets the table. His mother's miming the words "She's adorable" conveys as much about her character as the words convey her feeling at the moment. The way Harold puts his arm around Jonathan during the visit to the cemetery shows him to be a warm and reliable person, supportive but not intrusive.

Symbolic Imagery

Doctorow wrote in *The Book of Daniel*, "Images are what things mean." In "The Writer in the Family," through quick images of his characters, Doctorow elicits their attitudes and characteristics. In his first letter, Jonathan, as his father, describes "peculiar crooked trees that look like men holding their arms out." Without having to give any psychological analysis of his father, Jonathan allows the idea of tormented longing to attach itself to the reader's idea of his father, a man whose dreams were thwarted and whose life was narrowed. When speaking of his father's grave, Jonathan mentions that it has no headstone because the stonecutters were on strike. The missing headstone suggests an incomplete death, as Jonathan himself suggests, and it reinforces the central conceit of the story, Jack's sisters' efforts to conceal and thus deny his death, as well as its antithesis, Jonathan's ability to accomplish his father's death and to free himself from the shadow of his father's failures. The image of Jonathan trying on his father's suit suggests a presence of his father from which he has not freed himself. In his final letter, Jonathan gives the word "desert" resonance as an image. He uses the word, ostensibly, to refer to Arizona, the desert his sisters have consigned him to, but the word takes on much more encompassing meaning. The desert is the place without water; it signifies the quality of Jack's life. The actual desert of Arizona reflects, as an image, the barren desert of Jack's mis-lived life, and it suggests the absence of the sea that Jack endured by not being a sailor.

HISTORICAL CONTEXT

Upward Mobility

After defeating Fascist Germany in 1945, the United States entered a period defined by economic growth and increasing chances for working-class people to rise from blue-collar factory jobs to white-collar professional jobs. With the new upward mobility, there was also a massive exodus from cities to suburbs. The idea of "keeping up with the Joneses"—showing that one had as much wealth as one's neighbors, if not more—became an important mark of success. This led to the social habit of conspicuous consumption, buying expensive things in order to show anyone paying attention just how successful one had become. In "The Writer in the Family," Jack did not succeed in moving up to the professional class, and that was cause for condescension on the part of his family. Similarly, Jack and his family continued to live in the Bronx, unlike his sister Frances, whose husband is a lawyer and has a house in Larchmont, a wealthy suburb located on the shore of the Long Island Sound.

The Nuclear Family

The co-residence of the nuclear family, a household comprising mother, father, and children, was the norm in the 1950s. The independent functioning of the nuclear family replaced what has commonly been called the extended family, comprising the nuclear family plus a mixture of grandparents, aunts, uncles, cousins, or adult siblings, living under the same roof and sharing the same economic circumstances. This had been a common living arrangement before the 1950s. The breakdown of the extended family caused social division among family members who were no longer interdependent. Increases in the number of households composed only of the nuclear family were often associated with the placement of older or infirm members of the family in nursing homes.

The Death of Russ Columbo

Russ Columbo (1908–1934) was an American crooner of the twenties and thirties, famous particularly for writing and performing the pop song "Prisoner of Love." When Columbo died in 1934 in a gun accident, Doctorow was three years old. Columbo's sixty-eight-year-old mother, Julia, was in the hospital with a serious heart condition at the time of her son's death. Her doctors, worried about the potential effect of the news of her son's death on her, kept the news from her. Her family, in turn, told her that Columbo had flown to New York and was married there to the actress Carole Lombard. Telegrams from New York, signed by Colombo and Lombard, were sent to Columbo's mother, and she was told they were flying to England. She was then told that Colombo would remain in Europe and tour extensively. From time to time

COMPARE & CONTRAST

- **1950s:** New York City, especially Lower Manhattan, looks rather the way it has looked for over a century, a city of old buildings and narrow streets. Wealthy families are leaving the city for the openness and prestige of the suburbs.

  1980s: Fueled by the neglect of social services by the administration of President Ronald Reagan and the boom in corporate wealth, New York is a city with sharp class divisions in which numerous homeless people live, beg, and sleep on its streets. Old buildings are being demolished, the bank of the Hudson River is being transformed into landfill on the Lower West Side, and office towers and luxury apartment buildings are going up.

  Today: New York City has been radically altered by the demolition of old buildings, the redesign of streets and waterfronts, and the construction of new skyscrapers and luxury residences. Affluent families are resettling in the city, including boroughs like Harlem. The number of homeless people living on the street has been greatly reduced.

- **1950s:** Women generally do not work once they are married. Like Jonathan's mother, they often seek employment in secondary positions only when desperate family circumstances compel them to.

  1980s: Feminism has brought women into the workforce in large numbers, and women can be seen doing many jobs that were once exclusively done by males.

  Today: Women constitute a significant portion of the modern American workforce. Some hold high executive positions.

- **1950s:** Letter writing is the primary way for people to communicate over long distances. Long-distance telephone calls are expensive and require operator assistance. In emergencies, people use telegrams.

  1980s: While people still write letters and postcards, telephones have become the favored means of communication. Businesses use fax machines.

  Today: The Internet has enabled instantaneous communication among people using a variety of media, including text, pictures, voice, and video. E-mail has essentially replaced letter writing, and the mobile phone has come to dominate interpersonal communications via voice, text message, and mobile e-mail.

Julia received letters, and even money, supposedly from her son. Newspaper articles about his death, as well as about Lombard's later marriage to the movie actor Clark Gable, were kept from her. This pretense went on for ten years, until Julia Columbo's death. It is likely that Doctorow, whose acquaintance with pop culture is extensive, was aware of this story.

CRITICAL OVERVIEW

Being a short story by a writer whose reputation rests on his recognition as one of the major novelists of the latter part of the twentieth century, "The Writer in the Family" has not been given the critical attention that Doctorow's major works have been afforded. Nevertheless, the critical attention it has received has extended it the same regard that works like *The Book of Daniel* and *Ragtime* have enjoyed. Christopher Lehmann-Haupt, reviewing *Lives of the Poets: Six Stories and a Novella*—the work that includes "The Writer in the Family"—in the *New York Times* in November 1984, calls it "a thoroughly charming but somewhat conventional piece." Benjamin Demott, writing in the *New York Times* a few days later, calls the entire work Doctorow's "subtlest work of fiction," noting that it offers "an account of one man's search for seriousness—and for human connection and truth." Demott sees "The Writer in the Family" as a story of how a boy "awakens to the self-centeredness and disloyalty of" subordinating his gift as a writer to his aunt's demands, thus "showing the writer in the family to be not a technician but a truth-teller, a scribe directing his imagination to the service of reality and thereby recovering integrity and pride."

The importance of "The Writer in the Family" to the novella *Lives of the Poets* and of the novella to the story is emphasized by Carol C. Harter and James R. Thompson, who remark in *E. L. Doctorow* that "what appears to be a collection of only vaguely related pieces may be read as a spatially constructed novel of sorts." They cite as an example the instance in the novella when on Jonathan's fiftieth birthday his mother "admits that she was at least partially responsible for his father's unfulfilled life," altering the reader's perception of her. In the opening story she appears as the victim of her husband's sisters' apparently unjust criticism, but perhaps the criticism is actually, or partially, warranted.

Stephen Matterson, in his 1993 *Critique: Studies in Contemporary Fiction* essay "Why Not Say What Happened? E. L. Doctorow's *Lives of the Poets*," argues that the story "establishes within the book, a set of fundamental questions and observations about writing and the role of the writer." Noting "his refusal to use writing for deceit," Matterson concludes that "Jonathan actually comes to a truthful image of his father by writing the letters through the fiction that he makes up," such that "he uncovers two kinds of truth about his father, the factual and the psychological."

CRITICISM

Neil Heims

Heims is the author of over two dozen books on literature and literary figures. In the following essay, Heims discusses "The Writer in the Family" as a work showing how the writer of the story became a writer.

In "The Writer in the Family," E. L. Doctorow has fashioned a narrative account of a youth's transformation into a man and a writer that not only tells of his metamorphosis but also graphically demonstrates its success. "The Writer in the Family" is a story of a rite of passage and itself stands as an outgrowth and example of its narrator and central character Jonathan's successful accomplishment of that passage.

"IF ONE CONSIDERS JONATHAN AS THE AUTHOR OF THE STORY, THEN THE STORY ITSELF IS THE PROOF OF THE SUCCESS OF THE PROCESS IT DESCRIBES."

Focusing on a series of external events, Doctorow presents the moment of a boy's psychological metamorphosis. It is a significant moment in the fundamental development of Jonathan's understanding, in the formulation of his integrity, and in the definition of his character. Jonathan is not only the main character in "The Writer in the Family" but also, inside the fictional world of *Lives of the Poets*, the author of the story. Consequently, because the story is a representative piece of Jonathan's work, in addition to being a tale recounting an episode in the narrator's youth, it is a story about how the narrator came to be an author—the author of the very story the reader is reading. Jonathan is faced, in the telling of the story, with an implicit and essential task. He must show convincingly that the outer circumstances of the story he tells, the events to which he was forced to respond, contributed not only to the development of his consciousness as a person but to his understanding of what a writer is and to the development of his craft as a writer. If one considers Jonathan as the author of the story, then the story itself is the proof of the success of the process it describes.

Jonathan's growth as a writer and his transformation from a boy living in the shadow of his dead father into a man who by reimagining his father releases himself from him—and at the same time releases his father from his father's own false life—are the results of the intersection of events in the world and of his own developing response to those events. His maturation is a function not only of how he comes to terms with his place in the world, as that place has been defined by his role in his family, but also of how he develops the ability to redefine his place in the world and not accept others' definitions, whether his aunt's or his father's, of what he is, where he belongs, and what he does. When

WHAT DO I READ NEXT?

- In Paul Goodman's story "The Home-made Sweater," originally published in 1949 and available in the 1979 collection *The Facts of Life: Stories, 1940–1949*, Goodman presents the psychology of the realization that occurs when a seven-year-old girl intuits that the objects in the world are actually made by people and are not mysteriously preexisting things.
- In "On Being a Son: A Story of the Fifties," by George Dennison, published in *New American Review*, Vol. 8, in 1969, Dennison transports his hero from within the context of the bohemian milieu of 1950s Greenwich Village to his hometown in Pennsylvania and explores the family conflicts that haunt him and how he comes to terms with his conflicting feelings about his mother.
- "The Locking Gas-Cap," by Meyer Liben, published in *Justice Hunger* in 1957, explores the neurotic relationship a man has with his fiancée, who has a neurotic attachment to her mother and her dead father, through an anecdote concerning the car they own together.
- Grace Paley's "Goodbye and Good Luck," originally published in 1959 and reprinted in *The Little Disturbances of Man* in 1968, tells the story of a spinster who relates her life history as the mistress of a great actor in the Yiddish theater to the daughter of her condescending sister on the day that she finally marries the actor. As in Doctorow's story, Paley uses a first-person narrator who draws on past experience to show how her present condition has evolved.
- In "Uncle Wiggly in Connecticut," by J. D. Salinger, originally published in 1948 and reprinted in *Nine Stories* in 1966, two women who were friends in college spend an afternoon together getting drunk and remembering their past. The family tensions that are explicit in Doctorow's story are implicit in Salinger's, as revealed in the conversation between the two women.
- In *The Vanishing Adolescent*, by Edgar Z. Friedenberg, published in 1959, the author presents a study of adolescent development focusing on self-definition, conflict, and the establishment of self-esteem in boys.

his aunt Frances calls him "the writer in the family," the reader may cringe a bit, feeling the force of condescension in her words. She seems to be patronizing Jonathan, drawing on his power and on his resources for her own sake. She is using him. She does not consider the character of a writer as something beholden to itself but reduces writing to a servile act, a clever ability to dissemble and create illusions. Frances turns writing into a technical skill and is oblivious to the craft as a sacred calling. Consequently, she indifferently diminishes Jonathan's authenticity and authority as a writer, which depends upon his sense of duty and loyalty to the truth as he perceives and understands it. Similarly, being enthralled by his father's failure lessens Jonathan's sense of himself and of the integrity of his vocation. The dramatic action of the story is found in the way Jonathan transcends his father's hold upon him as well as his aunt's condescension, which also had his father and mother as its object. In the process he also escapes his aunt's usurpation of his talent and identity and becomes truly a writer. He forcefully dedicates himself to his own vision of truth and avoids becoming his aunt's factotum.

"The Writer in the Family," is, consequently, not only a story about the events that Jonathan relates, although they are its manifest content. It is as much a story about how those events affected him then and how they determined what he and his work are like now, at the time he is telling the story, as an adult writer of published work. As an example of his work, the story is an exhibit in his defense against his aunt's criticism of him for asserting his vision over her wishes in his last letter from his father to his grandmother.

In order to demonstrate how he was affected by the events he is narrating, Jonathan must present those events to the reader in such a way that the reader experiences them as he did. By making Jonathan the narrator of his own story, rather than using a limited and removed third-person narrator, Doctorow demonstrates Jonathan's power as a writer, his achievements as a writer and as a son, and his sensitivity as a person. Indeed, the narrative is effective as a story of enlightenment. Making Jonathan the narrator of his own experience also shows the importance of that experience for him: his skill as a storyteller, his decorum as a narrator, and the control of his material demonstrate his accomplishment. As such, they validate the importance of his having written the letter that Frances deplored. That letter was his declaration of independence as a son, as a nephew, and as a writer—his liberation from dependency and his first step in the direction of the authority it takes a writer to be an actual author. What Aunt Frances piously tells him to do when she returns his letter, to think about "what you've done," is really what the reader must do, and in so doing the reader will see that to be a writer is to find the truth of the other, as young Jonathan found the truth of his father. Because of that early discovery, which made him into a writer, the readers of the story can sense that the truths of the other characters—Frances, his mother, his brother—have also been found by the older Jonathan now telling the story.

Jonathan found the truth of his father in the very act of attempting to become his father imaginatively and fictitiously through writing letters in his name. Before discovering that truth, he was dwarfed and disturbed by unburied remnants of his father. Symbolically, his discomfort and his sense of being less than his father are represented by his feeling uneasy when he tries on his father's too-large suit jacket. Moreover, Jonathan begins, after he has begun to write the letters in his father's voice, to be haunted by his father. He dreams of him, with his dreams so fraught with disturbance that they keep him awake. Since he is sensitized in this way, the picture of his seafaring father that is discovered toward the end of the story—a photograph that reveals a truth about his father of which he had been ignorant—penetrates his understanding. This photo, a frozen representation of his father as a young man, thaws out in his consciousness and replaces the phantom figure of a disturbing ghost with a warm figure whose secret meanings he becomes empowered to express the way his father never had been free to. He meets his father, and in the process, he meets himself—that is, he participates in the process of creating, of fathering, himself by giving his father his true life.

The living characters in "The Writer in the Family" are revealed as full human beings glimpsed as they are displaying particular aspects of their character. Doctorow endows Jonathan with the skill to elicit people who are both types and individuals. The portraits Jonathan draws catch and present his characters in their essence. The depiction of Aunt Frances sitting in her Buick, for example—at which time, though the car is parked, she keeps her hands on the steering wheel and looks straight ahead as she reprimands Jonathan for what she calls the cruelty of his letter—shows the woman that she is: a woman who has taken her place in the driver's seat. She reflects the social proprieties that she has identified with and that Jonathan must reject in order truly to be a writer. Jonathan's description of his mother slamming the telephone and crying out in anger that her husband "can't even die when he wants to" is another quick portrait that reveals something about her that is always with her, a sense of frustration at having to struggle as hard as she does to keep living despite the burdens she has had to bear. There are other quick pictures—Jonathan's brother putting his arm about him at his father's grave, for example. His brother's girlfriend's astonishment at the number of books in their apartment not only quickly shows her to the reader but also gives an impression of the apartment and their culture. The scene shows one of the roots of Jonathan's desire to be a writer.

Often Jonathan renders portraits through what may be called verbal images, in other words, through tonality. The tone of Frances's voice and the nature of her diction on the phone reveal the psychology of her personality. She must command and control. Jonathan's apparently objective, almost photographic representation of her corroborates his mother's subjective dislike of her. The reader can hear Frances when she speaks. In few words, Jonathan presents the cloying sweetness that both conceals and reveals her passive aggressivity. She hardly speaks, yet she is a firm and full presence. Similarly, his mother is revealed as the tired, frustrated, and thwarted yet good-hearted and clear-sighted woman she is with quick strokes, such as with her complaints about Jack's family at the cemetery and her muffled appreciation of Harold's girlfriend, Susan. Similarly, although Jack does not appear in the story, his spirit is conveyed by Jonathan's recollection of how he called him "matey" as well as by the old photograph of him in the navy. Already dead and only a memory, Jack nevertheless appears as a complex person in the story. The photograph of Jack on the deck of a ship toward the end of World War I, a classic image of sailors with their mops, in part reveals his inner life. And the juxtaposition of that photograph with Jonathan's description of his later life gives the reader a sense of the man's deepest longings and disappointments and even a sense of his heroism. He lived a painfully thwarted life as authentically as he could.

Through the accumulation of graphic details, like the way his father called him "matey," the way his aunt sits in the car, the way his mother hangs up the phone, the way he dreams about his father, or the way his brother consoles and advises him, Jonathan not only brings together a narrative of his early life but also shows how the forces around him are fragments that he has assembled into one complete, unified art work. They show a portrait of himself, a portrait of the artist in the process of becoming an artist.

Source: Neil Heims, Critical Essay on "The Writer in the Family," in *Short Stories for Students*, Gale, Cengage Learning, 2009.

Michelle M. Tokarczyk

In the following excerpt, Tokarczyk examines the character of Jonathan in "The Writer in the Family" and the class status of his family.

In many of his essays, Doctorow addresses the situation of contemporary American writers, but he most clearly articulates his view of contemporary fiction and its reception in "The Beliefs of Writers." Here he laments what he sees as a lack of passion in contemporary writing and a related inability of writers to represent politics. In contrasting American writers with Europeans he finds his cohorts, "With certain exceptions . . . less fervent about the social value of art and therefore less vulnerable to crises of conscience" (*Jack London* 106). He further argues that withdrawal from and distrust of society has been prominent in American fiction since Hemingway's *For Whom the Bell Tolls*, and that fiction suffers from a "reduced authority" because it neglects the issues that are critical to contemporary life. Moreover, critics have not developed a way of writing about social and political fiction: "There is no poetics yet devised by American critics that would treat engagement as anything more than an understandable but nevertheless deplorable breakdown of form" (112). Doctorow ends this essay with a charge to writers themselves to write books about, "the way power works in our society, who has it, and how it is making history" (116).

"IN THIS STORY, AS IN SOME OF DOCTOROW'S OTHER WORK, THE FATHER'S STRAINED 'LINKAGE' IS RELATED TO HIS ROLE AS BREADWINNER. THE FATHER'S FINANCIAL IRRESPONSIBILITY PUTS A BARRIER BETWEEN HIMSELF AND HIS SON THAT, THE BOY DISCOVERS, WRITING HELPS DISSOLVE."

Each of Doctorow's novels, I believe, attempts to address this imperative, but in fleshing out the conflicts contemporary writers face and the difficulties of formulating an acceptable aesthetic and praxis, it is instructive to begin by examining his two autobiographical works, *Lives of the Poets: A Novella and Six Stories* and *World's Fair*. In his interview with Larry McCaffery, Doctorow stated that his first attempted novel was autobiographical, but that he quickly realized this type of writing was not his strength ("Spirit" 34). As a middle-aged man, however, he was perhaps better able to return to the subject of his life not as an example of isolated, atomistic experiences, but rather as a "case study" (to use a social science term admittedly too impersonal for Doctorow's fiction) of the writer's place in American society. In both *Lives of the Poets: A Novella and Six Stories* and *World's Fair*, Doctorow grapples with the boundaries between art and practice, between individual and community, that will inform all of his fiction.

Nowhere is the artist's position to his society, the artist's role as witness, more clearly articulated.

Like Doctorow's other fiction, *Lives of the Poets* and *World's Fair* are in many ways specific to time, class, and region. Both works are set in New York City, where Doctorow has spent the majority of his life and with which he strongly identifies. Class mobility is prominent in each work, although in *Lives of the Poets* the protagonist has moved up while in *World's Fair* the family is downwardly mobile. Furthermore, as in much of his fiction, the search for a father-figure to complement or replace an inadequate one is an important theme which is, in each work, resolved through the representation of writing as the ideal parent.

Lives of the Poets is composed of six short stories and a novella that is supposedly about the author of these stories. Hence, while the prose in this book is not generally experimental, especially when compared with *Ragtime* or *Loon Lake*, the book's composition is distinctly self-reflexive, reflecting the postmodernist bent in Doctorow's writing. The stories' subjects are very different, but all feature characters who are outsiders, misunderstood and often thwarted; appropriately Harter and Thompson see dereliction as a motif in this work, for many characters face actual or emotional abandonment (105). Significantly, the collection begins with "The Writer in the Family," which is about a boy whose father has died and whose family is afraid to break this news to the ailing grandmother. Because of his letter-writing skills, young Jonathan is enlisted to write "fictional" letters from his deceased father. The boy makes up adventures for his less-than-successful father of whom the narrator tells us, "In his generation the great journey was from the working class to the professional class. He hadn't managed that either." Eventually, Jonathan learns his father had been in the navy and realizes the man's dreams were to be at sea. Angry at himself for not recognizing his father's dreams earlier, the boy drafts a letter from the father stating he has a fatal disease, should never have traveled to Arizona, and wishes his ashes to be scattered at sea. As a writer, the boy, like many Doctorow characters, bears witness to the emotional rather than the literal truth.

In its focus on a boy estranged from his father, "The Writer in the Family" is typical of Doctorow's work. Ellen G. Friedman has argued that a preoccupation with the father is characteristic of much male fiction that features a missing father and often represents Oedipal conflicts, "The missing father is the link to the past that, for the protagonists, determines identity" (241). While Friedman's formulation cannot be applied to *Ragtime*, in which Father often appears as an outdated buffoon, it is useful in considering most of Doctorow's fiction, including "The Writer in the Family." In this story, as in some of Doctorow's other work, the father's strained "linkage" is related to his role as breadwinner. The father's financial irresponsibility puts a barrier between himself and his son that, the boy discovers, writing helps dissolve. As Doctorow says in discussing this story, writing leads Jonathan to the truth about his father's desires and causes for his failures (Morris "Fiction" 448). Presumably, this story is an autobiographical piece by the writer Jonathan in *Lives of the Poets* and might shed some light on him.

"Willi" also focuses on childhood experiences, but they are recalled by an old man years later (a technique repeatedly employed by Doctorow). The eastern European narrator remembers his mother's repeated infidelities for which his father beat and finally murdered her. There is a tension in the text between the child's romantic vision, "I imagined the earth's soul lifting to the warmth of the sun and mingling me in some divine embrace" and the harsh realities of his life, a tension reminiscent of the polarities associated with American romance but present in other fictional forms as well. Furthermore, there is an irony in the story being set in the early twentieth century, for at the end the narrator points out, "This was in Galicia in the year 1910. All of it was to be destroyed anyway, even without me." Like so much of Doctorow's work, "Willi" suggests the impossibility of isolating private tragedy from political turmoil.

While most of Doctorow's fiction is about males and often about male themes (such as searching for a father figure), as Harter and Thompson point out "The Hunter" is unusual in that it is written from a woman's point of view (107). The female voice and experience of becoming interested in a man who sees her only as a sex object are gender specific, but her loneliness and alienation are common to many of the male characters in this book....

It is easy to see the outlines of Doctorow's life in Jonathan's New York suburban lifestyle, in his age and profession, and in the writers described who resemble some of Doctorow's colleagues, such as Norman Mailer. However, it is also easy to see why Doctorow would disavow claims that the narrator is actually based on himself, for the lives described here represent some of the problems contemporary writers face as well as Jonathan's shortcomings (McInerney 152–55). In a sense *Lives of the Poets* is not Doctorow's or even Jonathan's life; rather it is the collective life of contemporary successful male authors. Samuel Johnson's *Lives of the Poets*, in contrast, focused on individual lives. Interestingly, scholars have pointed out that the critical judgments in Johnson's biographies obviously bear the stamp of his neoclassical time (Hardy vii–xv). Hence, the allusion to Johnson's work suggests that the writer is constructed by his time and his literary cohorts.

Lives of the Poets might be read as a model, or perhaps a parody, of the diminished fiction against which Doctorow has cautioned. Private angst certainly dominates Jonathan's life. As the novella begins he complains of minor physical ailments that characterize middle age. Additionally, he focuses on his own and his colleagues' marital difficulties and his need for isolation. At the core of many problems is a conflict between a need for autonomy and a need for solidarity with other people—not just for companionship but for a sense of shared human purpose. Marital problems become symbolic of the conflict between the need for bonding with another person and the need for freedom and isolation; Jonathan describes the many marriages between couples not divorced but not entirely together (such as himself and his wife) as wavering between two "archetypes," touching on both but committing to neither. These problems also represent Jonathan's doubts about his self-worth as a man, doubts that might stem from his relationship with and opinion of his father. When his wife Angel goes into a tirade against male perfidy, Jonathan reinforces her views. His willingness to condemn males partially reflects an insecurity rooted in his relationship with his own father. Again, it is useful to consider "The Writer in the Family" as a story reflecting the childhood experiences of its fictitious writer with his own father as well as those of Doctorow himself. (For one, the father in "Writer," reportedly loved the city—a trait Jonathan in *Lives* and Doctorow share.) As the Jonathan of the novella remembers his father, he recalls, "How I loved him. The man who disappointed millions. Make promises, fail to keep them." Clearly, Jonathan tries to distance himself from his father, for he reflects on both his success and his financial responsibility. Moreover, he points out that he is a "true Capricorn," an earth sign implying a stable character as opposed to the father who loved the sea in "The Writer in the Family." In a sense, Jonathan has achieved the American Dream constructed as a child economically surpassing his parents. Yet achieving or even striving for this dream can have many dark sides. In their study *The Hidden Injuries of Class* sociologists Richard Sennett and Jonathan Cobb analyze the often-hidden costs of the assumption that in the United States everyone who works hard can be at least middle class. One of the more detrimental effects of this ideology upon working-class families is parents' tendency to in effect tell their children not be like them and for working-class children to see their parents as failures. Hence, the child may be encouraged to "desert [his/her past] . . . leave it and the parents who have sacrificed for it behind" (131). But those who alienate themselves from their parents and their pasts are likely to feel guilty. So it is not surprising that Jonathan sees his financial responsibility as atonement for success. Most likely, other actions are also penances.

For one, Jonathan's isolation is self-inflicted. New York City functions as a metaphor for this isolation and as an ironic preserver of it. According to some social critics and historians, a common theme among writers and historians from the nineteenth century until today has been the sense of estrangement urban inhabitants feel—estrangement from their surroundings, themselves, and from people of other classes (Vidler 11). The urban landscape itself and the particularly dense population of New York City can foster a sense of anonymity and isolation. For this reason among others, cities have in postmodern novels often been represented as labyrinths where memory is cut off from experience (Lehan 240–45). While Jonathan is perhaps better at connecting memory and experience than are the characters in *White Noise* or *The Crying of Lot 49*, he is no more able to learn from experience. In addition, he is unable to connect with other people in any meaningful way. Throughout the novella there are images of the body as fort; while riding the subway he sees his skin as a border. He condemns people who talk too much, thereby violating their own privacy. These images suggest that the city functions both to isolate and to insulate. Jonathan's neighborhood, Greenwich Village, is a former bohemian haunt. Yet in the 1980s much of the housing is affordable only to the affluent. Hence, Jonathan, like most New Yorkers, lives in close proximity to the poor, but otherwise removed from their lives. In stating that most of his acquaintances eventually switched from riding the subways to taking taxis, he is referring to the class mobility among his peers and to their growing reluctance to mingle with other classes.

While there are economic and psychological roots of Jonathan's isolation, there are also important ones in his being a writer. Writers require isolation; to write novels they must, in most cases, work alone for several hours a day. Moreover, the writer is often working on something of dubious value; in interviews with me and with Christopher Morris, Doctorow talked of how the author is often filled with doubts about the value of his work, of how difficult it is to determine the worth of literary labor as compared with other kinds of labor (Tokarczyk 36–37; Morris 455). Such anxieties are likely related to the increasing commodification in American society—especially in the 1980s when some artists in all fields became stars and visual artists in particular sometimes had six-figure annual incomes. It is perhaps these concerns taken together that prompt Jonathan to refer to writing as "like a sentence—it's a prison image. It's an exclusionary image as far as I'm concerned." The exclusion here refers both to non-writers being excluded and to the author being excluded from everyday society. As Fred Pfeil stated, the writer's engagement with others seems "indirect, incomplete, filtered through this premeditated skein of words, a process by which what I do now, writing the words, loses the name of action" (25). Like *Ragtime's* Houdini, the author here laments not being [able] to create, a "real world act"; fiction, despite the substantial power Doctorow assigns it, does not have the immediacy of many forms of communication. Moreover, in the act of writing fiction the sources of the fiction are lost or mutated; hence, in a desperate tone Jonathan tells a friend "each book has taken me further and further out so that the occasion itself is extenuated, no more than a weak signal from the home station, and even that may be fading." Jonathan is not only isolated and alienated from others, but to an extent from his own work, which may explain his inconsolable nature.

But Jonathan's problems are the problems of contemporary American writers and to some extent other intellectuals; as was discussed earlier, the book is titled for "poets," all writers, not Jonathan as an individual. As such, the book questions not only how writers should respond to their own dilemmas, but also how they should address the social and political realities in society. John Williams argues that often Doctorow's characters are escapees from a social power structure who try to assert writing as resistance to life-denying forces in culture (11–12). This is certainly the role into which the Jonathan of "The Writer in the Family" falls, and, as we will see, one which Edgar of *World's Fair* discovers. But it is not one into which Jonathan has found entrée. He has not yet been able to finish his work *Lives of the Poets*, perhaps because he has not found the kind of fiction he wants to write, a fiction similar to that endorsed by Doctorow in "The Beliefs of Writers."

Because he has not found a way to address his own problems or those of his society, he adapts a stance similar to that of a modern cynic as conceptualized by Peter Sloterdijk. According to Sloterdijk, contemporary culture is marked by a universal, pervasive cynicism. "Modern cynicism presents itself as that state of consciousness that follows after naïve ideologies and their enlightenment." In other words, cynicism results from the exhaustion of seemingly failed ideologies and social institutions. This pervasive modern figure has its roots in ancient culture in which the cynic, typified in Diogenes, is "a lone owl" and "an urban figure who maintains his cutting edge in the goings on of the ancient metropolises." In the modern world the city becomes a fertile breeding ground for cynics, for in this anonymous setting cynics can perform their daily duties, apparently effectively blending into society, while having little faith in this society. This performance aspect is crucial, for Sloterdijk sees cynics as having enlightened false consciousness. In traditional Marxist ideology, false consciousness described the state of the proletariat identifying with the ruling class and actually believing that it shares in the upper class's benefits. The cynic, in contrast, knows that many social policies and institutions are meaningless, but nonetheless goes through the motions of accepting them. What might appear to be false consciousness is then "a constitution of consciousness afflicted with enlightenment that, having learned from historical experience, refuses cheap optimism." Indeed, according to Sloterdijk one of the hallmarks of cynics is their ability to work and be successful, even though they are often borderline melancholics. The distinction between cynicism and skepticism, I would argue, is the degree to which one accepts enlightened false consciousness.

In many respects Jonathan fits Sloterdijk's profile. He is an urban figure on the periphery of society; he might also be seen as a melancholic nonetheless able to control symptoms and work, if with reduced efficiency. Jonathan withdraws from his society in what Sloterdijk describes as "mournful detachment." His sense of existential absurdity is to him something to be ashamed of, so it is repressed and internalized and consequently useless for taking preemptive action. Possibly he perceives himself as being more marginal to society than he actually is. Having shown some fascinations with derelicts—those without home or work who live on the edge, he reflects "between the artist and simple dereliction there is a very fine line." Furthermore, he believes that dereliction is a state of mind common to middle-aged men, but not women. We might speculate that to the extent this perception rings true it does because, as theorists such as Carol Gilligan, Nancy Chodorow, and Mary Belenkey have in various ways shown, women tend to value connection over individuation, while men have contrary priorities. Hence, intimacy and connectedness are often threatening to men; they may avoid these states and thus become isolated.

Although Jonathan is relatively isolated in his society, he is far from apathetic. In particular he laments the plight of refugees and the actions of the U.S. government that made the refugees' lands unlivable. Furthermore, he refers to the U.S. president embracing sociopathic murderers, and at this point contemplates whether he has become "estranged" from his calling. Such estrangement is presumably what prompts him to offer his home as sanctuary to illegal aliens, an act a local minister calls "bearing witness"—a term Doctorow might use to describe the writer's art.

Despite his fears of commitment, he decides to take the leap of becoming a political activist and returning to live with his wife. In typing with the alien boy, relying on the child to reach his quota of pages, he is resolving his father-son issues by realizing that his battle with his own father is over and it is time for him to be a father figure. Rather than wish for a son to surpass him economically, he will "adopt" an "orphan" and try to give that boy a new life.

In discussing American literature, Katherine Newman argues that its governing theme is not the American Dream, but rather the selection of a cultural model that will satisfy spiritual and emotional needs. Novels are often about choices of assimilation, accommodation, and successful rebellion. Despite concern about the legal ramifications of his actions, Jonathan, who had the guise of an assimilationist, chooses to rebel against his society, and despite his ideals of writerly detachment, Jonathan gets involved; he changes from cynic to activist.

In theorizing Jonathan's action, it is useful to consider Frank Lentricchia's *Criticism and Society* in which the author argues that society is unreasonable, most critics recognize this is so, and it is the intellectual's task to go about transforming society. To do so, one must keep in mind a fact that might seem like a commonplace [one], but nonetheless has powerful implications: that the ruling culture does not define all culture; it excludes marginalized voices that the oppositional critic must work to amplify. In teaching the young boy to write, Jonathan is enabling him to someday voice his own concerns. In his essay "Foucault's Legacy," Lentricchia speculates that the central if unacknowledged desire for historicism is to find a space of freedom in which people are not forced to become what they do not wish to become. Drawing on Raymond Williams's notion that determinism is a complex and interrelated process of limits and pressures in the social process, we might see the pressures for commitment conflicting with those for isolation, the fact that Jonathan, for his weaknesses, is not emotionally crippled, and understand his willingness to commit on various levels. We might also utilize Barbara Eckstein's concept of complicity. She explains that in the *OED* complicity is related both to "complicate" and "accomplice," and that its roots ("com" and "plic") mean to "fold together." In contemporary definitions "complicity" means both "being an accomplice" and "[the] state of being complex and involved." Hence, "If evil befalls the other, the self is not simply guilty, to blame, but rather complicit in a network of personal, social, political, even aesthetic conditions which perpetuate the stereotypes and which, in turn, rationalize the suffering. The self is an accomplice in this complexity. But in the web of complicity the self also suffers" (32–33). It might be argued that Jonathan becomes acutely aware of his inevitable complicity, and then decides to undermine immoral policies of the country to which he nonetheless owes allegiance and supports with his taxes.

While the previous analyses are appealing, some critics have found the ending of *Lives of the Poets* unconvincing. It is indeed difficult to believe that Jonathan could so quickly commit to his wife and become an activist who takes legal risks. That the ending is strained most likely reflects Doctorow's continued ambivalence concerning the writer and political activism, an ambivalence attributable both to a solitary nature and to a New Critical schooling. The move to activism in this novel is perhaps best seen as an ideal that the writer is still struggling to envision a way to achieve. . . .

Source: Michelle M. Tokarczyk, "Praxis, Identity, and the American Writer: *Lives of the Poet* and *World's Fair*," in *E. L. Doctorow's Skeptical Commitment*, Peter Lang, 2000, pp. 27–45.

Stephen Matterson

In the following excerpt, Matterson argues that "The Writer in the Family" sets up a central concern in the collection Lives of the Poets*—that fiction, although by definition not true, can nonetheless reveal important truths.*

Lives of the Poets, E. L. Doctorow's seventh work, first published in 1984, occupies a unique space in his writings. Its most obvious difference from the other work is announced in its subtitle, *A Novella and Six Stories*, because, apart from the 1979 play, *Drinks Before Dinner*, Doctorow's previous work had been in the novel form. A case could be made for considering *Lives of the Poets* almost an aberration within the Doctorow canon. Among its diverse themes and settings the collection becomes an exploration of the nature of writing itself and of the relation of writing to the life of its author. Doctorow had never before treated this issue so explicitly, though a debate about the reliability of fiction had often been implicitly present in his work. The style of the book is also markedly different from the other work. Doctorow appears willing to allow his self and voice to emerge more fully than they ever had before. *Lives of the Poets* could also be said to lack something of the ambitious breadth of Doctorow's novels. The multiple plotting and discontinuities that might be considered typical of Doctorow's writing are here apparently disregarded in favor of a series of self-contained stories. Doctorow's typically sustained focus on a particular time period is also absent. Whether writing of the 1870s, the turn of the century, the 1960s or the 1930s, Doctorow had maintained the focus on that time even while diffusing the action. In contrast, the short stories here range broadly in time and setting. However, in spite of the elements that would make *Lives of the Poets* an oddity among Doctorow's works, the book illuminates and adds much to our understanding of the novels. It may remain an aberration, but one that it was essential for Doctorow to write and that is in itself a major achievement.

"FOR ALL OF ITS DARKLY COMIC SITUATION, 'THE WRITER IN THE FAMILY' CONCLUDES SUBTLY WITH A COMPLEX AND DUAL MESSAGE: ALTHOUGH FICTION IS DECEIT, MADE-UP STORIES, IT CAN REVEAL TRUTHS THAT FACTS ALONE CANNOT."

For the reader to appreciate fully the unfolding of its meanings, *Lives of the Poets* must be read in sequence. It would be possible to detach particular stories and consider them complete in themselves, but Doctorow's achievement in the book is an overall one in which the stories are interdependent and contribute to a developing meaning. *Lives of the Poets* works in part through a series of correspondences that are established in the first story and are developed by the others.

These correspondences achieve two effects. First, they establish a series of connections, which, when taken together, make up the theme of the whole book. Second, the correspondences between this book and Doctorow's other writing indicate the seriousness and urgency of the themes and issues it raises. It addresses fundamental questions about the nature and function of the writer, questions that Doctorow is applying to himself and to his already published work. In some respects, chiefly through what it reveals about the writer and the need to write, *Lives of the Poets* could be said to alter our understanding of Doctorow's preceding novels. After reading this work we reconsider some aspects of *Welcome to Hard Times*, *The Book of Daniel*, *Ragtime*, and *Loon Lake*. *Lives of the Poets* is an outstanding example of the supposition that T. S. Eliot made in 1917: "The existing order is complete before the new work arrives; for order to persist after the supervention of novelty, the *whole* existing order must be, if ever so slightly, altered" (5). Indeed, it can be argued that one of the urges driving *Lives of the Poets* is Doctorow's need to re-examine some of the ideas that Eliot originated in that essay....

The situation established in the book's first story, "The Writer in the Family," is important for appreciating this dual series of connections. The narrator, Jonathan, is in his early teens when his father dies, leaving a widow and two sons, Jonathan and his older brother Harold. The father's elderly mother, however, is still living, in a nursing home. Fearing that the shock of her son's death will be too much for the old lady, the narrator's wealthy Aunt Frances persuades Jonathan to write a letter purporting to come from his father, pretending that the family has moved to Arizona. Aunt Frances is delighted with the letter and prevails upon Jonathan to write more. Eventually the deceit disturbs the boy and to end the letters, he writes one that he knows Aunt Frances cannot show her mother.

Because of the dual system of correspondences in *Lives of the Poets*, "The Writer in the Family" is not a self-contained, straightforward story. It establishes within the book, a set of fundamental questions and observations about writing and the role of the writer. It is suggested that Jonathan has to give up the letters because they are dishonest. In anticipation of the novella *"Lives of the Poets,"* young Jonathan is already haunted by Robert Lowell's question from the poem "Epilogue," quoted in the novella: "Yet why not say what happened?" On one level, "The Writer in the Family" is about the boy's almost heroic stand, his refusal to use writing for deceit. Yet the story introduces other, potentially more important, areas. First, in spite of the deceit involved, Jonathan actually comes to a truthful image of his father by writing the letters through the fiction that he makes up. Thus, in the final letter, he invents the father's longing for the sea, and, in so doing, he uncovers two kinds of truth about his father, the factual and the psychological. His father actually was, as Jonathan later discovers, in the navy for a year. Psychologically, the father was restless and unsatisfied, a man for whom living in Arizona would have been a kind of death.

The second significant point about the fictive letters is that they come to have a function far beyond their ostensible one of deceiving the grandmother. Their immediate effect is somehow to keep the father's memory alive, to keep him real and living to the boy (he has a vivid dream that his father is still alive), and to Aunt Frances. The first brief letter has a profound effect on Aunt Frances:

> My aunt called some days later and told me it was when she read this letter aloud to the old lady that the full effect of Jack's death came over her. She had to excuse herself and went out in the parking lot to cry. "I wept so," she said. "I felt such terrible longing for him. You're so right, he loved to go places, he loved life, he loved everything."

The talent of the young writer has given the father a truth, a reality, that keeps him alive for others. Jonathan never really grasps this fact, and Aunt Frances' motives are misunderstood. His brother, Harold, points out that the letters are unnecessary: "Grandma is almost totally blind, she's half deaf and crippled. Does the situation call for a literary composition? Does it need verisimilitude? Would the old lady know the difference if she was read the phone books?" Both the brothers misunderstand Aunt Frances because they fail to realize how much the letters help in dealing with the loss of her brother.

For all of its darkly comic situation, "The Writer in the Family" concludes subtly with a complex and dual message: although fiction is deceit, made-up stories, it can reveal truths that facts alone cannot. Jonathan is as yet too young to grasp this fully; to him the letters are deceptions that he cannot continue. It is significant here to suggest the ways in which this dual approach to fictions pervades Doctorow's other works. "The Writer in the Family" forces the reader to recognize how much of Jonathan's situation has been repeated in the novels. This happens most obviously in *World's Fair*, which followed *Lives of the Poets*; there, Aunt Frances and the family all reappear at much greater length. There are particular changes; for instance, the brother Harold is renamed Donald, and the family situation is amplified from "The Writer in the Family." Edgar in *World's Fair*, who wins a prize in an essay contest, resembles Jonathan in the earlier story. Though absent in "The Writer in the Family," the father is a prominent figure in *World's Fair*, and his longing for the sea is further outlined, appropriately enough, by Aunt Frances herself (240–41)....

Source: Stephen Matterson, "Why Not Say What Happened? E. L. Doctorow's *Lives of the Poets*," in *Critique*, Vol. 34, No. 2, January 1993, pp. 113–25.

SOURCES

DeMott, Benjamin, "Pilgrim among the Culturati," in the *New York Times*, November 11, 1984, Section 7, p. 1.

Doctorow, E. L., *The Book of Daniel*, Random House, 1971, p. 71.

———, "The Writer in the Family," in *Lives of the Poets: Six Stories and a Novella*, Random House, 1984, pp. 3–20.

Fowler, Douglas, "E. L. Doctorow," in *Dictionary of Literary Biography*, Vol. 173: *American Novelists Since World War II, Fifth Series*, Gale Research, 1996, pp. 54–72.

Harter, Carol C., and James R. Thompson, *E. L. Doctorow*, Twayne Publishers, 1990, pp. 100, 103.

Lehmann-Haupt, Christopher, Review of *Lives of the Poets: Six Stories and a Novella*, in the *New York Times*, November 6, 1984.

Matterson, Stephen, "Why Not Say What Happened? E. L. Doctorow's *Lives of the Poets*," in *Critique: Studies in Contemporary Fiction*, Vol. 34, No. 2, Winter 1993, pp. 113–25.

Pierce, Max, "Russ Columbo: Hollywood's Tragic Crooner" in *Classic Images*, Vol. 286, April 1999, http://www.classicimages.com/past_issues/view/?x=1999/april99/columbo.htmlin (accessed August 19, 2008).

FURTHER READING

Doctorow, E. L., *Jack London, Hemingway, and the Constitution: Selected Essays, 1977–1992*, Random House, 1993.

Although predominantly a writer of fiction, Doctorow uses the essay form, such as with those presented here, to discuss literary, cultural, and political issues of concern to him.

———, *World's Fair*, Random House, 1985.

Published a year after Lives of the Poets, World's Fair extends, amplifies, and deepens the situation Doctorow presented in "The Writer in the Family." Jack, for example, is a living character in this work.

Fowler, Douglas, *Understanding E. L. Doctorow*, University of South Carolina Press, 1992.

Fowler examines Doctorow's work, style, themes, and development, starting with Welcome to Hard Times (1960) and going through Billy Bathgate (1989).

Rosenberg, Bernard, and Ernest Goldstein, eds., *Creators and Disturbers: Reminiscences by Jewish Intellectuals of New York*, Columbia University Press, 1982.

In a series of interviews with New York Jewish intellectuals, the editors give a sense of the cultural context of midcentury America in New York City.

Zlateh the Goat

ISAAC BASHEVIS SINGER

1966

The short story "Zlateh the Goat," written by the Yiddish author Isaac Bashevis Singer, was first published in 1966 in *Zlateh the Goat, and Other Stories*. The collection is based on old Jewish folktales and is narrated just as a traditional folktale would be. Unlike many of the other stories in the collection, "Zlateh the Goat" is a realistic story that contains no magical or miraculous elements. At the same time, this story sits squarely within the Singer canon in its Jewish and folkloric overtones, which appear not only in *Zlateh the Goat, and Other Stories* but in virtually all of Singer's work. Indeed, Singer is best known as an author writing in the Jewish American or Yiddish literary tradition. His work is mostly written for adults, though he has written numerous short stories for younger readers.

Zlateh the Goat, and Other Stories was met with popular and critical acclaim, winning a prestigious Newbery Honor in 1967. The story is ostensibly about a young boy who, due to circumstance, must take the beloved family goat to the butcher, but the boy and the goat are lost in a blizzard on their way there. The story, though written for children, has also captivated older readers. A 1984 edition of *Zlateh the Goat, and Other Stories* is still in print.

AUTHOR BIOGRAPHY

Isaac Bashevis Singer was born Icek-Hersz Zynger on, according to some sources, July 14,

Isaac Bashevis Singer (© Getty Images)

1904, in Radzymin, Poland, near Warsaw. Some sources claim that Singer was born on November 21, 1902, in Leoncin, Poland, and that his 1904 birth date was a fabrication meant to help him avoid the draft. Singer's father, Pinchos Menachem, was a rabbi, and his mother, Bathsheba (Zylberman) Singer, was the daughter of a rabbi. Singer had a younger brother and two elder siblings (a sister and a brother), both of whom were also writers. The family often moved around Poland, depending upon Pinchos Menachem's changing positions as a rabbi, and in 1908 they settled in Warsaw, where Singer spent most of his childhood, receiving a traditional Jewish education. The upheaval that came with World War I caused the family to separate, and Singer moved with his mother and younger brother to Bilgoraj (or Bilgoray), his mother's hometown.

By 1921, Singer had returned to Warsaw, entering the Tachkemoni Rabbinical Seminary. He dropped out in 1923, deciding that he was not cut out to be a rabbi. Instead, Singer followed in the footsteps of his elder siblings, even working for his brother as a proofreader for the *Literarische Bleter*. By the age of twenty-three, Singer had published his first short story, was translating German works into Yiddish, and was working as a journalist. His first novel, *Der Sotn in Goray* (later translated as *Satan in Goray*), was published in 1935. That same year, Singer fled the rising Fascism and anti-Semitism in Poland, immigrating to New York City and parting ways with his first wife, Rachel, and their son, Israel, in the process. Singer married his second wife, Alma Haimann, on February 14, 1940. The couple did not have any children. Shortly after their marriage, in 1943, Singer became an American citizen.

Singer's first novel published in English was *The Family Moskat* (1950). Other well-known novels include *The Magician of Lublin* (1960), *The Manor* (1967), and *Shosha* (1978). His first, and most renowned, collection of short stories, *Gimpel the Fool, and Other Stories*, was published in 1957. Other notable short story collections include *The Spinoza of Market Street* (1961), *A Friend of Kafka* (1970), and *The Death of Methuselah* (1988). His 1973 collection titled *A Crown of Feathers, and Other Stories* won the National Book Award for fiction in 1974. Four years later, Singer was awarded the Nobel Prize for Literature.

Singer also wrote several books and collections of short stories for children. *Zlateh the Goat, and Other Stories* (1966), in which "Zlateh the Goat" first appeared, won a 1967 Newbery Honor (awarded to runners-up to the Newbery Medal, one of the most prestigious awards for children's books). In fact, Singer won a Newbery Honor for three years straight, receiving it again in 1968 and 1969 for *The Fearsome Inn* and *When Shlemiel Went to Warsaw, and Other Stories*, respectively. Singer's 1969 autobiography for children, *A Day of Pleasure: Stories of a Boy Growing up in Warsaw*, which was published under the pseudonym Isaac Warshofsky, won the National Book Award for children's literature in 1970.

Singer's prolific writing career was mainly sustained after he immigrated to America, yet he continued to write in Yiddish throughout his life. Only late in his career did he begin to translate his own Yiddish stories, usually with the help of other English translators. Singer died in Surfside, Florida, on July 24, 1991, following a series of strokes. He is buried at Beth-El Cemetery, in Washington Township, New Jersey.

PLOT SUMMARY

Much like a fairy tale, "Zlateh the Goat" takes place at an unknown time in an unknown place, which makes the story seem more universal, existing largely outside of the constraints of history or nationality. The Jewish holiday Hanukkah has almost arrived, but the snow has not begun to fall, and the winter thus far has been an unusually "mild one." Because of this, Reuven's business is not doing well. Reuven lives in the village and is a furrier, which means that he sells, makes, and repairs furs. People do not need furs when the weather is warm, and since the winter has been mild, Reuven is having a "bad year"; he will not be able to afford all of the Hanukkah "holiday necessaries," such as candles, latkes (potato pancakes), and gifts. Because of this, Reuven decides to sell the beloved family goat, Zlateh, to Feivel, a butcher who lives in the town. Zlateh is old and no longer has much milk, so to Reuven, she is worth more dead than alive. The proceeds from selling Zlateh to the butcher will help Reuven pay for the latkes and Hanukkah candles that he cannot yet afford.

Reuven tells his oldest son, Aaron, to take Zlateh to the town butcher. Although Aaron does not want to, he "had to obey his father." The whole family is upset by the thought of losing Zlateh. Aaron's mother, Leah, and his sisters, Anna and Miriam, start to cry when they hear the news. As Aaron prepares to leave with Zlateh, the goat waits for him serenely: "Zlateh trusted human beings. She knew that they always fed her and never did her any harm." Nevertheless, Zlateh is soon "astonished" to be led towards town, although she quickly accepts this turn of events because she "seemed to come to the conclusion that a goat shouldn't ask questions." Aaron and Zlateh gradually make their way toward town, and Aaron chases away a stray dog.

The mild, sunny weather changes without warning as storm clouds roll in and a hail shower begins, which is rather unusual since it is winter and hail tends to fall in the summer. The storm blocks out the sunlight, and the hail turns into snow. Aaron, who is twelve years old, has never seen a storm like this one, and soon the winding road to town is covered in snow so that Aaron cannot tell the difference between the road and the surrounding farmland. Zlateh, who is also twelve years old, accepts the situation at first, but as the snow gets thicker and deeper, "her mild eyes seemed to ask, 'Why are we out in such a storm?'" In the midst of the foul weather, Aaron keeps an eye out for passing carts, but none appear.

Aaron realizes that he is no longer walking on the road and that he has strayed into a pasture. He cannot tell where he is or what direction he is going in, and he knows that he and Zlateh are in danger of freezing to death, lost in the snow. Zlateh, who has gone along with the adventure up until now, "anchored her cleft hooves in the earth and bleated as if pleading to be taken home." Aaron begins to look for a shelter in the storm, which is now a full blizzard. Zlateh's bleats begin to sound like human cries, as "those humans in whom she had so much confidence had dragged her into a trap." Aaron begins to pray for himself and "the innocent animal."

Aaron makes out a strange hill in the distance and wonders what it could be, when he realizes that it is a haystack covered in snow. It occurs to Aaron that he and Zlateh can burrow into the haystack to survive the blizzard: "He was a village boy and knew what to do." The hay in the nest also provides food for Zlateh, who quickly begins to eat and is immediately "contented." Indeed, "Zlateh, having eaten her

MEDIA ADAPTATIONS

- "Zlateh the Goat" was adapted as a short film by the same title by Weston Woods Studios in 1973.
- Part of the Jewish Heritage Video Collection, the short film *Stories from the Jewish Tradition: "In the Month of Kislev" and "Zlateh the Goat"* was released in 1995.
- *Zlateh the Goat, and Other Stories* was adapted as an audiobook of the same title in 1974, produced by Newbery Award Records and narrated by Eli Wallach.

fill . . . seemed to have regained her confidence in man." The snow covers over Aaron and Zlateh's nest, so Aaron pokes a hole in the snow to make sure they can breathe. Then he begins to eat the lunch that he had brought for his journey to town. When he finishes, Aaron is still hungry and notices that Zlateh's udders are full, so he scoots under Zlateh and begins to milk her straight into his mouth. This seems a little odd to Zlateh, but she accepts it, even appearing as if she is "eager to reward Aaron" for finding her a nest made entirely of food.

Aaron and Zlateh settle in to wait out the blizzard. Zlateh eats hay, and Aaron snuggles with Zlateh to keep warm. Aaron "had always loved Zlateh, but now she was like a sister." Aaron even begins to talk to Zlateh, asking her questions. Her response to each question is the same: "Maaaa." Despite the rather limited conversation, Aaron says, "You can't speak, but I know you understand. I need you and you need me. Isn't that right?" Zlateh in turn simply responds as she always does.

Aaron and Zlateh stay in the haystack for three days as the storm rages, with Zlateh surviving on the surrounding hay and Aaron surviving on Zlateh's milk. Aaron's love for Zlateh continues to grow. He tells her stories, and her ears perk up as she listens to him. Zlateh licks Aaron when he pets her and says "Maaaa." This time, Aaron knows that the sound Zlateh makes means "I love you, too."

Over the three days, Aaron imagines that he and Zlateh have no family and no past, that they are instead "born of the snow." It is silent in the haystack buried beneath the snow, and Aaron sleeps, dreaming of summer. On the third night, the snow stops, and Aaron waits for daylight before venturing out and attempting to find his way back to the road. In the meantime, he gazes at the transformed landscape, "dreaming dreams of heavenly splendor."

In the morning, Aaron hears sleigh bells, and he realizes that they cannot be far from the road after all. The peasant in the sleigh points him home toward the village. Aaron will not continue to town to the butcher's, as he "had decided in the haystack that he would never part with Zlateh."

While Aaron and Zlateh were sheltered in the haystack, search parties unsuccessfully attempted to find them. Aaron's family had assumed that Aaron and Zlateh were dead—lost forever in the storm—and they are overjoyed when the boy and the goat miraculously return. When the family hears how Zlateh kept Aaron warm and fed, Aaron's sisters embrace the goat, feeding Zlateh "a special treat of chopped carrots and potato peels." The family will never again try to sell Zlateh, and because of the blizzard, Reuven's furrier business is booming once again. Now, even without selling Zlateh, the family will have enough money for potato pancakes and other Hanukkah sundries. Even Zlateh gets some potato pancakes.

Although Zlateh lives in a pen, she comes to the kitchen door and knocks with her horns. The family lets her in. While Aaron and his sisters play dreidel (a Hanukkah game), Zlateh lays in the kitchen and watches the Hanukkah candles as they burn. As time goes by, Aaron occasionally talks to Zlateh, asking her if she remembers the time they spent in the haystack. Zlateh responds as she always has, "with the single sound which expressed all her thoughts, and all her love."

CHARACTERS

Aaron

Aaron is the twelve-year-old son of Reuven and Leah. His sisters are Anna and Miriam. When Reuven the furrier must sell Zlateh in order to afford the Hanukkah necessities, Reuven instructs Aaron to take the goat to Feivel, the town butcher. Although Aaron does not want to take the goat to be slaughtered, he "had to obey his father." Aaron packs a lunch, wears some warm clothing, and prepares to set off toward town, where he will spend the night before returning the next day with the money from the butcher. On the way to town, Aaron chases away a stray dog.

When the weather suddenly changes from mild and sunny to stormy with hail, Aaron is perplexed. As the impending storm darkens the sky and turns to snow, he becomes worried. The road and the surrounding fields become covered in snow, and it is hard to tell which way he and Zlateh are going. Aaron hopes that a cart will come by, but he and Zlateh are alone, lost in the snowstorm. When Aaron realizes that he and Zlateh have strayed from the road, he begins to fear for their lives. He knows that he and Zlateh may freeze to death in the storm. Aaron begins to pray for himself and for the goat.

Luckily, Aaron finds a haystack covered in snow, and he knows that he and Zlateh can burrow inside of the haystack for shelter and warmth. After making a nest for himself and the goat, Aaron is sure to make a hole for air so that they can breathe while waiting for the storm to end. Aaron eats his lunch, and Zlateh eats the hay, but Aaron is still hungry, so he lays under Zlateh and milks her straight into his mouth. Aaron and Zlateh settle in to wait out the blizzard, and Aaron snuggles with Zlateh to keep warm.

Aaron "had always loved Zlateh, but now she was like a sister." Aaron even begins to talk to Zlateh, asking her questions. Her response to each question is the same: "Maaaa." Aaron says to Zlateh: "You can't speak, but I know you understand. I need you and you need me. Isn't that right?"

Aaron and Zlateh stay in the haystack for three days. To pass the time, Aaron tells Zlateh stories, and her ears perk up as she listens to him. Zlateh licks Aaron when he pets her and says "Maaaa." At one point Aaron thinks that the sound Zlateh makes means "I love you, too." Aaron sleeps and dreams of summer, and when he is awake, he imagines that he and Zlateh are pure, without a past or a family—"born of the snow."

When the snow stops and Aaron and Zlateh are able to leave the shelter of the haystack, Aaron leads Zlateh back to the village instead of continuing his journey toward town, to Feivel the butcher. Aaron "had decided in the haystack that he would never part with Zlateh."

Aaron's family is happy to see him and Zlateh, as they had thought he and the goat might have died in the snowstorm. Of course, no one mentions selling Zlateh after Aaron tells how she kept him warm and fed.

It could be argued that Aaron is the protagonist of "Zlateh the Goat"; however, it seems that much more is made of Zlateh and her actions and reactions throughout the narration of the story. Furthermore, the title of the story may indicate that Aaron is not the protagonist.

Anna

Anna is one of Aaron's younger sisters, a daughter of Leah and Reuven. Anna cries when Zlateh is to be taken to the butcher, and she also cries when her brother and the family goat are presumed to have frozen to death in the snowstorm. When Aaron and Zlateh return and Anna hears how Zlateh fed Aaron in the haystack, Anna and her sister, Miriam, kiss and hug the goat. The sisters feed Zlateh "a special treat of chopped carrots and potato peels." During the Hanukkah festivities, Anna plays dreidel with her brother and sister. Anna is only mentioned a few times in the story, and only in concert with her sister. In fact, Anna's character is identical to, and interchangeable with, that of her sister, Miriam.

Feivel

Feivel is the town butcher; he wants to buy and slaughter Zlateh for her meat, which he can then sell. For the goat, Feivel offers Reuven eight gulden, apparently enough money to help Reuven pay for all of the potato pancakes, gifts, candles, and other Hanukkah supplies that his family needs. Reuven agrees to sell the goat to Feivel, but the butcher never receives Zlateh, as she and Aaron are trapped in a snowstorm on the way from their village to the town. Feivel is only mentioned at the beginning of the story, and he is not referred to after Zlateh and Aaron return to the village. No one seems to care whether Feivel is still waiting for the goat.

Leah

Leah is the mother of Aaron and his younger sisters, Anna and Miriam, and the wife of Aaron's father, Reuven the furrier. Leah cries when she hears that Aaron must take Zlateh to the butcher. Leah also cries when her son and the family goat are presumed to have frozen to death in the snowstorm. Leah is only mentioned a few times throughout the entire story, and in those instances she is either crying or cooking. Upon Aaron and Zlateh's safe return, Leah makes potato pancakes every night of the Hanukkah holiday.

Miriam

Miriam is one of Aaron's younger sisters, a daughter of Leah and Reuven. Miriam cries when Zlateh is to be taken to the butcher, and she also cries when her brother and the family goat are presumed to have frozen to death in the snowstorm. When Aaron and Zlateh return and Miriam hears how Zlateh fed Aaron in the haystack, Miriam and her sister, Anna, kiss and hug the goat. The sisters feed Zlateh "a special treat of chopped carrots and potato peels." During the Hanukkah festivities, Miriam plays dreidel with her brother and sister. Miriam is only mentioned a few times in the story, and only in concert with her sister. Miriam's character is identical to, and interchangeable with, that of her sister, Anna.

Neighbors

Aaron's neighbors search for Aaron and Zlateh when they are burrowed in the haystack. The neighbors do not find them, and Aaron and Zlateh are presumed dead.

Peasant

After spending three days burrowed in the haystack, Aaron hears sleigh bells and realizes that he has not wandered far from the road after all. The peasant in the sleigh tells Aaron which direction to take to head home toward the village.

Reuven

Reuven is the father of Aaron and his younger sisters, Anna and Miriam, and the husband of Leah. Reuven is a furrier, someone who makes, sews, and repairs furs. Thus, his livelihood is dependent upon the cold weather, as that is when the other villagers need furs. Because the winter has been a warm one, Reuven's business is not going well, and he will not be able to afford potato pancakes, oil, candles, and gifts for the family for Hanukkah. Because of this, Reuven decides, "after long hesitation," to sell the family goat, Zlateh, to Feivel, the town butcher. Reuven knows that the money from the sale will allow him to pay for the Hanukkah supplies. He tells his eldest son, Aaron, to take Zlateh to the butcher.

Even though Aaron does not want to, he knows he must "obey his father." Even though Reuven's family loves Zlateh, and even though his wife and daughters cry at the thought of losing her, no one dares to challenge Reuven's decision. In a traditional Jewish family like this one, the father is the head of the family, and thus Reuven's decision must be obeyed without question. Zlateh licks Reuven's hand before Aaron begins to lead her toward town.

Although Aaron's mother and sisters cry when they believe that he and Zlateh are dead, Reuven does not cry but instead turns "silent and gloomy." The whole family, including Reuven, is of course happy at the boy and goat's return. No one ever thinks to sell Zlateh again, and Reuven does not insist that his original orders be obeyed, nor does he remark upon the fact that they were not obeyed in the first place. Reuven's furrier business resumes thanks to the very storm that stranded Aaron and Zlateh, and Reuven is able to afford the Hanukkah supplies without selling the family goat. Curiously, this is the last specific mention of Reuven in the story. He is not pictured as taking part in the ensuing Hanukkah festivities.

Zlateh

Zlateh is the beloved family goat who loves and trusts her family in return. Zlateh, like Aaron, is twelve years old. She is blissfully unaware of the family's plans to sell her to the butcher. She stands, "patiently and good-naturedly as ever," as Aaron puts a rope around her neck to lead her to town. She even licks the hands of the man who has sentenced her to her fate, as she "trusted human beings. She knew that they always fed her and never did her any harm." Zlateh is soon "astonished" by the trip toward town, but she later "seemed to come to the conclusion that a goat shouldn't ask questions."

At first, Zlateh accepts the sudden onset of the snowstorm, but as the snow gets deeper "her mild eyes seemed to ask, 'Why are we out in such a storm?'" Eventually she stops moving, and her bleats "sound like crying," as if she is "pleading to be taken home." Aaron prays for himself and for Zlateh, who is described as an "innocent animal."

As soon as Aaron makes the nest in the haystack, Zlateh is immediately "contented," and she begins to nibble on the hay. Then, "Zlateh, having eaten her fill...seemed to have regained her confidence in man." Aaron then milks Zlateh into his mouth, which astonishes the goat, though she quickly accepts it, even appearing as if she is "eager to reward Aaron" for making her a nest made entirely of food.

In the haystack, Aaron speaks to Zlateh, telling her stories and asking her questions, and she responds with "Maaaa," the only response she can give. Aaron says, "You can't speak, but I know you understand. I need you and you need me. Isn't that right?" Zlateh simply responds as she always does. Each time Zlateh bleats, Aaron understands it differently: "Yes, Zlateh's language consisted of only one word, but it meant many things. Now she was saying, 'We must accept all that God gives us—heat, cold, hunger, satisfaction, light, and darkness.'" Later, Zlateh licks Aaron when he pets her and says "Maaaa," and this time Aaron believes that the sound means "I love you."

Over the three days that Zlateh and Aaron shelter in the haystack waiting for the storm to end, Aaron imagines that he and Zlateh have no family and no past, that they are instead "born of the snow." When the storm finally ends, Aaron leads Zlateh back toward the village rather than continue toward town to sell Zlateh to the butcher. He "had decided in the haystack that he would never part with Zlateh."

As Zlateh and Aaron were presumed to have been lost in the storm, their family is overjoyed to see them. When the family hears how Zlateh kept Aaron warm and fed, Aaron's sisters embrace the goat, feeding Zlateh "a special treat of chopped carrots and potato peels." The family never again thinks to sell Zlateh, even letting her into the house whenever she knocks on the kitchen door with her horns. In the house, Zlateh sits by the stove and watches the children play dreidel. As time goes by, Aaron occasionally asks her about the time they spent together in the haystack, and she replies as she always does, "with the single sound which expressed all her thoughts, and all her love."

Although it could be argued that Aaron is the protagonist of "Zlateh the Goat," it seems that much more is made of Zlateh and her actions and reactions throughout the narration of the story. Furthermore, the title of the story may indicate that Zlateh is indeed the protagonist.

TOPICS FOR FURTHER STUDY

- Do you think that Zlateh or Aaron is best labeled the main protagonist of "Zlateh the Goat"? Write an essay explaining your choice, and be sure to cite passages from the story.
- Research Jewish shtetls (towns or villages) in Poland and in the rest of eastern Europe from the late 1800s to the 1930s. What was life generally like in shtetls? How was it similar to or different from the lifestyle described in "Zlateh the Goat"? Give a presentation on your findings.
- Using a Yiddish-English dictionary, translate your favorite passage from "Zlateh the Goat" into Yiddish and read your translation aloud to the class. Discuss how the process of translating and your translation itself changed your interpretation of the story.
- Read one of Singer's short stories written for adults. In an essay, compare and contrast the story you read with "Zlateh the Goat." Do you think that there are significant differences between Singer's stories for children and his stories for adults? Why or why not?

THEMES

Love and Loyalty

Much can be said about love and loyalty in "Zlateh the Goat." Although the family loves Zlateh, they are willing to sell her to the town butcher in order to pay for Hanukkah supplies. The family is not happy to do this, but given the society in which they live, animals are seen as tools for survival, not pets. This does not mean that the family loves Zlateh any less than they would a pet. Perhaps once could argue that they love her more because they depend on her for milk and income. Nevertheless, they do not show any loyalty to her when they decide to sell her to the butcher.

Zlateh clearly loves her family. She licks Reuven's hand as she is being sent to the butcher, and although she seems to question her strange journey, she accepts it because she trusts her family and because she is loyal to them. Although she protests at the thickening snow, she becomes immediately "contented" once Aaron makes them a nest in the haystack. She shows her loyalty when she is "eager to reward" Aaron for finding a shelter. While Aaron and Zlateh are lost in the snow, Aaron prays not only for himself but also for Zlateh, who is described as an "innocent animal." Here, Aaron does show loyalty to Zlateh, as he continues to take care of her even when his own life is in danger.

Zlateh and Aaron depend upon each other through their ordeal, keeping each other warm and fed. Aaron goes from having love for Zlateh

Painting of haystacks in winter (© Peter Harholdt / Corbis)

to loving her as if she were a sister. Aaron talks to Zlateh, and though Zlateh can only respond as a goat, saying "Maaaa," Aaron understands that Zlateh is trying to tell him that she loves him as well. Zlateh "comforted" Aaron in the haystack, and "in these three days he loved her more and more."

By the end of the storm, Aaron's love for Zlateh has grown to such proportions that he returns to the village with her, having decided "that he would never part with Zlateh." Aaron's family, who thought that Aaron and Zlateh had died in the snowstorm, are overjoyed to see them. Because Zlateh saved Aaron from starvation, their love for her also grows, and she achieves the status of a family pet. Now Aaron and his family demonstrate the loyalty that was missing at the beginning of the story. Zlateh has helped Aaron through the storm, and they will forever remain loyal to her for this. From then on, Zlateh is "always admitted" into the house as she pleases, and she lies by the stove watching the children play when she visits. Whenever Aaron asks her about their ordeal, she can only answer as she always does, "with the single sound which expressed all her thoughts, and all her love."

Religion

Religion drives the narration of "Zlateh the Goat," and there are even a few strong but subtle references to God's will in the story. Aaron and his family are Jews, and this fact defines their life and family structure. The reason that Reuven decides to sell Zlateh is so that they will have the money they need for Hanukkah supplies. Because traditional Jewish families, like Aaron's, have a patriarchal structure, no one openly objects to Reuven's decision. Leah, Anna, and Miriam only cry when they hear of what will happen. Aaron knows that he must take Zlateh to the butcher because he must "obey his father"—one of the Old Testament's Ten Commandments, which Jews live by.

Only a few references to God can be found in the story, but they have a strong impact on the narrative. When Aaron and Zlateh are lost in the snow, "Aaron began to pray to God for himself and for the innocent animal." Immediately following his prayer, Aaron sees a shape in the snow.

This shape turns out to be the haystack that will save his and the goat's lives. As Aaron and Zlateh huddle in the hay, the wind outside is described as having "the sound of devilish laughter."

While in the hay, Aaron has what could be described as a religious experience. He becomes "born of the snow," as does Zlateh. On the night when the storm ends, as Aaron waits for morning so that he and Zlateh can return to the village, the world is "all white, quiet, dreaming dreams of heavenly splendor."

Coincidentally, the very storm that prevented Zlateh from being sold to the butcher is also responsible for reviving Reuven's furrier business. Thus, even without selling Zlateh, the family can now celebrate Hanukkah properly. It seems as if some religious lesson can be gleaned from this turn of events. Perhaps that lesson, as Zlateh's bleating during the storm seems to indicate to Aaron, is precisely that "we must accept all that God gives us—heat, cold, hunger, satisfaction, light, and darkness."

STYLE

Anthropomorphism

Anthropomorphism is a term for the giving of human traits to animals. There is a great deal of anthropomorphism in "Zlateh the Goat." Zlateh is usually discussed in human terms, not animal terms. At the beginning of the story, she is described as patient, good natured, trusting, and loving. She is credited with knowing how humans treat her. When Aaron begins to lead Zlateh toward town, the goat looks "astonished," but then she appears to "have come to the conclusion that a goat shouldn't ask questions." All of these feelings and qualities, and the ability to reason, are human traits. Even Zlateh's bleating in the snow takes on the sound of "crying."

Zlateh's conversations with Aaron in the haystack are also entirely humanized. In the haystack, Zlateh seems to tell Aaron that she loves him and that "we must accept all that God gives us." In the last line of the story, Zlateh is anthropomorphized once again: she bleats at Aaron "with the single sound which expressed all her thoughts, and all her love."

Indeed, nearly all of Zlateh's looks and bleats are ascribed with human feeling and meaning. In fact, the human characters in "Zlateh the Goat" are not given nearly as much attention in the narrative as the goat is given. Aside from Zlateh, only Aaron's thoughts and feelings are acknowledged by the narrator. None of the other character's inner thoughts are even mentioned.

Folktale

"Zlateh the Goat" is based on old Jewish folktales, and the story retains much from its original folk roots. The story has religious or moral lessons embedded within it, as most folktales do, and these moral lessons are of a traditional nature, touching on love, loyalty, and survival in the face of powerful forces. The third-person narrator is omniscient, able to report on the inner thoughts of the story's characters, and this stylistic trait is also typical of folktales. The diction, or language style, is simple and straightforward, like a fairy tale in its generic tone. The story opens with a phrase that is akin to the classic "Once upon a time" beginning; the opening phrase of "Zlateh the Goat" is "At Hanukkah time."

Folktales are meant to be universal, transcendent of time and place, and "Zlateh the Goat" adheres to this tradition. The town and the village are not named, and even the era in which the story takes place is unknown. The people in the story are not complex; their reactions are especially simple, as they are mostly described as being sad, scared, or happy. Much like a traditional folk or fairy tale, this story has a happy ending. Aaron and Zlateh survive the storm, and the family is able to buy Hanukkah supplies even without selling Zlateh to the butcher.

HISTORICAL CONTEXT

Yiddish and Eastern European Jews

Long after Singer immigrated to America, he continued to write in Yiddish, and his stories were translated into English before publication. Singer is known as a Yiddish writer, and his writing is part of the canon of Yiddish literature. Yiddish is a very interesting language because it is not the official language of any one country, though it was once almost the official language of an entire religion, spoken throughout Europe by most Jews. It is also relatively singular in that it contains word parts from many other languages. Its idioms, or sayings, are also known

COMPARE & CONTRAST

- **Early 1900s:** European Jews live in shtetls and speak Yiddish. They are effectively segregated from the non-Jewish populace.

  1960s: The majority of European Jews who were not killed in the Holocaust have immigrated to America and Israel.

  Today: Most survivors of the Holocaust have died from old age. Their descendants rarely speak Yiddish.

- **Early 1900s:** Hanukkah is not the most holy or important of the Jewish holidays.

  1960s: In America, the growing commercialization of Christmas begins to affect Hanukkah as well. Both holidays occur at the same time, and the celebration of Hanukkah becomes more prominent as a result of this coincidence.

  Today: Gift exchanges on Hanukkah are exceedingly common, although this is not a traditional part of the holiday celebration.

- **Early 1900s:** A lifestyle like that of Aaron and his family—one that entails living in the country, raising and selling livestock, practicing a trade (making furs), and traveling by foot—is not uncommon. There are no cell phones, cars, or televisions.

  1960s: More and more people move to cities or suburbs and enjoy reliable transportation via automobile; they have telephones and televisions, and fewer people farm or raise livestock.

  Today: Urban and suburban lifestyles predominate in the developed world, and the now-foreign country life is often romanticized by city dwellers. Given the availability of cars and cell phones, few would find themselves trapped in a snowstorm like Aaron and Zlateh.

---

for being very colorful, which makes it an ideal language for writing literature.

The history of the Yiddish language also reflects the history of Jews and their migrations as a population. Several theories about this process abound, but it seems certain that many among the Jewish population in Eastern Europe were the descendants of migratory Jews who had been exiled from Jerusalem by the Romans over the first few centuries of the Common Era. Another large portion emigrated from Western Europe in the Middle Ages during the Black Plague (for which they were blamed) and the Crusades. Yiddish emerged as a language in these populations, an amalgamation of Arabic, Hebrew, German, and romance languages.

During the late nineteenth and early twentieth centuries, large populations of Jews in Eastern Europe lived in shtetls that were exclusively Jewish. Even in the larger towns, Jews lived in segregated neighborhoods. All spoke Yiddish on a day-to-day basis. Hebrew was considered a language of religion, much like Latin is to Christians, and while most Jews also spoke their national languages, such as Polish, Russian, and German, they were able to transcend national boundaries because of their common language as Jews. When early twentieth-century Jews across Eastern Europe were exterminated in pogroms (acts of violence perpetrated against individual villages) and through the Holocaust, Yiddish began to die out. After survivors emigrated, their children did not continue to speak the language. In the present day, Yiddish is considered a near-dead language. Singer, who was himself a Jewish emigrant, was aware of the slow death of Yiddish, and this is why he chose to continue writing in the language, telling tales of Jewish life in Europe before the Holocaust. In a journal article, Jill P. May quotes Melvin Maddock's interview with Singer in *Isaac Bashevis Singer: Conversations*: "By his own admission he writes 'as if none of the terrible things that happened to the Jewish people during the last two decades really did occur.'"

Hanukkah

The Jewish holiday of Hanukkah takes a prominent role in "Zlateh the Goat." Reuven decides to sell Zlateh so that he can afford oil, potato pancakes, and other sundries necessary for the celebration. Hanukkah, or the Festival of Lights, is a holiday that is celebrated over eight days and nights, beginning annually on the twenty-fifth of Kisev on the Jewish calendar. Because the Jewish calendar is a lunar calendar, the holiday begins on a different day of the Western calendar each year. For the most part, however, the holiday takes place in December, and it has gained significance in the Western world as a holiday that is the Jewish equivalent of Christmas.

Sometime around 167 BCE, the Greeks desecrated the holy temple in Jerusalem. The Jews fought back, and after expelling the Greeks, they returned to the temple in hopes of relighting the menorah, which was meant to burn ceaselessly as a symbolic reminder of God's eternal presence and of the Jews' covenant with God as a chosen people. The Jews found only enough oil to light the lamp for one day, but miraculously, the lamp burned for eight days and eight nights until more oil could be found.

In celebration of this miracle, Jews light a menorah each year at Hanukkah for eight nights. Traditional foods eaten during Hanukkah include potato pancakes and donuts, which are made by being fried in oil. Another holiday tradition is playing dreidel with gelt (money). A dreidel is a four-sided top with a different symbol on each side. Each symbol indicates an action, such as taking half the money in the community pile, adding money to the pile, and so on. It is essentially a gambling game. When the Greeks occupied Jerusalem, they forbade Jews from studying the Torah. Jews gathered to study anyhow, and to avoid detection they would appear to be playing dreidel, tricking the Greeks into thinking that they were not studying but gambling instead.

CRITICAL OVERVIEW

Singer and his work are almost universally lauded, and *Zlateh the Goat, and Other Stories*, in which "Zlateh the Goat" first appeared, is no exception. The collection won a prestigious Newbery Honor in 1967. By that time, Singer was already well established as a writer for adults; *Zlateh the Goat, and Other Stories* was his first book for children. Writing about this transition in the *Dictionary of Literary Biography*, Joseph Sherman comments that "the stories enable Singer to be openly didactic in a way he rarely was in fiction addressed to adults." Indeed, Sherman goes on to note that Singer's stories for children contain "unambiguous wish-fulfillment tales in which the good are rewarded and the wicked punished." Sherman furthermore states that Singer's "work for children also allowed him to express, for the first time in English, a poignant nostalgia for his own childhood and for the Poland in which it had been spent."

Writing specifically of "Zlateh the Goat," the critic Eric A. Kimmel, referencing Anton Chekhov's famous play *The Cherry Orchard*, notes in *Twentieth-Century Children's Writers* that the story's "smells and textures are so rich they might have been wafted from the Cherry Orchard." Grace Farrell Lee, writing in the *Hollins Critic*, calls Singer a "master story teller," observing that "in large measure Jewish mysticism and folklore structure his vision and determine his style." Jill P. May, writing about the story in the *Journal of the Midwest Modern Language Association*, quotes Alida Allison's *Isaac Bashevis Singer: Children's Stories and Childhood Memoirs*, in which Allison states that in *Zlateh the Goat, and Other Stories*, Singer "demarcated and transmitted his lively world in full dimension, establishing from the first page . . . the complexity and originality of his use of his native material." Writing of the collection's title story, the *Washington Post Book World* contributor Michael Dirda calls the tale "a little masterpiece" in which Zlateh's "bleating comes to embody a love, devotion and understanding beyond mere words."

CRITICISM

Leah Tieger

Tieger is a freelance writer and editor. In the following essay, she explores the religious undertones, themes, and symbols in "Zlateh the Goat."

"Zlateh the Goat" is unlike much of Singer's other work because it is not overtly religious or mystical. The religious themes in "Zlateh the Goat" may be subtle, but they are nonetheless powerful. Indeed, they are so powerful that school textbooks reprinting the story have attempted to

WHAT DO I READ NEXT?

- Singer's memoirs are collected in *Love and Exile: A Memoir* (1984), which sheds much insight on Singer and his work. The collection includes his three full-length autobiographical works, *A Little Boy in Search of God: Mysticism in a Personal Light*, *A Young Man in Search of Love*, and *Lost in America*.
- A notable Yiddish writer who influenced Singer is Sholem Aleichem. A good introduction to this renowned author's work is *The Best of Sholom Aleichem*, which was published in 1979.
- Another Yiddish literary great who is one of Singer's predecessors is I. L. Peretz. His *Selected Stories* (1974) provides a good starting place for familiarizing oneself with Yiddish literature.
- Edited by Marvin Herzog and others, the three-volume set *The Language and Culture Atlas of Ashkenazic Jewry* was published from 1992 to 2000. The series presents a comprehensive overview of Yiddish and its rise and fall as a language.

"WHAT AT FIRST GLANCE APPEARS TO BE A SIMPLE TALE ABOUT A BOY AND HIS GOAT (REPLETE WITH A 'ONCE UPON A TIME' BEGINNING AND OBLIGATORY HAPPY ENDING) IS, AT SECOND GLANCE, A RELIGIOUS PARABLE ABOUT FAITH AND LOVE."

gloss over, or downplay, the religious content. For instance, the *New York Times* contributor Edward B. Fiske reports that a version of "Zlateh the Goat" that was reprinted in *Catch the Wind*, a 1975 Macmillan textbook, had all references to God removed. One of the key phrases in the story, one that could in fact be described as summing up the story's theme, is "We must accept all that God gives us." According to Fiske, the Macmillan textbook changed the phrase to "We must accept all that is given us."

Even more astounding is the fact that the change was made without Singer's knowledge or permission. Fiske relates that Singer called the deletions "barbarism" and felt "ashamed that [the publishers] are doing that." Singer's response to the changes themselves shed further light on the religiosity inherent in "Zlateh the Goat": "In all my stories there is an element of faith in God. To take out the idea that there is a plan in creation means to take away the very essence of the story." This is a very telling statement. What at first glance appears to be a simple tale about a boy and his goat (replete with a 'once upon a time' beginning and obligatory happy ending) is, at second glance, a religious parable about faith and love.

One could claim, of course, that the bond between Aaron and Zlateh is closely related to "the idea that there is a plan in creation." The bond would be a part of that plan, but it could also be considered a response to or result of that plan. It seems obvious enough that Aaron and Zlateh's bond grows because they must weather the blizzard together, relying on one another for survival. But what is the blizzard in the story if not a symbol of God's will? The snowstorm is undeniably imbued with many supernatural qualities. It arrives unexpectedly, delivering a hailstorm out of season. Furthermore, the storm is unlike anything Aaron or Zlateh has ever seen. The flurries of snow appear "as if white imps were playing tag on the fields." Other mystical elements are also attached to the storm; the wind "wailed, first with one voice and then with many," and it occasionally resembled "devilish laughter."

It is during this storm that one of Zlateh's bleats is interpreted as meaning "We must accept all that God gives us—heat, cold, hunger, satisfaction, light, and darkness." This statement, the story's greatest lesson (and the one censored by Macmillan), is delivered by the circumstances of the storm. As if to stress this point, the ordeal of the storm is given further religious undertones when Aaron perceives himself and Zlateh as being "born of the snow." This symbolic purification and rebirth are typical of religious epiphanies and experiences. When the storm is over, the world, too, is purified; it is "all white, quiet, dreaming dreams of heavenly splendor."

Other religious elements in the story are more straightforward. When Aaron and Zlateh are lost in the snow, Aaron begins "to pray to God for himself and for the innocent animal." Immediately following his prayer, Aaron sees a shape in the snow. This shape turns out to be the haystack that will provide Aaron and Zlateh with shelter, and Aaron knows that he and his goat are now "saved." Shortly after settling into the hay, the narrator notes, "Thank God that in the hay it was not cold."

Yet another important religious component in the story is faith, as Singer himself notes. Zlateh is almost a paragon of faith; she "trusted human beings," unsuspectingly licking the hand of the very man who has sentenced her to her death. Zlateh's faith in people could be seen as a metaphor for faith in God. Zlateh cannot truly understand humans or their plans for her, just as humans cannot understand God or God's plan for them. Other evidence of her faith is that she decides "she shouldn't ask questions" of what comes her way. This mirrors the relatively traditional religious teaching that people should not question God's will.

Religious faith is often coupled with religious love. Traditionally, people with faith in God also love God, and, according to some religious teachings, God loves those who love him in return. This religious tenet is reflected in Zlateh's relationship with Aaron. Zlateh's bleats may mean many things, but in one of the story's more significant moments, Aaron knows that she is saying, "I love you." Zlateh's ability to communicate her love for Aaron is reiterated in the last words of the story, as she makes "the single sound which expressed all her thoughts, and all her love." Aaron, like God, returns the love of the faithful. As Aaron and Zlateh survived together in the hay, "he loved her more and more."

Following this same chain of reasoning, one could also claim that Zlateh experiences a crisis of faith and that Aaron's growing love for Zlateh is a result of Zlateh's return to faith. Indeed, there is a famous religious parable that describes God as a shepherd. This same parable holds that God loves the sheep who get lost from the flock but return even more than those who never leave the flock in the first place. Certainly, the idea of Zlateh as a figure whose faith is lost and then found again is reinforced by Aaron's growing love for the goat, for where "he had always loved Zlateh . . . now she was like a sister." But what, exactly, is Zlateh's crisis of faith?

Zlateh appears "somewhat astonished" as Aaron leads her toward town, and she looks at him "questioningly." Nevertheless, she ultimately concludes "that a goat shouldn't ask questions." This episode is the first evidence of Zlateh's fragile faith. When the snow begins to fall, Zlateh accepts the situation at first, but then her faith falters once again, and "her mild eyes seemed to ask, 'Why are we out in such a storm?'" Eventually, she gives up entirely: "she anchored her cleft hooves in the earth and bleated as if pleading to be taken home." Her bleats begin "to sound like crying," and it is implied that she feels as if "those humans in whom she had so much confidence had dragged her into a trap." This latter sentiment shows not only a loss of faith but also a sliver of blame or accusation.

Aaron, however, shows no such tendencies. He reacts to the storm with surprise but keeps calm and does not panic. He accepts the storm's presence and is practical about it, vainly hoping to run into a villager in a cart. Even when Aaron realizes that he and Zlateh are lost, he does not panic (and it is at this point that Zlateh does panic). Aaron, knowing the serious situation that they are in, is hardly even able to "admit the danger" that he and Zlateh face. While Zlateh cries, Aaron prays "to God for himself and for the innocent animal." His prayers are immediately answered in the form of a haystack.

Zlateh's crisis of faith ends only when her fear, cold, and hunger are assuaged, and yet she is later portrayed as communicating to Aaron that these are the very discomforts that "we must accept." Once in the haystack Zlateh is again "contented," having "seemed to regain her confidence in man." Like a penitent sheep returning to her flock, Zlateh appears "eager to reward" her savior. Lost in the snow, Zlateh must place her faith in Aaron, and she fails, recovering her faith only when she is led toward food and shelter. Aaron, however, cannot put his faith in a goat; he can only put his faith in God, and he does not fail. This is the essential difference between Zlateh and Aaron. It is all the more interesting, then, that Zlateh is the character who seems to tell Aaron that "we must accept all that God gives us." What one says with a bleat, the other does in deed.

Source: Leah Tieger, Critical Essay on "Zlateh the Goat," in *Short Stories for Students*, Gale, Cengage Learning, 2009.

Suzanne Rahn

In the following excerpt, Rahn argues that through works such as "Zlateh the Goat," Singer contributed to the increasing visibility of Jewish characters in children's literature.

In 1986 the celebrated illustrator Trina Schart Hyman delivered a plenary address at the thirteenth annual conference of the Children's Literature Association. Instead of a formal presentation, Hyman gave her audience an insider's look at the picture book she had just completed, *The Water of Life*, with slides displaying her illustrations. The text was a straightforward adaptation by Barbara Rogasky of the German folktale in which a prince seeks for the Water of Life and finds a princess in an enchanted castle; the illustrations, on the other hand, like those in Hyman's *Snow White* (1974), *The Sleeping Beauty* (1977), and *Saint George and the Dragon* (1984), expressed an interpretation very much her own. Her princess, for example, was depicted as, in Hyman's words, "an equal opportunity employer," with illustrations showing "a black guy and a woman as the heads of her guards" (10). One of the enchanted princes in another illustration was also black. Most remarkable, however, was the beautiful, dark-haired princess herself, first seen as the hero discovers her in her room, studying books and maps. "Now I'll have you know that this is a Jewish princess," Hyman announced.

> This princess went to Bennington and Sarah Lawrence, and she's smart as well as beautiful. I mean, she hasn't just been sitting around this castle waiting to be rescued. She's been reading books and trying to find out how to break the spell herself.... And those are her books, and all her Christian symbols up on the bookshelf. After all, if you were a Jewish princess in those days, you had to disguise the fact pretty well. (8)

The "Christian symbols," incidentally, are icons, including one of the Virgin and Child.

Hyman's odd decision to create a Jewish heroine known as such only to her (and to several hundred members of the Children's Literature Association) may be seen as one idiosyncratic manifestation of a much larger phenomenon—the widespread "invisibility" of Jewish characters in mainstream English-language children's literature. This has been, for the most part, an invisibility of absence; until thirty years ago, Jewish

> "MAJOR CHANGE IN THE DEPICTION OF JEWISH CHARACTERS, HOWEVER, DID NOT TAKE PLACE UNTIL THE 1960S, WHEN THE ENTIRE FIELD OF CHILDREN'S LITERATURE WAS BEGINNING TO BREAK THROUGH THE TABOOS OF THE 1950S AND EXPAND IN NEW DIRECTIONS."

characters of any sort were extremely rare. Often, however, their invisibility has resembled that of Hyman's princess. Jewish characters, whatever the author's private intention, were not explicitly identified as "Jewish," which meant that as far as most young readers were concerned, they might as well not be Jewish at all. Clues of physical appearance, speech, dress, and nomenclature which—often stereotypically—might spell Jewishness to an adult reader would be illegible to most children....

Major change in the depiction of Jewish characters, however, did not take place until the 1960s, when the entire field of children's literature was beginning to break through the taboos of the 1950s and expand in new directions. Internationalism flourished once more; stories set in foreign—and often non-European—countries became more common, as did stories translated from other languages. Israel, past and present, became a familiar setting (Posner 123–24). In 1966, Isaac Bashevis Singer's *Zlateh the Goat and Other Stories*, with its poignant illustrations by Maurice Sendak, became the Newbery Award's first Jewish Honor Book. Historical novels were widening their range as well, giving children the opportunity to see Jewish characters in a variety of historical contexts. British author Josephine Kamm, for example, in *Return to Freedom* (1962), introduced children to the plight of English Jews in the Middle Ages; in *Red Towers of Granada* (1966), another British novelist, Geoffrey Trease, contrasted the treatment of Jews in thirteenth-century England with that in Moorish Spain, where religious tolerance resulted in a unique flowering of civilization. Jewish-American author Shulamith Ish-Kishor painted a dark but memorable picture of life in a sixteenth-century

Jewish ghetto in *A Boy of Old Prague* (1963). In its unrelenting portrayal of prejudice and persecution, and in its tragic ending, *A Boy of Old Prague* foreshadows novels of the Holocaust to be written in the 1970s, '80s, and '90s by such children's authors as Jane Yolen and Myron LeVoy.

> The raging beasts of the mob had made a human bonfire. They had dragged the Jews out of their houses, men, women, and children, and brought them down to the market place. Scores of bodies were found in a heap, outside a mass of ruined houses. When I went there the wind was blowing the black flakes and fragments here and there. (88)

Yet invisibility still recurs in the children's books of this period. In *The Winged Watchman* (1962) by Hilda Van Stockum, an engrossing story of the Nazi occupation of Holland, a boy and his mother watch an entire family being loaded by S.S. men into a van:

> Mother flung her apron over Joris' head—he was still very small then—but he peeked underneath and saw it all. The old grandfather, who could hardly walk, was taken. He had a little black cap on his head and a big yellow star on his coat. Then came Mr. Groen, two boys and a little girl, all wearing stars. Last of all came Mrs. Groen, and Joris would never forget her face. When she saw Mother she made a sign to her, pointing to her garden. (58)

When the van has gone, Joris's mother finds the baby that Mrs. Groen had hidden in the bushes, takes it home with her, and raises the little girl as her own child. The word "Jew," however, is never used in this moving scene, nor at the end of the book, when Mrs. Groen returns—the only survivor—and little Rachel is given back to her.

By the 1970s, however, the invisibility that had hung like a mist over Jewish characters for nearly a hundred years had finally dissipated for good. Hilda Van Stockum herself, in a second novel set in Nazi-occupied Holland, *The Borrowed House*, confronted anti-Semitism in 1975 far more directly than she had in 1963. In this story, it is the young protagonist who is a Nazi, a dedicated member of the Hitler Youth who sincerely believes that Jews are evil, though (as far as she knows) she has never seen one. "'I think they're like the *Nibelungen* dwarfs in our play . . . sly and dangerous,'" she naively informs her friend Greta. "'It's the Jews in England and America that are fighting us'" (10). Janna's gradual enlightenment, when she makes friends with a Jewish boy hiding in the house her parents have commandeered, is what this book is about. At first, she does not perceive Sef's Jewishness, because he does not fit her stereotype; she assumes he is merely a member of the Resistance. Then, when she discovers his yellow star, she is horrified and must overcome her own longheld beliefs. Finally, she accepts and loves Sef for what he truly is. Though he must still stay hidden until the war is over, the Jew is no longer invisible to Janna, or to the reader.

The invisibility of Jewishness in characters clearly envisioned as Jewish by such children's authors as Hilda Van Stockum, Robert Heinlein, and Noel Streatfeild seems related to the issue of Jewish assimilation with which so many Jewish-American authors have been concerned (see, for example, the articles by June Cummins, Jonathan Krasner, and Leslie Tannenbaum in this issue). Invisibility made it possible to imply, for an audience of non-Jewish children (though not for their parents), that Jews were essentially no different from themselves, helping to ensure that these children would grow up free from the prejudices of the parents, or even of the authors. At the same time, British and American authors who believed that the best possible outcome for British and American Jews was to be wholly assimilated into the mainstream culture could thus create a kind of assimilation before the fact.

However, the growing cultural prominence of ethnic identity, encouraged in America by the civil rights movement and in Britain by immigration from former colonies, has led to a new openness about ethnicity, and to the increased presence of all ethnic groups in English-language children's literature. Since the 1980s, the publicity given the Holocaust and its incorporation into school curricula has made Jewishness particularly visible. Most importantly, a new array of Jewish children's authors has not only identified itself as Jewish but produced a wonderful variety of characters who are Jewish, too. Isaac Bashevis Singer, Kathryn Lasky, Uri Shulevitz, Maurice Sendak, Marilyn Sachs, Eric Kimmel, Lynne Reid Banks, Maxine Rose Schur, Sonia Levitin, and many more fine authors and illustrators have vastly expanded the range of Jewish experience depicted in mainstream English-language children's literature. Today, Jewish characters are no longer exceptional—or invisible—and young readers, Jewish and non-Jewish, are free to share their imaginary lives.

"SINGER NEVER SUGGESTED THAT HIS STORIES WERE SIMPLE ADAPTATIONS OF THE STORIES HE LEARNED AS A CHILD, BUT THERE ARE OBVIOUS STRANDS OF HIS CHILDHOOD READING AND HIS JEWISH UPBRINGING IN HIS WRITING FOR CHILDREN."

Source: Suzanne Rahn, "'Like a Star Through Flying Snow': Jewish Characters, Visible and Invisible," in *The Lion and the Unicorn*, Vol. 27, No. 3, September 2003, pp. 303–23.

Jill P. May

In the following excerpt, May provides an analysis of the relationship between Singer and Maurice Sendak, the illustrator of Zlateh the Goat and Other Stories, *suggesting that each man attempted to "revive the dead" in their work.*

Maurice Sendak and Isaac Singer devoted much of their careers to the recreation of a Polish community, hoping to bring alive lost villages and people for a youthful audience. At the same time, both men sought resolutions for their past, and they "revived the dead" in order to answer personal questions about ethnic survival and religious annihilation. These two men returned to earlier stories from Polish villages and recreated their Jewish families in these isolated communities.

Neither Singer nor Sendak lived in Poland when it came under Nazi rule. Sendak was born in Brooklyn; Singer fled Poland prior to World War II and re-settled in New York City. As a youth, Sendak heard stories about his family's past in Poland, while Singer remembered the country of his childhood and his youth. Sendak's Poland is dominated by relatives who would never make it out alive. Because he was a boy growing up in America during World War II, Sendak's Jewish community extends beyond the boundaries of Europe and Nazi occupation. It has much to do with an American childhood in New York City. Singer left contemporary Poland and the Nazi regime behind him when he arrived in the United States. Written at the end of his career, his children's literature most often contains adolescents struggling with making sense of their world within their Jewish villages, and the events end prior to World War II. Singer rarely depicts the Nazi regime in his literature written specifically for children. Their journeys, therefore, reflect two different perspectives of the Jewish experience, and the worlds they bring alive hold a different sense of realism for their youthful audiences.

I.

Isaac Singer won the Nobel Peace prize for his writing in 1978. By then he had received the Newbery Honors for *Zlatech the Goat and Other Stories*, *The Fearsome Inn* and *When Shlemiel Went to Warsaw* and was awarded the National Book Award in Children's Literature for *A Day of Pleasure*. Singer never won the coveted Newbery Award, and his Nobel Prize was not given to him because he was a children's author. As an author of adult literature prior to turning to children's literature, Singer won his Nobel Prize for "his impassioned narrative art which, with its roots in Polish-Jewish cultural tradition, brings universal human conditions to life" (Noble 162).

When asked what caused him to write about Poland, he reasoned: "the lost world is the world of my childhood, of my younger days. . . . We are bound to write about the things of our younger days and to remember them better than the things that happened yesterday or the day before. . . . I write about people from Poland—Yiddish-speaking Poles, Jews—I do this to be sure that I write about people I know best" (Teicholz 219–220). Singer left Poland when the country was on the ebb of war; it was not yet a country with the political practice of Jewish termination. He was a young man who had fathered a son and divorced his wife. Singer and his older brother Joseph, also a writer, chose to immigrate in the mid-thirties, and they settled in New York City.

Once in America, Isaac Singer did not immediately feel comfortable. His memories of a vibrant Jewish community with a rich heritage led him to have certain language and cultural expectations. Singer later explained: "When I came to this country I lived through a terrible disappointment. I felt then—more than I do now—that Yiddish had no future in this country. In Poland, Yiddish was still very much alive" (Blocker and Elman 14). Although he chose to emigrate to America over going to Israel or Russia, Singer remained an exiled Jew for the major part of his life. After visiting Singer in 1967, Melvin Naddocks observed:

> What a strange amalgam Singer is! Hunched over a 32-year-old Yiddish typewriter in New York City, in 1967, he writes of the Polish past—of dybbuks he does not believe in and of shetls (East European Jewish villages) long disappeared. By his own admission he writes "as if none of the terrible things that happened to the Jewish people during the last two decades really did occur." (33)

Singer is thus depicted as an alienated Jew who lives in his past, in a time prior to World War II, and who refuses to acknowledge that the people he left behind are truly dead.

Singer's fiction was first published in the *Jewish Daily Forward*, New York's Yiddish-language newspaper; throughout his career, Singer wrote in Yiddish. He once quipped: "Yiddish is a sick language because the young people don't speak it. And many consider it a dead language. But in our history between being sick and dying is a long way" (Anderson 101). Singer admitted in *A Little Boy in Search of God* that he was aware of injustice throughout his life:

> I had heard about the cruelties perpetrated by Chmielnicki's Cossacks. I had read about the Inquisition. I knew about the pogroms on Jews in Russia and Spain. I lived in a world of cruelty. I was tormented not only by the sufferings of men but by the sufferings of beasts, birds, and insects as well. Hungry wolves attacked lambs. Lions, tigers, and leopards had to devour other creatures or die from hunger. The squires wandered through forests and shot deer, hares, and pheasants for pleasure. I bore resentment against not only man but against God, too.... It was He who had made man a blood thirsty creature ready to do violence at every step. I was a child, but I had the same view of the world that I have today—one huge slaughterhouse, one enormous hell.

Born in Radzymin, Poland, on July 14, 1904, Isaac Singer grew up hearing two kinds of stories. From his father, Rabbi Pinchos Menachem, he heard stories with a moral, stories about religious beliefs and practices. From his mother he heard tales "so pointless that you really could learn nothing from them" (*Children's Literature* 9). Although the expectations for their listeners were different, both parents would be considered to be excellent storytellers throughout Singer's life. Oral storytelling and community traditions became significant elements to Singer in his own storymaking. Often, during interviews, Singer would talk of his family's conversations about religion and of his parents' fear that he and his older brother were becoming too cosmopolitan. Both boys read secular novels and European philosophy that had been translated into Hebrew and Yiddish. When asked once if his parents approved of his writing fiction, Singer replied: "They considered all the secular writers to be heretics, all unbelievers.... Everybody who read such books sooner or later became a worldly man and forsook the traditions. In my family, of course, my brother had gone first, and I went after him. For my parents, this was a tragedy" (Blocker and Elman 13).

When Isaac Singer left Poland he chose to break with his rabbinical heritage, but he did not lose his belief in the Jewish traditions he grew up in or his need to be thought of as an Eastern European Jewish writer. At one point he explained the significant difference between western literature and Yiddish literature as one of characterization, noting that the western hero "is the Superman, the Prometheus character" while the Yiddish hero is "the little man. He's poor but proud, always struggling against his personal, financial, and political odds to maintain his dignity and status" (Flender 42–43). Singer never suggested that his stories were simple adaptations of the stories he learned as a child, but there are obvious strands of his childhood reading and his Jewish upbringing in his writing for children. Shlemiel is a prominent character in his stories, as are witches and spirits; many of the stories also take place in Chelm where the wise men live. Concerning those elements found in all of Singer's writing, Howard Scwartz commented:

> Singer was born into a rabbinic family in Leoncin, a village in Poland, in 1904 and grew up in Warsau, where he began his writing career in 1925. It is important to emphasize the crucial role played by his older brother ... in the career of his younger brother.
>
> Singer's emigration to the United States in 1935 and the subsequent destruction of the Polish Jewish communities by the Nazis in World War II created a situation in which he had to turn, of necessity, to his memory and imagination for subject matter. So great was his success that for many readers Singer's descriptions of life in prewar Poland form the basis for their conception of this period. To his detractors, Singer's character portraits ... are overworked and exaggerated. But Singer has always emphasized the primary role of the imagination in his stories and novels. (184)

Singer liked to talk about his need to write beyond orthodoxy. In one interview he attested: "The truth is that the Yiddishists don't consider me a writer who writes in their tradition. Neither do I consider myself a writer in their tradition. I consider myself a writer in the Jewish tradition but not exactly the Yiddish tradition" (Howe 126). Singer maintained that stories are not universal creations, that each person's rendition is his own, and this gave his writing personal impetus: "After all, these folktales were invented by someone; the people did not tell them all.... I say to myself, 'I am a part of the folk myself. Why can't I invent stories?'...Sometimes I hear a little story, a spark of a story, and then I make from the spark a fire" (*Children's Literature* 11). Efraim Sicher explains Singer's need for a personal sense of creativity within a Jewish folklore tradition as his haunting by a legendary dybbuk, "a wandering spirit of a deceased person who returns to fulfill some uncompleted task or undo a wrong" (56). As a folkloric figure, the dybbuk seeks *tikkum*. Sicher feels that *tikkum* forced Singer to "grapple with the past, with the unprecedented revelation of evil in the Holocaust." Thus, he reasons, Singer's creative freedom caused him to consider that "the demonic existed in the lost East European community of belief" and allowed him to "exorcise" his past through his writing, admitting his "schizophrenia" between his desire for spiritual perfection and acknowledgment of human defilement (57).

Singer hoped to keep his Jewish heritage intact. Once, in an interview, he argued: "If we reach a time when Yiddish and Yiddish customs and folklore are forgotten, Hitler will have succeeded not only physically but also spiritually.... I wish Yiddish could be as alive today as when I was a child and that there were many young talents writing in Yiddish" (Lottman 123). Because he lost those who remained behind in Poland, Singer was forced to recreate that other time and place, to resolve the loss of a spiritual and intellectual community.

Throughout his life, Singer tied reading and religion together. At one point he argued that one need not worry about the particular social system where one lived as much as why God "created the world the way it is," adding, "It's He who has caused all these troubles, and I often rebel against Him. But the fact that I rebel against Him shows that I believe in Him and I really do" (Anderson 106). Grace Farrell Lee observes,

> ...while Singer fills his fiction with a wide variety of folk figures—comic angels and imps, maliciously demonic narrators, dream phantoms and apparitions—the significance of the demonic in his fiction is always related, not to traditional notions of sin and retribution, but to his major theme of exile and the problem of meaning. (32)

Singer's sense of injustice would not allow him to create an idealized world. All of his writing, even that written specifically for children, contains links between local customs and provincial attitudes within the everyday lives of simple peasants and the cabalistic spiritual world. Singer's children's literature falls into two categories: that built around the mundane events of a Yiddish Polish village and that inhabited by spirits. The mundane stories depict the Jewish peasants in the small village where as a teen he lived with his mother. This community is isolated and seems oblivious to the dangers without. Humor is often found in Singer's village. Yet, it is barbed humor, usually pointing out the foibles of blind trust and the worries of persecution from those who live just beyond the village, while relating the humorous escapades of a likable anti-hero.

In *Zlateh the Goat*, Singer writes: "Literature helps us remember the past with its many moods. To the storyteller yesterday is still here as are the years and the decades gone by.... For the writer and his readers all creatures go on living forever" (xi). Within this collection, logic is often misconstrued as simple faith in what one is told....

In her book-length study of Singer's children's fiction, Alida Allison calls *Zlateh the Goat* Singer's "standard" children's work, adding, "In it he demarcated and transmitted his lively world in full dimension, establishing from the first page...the complexity and originality of his use of his native material" (31). When discussing his writing for children, Singer once commented: "In real life many of the people that I describe no longer exist, but to me they remain alive... with their wisdom, their strange beliefs, and sometimes their foolishness" (Toothaker 532). While he was alive, Singer's writings were defined by Leo W. Schwarz as stories tied to "a pre-modern culture" and he concluded: "Singer has come to terms with himself; he is committed to the hallowing of man and life" (12).

II.

Maurice Sendak is probably the best-known children's illustrator of the twentieth century. Although his fame has evolved from his illustrative work in the United States, his talents are not limited to this genre. Sendak had been described as the Picasso of children's literature in the popular press, as an American artist whose work looks "like something out of Brueghal" by Paul Heins, one of the early authoritative reviewers for *Horn Book Magazine*, and as an illustrator who has manipulated the heroic journey towards self discovery in his psychological fantasies, by Canadian children's literature critic Roderick McGillis. His contributions also reflect a Jewish author/illustrator who lived through World War II and, as an adult, determined to write and illustrate books for the American city child he had watched belittled as he grew up in New York City. . . .

Sendak has admitted that when he was young he knew there was a war going on, but he believes he better appreciated the darkness in Disney's *Pinocchio*. "I was only a child," he recalls, "but I knew something dreadful was happening in the world, and that my parents were worried to death. And it seems to me that something of the quality of that terrible, anxious time is reflected in the very color and dramatic power of *Pinocchio*" (*Caldecott & Co.* 112). Unlike Jack Zipes, who writes that Disney reshaped the material to "'Americanize' the representation of boyhood itself; and to simplify the plot so that his moral code of success based on conforming to the dictates of good behavior and diligence could be transmitted through story, dance, and rounded images of tranquillity" (83), Sendak has called the film a wonderful re-write of the Italian classic. . . .

His personal memories of *Pinocchio* suggest that the fantasy provided him an alternative ending for his family's reality. In 1941, on the day of his bar mitzvah, his father received a letter informing him that his own father was dead. Sendak ties his growing up to his cognizance that those ancestors his parents worried about might ultimately be killed. Later, he revived the lost relatives:

> Both my parents lost everybody, practically, in the Holocaust. . . . And many of the pictures in *Zlateh* [*the Goat*] are portraits taken from photograph albums of people I never knew, because they died in concentration camps. . . . I gave some of the characters their faces so I could surprise my parents. They were deeply touched because they recognized this one and that one. Those lost people were alive again in the book, they would always be alive in the book, they would always be characters in Isaac Singer stories. (*Sendak's Western Canon* 1)

Sendak has commented that his bar mitzvah was a day of happiness and resentment for him. His celebration was a somber time for his parents, and the war continued to affect his family. His sister lost her fiancé in the war, and his brother was sent to the Pacific (Lanes 23).

Sendak lived in a neighborhood inhabited by Eastern Jews and Italians. Within the books, magazines and newspapers being published, Sendak's ethnic world was being negatively discussed as a replication of "the life which the Jews had led in eastern Europe" (Hendrick 108). In *The Jews in America*, first published by Doubleday in 1922, Burton Jesse Hendrick discussed the ethnicity of the eastern Jewish community in America, and he concluded: "the process of 'Americanization' is going to be slow and more difficult with this class of immigrants than with any other, except perhaps the Southern Italians. . . . Until this mass is brought into harmony with American traditions and American instincts it would certainly be folly to add considerably to it" (170–171). Such assertions would cause anxiety for Sendak's family. Indeed, the possibility of their relatives immigrating to America would have been bleak. . . .

Sendak's work relies on his childhood memories and on his understanding of the child's integration of popular culture images, modern song and dance, and community adult attitudes, reflected in their fears and pleasures when they are parents. His Jewish neighborhood is a replica of the one in America that was inhabited by the "unchosen" in the American social ambiance of the thirties and the forties.

III.

The works of Isaac Singer and Maurice Sendak resolve the reverie of an immigrant survivor by allowing the artist to return to his family traditions and redefine his loss of ethnic heritage by preserving his family in art. As they wrote and illustrated the Jewish life that was ostracized and destroyed in Poland, ignored and diminished in America, Singer and Sendak documented Polish Jewish families who faced cultural extinction within socially sanctioned policies, both in and outside the United States. As they worked with their skeletons of religious doubt and persecution and publicly acknowledged the personal sufferings of their families, they conveyed a new sense of the Holocaust and of Shoah. Efraim Sicher has spoken about narrative as a way to revisit the Holocaust's "blanks and disorder" and redefine the writer's life within his collapsed family and society (6). Leo Schwarz has commented that within the best Jewish works there is "a sense of immediacy and warmth in human association... rooted in the Jewish tradition of their childhood" (17). Schwarz argues: "Jewish education taught them, not merely about Judaism, but, above all, to be a Jew.... This means, not copulating with death but coping with life, and this, in turn, means facing the crises and paradoxes of existence and making hard decisions on questions of right and wrong" (17). Alan Berger has disclosed the need for second-generation Americans who suffered the Holocaust and Shoah by observing their families to produce art, explaining, "For example, many feel guilty for not having been in the Shoah. Others feel guilt, quite undeservedly, for the fact that their parents suffered during the Holocaust. Still others feel a sense of guilt for not being able to comprehend the meaning of their parents' suffering and their own Holocaust legacy" (65).

Singer, the grandson and son of rabbis, escaped Poland, and while he saw the world skeptically, he believed in God's goodness. At one point, he commented: "No man in his right mind unless he is a silly liberal believes that we can change the world.... But I feel that the cosmos cannot be all evil, that the creator of all these galaxies could not just be an ice cold sadist who plays around with little creatures. There must be something great, good, eternal" (Farrell 135). Singer refused to revisit the destruction of his people in books for youthful readers. Instead, he rebuilt the Polish villages as they existed when he was young in short fiction for children. Sendak has continually regarded his parents, siblings and himself as lucky survivors. He recently remembered his journey to Amsterdam where he visited Anne Frank's home, and he admitted: "I had the uneasy, chilly feeling that I could get on a plane and go home, but for her there had been no escape. And that kept reminding me of my father and my mother, and the whimsicality of their coming here. I had cousins who died in the Holocaust the year of my bar mitzvah; they had no bar mitzvah, and I knew all the time that it was luck" (*Sendak's Western Canon* 11). Sendak's Jewish community lived in New York City during the war; they faced the prejudice of people like Burton Hendrick in their everyday lives. They held few hopes that their relatives would get help to flee Nazi persecution. Sendak's work is defined by Alan Berger's suggestion that second-generation artists have not forgotten the past. Rather, they are trying to remember and mourn the dead, express their personal sense of loss, and live as Jews after facing the twentieth century's indifference about earlier plans for Jewish annihilation (19).

"ELIZABETH SHUB REMEMBERS WHEN SINGER FINALLY AGREED TO TRY HIS HAND AT WRITING FOR CHILDREN. HE BROUGHT HIS FIRST ATTEMPTS, HANUKKAH POEMS, TO HER APARTMENT. IT TOOK HER UNTIL THE NEXT DAY TO FIND THE COURAGE TO REJECT THE POEMS, A RESPONSE SINGER WASN'T AT ALL PLEASED ABOUT."

Source: Jill P. May, "Envisioning the Jewish Community in Children's Literature: Maurice Sendak and Isaac Singer," in *Midwest Modern Language Association*, Vol. 33, No. 3, Autumn, Winter 2000/2001, pp. 137–51.

Alida Allison

In the following excerpt, Allison describes the role of Singer's translator, Elizabeth Shub, in the writing of "Zlateh the Goat," a story that "would never have come into existence" without Shub's persuasion.

In an essay reprinted by the American P.E.N. Center in its 1987 book *On the World of Translation*, Isaac Bashevis Singer makes a joke. Someone, he writes, once asked him at a lecture, "What would you do if you met God face to face?" Says Singer, "My answer was, 'I would ask him to collaborate with me on some translations.'" Tellingly, he adds, "I would not trust him to do it himself." Beyond linguistic and creative considerations, the topics of metaphysical translation, the inevitability of error, and the struggle to get it right—all were of interest to the philosophical Singer.

In regard to Singer's children's stories, there was a highly noteworthy collaboration: not with *the* God, but with *the* translator, Elizabeth Shub. Without her, "Zlateh the Goat," Singer's first venture for children, would never have come into existence. Singer had many translators in his long career, from Saul Bellow to his own nephew Joseph Singer. But only Shub thought of him in regard to children's books. As Singer recalls:

> I had been writing for forty years and it never occurred to me that I would ever write for children.... But my friend, Elizabeth Shub, who was then an editor of juvenile books at Harper, had different ideas. For a long time she tried to persuade me...that I was, at least potentially, a writer for children.
>
> The net result was that she translated many stories into English from Yiddish and now, whenever I get a check, she gets a check. Which proves that sometimes altruism pays off.

Translation had always been crucial for Singer. Yiddish was a minority language if ever there was one, and his worldwide fame rested on his works in translation. Once he acquired an English-reading audience, he became, as he says, "one of those rare writers who works with his translators...I check my translators constantly—I mean those who translate me into English or Hebrew. What happens to me in Italian, Portuguese or Finnish I will never know."

Elizabeth Shub had known Singer since she was a teenager and he a young new immigrant to New York. Singer spoke no English when he arrived in 1935. By the time he began writing for children 30 years later, his English was fluent. But his was not native English; Shub's was. "It just seemed natural," Shub said, "when he asked me to translate for him." In addition, Shub worked in and knew children's literature; Singer did not; as he observed, "It did not exist among the Jewish people in my time." Shub's skills, her already having translated many of his adult stories, her tact with Singer, and, significantly, her familiarity (though second generation) with the world Isaac Singer had come from—all contributed to a solid working friendship.

Oddly enough, however, there was one thing Elizabeth Shub could not do; she could not read Isaac Singer's handwriting. "Other translators of Singer, such as Mirra Ginsburg, worked alone," Shub said. "Her Yiddish was better and she could read everything." Shub spoke Yiddish and read it in typeset, but Singer's longhand was beyond her. As a consequence, Shub says:

> The way we mostly worked, at least on the first draft, is that he would come to my house and read it to me in Yiddish. He would sit in a nice easy chair and I would sit at the typewriter and do a rough immediate translation. If there was a word I didn't understand, he was there to help me. Then I would read it to him and he would correct whatever he didn't think was right. Then I would type the whole thing out clean and I would edit it to correct anything that I thought was wrong. And then he would go over it and correct anything he didn't like. Then I would read it to him and he would make corrections again or if I felt something wasn't working, he would immediately, if he agreed, fix it.
>
> Bringing the manuscript over didn't mean that as he read to me he didn't change things. He never felt that the manuscripts he brought over were just as they had to be. Once it was done, however, it was done. He wasn't a writer, like some of my others, who went back and said, "Oh, I hate this."
>
> Until I got used to working with him I would sometimes not understand what he was doing. I would have a questioning look or frown a little bit. He'd get very angry and he would say "Why do you look like that? How can I work when you look like that?..." I would smile and say, "I'm sorry." And then, by the end of the story, usually he had pulled it together and what didn't have any meaning to me in the middle certainly meant exactly what he wanted it to at the end. And that was a lesson I learned...not to take anything for granted till the story was finished. His instinct for the right word in another language was very, very keen.

The spontaneous oral exchange between author and translator drew out the best of Singer's storytelling ability. Alternately he and Shub served as on-site audience. "My translators," says Singer, "are my best critics. I can tell by their expressions when they don't like a story of mine or any part of it." Telling the stories aloud also drew out from him what Roderick McGillis calls "the speaking voice" of literature, the narrative cadences of his young days in Eastern Europe as the son of a rabbi to whose drawing room all kinds of people came to tell their stories. Singer has often depicted himself in his memoirs as a child who listened carefully and consciously to the ways in which people told their stories.

Elizabeth Shub remembers when Singer finally agreed to try his hand at writing for children. He brought his first attempts, Hanukkah poems, to her apartment. It took her until the next day to find the courage to reject the poems, a response Singer wasn't at all pleased about.

Shub continues, "It was maybe a day and a half later when I got this phone call. He said, 'I wrote another story.' 'Oh great, that's wonderful, do you want to come to my house?' 'No, meet me at Famous' (his favorite deli on 72nd Street). So I met him in the cafeteria and he handed me 'Zlateh the Goat' and that's how we got started."

Since Singer's debut as a children's writer won the first of his three Newbery Honor Medals—all three won for books Shub translated with him—theirs was a very good start indeed.

Briefly, "Zlateh the Goat" is about the Russian Jewish family of Reuven, the furrier. An unusually warm winter spells disaster for them, and reluctantly they are forced to sell their beloved old goat Zlateh to raise a few gulden for necessities. The task of taking her to the town butcher is laid upon young Aaron, but no sooner do he and Zlateh set off than they are caught in a blizzard. Their salvation appears in the form of a mound of snow, covering, Aaron realizes, a large haystack. He tunnels a way in for him and Zlateh and, during the three days they share there, they converse in their own way as Zlateh eats the hay and Aaron drinks her milk. The family is overjoyed when they return. The snow has alleviated the economic situation and Zlateh remains at home. The elements of Singer's own roots, family love and sacrifice, human/animal dependence, the warmth of the holiday, and harsh reality—economic and environmental—are all part of his first children's story.

New York University's Fales Library holds all the original English drafts of the seven stories of *Zlateh the Goat*, plus the stories Singer wrote specifically for *A Day of Pleasure*, his National Book Award–winning autobiography of childhood in Poland. The drafts are concrete documentation of a creative process that word processing has rendered quaint. Figures 1 through 3 reproduce draft pages from *Zlateh the Goat*. . . .

There is very little editing on figure 1. The large signature on top is Singer's, appended when he donated the manuscripts; interestingly, it looks as if he spelled his last name wrong. The rest of the handwriting is Elizabeth Shub's. The editorial improvement is clear: midpage, "For that money one could buy Hanukkah candles" becomes the more resonant "Such a sum would buy Hanukkah candles," and below, "began to cry out" becomes "cried out loud," and finally "cried loudly."

In figure 2, the collaborative translating is more evident; there is much more revision in Shub's hand. Midpage, one sees the dramatic "She could walk no longer" replacing the bulky and flat "She no longer wanted to or was able to walk"; the strongly cadenced "did not want to admit the danger" replaces the polysyllabic "was reluctant to admit the danger." And at the bottom of the page, "a large hay stack which the snow had blanketed" is the revised version of the bland "a large stack of hay covered with snow." The final page of the manuscript, figure 3, shows how spontaneous the working out of the story had become. In Shub's hand is written the final flawless paragraph of Zlateh: one can see "utter bleat" crossed out, replaced with "come out with a single sound which expressed," and the perfect last sentence is refined through crossings out from "all her feelings, all her thoughts, and all her love" to "all her thoughts, and all her love." Love *is* a feeling, after all, so why be repetitious?

There is a particularly lively page from one of the several draft versions in Shub's possession of Singer's 1983 *The Fools of Chelm and Their History*. The novella is an Orwellian Yiddish political comedy about the famous folklore fools, the so-called sages of Chelm, and the consequences of their harebrained imperialism. Humor is notoriously difficult to translate, and as Singer says, "Yiddish is a language with a built-in humor . . . [it] can take a lot of overstatement . . . English or French must be much more precise, logical, lean." The deadpan and parody that begin with the inflated opening of the "history" of Chelm, that "God said, 'Let there be Chelm.' And there was Chelm" does translate, in no small part because of the tightening, the precision, of the editing. Artist Uri Shulevitz told me he was so tickled by Singer's opening that he chose to expand upon it in his illustration, which is the frontispiece of the published book: the illustration "Let there be Chelm." About two-thirds down the page in question, for example, is humor that takes on evolution itself—all of history, from sea creature to Chelmite, is seen to have happened only to provide an explanation of why Chelmites like gefilte fish. At the bottom of the page, sentence structure and delivery are refined: "It is said that the first Chelmites were primitive people, or maybe just fools" becomes "It is said that the earliest Chelmites were primitive people. Some said they were just plain fools." Wording is definitely punchier the second time around. Singer's stories are good enough to be good in any language, but Elizabeth Shub made them good in *English*.

A theory of language contained in *The Fools of Chelm and Their History* effects a transition from a study of primary sources to a few preliminary Singeresque speculations about Language and Translation as metaphors for human—and divine—struggle. Indeed, language and translation were more than practical and artistic issues for Isaac Singer; they were central metaphors imbued with cosmological meaning.

Describing living and cultural conditions in Chelm, Singer writes:

> They walked around naked and barefoot... and hunted animals with axes of stone.... They often starved or were sick. [And this is Shub's writing] But since the word problem did not exist as yet, there were no problems and no one tried to solve them.
>
> After many years the Chelmites became civilized. They learned to read and write and such words as problem and crisis were created. The moment the word "crisis" appeared in the language, the people realized there was a crisis in their town.

These are the same Chelmite sages who, in another Singer story set during a year of deprivation when there is no sour cream for Hanukkah but plenty of water, solve the problem by decreeing that everyone call sour cream "water" and water "sour cream." Thus, there is plenty of sour cream, and who cares if there's no water?

We—who are of course not fools—we know water is not sour cream no matter what it is called, and that the crisis exist whether we name it or not. But such is the manipulability of words and the possibility of confusion within one language—much less among languages—that words are associated literally and metaphorically not only with great power but with mistakes as well. Singer's example of a translator's error is the rendering of "She cried like a woman in labor" as "She cried like a woman in the Histadruth (union movement)," which has a certain logic to it, ultimately, but is nonetheless wrong. With word, with existence, with the creation of the actual, comes the probability of error.

Singer had a lifelong passion for mystic ideas that embodied what George Steiner calls (in the "Language and Gnosis" chapter of *After Babel*) the affinity between Judaism and mystical linguistics: "Starting with Genesis 11.11 (the story of the tower of Babel)... Jewish thought has played a pronounced role in linguistic mystique, scholarship, and philosophy."

In his Flora Levy Lecture, "My Personal Conception of Religion," Singer uses the mystical metaphor of God as primal writer of the universe, an idea derived from the *Sefer Yezirah*. Grace Farrell discusses this in her essay "Belief and Disbelief: The Kabbalic Basis of I. B. Singer's Secular Vision." Singer writes in his Levy lecture that, as an artist, God is prone to all the strengths and weaknesses of authorship; Singer's God "experiments eternally... He creates and he fails—perhaps. He makes artistic errors, then rectifies them... God keeps on improving Himself... Godliness *is* struggle."

In a typically Jewish fashion, I would like to base my conclusion on a quotation. This one is from an 18th-century Hasidic master whom young Singer would certainly have read, one Menahem Mendl of Vibetsk. Rebbe Mendl said: "Man is the language of God." A beautiful and thought-provoking statement, it is based on a belief in the primacy of language and humanity in the divine scheme. A Taoist teacher in Hong Kong compressed the same idea into three characters: Yun Yan Ji—"Profound ('s) Seal Man"—With "seal" in the Chinese sense of a carved signature. In other words, humanity is the imprint of God. Existence is the Creator talking.

Typically Jewish, however, as opposed to Taoist, is the idea of a screw-up somewhere along the line. This experience-based attitude complements the exaltation of "Man is the language of God" with a resigned "So?—if man is the language of God, maybe it would have been better all around if God had kept his mouth shut."

But God did say, "Let there be," and from that a chain of linguistic imagery follows. For, if, as Mendl says, man is the language of God, then we can say that the writer, the author, is the language of man, the one who actualizes the human experience of existence, puts it into words and thus into memory and thus into as close to immortality as we humans can get. Steiner points out that language is a strange combination of the ineffable with the corporeal. God chose to express his creative power through the medium of flesh and bone, the stuff of speaking, vocal cords and tongues, while the author requires the things of the flesh to give concrete form to his or her creativity. The writer imagines what he or she will, but to put that vision onto paper requires exactly that, paper, pen, hands typing, synapses coordinating: these are necessary . . . but they are prone to error.

To stretch this metaphorical string, if man is the language of God and the author is the language of humanity, can we then say the translator is the language of the author? The author requires the physical agency of another being in order to speak, to actualize, in another tongue. Singer understands translation in the broadest sense, as does Steiner, as the communicating not only of language but of ideas and arts: "In every field of human endeavor we are in need of translations." Man is dependent on God, the author is dependent on humanity, and the translator is dependent upon the author, for the material circumstance. But God is dependent upon humanity to be expressed in a new world, and authors are dependent upon translators to make them exist in another universe of readership. But at the same time he or she opens a world, the translator creates the possibility for more error.

The world as a Translated Text is, as Singer's famous fool Gimpel says, at least once removed from the true world; this secondary world is one of flaws and deceptions. In his essay "On Translating My Books," Singer brings the metaphorical and the mundane acts of translation together: "I sometimes suspect that the Universe is nothing but a bad translation from God's original. My cabalistic theory is that God trusted Satan to translate His creation and it was published before He had a chance to correct the proofs."

Steiner says that translation is doubly removed from God—once because humanity has been exiled from the garden in which Adam spoke the language of God and himself named the animals, and again after Babel when humanity's linguistic oneness was forfeit to its arrogance. The fact that we don't speak the same language reveals a spiritual state distanced from not only direct communication, but communion and community. How do we humans—and here the typically Jewish moral aspect entwines with the metaphorical and metaphysical—how do we get that already-once-translated world as right as possible yet again? How do we avoid error? More practically still, how do we live with inevitable error?

Just as these questions occupied Singer, they will continue to occupy Singer scholars, philosophers, and translators. Singer was not as trusting as God in regard to translation; "I am not going to make the same blunder," he wrote; "all translators must be closely watched." Struggling with his translators personally to get it right was Singer's way of watching. For Singer, whose native tongue necessitated translation and whose career depended upon it, the ultimate justification, however, for struggling so much with translation was not so much fear of being misunderstood, or as he put it, "that if I'm going to be translated one day into Chinese that no one will understand what a Hasid is and what a rabbi is." Singer desired—as directly as possible—to speak his own creation into being in another tongue: "What I do worry about," writes the Nobel Prize winner, "is that my work will be good enough to be translated or to be read, and I work accordingly."

Source: Alida Allison, "Manuscript and Metaphor: Translating Isaac Bashevis Singer's Children's Stories," in *Critical Essays on Isaac Bashevis Singer*, edited by Grace Farrell, G. K. Hall, 1996, pp. 180–90.

SOURCES

Dirda, Michael, "Tales for a Winter Night," in *Washington Post Book World*, December 9, 1984, p. 8.

Fiske, Edward B., "The Push for Smarter Schoolbooks," in *New York Times*, August 2, 1987, Section 12, p. 20.

Johnson, George, "Scholars Debate Roots of Yiddish, Migration of Jews," in *New York Times*, October 29, 1996, p. C1.

Kimmel, Eric A., "Isaac Bashevis Singer: Overview," in *Twentieth-Century Children's Writers*, 4th ed., edited by Laura Standley Berger, St. James Press, 1995.

Lee, Grace Farrell, "The Hidden God of Isaac Bashevis Singer," in *Hollins Critic*, Vol. 10, No. 6, December 1973, pp. 1–15.

May, Jill P., "Envisioning the Jewish Community in Children's Literature: Maurice Sendak and Isaac Singer," in *Journal of the Midwest Modern Language Association*, Vol. 33, No. 3, Autumn 2000–Winter 2001, pp. 137–51.

Sherman, Joseph, "Isaac Bashevis Singer," in *Dictionary of Literary Biography*, Vol. 333: *Writers in Yiddish*, edited by Joseph Sherman, Thomson Gale, 2007, pp. 278–89.

Singer, Isaac Bashevis, "Zlateh the Goat," in *Stories for Children*, translated by Elizabeth Shub and Isaac Bashevis Singer, Farrar, Straus and Giroux, 1984, pp. 45–52.

FURTHER READING

Gold, Ben-Zion, *The Life of Jews in Poland before the Holocaust: A Memoir*, University of Nebraska Press, 2007.

Several of Singer's stories attempt to recapture the world of Polish Jews that was irrevocably lost following the Holocaust. Like Singer, Gold was a Polish Jew, and he portrays this same world in his memoir.

Hadda, Janet, *Isaac Bashevis Singer: A Life*, Oxford University Press, 1997.

In one of the more recent biographies of Singer, Hadda takes a psychological approach to the author's life and work, declaring that he was a neurotic individual.

Scharfstein, Sol, *Understanding Jewish Holidays and Customs: Historical and Contemporary*, Ktav, 1999.

This volume offers a great overview of Jewish holidays, beginning with each holiday's history and attendant customs and moving into a discussion of how those ancient customs have evolved through the present day.

Singer, Isaac Bashevis, *Gimpel the Fool, and Other Stories*, Noonday Press, 1957.

This collection of short stories was the first that Singer published in English, and it remains one of his most renowned. The title story is still held as a shining example of Singer's oeuvre in particular and of Yiddish literature in general.

Glossary

A

Aestheticism: A literary and artistic movement of the nineteenth century. Followers of the movement believed that art should not be mixed with social, political, or moral teaching. The statement "art for art's sake" is a good summary of aestheticism. The movement had its roots in France, but it gained widespread importance in England in the last half of the nineteenth century, where it helped change the Victorian practice of including moral lessons in literature. Oscar Wilde and Edgar Allan Poe are two of the best-known "aesthetes" of the late nineteenth century.

Allegory: A narrative technique in which characters representing things or abstract ideas are used to convey a message or teach a lesson. Allegory is typically used to teach moral, ethical, or religious lessons but is sometimes used for satiric or political purposes. Many fairy tales are allegories.

Allusion: A reference to a familiar literary or historical person or event, used to make an idea more easily understood. Joyce Carol Oates's story "Where Are You Going, Where Have You Been?" exhibits several allusions to popular music.

Analogy: A comparison of two things made to explain something unfamiliar through its similarities to something familiar, or to prove one point based on the acceptance of another. Similes and metaphors are types of analogies.

Antagonist: The major character in a narrative or drama who works against the hero or protagonist. The Misfit in Flannery O'Connor's story "A Good Man Is Hard to Find" serves as the antagonist for the Grandmother.

Anthology: A collection of similar works of literature, art, or music. Zora Neale Hurston's "The Eatonville Anthology" is a collection of stories that take place in the same town.

Anthropomorphism: The presentation of animals or objects in human shape or with human characteristics. The term is derived from the Greek word for "human form." The fur necklet in Katherine Mansfield's story "Miss Brill" has anthropomorphic characteristics.

Anti-hero: A central character in a work of literature who lacks traditional heroic qualities such as courage, physical prowess, and fortitude. Anti-heroes typically distrust conventional values and are unable to commit themselves to any ideals. They generally feel helpless in a world over which they have no control. Anti-heroes usually accept, and often celebrate, their positions as social outcasts. A well-known anti-hero is Walter Mitty in James Thurber's story "The Secret Life of Walter Mitty."

Archetype: The word archetype is commonly used to describe an original pattern or model from which all other things of the same kind are made. Archetypes are the literary images that grow out of the "collective unconscious," a theory proposed by psychologist Carl Jung. They appear in literature as incidents and plots that repeat basic patterns of life. They may also appear as stereotyped characters. The "schlemiel" of Yiddish literature is an archetype.

Autobiography: A narrative in which an individual tells his or her life story. Examples include Benjamin Franklin's *Autobiography* and Amy Hempel's story "In the Cemetery Where Al Jolson Is Buried," which has autobiographical characteristics even though it is a work of fiction.

Avant-garde: A literary term that describes new writing that rejects traditional approaches to literature in favor of innovations in style or content. Twentieth-century examples of the literary avant-garde include the modernists and the minimalists.

B

Belles-lettres: A French term meaning "fine letters" or" beautiful writing." It is often used as a synonym for literature, typically referring to imaginative and artistic rather than scientific or expository writing. Current usage sometimes restricts the meaning to light or humorous writing and appreciative essays about literature. Lewis Carroll's *Alice in Wonderland* epitomizes the realm of belles-lettres.

Bildungsroman: A German word meaning "novel of development." The *bildungsroman* is a study of the maturation of a youthful character, typically brought about through a series of social or sexual encounters that lead to self-awareness. J. D. Salinger's *Catcher in the Rye* is a *bildungsroman*, and Doris Lessing's story "Through the Tunnel" exhibits characteristics of a *bildungsroman* as well.

Black Aesthetic Movement: A period of artistic and literary development among African Americans in the 1960s and early 1970s. This was the first major African-American artistic movement since the Harlem Renaissance and was closely paralleled by the civil rights and black power movements. The black aesthetic writers attempted to produce works of art that would be meaningful to the black masses. Key figures in black aesthetics included one of its founders, poet and playwright Amiri Baraka, formerly known as Le Roi Jones; poet and essayist Haki R. Madhubuti, formerly Don L. Lee; poet and playwright Sonia Sanchez; and dramatist Ed Bullins. Works representative of the Black Aesthetic Movement include Amiri Baraka's play *Dutchman,* a 1964 Obie award-winner.

Black Humor: Writing that places grotesque elements side by side with humorous ones in an attempt to shock the reader, forcing him or her to laugh at the horrifying reality of a disordered world. "Lamb to the Slaughter," by Roald Dahl, in which a placid housewife murders her husband and serves the murder weapon to the investigating policemen, is an example of black humor.

C

Catharsis: The release or purging of unwanted emotions—specifically fear and pity—brought about by exposure to art. The term was first used by the Greek philosopher Aristotle in his *Poetics* to refer to the desired effect of tragedy on spectators.

Character: Broadly speaking, a person in a literary work. The actions of characters are what constitute the plot of a story, novel, or poem. There are numerous types of characters, ranging from simple, stereotypical figures to intricate, multifaceted ones. "Characterization" is the process by which an author creates vivid, believable characters in a work of art. This may be done in a variety of ways, including (1) direct description of the character by the narrator; (2) the direct presentation of the speech, thoughts, or actions of the character; and (3) the responses of other characters to the character. The term "character" also refers to a form originated by the ancient Greek writer Theophrastus that later became popular in the seventeenth and eighteenth centuries. It is a short essay or sketch of a person who prominently displays a specific attribute or quality, such as miserliness or ambition. "Miss Brill," a story by Katherine Mansfield, is an example of a character sketch.

Classical: In its strictest definition in literary criticism, classicism refers to works of ancient Greek or Roman literature. The term may also be used to describe a literary work of recognized importance (a "classic") from any time period or literature that exhibits the traits of classicism. Examples of later works and authors now described as classical include French literature of the seventeenth century, Western novels of the nineteenth century, and American fiction of the mid-nineteenth century such as that written by James Fenimore Cooper and Mark Twain.

Climax: The turning point in a narrative, the moment when the conflict is at its most intense. Typically, the structure of stories, novels, and plays is one of rising action, in which tension builds to the climax, followed by falling action, in which tension lessens as the story moves to its conclusion.

Comedy: One of two major types of drama, the other being tragedy. Its aim is to amuse, and it typically ends happily. Comedy assumes many forms, such as farce and burlesque, and uses a variety of techniques, from parody to satire. In a restricted sense the term comedy refers only to dramatic presentations, but in general usage it is commonly applied to nondramatic works as well.

Comic Relief: The use of humor to lighten the mood of a serious or tragic story, especially in plays. The technique is very common in Elizabethan works, and can be an integral part of the plot or simply a brief event designed to break the tension of the scene.

Conflict: The conflict in a work of fiction is the issue to be resolved in the story. It usually occurs between two characters, the protagonist and the antagonist, or between the protagonist and society or the protagonist and himself or herself. The conflict in Washington Irving's story "The Devil and Tom Walker" is that the Devil wants Tom Walker's soul but Tom does not want to go to hell.

Criticism: The systematic study and evaluation of literary works, usually based on a specific method or set of principles. An important part of literary studies since ancient times, the practice of criticism has given rise to numerous theories, methods, and "schools," sometimes producing conflicting, even contradictory, interpretations of literature in general as well as of individual works. Even such basic issues as what constitutes a poem or a novel have been the subject of much criticism over the centuries. Seminal texts of literary criticism include Plato's *Republic,* Aristotle's *Poetics*, Sir Philip Sidney's *The Defence of Poesie,* and John Dryden's *Of Dramatic Poesie.* Contemporary schools of criticism include deconstruction, feminist, psychoanalytic, poststructuralist, new historicist, postcolonialist, and reader-response.

D

Deconstruction: A method of literary criticism characterized by multiple conflicting interpretations of a given work. Deconstructionists consider the impact of the language of a work and suggest that the true meaning of the work is not necessarily the meaning that the author intended.

Deduction: The process of reaching a conclusion through reasoning from general premises to a specific premise. Arthur Conan Doyle's character Sherlock Holmes often used deductive reasoning to solve mysteries.

Denotation: The definition of a word, apart from the impressions or feelings it creates in the reader. The word "apartheid" denotes a political and economic policy of segregation by race, but its connotations—oppression, slavery, inequality—are numerous.

Denouement: A French word meaning "the unknotting." In literature, it denotes the resolution of conflict in fiction or drama. The *denouement* follows the climax and provides an outcome to the primary plot situation as well as an explanation of secondary plot complications. A well-known example of *denouement* is the last scene of the play *As You Like It* by William Shakespeare, in which couples are married, an evildoer repents, the identities of two disguised characters are revealed, and a ruler is restored to power. Also known as "falling action."

Detective Story: A narrative about the solution of a mystery or the identification of a criminal. The conventions of the detective story include the detective's scrupulous use of logic in solving the mystery; incompetent or ineffectual police; a suspect who appears guilty at first but is later proved innocent; and the detective's friend or confidant—often the narrator—whose slowness in interpreting clues emphasizes by contrast the detective's brilliance. Edgar Allan Poe's "Murders in the Rue Morgue" is commonly regarded as the earliest example of this type of story. Other practitioners are Arthur Conan Doyle, Dashiell Hammett, and Agatha Christie.

Dialogue: Dialogue is conversation between people in a literary work. In its most restricted sense, it refers specifically to the speech of characters in a drama. As a specific literary genre, a "dialogue" is a composition in which characters debate an issue or idea.

Didactic: A term used to describe works of literature that aim to teach a moral, religious, political, or practical lesson. Although didactic elements are often found inartistically pleasing works, the term "didactic" usually refers to literature in which the message is more important than the form. The term may also be used to criticize a work that the critic finds "overly didactic," that is, heavy-handed in its delivery of a lesson. An example of didactic literature is John Bunyan's *Pilgrim's Progress*.

Dramatic Irony: Occurs when the reader of a work of literature knows something that a character in the work itself does not know. The irony is in the contrast between the intended meaning of the statements or actions of a character and the additional information understood by the audience.

Dystopia: An imaginary place in a work of fiction where the characters lead dehumanized, fearful lives. George Orwell's *Nineteen Eighty-four,* and Margaret Atwood's *Handmaid's Tale* portray versions of dystopia.

E

Edwardian: Describes cultural conventions identified with the period of the reign of Edward VII of England (1901–1910). Writers of the Edwardian Age typically displayed a strong reaction against the propriety and conservatism of the Victorian Age. Their work often exhibits distrust of authority in religion, politics, and art and expresses strong doubts about the soundness of conventional values. Writers of this era include E. M. Forster, H. G. Wells, and Joseph Conrad.

Empathy: A sense of shared experience, including emotional and physical feelings, with someone or something other than oneself. Empathy is often used to describe the response of a reader to a literary character.

Epilogue: A concluding statement or section of a literary work. In dramas, particularly those of the seventeenth and eighteenth centuries, the epilogue is a closing speech, often in verse, delivered by an actor at the end of a play and spoken directly to the audience.

Epiphany: A sudden revelation of truth inspired by a seemingly trivial incident. The term was widely used by James Joyce in his critical writings, and the stories in Joyce's *Dubliners* are commonly called "epiphanies."

Epistolary Novel: A novel in the form of letters. The form was particularly popular in the eighteenth century. The form can also be applied to short stories, as in Edwidge Danticat's "Children of the Sea."

Epithet: A word or phrase, often disparaging or abusive, that expresses a character trait of someone or something. "The Napoleon of crime" is an epithet applied to Professor Moriarty, arch-rival of Sherlock Holmes in Arthur Conan Doyle's series of detective stories.

Existentialism: A predominantly twentieth-century philosophy concerned with the nature and perception of human existence. There are two major strains of existentialist thought: atheistic and Christian. Followers of atheistic existentialism believe that the individual is alone in a godless universe and that the basic human condition is one of suffering and loneliness. Nevertheless, because there are no fixed values, individuals can create their own characters—indeed, they can shape themselves—through the exercise of free will. The atheistic strain culminates in and is popularly associated with the works of Jean-Paul Sartre. The Christian existentialists, on the other hand, believe that only in God may people find freedom from life's anguish. The two strains hold certain beliefs in common: that existence cannot be fully understood or described through empirical effort; that anguish is a universal element of life; that individuals must bear responsibility for their actions; and that there is no common standard of behavior or perception for religious and ethical matters. Existentialist thought figures prominently in the works of such authors as Franz Kafka, Fyodor Dostoyevsky, and Albert Camus.

Expatriatism: The practice of leaving one's country to live for an extended period in another country. Literary expatriates include Irish author James Joyce who moved to Italy and France, American writers James Baldwin, Ernest Hemingway, Gertrude Stein, and F. Scott Fitzgerald who lived and wrote in Paris, and Polish novelist Joseph Conrad in England.

Exposition: Writing intended to explain the nature of an idea, thing, or theme. Expository writing is often combined with description, narration, or argument.

Expressionism: An indistinct literary term, originally used to describe an early twentieth-century school of German painting. The term applies to almost any mode of unconventional, highly subjective writing that distorts reality in some way. Advocates of Expressionism include Federico Garcia Lorca, Eugene O'Neill, Franz Kafka, and James Joyce.

F

Fable: A prose or verse narrative intended to convey amoral. Animals or inanimate objects with human characteristics often serve as characters in fables. A famous fable is Aesop's "The Tortoise and the Hare."

Fantasy: A literary form related to mythology and folklore. Fantasy literature is typically set in non-existent realms and features supernatural beings. Notable examples of literature with elements of fantasy are Gabriel Gárcia Márquez's story "The Handsomest Drowned Man in the World" and Ursula K. Le Guin's "The Ones Who Walk Away from Omelas."

Farce: A type of comedy characterized by broad humor, outlandish incidents, and often vulgar subject matter. Much of the comedy in film and television could more accurately be described as farce.

Fiction: Any story that is the product of imagination rather than a documentation of fact. Characters and events in such narratives may be based in real life but their ultimate form and configuration is a creation of the author.

Figurative Language: A technique in which an author uses figures of speech such as hyperbole, irony, metaphor, or simile for a particular effect. Figurative language is the opposite of literal language, in which every word is truthful, accurate, and free of exaggeration or embellishment.

Flashback: A device used in literature to present action that occurred before the beginning of the story. Flashbacks are often introduced as the dreams or recollections of one or more characters.

Foil: A character in a work of literature whose physical or psychological qualities contrast strongly with, and therefore highlight, the corresponding qualities of another character. In his Sherlock Holmes stories, Arthur Conan Doyle portrayed Dr. Watson as a man of normal habits and intelligence, making him a foil for the eccentric and unusually perceptive Sherlock Holmes.

Folklore: Traditions and myths preserved in a culture or group of people. Typically, these are passed on by word of mouth in various forms—such as legends, songs, and proverbs—or preserved in customs and ceremonies. Washington Irving, in "The Devil and Tom Walker" and many of his other stories, incorporates many elements of the folklore of New England and Germany.

Folktale: A story originating in oral tradition. Folk tales fall into a variety of categories, including legends, ghost stories, fairy tales, fables, and anecdotes based on historical figures and events.

Foreshadowing: A device used in literature to create expectation or to set up an explanation of later developments. Edgar Allan Poe uses foreshadowing to create suspense in "The Fall of the House of Usher" when the narrator comments on the crumbling state of disrepair in which he finds the house.

G

Genre: A category of literary work. Genre may refer to both the content of a given work—tragedy, comedy, horror, science fiction—and to its form, such as poetry, novel, or drama.

Gilded Age: A period in American history during the 1870s and after characterized by political corruption and materialism. A number of important novels of social and political criticism were written during this time. Henry James and Kate Chopin are two writers who were prominent during the Gilded Age.

Gothicism: In literature, works characterized by a taste for medieval or morbid characters and situations. A gothic novel prominently features elements of horror, the supernatural, gloom, and violence: clanking chains, terror, ghosts, medieval castles, and unexplained phenomena. The term "gothic novel" is also applied to novels that lack elements of the traditional Gothic setting but that create a similar atmosphere of terror or dread. The term can also be applied to stories, plays, and poems. Mary Shelley's *Frankenstein* and Joyce Carol Oates's *Belle fleur* are both gothic novels.

Grotesque: In literature, a work that is characterized by exaggeration, deformity, freakishness, and disorder. The grotesque often includes an element of comic absurdity. Examples of the grotesque can be found in the works of Edgar Allan Poe, Flannery O'Connor, Joseph Heller, and Shirley Jackson.

H

Harlem Renaissance: The Harlem Renaissance of the 1920s is generally considered the first significant movement of black writers and artists in the United States. During this period, new and established black writers, many of whom lived in the region of New York City known as Harlem, published more fiction and poetry than ever before, the first influential black literary journals were established, and black authors and artists received their first widespread recognition and serious critical appraisal. Among the major writers associated with this period are Countee Cullen, Langston Hughes, Arna Bontemps, and Zora Neale Hurston.

Hero/Heroine: The principal sympathetic character in a literary work. Heroes and heroines typically exhibit admirable traits: idealism, courage, and integrity, for example. Famous heroes and heroines of literature include Charles Dickens's Oliver Twist, Margaret Mitchell's Scarlett O'Hara, and the anonymous narrator in Ralph Ellison's *Invisible Man*.

Hyperbole: Deliberate exaggeration used to achieve an effect. In William Shakespeare's *Macbeth,* Lady Macbeth hyperbolizes when she says, "All the perfumes of Arabia could not sweeten this little hand."

I

Image: A concrete representation of an object or sensory experience. Typically, such a representation helps evoke the feelings associated with the object or experience itself. Images are either "literal" or "figurative." Literal images are especially concrete and involve little or no extension of the obvious meaning of the words used to express them. Figurative images do not follow the literal meaning of the words exactly. Images in literature are usually visual, but the term "image" can also refer to the representation of any sensory experience.

Imagery: The array of images in a literary work. Also used to convey the author's overall use of figurative language in a work.

In medias res: A Latin term meaning "in the middle of things." It refers to the technique of beginning a story at its midpoint and then using various flashback devices to reveal previous action. This technique originated in such epics as Virgil's *Aeneid.*

Interior Monologue: A narrative technique in which characters' thoughts are revealed in a way that appears to be uncontrolled by the author. The interior monologue typically aims to reveal the inner self of a character. It portrays emotional experiences as they occur at both a conscious and unconscious level. One of the best-known interior monologues in English is the Molly Bloom section at the close of James Joyce's *Ulysses.* Katherine Anne Porter's "The Jilting of Granny Weatherall" is also told in the form of an interior monologue.

Irony: In literary criticism, the effect of language in which the intended meaning is the opposite of what is stated. The title of Jonathan Swift's "A Modest Proposal" is ironic because what Swift proposes in this essay is cannibalism—hardly "modest."

J

Jargon: Language that is used or understood only by a select group of people. Jargon may refer to terminology used in a certain profession, such as computer jargon, or it may refer to any nonsensical language that is not understood by most people. Anthony Burgess's *A Clockwork Orange* and James Thurber's "The Secret Life of Walter Mitty" both use jargon.

K

Knickerbocker Group: An indistinct group of New York writers of the first half of the nineteenth century. Members of the group were linked only by location and a common theme: New York life. Two famous members of the Knickerbocker Group were Washington Irving and William Cullen Bryant. The group's name derives from Irving's *Knickerbocker's History of New York*.

L

Literal Language: An author uses literal language when he or she writes without exaggerating or embellishing the subject matter and without any tools of figurative language. To say "He ran very quickly down the street" is to use literal language, whereas to say "He ran like a hare down the street" would be using figurative language.

Literature: Literature is broadly defined as any written or spoken material, but the term most often refers to creative works. Literature includes poetry, drama, fiction, and many kinds of nonfiction writing, as well as oral, dramatic, and broadcast compositions not necessarily preserved in a written format, such as films and television programs.

Lost Generation: A term first used by Gertrude Stein to describe the post-World War I generation of American writers: men and women haunted by a sense of betrayal and emptiness brought about by the destructiveness of the war. The term is commonly applied to Hart Crane, Ernest Hemingway, F. Scott Fitzgerald, and others.

M

Magic Realism: A form of literature that incorporates fantasy elements or supernatural occurrences into the narrative and accepts them as truth. Gabriel Gárcia Márquez and Laura Esquivel are two writers known for their works of magic realism.

Metaphor: A figure of speech that expresses an idea through the image of another object. Metaphors suggest the essence of the first object by identifying it with certain qualities of the second object. An example is "But soft, what light through yonder window breaks? / It is the east, and Juliet is the sun" in William Shakespeare's *Romeo and Juliet*. Here, Juliet, the first object, is identified with qualities of the second object, the sun.

Minimalism: A literary style characterized by spare, simple prose with few elaborations. In minimalism, the main theme of the work is often never discussed directly. Amy Hempel and Ernest Hemingway are two writers known for their works of minimalism.

Modernism: Modern literary practices. Also, the principles of a literary school that lasted from roughly the beginning of the twentieth century until the end of World War II. Modernism is defined by its rejection of the literary conventions of the nineteenth century and by its opposition to conventional morality, taste, traditions, and economic values. Many writers are associated with the concepts of modernism, including Albert Camus, D. H. Lawrence, Ernest Hemingway, William Faulkner, Eugene O'Neill, and James Joyce.

Monologue: A composition, written or oral, by a single individual. More specifically, a speech given by a single individual in a drama or other public entertainment. It has no set length, although it is usually several or more lines long. "I Stand Here Ironing" by Tillie Olsen is an example of a story written in the form of a monologue.

Mood: The prevailing emotions of a work or of the author in his or her creation of the work. The mood of a work is not always what might be expected based on its subject matter.

Motif: A theme, character type, image, metaphor, or other verbal element that recurs throughout a single work of literature or occurs in a number of different works over a period of time. For example, the color white in Herman Melville's *Moby Dick* is a "specific" motif, while the trials of star-crossed lovers is a "conventional" motif from the literature of all periods.

N

Narration: The telling of a series of events, real or invented. A narration may be either a simple narrative, in which the events are recounted chronologically, or a narrative with a plot, in which the account is given in a style reflecting the author's artistic concept of the story. Narration is sometimes used as a synonym for "storyline."

Narrative: A verse or prose accounting of an event or sequence of events, real or invented. The term is also used as an adjective in the sense "method of narration." For example, in literary criticism, the expression "narrative technique" usually refers to the way the author structures and presents his or her story. Different narrative forms include diaries, travelogues, novels, ballads, epics, short stories, and other fictional forms.

Narrator: The teller of a story. The narrator may be the author or a character in the story through whom the author speaks. Huckleberry Finn is the narrator of Mark Twain's *The Adventures of Huckleberry Finn.*

Novella: An Italian term meaning "story." This term has been especially used to describe fourteenth-century Italian tales, but it also refers to modern short novels. Modern novellas include Leo Tolstoy's *The Death of Ivan Ilich,* Fyodor Dostoyevsky's *Notes from the Underground,* and Joseph Conrad's *Heart of Darkness.*

O

Oedipus Complex: A son's romantic obsession with his mother. The phrase is derived from the story of the ancient Theban hero Oedipus, who unknowingly killed his father and married his mother, and was popularized by Sigmund Freud's theory of psychoanalysis. Literary occurrences of the Oedipus complex include Sophocles' *Oedipus Rex* and D. H. Lawrence's "The Rocking-Horse Winner."

Onomatopoeia: The use of words whose sounds express or suggest their meaning. In its simplest sense, onomatopoeia may be represented by words that mimic the sounds they denote such as "hiss" or "meow." At a more subtle level, the pattern and rhythm of sounds and rhymes of a line or poem may be onomatopoeic.

Oral Tradition: A process by which songs, ballads, folklore, and other material are transmitted by word of mouth. The tradition of oral transmission predates the written record systems of literate society. Oral transmission preserves material sometimes over generations, although often with variations. Memory plays a large part in the recitation and preservation of orally transmitted material. Native American myths and legends, and African folktales told by plantation slaves are examples of orally transmitted literature.

P

Parable: A story intended to teach a moral lesson or answer an ethical question. Examples of parables are the stories told by Jesus Christ in the New Testament, notably "The Prodigal Son," but parables also are used in Sufism, rabbinic literature, Hasidism, and Zen Buddhism. Isaac Bashevis Singer's story "Gimpel the Fool" exhibits characteristics of a parable.

Paradox: A statement that appears illogical or contradictory at first, but may actually point to an underlying truth. A literary example of a paradox is George Orwell's statement "All animals are equal, but some animals are more equal than others" in *Animal Farm.*

Parody: In literature, this term refers to an imitation of a serious literary work or the signature style of a particular author in a ridiculous manner. Atypical parody adopts the style of the original and applies it to an inappropriate subject for humorous effect. Parody is a form of satire and could be considered the literary equivalent of a caricature or cartoon. Henry Fielding's *Shamela* is a parody of Samuel Richardson's *Pamela.*

Persona: A Latin term meaning "mask." Personae are the characters in a fictional work of literature. The persona generally functions as a mask through which the author tells a story in a voice other than his or her own. A persona is usually either a character in a story who acts as a narrator or an "implied author," a voice created by the author to act as the narrator for himself or herself. The persona in Charlotte Perkins Gilman's story "The Yellow Wallpaper" is the unnamed young mother experiencing a mental breakdown.

Personification: A figure of speech that gives human qualities to abstract ideas, animals, and inanimate objects. To say that "the sun is smiling" is to personify the sun.

Plot: The pattern of events in a narrative or drama. In its simplest sense, the plot guides the author in composing the work and helps the reader follow the work. Typically, plots exhibit causality and unity and have a beginning, a middle, and an end. Sometimes, however, a plot may consist of a series of disconnected events, in which case it is known as an "episodic plot."

Poetic Justice: An outcome in a literary work, not necessarily a poem, in which the good are rewarded and the evil are punished, especially in ways that particularly fit their virtues or crimes. For example, a murderer may himself be murdered, or a thief will find himself penniless.

Poetic License: Distortions of fact and literary convention made by a writer—not always a poet—for the sake of the effect gained. Poetic license is closely related to the concept of "artistic freedom." An author exercises poetic license by saying that a pile of money "reaches as high as a mountain" when the pile is actually only a foot or two high.

Point of View: The narrative perspective from which a literary work is presented to the reader. There are four traditional points of view. The "third person omniscient" gives the reader a "godlike" perspective, unrestricted by time or place, from which to see actions and look into the minds of characters. This allows the author to comment openly on characters and events in the work. The "third person" point of view presents the events of the story from outside of any single character's perception, much like the omniscient point of view, but the reader must understand the action as it takes place and without any special insight into characters' minds or motivations. The "first person" or "personal" point of view relates events as they are perceived by a single character. The main character "tells" the story and may offer opinions about the action and characters which differ from those of the author. Much less common than omniscient, third person, and first person is the "second person" point of view, wherein the author tells the story as if it is happening to the reader. James Thurber employs the omniscient point of view in his short story "The Secret Life of Walter Mitty." Ernest Hemingway's "A Clean, Well-Lighted Place" is a short story told from the third person point of view. Mark Twain's novel *Huckleberry Finn* is presented from the first person viewpoint. Jay McInerney's *Bright Lights, Big City* is an example of a novel which uses the second person point of view.

Pornography: Writing intended to provoke feelings of lust in the reader. Such works are often condemned by critics and teachers, but those which can be shown to have literary value are viewed less harshly. Literary works that have been described as pornographic include D. H. Lawrence's *Lady Chatterley's Lover* and James Joyce's *Ulysses.*

Post-Aesthetic Movement: An artistic response made by African Americans to the black aesthetic movement of the 1960s and early 1970s. Writers since that time have adopted a somewhat different tone in their work, with less emphasis placed on the disparity between black and white in the United States. In the words of post-aesthetic authors such as Toni Morrison, John Edgar Wideman, and Kristin Hunter, African Americans are portrayed as looking inward for answers to their own questions, rather than always looking to the outside world. Two well-known examples of works produced as part of the post-aesthetic movement are the Pulitzer Prize–winning novels *The Color Purple* by Alice Walker and *Beloved* by Toni Morrison.

Postmodernism: Writing from the 1960s forward characterized by experimentation and application of modernist elements, which include existentialism and alienation. Postmodernists have gone a step further in the rejection of tradition begun with the modernists by also rejecting traditional forms, preferring the anti-novel over the novel and the anti-hero over the hero. Postmodern writers include Thomas Pynchon, Margaret Drabble, and Gabriel Gárcia Márquez.

Prologue: An introductory section of a literary work. It often contains information establishing the situation of the characters or presents information about the setting, time period, or action. In drama, the prologue is spoken by a chorus or by one of the principal characters.

Prose: A literary medium that attempts to mirror the language of everyday speech. It is distinguished from poetry by its use of unmetered, unrhymed language consisting of logically related sentences. Prose is usually grouped into paragraphs that form a cohesive whole such as an essay or a novel. The term is sometimes used to mean an author's general writing.

Protagonist: The central character of a story who serves as a focus for its themes and incidents and as the principal rationale for its development. The protagonist is sometimes referred to in discussions of modern literature as the hero or anti-hero. Well-known protagonists are Hamlet in William Shakespeare's *Hamlet* and Jay Gatsby in F. Scott Fitzgerald's *The Great Gatsby.*

R

Realism: A nineteenth-century European literary movement that sought to portray familiar characters, situations, and settings in a realistic manner. This was done primarily by using an objective narrative point of view and through the buildup of accurate detail. The standard for success of any realistic work depends on how faithfully it transfers common experience into fictional forms. The realistic method may be altered or extended, as in stream of consciousness writing, to record highly subjective experience. Contemporary authors who often write in a realistic way include Nadine Gordimer and Grace Paley.

Resolution: The portion of a story following the climax, in which the conflict is resolved. The resolution of Jane Austen's *Northanger Abbey* is neatly summed up in the following sentence: "Henry and Catherine were married, the bells rang and every body smiled."

Rising Action: The part of a drama where the plot becomes increasingly complicated. Rising action leads up to the climax, or turning point, of a drama. The final "chase scene" of an action film is generally the rising action which culminates in the film's climax.

Roman a clef: A French phrase meaning "novel with a key." It refers to a narrative in which real persons are portrayed under fictitious names. Jack Kerouac, for example, portrayed various friends under fictitious names in the novel *On the Road.* D. H. Lawrence based "The Rocking-Horse Winner" on a family he knew.

Romanticism: This term has two widely accepted meanings. In historical criticism, it refers to a European intellectual and artistic movement of the late eighteenth and early nineteenth centuries that sought greater freedom of personal expression than that allowed by the strict rules of literary form and logic of the eighteenth-century neoclassicists. The Romantics preferred emotional and imaginative expression to rational analysis. They considered the individual to be at the center of all experience and so placed him or her at the center of their art. The Romantics believed that the creative imagination reveals nobler truths—unique feelings and attitudes—than those that could be discovered by logic or by scientific examination. "Romanticism" is also used as a general term to refer to a type of sensibility found in all periods of literary history and usually considered to be in opposition to the principles of classicism. In this sense, Romanticism signifies any work or philosophy in which the exotic or dreamlike figure strongly, or that is devoted to individualistic expression, self-analysis, or a pursuit of a higher realm of knowledge than can be discovered by human reason. Prominent Romantics include Jean-Jacques Rousseau, William Wordsworth, John Keats, Lord Byron, and Johann Wolfgang von Goethe.

S

Satire: A work that uses ridicule, humor, and wit to criticize and provoke change in human nature and institutions. Voltaire's novella *Candide* and Jonathan Swift's essay "A Modest Proposal" are both satires. Flannery O'Connor's portrayal of the family in "A Good Man Is Hard to Find" is a satire of a modern, Southern, American family.

Science Fiction: A type of narrative based upon real or imagined scientific theories and technology. Science fiction is often peopled with alien creatures and set on other planets or in different dimensions. Popular writers of science fiction are Isaac Asimov, Karel Capek, Ray Bradbury, and Ursula K. Le Guin.

Setting: The time, place, and culture in which the action of a narrative takes place. The elements of setting may include geographic location, characters's physical and mental environments, prevailing cultural attitudes, or the historical time in which the action takes place.

Short Story: A fictional prose narrative shorter and more focused than a novella. The short story usually deals with a single episode and often a single character. The "tone," the author's attitude toward his or her subject and audience, is uniform throughout. The short story frequently also lacks *denouement*, ending instead at its climax.

Signifying Monkey: A popular trickster figure in black folklore, with hundreds of tales about this character documented since the 19th century. Henry Louis Gates Jr. examines the history of the signifying monkey in *The Signifying Monkey: Towards a Theory of Afro-American Literary Criticism,* published in 1988.

Simile: A comparison, usually using "like" or "as," of two essentially dissimilar things, as in "coffee as cold as ice" or "He sounded like a broken record." The title of Ernest Hemingway's "Hills Like White Elephants" contains a simile.

Socialist Realism: The Socialist Realism school of literary theory was proposed by Maxim Gorky and established as a dogma by the first Soviet Congress of Writers. It demanded adherence to a communist worldview in works of literature. Its doctrines required an objective viewpoint comprehensible to the working classes and themes of social struggle featuring strong proletarian heroes. Gabriel Gárcia Márquez's stories exhibit some characteristics of Socialist Realism.

Stereotype: A stereotype was originally the name for a duplication made during the printing process; this led to its modern definition as a person or thing that is (or is assumed to be) the same as all others of its type. Common stereotypical characters include the absent-minded professor, the nagging wife, the troublemaking teenager, and the kindhearted grandmother.

Stream of Consciousness: A narrative technique for rendering the inward experience of a character. This technique is designed to give the impression of an ever-changing series of thoughts, emotions, images, and memories in the spontaneous and seemingly illogical order that they occur in life. The textbook example of stream of consciousness is the last section of James Joyce's *Ulysses.*

Structure: The form taken by a piece of literature. The structure may be made obvious for ease of understanding, as in nonfiction works, or may obscured for artistic purposes, as in some poetry or seemingly "unstructured" prose.

Style: A writer's distinctive manner of arranging words to suit his or her ideas and purpose in writing. The unique imprint of the author's personality upon his or her writing, style is the product of an author's way of arranging ideas and his or her use of diction, different sentence structures, rhythm, figures of speech, rhetorical principles, and other elements of composition.

Suspense: A literary device in which the author maintains the audience's attention through the buildup of events, the outcome of which will soon be revealed. Suspense in William Shakespeare's *Hamlet* is sustained throughout by the question of whether or not the Prince will achieve what he has been instructed to do and of what he intends to do.

Symbol: Something that suggests or stands for something else without losing its original identity. In literature, symbols combine their literal meaning with the suggestion of an abstract concept. Literary symbols are of two types: those that carry complex associations of meaning no matter what their contexts, and those that derive their suggestive meaning from their functions in specific literary works. Examples of symbols are sunshine suggesting happiness, rain suggesting sorrow, and storm clouds suggesting despair.

T

Tale: A story told by a narrator with a simple plot and little character development. Tales are usually relatively short and often carry a simple message. Examples of tales can be found in the works of Saki, Anton Chekhov, Guy de Maupassant, and O. Henry.

Tall Tale: A humorous tale told in a straightforward, credible tone but relating absolutely impossible events or feats of the characters. Such tales were commonly told of frontier adventures during the settlement of the west in the United States. Literary use of tall tales can be found in Washington Irving's *History of New York,* Mark Twain's *Life on the Mississippi,* and in the German R. F. Raspe's *Baron Munchausen's Narratives of His Marvellous Travels and Campaigns in Russia.*

Theme: The main point of a work of literature. The term is used interchangeably with thesis. Many works have multiple themes. One of the themes of Nathaniel Hawthorne's "Young Goodman Brown" is loss of faith.

Tone: The author's attitude toward his or her audience maybe deduced from the tone of the work. A formal tone may create distance or convey politeness, while an informal tone may encourage a friendly, intimate, or intrusive feeling in the reader. The author's attitude toward his or her subject matter may also be deduced from the tone of the words he or she uses in discussing it. The tone of John F. Kennedy's speech which included the appeal to "ask not what your country can do for you" was intended to instill feelings of camaraderie and national pride in listeners.

Tragedy: A drama in prose or poetry about a noble, courageous hero of excellent character who, because of some tragic character flaw, brings ruin upon him- or herself. Tragedy treats its subjects in a dignified and serious manner, using poetic language to help evoke pity and fear and bring about catharsis, a purging of these emotions. The tragic form was practiced extensively by the ancient Greeks. The classical form of tragedy was revived in the sixteenth century; it flourished especially on the Elizabethan stage. In modern times, dramatists have attempted to adapt the form to the needs of modern society by drawing their heroes from the ranks of ordinary men and women and defining the nobility of these heroes in terms of spirit rather than exalted social standing. Some contemporary works that are thought of as tragedies include *The Great Gatsby* by F. Scott Fitzgerald, and *The Sound and the Fury* by William Faulkner.

Tragic Flaw: In a tragedy, the quality within the hero or heroine which leads to his or her downfall. Examples of the tragic flaw include Othello's jealousy and Hamlet's indecisiveness, although most great tragedies defy such simple interpretation.

U

Utopia: A fictional perfect place, such as "paradise" or "heaven." An early literary utopia was described in Plato's *Republic,* and in modern literature, Ursula K. Le Guin depicts a utopia in "The Ones Who Walk Away from Omelas."

V

Victorian: Refers broadly to the reign of Queen Victoria of England (1837-1901) and to anything with qualities typical of that era. For example, the qualities of smug narrow-mindedness, bourgeois materialism, faith in social progress, and priggish morality are often considered Victorian. In literature, the Victorian Period was the great age of the English novel, and the latter part of the era saw the rise of movements such as decadence and symbolism.

Cumulative Author/Title Index

A

A & P (Updike): V3
Achebe, Chinua
Civil Peace: V13
Vengeful Creditor: V3
Adams, Alice
Greyhound People: V21
The Last Lovely City: V14
African Passions (Rivera): V15
Africans (Kohler): V18
Aftermath (Waters): V22
After Twenty Years (Henry): V27
Agüeros, Jack
Dominoes: V13
Aiken, Conrad
Silent Snow, Secret Snow: V8
The Aleph (Borges): V17
Alexie, Sherman
Because My Father Always Said He Was the Only Indian Who Saw Jimi Hendrix Play "The Star-Spangled Banner" at Woodstock: V18
All the Years of Her Life (Callaghan): V19
Allen, Woody
The Kugelmass Episode: V21
Allende, Isabel
And of Clay Are We Created: V11
The Gold of Tomás Vargas: V16
Alvarez, Julia
Liberty: V27
America and I (Yezierska): V15
American History (Cofer): V27
And of Clay Are We Created (Allende): V11
Anderson, Sherwood
Death in the Woods: V10
Hands: V11
Sophistication: V4
Animal Stories (Brown): V14
Anxiety (Paley): V27
The Arabian Nights (Burton): V21
Araby (Joyce): V1
Art Work (Byatt): V26
Asimov, Isaac
Nightfall: V17
Astronomer's Wife (Boyle): V13
Atwood, Margaret
Happy Endings: V13
Rape Fantasies: V3
Average Waves in Unprotected Waters (Tyler): V17
Axolotl (Cortázar): V3

B

Babel, Isaac
My First Goose: V10
Babette's Feast (Dinesen): V20
Babylon Revisited (Fitzgerald): V4
Baida, Peter
A Nurse's Story: V25
Baldwin, James
The Rockpile: V18
Sonny's Blues: V2
Balzac, Honore de
La Grande Bretèche: V10
Bambara, Toni Cade
Blues Ain't No Mockin Bird: V4
Gorilla, My Love: V21
The Lesson: V12
Raymond's Run: V7
Barn Burning (Faulkner): V5
Barnes, Julian
Melon: V24
Barrett, Andrea
The English Pupil: V24
Barth, John
Lost in the Funhouse: V6
Barthelme, Donald
The Indian Uprising: V17
Robert Kennedy Saved from Drowning: V3
Bartleby the Scrivener, A Tale of Wall Street (Melville): V3
Bates, H. E.
The Daffodil Sky: V7
The Bear (Faulkner): V2
The Beast in the Jungle (James): V6
Beattie, Ann
Imagined Scenes: V20
Janus: V9
Because My Father Always Said He Was the Only Indian Who Saw Jimi Hendrix Play "The Star-Spangled Banner" at Woodstock (Alexie): V18
Beckett, Samuel
Dante and the Lobster: V15
The Beginning of Homewood (Wideman): V12
Bellow, Saul
Leaving the Yellow House: V12
A Silver Dish: V22
Bender, Aimee
The Rememberer: V25
Benet, Stephen Vincent
An End to Dreams: V22

Berriault, Gina
The Stone Boy: V7
Women in Their Beds: V11
The Best Girlfriend You Never Had (Houston): V17
Bierce, Ambrose
The Boarded Window: V9
A Horseman in the Sky: V27
An Occurrence at Owl Creek Bridge: V2
Big Black Good Man (Wright): V20
Big Blonde (Parker): V5
The Birds (du Maurier): V16
Bisson, Terry
The Toxic Donut: V18
Black Boy (Boyle): V14
The Black Cat (Poe): V26
Black Is My Favorite Color (Malamud): V16
Blackberry Winter (Warren): V8
Bliss (Mansfield): V10
Blood-Burning Moon (Toomer): V5
Bloodchild (Butler): V6
The Bloody Chamber (Carter): V4
Bloom, Amy
Silver Water: V11
Blues Ain't No Mockin Bird (Bambara): V4
The Blues I'm Playing (Hughes): V7
The Boarded Window (Bierce): V9
Boll, Heinrich
Christmas Not Just Once a Year: V20
Borges, Jorge Luis
The Aleph: V17
The Circular Ruins: V26
The Garden of Forking Paths: V9
Pierre Menard, Author of the Quixote: V4
Borowski, Tadeusz
This Way for the Gas, Ladies and Gentlemen: V13
Boule de Suif (Maupassant): V21
Bowen, Elizabeth
A Day in the Dark: V22
The Demon Lover: V5
Bowles, Paul
The Eye: V17
A Boy and His Dog (Ellison): V14
Boyle, Kay
Astronomer's Wife: V13
Black Boy: V14
The White Horses of Vienna: V10
Boyle, T. Coraghessan
Stones in My Passway, Hellhound on My Trail: V13
The Underground Gardens: V19
Boys and Girls (Munro): V5
Bradbury, Ray
There Will Come Soft Rains: V1
The Veldt: V20
Brazzaville Teen-ager (Friedman): V18
Bright and Morning Star (Wright): V15
Brokeback Mountain (Proulx): V23
Brown, Jason
Animal Stories: V14
Brownies (Packer): V25
Burton, Richard
The Arabian Nights: V21
Butler, Octavia
Bloodchild: V6
Butler, Robert Olen
A Good Scent from a Strange Mountain: V11
Titanic *Survivors Found in Bermuda Triangle:* V22
Byatt, A. S.
Art Work: V26

C

Callaghan, Morley
All the Years of Her Life: V19
Calvino, Italo
The Feathered Ogre: V12
Camus, Albert
The Guest: V4
The Canal (Yates): V24
The Canterville Ghost (Wilde): V7
Capote, Truman
A Christmas Memory: V2
Caroline's Wedding (Danticat): V25
Carter, Angela
The Bloody Chamber: V4
The Erlking: V12
Carver, Raymond
Cathedral: V6
Errand: V13
A Small, Good Thing: V23
What We Talk About When We Talk About Love: V12
Where I'm Calling From: V3
The Cask of Amontillado (Poe): V7
The Catbird Seat (Thurber): V10
Cathedral (Carver): V6
Cather, Willa
The Diamond Mine: V16
Neighbour Rosicky: V7
Paul's Case: V2
A Wagner Matinee: V27
The Celebrated Jumping Frog of Calaveras County (Twain): V1
The Centaur (Saramago): V23
The Challenge (Vargas Llosa): V14
Chandra, Vikram
Dharma: V16
Charles (Jackson): V27
Cheever, John
The Country Husband: V14
The Swimmer: V2
Chekhov, Anton
The Darling: V13
Gooseberries: V14
Gusev: V26
The Lady with the Pet Dog: V5
Chesnutt, Charles Waddell
The Goophered Grapevine: V26
The Sheriff's Children: V11
Children of the Sea (Danticat): V1
Chopin, Kate
Désirée's Baby: V13
A Point at Issue!: V17
The Storm: V26
The Story of an Hour: V2
A Christmas Memory (Capote): V2
Christmas Not Just Once a Year (Böll): V20
The Chrysanthemums (Steinbeck): V6
A Circle in the Fire (O'Connor): V19
The Circular Ruins (Borges): V26
Cisneros, Sandra
Eleven: V27
Little Miracles, Kept Promises: V13
Woman Hollering Creek: V3
Civil Peace (Achebe): V13
Clarke, Arthur C.
"If I Forget Thee, O Earth . . .": V18
The Star: V4
A Clean, Well-Lighted Place (Hemingway): V9
Cofer, Judith Ortiz
American History: V27
Connell, Richard
The Most Dangerous Game: V1
Conrad, Joseph
Heart of Darkness: V12
The Secret Sharer: V1
Conscience of the Court (Hurston): V21
A Conversation from the Third Floor (El-Bisatie): V17
A Conversation with My Father (Paley): V3
The Conversion of the Jews (Roth): V18
Cortázar, Julio
Axolotl: V3
The Pursuer: V20
The Country Husband (Cheever): V14
Crane, Stephen
The Open Boat: V4
Crazy Sunday (Fitzgerald): V21
The Curing Woman (Morales): V19

D

The Daffodil Sky (Bates): V7
Dahl, Roald
Lamb to the Slaughter: V4
Dante and the Lobster (Beckett): V15

Danticat, Edwidge
Caroline's Wedding: V25
Children of the Sea: V1
The Darling (Chekhov): V13
Davies, Peter Ho
Think of England: V21
Davis, Rebecca Harding
Life in the Iron Mills: V26
A Day in the Dark (Bowen): V22
de Balzac, Honore
La Grande Bretèche: V10
de Unamuno, Miguel
Saint Emmanuel the Good, Martyr: V20
The Dead (Joyce): V6
Death in the Woods (Anderson): V10
Death in Venice (Mann): V9
The Death of Ivan Ilych (Tolstoy): V5
Debbie and Julie (Lessing): V12
The Deep (Swan): V23
The Demon Lover (Bowen): V5
Desiree's Baby (Chopin): V13
The Destructors (Greene): V14
The Devil and Tom Walker (Irving): V1
Devlin, Anne
Naming the Names: V17
Dharma (Chandra): V16
The Diamond as Big as the Ritz (Fitzgerald): V25
The Diamond Mine (Cather): V16
Diaz, Junot
The Sun, the Moon, the Stars: V20
The Difference (Glasgow): V9
Dinesen, Isak
Babette's Feast: V20
The Ring: V6
The Sailor-Boy's Tale: V13
Sorrow-Acre: V3
Disorder and Early Sorrow (Mann): V4
Divakaruni, Chitra Banerjee
Meeting Mrinal: V24
Mrs. Dutta Writes a Letter: V18
Doctorow, E. L.
The Writer in the Family: V27
Doerr, Anthony
The Shell Collector: V25
The Dog of Tithwal (Manto): V15
Dominoes (Agüeros): V13
Don't Look Now (du Maurier): V14
The Door in the Wall (Wells): V3
Dostoevsky, Fyodor
The Grand Inquisitor: V8
Doyle, Arthur Conan
The Red-Headed League: V2
du Maurier, Daphne
The Birds: V16
Don't Look Now: V14
Dubus, Andre
The Fat Girl: V10
Dybek, Stuart
Hot Ice: V23

E

The Eatonville Anthology (Hurston): V1
Edwards, Kim
The Way It Felt to Be Falling: V18
Eisenberg, Deborah
Someone to Talk To: V24
El-Bisatie, Mohamed
A Conversation from the Third Floor: V17
Elbow Room (McPherson): V23
The Elephant Vanishes (Murakami): V23
Eleven (Cisneros): V27
Eliot, George
The Lifted Veil: V8
Ellison, Harlan
A Boy and His Dog: V14
I Have No Mouth, and I Must Scream: V15
Jeffty Is Five: V13
"Repent, Harlequin!" Said the Ticktockman: V21
Ellison, Ralph
The Invisible Man, or Battle Royal: V11
King of the Bingo Game: V1
The End of Old Horse (Ortiz): V22
An End to Dreams (Benét): V22
The English Pupil (Barrett): V24
Erdrich, Louise
Fleur: V22
The Red Convertible: V14
The Erlking (Carter): V12
Errand (Carver): V13
The Eskimo Connection (Yamamoto): V14
Eveline (Joyce): V19
Everyday Use (Walker): V2
Everything That Rises Must Converge (O'Connor): V10
Exchanging Glances (Wolf): V14
The Eye (Bowles): V17
Eyes of a Blue Dog (García Márquez): V21

F

The Fall of Edward Barnard (Maugham): V17
The Fall of the House of Usher (Poe): V2
The Far and the Near (Wolfe): V18
Far, Sui Sin
Mrs. Spring Fragrance: V4
The Fat Girl (Dubus): V10
Faulkner, William
Barn Burning: V5
The Bear: V2
Race at Morning: V27
A Rose for Emily: V6
That Evening Sun: V12
The Feathered Ogre (Calvino): V12
Ferrell, Carolyn
Proper Library: V23
Fever (Wideman): V6
The First Seven Years (Malamud): V13
Fish (McCorkle): V24
Fitzgerald, F. Scott
Babylon Revisited: V4
Crazy Sunday: V21
The Diamond as Big as the Ritz: V25
Winter Dreams: V15
Flaubert, Gustave
A Simple Heart: V6
Fleur (Erdrich): V22
Flight (Steinbeck): V3
Flowering Judas (Porter): V8
Fountains in the Rain (Mishima): V12
Four Summers (Oates): V17
Freeman, Mary E. Wilkins
A New England Nun: V8
Old Woman Magoun: V26
The Revolt of 'Mother': V4
Friedman, Bruce Jay
Brazzaville Teen-ager: V18

G

Gaines, Ernest
The Sky is Gray: V5
Galsworthy, John
The Japanese Quince: V3
García Márquez, Gabriel
Eyes of a Blue Dog: V21
The Handsomest Drowned Man in the World: V1
A Very Old Man with Enormous Wings: V6
The Woman Who Came at Six O'Clock: V16
The Garden of Forking Paths (Borges): V9
The Garden Party (Mansfield): V8
Gardner, John
Redemption: V8
Gibson, William
Johnny Mnemonic: V26
The Gift of the Magi (Henry): V2
Gilchrist, Ellen
Victory Over Japan: V9
The Gilded Six-Bits (Hurston): V11
Gilman, Charlotte Perkins
Three Thanksgivings: V18
The Yellow Wallpaper: V1
Gimpel the Fool (Singer): V2
Girl (Kincaid): V7
A Girl like Phyl (Highsmith): V25
The Girls (Williams): V25
Glasgow, Ellen
The Difference: V9
Glaspell, Susan
A Jury of Her Peers: V3

Gogol, Nikolai
The Overcoat: V7
The Gold of Tomás Vargas (Allende): V16
The Good Doctor (Haslett): V24
A Good Man Is Hard to Find (O'Connor): V2
A Good Scent from a Strange Mountain (Butler): V11
The Good Shopkeeper (Upadhyay): V22
Goodbye, Columbus (Roth): V12
The Goophered Grapevine (Chesnutt): V26
Gooseberries (Chekhov): V14
Gordimer, Nadine
Town and Country Lovers: V14
The Train from Rhodesia: V2
The Ultimate Safari: V19
Gorilla, My Love (Bambara): V21
The Grand Inquisitor (Dostoevsky): V8
The Grave (Porter): V11
A Great Day (Sargeson): V20
Great Day (Malouf): V24
Greatness Strikes Where It Pleases (Gustafsson): V22
The Green Leaves (Ogot): V15
Greene, Graham
The Destructors: V14
Greyhound People (Adams): V21
The Guest (Camus): V4
Guests of the Nation (O'Connor): V5
A Guide to Berlin (Nabokov): V6
Gusev (Chekhov): V26
Gustafsson, Lars
Greatness Strikes Where It Pleases: V22

H

Half a Day (Mahfouz): V9
The Half-Skinned Steer (Proulx): V18
Han's Crime (Naoya): V5
Hands (Anderson): V11
The Handsomest Drowned Man in the World (García Márquez): V1
Happy Endings (Atwood): V13
Harrison Bergeron (Vonnegut): V5
Harte, Bret
The Outcasts of Poker Flat: V3
The Harvest (Rivera): V15
Haslett, Adam
The Good Doctor: V24
Hawthorne, Nathaniel
The Minister's Black Veil: A Parable: V7
My Kinsman, Major Molineux: V11
The Wives of the Dead: V15
Young Goodman Brown: V1
He (Porter): V16
Head, Bessie
Life: V13
Snapshots of a Wedding: V5
Heart of Darkness (Conrad): V12
Heinlein, Robert A.
Waldo: V7
Helprin, Mark
Perfection: V25
Hemingway, Ernest
A Clean, Well-Lighted Place: V9
Hills Like White Elephants: V6
In Another Country: V8
The Killers: V17
The Short Happy Life of Francis Macomber: V1
The Snows of Kilimanjaro: V11
Soldier's Home: V26
Hemon, Aleksandar
Islands: V22
Hempel, Amy
In the Cemetery Where Al Jolson Is Buried: V2
Hendel, Yehudit
Small Change: V14
Henne Fire (Singer): V16
Henry, O.
After Twenty Years: V27
The Gift of the Magi: V2
Mammon and the Archer: V18
Here's Your Hat What's Your Hurry (McCracken): V25
Highsmith, Patricia
A Girl like Phyl: V25
Hills Like White Elephants (Hemingway): V6
The Hitchhiking Game (Kundera): V10
Hoeg, Peter
Journey into a Dark Heart: V18
Holiday (Porter): V23
A Horse and Two Goats (Narayan): V5
A Horseman in the Sky (Bierce): V27
Hot Ice (Dybek): V23
Houston, Pam
The Best Girlfriend You Never Had: V17
How I Contemplated the World from the Detroit House of Correction and Began My Life Over Again (Oates): V8
How to Tell a True War Story (O'Brien): V15
Hughes, Langston
The Blues I'm Playing: V7
Slave on the Block: V4
A Hunger Artist (Kafka): V7
Hurst, James
The Scarlet Ibis: V23
Hurston, Zora Neale
Conscience of the Court: V21
The Eatonville Anthology: V1
The Gilded Six-Bits: V11
Spunk: V6
Sweat: V19

I

I Have No Mouth, and I Must Scream (Ellison): V15
I Stand Here Ironing (Olsen): V1
If I Forget Thee, O Earth . . ." (Clarke): V18
If You Sing like That for Me (Sharma): V21
Imagined Scenes (Beattie): V20
Immigration Blues (Santos): V19
Immortality (Yiyun Li): V24
In Another Country (Hemingway): V8
In the Cemetery Where Al Jolson Is Buried (Hempel): V2
In the Garden of the North American Martyrs (Wolff): V4
In the Kindergarten (Jin): V17
In the Middle of the Fields (Lavin): V23
In the Penal Colony (Kafka): V3
In the Shadow of War (Okri): V20
In the Zoo (Stafford): V21
The Indian Uprising (Barthelme): V17
The Interlopers (Saki): V15
The Invalid's Story (Twain): V16
The Invisible Man, or Battle Royal (Ellison): V11
Irving, Washington
The Devil and Tom Walker: V1
The Legend of Sleepy Hollow: V8
Rip Van Winkle: V16
Islands (Hemon): V22

J

Jackson, Shirley
Charles: V27
The Lottery: V1
Jacobs, W. W.
The Monkey's Paw: V2
James, Henry
The Beast in the Jungle: V6
The Jolly Corner: V9
Janus (Beattie): V9
The Japanese Quince (Galsworthy): V3
Jeeves Takes Charge (Wodehouse): V10
Jeffty Is Five (Ellison): V13
Jewett, Sarah Orne
A White Heron: V4
The Jilting of Granny Weatherall (Porter): V1
Jim Baker's Blue Jay Yarn (Twain): V27
Jin, Ha
In the Kindergarten: V17
Johnny Mnemonic (Gibson): V26

Johnson, Charles
Menagerie, a Child's Fable: V16
The Jolly Corner (James): V9
Jones, Thom
The Pugilist at Rest: V23
Journey into a Dark Heart (Høeg): V18
Joyce, James
Araby: V1
The Dead: V6
Eveline: V19
Julavits, Heidi
Marry the One Who Gets There First: V23
A Jury of Her Peers (Glaspell): V3

K

Kafka, Franz
A Hunger Artist: V7
In the Penal Colony: V3
The Metamorphosis: V12
Kew Gardens (Woolf): V12
The Killers (Hemingway): V17
Kincaid, Jamaica
Girl: V7
What I Have Been Doing Lately: V5
King of the Bingo Game (Ellison): V1
Kingston, Maxine Hong
On Discovery: V3
Kipling, Rudyard
Mowgli's Brothers: V22
Mrs. Bathurst: V8
Rikki-Tikki-Tavi: V21
Kitchen (Yoshimoto): V16
Kohler, Sheila
Africans: V18
The Kugelmass Episode (Allen): V21
Kundera, Milan
The Hitchhiking Game: V10

L

La Grande Bretèche (Balzac/de Balzac): V10
The Lady with the Pet Dog (Chekhov): V5
The Lady, or the Tiger? (Stockton): V3
Lagerlöf, Selma
The Legend of the Christmas Rose: V18
Lahiri, Jhumpa
A Temporary Matter: V19
This Blessed House: V27
Lamb to the Slaughter (Dahl): V4
Last Courtesies (Leffland): V24
The Last Lovely City (Adams): V14
Last Night (Salter): V25
Lavin, Mary
In the Middle of the Fields: V23
Lawrence, D. H.
Odour of Chrysanthemums: V6
The Rocking-Horse Winner: V2
Le Guin, Ursula K.
The Ones Who Walk Away from Omelas: V2
Leaving the Yellow House (Bellow): V12
Lee, Don
The Price of Eggs in China: V25
Leffland, Ella
Last Courtesies: V24
The Legend of Sleepy Hollow (Irving): V8
The Legend of the Christmas Rose (Lagerlöf): V18
Lessing, Doris
Debbie and Julie: V12
A Mild Attack of Locusts: V26
Through the Tunnel: V1
To Room Nineteen: V20
The Lesson (Bambara): V12
Li, Yiyun
Immortality: V24
Liberty (Alvarez): V27
Life (Head): V13
Life in the Iron Mills (Davis): V26
The Life You Save May Be Your Own (O'Connor): V7
The Lifted Veil (Eliot): V8
Little Miracles, Kept Promises (Cisneros): V13
London, Jack
To Build a Fire: V7
Long Distance (Smiley): V19
The Long-Distance Runner (Paley): V20
Lost in the Funhouse (Barth): V6
The Lottery (Jackson): V1
Lullaby (Silko): V10

M

The Magic Barrel (Malamud): V8
Mahfouz, Naguib
Half a Day: V9
Malamud, Bernard
Black Is My Favorite Color: V16
The First Seven Years: V13
The Magic Barrel: V8
Malouf, David
Great Day: V24
Mammon and the Archer (Henry): V18
The Man That Corrupted Hadleyburg (Twain): V7
The Man to Send Rain Clouds (Silko): V8
The Man Who Lived Underground (Wright): V3
The Man Who Was Almost a Man (Wright): V9
The Management of Grief (Mukherjee): V7
Mann, Thomas
Death in Venice: V9
Disorder and Early Sorrow: V4
Mansfield, Katherine
Bliss: V10
The Garden Party: V8
Marriage à la Mode: V11
Miss Brill: V2
Manto, Saadat Hasan
The Dog of Tithwal: V15
A Map of Tripoli, 1967 (Wetzel): V17
Marriage à la Mode (Mansfield): V11
Marry the One Who Gets There First (Julavits): V23
Marshall, Paule
To Da-duh, in Memoriam: V15
Mason, Bobbie Ann
Private Lies: V20
Residents and Transients: V8
Shiloh: V3
The Masque of the Red Death (Poe): V8
Mateo Falcone (Merimee): V8
Maugham, W. Somerset
The Fall of Edward Barnard: V17
Maupassant, Guy de
Boule de Suif: V21
The Necklace: V4
McCorkle, Jill
Fish: V24
McCracken, Elizabeth
Here's Your Hat What's Your Hurry: V25
McCullers, Carson
Wunderkind: V5
McPherson, James Alan
Elbow Room: V23
Meeting Mrinal (Divakaruni): V24
Melanctha (Stein): V5
Melon (Barnes): V24
Melville, Herman
Bartleby the Scrivener, A Tale of Wall Street: V3
Menagerie, a Child's Fable (Johnson): V16
Meneseteung (Munro): V19
Merimee, Prosper
Mateo Falcone: V8
The Metamorphosis (Kafka): V12
The Middleman (Mukherjee): V24
A Mild Attack of Locusts (Lessing): V26
The Minister's Black Veil: A Parable (Hawthorne): V7
Mishima, Yukio
Fountains in the Rain: V12
Swaddling Clothes: V5
Miss Brill (Mansfield): V2
Mistry, Rohinton
Swimming Lessons: V6
The Monkey's Paw (Jacobs): V2
Moon Lake (Welty): V26
Moore, Lorrie
You're Ugly, Too: V19

Morales, Alejandro
The Curing Woman: V19
Morrison, Toni
Recitatif: V5
The Most Dangerous Game (Connell): V1
Mowgli's Brothers (Kipling): V22
Mphahlele, Es'kia (Ezekiel)
Mrs. Plum: V11
Mrs. Bathurst (Kipling): V8
Mrs. Dutta Writes a Letter (Divakaruni): V18
Mrs. Plum (Mphahlele): V11
Mrs. Spring Fragrance (Far): V4
Mukherjee, Bharati
The Management of Grief: V7
The Middleman: V24
Munro, Alice
Boys and Girls: V5
Meneseteung: V19
Walker Brothers Cowboy: V13
Murakami, Haruki
The Elephant Vanishes: V23
My First Goose (Babel): V10
My Kinsman, Major Molineux (Hawthorne): V11
My Life with the Wave (Paz): V13

N

Nabokov, Vladimir
A Guide to Berlin: V6
That in Aleppo Once . . . : V15
Naming the Names (Devlin): V17
Naoya, Shiga
Han's Crime: V5
Narayan, R. K.
A Horse and Two Goats: V5
The Necessary Grace to Fall (Ochsner): V24
The Necklace (Maupassant): V4
Neighbour Rosicky (Cather): V7
The New Dress (Woolf): V4
A New England Nun (Freeman): V8
The News from Ireland (Trevor): V10
The Night the Ghost Got In (Thurber): V19
Night (Tolstaya): V14
Nightfall (Asimov): V17
No. 44, The Mysterious Stranger (Twain): V21
A Nurse's Story (Baida): V25

O

O'Brien, Tim
How to Tell a True War Story: V15
The Things They Carried: V5
O'Connor, Flannery
A Circle in the Fire: V19
Everything That Rises Must Converge: V10
A Good Man Is Hard to Find: V2
The Life You Save May Be Your Own: V7
O'Connor, Frank
Guests of the Nation: V5
O'Flaherty, Liam
The Sniper: V20
The Wave: V5
Oates, Joyce Carol
Four Summers: V17
How I Contemplated the World from the Detroit House of Correction and Began My Life Over Again: V8
Where Are You Going, Where Have You Been?: V1
An Occurrence at Owl Creek Bridge (Bierce): V2
Ochsner, Gina
The Necessary Grace to Fall: V24
Odour of Chrysanthemums (Lawrence): V6
Ogot, Grace
The Green Leaves: V15
Okri, Ben
In the Shadow of War: V20
Old Woman Magoun (Freeman): V26
Olsen, Tillie
I Stand Here Ironing: V1
On Discovery (Kingston): V3
One Day in the Life of Ivan Denisovich (Solzhenitsyn): V9
The Ones Who Walk Away from Omelas (Le Guin): V2
The Open Boat (Crane): V4
The Open Window (Saki): V1
Orringer, Julie
The Smoothest Way Is Full of Stones: V23
Ortiz, Simon J.
The End of Old Horse: V22
Orwell, George
Shooting an Elephant: V4
The Outcasts of Poker Flat (Harte): V3
The Overcoat (Gogol): V7
Ozick, Cynthia
The Pagan Rabbi: V12
Rosa: V22
The Shawl: V3

P

Packer, ZZ
Brownies: V25
The Pagan Rabbi (Ozick): V12
Paley, Grace
Anxiety: V27
A Conversation with My Father: V3
The Long-Distance Runner: V20
Paris 1991 (Walbert): V24
Parker, Dortothy
Big Blonde: V5
Paul's Case (Cather): V2
Paz, Octavio
My Life with the Wave: V13
The Pearl (Steinbeck): V22
A Perfect Day for Bananafish (Salinger): V17
Perfection (Helprin): V25
Phillips, Jayne Anne
Souvenir: V4
Pierre Menard, Author of the Quixote (Borges): V4
Poe, Edgar Allan
The Black Cat: V26
The Cask of Amontillado: V7
The Fall of the House of Usher: V2
The Masque of the Red Death: V8
The Purloined Letter: V16
The Tell-Tale Heart: V4
A Point at Issue! (Chopin): V17
Pomegranate Seed (Wharton): V6
Porter, Katherine Anne
Flowering Judas: V8
The Grave: V11
He: V16
Holiday: V23
The Jilting of Granny Weatherall: V1
Powell, Padgett
Trick or Treat: V25
The Price of Eggs in China (Lee): V25
Private Lies (Mason): V20
Proper Library (Ferrell): V23
Proulx, E. Annie
Brokeback Mountain: V23
The Half-Skinned Steer: V18
The Pugilist at Rest (Jones): V23
The Purloined Letter (Poe): V16
The Pursuer (Cortázar): V20
Pushkin, Alexander
The Stationmaster: V9

R

Race at Morning (Faulkner): V27
Rape Fantasies (Atwood): V3
Raymond's Run (Bambara): V7
Recitatif (Morrison): V5
The Red Convertible (Erdrich): V14
The Red-Headed League (Doyle): V2
Redemption (Gardner): V8
The Rememberer (Bender): V25
Repent, Harlequin!" Said the Ticktockman (Ellison): V21
The Replacement (Robbe-Grillet): V15
Residents and Transients (Mason): V8
Resurrection of a Life (Saroyan): V14
The Revolt of 'Mother' (Freeman): V4
Rikki-Tikki-Tavi (Kipling): V21
The Ring (Dinesen): V6
Rip Van Winkle (Irving): V16

Rivera, Beatriz
African Passions: V15
Rivera, Tomás
The Harvest: V15
Robbe-Grillet, Alain
The Replacement: V15
Robert Kennedy Saved from Drowning (Barthelme): V3
The Rocking-Horse Winner (Lawrence): V2
The Rockpile (Baldwin): V18
Roman Fever (Wharton): V7
Rosa (Ozick): V22
A Rose for Emily (Faulkner): V6
Roselily (Walker): V11
Roth, Philip
The Conversion of the Jews: V18
Goodbye, Columbus: V12
Rules of the Game (Tan): V16

S

The Sailor-Boy's Tale (Dinesen): V13
Saint Emmanuel the Good, Martyr (Unamuno/de Unamuno): V20
Saki
The Interlopers: V15
The Open Window: V1
Salinger, J. D.
A Perfect Day for Bananafish: V17
Salter, James
Last Night: V25
Santos, Bienvenido
Immigration Blues: V19
Saramago, José
The Centaur: V23
Sargeson, Frank
A Great Day: V20
Saroyan, William
Resurrection of a Life: V14
Sartre, Jean-Paul
The Wall: V9
Say Yes (Wolff): V11
Sayers, Dorothy L.
Suspicion: V12
The Scarlet Ibis (Hurst): V23
Scott, Sir Walter
Wandering Willie's Tale: V10
The Secret Life of Walter Mitty (Thurber): V1
The Secret Sharer (Conrad): V1
Sharma, Akhil
If You Sing like That for Me: V21
The Shawl (Ozick): V3
The Shell Collector (Doerr): V25
The Sheriff's Children (Chesnutt): V11
Shiloh (Mason): V3
Shooting an Elephant (Orwell): V4
The Short Happy Life of Francis Macomber (Hemingway): V1
Silent Snow, Secret Snow (Aiken): V8
Silko, Leslie Marmon
Lullaby: V10
The Man to Send Rain Clouds: V8
Storyteller: V11
Yellow Woman: V4
Silver, Marisa
What I Saw from Where I Stood: V25
A Silver Dish (Bellow): V22
Silver Water (Bloom): V11
A Simple Heart (Flaubert): V6
Singer, Isaac Bashevis
Gimpel the Fool: V2
Henne Fire: V16
The Spinoza of Market Street: V12
Zlateh the Goat: V27
The Sky is Gray (Gaines): V5
Slave on the Block (Hughes): V4
The Slump (Updike): V19
Small Change (Hendel): V14
A Small, Good Thing (Carver): V23
Smiley, Jane
Long Distance: V19
The Smoothest Way Is Full of Stones (Orringer): V23
Snapshots of a Wedding (Head): V5
The Sniper (O'Flaherty): V20
The Snows of Kilimanjaro (Hemingway): V11
Soldier's Home (Hemingway): V26
Solzhenitsyn, Alexandr
One Day in the Life of Ivan Denisovich: V9
Someone to Talk To (Eisenberg): V24
Sonny's Blues (Baldwin): V2
Sontag, Susan
The Way We Live Now: V10
Sophistication (Anderson): V4
Sorrow-Acre (Dinesen): V3
Souvenir (Phillips): V4
The Spinoza of Market Street (Singer): V12
A Spinster's Tale (Taylor): V9
Spunk (Hurston): V6
Stafford, Jean
In the Zoo: V21
The Star (Clarke): V4
The Stationmaster (Pushkin): V9
Stein, Gertrude
Melanctha: V5
Steinbeck, John
The Chrysanthemums: V6
Flight: V3
The Pearl: V22
Stockton, Frank R.
The Lady, or the Tiger?: V3
The Stone Boy (Berriault): V7
Stones in My Passway, Hellhound on My Trail (Boyle): V13
The Storm (Chopin): V26
The Story of an Hour (Chopin): V2
Storyteller (Silko): V11
The Sun, the Moon, the Stars (Díaz): V20
Suspicion (Sayers): V12
Swaddling Clothes (Mishima): V5
Swan, Mary
The Deep: V23
Sweat (Hurston): V19
The Swimmer (Cheever): V2
Swimming Lessons (Mistry): V6

T

Tan, Amy
Rules of the Game: V16
Two Kinds: V9
Taylor, Peter
A Spinster's Tale: V9
The Tell-Tale Heart (Poe): V4
A Temporary Matter (Lahiri): V19
That Evening Sun (Faulkner): V12
That in Aleppo Once . . . (Nabokov): V15
There Will Come Soft Rains (Bradbury): V1
The Things They Carried (O'Brien): V5
Think of England (Davies): V21
This Blessed House (Lahiri): V27
This Way for the Gas, Ladies and Gentlemen (Borowski): V13
Three Thanksgivings (Gilman): V18
Through the Tunnel (Lessing): V1
Thurber, James
The Catbird Seat: V10
The Night the Ghost Got In: V19
The Secret Life of Walter Mitty: V1
Titanic *Survivors Found in Bermuda Triangle* (Butler): V22
To Build a Fire (London): V7
To Da-duh, in Memoriam (Marshall): V15
To Room Nineteen (Lessing): V20
Tolstaya, Tatyana
Night: V14
Tolstoy, Leo
The Death of Ivan Ilych: V5
Toomer, Jean
Blood-Burning Moon: V5
Town and Country Lovers (Gordimer): V14
The Toxic Donut (Bisson): V18
The Train from Rhodesia (Gordimer): V2
Trevor, William
The News from Ireland: V10
Trick or Treat (Powell): V25
Twain, Mark
The Celebrated Jumping Frog of Calaveras County: V1
The Invalid's Story: V16
Jim Baker's Blue Jay Yarn: V27

The Man That Corrupted Hadleyburg: V7
No. 44, The Mysterious Stranger: V21
Two Kinds (Tan): V9
Tyler, Anne
Average Waves in Unprotected Waters: V17

U

The Ultimate Safari (Gordimer): V19
Unamuno, Miguel de
Saint Emmanuel the Good, Martyr: V20
The Underground Gardens (Boyle): V19
Upadhyay, Samrat
The Good Shopkeeper: V22
Updike, John
A & P: V3
The Slump: V19
The Use of Force (Williams): V27

V

Vargas Llosa, Mario
The Challenge: V14
The Veldt (Bradbury): V20
Vengeful Creditor (Achebe): V3
A Very Old Man with Enormous Wings (García Márquez): V6
Victory Over Japan (Gilchrist): V9
Vonnegut, Kurt
Harrison Bergeron: V5

W

A Wagner Matinee (Cather): V27
Walbert, Kate
Paris 1991: V24
Waldo (Heinlein): V7
Walker Brothers Cowboy (Munro): V13
Walker, Alice
Everyday Use: V2
Roselily: V11
The Wall (Sartre): V9
Wandering Willie's Tale (Scott): V10
Warren, Robert Penn
Blackberry Winter: V8
Waters, Mary Yukari
Aftermath: V22
The Wave (O'Flaherty): V5
The Way It Felt to Be Falling (Edwards): V18
The Way We Live Now (Sontag): V10
Wells, H. G.
The Door in the Wall: V3
Welty, Eudora
Moon Lake: V26
Why I Live at the P.O.: V10
A Worn Path: V2
Wetzel, Marlene Reed
A Map of Tripoli, 1967: V17
Wharton, Edith
Pomegranate Seed: V6
Roman Fever: V7
What I Have Been Doing Lately (Kincaid): V5
What I Saw from Where I Stood (Silver): V25
What We Cannot Speak About We Must Pass Over in Silence (Wideman): V24
What We Talk About When We Talk About Love (Carver): V12
Where Are You Going, Where Have You Been? (Oates): V1
Where I'm Calling From (Carver): V3
A White Heron (Jewett): V4
The White Horses of Vienna (Boyle): V10
Why I Live at the P.O. (Welty): V10
Wideman, John Edgar
The Beginning of Homewood: V12
Fever: V6
What We Cannot Speak About We Must Pass Over in Silence: V24
Wilde, Oscar
The Canterville Ghost: V7
Williams, Joy
The Girls: V25
Williams, William Carlos
The Use of Force: V27
Winter Dreams (Fitzgerald): V15
The Wives of the Dead (Hawthorne): V15
Wodehouse, Pelham Grenville
Jeeves Takes Charge: V10
Wolf, Christa
Exchanging Glances: V14
Wolfe, Thomas
The Far and the Near: V18
Wolff, Tobias
In the Garden of the North American Martyrs: V4
Say Yes: V11
Woman Hollering Creek (Cisneros): V3
The Woman Who Came at Six O'Clock (García Márquez): V16
Women in Their Beds (Berriault): V11
Woolf, Virginia
Kew Gardens: V12
The New Dress: V4
A Worn Path (Welty): V2
Wright, Richard
Big Black Good Man: V20
Bright and Morning Star: V15
The Man Who Lived Underground: V3
The Man Who Was Almost a Man: V9
The Writer in the Family (Doctorow): V27
Wunderkind (McCullers): V5

Y

Yamamoto, Hisaye
The Eskimo Connection: V14
Yates, Richard
The Canal: V24
The Yellow Wallpaper (Gilman): V1
Yellow Woman (Silko): V4
Yezierska, Anzia
America and I: V15
Yiyun Li
Immortality: V24
Yoshimoto, Banana
Kitchen: V16
You're Ugly, Too (Moore): V19
Young Goodman Brown (Hawthorne): V1

Z

Zlateh the Goat (Singer): V27

Cumulative Nationality/Ethnicity Index

African American

Baldwin, James
The Rockpile: V18
Sonny's Blues: V2
Bambara, Toni Cade
Blues Ain't No Mockin Bird: V4
Gorilla, My Love: V21
The Lesson: V12
Raymond's Run: V7
Butler, Octavia
Bloodchild: V6
Chesnutt, Charles Waddell
The Goophered Grapevine: V26
The Sheriff's Children: V11
Ellison, Ralph
King of the Bingo Game: V1
Hughes, Langston
The Blues I'm Playing: V7
Slave on the Block: V4
Hurston, Zora Neale
Conscience of the Court: V21
The Eatonville Anthology: V1
The Gilded Six-Bits: V11
Spunk: V6
Sweat: V19
Marshall, Paule
To Da-duh, in Memoriam: V15
McPherson, James Alan
Elbow Room: V23
Toomer, Jean
Blood-Burning Moon: V5
Walker, Alice
Everyday Use: V2
Roselily: V11
Wideman, John Edgar
The Beginning of Homewood: V12
Fever: V6
What We Cannot Speak About We Must Pass Over in Silence: V24
Wright, Richard
Big Black Good Man: V20
Bright and Morning Star: V15
The Man Who Lived Underground: V3
The Man Who Was Almost a Man: V9

American

Adams, Alice
Greyhound People: V21
The Last Lovely City: V14
Agüeros, Jack
Dominoes: V13
Aiken, Conrad
Silent Snow, Secret Snow: V8
Alexie, Sherman
Because My Father Always Said He Was the Only Indian Who Saw Jimi Hendrix Play "The Star-Spangled Banner" at Woodstock: V18
Allen, Woody
The Kugelmass Episode: V21
Alvarez, Julia
Liberty: V27
Anderson, Sherwood
Death in the Woods: V10
Hands: V11
Sophistication: V4
Asimov, Isaac
Nightfall: V17
Baida, Peter
A Nurse's Story: V25
Baldwin, James
The Rockpile: V18
Sonny's Blues: V2
Bambara, Toni Cade
Blues Ain't No Mockin Bird: V4
Gorilla, My Love: V21
The Lesson: V12
Raymond's Run: V7
Barrett, Andrea
The English Pupil: V24
Barth, John
Lost in the Funhouse: V6
Barthelme, Donald
The Indian Uprising: V17
Robert Kennedy Saved from Drowning: V3
Beattie, Ann
Imagined Scenes: V20
Janus: V9
Bellow, Saul
Leaving the Yellow House: V12
A Silver Dish: V22
Bender, Aimee
The Rememberer: V25
Benet, Stephen Vincent
An End to Dreams: V22
Berriault, Gina
The Stone Boy: V7
Women in Their Beds: V11
Bierce, Ambrose
The Boarded Window: V9
A Horseman in the Sky: V27
An Occurrence at Owl Creek Bridge: V2
Bisson, Terry
The Toxic Donut: V18

Bloom, Amy
Silver Water: V11
Bowles, Paul
The Eye: V17
Boyle, Kay
Astronomer's Wife: V13
Black Boy: V14
The White Horses of Vienna: V10
Boyle, T. Coraghessan
Stones in My Passway, Hellhound on My Trail: V13
The Underground Gardens: V19
Bradbury, Ray
There Will Come Soft Rains: V1
The Veldt: V20
Brown, Jason
Animal Stories: V14
Butler, Octavia
Bloodchild: V6
Butler, Robert Olen
A Good Scent from a Strange Mountain: V11
Titanic *Survivors Found in Bermuda Triangle:* V22
Capote, Truman
A Christmas Memory: V2
Carver, Raymond
Cathedral: V6
Errand: V13
A Small, Good Thing: V23
What We Talk About When We Talk About Love: V12
Where I'm Calling From: V3
Cather, Willa
The Diamond Mine: V16
Neighbour Rosicky: V7
Paul's Case: V2
A Wagner Matinee: V27
Cheever, John
The Country Husband: V14
The Swimmer: V2
Chesnutt, Charles Waddell
The Goophered Grapevine: V26
The Sheriff's Children: V11
Chopin, Kate
Désirée's Baby: V13
A Point at Issue!: V17
The Storm: V26
The Story of an Hour: V2
Cisneros, Sandra
Eleven: V27
Little Miracles, Kept Promises: V13
Woman Hollering Creek: V3
Cofer, Judith Ortiz
American History: V27
Connell, Richard
The Most Dangerous Game: V1
Crane, Stephen
The Open Boat: V4
Davies, Peter Ho
Think of England: V21
Davis, Rebecca Harding
Life in the Iron Mills: V26
Diaz, Junot
The Sun, the Moon, the Stars: V20
Doctorow, E. L.
The Writer in the Family: V27
Doerr, Anthony
The Shell Collector: V25
Dubus, Andre
The Fat Girl: V10
Dybek, Stuart
Hot Ice: V23
Edwards, Kim
The Way It Felt to Be Falling: V18
Eisenberg, Deborah
Someone to Talk To: V24
Ellison, Harlan
A Boy and His Dog: V14
I Have No Mouth, and I Must Scream: V15
Jeffty Is Five: V13
"Repent, Harlequin!" Said the Ticktockman: V21
Ellison, Ralph
The Invisible Man, or Battle Royal: V11
King of the Bingo Game: V1
Erdrich, Louise
Fleur: V22
The Red Convertible: V14
Faulkner, William
Barn Burning: V5
The Bear: V2
Race at Morning: V27
A Rose for Emily: V6
That Evening Sun: V12
Ferrell, Carolyn
Proper Library: V23
Fitzgerald, F. Scott
Babylon Revisited: V4
Crazy Sunday: V21
The Diamond as Big as the Ritz: V25
Winter Dreams: V15
Freeman, Mary E. Wilkins
A New England Nun: V8
Old Woman Magoun: V26
The Revolt of 'Mother': V4
Friedman, Bruce Jay
Brazzaville Teen-ager: V18
Gaines, Ernest
The Sky is Gray: V5
Gardner, John
Redemption: V8
Gibson, William
Johnny Mnemonic: V26
Gilchrist, Ellen
Victory Over Japan: V9
Gilman, Charlotte Perkins
Three Thanksgivings: V18
The Yellow Wallpaper: V1
Glasgow, Ellen
The Difference: V9
Glaspell, Susan
A Jury of Her Peers: V3
Harte, Bret
The Outcasts of Poker Flat: V3
Haslett, Adam
The Good Doctor: V24
Hawthorne, Nathaniel
The Minister's Black Veil: A Parable: V7
My Kinsman, Major Molineux: V11
The Wives of the Dead: V15
Young Goodman Brown: V1
Heinlein, Robert A.
Waldo: V7
Helprin, Mark
Perfection: V25
Hemingway, Ernest
A Clean, Well-Lighted Place: V9
Hills Like White Elephants: V6
In Another Country: V8
The Killers: V17
The Short Happy Life of Francis Macomber: V1
The Snows of Kilimanjaro: V11
Soldier's Home: V26
Hempel, Amy
In the Cemetery Where Al Jolson Is Buried: V2
Henry, O.
After Twenty Years: V27
The Gift of the Magi: V2
Mammon and the Archer: V18
Highsmith, Patricia
A Girl like Phyl: V25
Houston, Pam
The Best Girlfriend You Never Had: V17
Hughes, Langston
The Blues I'm Playing: V7
Slave on the Block: V4
Hurst, James
The Scarlet Ibis: V23
Hurston, Zora Neale
Conscience of the Court: V21
The Eatonville Anthology: V1
The Gilded Six-Bits: V11
Spunk: V6
Sweat: V19
Irving, Washington
The Devil and Tom Walker: V1
The Legend of Sleepy Hollow: V8
Rip Van Winkle: V16
Jackson, Shirley
Charles: V27
The Lottery: V1
James, Henry
The Beast in the Jungle: V6
The Jolly Corner: V9
Jewett, Sarah Orne
A White Heron: V4
Johnson, Charles
Menagerie, a Child's Fable: V16

Jones, Thom
The Pugilist at Rest: V23
Julavits, Heidi
Marry the One Who Gets There First: V23
Kincaid, Jamaica
Girl: V7
What I Have Been Doing Lately: V5
Kingston, Maxine Hong
On Discovery: V3
Lahiri, Jhumpa
A Temporary Matter: V19
This Blessed House: V27
Lavin, Mary
In the Middle of the Fields: V23
Le Guin, Ursula K.
The Ones Who Walk Away from Omelas: V2
Lee, Don
The Price of Eggs in China: V25
Leffland, Ella
Last Courtesies: V24
London, Jack
To Build a Fire: V7
Malamud, Bernard
Black Is My Favorite Color: V16
The First Seven Years: V13
The Magic Barrel: V8
Marshall, Paule
To Da-duh, in Memoriam: V15
Mason, Bobbie Ann
Private Lies: V20
Residents and Transients: V8
Shiloh: V3
McCorkle, Jill
Fish: V24
McCracken, Elizabeth
Here's Your Hat What's Your Hurry: V25
McCullers, Carson
Wunderkind: V5
McPherson, James Alan
Elbow Room: V23
Melville, Herman
Bartleby the Scrivener, A Tale of Wall Street: V3
Moore, Lorrie
You're Ugly, Too: V19
Morales, Alejandro
The Curing Woman: V19
Morrison, Toni
Recitatif: V5
Mukherjee, Bharati
The Management of Grief: V7
The Middleman: V24
Nabokov, Vladimir
A Guide to Berlin: V6
That in Aleppo Once . . .: V15
O'Brien, Tim
How to Tell a True War Story: V15
The Things They Carried: V5
O'Connor, Flannery
A Circle in the Fire: V19
Everything That Rises Must Converge: V10
A Good Man Is Hard to Find: V2
The Life You Save May Be Your Own: V7
Oates, Joyce Carol
Four Summers: V17
How I Contemplated the World from the Detroit House of Correction and Began My Life Over Again: V8
Where Are You Going, Where Have You Been?: V1
Ochsner, Gina
The Necessary Grace to Fall: V24
Olsen, Tillie
I Stand Here Ironing: V1
Orringer, Julie
The Smoothest Way Is Full of Stones: V23
Ortiz, Simon J.
The End of Old Horse: V22
Ozick, Cynthia
The Pagan Rabbi: V12
Rosa: V22
The Shawl: V3
Packer, ZZ
Brownies: V25
Paley, Grace
Anxiety: V27
A Conversation with My Father: V3
The Long-Distance Runner: V20
Parker, Dortothy
Big Blonde: V5
Phillips, Jayne Anne
Souvenir: V4
Poe, Edgar Allan
The Black Cat: V26
The Cask of Amontillado: V7
The Fall of the House of Usher: V2
The Masque of the Red Death: V8
The Purloined Letter: V16
The Tell-Tale Heart: V4
Porter, Katherine Anne
Flowering Judas: V8
The Grave: V11
He: V16
Holiday: V23
The Jilting of Granny Weatherall: V1
Powell, Padgett
Trick or Treat: V25
Proulx, E. Annie
Brokeback Mountain: V23
The Half-Skinned Steer: V18
Rivera, Beatriz
African Passions: V15
Rivera, Tomás
The Harvest: V15
Roth, Philip
The Conversion of the Jews: V18
Goodbye, Columbus: V12
Salinger, J. D.
A Perfect Day for Bananafish: V17
Salter, James
Last Night: V25
Santos, Bienvenido
Immigration Blues: V19
Saroyan, William
Resurrection of a Life: V14
Sharma, Akhil
If You Sing like That for Me: V21
Silko, Leslie Marmon
Lullaby: V10
The Man to Send Rain Clouds: V8
Storyteller: V11
Yellow Woman: V4
Silver, Marisa
What I Saw from Where I Stood: V25
Singer, Isaac Bashevis
Gimpel the Fool: V2
Henne Fire: V16
The Spinoza of Market Street: V12
Zlateh the Goat: V27
Smiley, Jane
Long Distance: V19
Sontag, Susan
The Way We Live Now: V10
Stafford, Jean
In the Zoo: V21
Stein, Gertrude
Melanctha: V5
Steinbeck, John
The Chrysanthemums: V6
Flight: V3
The Pearl: V22
Stockton, Frank R.
The Lady, or the Tiger?: V3
Tan, Amy
Rules of the Game: V16
Two Kinds: V9
Taylor, Peter
A Spinster's Tale: V9
Thurber, James
The Catbird Seat: V10
The Night the Ghost Got In: V19
The Secret Life of Walter Mitty: V1
Toomer, Jean
Blood-Burning Moon: V5
Twain, Mark
The Celebrated Jumping Frog of Calaveras County: V1
The Invalid's Story: V16
Jim Baker's Blue Jay Yarn: V27
The Man That Corrupted Hadleyburg: V7
No. 44, The Mysterious Stranger: V21

Tyler, Anne
Average Waves in Unprotected Waters: V17
Updike, John
A & P: V3
The Slump: V19
Vonnegut, Kurt
Harrison Bergeron: V5
Walbert, Kate
Paris 1991: V24
Walker, Alice
Everyday Use: V2
Roselily: V11
Warren, Robert Penn
Blackberry Winter: V8
Waters, Mary Yukari
Aftermath: V22
Welty, Eudora
Moon Lake: V26
Why I Live at the P.O.: V10
A Worn Path: V2
Wetzel, Marlene Reed
A Map of Tripoli, 1967: V17
Wharton, Edith
Pomegranate Seed: V6
Roman Fever: V7
Wideman, John Edgar
The Beginning of Homewood: V12
Fever: V6
What We Cannot Speak About We Must Pass Over in Silence: V24
Williams, Joy
The Girls: V25
Williams, William Carlos
The Use of Force: V27
Wolfe, Thomas
The Far and the Near: V18
Wolff, Tobias
In the Garden of the North American Martyrs: V4
Say Yes: V11
Wright, Richard
Big Black Good Man: V20
Bright and Morning Star: V15
The Man Who Lived Underground: V3
The Man Who Was Almost a Man: V9
Yamamoto, Hisaye
The Eskimo Connection: V14
Yates, Richard
The Canal: V24
Yezierska, Anzia
America and I: V15

Antiguan

Kincaid, Jamaica
Girl: V7
What I Have Been Doing Lately: V5

Argentinian

Borges, Jorge Luis
The Aleph: V17
The Circular Ruins: V26
The Garden of Forking Paths: V9
Pierre Menard, Author of the Quixote: V4
Cortázar, Julio
Axolotl: V3
The Pursuer: V20

Asian American

Kingston, Maxine Hong
On Discovery: V3
Lee, Don
The Price of Eggs in China: V25
Tan, Amy
Rules of the Game: V16
Two Kinds: V9
Yamamoto, Hisaye
The Eskimo Connection: V14

Australian

Malouf, David
Great Day: V24

Austrian

Kafka, Franz
A Hunger Artist: V7
In the Penal Colony: V3
The Metamorphosis: V12

Bosnian

Hemon, Aleksandar
Islands: V22

Canadian

Atwood, Margaret
Happy Endings: V13
Rape Fantasies: V3
Bellow, Saul
A Silver Dish: V22
Callaghan, Morley
All the Years of Her Life: V19
Mistry, Rohinton
Swimming Lessons: V6
Mukherjee, Bharati
The Management of Grief: V7
The Middleman: V24
Munro, Alice
Boys and Girls: V5
Meneseteung: V19
Walker Brothers Cowboy: V13
Swan, Mary
The Deep: V23

Chilean

Allende, Isabel
And of Clay Are We Created: V11
The Gold of Tomás Vargas: V16

Chinese

Jin, Ha
In the Kindergarten: V17
Yiyun Li
Immortality: V24

Colombian

García Márquez, Gabriel
Eyes of a Blue Dog: V21
The Handsomest Drowned Man in the World: V1
A Very Old Man with Enormous Wings: V6
The Woman Who Came at Six O'Clock: V16

Cuban

Calvino, Italo
The Feathered Ogre: V12
Rivera, Beatriz
African Passions: V15

Czech

Kafka, Franz
A Hunger Artist: V7
In the Penal Colony: V3
The Metamorphosis: V12
Kundera, Milan
The Hitchhiking Game: V10

Danish

Dinesen, Isak
Babette's Feast: V20
The Ring: V6
The Sailor-Boy's Tale: V13
Sorrow-Acre: V3
Høeg, Peter
Journey into a Dark Heart: V18

Dominican

Alvarez, Julia
Liberty: V27
Díaz, Junot
The Sun, the Moon, the Stars: V20

Egyptian

El-Bisatie, Mohamed
A Conversation from the Third Floor: V17
Mahfouz, Naguib
Half a Day: V9

English

Barnes, Julian
Melon: V24
Bates, H. E.
The Daffodil Sky: V7
Bowen, Elizabeth
The Demon Lover: V5

Burton, Richard
The Arabian Nights: V21
Byatt, A. S.
Art Work: V26
Carter, Angela
The Bloody Chamber: V4
The Erlking: V12
Clarke, Arthur C.
"If I Forget Thee, O Earth . . .": V18
The Star: V4
Conrad, Joseph
Heart of Darkness: V12
The Secret Sharer: V1
Davies, Peter Ho
Think of England: V21
du Maurier, Daphne
The Birds: V16
Don't Look Now: V14
Eliot, George
The Lifted Veil: V8
Far, Sui Sin
Mrs. Spring Fragrance: V4
Galsworthy, John
The Japanese Quince: V3
Greene, Graham
The Destructors: V14
Jacobs, W. W.
The Monkey's Paw: V2
Kipling, Rudyard
Mowgli's Brothers: V22
Mrs. Bathurst: V8
Rikki-Tikki-Tavi: V21
Lahiri, Jhumpa
A Temporary Matter: V19
This Blessed House: V27
Lawrence, D. H.
Odour of Chrysanthemums: V6
The Rocking-Horse Winner: V2
Lessing, Doris
Debbie and Julie: V12
A Mild Attack of Locusts: V26
Through the Tunnel: V1
To Room Nineteen: V20
Maugham, W. Somerset
The Fall of Edward Barnard: V17
Okri, Ben
In the Shadow of War: V20
Orwell, George
Shooting an Elephant: V4
Saki
The Interlopers: V15
The Open Window: V1
Sayers, Dorothy L.
Suspicion: V12
Wells, H. G.
The Door in the Wall: V3
Williams, William Carlos
The Use of Force: V27
Wodehouse, Pelham Grenville
Jeeves Takes Charge: V10
Woolf, Virginia
Kew Gardens: V12
The New Dress: V4

Eurasian

Far, Sui Sin
Mrs. Spring Fragrance: V4

French

Balzac, Honore de
La Grande Bretèche: V10
Beckett, Samuel
Dante and the Lobster: V15
Camus, Albert
The Guest: V4
Cortázar, Julio
Axolotl: V3
The Pursuer: V20
Flaubert, Gustave
A Simple Heart: V6
Maupassant, Guy de
Boule de Suif: V21
The Necklace: V4
Merimee, Prosper
Mateo Falcone: V8
Robbe-Grillet, Alain
The Replacement: V15
Sartre, Jean-Paul
The Wall: V9

German

Böll, Heinrich
Christmas Not Just Once a Year: V20
Mann, Thomas
Death in Venice: V9
Disorder and Early Sorrow: V4
Wolf, Christa
Exchanging Glances: V14

Haitian

Danticat, Edwidge
Caroline's Wedding: V25
Children of the Sea: V1

Hispanic

Allende, Isabel
And of Clay Are We Created: V11
The Gold of Tomás Vargas: V16
Alvarez, Julia
Liberty: V27
Cisneros, Sandra
Eleven: V27
Little Miracles, Kept Promises: V13
Woman Hollering Creek: V3
Cofer, Judith Ortiz
American History: V27
García Márquez, Gabriel
Eyes of a Blue Dog: V21
The Handsomest Drowned Man in the World: V1
A Very Old Man with Enormous Wings: V6
The Woman Who Came at Six O'Clock: V16
Morales, Alejandro
The Curing Woman: V19
Rivera, Beatriz
African Passions: V15
Rivera, Tomás
The Harvest: V15

Indian

Chandra, Vikram
Dharma: V16
Divakaruni, Chitra Banerjee
Meeting Mrinal: V24
Mrs. Dutta Writes a Letter: V18
Lahiri, Jhumpa
A Temporary Matter: V19
This Blessed House: V27
Manto, Saadat Hasan
The Dog of Tithwal: V15
Mistry, Rohinton
Swimming Lessons: V6
Mukherjee, Bharati
The Management of Grief: V7
The Middleman: V24
Narayan, R. K.
A Horse and Two Goats: V5
Sharma, Akhil
If You Sing like That for Me: V21

Irish

Beckett, Samuel
Dante and the Lobster: V15
Bowen, Elizabeth
A Day in the Dark: V22
The Demon Lover: V5
Devlin, Anne
Naming the Names: V17
Joyce, James
Araby: V1
The Dead: V6
Eveline: V19
Lavin, Mary
In the Middle of the Fields: V23
O'Connor, Frank
Guests of the Nation: V5
O'Flaherty, Liam
The Sniper: V20
The Wave: V5
Trevor, William
The News from Ireland: V10
Wilde, Oscar
The Canterville Ghost: V7

Israeli

Hendel, Yehudit
Small Change: V14

Italian

Calvino, Italo
The Feathered Ogre: V12

Japanese

Mishima, Yukio
Fountains in the Rain: V12
Swaddling Clothes: V5
Murakami, Haruki
The Elephant Vanishes: V23
Naoya, Shiga
Han's Crime: V5
Waters, Mary Yukari
Aftermath: V22
Yoshimoto, Banana
Kitchen: V16

Jewish

Asimov, Isaac
Nightfall: V17
Babel, Isaac
My First Goose: V10
Bellow, Saul
Leaving the Yellow House: V12
A Silver Dish: V22
Berriault, Gina
The Stone Boy: V7
Women in Their Beds: V11
Doctorow, E. L.
The Writer in the Family: V27
Eisenberg, Deborah
Someone to Talk To: V24
Friedman, Bruce Jay
Brazzaville Teen-ager: V18
Helprin, Mark
Perfection: V25
Kafka, Franz
A Hunger Artist: V7
In the Penal Colony: V3
The Metamorphosis: V12
Malamud, Bernard
Black Is My Favorite Color: V16
The First Seven Years: V13
The Magic Barrel: V8
Orringer, Julie
The Smoothest Way Is Full of Stones: V23
Ozick, Cynthia
The Pagan Rabbi: V12
Rosa: V22
The Shawl: V3
Paley, Grace
Anxiety: V27
A Conversation with My Father: V3
The Long-Distance Runner: V20
Roth, Philip
The Conversion of the Jews: V18
Goodbye, Columbus: V12
Salinger, J. D.
A Perfect Day for Bananafish: V17
Singer, Isaac Bashevis
Gimpel the Fool: V2
Henne Fire: V16
The Spinoza of Market Street: V12
Zlateh the Goat: V27
Stein, Gertrude
Melanctha: V5

Kenyan

Ogot, Grace
The Green Leaves: V15

Mexican

Paz, Octavio
My Life with the Wave: V13

Native American

Alexie, Sherman
Because My Father Always Said He Was the Only Indian Who Saw Jimi Hendrix Play "The Star-Spangled Banner" at Woodstock: V18
Erdrich, Louise
Fleur: V22
The Red Convertible: V14
Ortiz, Simon J.
The End of Old Horse: V22
Silko, Leslie Marmon
Lullaby: V10
The Man to Send Rain Clouds: V8
Storyteller: V11
Yellow Woman: V4

Nepalese

Upadhyay, Samrat
The Good Shopkeeper: V22

New Zealander

Mansfield, Katherine
Bliss: V10
The Garden Party: V8
Marriage à la Mode: V11
Miss Brill: V2
Sargeson, Frank
A Great Day: V20

Nigerian

Achebe, Chinua
Civil Peace: V13
Vengeful Creditor: V3
Okri, Ben
In the Shadow of War: V20

Peruvian

Vargas Llosa, Mario
The Challenge: V14

Philippine

Santos, Bienvenido
Immigration Blues: V19

Polish

Borowski, Tadeusz
This Way for the Gas, Ladies and Gentlemen: V13
Conrad, Joseph
Heart of Darkness: V12
The Secret Sharer: V1
Singer, Isaac Bashevis
Gimpel the Fool: V2
Henne Fire: V16
The Spinoza of Market Street: V12
Zlateh the Goat: V27

Portuguese

Saramago, José
The Centaur: V23

Puerto Rican

Cofer, Judith Ortiz
American History: V27
Williams, William Carlos
The Use of Force: V27

Russian

Asimov, Isaac
Nightfall: V17
Babel, Isaac
My First Goose: V10
Chekhov, Anton
The Darling: V13
Gooseberries: V14
Gusev: V26
The Lady with the Pet Dog: V5
Dostoevsky, Fyodor
The Grand Inquisitor: V8
Gogol, Nikolai
The Overcoat: V7
Nabokov, Vladimir
A Guide to Berlin: V6
That in Aleppo Once . . . : V15
Pushkin, Alexander
The Stationmaster: V9
Solzhenitsyn, Alexandr
One Day in the Life of Ivan Denisovich: V9
Tolstaya, Tatyana
Night: V14
Tolstoy, Leo
The Death of Ivan Ilych: V5
Yezierska, Anzia
America and I: V15

Scottish

Doyle, Arthur Conan
The Red-Headed League: V2

Scott, Sir Walter
Wandering Willie's Tale: V10

South African

Gordimer, Nadine
Town and Country Lovers: V14
The Train from Rhodesia: V2
The Ultimate Safari: V19
Head, Bessie
Life: V13
Snapshots of a Wedding: V5
Kohler, Sheila
Africans: V18
Mphahlele, Es'kia (Ezekiel)
Mrs. Plum: V11

Spanish

Unamuno, Miguel de
Saint Emmanuel the Good, Martyr: V20
Vargas Llosa, Mario
The Challenge: V14

Swedish

Gustafsson, Lars
Greatness Strikes Where It Pleases: V22
Lagerlöf, Selma
The Legend of the Christmas Rose: V18

Welsh

Dahl, Roald
Lamb to the Slaughter: V4

West Indian

Kincaid, Jamaica
Girl: V7
What I Have Been Doing Lately: V5

Subject/Theme Index

Boldfaced
Denotes discussion in *Themes* section

A

Activism
The Writer in the Family: 280–281
Admiration
The Use of Force: 227–228
Adolescence
American History: 31
Adulthood
American History: 31
Eleven: 92
The Writer in the Family: 273
Age
Eleven: 89
Aggression
The Use of Force: 228
Agriculture, Decline in
Race at Morning: 195–196
Alienation
Charles: 80
This Blessed House: 222
Allegory
A Horseman in the Sky: 115
Allusion
After Twenty Years: 18–19, 22
Alter Ego
Charles: 72, 73
Ambiguity
The Use of Force: 231
The Writer in the Family: 267
Ambivalence
A Wagner Matinee: 256
American Dream
This Blessed House: 212
The Writer in the Family: 278
American Northeast
American History: 25, 30
A Wagner Matinee: 250–253, 255, 256
American South
Jim Baker's Blue Jay Yarn: 146
Race at Morning: 176, 178, 186–188, 190, 191, 194, 202–204
American West
After Twenty Years: 7–8
Jim Baker's Blue Jay Yarn: 154–157
A Wagner Matinee: 250–253, 255, 256
Analogy
After Twenty Years: 16
Anger
The Use of Force: 227, 232
Animals
Jim Baker's Blue Jay Yarn: 153
Race at Morning: 181
Anthropomorphism
Zlateh the Goat: 292
Anti-war Sentiment
A Horseman in the Sky: 128–132
Antisocial Behavior
Charles: 80
Anxiety
Anxiety: 50–51
Apocalypse
Race at Morning: 197–198
Appearances
This Blessed House: 209, 216, 221
Art and the Artist
A Wagner Matinee: 248–249, 252–253, 255–258, 258–260, 261–262
The Writer in the Family: 263, 276
Assimilation
This Blessed House: 211, 216–217
Authority
Anxiety: 48, 51, 58–59
The Use of Force: 239
Autobiography
Liberty: 168–169
A Wagner Matinee: 250
Autonomy
This Blessed House: 213–214
The Writer in the Family: 278

B

Battle of Wills
This Blessed House: 211
Battlefield Experience
A Horseman in the Sky: 130
Beauty
A Wagner Matinee: 259
Bildungsroman
Charles: 76
Bilingualism
Eleven: 86
Bleakness
A Wagner Matinee: 260
Body Image
American History: 28

C

Care
This Blessed House: 218–219, 220
Cautionary Figures
Anxiety: 58

Change
Race at Morning: 183, 185–186, 187–188, 190
Characterization
After Twenty Years: 21
Eleven: 110
A Horseman in the Sky: 134
A Wagner Matinee: 250
The Writer in the Family: 270–271
Chase
Race at Morning: 201
Childhood, Loss of
Eleven: 103
Children, Protection of
Anxiety: 58
Children's Literature
Zlateh the Goat: 298, 301, 304–305
Child's Point of View
Liberty: 164, 167
Civic duty
After Twenty Years: 5–6
Civil War
A Horseman in the Sky: 117
Civil War
A Horseman in the Sky: 118, 120–122, 124–126, 126–128
Civilization
Race at Morning: 198–200
Classical Allusion
After Twenty Years: 18–19
Classical Music
A Wagner Matinee: 248–249, 252–253
Classicism
A Horseman in the Sky: 120
Coincidence
A Horseman in the Sky: 131, 136
Cold War
Charles: 76–77
Coldness
American History: 28, 30–31
Coming of Age
American History: 24, 31
Eleven: 92, 96
Race at Morning: 190
The Writer in the Family: 263, 273
Commitment
The Writer in the Family: 280
Communication
Jim Baker's Blue Jay Yarn: 139, 142
This Blessed House: 223
Community
This Blessed House: 220–221, 222–223
The Writer in the Family: 276–277
Companionship
The Writer in the Family: 278
Compassion
The Use of Force: 230
Compassion
The Use of Force: 237
Complicity
The Writer in the Family: 280–281
Compromise
This Blessed House: 211
Concern
The Use of Force: 227–228, 228
Condescension
A Wagner Matinee: 251
Conformity
Charles: 73
Connection
This Blessed House: 222
The Writer in the Family: 282
Consciousness
The Writer in the Family: 279–280
Conservatism
Charles: 77–78
Consumption
A Wagner Matinee: 256
Contempt
The Use of Force: 236
Contrasting Perspectives
American History: 31
Control
This Blessed House: 206, 210–211, 213–214
A Wagner Matinee: 261–262
The Writer in the Family: 270
Conventionalism
A Wagner Matinee: 254
Correspondence
The Writer in the Family: 282
Creative Imagination and the Fictionalization of Self
Charles: 73
Creativity
This Blessed House: 221
A Wagner Matinee: 256, 258–260
Zlateh the Goat: 305
Crime
After Twenty Years: 5
Cultural Identity
Eleven: 96, 99–101, 102–104
This Blessed House: 222–223
Culture
A Wagner Matinee: 250, 253–260
The Writer in the Family: 279
Culture Clash and the Immigrant Experience
American History: 42
Eleven: 97–99, 110
This Blessed House: 222–223
Culture Clash and the Immigrant Experience
Eleven: 90
Cynicism
A Horseman in the Sky: 121–122
The Writer in the Family: 279–280

D

Danger
Anxiety: 49, 51
Death
The Writer in the Family: 271
Deceit
The Writer in the Family: 282
Defeat
The Use of Force: 228, 230
Depression (era)
The Use of Force: 232
Description
After Twenty Years: 21–22
Desire
Race at Morning: 182, 186
Despair
Race at Morning: 199
Destruction and Renewal
Race at Morning: 194–195
Detachment
Charles: 81
The Use of Force: 231, 236–237
Detail, Suppression of
After Twenty Years: 20
Determination
Jim Baker's Blue Jay Yarn: 139, 148–151
Race at Morning: 182
The Use of Force: 227
Determination
Jim Baker's Blue Jay Yarn: 143–144
Determinism
A Horseman in the Sky: 135
Dialogue
After Twenty Years: 16
Charles: 78
Differences, Interpersonal
This Blessed House: 216
Disapproval
A Wagner Matinee: 251, 252
Discipline
American History: 38
Disease
The Use of Force: 225, 232–233
Displacement
Eleven: 87
This Blessed House: 217–218
Dissociation
Charles: 80
Disturbed Causality
A Horseman in the Sky: 131
Domestic Realism
Charles: 70, 75–76
Domesticity
Charles: 82, 84
Dramatic Irony
Charles: 75
Dreams
The Writer in the Family: 275
Dual Cultural Life of the Immigrant
Eleven: 99–101, 104–106, 110

Dual Cultural Life of the Immigrant
This Blessed House: 211–212
Duality
A Horseman in the Sky: 119–120
A Wagner Matinee: 255–256
Duty
A Horseman in the Sky: 114, 115, 116, 118, 126, 128
Duty and Responsibility
After Twenty Years: 5–6

E

Economy of Language
After Twenty Years: 20
American History: 37
Efficiency
This Blessed House: 209
Ego
The Use of Force: 238–240
Ekphrasis
A Horseman in the Sky: 115, 120
Emigration
Liberty: 161, 167
Emotional Conflict
The Use of Force: 226–227, 236, 238, 240
Emotionalism
The Use of Force: 225
Empathy
Race at Morning: 181
The Use of Force: 230–231, 235–236
Emptiness
Jim Baker's Blue Jay Yarn: 154–157
Enlightenment
The Writer in the Family: 275, 279–280
Environmental Change
Race at Morning: 190–197, 199, 202
Estrangement
The Writer in the Family: 278, 280
Ethnic Identity
American History: 42–43
Anxiety: 47
Zlateh the Goat: 298, 302–303
Evil
Charles: 69, 78, 80
Race at Morning: 195
The Use of Force: 238
Evil, The Nature of
Charles: 75
Exaggeration
Jim Baker's Blue Jay Yarn: 145

F

Fable
Jim Baker's Blue Jay Yarn: 139
Faith
Zlateh the Goat: 295, 296
False Consciousness
The Writer in the Family: 279–280
Family Conflict
The Writer in the Family: 263, 265
Family Conflict
The Writer in the Family: 268–269
Family Duty
A Horseman in the Sky: 118, 126
Family Life
Charles: 74–75, 78, 81, 84
Liberty: 167
Family Relationships
Charles: 74–75
Fantasy
American History: 35
Fascism
American History: 24
Fatalism
A Horseman in the Sky: 134–137
Father-Son Relationship
The Writer in the Family: 273, 275, 277, 278, 280
Fatherhood
Anxiety: 48, 52, 54
Feminine Identity
Eleven: 96, 101–104
Feminism
This Blessed House: 214–215
Fiction, The Nature of
The Writer in the Family: 269–270
Fiction, The Nature of
The Writer in the Family: 279, 281–282
Fictionalized Self
Charles: 69, 72
Figurative Comparisons
After Twenty Years: 19
Figurative Language
Jim Baker's Blue Jay Yarn: 142
First-person Narration
American History: 30
Anxiety: 51–52
Eleven: 89, 93
Race at Morning: 186
A Wagner Matinee: 247–248
The Writer in the Family: 270
Folk Narrators
Jim Baker's Blue Jay Yarn: 153–154
Folk Tales
Zlateh the Goat: 284, 292, 301
Food
American History: 43
This Blessed House: 216, 218, 220
Frame Narrative
Jim Baker's Blue Jay Yarn: 145, 153
Freudian Psychology
A Horseman in the Sky: 126
The Use of Force: 238–240
Friendship
After Twenty Years: 4–5
Friendship
After Twenty Years: 6
Frontier Life
A Wagner Matinee: 241, 246–248, 250–253, 254–255, 258–260
Frontier Life
A Wagner Matinee: 245
Frustration
A Horseman in the Sky: 136

G

Gender
Eleven: 101–104
Gender Roles
Anxiety: 54
This Blessed House: 214–216
The Use of Force: 236
A Wagner Matinee: 254, 256–257
Genuineness
A Wagner Matinee: 257
God
Zlateh the Goat: 295, 296, 306–307
Goodness
Race at Morning: 183
Grandmotherhood
Anxiety: 54–55

H

Hanukkah
Zlateh the Goat: 294
Happiness
This Blessed House: 223
Happy Ending
Zlateh the Goat: 292
Harmony
After Twenty Years: 22
Hatred
The Use of Force: 227
Helplessness
A Horseman in the Sky: 136
Hispanic Americans
American History: 24, 28, 33–34, 39–40
Eleven: 86, 94–96, 99–106, 107–108, 110
Liberty: 166, 170–172
Holocaust
Charles: 76
Zlateh the Goat: 302–303
Homesteading
A Wagner Matinee: 248
Honesty
The Use of Force: 237
Hope
American History: 31
Race at Morning: 199
Human Condition
After Twenty Years: 1
A Horseman in the Sky: 134–137
Human Connection
The Writer in the Family: 273

Subject/Theme Index

Human Nature
Jim Baker's Blue Jay Yarn: 139
The Use of Force: 238–240
Humanity
This Blessed House: 223
Humans' Relationship with the Land
Race at Morning: 190–197
Humiliation
Eleven: 88, 92, 98–99
Humiliation
The Use of Force: 230–231
Humor
After Twenty Years: 21–22
Charles: 69, 78
Jim Baker's Blue Jay Yarn: 139, 153, 154–157
Race at Morning: 182, 201
Zlateh the Goat: 301, 305
Hunting
Race at Morning: 176, 178–181, 188, 189, 190–197, 201, 202
Hypocrisy
A Horseman in the Sky: 112, 113, 121, 125

I

Id
The Use of Force: 238–240
Identity
American History: 42–43
Imagery
American History: 30–31
Eleven: 93, 96, 109
Jim Baker's Blue Jay Yarn: 145
This Blessed House: 212
The Writer in the Family: 271
Imagism
The Use of Force: 225, 233–234
Immigrants
American History: 24, 25, 27
Anxiety: 57
Eleven: 94–95
This Blessed House: 206, 212–213, 216–217, 218
Impatience
The Use of Force: 229
Impulsivity
This Blessed House: 209–210
In Medias Res
A Horseman in the Sky: 120
Independence
The Writer in the Family: 275
Individual Growth
The Writer in the Family: 263
Individuality
This Blessed House: 223
The Writer in the Family: 276–277
Integrity
The Writer in the Family: 268
Integrity
The Writer in the Family: 273, 274
Invisibility
Eleven: 86
Irony
After Twenty Years: 6–7, 11, 13
Charles: 69, 74, 75
A Horseman in the Sky: 112, 114, 122, 127, 128, 130, 132–134
Isolation
American History: 34–36
A Wagner Matinee: 250
The Writer in the Family: 278, 279, 280

J

Jewish Americans
Zlateh the Goat: 284, 291, 292–293, 297–298, 302–303
Jewish Mothers
Anxiety: 56–59
Joie de Vivre
This Blessed House: 221
Justice and Injustice
Eleven: 90–91

L

Language
After Twenty Years: 13–14, 15, 22
American History: 37
Eleven: 109
A Horseman in the Sky: 119–120, 123
Jim Baker's Blue Jay Yarn: 139, 142, 155
Zlateh the Goat: 292–293, 300, 306
Language
Jim Baker's Blue Jay Yarn: 144–145
Latin Americans
American History: 42–43
Liberation
The Writer in the Family: 275
Liberty
Liberty: 162–163, 169
Liberty
Liberty: 169
Loss
This Blessed House: 222
Loss of Innocence
Liberty: 163–164
Race at Morning: 185–186
Loss of Innocence
Race at Morning: 176
Loss of Love
Anxiety: 63
Love
Eleven: 109
This Blessed House: 209
The Use of Force: 227, 236
Zlateh the Goat: 295, 296
Love and Loyalty
Zlateh the Goat: 290–291

M

Magic realism
A Horseman in the Sky: 118–119, 123–125
Male Themes
The Writer in the Family: 277
Marginalization
Eleven: 90, 96–99, 97–99, 101
Marriage
This Blessed House: 206, 210–211, 213–217, 219
Martial Spirit
A Horseman in the Sky: 128–132
Martyrdom
A Wagner Matinee: 252, 260
Meaning, Duality of
A Horseman in the Sky: 119–120
Memory
A Horseman in the Sky: 116
Metaphor
After Twenty Years: 16
A Horseman in the Sky: 120, 136
Jim Baker's Blue Jay Yarn: 153, 155
This Blessed House: 218
Middle Class
The Writer in the Family: 278
Military Duty
A Horseman in the Sky: 118, 126, 128
Minority Culture
Eleven: 86, 89, 98, 99–101
Morality
A Horseman in the Sky: 126
Race at Morning: 183, 190, 199
Zlateh the Goat: 292
Motherhood
Anxiety: 48, 56–59
Mourning
This Blessed House: 219–220
Multigenerational Parenting
Anxiety: 54–55
Music
A Wagner Matinee: 248–249, 252–253
Mystical Elements
Zlateh the Goat: 295, 306

N

Narrative Technique
Jim Baker's Blue Jay Yarn: 151–152
Native American Belief System
Race at Morning: 194–195
Nature
Race at Morning: 190–197, 197–200
Neglect
This Blessed House: 218–219, 220

Nuclear Family
The Writer in the Family: 271
Numbness
A Wagner Matinee: 245, 252

O

Observation
Anxiety: 49
Oedipus Complex
A Horseman in the Sky: 126
Omniscient Narration
A Horseman in the Sky: 120
Opposition
American History: 42
A Wagner Matinee: 255
Ordeal
Zlateh the Goat: 295–296

P

Pacifism
Anxiety: 45
Pain Avoidance
The Use of Force: 239
Parental Love
Anxiety: 51
Parenthood
Anxiety: 51, 54–55
Charles: 75
The Use of Force: 239
Parody
After Twenty Years: 13, 15, 16
Past Tense
Liberty: 164
Patriarchy
Eleven: 100
Patricide
A Horseman in the Sky: 116, 125, 128
Patricide
A Horseman in the Sky: 117–118
Patriotism
A Horseman in the Sky: 127
Perseverance
Race at Morning: 182
Personal and Professional Contempt
The Use of Force: 231
Philistine World
A Wagner Matinee: 255–256
Phoniness
The Use of Force: 237
Physicality
The Writer in the Family: 270–271
Pity
A Wagner Matinee: 244–245, 246, 252
Plain style
A Horseman in the Sky: 123
Pleasure
The Use of Force: 239
Poetry
Eleven: 109–110
Political Activism
Anxiety: 64–66
Political Oppression
Liberty: 163, 165–166, 167–169, 173
Politics
A Wagner Matinee: 248
Possibility
Race at Morning: 186
Postmodernism
The Writer in the Family: 277
Power and Powerlessness
Eleven: 99
The Use of Force: 230
The Writer in the Family: 279
Prayer
Zlateh the Goat: 296
Prejudice
American History: 24, 28, 31, 42
Charles: 73
Prejudice
American History: 29–30
Charles: 74
Present Tense
Liberty: 164
Professionalism
The Use of Force: 227, 236–237
Projection
Charles: 69, 76, 79–80
Protest Literature
Anxiety: 45, 52
Psychology
A Horseman in the Sky: 126
The Use of Force: 238–240
Pure English
A Horseman in the Sky: 123
Purification
Zlateh the Goat: 295–296
Purpose
The Writer in the Family: 278

Q

Quotation, Use of
After Twenty Years: 15
Quotation Marks, Absence of
The Use of Force: 231, 237

R

Racial Segregation
Race at Morning: 197
Realism
A Horseman in the Sky: 112–113, 118–119, 121–122, 123–124
Jim Baker's Blue Jay Yarn: 146–147
A Wagner Matinee: 247
Reason
A Horseman in the Sky: 132–134
The Use of Force: 240
Rebirth
Race at Morning: 194–195
Zlateh the Goat: 295–296
Regret
A Wagner Matinee: 245–247
Religion
A Horseman in the Sky: 118
Zlateh the Goat: 291–292
Religion
This Blessed House: 212, 223
Zlateh the Goat: 294–296
Religion and Death
American History: 28–29
Renewal
Race at Morning: 194–195
Resilience
American History: 27, 31
Race at Morning: 197
Respect
Race at Morning: 182, 183
Respect
Race at Morning: 184–185
The Use of Force: 236
Revision
Zlateh the Goat: 304–305
Revulsion
A Wagner Matinee: 244–245
Rite of Passage
The Writer in the Family: 273
Ritual
This Blessed House: 218, 220

S

Sacrifice
A Wagner Matinee: 252
Satire
Charles: 76
A Horseman in the Sky: 113, 132–134
Jim Baker's Blue Jay Yarn: 153
Savagery
The Use of Force: 238
Science and Technology
Anxiety: 51
Scientific Determinism
A Horseman in the Sky: 135
Secrecy
The Use of Force: 227, 238
Segregation
American History: 24
Self-assertion
The Writer in the Family: 263
Self-identity
Charles: 69, 72–73
Self-knowledge
This Blessed House: 222–223

Sensory Imagery
Eleven: 109
Sentences
Anxiety: 63
Setting
American History: 30–31
Race at Morning: 202–204
Sexual Conquest
The Use of Force: 238
Shame
American History: 28
Shame
American History:
Eleven: 92
Silencing
Eleven: 88, 98
Simile
Jim Baker's Blue Jay Yarn: 140
Situational Irony
After Twenty Years: 6–7
Charles: 75
Skepticism
The Use of Force: 229
Slice-of-life
After Twenty Years: 13
Social Activism
Anxiety: 52, 64–68
Social Class
Eleven: 98
The Use of Force: 236
The Writer in the Family: 271, 277, 278, 279
Solidarity
The Writer in the Family: 278
South America
Liberty: 165–166, 174
Stereotypes
American History: 43
Anxiety: 56–58
Eleven: 103
Sterility
A Wagner Matinee: 259–260
Storytelling
American History: 37–38, 41–42
Race at Morning: 199
Zlateh the Goat: 300, 301
Strength
Anxiety: 58–59
Struggle for Dominance
This Blessed House: 210–211
Stubbornness
The Use of Force: 227
Suffering
Eleven: 101
A Horseman in the Sky: 137
Suggestive Description
After Twenty Years: 21–22
Super-ego
The Use of Force: 238–240
Supernatural
A Horseman in the Sky: 123
Survival
Zlateh the Goat: 303
Symbolism
American History: 31
A Horseman in the Sky: 112, 118, 119, 120, 125
Liberty: 164, 169
Race at Morning: 186, 195, 201
This Blessed House: 221
The Use of Force: 231–232, 238
A Wagner Matinee: 258–259
The Writer in the Family: 271, 275
Zlateh the Goat: 295–296
Sympathy
The Use of Force: 237

T

Tall Tales
Jim Baker's Blue Jay Yarn: 145, 152–153, 154
Technology
Anxiety: 51, 52
Tenderness
The Use of Force: 228
Tenement Life
Anxiety: 47, 49, 57
Third-person Narration
After Twenty Years: 7
This Blessed House: 212
Zlateh the Goat: 292
Tidiness
This Blessed House: 209
Tone
After Twenty Years: 22
The Writer in the Family: 275
Transformation
Eleven: 92, 93, 97, 99
The Writer in the Family: 273
Translation
Zlateh the Goat: 304–307
Treason
A Horseman in the Sky: 114
Truth
American History: 42, 43
The Writer in the Family: 270, 273, 274, 275, 277, 282
Twist of Fate
After Twenty Years: 1, 9–11, 15, 21

U

Unfulfilled Life
The Writer in the Family: 268, 271, 273
Universality
This Blessed House: 223
Zlateh the Goat: 292
Unjust Criticism
The Writer in the Family: 273
Unreliable Narrator
Race at Morning: 186
Upward Mobility
The Writer in the Family: 271
Urban Life
Anxiety: 47, 49, 57
The Writer in the Family: 278–279
Urgency
The Use of Force: 237, 240

V

Value of Life
Race at Morning: 202
Vernacular
Race at Morning: 176, 178, 186
Violence
The Use of Force: 235–236, 236, 238, 240
Violence as a Useful Function
The Use of Force: 229–230
Vocation
A Wagner Matinee: 256
Voice
Anxiety: 62–64
Eleven: 104–106, 107
Jim Baker's Blue Jay Yarn: 145–146
Vulnerability
Eleven: 101–104

W

War
Anxiety: 52
A Horseman in the Sky: 112–113, 116, 119, 123, 128–132, 132–134, 136–137
Warning
Anxiety: 48, 49, 58
Wilderness
Race at Morning: 189–201
Wildness
Race at Morning: 182
This Blessed House: 209–210
Withdrawal
American History: 35
Womanhood
American History: 42
Women
Charles: 78
Writing and Writers
After Twenty Years: 14, 20
American History: 39–40
Anxiety: 61–62
Eleven: 108
The Writer in the Family: 273, 274, 275, 278, 279, 281–282
Zlateh the Goat: 306–307

Y

Yarns
Jim Baker's Blue Jay Yarn: 145
Yiddish
Zlateh the Goat: 284, 292–293, 300, 301, 304–307